T0367229

UNMASKING THE KLANSMAN

Also by Dan T. Carter

Scottsboro: A Tragedy of the American South (1969)

When the War Was Over: Self-Reconstruction in the South, 1865–1867 (1985)

The Politics of Rage: George Wallace, the Origins of the New Conservatism and the Transformation of American Politics (1995)

From George Wallace to Newt Gingrich: Race in the Conservative Counterrevolution, 1963–1994 (1996)

UNMASKING

KLANSMAN

The Double Life of Asa and Forrest Carter

DAN T. CARTER

NEWSOUTH BOOKS
an imprint of
The University of Georgia Press
Athens

NSB

Published by NewSouth Books
an imprint of the University of Georgia Press
Athens, Georgia 30602
https://ugapress.org/imprints/newsouth-books/

Designed by Randall Williams
Cover designed by Erin Kirk
Printed and bound by Books International, Inc.

Most NewSouth/University of Georgia Press titles
are available from popular ebook vendors.

Library of Congress Control Number: 2023931098
ISBN: 9781588384812 (hardback)
ISBN: 9781588384829 (ebook)

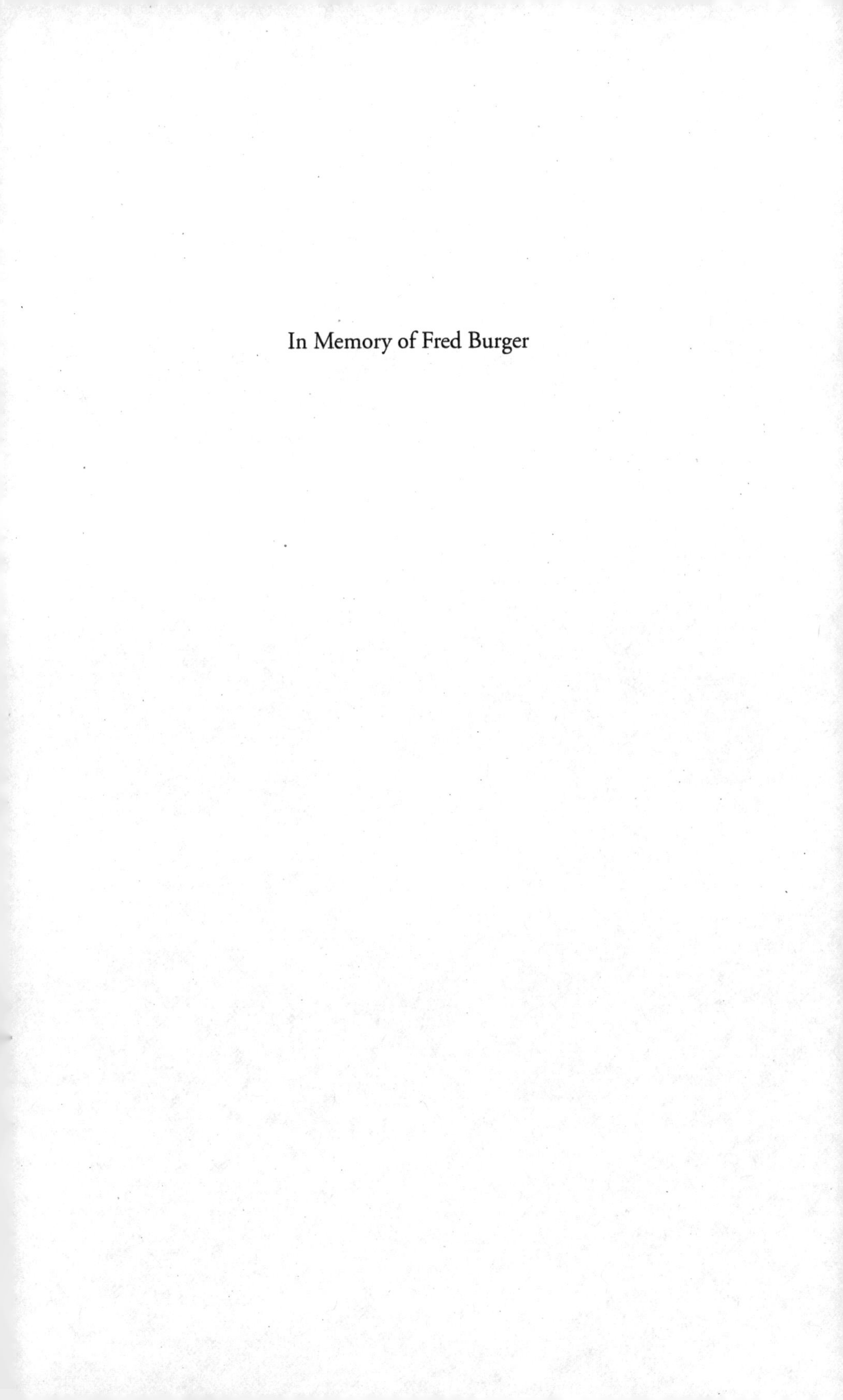

In Memory of Fred Burger

Contents

Contents

Preface

The Speech of a Lifetime

January 8, 1963. For weeks, George Wallace's press secretary, Bill Jones, had been on the phone, cajoling the national television networks, *Time* and *Newsweek* magazines, the *New York Times*, and other major newspapers into covering the inauguration of the Alabama governor-elect rather than relying on AP and UPI stringers. When *Los Angeles Times* Southern correspondent Jack Nelson responded that state governors' inauguration ceremonies seldom received such national attention, Jones promised that the new governor planned to deliver a fiery challenge to John Kennedy's civil rights policies with a "helluva speech. History is going to be made," he told Nelson. "You're going to be sorry if you don't show up."[1]

But with the clock running out, there was no "helluva speech"; not a word had been written by the governor-elect's secret speech-writer, Asa Earl Carter. In the weeks leading up to the inauguration, Carter had avoided a frantic Jones and other Wallace aides as he worked a lucrative con. Without approval from the campaign, Carter had approached businessmen with state contracts, emphasizing his close contacts with Wallace and urging them to buy advertisements for what he described as the "official" inauguration program. With ads running as high as $400, a local printing company churned out 20,000 glossy programs to be sold at $2.50, eventually netting Carter more than $25,000 ($200,000 in 2023 dollars).[2]

Frustrated and angry, the top aide to and self-described "son-of-a-bitch for Wallace" finally cornered Carter at his hotel room in Montgomery's Jefferson Davis Hotel. "I told him he was finished if he didn't get to work," said Seymore Trammell, who claimed that he locked Carter in his hotel room with room service on call, a carton of Pall Mall cigarettes, two bottles of Jack Daniels, and a stack of paper for his portable Underwood typewriter.

Wallace had given him a few suggestions, but over the next two days

Carter wrote 90 percent of the speech, using phrases and arguments from material he had published in his white supremacy magazine, *The Southerner*, as well as more than a hundred radio commentaries he had delivered in the 1950s and 1960s.

A Wallace friend recalled the moment when an unshaven, disheveled, and hungover Carter rode the elevator up to the governor-elect's suite twenty-four hours before the inauguration. As he handed the speech to Wallace, he turned to page three and pointed his finger: "segregation today . . . segregation tomorrow . . . segregation forever." "Here are the lines that are going to catch everybody," he said. Montgomery journalist Bob Ingram, who spent much of the next day with the incoming governor, remembered Wallace's enthusiasm. "I like that line, I like it," he kept saying as he chewed on one of his ever-present (and unlit) cigars.[3]

THE FOLLOWING MONDAY, DESPITE the coldest Montgomery temperatures in eighty years, huge crowds filled the streets, many wearing white carnations that had become symbols of their new governor's devotion to white supremacy. As state employees hastily rounded up electric heaters for the parade review stand, others added more loudspeakers to

George Wallace being sworn in for his first term, January 14, 1963.

accommodate the growing crowd. The new governor's press secretary delivered hot coffee and donuts to half-frozen television crews as they checked their cameras and microphones. ("I thought this was the Deep South," grumbled one lightly-dressed CBS cameraman who had flown in from New York.)

Among the thousands of white spectators, three black men, James Arrington and Stevens and John Walters, stood at a distance. But they never heard the new governor's speech. Minutes after they arrived, Montgomery police arrested and charged them with disorderly conduct, claiming they had "brushed against a white woman" who had to step off the sidewalk and into the street.[4]

As his brother Jack held the family Bible, Wallace removed his top hat and took the oath of office above a banner reading "In God We Trust." And then he launched into the speech that would make him a national figure:

> Today I have stood, where once Jefferson Davis stood, and took an oath to my people. It is very appropriate then that from this Cradle of the Confederacy, this very Heart of the Great Anglo-Saxon Southland, that today we sound the drum for freedom . . . In the name of the greatest people that have ever trod this earth, I draw the line in the dust and toss the gauntlet before the feet of tyranny . . . and I say . . . segregation now . . . segregation tomorrow . . . segregation forever.[5]

A roar of approval almost drowned out his last words. Asa Carter had been right: "segregation now . . . segregation tomorrow . . . segregation forever" became the lead in AP and UPI stories, in *Time* and *Newsweek,* and in the news broadcasts on the nation's three major networks.

Carter had produced the promised "helluva speech."

In later years, George Wallace's passionate embrace of segregation would limit his national aspirations, but if state and national media had given coverage to the even more extreme parts of Carter's speech, the consequences would have been worse (only the Montgomery-based *Alabama Journal* published the entire speech). At a time when most white Americans outside the South favored the right of blacks to vote, Carter's speech bitterly attacked the Fourteenth Amendment to the Constitution which had granted equal protection of the law to emancipated slaves in the aftermath of the Civil War. That "illegal" addition to our founding document had allowed the growth of "insipid bloc voters" (i.e., black voters), Carter had written for Wallace. Nothing was more irresponsible than the misguided belief that "everyone has voting rights."

In an attempt to appeal to white supporters outside the South, Carter embraced the boiler-plate rhetoric of 1950s right-wing conservatism: The American free enterprise system faced an existential threat from communists and from liberals who scorned "the basic law of our fathers that governments do not produce wealth . . . people produce wealth . . . free people." An increasingly socialistic central government penalized individuals' initiative and ambition and drove the country toward bankruptcy.

Carter had learned from bitter personal experience to avoid references to one of his primary obsessions: the threat posed by an international cabal of Jewish financial interests. Instead, he described the danger of a post-colonial upsurge of violence from the primitive darker races that would only lead to violence against whites and eventually racial amalgamation in the United States, replacing a "race of honor with a mongrel race" under the boot of an all-powerful federal government.

Asa Carter's creation unified the strands of traditional racism, the danger posed by immigrants of color, the threat of international communism, and a defense of traditional white Christian conservatism that foreshadowed today's white Christian nationalism: the belief that "whiteness" is the marker of true national identity.

A DECADE LATER, A dark-haired man wearing blue jeans, a western shirt, a denim jacket, and a black Stetson with a feather in the hatband walked into the largest bookstore in Abilene, Texas. "My name is Forrest Carter," he said as he held out his hand to the owner, Chuck Weeth. "I'd like to talk with you about a book I've written called *Gone to Texas*."

Like so many people who met Asa/Forrest Carter during these years, Weeth was captivated by this self-described "Cherokee cowboy." From the time they met, he never had any doubt about Carter's Indian heritage: "Dark eyes, native American appearance, and a composure about himself that said, 'I am centered. I know who I am.'"[6]

Forrest Carter soon would become known across Texas and the Southwest as a promising western writer, a powerful public speaker, and an early "New Age" native American prophet and defender of Indian rights. From 1973 to 1979, he gave dozens of speeches and book-signings in Texas and nearby states in connection with his novels, *The Rebel Outlaw: Josey Wales* (originally titled *Gone to Texas*), *The Vengeance Trail of Josey Wales, Watch for Me on the Mountain,* and *The Education of Little Tree* (the latter a "memoir" of his Cherokee childhood in the mountains of east Tennessee). No one ever questioned his authenticity as a native American or suspected that he might have a quite different history.

Stories of switched identities are as old as the Biblical account of Joseph's deception of his brothers who had sold him into slavery. Over the centuries, novelists, playwrights, screenwriters, and operatic composers have created dual identities for comic purposes but also to explore class conflict, the differences between men and women, and the complexity of human behavior. At least since the eighteenth century there have been repeated examples of authors who assumed fake personae to claim "authenticity" in their writings.[7]

Such tales and performances usually end with a dramatic resolution, but *Unmasking the Klansman* is not a novel in which I am free to use my imagination to bring Asa Carter's life to a satisfying conclusion. I can only try to tell, as best I can, the story of a fabulist and brilliant con artist who embarked at age eighteen on a lifetime of concealment.

I initially encountered Asa Carter thirty years ago as I began a study of Alabama Governor George Wallace and his role in American politics during the 1960s and early 1970s. At first, Carter was simply a footnote to a question of rhetorical provenance. Wallace's 1963 inaugural speech promising "segregation forever" contained the most memorable words of his long political career, and I soon confirmed that Asa Carter wrote those words, although George Wallace denied that he even knew the former Klansman, violent white supremacist, and passionate anti-Semite.[8]

If that was the beginning, it was not to be the end of my encounter with Carter. In almost every interview I conducted with old Wallace hands and political observers, they kept returning to the racist rabble-rouser from North Alabama. By the end of the 1980s, Carter had been dead for a decade, but any mention of his name always evoked an uneasiness, even apprehension. Several interviewees recalled his mercurial moods and the way he could instantly shift from pleasant small talk to murderous threats and rage. Three described the long-barreled .38 revolver Carter often carried, the same gun he was wearing the night of an infamous 1957 gunfight that erupted after two fellow Klansmen suggested that he had stolen money from the klavern's treasury.*

Seymore Trammell, a handsome redhead with a fiery temper, climbed briefly to the top of the political ladder in Alabama, enthusiastically playing the role of George Wallace's enforcer in the 1960s. By the time I came to know Trammell in the late 1980s and early 1990s, he hardly fit that description. Whatever had changed him—a stint in federal prison for tax evasion, his recovery from alcohol abuse, or simply the passage of time—I found him genial, open to good-natured disagreements, and willing to reflect upon his past failings as we sat in his small Montgomery apartment and talked for hours. "I was George Wallace's son-of-a-bitch," he told me in a 1989 interview. "It came natural: back then, I had an angry streak, and I wasn't scared of anyone."

But even Trammell had been wary of Asa Carter. In October 1989, over coffee and after a lengthy recital of his take-no-quarter approach to dealing with opponents, Trammell looked out his window. "*If* I was afraid of anyone," he said, "it would be Ace—particularly when he was drunk."

In one of our first interviews, I expressed to Trammell one of the things I found so bewildering about Carter. How, I asked, could this ex-Klansman—a

---

* Local Ku Klux Klan chapters were called "klaverns," in keeping with a grandiose set of terms created in the mid 1860s, shortly after the end of the civil war, by the original Klan founders to describe the officers ("grand dragon," "grand scribe," "grand titan," "grand cyclops," etc.) and organizational structure ("the empire," "the realm," "the dominion," the "province," the "den" and "the klavern"). Despite the elaborate nomenclature, the organization was never tightly controlled from the top down. "Revised and Amended Prescript of the Order of the Ku Klux Klan, 1868," *The American Historical Magazine*, January 1900.

high school graduate who had flunked out of Officer Candidate School in World War II and out of the University of Colorado in one semester—become such a successful speechwriter for Wallace?

"You know he could really write," replied Trammell. "He published that magazine, and he also wrote a bunch of novels they made into movies. You knew that didn't you?"

I knew about Carter's racist magazine, *The Southerner,* but a novelist whose books had been turned into movies? No, I cautiously replied, secretly wondering if I could rely upon the memory of the seventy-year-old Trammell.

Later that year, however, I sat in the den of my Atlanta home as my son and I watched a video of Clint Eastwood's 1976 film, *The Outlaw Josey Wales*, the movie that marked the actor's transition from spaghetti westerns to more serious films. ("When I saw that picture for the fourth time," said Orson Welles, "I realized that it belongs with the great Westerns. You know, the great Westerns of Ford and Hawks. . . ."[9]) As the credits rolled across the screen, I saw the name of the author and book on which it was based: Forrest Carter, *Gone to Texas.*[10] Remembering Trammell's claim that Carter had written a book made into a film, I rewound the videotape and jotted down the name and title, but it was the next day before the meaning of the author's name suddenly struck me: "*Forrest* Carter."

Asa Carter worshipped Nathan Bedford Forrest, the Confederate cavalry commander and leader of the first Ku Klux Klan during Reconstruction. It required little research to discover that, under the pseudonym "Forrest Carter," George Wallace's former ghostwriter had churned out three popular novels and a fake autobiography between 1972 and his death seven years later.

In the spring of 1991, on research leave collecting material for my Wallace biography, I watched an extraordinary publishing phenomenon. *The Education of Little Tree,* written by Forrest Carter, claimed to be the story of his childhood as a half-Cherokee orphan raised by his Cherokee grandparents. Long out of print, the memoir was republished in 1986 by the University of New Mexico Press as the "true story" of how a young half-Indian boy came to know the wisdom of his Native American ancestors.

With only word-of-mouth support, the book's sales rose to more than a quarter million copies by the spring of 1991, when the American Booksellers Association gave it the newly created "Abby" Award (honoring the "hidden treasures" that ABA bookstore members most enjoyed recommending to their customers). The award boosted *The Education of Little Tree* onto the *New York Times* bestsellers list.[11]

UNABLE TO FIND MUCH information on Carter, I took a short break from my Wallace research in the late spring of 1991 and drove up into northeastern Alabama to Carter's home near Anniston. A helpful librarian in the Anniston-Calhoun County Library found his 1943 senior high school annual, and after an hour with it and combing through the local telephone directory I found three of his former classmates. One spoke to me and then, as if he thought better of it, abruptly ended our conversation. The other two were willing to talk briefly, but only if I promised I would not use their names.

Frustrated, I made the short drive out of Anniston to the rural area where he had grown up and lived for many years. Since I had not been able to find his exact address on Choccolocco Road, I went from house to house to see if I could identity any of Carter's childhood friends and former neighbors from the 1950s and 1960s.

White Alabamians are generally unguarded and friendly—particularly to anyone of the right color with a Southern accent—and ready to respond to a request for information or gossip. "Hello, my name is Dan Carter," I would begin. My pitch was a truthful if incomplete explanation for my interest in Carter. I was, I explained, interested in the background of Anniston's most famous writer. "I'm trying to find folks that knew the late Asa Carter who grew up and lived in this community until the 1970s."

But when I mentioned Carter's name, particularly when talking to older people, the response was often immediate and hostile. One woman who greeted me at the door with a smile and an assurance that she knew "everybody who lived around here," visibly recoiled at the first mention of Carter's name and slammed the door in my face in mid-sentence. Another man in his fifties grimly asked if I was a "government man" and—without waiting for my response—closed his door. Residents of the tight-knit rural community, I learned, had always resented that FBI agents openly staked out Carter's house in the late 1950s and 1960s.

After a gruff rebuff by the owner of a small-engine repair shop, I walked out to my car and turned to see an older, grease-stained mechanic approach from the rear of the building. He motioned me over as he looked around apprehensively. "I wasn't one of Asa's men," he told me, "but I can tell you where to find a local boy who is a good friend of one of Asa's sons." The "local boy" turned out to be in his late thirties. A half hour later I stood in his comfortable living room, introduced myself and explained that I wanted to ask him about Asa Carter, the father of his long-time friend, Asa Jr. He responded with stony silence and, without a word, turned and went upstairs. In the distance I could hear the murmur of his voice on the telephone. As I waited uneasily, his wife (who seemed bewildered by her husband's reaction) turned and walked halfway up the stairs and listened. A moment later, she hurried down the steps with a look of panic on her face. "Get out," she said. "Leave—right now." When I began asking what was wrong, she took my arm and pushed me toward the door. "Please," she said. "Please, leave and don't come back." I left.

Asa Carter, I realized, was not a conventional research subject.

Those experiences only increased my interest in Carter. He lived a life so audacious, so filled with twists and turns, it could easily be dismissed as pulp fiction. But even as I became more fascinated with his life story and collected more research material, I came to see the enormous obstacles of writing a biography. Twice I abandoned the project. Operating in an underground world of terrorists and under constant surveillance by the FBI, Asa Carter left few records—even fewer that can be trusted. Perhaps I was also chastened by my wife's concern over my mental health ("Do you really want to spend years getting inside the skin of Asa Carter?").

It has been difficult to explore the world in which Carter lived, a world of cruel and vicious attacks on black (and Jewish) Americans. But as new material emerged over the years I became convinced that there was something to be learned by following Asa Carter's journey from Alabama farm boy to Klan rabble-rouser to speech writer for George Wallace's white backlash and finally to successful New Age author. In *Requiem for a Nun,* William Faulkner's character Temple Drake spoke one of the best-known lines in American literature: "The past is never dead. It's not even past." If we have learned anything from watching American politics during the last few decades, it is that Carter's ideas—however extreme—have not been consigned to the dustbin; in different forms they have moved into the mainstream of American politics.

The English/Italian historian Iris Origo warned of the three "insidious temptations" that face every biographer: suppressing material that contradicts your own point of view, sitting in lofty judgment on your subject, and, above all, invention in any form.[12] I have tried to avoid those three temptations and ground Asa Carter's life in a web of facts and reasonable assumptions, but I am all too conscious that there is no such thing as a definitive history. However intent upon fairness and empathy in dealing with the past, I am telling "a" story. And as Louis Menand, the American critic and essayist recently pointed out, whether a historian writes to indoctrinate, to entertain, to warn, to justify, or to condemn, "it is, almost always, because it matters to the historian. . . ."[13]

While I hope I have not written to indoctrinate, this biography and the broader context of Asa Carter's life is important to me. But, because I am all too aware of the connections between my own values and my efforts to write about Asa Carter, I have stepped away from some of the guideposts that marked my life as an academic historian.

My first graduate school adviser always handed out his parody of Moses's Ten Commandments: "The Commandments of Clio, the Muse of History." William Hesseltine's list of do's and don'ts emphasized the rules of research and writing every professional historian should follow. The first commandment: "Thou shalt not use first-person pronouns—I, we, me, us, our—for they are an abomination to the Muse." Or as he put it in a scrawled red correction to one of my first graduate essays, "Learn to keep your hands under the table!"

Despite his warning, I have put aside what almost all historians now recognize as fiction: the belief that the role of omniscient narrator allows writers to separate their own assumptions and values from their work. In a way that I hope is not too intrusive, I have inserted some of my own experiences as I grew up in the same rural world of the pre-civil rights South where a regional culture that mixed kindness and cruelty shaped both my and Asa's lives.

"We may suspect that the voices we hear are an echo of our own, and the movement we see is our own shadow," said historical novelist Hilary Mantel. "But we sense the dead have a vital force still—they have something to tell us, something we need to understand."[14] For me, that conversation with voices past can become, as Leo Tolstoy said, a form of moral reflection. And the story of Asa Carter and the history he lived might also help us make choices about how we *should* live, even if it means exploring some of the darkest corners of our history.

Acknowledgments

In the years after I began intensive research on Asa Carter in 1996, I abandoned the project twice. Even though there have been lengthy interruptions in this journey, I have accumulated a long list of individuals who richly deserve my thanks. My apologies for omitting those whose names I may have forgotten.

In the late 1990s, at a time when the digitization of newspapers had scarcely begun, Virginia Shadron and Chris Lutz tediously scrolled through miles of census data, government records, and newspaper and magazine microfilm to uncover the public record of Asa/"Forrest" Carter. Virginia was particularly resourceful in collecting critical materials from courthouses and state archives. The detailed timeline they created helped me shape the initial structure of his story.

Cornelius ("Kees") van Minnen, then director of the Roosevelt Center in Middelberg, the Netherlands, arranged an idyllic semester in that beautiful old Dutch city, where I was able to begin my first efforts at writing an account of Carter's life.

"Whoever you are—I have always depended on the kindness of strangers," said Blanche DuBois in the last lines of *A Streetcar Named Desire.* It's a phrase I have come to know well as one individual after another has answered my emails and letters with a generosity that belies our cynical age.

In addition to my help from the Anniston-Calhoun County library staff, my friends Theresa Shadrix and Carol Puckett have responded to my last minute requests for research help in Alabama, while Josie Ayers, publisher of the *Anniston Star* (and long-time friend), has been a cheerleader on this project from the beginning.

Alec Marsh, who wrote *John Kasper and Ezra Pound,* not only responded to my questions but mailed me copies of the extensive correspondence he had collected between the two men. With equal generosity, Gary Sprayberry sent me research materials he had used for his excellent dissertation on Anniston, Alabama. And Laura Browder, author of a perceptive essay on Carter and co-producer of the documentary *The Reconstruction of Asa Carter*, put me in touch with Marco Ricci, the film's director. Marco excavated his attic files to find and send me the extensive video outtakes from the thirty-two individuals interviewed for the film. Garret Freymann-Weyr, David Kopel, John Green, and the family of Linda Sollinger took the time to locate and send photographs for the book. And when I visited Abilene, Texas, Taylor County Judge Samuel Matta reviewed the sealed investigation into Carter's 1979 death and then ingeniously managed to allow me access.

Among the many individuals I interviewed was filmmaker Mickey Grant. Just starting out in his career in the mid-1970s, he became the key figure in the ill-fated effort to film Carter's second book, *The Vengeance Trail of Josey Wales*. I was unable to do justice to the rich and darkly humorous story of his adventures, but I am grateful for the time he spent describing what could be its own documentary.

In searching for materials—particularly elusive photographs—these are only some of the individuals who swiftly responded: Amelia Chase, Meredith McDonough, and Ken Barr at the Alabama Department of Archives and History; Jim Baggett, head of the Archives at the Birmingham Public Library; Katelyn Morgan at the University of Minnesota Archives; Courtney Matthews at the Library of Congress; and the staff of the University of Tennessee Archives.

Two other libraries have been critical to my research:

Tom Mullins, head of the Anniston-Calhoun County library's Alabama Room collection, arranged for the donation of Fred Burger's research materials in 2018. Since then, Library Director Teresa Kiser, Linda Duke, Shane Spears, and Steven Barnett have generously tolerated my presence and responded to what others might see as unreasonable requests for special assistance.

And then there is the Transylvania County Library. When I renewed work on this book after I retired and moved to the small mountain town of Brevard, North Carolina, I feared that I would have to make regular three-hour trips to the University of South Carolina library in Columbia.

Instead, I learned why my hometown public library is considered one of the best in the state. Again, I hesitate to list those who have done so much to make my life easier, because almost everyone on the staff has assisted me at some point. But I particularly want to thank Director Rishara Finsel, Lisa Sheffield, Susan Chambers, Kris Blair, Laura Sperry, Hale Durant, and Marcia Thompson.

Over the years, a number of friends encouraged me to continue with this project when I became discouraged. I came to know Paul Stekler in the 1990s when we worked together on *Settin' the Woods on Fire,* his prize-winning documentary on Alabama Governor George Wallace. Over the years Paul has read drafts of troublesome sections and made suggestions while insisting that there was a story worth telling in the six file drawers of research and thousands of research files that seemed so overwhelming. Andy Delbanco, Tony Badger, Steve Channing, Elaina Plott Calabro, and my son David Carter also read portions of the manuscript and made helpful suggestions.

Once finished, I was extraordinarily fortunate to have the guiding hand of editor Randall Williams and publisher Suzanne La Rosa of NewSouth Books. I have had other editors, some of them very good, some less so, but none combined Randall's superb copyediting skills, his eye for chronology and details, and his broad knowledge of the history of this era. He and reader Joel Sanders improved the manuscript and repeatedly saved me from embarrassment.

I will never be able to express my deepest thanks for the contribution of Fred Burger. Over the years, Fred worked as a journalist at a number of newspapers including the *Miami Herald,* but he spent the last part of his career as a reporter at the *Anniston Star.* Like me, he was fascinated with Asa Carter, and I knew that he was working on a biography on the one occasion we met. It could have been an awkward conversation; it wasn't. Like many of his friends, I was stunned to receive news in 2018 that Fred—only sixty-eight—had unexpectedly died. In the following months, his brother John arranged to have all of Fred's research materials donated to the Anniston-Calhoun County Library. In an example of extraordinary generosity, John encouraged me to use his late brother's materials in my book. Because of my role in exposing Asa Carter's true background, I had never been able to persuade any of Carter's family or close friends to speak with me. But my discovery in Fred's collection of more than two hundred hours of cassette recordings of interviews, including several with Asa's two brothers, his sister-in-law, and a niece and nephew, finally convinced me that I could finish Burger's story.

I have dedicated this book to Fred's memory. I hope the final result does justice to the gift I was given.

And then there is Jane. No one has lived with this project as long as my wife. Ignoring my whines and complaints, she encouraged me as she read my drafts, corralling wandering antecedents and removing inappropriate metaphors with only a lifted eyebrow. And a ruthless red pen. How lucky I am to have her as my editor and my lifelong soul mate.

~

Photo Sources

Except as noted, all images are from the holdings of the Alabama Department of Archives and History.

Chapter 1: Page *7*, William Luke Grave Marker courtesy of David Hamilton, Dan T. Carter Research Collection, hereafter cited as DC; ***9***, Main Street, Anniston, Alabama, 1910, Public Library of Anniston-Calhoun County, Alabama, hereinafter cited as PLAC; ***11***, Asa Carter and Childhood Home, Fred Burger Research Collection, PLAC, hereafter cited as FBRC; ***13***, Anniston 1941 Street Scene, PLAC; ***14***, Oxford Football Team, 1941, Oxford High 1943 Yearbook, DC Collection; ***15***, Asa Carter Photo, Oxford High 1943 Yearbook, DC Collection. **Chapter 2:** ***17***, Thomas Nast Cartoons, Library of Congress Prints and Photographs, hereinafter cited as LCPP; ***23***, Asa Carter Photo, FBRC; ***24***, USS Appling, US Navy Photo, DC Collection; ***25***, Calisphere Bar Photo, UC San Diego Special Collections and Archives; ***28***, Landing Craft, US Navy Photo, DC Collection; ***32***, Gerald L. K. Smith with supporters,

University, Bentley Historical Library, University of Michigan; 37, Nagasaki Photo, FBRC. **CHAPTER 3:** ***41***, John Rath Photo, University of Minnesota Library Archives; ***41***, Asa Carter Photo, FBRC; ***47***, Jerry Kopel, courtesy of David Kopel, DC Collection; ***50***, KKK Denver March, LCPP; ***51***, Asa Carter Photo, FBRC. **CHAPTER 4:** ***57***, Fulton J. Lewis Photo, Alamy; **CHAPTER 5:** ***69***, Birth of a Nation Poster, DC Collection; ***69***, Black Legislators in *Birth of a Nation,* screenshot, DC Collection; ***72***, Nathan Bedford Forrest Photo, LCPP. **CHAPTER 6:** ***85***, Thomas Brady Photo, McCain Library and Archives, the University of Southern Mississippi; 88, James Eastland Photo, LCPP. **CHAPTER 7:** ***110***, J. B. Stoner, Florida Photographic Collection, State Archives of Florida; ***119***, Autherine Lucy, DC Collection; ***122***, Students Protesting, LCPP; ***126***, John Crommelin Photo, DC Collection. **CHAPTER 9:** ***147***, Nat King Cole Trio Photo, *Billboard Magazine*; ***153***, Nat King Cole Photo, DC Collection; ***159***, John Kasper Photo, DC Collection; ***159***, Ezra Pound Photo, US Army Photo; ***165***, Sarah Patton Boyle Photo, Courtesy of Family. **CHAPTER 10:** ***168***, African American Students at Clinton High, Alamy; ***169***, John Kasper Photo, DC Collection; ***172*** Asa Carter Photo, University of Tennessee, Knoxville, Libraries; ***174***, Mob attacking car with Black passengers, LCPP. **CHAPTER 12:** ***198***, Carter Family Photo, DC Collection; ***201***, Fred Shuttlesworth Mug Shot, DC Collection. **CHAPTER 16:** ***264***, Robert Shelton, DC Collection. **CHAPTER 17:** ***283***, Sam Bowers Photo, Mississippi Department of Archives and History; ***287***, Asa Carter Screen Shot, 1970 Television Commercial, DC Collection. **CHAPTER 19:** ***313***, "Forrest" Carter Photo, DC Collection; ***314***, Don Josey Photo, Courtesy Family of Linda Sollinger; ***318***, Rhoda Weyr Photo, courtesy of Garrett Weyr. **CHAPTER 20:** ***328***, Eleanor Kask Friede Photo, DC Collection; ***331***, "Forrest" Carter Photo, DC Collection; ***332***, "Forrest Carter" book signing Photo, FB. **CHAPTER 21:** ***340***, Barbara Walters and Frank McGee, Screen Capture of The Today Show, DC Collection. **CHAPTER 22:** ***357***, Louise Green Photo, courtesy of John Green; ***363***, "Forrest" Carter Photo, DC Collection. **CODA:** ***389***, publicity still from *The Outlaw Josey Wales*, DC Collection.

UNMASKING THE KLANSMAN

1

'The Past Is Never Past'

All of us labor in webs spun long before we were born, webs of heredity and environment, of desire and consequence, of history and eternity. Haunted by wrong turns and roads not taken, we pursue images perceived as new but whose providence dates to the dim dramas of childhood, which are themselves but ripples of consequence echoing down the generations.

— Greg Isles[15]

Asa Carter. Born, September 4, 1925, D'Armanville, Calhoun County, Alabama.

His mother, Hermione, had been a Weatherly, her mother, a Pinson, names that reached back to the first pioneers of eastern Alabama. In March of 1834, Hermione's great-great-grandparents, Joseph and Mary Pinson, loaded a covered wagon with a few pieces of furniture and their most treasured family possession, the family Bible, as they headed west through Georgia and into north Alabama on the Great Wagon Road. Joseph Pinson's father, a Revolutionary War veteran, had received a small land grant from the federal government in the 1780s, but as the younger son, Joseph saw little future working on his father's farm in upcountry South Carolina. Their journey reflected the steady migration of white and enslaved Americans as they moved westward from the depleted soils of Virginia, the Carolinas, and Georgia bound for Alabama, Mississippi, Louisiana, and east Texas, into lands occupied for centuries by the Cherokees, Chickasaws, Choctaws, and Creeks.[16]

During that same spring of 1834, the English-born geographer George Featherstonhaugh traveled eastward along one of the many trails that ended in Alabama and Mississippi. Day after day, he met an almost unbroken train of wagons, many containing the families of planters, as they lurched over the rutted roads and forded stream after stream. Enslaved women and their small children sat in packed wagons while following behind were hundreds of male slaves soaked from wading across streams and shallow rivers, "shivering with cold . . . trudging on foot and worn down with fatigue."[17] In two short decades from 1820 to 1840, Alabama's white population would grow from less than 100,000 to 335,000, while the enslaved population increased to 250,000.[18]

Southern politicians and ardent defenders of slavery saw this migration as their own version of Manifest Destiny, a hedge against the western movement of settlers into the new free states of the North. Like many white emigrants, Pinson sought to better his condition and, if possible, to acquire slaves and land.

Eighteenth- and early nineteenth-century treaties forced the Creeks to cede millions of acres to the wave of white settlers, and the 1832 Treaty of Cusseta ended the communal structure of Indian settlements. It did allocate some of their remaining land to "chiefs" (320 acres) and heads of households (160 acres) who remained in the new state. As usual, such promises proved fleeting as waves of land-hungry whites pressed in on the new Creek and Cherokee landowners.

Three months after the treaty-signing, twenty-six-year-old Joseph Pinson stopped in a fertile field southeast of present-day Anniston, Alabama, met with several Creeks and bought some six hundred acres for a bag of thirty silver dollars.[19] With prices for former Indian land selling for an average of three dollars an acre, Pinson purchased his farmland for a fraction of its actual worth.[20]

Just six years after Joseph Pinson purchased his farm, President Andrew Jackson's administration ignored the treaty and ordered the expulsion of Alabama's fifteen thousand remaining Creeks on the grounds of "military necessity." In January 1839, the great American naturalist and painter James Audubon traveled through Alabama on horseback, moving past more than two thousand Creek men, women, and children walking along, wading barefoot across icy streams under an escort of armed militia, "destined for distant and unknown lands," he wrote in his diary, "where their future and latter days must be spent in the deepest of sorrows . . ." A handful of Creeks evaded capture and remained in Alabama. Most were forced to join the thirty thousand Cherokees, Choctaws, Chickasaws, and Seminoles in the infamous "Trail of Tears" that stretched twelve hundred miles from western North Carolina to Fort Gibson, Oklahoma.[21]

By the time he died of tuberculosis in 1852, Pinson—like many of these new emigrants—had become a substantial landowner with more than ninety slaves. Hermione Carter's Weatherly ancestors on her father's side were equally prosperous mid-level slave owners with several hundred acres of cotton land.[22]

It was rich soil, but a harsh land. The 1930s slave narrative project undertaken during the New Deal collected more than two thousand interviews from elderly former slaves who had come of age before the Civil War. Like prisoners in a gulag, enslaved African Americans recalled their years as chattel. They developed a keen sense of the differences among those who held them in bondage. "Good masters" avoided or minimized the lash and treated them with some degree of humanity. "Bad masters" seemed to take pleasure in reaching for the cat o' nine tails at the slightest real or imagined provocation. But all of the enslaved men and women knew full well the difference between slavery and freedom.

And after emancipation, they lacked even the protection of their value as property.

Lynching is often associated with the late nineteenth century, but the thousands who died at the hands of whites during that period were part of the continuum of violence in the post-war years. During the Reconstruction era, vigilantes led by the Ku Klux Klan directed much of that violence against Black political activists and their white allies. The large white majority in Calhoun County allowed whites to maintain control of county offices, but bitterness over the creation of a biracial government in Montgomery and concern over what was seen as the growing assertiveness of newly enfranchised Black male voters strengthened the commitment of whites to maintaining absolute supremacy. Calhoun and surrounding counties became the home of numerous Klan "klaverns" that joined in a statewide campaign of violent white resistance.[23]

Many of these acts went unreported, but in 1870 the county became notorious as the site of a mass lynching that attracted national attention and a hearing before Congress, probably because it involved a white Northerner. In 1869, Canadian Methodist minister William Luke had traveled south and settled just outside the small village of Cross Plains (now Piedmont, Alabama) in Calhoun County, north of Asa Carter's birthplace. Luke felt a sacred calling to "lift up" the former slaves through education, and with the financial support of the Northern owners of the Selma, Rome and Dalton Railroad, he set up a one-room school for emancipated children. Even though he avoided discussing politics, rumors spread that he had publicly preached racial equality and other heretical Yankee doctrines. He became aware of the growing hostility of local whites when unknown gunmen fired into the small house where he boarded with a Black family. Whites spurned him and he suffered the isolation shared by almost all Northern educational missionaries who traveled to the South. These teachers, said the editor of the *Montgomery Advertiser*, were drawn from "a class of people destitute either of money, character, or virtue . . ."

Still, Luke persisted, confident that he was "about my Father's business."[24]

In mid July of that year, a fight on the streets of Cross Plains escalated to a brief but pitched exchange of gunfire between more than a dozen Black and white participants. While no one was injured and the Black gunmen fled, rumors spread that a mob of local Black men were planning an assault on the sleepy little village. After deputizing several dozen whites to safeguard the hamlet, Cross Plains magistrate "Major" Andrew Bailey, a former Confederate officer, arrested Jacob Moore, Tony Cliff, Berry Harris, Caesar Frederick, and William Hall, accusing them of provoking the gunfight.

Although Luke had not been involved, he felt obligated to represent the Black defendants in a hastily arranged hearing. In the raucous interview that followed, Luke became the object of the interrogation. He admitted that he had purchased pistols for several Black farmers in the county who had been threatened by the KKK and, while he denied any teachings of social equality, he acknowledged that he believed Blacks and whites were equal in God's eyes. Equally damaging was his admission that he had told Black wage earners and farmers they should ask to be paid the same as whites.

By midnight more than fifty hooded Klansmen had gathered from nearby klaverns. They brushed Magistrate Bailey aside, roping together and dragging Luke, Cliff, Harris, Frederick, and Hall through the unpaved main street of Cross Plains and down the road to an oak grove on the grounds of a small church. There, one by one, the Klansmen hanged the four Black men.

Surrounded by burning torches, William Luke pleaded to be allowed to write a final letter to his wife. As Luke began to scrawl his farewell, two of the four hanged men continued to struggle at the end of their ropes and Klansmen stepped forward, placed pistols at the back of their heads and administered the *coup de grâce*.

Luke began his brief note on a piece of paper he had found in his coat pocket. "I die tonight," he wrote his wife:

> It has been so determined by those who think I deserve it. God only knows I feel myself entirely innocent of the charge. I have only sought to educate the negro. I little thought when leaving you that we should thus part forever so far distant from each other.

William Luke's body was retrieved the next day and taken by wagon fifty miles south to the newly created black Talladega College where he had briefly worked. After Luke's funeral on the campus, he was buried in the black section of Talladega's Oak Hill Cemetery. The graves of the six black men killed by the Klan are unmarked.

But God's will be done . . . God of mercy bless and keep you ever dear, dear wife and children. Your William.

He struggled at the end of a rope for several minutes before death. His murderers cut him down and laid him out on the ground, side by side with the men he had sought to defend.[25] Not satisfied with the lynching at Cross Plains, Klansmen hanged Essex Hendricks and Green Little, two other Black locals suspected of taking part in the original brawl.

While most newspapers in Alabama and surrounding Deep South states ignored the Black victims, they went out of their way to justify the hanging of Luke. As Georgia's *Rome Daily* concluded, Luke was a "fanatic of the deepest dye" who had provoked local "negroes" against the white people of the community. He deserved his fate.[26]

After Alabama's Reconstruction government collapsed in 1874, the list of Black lynching victims grew in Calhoun County: John Brooks, in 1882, John Jones in 1890, Jack Brownlee in 1894, John Calloway in 1898, Bunk Richardson in 1906, and other African American men whose names were never published.[27] Their alleged crimes? Engaging in politics, "assaulting" a white man, attempted rape, robbery, attempted murder, and "sassing" a white landowner."

Between 1870 and 1906, Calhoun County, with less than 1 percent of the state's Black population, was responsible for 5 percent of the recorded lynchings in the state, a much higher percentage than any of the five surrounding counties.[28]

The more respectable town-folk of Anniston—which became the largest town in the county in the late nineteenth century—privately acknowledged the regrettable tendency of rural folk to take the law into their own hands, but they saw themselves as a world apart from the raw countryside. The post-Civil War creation of Samuel Noble, an English-born ironmaster and Union General Daniel Taylor, Anniston—called "The Model City"—became the home of a carefully planned community with paved, tree-lined streets, well-built worker-cottages, a library, schools, and churches for its work force. The Woodstock Corporation created in 1872 succeeded beyond the expectations of its founders, becoming a widely publicized symbol of the

Anniston, Alabama, 1910.

possibilities of Southern industrialization. Within a decade, the foundry was in full production and the corporation soon built the largest cotton mill in Alabama to employ the wives and children of the ironworkers.

The foundry and the cotton mill restricted the relatively small number of Black workers to the lowest paying jobs, but Noble and Tyler supported the "sober and progressive elements" within the community in establishing a Black school in 1885. They constructed housing that, albeit segregated, was little different from that of whites. The historian of the town's founding aptly described their attitudes as a blend of "*noblesse oblige* and paternalism." However patronizing, it seemed preferable to the brutal suppression of Black lives that characterized much of the state's political leadership.[29] No wonder Henry Grady, the editor of the *Atlanta Constitution,* tirelessly promoted Anniston as a model for his vision of a New South that had turned its back on the past and marched into a new and prosperous industrial age.

After 1900, an open defense of lynch law declined, at least by respectable citizens, but even though the most violent of these events happened before Asa Carter was born in 1925, he came to adulthood in a culture steeped in white violence, much of it directed toward one goal: guaranteeing absolute Black subordination.

The considerable wealth of the Weatherly and Pinson families slipped away in the years that followed, diminished by the war, emancipation, recurring post-war agricultural recessions and repeated land subdivision among succeeding generations. By 1916, Asa Carter's Weatherly grandparents still owned several hundred acres and tenaciously clung to their standing as descendants of the first families of the county, but they could no longer claim a life of leisure. In 1917, with America mobilizing for war and many of the young men off to training camps, Asa's mother, Hermione, found a position as a "sales lady" in a dry goods store in Oxford, population fourteen hundred.

Three years later, she met Ralph Carter, a lanky, handsome twenty-year-old whose ancestry lacked the romance of her background. His great-grandparents and grandparents were part of the great Scotch-Irish migration that drifted southwestward from Pennsylvania across the Carolinas, through Georgia and into Alabama in the nineteenth century. Ralph Carter's grandfather, William Carter, acquired a small farm in Calhoun County, Georgia, in the 1850s, but sometime between 1880 and 1890, he lost his land and became a sharecropper. His son, Edwin (or "Wales" as he was more commonly called), moved to Alabama in the late 1890s. He and his wife, Josie, settled in Anniston, where Wales worked as an agricultural day laborer on nearby farms. To survive, the Carters rented two of their three bedrooms to boarders while the family slept in the remaining bedroom, the lean-to porch, and on pallets in the parlor.[30]

In the spring of 1921, Ralph Carter and Hermione exchanged wedding vows, but there was no church wedding. Without family members present, they drove to Anniston in a farm wagon where a Justice of the Peace performed the ceremony. Ralph, who had attended school less than six months, carefully signed the marriage license, but even though he seemed to have an instinctive mastery of his "sums," he could neither read nor write. In a phrase commonly used among class-conscious white Southerners, Hermione had "married down."

Seven-year-old Asa Carter. Above, his new childhood home.

Through the 1920s, the couple struggled to make ends meet as their family grew: first a daughter Marie (1924) and then Asa (1925). While Hermione remained a stay-at-home mother, Ralph raised cotton as a small tenant farmer just outside Oxford even as he spent long hours as a day laborer in nearby Anniston. With the patient tutoring of his wife, he mastered his ABC's well enough to read scripture aloud at the D'Armanville Methodist Church which the family religiously attended. And he gained the admiration of those who knew him for his ability to repair any equipment from a hay baler to a farm tractor.[31]

In 1931, when Asa was six years old and Marie eight, the death of Hermione's father transformed their lives. J. W. Weatherly left to his only daughter a sixty-acre piece of the old family farm that included the house he had built after World War I. In the years that followed, the Carters had two more sons, Douglas (1932) and Larry (1938). Ralph, a workaholic, developed a small dairy operation, worked forty hours a week as a driver for a soft-drink plant in Anniston, and opened a small country store. By the impoverished standards of Depression Alabama, the Carters were middle class when Asa moved from his rural elementary school to the "town" high school just a few miles away in the small village of Oxford.

Like all rural farm boys, Asa Carter had his list of chores, but the surrounding community offered ample diversions in his free time. Oxford lay at the foothills of the Appalachian Mountains in northeastern Alabama, half-way between Birmingham and Atlanta. Main Street offered a dry goods store, grocery, barber shop, and a handful of other stores frequented by local farmers. While train service had come to the larger nearby town of Anniston in the 1870s, as late as 1925 Oxford's streets ended at the city boundary with unpaved and often impassable roads stretching in every direction. But by the time Asa attended Oxford High in 1940, a string of newly paved highways heavily funded by Franklin Roosevelt's New Deal stretched east and west, north and south.

In the midst of the Great Depression, the federal government purchased nearly four hundred thousand acres around the town to create the Talladega National Forest, which became a favorite hunting area for locals. And despite the town's small size, an Oxford entrepreneur had converted the 1892 Knights of Pythias Lodge into a movie house, admission fifteen cents or twenty cents on weekends when viewers could typically see such double features as a Tom Mix cowboy film and a Tarzan adventure.[32]

In the months after Pearl Harbor, dozens of young area men signed up (or were soon drafted) into the military. Even as America's role in the war grew, however, it had little direct impact on the lives of locals beyond a boost to the regional economy. For high school teenagers, there was a fifteen-hundred-acre lake just outside Oxford where an enterprising developer built a park and "entertainment" center similar to the dozens of rural private parks developed near towns and cities in the late nineteenth century, often at the end of a street car or rail line. The boat house with rental canoes, a roped-off area for swimming, a merry-go-round, a race track, and an "opera house" featuring occasional vaudeville acts drew customers from miles away as well as soldiers from a nearby army training center.

Just six miles away and a fifteen-minute ride on the Dixie Coach line, Anniston offered even more entertainment: two five-and-dime stores as well as several department stores, two movie theaters, and three soda shops where teenagers gathered in the late afternoons. For those who lived in Oxford and the surrounding rural areas, however, Anniston might as well have been a day's ride away. It was "town"; they were "country." One of Asa's high school friends recalled the one attraction that sometimes drew his classmates to the town of twenty-five thousand: bellhops at a downtown hotel who offered bonded whiskey to the teenagers in a county where prohibition remained the law until the 1960s.

But there was always something to drink closer to home. Bootleggers openly sold white lightning for two dollars a pint outside the dance hall in Oxford. Even more affordable was the home-brewed beer made from ground corn which Asa and his friends mixed with yeast and brown sugar in five-gallon batches and let "age" for a week before they gathered in outbuildings for a weekend of drinking. It was a perilous enterprise for Asa. As his younger brother Larry recalled, "Mama could have been Carrie Nation." She hated

Anniston street scene, 1941.

alcohol because of the problems it had caused in her husband's family and repeatedly warned her sons that there would be dire consequences if they touched a drop of alcohol. "I was really scared of what might happen," said Larry. "I was probably twenty-seven or twenty-eight years old before I had a drink." For Asa and his brother, Doug, however, the weekend drinking sessions began their long struggles with alcoholism.[33]

None of these problems seemed obvious in Asa's early years. Academically, he had always seemed a cut above many of his fellow students and from elementary school on he effortlessly led the school honor roll. He wasn't particularly "bookish," his younger brother said. "But Bud [Asa] could wait till the morning when a report was due, get up early, write it out quickly, and get an A."[34] The only discussion of politics or current events that his classmate Margaret Ruhle could recall was in history class when their teacher would assign readings about world events, particularly as the war progressed in 1942 and 1943. Asa, she said, was always knowledgeable in class discussion. And she never heard him make any racial remarks. "I was just shocked when I [later] saw the things in the paper that he did."[35]

At Oxford High School, he was a class officer and leader and particularly popular among his coed classmates who were attracted to the darkly

Carter, circled at center, in his first year on his school's football team.

Carter, as high school senior.

handsome Carter. In the fall of 1941—his first year in high school—he tried out for the school's football team and made varsity despite the fact that he was still relatively small at age fifteen. Playing right end, his speed and aggressive play compensated for his lack of height. Although he suffered a serious knee injury half-way through the season and had to sit out the final five games, he had played enough to gain a coveted varsity jacket. With a growth spurt over the next year that saw him shoot up to 5'10", he became a key member of the team and a natural leader. In his last year in high school, fellow players elected him co-captain.

He was equally successful as the leading man in his high school's drama productions. His senior year he played a handsome young doctor in *Who's Crazy Now*, a typical 1930s farce designed for high school actors. Carter was the idealistic director of an "insane asylum" who decided to have several of his patients—former school teachers—educate other inmates who were only marginally more disturbed.[36] Years later a classmate remembered little of the play except the striking ease of Carter whose poised delivery seemed "like a real Hollywood actor" in comparison to his fellow cast members.[37]

When Carter attended public school in the late 1930s and early '40s, Alabama required that all students take two years of state history. In the fourth grade, Carter, like all Alabama elementary students, read *Know Alabama,* a text coauthored by the distinguished Vanderbilt historian, Frank Owsley. *Know Alabama* depicted the history of antebellum slavery through the eyes of a white child living on a plantation, reared by a "loyal Mammy." Kindly masters made slavery a "joyous institution" in a format that seemed to have been plucked directly from the more benign stories of Joel Chandler Harris's "Uncle Remus."[38]

For high school students, there was a much more extended and overtly political account of racial issues. In 1934 University of Alabama history professor Albert Burton Moore published an 834-page textbook summary of his massive three-volume *History of Alabama* (1927). It remained Alabama's high school state history text for the next forty years.[39]

Beneath mind-numbing historical minutiae, Moore constructed a defense of white supremacy that rested upon the foundation of the Old South. For Moore, antebellum white Southerners had created a racial peaceable kingdom in which slavery was an idyllic relationship administered by kindly paternal slave-owners. Moore wrote that owners' families treated their slaves as though they were members of the family, who were well cared for by physicians when ill and maintained in old age after they became too feeble to work in the fields.[40]

All was well until the tragic "War Between the States." To Moore, the conflict that consumed the lives of six hundred thousand men North and South, (more than thirty-five thousand from Alabama) had nothing to do with slavery; it was a conflict based upon "constitutional principles."[41] In the wake of Confederate defeat, a vengeful North not only emancipated the slaves, but, with the help of a few turncoat "scalawag" Southerners and greedy Northern "carpetbaggers," placed ignorant and uneducated Black people in power over a prostrate people. For the next decade, whites in Alabama witnessed the spectacle of a society suddenly turned "bottom side up" in which brutal and corrupt regimes humiliated whites as they looted the state.

Fortunately, Moore explained to his young readers, proud former Confederate soldiers refused to accept the "degradation and galling despotism" of Black domination. Together they rose and created the Ku Klux Klan a "regulator of society for the protection of women and children and property." Ultimately, the Klan reestablished white control of the state. And once the North had tired of its foolish efforts to elevate the freedmen to political equality, said Moore, whites passed laws that "relieved the State of an incubus of ignorance and vice" by disenfranchising the Black voters of Alabama.[42]

Once Black Alabamians had been safely removed from politics, they held little interest to Moore. "The political slogan of the white counties—'This is a white man's country'—was in a large sense as true of the economic life

The term "carpetbagger" is widely attributed to the editor of the Montgomery Advertiser. *The racist cartoons here, by* Harper's *Thomas Nast, who had originally supported Reconstruction, were widely distributed and sometimes reprinted in regional textbooks.*

of the State as it was of its politics," said Moore, who argued that Alabama's Black residents were destined to play "relatively an insignificant role in the up-building of the State."[43]

Distinguished national historians who wrote the textbooks of the era, men like John Hicks, Samuel Eliot Morison, Thomas Bailey, and Henry Steele Commager—all non-Southerners—shared Moore's distorted rendering of Southern history. They also spoke disparagingly, if not quite so crudely, of Black suffrage, depicted the Reconstruction era through the eyes of conservative white Southerners, and attributed only the basest motives to advocates of equal rights. The white South may have surrendered at Appomattox, but over the decades that followed, white Southerners won the war of memory, a vision of the Southern past made holy by white Southerners' dedication to the memory of the Lost Cause and redeemed in history by the "unsurpassed sacrifice and heroism of the Southern armies and civilian population—the proudest and most sacred tradition of the South . . ."[44]

However cruel and demeaning these official state histories were to Black children and teenagers, for most white students the history textbooks of the period were as interesting as telephone directories, significant only because they reflected as much as they shaped white Southerners' sense of their past. Outside the classroom, films, popular fiction, "patriotic" celebrations, hundreds of Confederate monuments constructed in the late nineteenth and early twentieth century, the street, school and building names of Southern towns and cities, even oft-hand conversations: all these shaped the mental landscape of the white South. That collective memory of Yankee perfidy, Confederate bravery, and Black degeneracy eased the sting of defeat, poverty, and backwardness even as it justified the daily cruelties of white supremacy and Black oppression. Asa Carter did not need to read a boring high school textbook to embrace a mythical past that white Southerners created.

And neither did I. The universe in which I lived as a child and a teenager was still that of the segregated South though I use the term "segregated" fully aware of the irony of the word. It was certainly an oppressive culture that relegated Blacks to the bottom rung of every economic ladder and barred them by law from the schools of my childhood and by ruthlessly enforced

custom from the ballot box of my community. But it was hardly segregated. I saw, talked with, played with (and occasionally fought) Black children from the time I can remember. Beginning the summer I was nine, I worked five days a week in the tobacco fields, side by side with Black men and women and girls and boys of my own age.

Still, there were disquieting moments. In the summer of 1952, I traveled to Charleston on a Greyhound bus for a week's visit with one of my favorite aunts. As we rolled through the flat land just east of Lake City, an older Black woman hailed the bus, and from a tightly bound handkerchief she carefully counted out the fare for her granddaughter (I presume) to ride to a small town less than thirty miles away. As we drove away, I watched in surprise as the eight- or nine-year-old girl tentatively sat down on the front seat of the nearly empty bus across from me. At first the driver did not see her; when he did, he gruffly mumbled "move on back." Either she didn't hear, or she didn't understand the taboo she had violated. When she remained seated, he suddenly pulled the bus to the side of the road, stood up, and towered over her: "I told you to move to the back of the bus," he shouted. Paralyzed with fear, she remained in her seat, crying softly. From the back of the bus an older and poorly dressed Black man moved up the aisle and gently took her hand: "Come on back here with me, honey," he said. Until she got off the bus thirty minutes later, I sat with eyes carefully averted as I heard her sobbing slowly subside. I remember this as vividly as anything from my childhood. My indignation, however, was not against a system that allowed such brutalities, but against the driver's bad manners. Even as a twelve-year-old, I knew that we were supposed to be "polite to colored people."

If Asa Carter absorbed the traditional racial views of his generation, there was little to suggest that politics concerned him or that he obsessed over matters of race during his childhood and early adolescence. John Jackson, a Black playmate from a nearby farm, recalled playing with him and several other whites during his youth. He could not ever remember "Bud," as Carter was called, denigrating him because he was Black. And almost every classmate *Anniston Star* reporter Fred Burger interviewed seemed surprised, even shocked, when told details of Carter's violent political activities in the

1950s. His classmates agreed that he was popular with girls, a talented actor in the school plays, and, in the words of one of his friends, the "smartest person in the class" who always made straight A's. None of the five classmates Burger interviewed could remember Carter ever expressing strong opinions on any subject except sports.[45]

Most white Southerners who grew up during these years did not become fanatical racists and ideologues, but the lessons of childhood were always in the background: Blacks were a child-like race that could never equal that of whites, and any attempt to rise above their place was a threat, one made more dangerous by the rise of outside agitators who sought to undermine the delicate balance of a society dominated by whites.

"Nothing in all creation is hidden from God's sight," wrote the unknown author of the New Testament book of Hebrews. "Everything is uncovered and exposed before the eyes of Him to whom we must give account." But in the absence of such omniscience we can never be certain about the forces that led Asa Carter into a life of deceit, violence, and deeply rooted ideological racism. We can only be satisfied with James Boswell's observation to his friend Samuel Johnson: "Men's hearts are concealed. But their actions are open to scrutiny."

2

The Critical Years: 1943–46

"The South will never free itself from the bondage of the political mongrelizers until it realizes that behind the mongrelizers stand the Jews . . . Anyone knows that the poor Negro is not smart enough or natively evil enough to be victorious over us."

— Gerald L. K. Smith[46]

"The satanic-plot to mix the blood of White Christian People of the South with Negroes is directed and financed by the Jewish-Communist conspiracy; . . . the ultimate objective of the Communist-Jewish conspirators is to use their world-wide control of money to destroy Christianity and set up a world Government in the framework of the United nations and erase all national boundaries and eliminate all racial distinction except the so-called Jewish race, which will then become the master race with headquarters in the state of Israel and in the United Nations in New York and from these to communication centers rule a slave like world population of copper-colored human mongrels. This is the Messianic dream of a Communist-Zionist Jews, but it is the unspeakable nightmare of the great White Christian Race."

— Rear Admiral John Crommelin (ret.)[47]

In mid-May of 1943 Asa Earl Carter joined forty-seven classmates as he graduated from Oxford High School in northeast Alabama. Like all healthy young men, Carter knew he had only two choices: enlistment or the draft. By that spring, the unbroken train of Axis victories had come to an end. In early February the Soviet Union had surrounded and destroyed Germany's 6th Army at Stalingrad while British, Commonwealth, and newly arrived American troops turned back General Erwin Rommel's three-year campaign to seize the Suez Canal and Egypt's rich oil fields. Six months earlier, America's Pacific fleet had inflicted a devastating defeat on the Japanese at the Battle of Midway. But Germany still controlled most of Europe, and even though American and allied forces in the Pacific inflicted heavy losses on Japanese air and naval forces, the successful but bloody assault on the island of Guadalcanal in the late winter of 1942 left thousands of American marines, soldiers, and sailors dead and wounded, twenty-nine ships sunk, and 615 aircraft destroyed. The war was far from over.

With his athletic and academic background and demonstrated leadership, Carter applied for admission to the first class of the Navy's V-12 officer training program. His selection to the demanding program brought pride to Oxford's tight-knit white community. The Daughters of the American Revolution began their June meeting with a tribute to Carter, reciting the DAR prize-winning poem "Old Glory" Asa had written shortly after the outbreak of the war, containing the line, "All hail the flag of glory, stained by the blood of heroes. . . ."[48]

On June 15, Ralph Carter rose before dawn to avoid the ninety-four degree midday heat and drove his son westward from Oxford sixty-five miles along old Highway 78 through the small marketing towns of Eastaboga, Lincoln, Cook Springs, Leeds, and on to Alabama's largest city, Birmingham. There Asa joined more than seven hundred young men as they officially enlisted in the Army, Navy and Marines before boarding buses and trains for training camps across the nation. For Carter, it was a short train ride to New Orleans for two weeks of orientation and then to the campus of Mississippi College, a small struggling Baptist school just west of Jackson, the state capital.

The Navy's daunting challenge was to condense more than two years of training into eight months to prepare 125,000 junior naval officers for the expanding US fleet in the Pacific and the Atlantic. Like the five hundred other candidates at Mississippi College, Carter began his training with a grueling thirty-day boot camp in the blistering July heat, run by Marine

Corps drill instructors who, one V-12 candidate later claimed, had been "trained in hell." After that first month, the physical regimen dropped from thirty to fifteen hours a week, but the candidates then faced seventeen hours a week of classes taught by military as well as civilian instructors. Those who successfully completed the first four months went on to four more months of classroom instruction before receiving their commissions as Navy ensigns and reporting for additional training before shipping out.[49]

But in early November, Mississippi College's V-12 director assembled Carter and forty other candidates and briskly informed them they had failed to qualify for the last half of the program. The great majority of the students had at least some college, and many came from stronger academic backgrounds than Carter. As his brother would later recall, "you're talking about a seventeen-year-old boy off the farm intimidated by more sophisticated and better-educated classmates."[50]

At the small Oxford High School (which ended after eleven years) there had been no courses beyond basic algebra and geometry. In the V-12 program, Carter repeatedly failed tests in the advanced algebra curriculum necessary for graduation. Under pressure, he began drinking heavily, and after two episodes in which he was found too drunk to attend classes, instructors showed little interest in reassigning him to remedial classes. He had left home the pride of Oxford, but when he returned for a short break before his reassignment to the enlisted Navy, the "Oxford Personal" column in the local newspaper described his return in one sentence: "Asa Carter, U.S.N.R., from Mississippi College, Clinton, Miss., is visiting his parents, Mr. and Mrs. Ralph Carter."[51]

Seaman 3rd Class Carter, 1943.

He would remain a Seaman Third Class for the remainder of his service.

Despite his V-12 washout, he applied for and received a coveted spot

The USS Appling, *August 1944.*

in the Navy's radio operator training program based at the University of Colorado, one of dozens of such sites scattered across the country. Mastering the mechanics of Morse Code required an ability to tap out the dots and dashes for each letter of the alphabet at a speed of at least sixty words a minute, a challenge which the majority of would-be operators failed to meet.[52] Carter proved extremely proficient, consistently earning an "excellent" rating in his training and performance while at sea.

NINE MONTHS LATER HE traveled to the Long Beach, California, Naval Base. He had looked forward to serving aboard one of the fighting destroyers, cruisers, battleships, and aircraft carriers. Instead, the Navy assigned him to the newly commissioned *USS Appling*, an unglamorous four thousand-ton ship designed to transport troops to combat zones in the Pacific. After a final fitting, the ship began training cruises in the huge San Diego harbor.[53]

The *Appling* proved to be a floating lemon. When Lieutenant Commander Alexander Stuart assumed command in August 1944, he found a thirty-page list of major construction and mechanical deficiencies. For the next month, the crew waited while workmen frantically sought to make the ship seaworthy. Even after repairs, the first shakedown cruise in September ended ignominiously when the main engine seized and the ship had to be towed seventy miles back to port. Commander Stuart responded stoically, according to a sailor who was on the bridge at the time. His chief engineer did not: "After two years in the Navy, I thought I had a pretty good vocabulary of cuss words," an engine room mechanic recalled. "But listening to the chief, I realized I was a pure amateur."[54]

During the 1990s, *Anniston Star* reporter Fred Burger located and interviewed more than a dozen of the 325 seamen from the *Appling*. Only two remembered Carter. Willis Robertson, a career seaman and one of the fourteen radio operators on the ship, vividly recalled several of his fellow radiomen, including a couple of Texans who were bigger (and louder) than life. But he never had more than a few words with Carter. The young Alabama sailor was tall and dark, recalled Robertson. Most of all, he remembered that "Ace" had been quiet, even withdrawn.[55]

One shipmate did come to know Carter. Radiomen generally had little to do with the "bilge rats" who worked in the engine room, but early in his deployment on the *Appling,* Gordon Lackey struck up a friendship with Carter. Lackey was a "nut buster" (mechanic) in the boiler room, a place that was, as he described it, "dirty, noisy and hot as hell." The two met during the weeks of repairs at San Diego Naval Base and regularly got together on shore leave. The downtown USO club furnished wholesome dances and social events; Carter and Lackey preferred the Gaslamp Quarter with its rows of bars, restaurants, and dance halls. Years later, Lackey still remembered their main haunts: the Paul Inn, the Calisphere, the Pacific Square Ballroom, the College Inn, and the well-known Rainbow Gardens where big bands played to a raucous dance floor and a crowded restaurant. The Calisphere bar soon became their favorite.

His impressions of Carter? He was a "nice looking guy," recalled Lackey,

Sailors and dates at the Calisphere Bar, San Diego, 1944.

"pretty quiet most of the time unless he had a few [drinks] too many. And that was pretty often." Then he would loosen up, "telling stories about growing up with his part-Indian grandparents" where he lived on the land and learned to hunt and shoot. "I thought some of it was bullshit, but then most of us were bullshitters."

On one occasion, "things got a little hairy," said Lackey. After a night of drinking, he and Carter ended up in a crowded bar on San Diego's Fourth Street next to a group of airmen from the Army Air Corps training base outside the city. As Lackey made small talk with the bartender, Carter leaped to his feet and into the midst of the airmen, shoving and shouting something about "a damn nigger." Surrounded and outnumbered, Lackey hastily pulled Carter out onto the street as he kept mumbling about that "nigger Joe Louis." "Somebody said something good about Louis and it really made Ace mad."[56]

Joe Louis, world heavyweight champion in the golden age of boxing, had carefully avoided the provocative behavior of his Black predecessor, Jack Johnson, who taunted his white opponents as he demolished them, married a white woman, and ultimately suffered imprisonment on a trumped-up charge of violating the Mann Act. In 1936, German boxer Max Schmeling knocked out an undefeated and overconfident Louis in twelve rounds. Two years later, Schmeling challenged Louis who had won the heavyweight title against James J. Braddock in 1937. It mattered little that Schmeling was not a passionate Nazi; he remained Adolf Hitler's favorite Aryan. But by 1938, in the wake of the Austrian *Anschluss* and Germany's increasing persecution of its Jewish population, growing numbers of Americans had become critical of Hitler's regime.

On June 2, 1938, seventy thousand fans packed Yankee Stadium while a world-wide radio audience of more than 150 million had scarcely settled down for the bout before Louis became America's hero, demolishing Schmeling in two minutes and four seconds. Within days after Pearl Harbor, December 7, 1941, Louis enlisted in the army and traveled across the country promoting the sale of war bonds and appearing in nearly one hundred boxing exhibitions before two million servicemen and women. In two major fights during the war, he donated his purses (millions in today's dollars) to the Army and Navy relief societies. Admired by many whites for his modest behavior (and worshipped by Black fans), the armed forces made Louis the face of unity despite the realities of a segregated military and a nation torn by racial strife.[57]

Among white Southerners, patriotism and American nationalism seemed to temporarily trump race. Writers like the sports editor of the *Birmingham News* celebrated the victory of Alabama's first national heavyweight champion who had "knocked Max back into Hitler's lap." In the leads of Deep South newspapers, there was little reference to Louis as a "Negro." He was a "brown-skinned American warrior," "tall, tan and terrific," and "America's Brown Bomber."[58]

But not to Asa Carter.

The drinking Lackey remembered, both at the Navy Officer's training program aboard ship and on shore leave, was another sign of Carter's long struggles with alcohol. Even before the *Appling* first set sail for San Diego, shipmates found him so drunk that he was unable to stand for reveille. He received a "Captain's Mast" (one step below a full court-martial) and had his pay docked. Only his skill as a radio operator protected him when, still under punishment from this drinking offense, a senior officer found him sound asleep on watch. Since the ship was not at sea, he was assigned additional extra duty and "counseled." Despite such reprimands, he received another Mast Report Slip the next month for arriving drunk and late from his first shore leave.[59]

From 1943 through 1944, allied forces had steadily moved toward the Japanese homeland: from Guadalcanal to Tarawa and on to the Marshalls, the Marianas, Eniwetok, Guam, and Tinian. In the fall of 1944 the *Appling* finally set sail for Papua New Guinea where Australian and US forces controlled the eastern end of the island, creating a staging base for American troops as they prepared to retake the Phillipines. In mid-January, Carter's ship went into a combat zone, unloading seven hundred Marines on the shores of the Lingayen Gulf, 150 miles north of Manila. The greatest threat to troop ships always came when they were stationary, off-loading 125 Marines at a time onto landing crafts for beach assaults. But with much of the

Japanese army retreating for a final defense of the Phillipines' capital city, their three trips from New Guinea from January to March passed without serious threats except from Japanese submarines.[60]

The island of Okinawa, less than a thousand miles from Japan, was to be the launching pad for the anticipated invasion of the homeland. In late March 1945, the *Appling* joined the massive fleet assembled for the assault that began on April 1. The initial landings met limited resistance; the Japanese were dug in further inland. But a week later as supply ships continued to offload troops and supplies, Japanese forces launched a wave of more than eight hundred Kamikaze aircraft. The "divine wind" would be the last desperate hope of the Empire to prevent the invasion of the mainland. The *Appling* began unloading its Marines just after the suicide attacks began. Anti-aircraft fire from a nearby destroyer brought down one Japanese plane just short of the *Appling*, but for two days crew members at their battle stations had clear views of direct hits on nearby ships.

Shipmate Willis Robertson had few recollections of Carter but admired his decision to serve as a radio operator aboard slow-moving landing craft which were targeted by suicide pilots and Japanese artillery. Over a seventy-two hour period, Carter made five trips to shore under heavy fire, maintaining radio contact between his landing craft, the *Appling*, and the shore command landing officer. Shrapnel from an exploding artillery shell critically injured one radioman on a nearby landing craft. Another seaman

Crowded deck of a US Navy troop landing craft, Okinawa, 1945.

"stuck his head above the side" and a Japanese machine gun "blew his head off," said Robertson. "It was pretty damn dangerous."[61]

Despite heightened tension during the unloading of troops in amphibious assaults, most of the *Appling*'s time was spent shuttling back and forth between combat zones and staging areas. With large areas set aside for transporting some seven hundred soldiers or Marines, the 326 enlisted men on the crew double-bunked on a vessel 425 feet long and less than sixty feet wide. Like other packed troop ships, the crew and their human cargo endured overcrowding and the stench of unwashed bodies made worse by backed up toilets and rough seas that sometimes left hundreds of soldiers vomiting in the close quarters.[62]

Most seamen on the *Appling* were on duty eight hours, followed by eight hours off, their days filled with watch duty or cleaning, polishing, and repairing equipment or in the dreaded "chipping detail" against the constant corrosion of salt water. Carter and other ship radio operators escaped the exhausting task of the chipping hammer, the wire brush, and the application of new layers of red and gray lead paint, "a labor of the damned" as one sailor described it.[63] For the most part the radio operators worked four-hour shifts monitoring traffic from shore stations and surrounding ships, followed by twenty hours of down time.

During these long stints moving through the Pacific at seventeen knots, the greatest enemy was often boredom. In his bestselling post-war novel, *Mr. Roberts*, Thomas Heggen—a naval officer on the cargo ship *The Virgo*—later described the maddening days of inactivity in the heat as they plowed through the vast Pacific waters. In one of the most oft-quoted lines in the 1955 film adaptation, Mr. Roberts (played by Henry Fonda) wrote to his shipmates that the "unseen enemy of this war is the boredom that eventually becomes a faith and therefore a terrible sort of suicide."[64] The monotony was broken by endless rounds of poker, cribbage, occasionally chess, acey-deucy (a card game of pure chance), and reminiscences of life back home before the war. Or sailors and Marines could find a private place and curl up with a book.

And books there were: one hundred and twenty-five million paperbacks. Less than four months after Pearl Harbor, key executives and editors from America's largest publishing houses met in New York to lay out ambitious plans for the distribution of inexpensive paperbacks to America's soldiers and sailors. Under the slogan, "Books are weapons in the war of ideas," they agreed to allow the Armed Forces publication division to print—with nominal royalties—more than thirteen hundred titles in cheap paperbacks for distribution to servicemen around the world.[65]

Ben Bradlee, managing editor of the *Washington Post* from 1965 to 1991, served on a navy destroyer in the same Pacific waters as Asa Carter. He described the rhythm of life aboard ship: from boring to exciting, dangerous, terrifying, and back to boring again. But forty-five years later, he could remember the eagerly anticipated arrival on board of the flimsy paperbacks. During his four years at Harvard he had dutifully read from the syllabi of his classes because, as he said, "I had to read books." But during his time aboard ship he came to appreciate works that had no academic purpose, only the relief of escaping from the present and imaginatively exploring life beyond his narrow world: David Cohn's *Love in America,* Philip Wylie's *A Generation of Vipers,* and Gladys Schmitt's now-forgotten stream-of-consciousness novel, *The Gates of Aulis.* Other sailors seemed far more interested in Edgar Rice Burroughs's *Tarzan of the Apes* or Kathleen Winsor's sexually adventurous (for the 1940s) bodice-ripper *Forever Amber.* Still, armed forces editors were surprised to discover that servicemen chose as their favorite book *A Tree Grows in Brooklyn,* Betty Smith's 1943 classic of a New York teenager's painful transition to adulthood.[66] Not all the servicemen came out of the war as serious readers, acknowledged a young English professor who had patriotically enlisted in the Navy, but many educated themselves widely and continued to read in the years that followed.[67]

WHILE CARTER HAD BEEN an excellent student in high school, none of his classmates or his two brothers would have described him as "bookish." But the evidence is clear that he became a voracious reader during his months at sea, a practice he would continue for the rest of his life. What is less explicable is the turn he took during the fifteen months he spent aboard the *USS Appling.* Early experiences and the environment of childhood have a major impact on adult attitudes, but a number of studies suggest that political and ideological attitudes tend to take shape in the late teens and early twenties, precisely the age when Carter came under the influence of a group of dedicated right-wing political activists aboard the *Appling*.[68]

Even for Americans knowledgeable about the nation's history, American fascism is vaguely remembered as an episode in the 1930s, mostly associated with the German-American Bund that dissolved in 1941.[69] Isolationists and non-isolationists had seemed to unite after the attack on Pearl Harbor, but not all who had admired Hitler and embraced an American-style fascism changed their underlying beliefs.

With the outbreak of the war, the Office of Naval Intelligence (ONI) focused its energies on assessing the threat from German propaganda. As the historian for the intelligence agency acknowledged, top-ranking officers in the ONI reflected racial prejudice as well as an "anti-leftish, . . . pro fundamentalist-Christian, anti-Jewish" bias, and they were unlikely to be hostile to right-wing attitudes among America's sailors. Still, intelligence officers in all services were concerned about an Axis "fifth column," and they regularly instructed senior officers to report any pro-German, pro-Japanese, or pro-Italian activities within the ranks.[70] While there was never evidence of such an active fifth column, and little if any support for the Japanese cause, a small number of Americans, and some servicemen, continued to believe that America had made a mistake in declaring war on Germany.

In early 1944, the ONI began compiling reports on a group of seamen aboard the *USS Appling* who had begun meeting informally to study the works of right-wing pro-fascist writers. When rumors of the group reached the ship's commanding officer, he arranged for a trusted crew member to join the discussions. According to naval intelligence, members of the informal study group passed around articles and publications, notably those written by the Reverend Gerald L. K. Smith, whose weekly magazine, *The Flag and the Cross*, attacked the "Japs" regularly and vaguely supported the war but avoided explicitly condemning Hitler.[71] Carter, the informant reported, was an active member.

Except for historians and a dwindling handful of diehard followers, Gerald L. K. Smith is little known today, but he was a major figure in right-wing American politics during the 1930s and '40s. The Wisconsin-born Disciples of Christ minister began his national career as a key adviser and

L. K. Smith, center, at a 1944 campaign rally in Michigan. Below, cover of one of his books.

organizer for Louisiana's Senator Huey Long during the 1930s. Traveling across the nation, Smith delivered hundreds of speeches promoting the Louisiana politician's "Share Our Wealth" plan and gradually established his own national following. A bemused H. L. Mencken had seen his share of demagogues by the 1930s, but Smith, he said, was America's "champion boob-bumper" and "the greatest rabbler-rouser . . . since Apostolic times!" Alabama journalist and novelist William Bradford Huie was less amused. Smith had "the passion of Billy Sunday," said Huie, and "the fire of Adolf Hitler. . . . He is the stuff of which Fuehrers are made."[72]

Initially Smith's speeches mirrored the economic populism promoted by Long. They were blunt, repetitious, and substance-free. Brandishing a Bible, he mixed quotes from Jesus and the Prophets with promises that Long's program would give followers a "real job, not a little old sow-belly, black-eyed pea job, but a real spending money, beefsteak and gravy, Chevrolet, Ford in the garage, new suit, Thomas Jefferson, Jesus Christ, red, white and blue job for every man."[73]

Despite his claim to be the "tribune of hard-working Americans," he privately had nothing but contempt for the men and women who idolized him. The "average voter runs an I.Q. of about eleven to twelve years of age," he told a friendly interviewer, and he cynically summarized how to attract such followers: "Religion and patriotism, keep going on that. It's the only way you can get them really 'het up.'"[74]

After Long's assassination in 1935, Smith veered sharply to the right. He had long sympathized with Europe's fascist movement and feared what he called "Semitic domination" in America. In the years that followed, he reprinted and tirelessly promoted the infamous "Protocols of the Elders of Zion," a 1903 Tsarist secret police forgery falsely claiming to be the minutes of late nineteenth-century conclaves of Jewish leaders who outlined their plans for world domination.[75]

By the summer of 1936, Smith, who had once campaigned for Huey P. Long's expansive federal social welfare proposals, bitterly opposed Roosevelt's New Deal and linked any social welfare to a stealthy form of despotism and communism.[76] Always ambitious, he may also have been influenced by the ease with which he raised funds from wealthy American businessmen who shared his sympathy for corporate-style European fascism: men like William Bell, president of the American Cyanamid Company, carmakers Henry Ford and Horace Dodge, as well as the corporate heads of such petroleum companies as Sun Oil, Kendall Refining, and Pennzoil.[77]

And Smith was only one of many such demagogues that sprang up during the Great Depression.

Gerald Winrod, a Kansas-born American fascist known as the "Jayhawk Nazi," combined antisemitism with fundamentalist religion in his widely read magazine, *The Defender*. "The same forces which crucified Christ nineteen hundred years ago are today trying to crucify His Church," he wrote in his 1935 book, *The Jewish Assault on Christianity*. "Many Christian leaders have not yet realized it, but Christianity is in the grip of a life and death struggle at the present time. International Jewish Communism, which has already undermined all nations, firmly expects to exterminate all Christians."[78]

Like Smith and Winrod, William Dudley Pelley, a successful Hollywood screen writer turned unstable spiritualist, become convinced that "international Jewry" linked with Soviet Communism formed a world-wide conspiracy. Impressed by the "energy" and charisma of Benito Mussolini and Adolf Hitler, he founded his pro-fascist "Silver Legion," commonly called the "Silver Shirts." Modeled on Mussolini's paramilitary backers *Camicia Nera* ("Black Shirts") and Hitler's Sturmabteilung ("Storm Detachment"), members were recognized by their brown denim shirts and swastika armbands as well as their enthusiasm for physically assaulting enemies of their leader.[79] From his headquarters in Asheville, North Carolina, he proposed the establishment of the United States as a formal "Christian Commonwealth," and in articles in the Legion's magazines, *Liberation* and *Silver Shirt Weekly*, Pelley laid out a plan for all Jews to be registered, confined to one city in each state, and removed from business, government, and cultural affairs.[80]

None of these demagogues proved as successful as the Catholic priest, Father Charles Coughlin. Broadcasting from his Detroit congregation, the Shrine of the Little Flower, he originally supported Franklin Roosevelt and embraced what he called the New Deal's "social justice" platform. But he soon found European-style fascism far more appealing. In 1936, he formally broke with Roosevelt and announced to a roaring audience of German-American Bundists: "I stand with fascism!"[81] Even when his broadcasts became virulently antisemitic, he continued to attract nearly twenty-nine million listeners, a broadcasting audience that has never been matched by any other radio or television political activist.

Smith had tried his hand at politics by joining with Coughlin and William Townsend to create an ill-fated "Union Party" to oppose Roosevelt in 1936; it had little impact on the election.[82] These pro-fascist groups always remained a minority, but a July 1939 Gallup poll found that one-third of Americans agreed with the statement that the federal government should adopt laws that would "prevent Jews from getting too much power in the business world." Even more disturbing was a poll that same year in which respondents were asked if they supported the deportation of all Jews "to some new homeland as fast as it can be done without inhumanity." Ten percent of Americans responded positively.[83]

With the attack on Pearl Harbor and the declaration of war against Germany and Italy, those who still supported Hitler learned to watch their language. In his writings and speeches, Gerald L. K. Smith expressed tepid support for the war even as he continued to warn that an unconditional defeat of Germany would only open Europe to Communist domination.

In his magazine, *The Sword and the Flag,* he defended Hitler as a "bible-believing Christian" and in private correspondence complained that the Nazi leader was the victim of the vast Jewish conspiracy intent on destroying the German people.[84]

If Smith came late to antisemitism, he had long been a racist. As a twenty-three-year-old church minister in the 1920s, he visited a Chicago dance hall (to evangelize the patrons, he insisted). There he watched in horror as white girls danced "cheek to cheek with black men," caught up in gyrations that "sickens one." He loved the "good, simple plantation niggers," he said, but they were a child race dominated by venereal diseases, barely "two hundred years out of cannibalism."[85] By the 1940s, he described the growing connection between communists, Blacks, and Jews as the greatest threat to American Christian civilization. Above all, he warned his followers, they should remember that "behind the mongrelizers stand the Jews. . . ."[86]

Reports from the Federal Bureau of Investigation refer to extensive files kept by Naval Intelligence on the pro-fascist sailors on the Appling who met to study the work of these American fascists, particularly Gerald L. K. Smith. The group's secret informant described Carter as one of the more active participants and a "follower" of Smith. Unfortunately, the Navy destroyed these files in the 1980s, and the remaining information comes from a brief summary of Carter's participation prepared by an FBI agent who read the files in the late 1940s.[87]

Whatever the precise details, something happened during his time aboard the *Appling.* During his high school years, Asa had shown no interest in politics or history, agreed his brother, Larry. Nor was there any evidence of a particular interest in—or aversion to—Jews. Most white Southerners in the area were either Baptist or Methodist and religious fears were far more likely to be directed against Catholics.

In May 1945, the *Appling* had made the long trip back to the Long Beach Naval Base for nearly a month of repairs and refitting in preparation for what everyone believed would be a land assault on the Japanese homeland. Carter made the long rail trip back home to spend a week with his family. His younger sibling, Larry, saw a transformed brother when Carter came home that May. "I remember so vividly," he recalled. "Momma and Daddy and I were sitting at the table" while "Bud" (as the family called Asa) paced back and forth "excitedly talking about Communism and the danger of it for what seemed like an hour." Many of his views seemed lifted directly from the pages of Gerald L. K. Smith's monthly magazine, *The Flag and the Cross*. Undeterred by the poor showing of the Union Party in 1936, Smith formed the "American First Party" in 1944, renaming it four years later as the "Christian Nationalist Party." Their platforms laid out the policies of isolationism, a bitter hostility toward the immigration of "inferior races," a demand that America expressly describe itself as a "Christian nation," and a commitment to racial segregation that called for the emigration of Black Americans to Africa. Running as the party's presidential candidate in 1948, Smith captured a pathetically small number of votes. His views resonated with Carter, who seemed most upset over what he described as the infiltration of communists into American society. "I had no idea what he was talking about," said Larry, but he was surprised by his brother's intensity. Later that night, he listened as Asa urged his fifteen-year-old brother, Doug, to read Adolf Hitler's call to arms, *Mein Kampf*, which he described as a "great book." Asa's conversations were more like lectures, and, after his father asked a few questions, he urged his family to subscribe to *The Flag and the Cross*.[88]

Within a few short months during his service in the Navy, Asa Carter had begun to embrace an outlook far more complex—and far more extreme—than the racial attitudes of most whites of his generation. To traditional white Southern racism he added the "international death struggle" between the forces of white Christian civilization and the darker races of the world—Black and brown people who were guided by Communists and Jews. "The nigger is the virus," he would later tell an Alabama police investigator, "but it's the Jews that use them to infect America."[89]

THE ATOMIC BOMBS DROPPED on Hiroshima and Nagasaki in early August 1945 forced the Japanese government to capitulate, but even before Japanese Foreign Minister Mamoru Shigemitsu and General Yoshijiro Umezu formally surrendered aboard the *USS Missouri*, the occupation had already begun. Five thousand lightly armed and apprehensive paratroopers from the 11th Airborne Division landed at an airfield outside Tokyo, a city in ruins from firestorms created by massive B-29 raids. Japanese military officials were there to meet them and, under orders from the Emperor, to cooperate in establishing their base outside Tokyo.[90]

With the war at an end, the *Appling* soon set out from Okinawa, carrying a work battalion of six hundred Marines to Japan. The crew had originally assumed they would be transporting occupation troops to Tokyo, a city that—despite its great devastation—offered the attraction of several dozen houses of prostitution set up within days after the first arrival of American troops. Under pressure from occupation authorities, local Japanese officials established brothels—restricted to American soldiers and seamen—where Japanese women, often driven to prostitution by destitution, "processed" twelve to fifteen GIs a day for which they were paid three hundred yen (about sixteen dollars in 2023).[91]

Instead, Carter and his shipmates found themselves on their way to Nagasaki, Japan, site of the second atomic bomb dropped on August 9, just three days after Hiroshima. Only six weeks after the blast, the *Appling* disembarked the Marine work battalion, while accompanying cargo ships unloaded bulldozers and heavy equipment. Over the following weeks, they cleared the debris without any protective gear and surrounded by clouds of radioactive dust. During the three days off-loading men and equipment, Carter and other sailors wandered one and a half miles from the harbor to the center of Nagasaki without restriction, surprised by the lack of resistance or hostility by the Japanese men and women digging through the rubble of their former homes. Alvin Kernan, author of the widely praised memoir, *Crossing the Line,* docked next to Carter's ship at the same time

From Nagasaki in 1945, Carter mailed home to his family this snapshot of the obliterated city.

and described how sailors and marines walked cavalierly around the city, oblivious to the dangers of radioactive poisoning. To him, the city looked little different from those flattened by massive conventional weapons. "We knew nothing of U-235, nor of the technology involved."

There for nearly a week, Carter mailed home a photo of Nagasaki's blasted center with a brief scrawled note on the back, but neither of his brothers could recall him talking about the city then or in the years that followed.[92]

From Nagasaki, the *Appling* made a long and roundabout voyage through the Pacific and ultimately back to the Portland, Oregon, naval yard in November 1945, where crewmen waited for months as the military bureaucracy slowly churned out discharge orders based on an elaborate formula that calculated years of service, time spent overseas, marital status, number of children, age, and decorations. With the war over and frustrated servicemen sitting around with few duties, patriotism "was a scarce commodity," wrote a young naval officer as he watched discipline collapse and widespread insubordination (and heavy drinking) increase aboard his ship.[93] Finally, in late March 1946, Carter boarded a train for the two-and-a-half day journey to Memphis, Tennessee, where he received his honorable discharge documents and last paycheck before taking a bus to Birmingham and going home to the family farm at White Plains.

BY THE TIME HE had arrived, the exuberant but brief celebrations of V-E and V-J days were long past. For those veterans returning home months after the war had ended, there were no parades and little attention to their sacrifices. "I think this must be the feeling of all veterans from Caesar's legions to the present," wrote one sailor. "The end of wars is anticlimactic; no one knows what to do or what to say."[94]

The three years Carter spent in the Navy proved critical in transforming him from a sometimes hell-raising high school student interested in sports and girls to the passionate far-right political activist he became during the 1950s and 1960s. Back home, he connected with few of his friends other than a former neighbor, playmate, and high-school friend, "Buddy Barnett." As children they had fished and swum together in a nearby creek. "I was a loner and Asa was a loner, even as a kid," said Barnett. While Carter seldom talked about his time in the navy, he made it clear to Barnett that he was glad that he had not had to fight Germany, "an Aryan nation." He was proud to "fight the Japs," but America had made a great mistake in dividing the white race by attacking the Germans.[95]

The main thing his family noticed was "how things would set him off": At the sound of a car horn or any sudden noises he would bolt from his chair. "He would also go from a calm conversation to an absolute tirade for no reason at all," said his brother, Larry. However concerned about his explosive outbursts, members of the family never openly discussed his behavior. His mother, Hermione, would call a halt to such talk, dismissing his rants as simply "bad nerves," a euphemistic expression that Southerners of her generation used to describe any emotional instability from nervous tics to schizophrenia.[96]

Weeks after he returned home, Carter began seeing Thelma Walker, a classmate one year older. They had never been "an item" at Oxford High, recalled several classmates, but she was clearly smitten with him, writing regularly during his time in the Navy. During the summer, he applied for a few jobs, but veterans discharged earlier had taken most of those and there was no civilian demand for a Navy code operator. Although he continued to help his father on the family farm, he had no desire to return to milking cows and repairing fences. Over that Christmas, his uncle Asa Weatherly drove up to visit the family from his home in Tallahassee, Florida. Weatherly, who drove a "sporty car," and ran a small soft-drink bottling company, soon convinced his namesake there was a great future in the bottling business.

After nine months home, twenty-one-year-old Asa had saved enough money to buy a used car, and two months after his uncle's visit, he packed his belongings and left Anniston for Tallahassee just before dawn on the morning of February 27, 1946. He did not tell his parents that he was picking up Thelma (or "India," as she would come to call herself). Three hours later, the couple stopped just north of Montgomery, paid six dollars for a marriage license, and repeated their vows before the local probate judge. From there, they made the four-hour drive south to Tallahassee to spend the first night of their marriage with Uncle Asa.[97]

3

Becoming an Activist

"Bud [Asa] was intent on making his place in history in a way that would change the world. He would be the next Lincoln or Lee . . . I don't know how to explain it, but hearing his conversations it was this grandiose ambition to be somebody."

—Larry Carter[98]

Five months in Tallahassee convinced Carter he had made a mistake. He had always liked his mother's brother, but Uncle Asa Weatherly turned out to be a drunk, preoccupied with spending the meager earnings of his small soft drink bottling company on good-quality Canadian whiskey. While Weatherly drove off to visit his "lady friends," his nephew worked six days a week in a small tin building, mixing the cola syrup with carbonated water and then delivering the product to small country stores from Ochlockonee to Capitola and south to Wakulla Springs.[99]

In the fall of 1947, Carter escaped Tallahassee with his new wife and drove to Boulder, Colorado, to enroll as a twenty-one-year-old freshman at the University of Colorado. It was familiar ground; he had received his naval training on campus as a radio technician and 40 percent of his fellow freshmen were World War II veterans. Like eight million veterans, he was the beneficiary of the 1944 G.I. Bill which paid for up to four years of room, board, and tuition, plus a small living allowance. By his second year, the number of veterans had increased to more than half of the university's students, many of them crowded into the campus "Vetville," a cluster of small travel trailers and quonset huts that had been thrown up for military trainees and then converted into post-war housing.

According to a university official interviewed by the FBI, Carter's IQ test, taken as part of his entrance application, showed an "extremely high intelligence." But from the first week of school he seemed little interested in the dreary duties of class attendance and studying for final exams. Registered as a journalism major, during his first semester he barely passed one course in the "Ethics of Journalism," failed a course in chemistry, and received C's in political science and English literature. He made one "B+" in a course on Austrian history.[100]

When his younger brother, Doug, visited him, Asa talked for hours about his"brilliant" history professor, John Rath, whose course was worth more than all the others combined. Asa's enthusiasm for a professor of Austrian history made little sense to Doug or to Asa's youngest brother, Larry.[101]

R. John Rath had returned from military service in World War II with a PhD from Columbia University and a passion for Austrian history. When Carter took his course, the thirty-seven-year-old assistant professor had just joined the university's history department, teaching half-time and serving as associate editor of the *Journal of Central European Affairs*. While he did not publish until a decade later his best-known work, on the abortive Viennese Revolution of 1848, he was hard at work on the project, and his early articles

Above, Carter by his trailer in "Vetville" at the University of Colorado, 1948. Left, Professor John Rath, 1949.

and academic papers explain why Carter was so taken with his lectures.

Fear, hatred, anger: all were powerful forces in bringing about massive, even revolutionary change in a society, argued Rath, but there must be more than hatred. There "must also be a bitter sense of oppression, whether real or imagined," and a sense that the existing political, social, or economic institutions were out of harmony with the great majority of the people. Change would come when the discontented rallied around a redeeming idea that would cleanse these evils and bring about a healthy and harmonious society. Initially, political tensions would increase, he said, as the "moderates" concluded that the growing turmoil was too unsettling; they would call for calm, lawful, and measured change—compromise. True believers understood—or believed they understood—that such compromises would simply lead to a failure to bring about their vision of a utopian future.[102]

Rath's research described the role of radical groups in the political upheavals of mid-nineteenth century Austria, but Asa found it a kind of universal explanation for radical change. And by this time, Asa had embraced the more extreme right-wing vision of a white Christian America free from Communists and Jews and the threat of the inferior races: Blacks in the South and ethnic minorities in the North. For an impressionable and relatively uninformed young white Southerner who longed to make his mark as a political activist and as an *intellectual,* Rath's analysis explained the inevitable struggle that Carter concluded would shape the future in the South: one between Yankee "outsiders" (the most dangerous of which were Jewish), the God-fearing, working class white Christians (in purest form in the American South), and the temporizing moderates who sought peace at any price.

Politics had become Asa Carter's passion.

For most individuals, the critical years for shaping political attitudes come at the end of adolescence and the beginning of adulthood. That was true for Asa Carter, and it was certainly true for me. When I graduated from my small rural high school in June 1958, I had planned to attend Clemson University. I vaguely thought about majoring in some form of engineering that would prepare me to work with my father, who was a small building contractor.

But when James Rogers, editor of the local newspaper, spoke at my graduation (nineteen students in my class), he urged me to consider enrolling in a recently established extension of the University of South Carolina. If I was interested, he said, I could work part-time as a reporter. During the next two years I attended night classes while I worked as at the Florence Morning News. *I started at twenty hours a week; by the end of my second month, I was working forty hours a week and taking a full load of classes. Most of my assignments were the usual regimen of a rookie reporter: writing obituaries, covering the local tobacco warehousemen's convention and the latest multiple-car accident. But on the eve of my employment at the newspaper, local Klansmen had driven editor Jack O'Dowd out of town for daring to argue that* Brown v. Board of Education *was the law of the land. If O'Dowd's successor, James Rogers, was more cautious in his editorial policies, he and most of my fellow reporters were disdainful of the threadbare rationale for white supremacy.*

I learned much during those two years. My editors, Dew James and Joe Dabney, struggled to teach me the pitfalls of adjectives and the superiority of active-voice verbs, but their greatest gift was to introduce me to the astonishing possibility that I could be critical of my culture without betraying its best values. On the surface, whites in the small town of Florence seemed united in their defense of segregation, but appearances were deceiving. Over endless cups of coffee at a downtown coffee shop, I came to know and to be instructed by men—and they were mostly men—who had a vision of a South without racism. Besides fellow newsmen, a couple of lawyers and a local Jewish businessman dropped in and out of our coffee breaks. In some cases, their openness to racial change sprang from deep religious conviction; others had served in the military or had lived outside the region. Some seemed to be innate nonconformists. ("I was born a square plug in a round hole," one group member would often say.) Publicly they may have spoken cautiously; privately they gently peeled away my half-hearted defenses of the "Southern way of life."

Among that group, a local lawyer made a particular impression. A decorated naval officer during World War II, Nicholas ("Nick") Zeigler graduated from Harvard Law School and returned to his hometown in Florence. I had never met a Harvard graduate and certainly no one who was as widely read in history and literature. It was Nick who loaned me a copy of Richard Wright's Native Son, *the first book I had ever read written by a Black author. It was Nick who urged me to read C. Vann Woodward's classic 1955 book,* The Strange Career of Jim Crow. *After a distinguished career in the South Carolina legislature, Zeigler took on the hopeless task of challenging US Senator Strom Thurmond in 1972. And lost badly. Most of all, I admired him for never losing his sense of commitment (or humor) as he tried to create a more humane society that saw the end of segregation as an opening for the liberation of white as well as Black South Carolinians.*

In the end, there would be no on-the-road-to-Damascus experience, but as a nineteen-year-old reporter in the spring of 1960, I stood in a Kress five-and-ten-cent store photographing raucous whites who muttered obscenities at the dozen well-dressed young Black men and women sitting quietly at the lunch counter. The tension was overwhelming. I was convinced that only the presence of a half dozen city policemen prevented onlookers from attacking the group.

Afterwards I interviewed two leaders of the demonstrators, the first time I had ever encountered Black college students. I was awed by their courage and their composure. "Which side are you on?" asks the old union rallying song. As I took those photographs and spoke to those two, there was no longer any doubt in my mind about which side I had chosen. In two short years, the racial moorings of a lifetime had been severed.

My next two years at the University of South Carolina in Columbia completed that transformation. Political pressure had led to the firing of two outspoken professors in the late 1950s for condemning segregation, yet a surprising number of faculty made little effort to hide their contempt for the state's commitment to maintaining white supremacy.

Within months after my arrival at the university, I gravitated toward a small group of students who openly challenged segregation, a system that most white students—there were no Black students at USC—accepted without questioning or, in some cases, saw as the bedrock of their world.

Although I was an undergraduate, I joined a house rental with graduate students Charles Joyner, Selden Smith, and Hayes Mizell. All would spend their careers provoking what John Lewis called "good trouble." At every step, we had the guidance and support of an earlier generation of activists who welcomed the dissenting voices of young students: Alice Spearman, the head of the South Carolina Council on Human Relations, Libby Ledeen of the University's YWCA, and James McBride Dabbs, the South Carolina writer whose book, The Southern Heritage *(1958) challenged white Southerners to see the civil rights movement as the best of that heritage.*

Encouraged by Spearman, Ledeen, and Dabbs, I joined a loose-knit group of fifty to sixty Black and white students from the state's colleges and universities. Rather grandly, we called ourselves the "South Carolina Student Council on Human Relations" and elected Joyner as our first president (he claimed it was because he could play the guitar and knew most of the words to the freedom songs). From the fall of 1960 until I went away to graduate school at the University of Wisconsin in 1962, there were Saturday evening meetings in Columbia and conferences and civil rights workshops at Highlander Folk School in Monteagle, Tennessee, the Southern Christian Leadership Conference Training School in Dorchester, Georgia, and Penn Community Center near Beaufort, South Carolina, where I met most of the Black and white civil rights activists of my generation. We hardly changed the world, but as I look back upon the young men and women I met, we changed ourselves.

Inspirational posters often quote some variation of the theme that "Life is not a matter of chance . . . It is a matter of choice." Perhaps, but chance is never absent from the choices we make.

For someone like Asa Carter who was anxious to engage in post-war politics, Denver, Colorado, was the place to be. From 1940 to 1945 Denver became one of many cities around the nation considered prime targets for Axis secret agents. During World War II, the federal government had established Amache, a camp southeast of the Colorado state capital to intern nearly seven thousand Japanese Americans. Military facilities and defense contracts mushroomed across the state, an expansion that showed no letup during the Cold War that followed. As fears of communist subversion replaced those of Axis spies, Colorado became the focus of dozens of covert internal security investigations by the federal government.

After World War I, the Federal Bureau of Investigation had assumed responsibility for the domestic surveillance of "subversive" groups, but in 1938—responding to the growth of a number of fascist organization in America—Franklin Roosevelt gave broad authority to the Military Intelligence Division of the War Department and the Navy's Office of Naval Intelligence to investigate domestic groups that posed a threat to the military. J. Edgar Hoover fought any policy that diminished the clout of his agency, but he reluctantly agreed to cooperate with military intelligence so long as the FBI was first among equals. By the late 1940s, twenty-five hundred members of the Army's Counter Intelligence Corps (CIC) operated in undercover surveillance. While these "G-2" agents were supposed to focus on armed forces personnel considered to be potential subversives, their investigations often surveilled civilian "radical" groups.[103]

In the spring of 1947, an army intelligence officer attended a meeting of a small group of what he called "pro-communist" activists in Denver. His attendance required no elaborate ruses. Desperate for allies, liberal and left-wing Popular Front activists welcomed the dwindling number of Communists to their meetings. Despite the presence of what he called "left-wing activists," the army's investigator found no evidence of subversion. Participants spent most of their time debating how to recruit new members and how to respond to the growing anti-communist fervor.

In compiling dossiers on the participants, the G-2 operative seemed confused about a University of Colorado freshman and former serviceman named Asa Carter who regularly showed up for meetings. Although there was nothing to indicate that the young man was a Communist Party member, he closely followed the discussions and repeatedly asked questions about how to effectively organize and recruit. After sending an inquiry to Washington, the agent received the naval intelligence report on Carter's role in the *Appling* group that documented his role as a follower of Gerald L. K. Smith. Shaped by the emerging cold war climate, the young intelligence officer found Carter's activities bewildering. Was this former seaman with a history of right-wing activism a double agent for the Communists, he asked his superiors?[104]

There was no mystery. Carter was simply following the example of other right-wing leaders and groups: know your enemy and emulate their best tactics. Despite the Ku Klux Klan's fierce anti-Catholicism, noted historian Richard Hofstadter, it "imitated Catholicism to the point of donning priestly vestments, developing an elaborate ritual and an equally elaborate hierarchy." Years later, in the same fashion, the "John Birch Society emulates Communist cells and quasi-secret operation through 'front' groups . . . along lines very similar to those it finds in the Communist enemy."[105]

Because Carter did not seem to be a key participant in the group's activities, the G-2 agent failed to follow up in his investigation. Army intelligence sent a copy of the Carter report to the FBI's internal security division in Washington, where it was catalogued and then filed away with thousands of similar reports documenting what the agency saw as the growing threat of Communist subversion. It was the first document in a file that would ultimately contain more than fifteen hundred pages.

In time, Jerry Kopel would become a prominent Denver journalist, newspaper columnist, attorney, and state legislator. In the fall of 1947, he was a nineteen-year-old freshman journalism major when he sat next to Carter at their orientation. Although Carter was only three years older, as a war-time vet and self-confident storyteller, he seemed far more sophisticated and worldly. He also shared Kopel's growing interest in politics. At least twice a week they left one of their journalism classes for coffee and long discussions about state and national issues.[106]

Jerry Kopel, 1948.

If the loquacious Alabamian had little interest in most of his classes, Kopel remembered seeing him carrying a musty translation of Friedrich Nietzschke's classic philosophical 1886 polemic, *Beyond Good and Evil,* as well as arcane volumes on political theory. "He could quote Karl Marx—who I had heard of—and a bunch of authors I didn't even know existed," said Kopel. But one of Carter's favorite books was a dog-eared pamphlet he had purchased from a used bookstore in Boulder. Kopel could not remember the exact title, but his new friend described it as a Communist manual on how to organize. "You can learn a lot of things from the enemy," Carter explained.[107]

The pamphlet was almost certainly J. Peters's 1935 booklet, *The Communist Party: A Manual on Organization.* "J. Peters," one of the many pseudonyms for Soviet spymaster Sándor Goldberger, illegally entered the United States in the 1920s. His first assignment had been to create fake US passports that would allow Soviet agents and sympathizers to enter the country. By the 1930s he had become the party's leading intellectual on how to organize "cadres" in the United States, and his manual became required reading for dedicated party members seeking to build a mass party that would overthrow American capitalism.

Carter had no use for Peters's theories of class revolution, reverence for the Soviet Union, or idolization of Joseph Stalin, but he read and re-read the description of revolutionary tactics and organization. It might be possible to cooperate publicly with other groups that shared common goals, the Hungarian-born activist argued. But given the ruthlessness and power of the enemy—capitalists and their bourgeois supporters—party leaders had to create secret cadres of dedicated followers, organized and operating according to strict military discipline. Interwoven with praise for Marx, Engels, Lenin, and Stalin, Peters offered practical tips on how to mobilize followers with down-to-earth forms of propaganda, how to vet potential party members, and, once accepted, how to make certain they were not "stool pigeons." Although Peters spoke of the need for "collective leadership," the existence of informers, and government agents, he required members to agree to accept without questioning the guidance of their leaders. In this life and death struggle, the party had no choice except to engage in secrecy. And duplicity.[108]

Carter had already developed skills in duplicity. During conversations with Kopel, he seldom mentioned his time in the Navy. Instead, he described a childhood of poverty and struggle in which his parents had died when he was seven. He said his mother's Cherokee parents had taken him to their Tennessee mountain cabin in the 1930s and introduced him to the wisdom of his Native American heritage as well as the rich literature of Shakespeare and the Bible. Carter's eloquent and emotional accounts of the lessons he said he had learned from his Indian ancestry seemed incongruous, since they were often by followed by remarks about ignorant Blacks and the dangers of racial mongrelization.

Kopel had little contact with African Americans before or during college, but Carter's racial views unnerved him. Even though he tried to excuse such comments as a "Southern thing," he learned to steer the conversation away from issues of race. But he never doubted Carter's claim of being raised by his Cherokee grandparents. Without knowing it, Kopel had become the friend of an accomplished fabulist who spent his lifetime blurring (or obliterating) the connections between truth and lies, myth and reality.[109]

Nor could Kopel—who was Jewish—ever recall that Carter had expressed the kind of virulent antisemitism that later came to dominate his writings. He did remember casual comments by Carter ("You Jews really know how to stick together") that some of his Christian friends seemed to think were compliments. As one of the few Jewish students at the University, he learned to shrug off similar remarks.[110]

On at least two occasions, Kopel suggested that Carter join classmates for a hike and picnic atop Sugarloaf Mountain ten miles west of the Boulder campus. Carter declined. Despite their many hours together on campus, Kopel knew nothing of his friend's private life. He had no idea that Carter had married his high school sweetheart, India Walker, who was living with him in "Vetville." Bewildered by his new friend's reticence and sometimes annoyed that Carter dominated their conversations with long-winded lectures, Kopel nevertheless found himself fascinated by his friend's wide-ranging discussion of politics and history. "He did know a lot more than I did about politics. I was pretty unsophisticated then. Only later did I come to realize how many of his ideas were ultra-right wing."[111]

If he was politically naive, Kopel came to see a darker side to his Alabama friend in the spring of 1948.

Politically, 1948 is remembered because of President Harry Truman's surprise upset of GOP nominee Thomas Dewey. But politics across the

A thousand KKK members paraded down Denver's main street in 1924.

nation had dissolved into fierce struggles as civil rights, communism, and the Cold War became divisive issues between conservatives and liberals in state and local campaigns across the country.

Far-right (and violent) politics had a long tradition in Colorado. During the 1920s, the state's Ku Klux Klan was the largest west of the Mississippi River, with more than fifty thousand members. In Denver alone, seventeen thousand residents paid their KKK dues and donned white robes—propelled by fears of Catholics, Blacks, and Mexican Americans. At their high-water mark, the Klan elected one of the state's US senators, its governor, and the majority of the state legislature, as well as dozens of city and county officials, including the mayor and city council of Denver.[112] Although the Klan went into nationwide decline in the late 1920s, its slide did not mark the end of political extremism in America. Or in Colorado.

In 1942, Pelley's Silver Shirts Legion collapsed after the Justice Department charged him with sedition, but many of his pro-fascist followers simply switched their allegiance to other far-right organizations: the Christian Nationalist Party, the Colorado Anti-Communist League, and the Christian Veterans Intelligence Service.[113]

To such toxic post-war politics, far-right ministers and their followers added religious zealotry. By 1946 charismatic "cowboy preacher" Harvey Springer had led his thousand-member church in suburban Denver out of the more liberal American Baptist Association. A friend and disciple of Gerald L. K. Smith, Springer distributed *The Sword and the Flag* as well as his weekly magazine, *The Western Voice*, to more than sixty thousand readers (he claimed) across the Rocky Mountain states. Every Sunday morning, he broadcast the worship services at the Englewood First Baptist Church over KVOD, the radio station where Asa Carter worked. His apocalyptic sermons warned of the threat posed by "secret forces" that had created the New Deal's "dictatorship" and joined hands with the "black forces of Communism and Modernism" arrayed against the "white forces of Christianity." Although Springer avoided explicit anti-Semitism in his radio broadcasts, his magazine described the danger of an "international Jewry" working closely with communists to make the United States subservient to an atheistic United Nations.[114]

Nor was Springer the only Denver proponent of this blend of racist theology, Christian nationalism, and right-wing politics. William Blessing, a former United Brethren minister, fell under the influence of Wesley Swift, a passionate Southern California adherent of Christian Identity theology and a leader in the movement as it emerged in the United States in the 1930s. Blessing moved from the west coast to Denver and spent the rest of his life promoting the small but influential movement.

Radio announcer Carter, 1950.

Christian Identity theology encompassed a range of religious and historical ideas so convoluted and irrational, it is not surprising that mainstream religious leaders (and the media) generally ignored the movement for much of its history. The American Christian Identity movement grew out of a small sect based in England, the so-called "British

Israelites." In the United States, this fringe movement created a version of premillennialist theology more political and overtly racist, giving a religious justification for such views to large numbers of followers.

According to the most common version of Identity Movement theology, Jesus was not Jewish, and so-called Jews were actually Mongolian-Turkish "Khazars," the children of Satan through the bloodline of Cain; Blacks were "mud people" without souls. The true Jews had crossed the Caucasus Mountains and founded the new Israel in the British Isles. Followers of the Identity Movement lived in preparation for the tribulation in which a "One-world government" would be created and ruled by the "Mother of Harlots"—the Antichrist. One of the most common variants of Christian Identity theology foretold a great battle led by a Christ returned to earth in which true Christians would defeat the forces of evil and usher in a new age in which "so-called" Jews would be exterminated and Blacks would become the permanent servants of whites.[115]

If Blessing shared the antisemitism of the Identity movement, he was equally concerned with the threat posed by the "colored races" and their refusal to "love and honor the white race," appointed by God to rule over all the earth. From Blessing's thousand-member congregation, the "House of Prayer for All People," he sought to establish Identity churches throughout the Southwest and Rocky Mountain states, with what one admirer called "unparalleled zeal." Blessing and his son, John David, served as guest ministers and distributed their monthly periodical, *Showers of Blessing,* as well as books and pamphlets written by Identity Church founders.[116]

Hitler's admirers and other right-wing antisemitic groups in America were crippled by their small numbers, their infighting, and the lack of a single charismatic influential who could shape American policy, but their views could hardly be dismissed as marginal. If the horrors of the Holocaust made antisemitism the third rail of mainstream political discussion, the underlying currents remained, often blending with racism and anti-communism in the post-war era.

Although Colorado had voted for Franklin Roosevelt in 1932 and 1936, it returned to its earlier Republican roots and drifted further to the right through the late 1930s. One of only ten states that favored Wendell Wilkie over FDR in the 1940 presidential campaign, Colorado led the way in anti-union legislation, becoming the first state to limit the power of labor with an early version of right-to-work laws that would quickly become a major goal of conservative business interests.[117]

In 1947, John Gunther, author of a series of journalistic surveys of state and national politics, visited Denver in preparation for his bestseller, *Inside U.S.A.* He described a right-wing current in Colorado far beyond the term "reactionary." Denver, said Gunther, was one of the few places in America filled with people who believed that subversives dominated the federal government and that Ray Clapper and Ernie Pyle—two admired World War II correspondents killed in the Pacific—were Communists.[118]

The undisputed kingpin of Colorado politics since the 1930s had been the jovial, glad-handing Ed Johnson, governor during the early 1930s and senator since 1934.[119] Technically a Democrat, he was far to the right on most issues and had consistently opposed Roosevelt and many of his policies in the 1930s. In 1940, he committed the ultimate political apostasy by endorsing Republican Wendell Wilkie; eight years later he made it clear he had little enthusiasm for his former fellow senator Harry Truman. Johnson combined support for the state's banking, mining, and industrial interests with contempt for organized labor and Mexican contract workers—or "aliens," as he always described them. A passionate anti-communist, by 1948 Johnson focused most of his speeches on the ever-present danger of "pinkos," a category that seemed to include almost anyone who did not share his reactionary politics.[120]

In the mid 1940s, Denver's Eugene Cervi, the mercurial editor and publisher of the *Rocky Mountain Journal,* emerged as Johnson's most persistent critic. Cervi's father, an Illinois coal miner, socialist, and supporter of labor activist Eugene Debs, named his first son after the four-time candidate for the presidency on the Socialist Party ticket. By the 1940s, the successful Denver newsman had lost his father's enthusiasm for socialism; he belonged to Denver's most prominent country club and liked the good life. ("I don't want to be a Republican," he told his friends. "I just want to live like one.") Still, he was an FDR liberal and a dedicated civil libertarian who believed that even Communists had civil rights. In editorial after editorial he needled Johnson over his right-wing voting record. When Cervi became state chairman of the Democratic Party and was unable to get anyone to run against Johnson, he impulsively decided to challenge the senator in the 1948 Democratic primary.

The Johnson-Cervi campaign would become one of many state and local races that showed the growing power of anti-communism in American politics. It also marked the end of Jerry Kopel's friendship with Asa Carter.

IN LATE MAY 1948, in the midst of the Johnson-Cervi primary campaign, Carter persuaded Kopel to join him on an early morning thirty-mile bus ride from Boulder to Denver with vague plans to attend a pro-Cervi rally. Kopel was surprised at Carter's suggestion; he remembered that his friend had repeatedly dismissed the Denver newsman as a "Communist sympathizer." But he went along, anxious to get a firsthand look at politics in action.

In Denver, however, Carter left Kopel with a promise to meet back at the lobby of the Cosmopolitan Hotel before the two o'clock rally. He said he had to attend a "political meeting" and made it clear that his young friend was not invited. Kopel waited four hours before giving up and catching a bus back to the university campus. On campus the next week, Carter made no apology for his disappearance and suggested that he had actually been protecting Kopel from getting involved. In fact, Carter had been with a group of anti-communist activists he cheerfully described as "Italian thugs"—local members of the Knights of Columbus—where they laid out plans to disrupt the Cervi rally. While Kopel was ecumenical in his political friendships and shrugged off Carter's virulent opposition to Cervi, he was appalled by the relish with which his classmate described assaulting Cervi's "pinko followers." A couple of shoves and a few punches, Carter bragged, sent them running "like a bunch of chickens."[121]

Their regular coffee sessions ended, recalled Kopel. And their friendship was over.

4

Right-Wing Radio Broadcaster: 1949–53

> *I think he [Asa] was either a communist or a communist sympathizer. He talked like a communist because of his theories concerning the rich capitalists and he always seemed to favor the down-trodden or poor people."*
>
> — David Highbaugh, owner, WAZF-AM[122]

In later years, Asa Carter sometimes claimed to have graduated from the University of Colorado; at other times, he acknowledged that he did not have a degree but said he had dropped out of school after marrying his high school girlfriend. In reality, he had little prospect of graduating. After two years, he had completed only four courses satisfactorily, his wife had given birth to their first child, Tara in June 1949, and he needed to make a living.

In December 1949, he officially withdrew from the University and used the G.I. Bill benefits to enroll in the "Spear Broadcasting Academy" in Los Angeles, California, one of dozens of such schools set up for aspiring disc jockeys and radio announcers in the heyday of American radio. The Los Angeles course lasted only three months, but long enough for the birth of their first son, Asa Jr. Although the school soon folded, Carter managed to get a job back in Denver as an announcer on local radio on the basis of his diploma and vague references to his time at the University of Colorado. In a small duplex apartment, Asa, Thelma, Tara, and Asa Jr. settled into life in the Mile High City. Carter's brother, Doug, was only seventeen and just out of high school, but Carter convinced the station to hire him as well, mainly to serve as a late-night announcer.

While KVOD billed itself as the "Voice of Denver" it remained in the shadow of other local stations, notably KOA-AM, whose fifty thousand-watt broadcasts could be heard across much of the Rocky Mountains in the evening.[123] The low-power KVOD, affiliated with the ABC radio network, appealed to local audiences with a combination of country and big band music, news commentary, and religious programming. ABC, the poorest of the major radio networks, relied heavily on freelance commentators and independently produced programs, most of which were conservative even by Cold War standards. The number and reach of extremely conservative broadcast commentators exploded after 1987 when the Federal Communications Commission abolished the "Fairness Doctrine" that required radio stations to present contrasting views. But the roots of the domination of far-right commentary lie in the broadcasts over hundreds of AM radio stations during the Cold War climate of the 1950s and 1960s.

For two years Carter broadcast under his middle name, Earl. He would later claim to have hosted a conservative political talk show, but Art Peterson, KVOD's news announcer in the post-war years, dismissed this claim. "He was just a fill-in announcer who did station breaks, read the wire-copy news," and occasionally played music during the late evenings. Peterson did remember Asa and Doug Carter, but not with fondness.

"I've always enjoyed the people I've worked with, but these guys definitely were exceptions." Without provocation, said Peterson, Asa and Doug would launch into "rants" about Blacks. "They were definitely racist, and you could tell as soon as they opened their mouth." Shortly after he joined the station, Doug began railing on about the threat of "niggers." When a KVOD office worker pushed back, Doug "threatened to throw him out the tenth-floor window," said Peterson. After that, "people at the station pretty much shied away from them."[124]

If Asa exaggerated his role as an early political broadcaster, he had ample opportunities to study and learn from conservative radio broadcasters on KVOD. George Sokolsky, a Hearst newspaper columnist and one-time Communist, launched his journalistic career as a bitter opponent of FDR's New Deal in the 1930s. By the early 1950s, his syndicated broadcasts were heard on KVOD and four hundred other AM stations across the nation.

Fulton J. Lewis, Carter's radio broadcasting model, 1949.

A Joseph McCarthy supporter in the early 1950s, Sokolsky railed against the "vast anti-American conspiracy" of "pinkos who have infiltrated America." While he denounced the "known Communists" operating in the state department, his primary crusade was to oust and blacklist anyone in Hollywood who failed to meet his standards of 100 percent Americanism.

Walter Winchell, another KVOD regular, by the late 1940s had more than twenty million regular listeners, a figure that topped the audience share for the major radio stars, Jack Benny and George Burns and Gracie Allen. Winchell, who was Jewish, began his newspaper career as a supporter of Franklin Roosevelt's New Deal, a defender of Black civil rights, and a bitter opponent of isolationists and pro-German figures like Charles Lindbergh and Gerald L. K. Smith (whom he always described as "Gerald Lucifer KKKodfish Smith"). By the late 1940s, however, Winchell had made a sharp right turn, embracing Joseph McCarthy and using his close friendship with FBI Director J. Edgar Hoover to defame liberals as "pinkos."[125]

Fulton J. Lewis also broadcast his "political commentaries" on KVOD and more than five hundred radio stations in the 1940s and 1950s.[126] The Washington-born former newsman began his career a supporter of Charles Lindbergh and the America First Movement, but swiftly shifted to the post-war anti-communist crusade, insisting that Communists "riddled the Truman Administration." Not surprisingly, he became one of Joe McCarthy's strongest supporters in the early 1950s. He did refuse to endorse the John Birch Society's 1950s national campaign to impeach Supreme Court Chief Justice Earl Warren. "I wouldn't impeach him," he said, "I'd lynch him."[127]

When Lewis died in 1996, conservative icon William J. Buckley praised him for his "saturation bombings" of the "liberal divinities: FDR, the

Supreme Court, various government bureaucratic agencies, and Radio Free Europe."[128]

Asa Carter shared the views of all these conservative commentators, but Doug Carter insisted that Lewis was his brother's model. Lewis's broadcasting style appealed to Carter. Chatty and informal, Lewis interspersed outraged political commentary with appealing and sometimes humorous personal stories. Occasionally he shared the stentorian style that characterized early radio broadcasters, but more common was a folksy tone of sarcasm and disgust at the foolishness of liberals in contrast to the average person's "common sense."[129]

Religious programming also distinguished KVOD from other Denver stations. At a time when radio and early television stations generally stuck to mainline religious broadcasts like "The Lutheran Hour" or radio broadcasts from local pastors, KVOD featured the Reverend Theodore Epp's "Back to the Bible" broadcasts, Charles Fuller's "Old Fashioned Revival Hour," and the Seventh Day Adventists' radio series, "Voice of Prophecy," with its warnings of the Biblical "tribulation." These fundamentalist radio programs seldom broadcast explicit partisan political content. But their constant warnings of the dangers of Communism and the threat proposed by religious liberalism reflected a deep suspicion of any forms of "modernism" and laid the foundations for the conservative religious theology that increasingly characterized the Christian broadcasting movement of the next half century.[130]

Carter's six-hour radio shifts allowed him time for his real passion: politics. Later he would claim to an FBI informant that he had attended thirty-five Communist Party meetings with the main purpose of learning how the party recruited strong supporters. FBI agents in Denver remained concerned about the threat posed by Communists but concluded that the gatherings attended by Carter were primarily composed of "left-wing" participants rather than members of the Communist Party.[131]

Frustrated by his inability to gain more than a minor broadcasting role at KVOD and unable to obtain employment in the city's larger stations, Carter left Denver in early 1952 and moved closer to his Alabama roots to become a disc jockey along the banks of the Yazoo River, in Yazoo City, Mississippi, long described as the northern gateway to the Mississippi Delta.

Here at last Carter had a chance to develop his ideas on the air. Between spinning country music records and reporting on hog futures, he launched his political broadcasting career with a series of fifteen-minute "liberty" essays: an eclectic mixture of commentaries that combined humorous (and often imaginary) stories about his childhood with reverent tributes to the greatness of Southern Confederate leaders, tales of the viciousness of carpetbaggers and scalawags during Reconstruction, and warnings of the dangers of integration as promoted by Communist "racial agitators."

Yazoo City gave Carter his first chance to become an on-air political commentator, and it proved fertile ground for his ideas. The town of twelve thousand later became the home of one of the largest Citizens' Councils in Mississippi. Local officials were known for their harsh response to Black civil rights activity. Still, the small town was no Denver. WAZF was a struggling low-power station that paid barely enough to feed and house Carter and his growing family. It was hardly the launching pad for an ambitious political activist.

Station owner and manager David Highbaugh had hired Carter on the basis of several audition recordings, but he soon actively disliked his new employee. Small-town radio announcers were expected to get out of the cramped studio and sell ad spots to local businesses. Carter spent every spare moment holed up in his small office, chain-smoking as he pored through books on politics and history, particularly Southern history. Frustrated with Carter's lackadaisical attitude toward recruiting advertisers, Highbaugh came to believe that his new DJ was a Communist sympathizer. He talked like a "Communist because of his theories concerning the rich capitalists" and "always seemed to favor the down-trodden or poor people."[132]

Highbaugh's confusion was understandable. In the post-Civil War South, economic elites sought to eradicate any discussion of class conflict among whites as they relentlessly promoted the argument that plantation owner and sharecropper, wealthy industrialist and worker were all equal in the struggle to maintain white supremacy. Despite occasional examples of what historian A. D. Kirwan called "a revolt of the rednecks," the insistence on white unity gave conservative political interests a powerful weapon that generally allowed them to maintain their political domination in the region.[133]

If unspoken, class tensions among whites always existed and lower-income white Southerners, particularly in rural communities, were acutely conscious of the condescending (and sometimes contemptuous) attitudes of their "betters." Sometimes it was trivial and inconsequential. Growing up on a farm in eastern South Carolina in the 1940s and 1950s, my family would be described as middle class, but many of my classmates at the small rural elementary and high school I attended were, by any definition, poor. Whatever our families' incomes, there were even clearer distinctions between our rural world and the "town." In high school, I met fellow teenagers from Florence (population 22,000) while playing in the city's high school marching band (my rural school was too small for such, too small even to have a football team). The town boys wore khakis and button-down shirts from Singleton's and Stein's men's specialty shops, and the more fashionably dressed girls shopped at Gladstone's or Furchgott's Millinery; my friends and I bought our clothes from Sears or J. C. Penney. As we imagined it, the "townies" spent their summer break lying around the country club swimming pool, while we worked six days a week in the blazing sun of the tobacco fields during the summer weeks of intensive harvesting and curing.

Of course, the parents of most students at McClenaghan High school did not belong to the Florence Country Club; many town students came from modest families and spent their summers working at various part-time jobs. But we country kids always sensed that we were viewed as unsophisticated at best, "hicks" at worst.

The really poor experienced more than a subtle difference in status. Journalist and memoirist Rick Bragg, the eloquent voice of white working-class Southerners, grew up just north of Asa Carter's home. Even though he was a generation younger than Carter, Bragg never forgot the contempt or, at best, well-meaning condescension he experienced. At age twelve, he and his brother were the beneficiaries of a Christmas party sponsored by the fraternities and sororities of nearby Jacksonville State University. The college students drove out into the country in their late-model cars—the males dressed in their blue blazers and penny loafers, smelling of after-shave lotion, the girls all beautiful, their sweaters casually thrown around their shoulders—to pass out gifts to the underprivileged white children of Possum Trot, Alabama. Bragg realized later these collegians were not truly rich, simply the privileged sons and daughters of small town bankers, real estate brokers, merchants, lawyers, and doctors. Still, "they were as alien to people like me as Eskimos and flying saucers," Bragg wrote. When he grew older, he came to resent such paternalistic gestures.[134]

His family may have been more secure, but Carter's background was similar, growing up on a dairy farm just outside the hamlet of Oxford and attending the town's small high school comprised—primarily—of students from the surrounding farms. Like Bragg, he seems to have resented the subtle disdain townies often had for rural and working-class white Southerners. As he became more politicized, he rebelled against the romantic images and stories of the Old South, an Arcadian utopia of courtly and gallant masters, beautiful wives and daughters, and faithful Black retainers. Albert Moore, Alabama's official historian at the time, captured that mythology of the old slave-holding aristocracy and their descendants: "generous, hospitable, courteous, courtly in manner and speech, natural, graceful, firm and manly," superior to the rest of the nation in the number of "gracious and charming women . . . [who] lived in the best social circles of Alabama and other Southern States."[135]

In Moore's telling, the poorer whites that Southern novelist Flannery O'Connor called "Good Country People" seldom appeared. When they did, the description of their lives was, to say the least, unflattering. Many rural whites were illiterate, Moore wrote in one disdainful passage, "baths were infrequent and tobacco chewing and snuff dipping were common habits even among women." Uncultured and uncouth, the great majority, he told his young readers, "possessed little of the world's knowledge. . . ."[136]

The wealthy Alabama antebellum lawyer, Daniel Hundley, foreshadowed such contempt account of poor whites in his 1860 classic, *Social Relations in Our Southern States*:

> Lank, lean, angular, and bony, with flaming red, or flaxen, or sandy, or carroty-colored hair, sallow complexion, awkward manners, and a natural stupidity or dullness of intellect that almost surpasses belief. All they seem

> to care for, is to live from hand to mouth; to get drunk, provided they can do so without having to trudge too far after their liquor; to shoot for beef; to hunt; to attend gander pullings; to vote at elections; to eat and to sleep.[137]

Fanny Kemble, the English actress who married an antebellum Georgia plantation owner, found her poor white neighbors "the most degraded race of human beings claiming an Anglo-Saxon origin that can be found on the face of the earth, —filthy, lazy, ignorant, brutal, proud, penniless savages . . ."[138]

Well-to-do Alabamians seldom expressed such feelings openly, but the proud subjects of their derision remained aware of their contempt. Rural families from Calhoun County as well as residents of the smaller communities—Jacksonville, Oxford, and Piedmont—shared with their Anniston betters a commitment to white supremacy. They might frequent the town's busy Noble Street shops, but a class and cultural divide always lay beneath the surface of white solidarity in Alabama.

Asa Carter's broadcasts captured that resentment as he praised uncouth Confederate leaders like Nathan Bedford Forrest and derided respectable upper and middle class Southerners for their reluctance to commit themselves to battle, whatever the cost. No wonder station manager David Highbaugh, Yazoo City civic booster and local chamber of commerce president, had no use for such talk.

Never content with his radio job in Yazoo City, Carter struggled to find a way to return to Alabama. Whenever possible, he would make the four and a half-hour trip eastward over the back roads of rural Mississippi through the small towns of Canton, Carthage, and Philadelphia and finally to Birmingham where he met with small but passionate white supremacy groups. For several months he attended meetings of the short-lived "Thomas Jefferson League," an anti-integration organization so extreme in its views that local officials barred it from meeting in any city facility.

An FBI informant reported that Carter also met at least twice with Birmingham followers of the National Renaissance Party (NRP), a neo-Nazi group created in 1949 and funded by a wealthy German-born New York real estate developer. The NRP never had more than a thousand active members, but for a brief period in the early 1950s the organization's newsletter, *National Renaissance,* had a circulation of twenty thousand and underwrote the books and writings of far-right and antisemitic authors. Under the banner "One Nation, One Race, One Leader," the NRP called for the creation of the US as an "Aryan state," which would be made possible by eliminating (in an unspecified manner) all Jews and racial minorities.[139] After Carter attended his second meeting in June of 1952 he apparently decided that there was little future in the splinter organization and, according to the FBI's informant, never joined.

Months later, Carter found a more promising outlet for his talents. In January 1954, six hundred prominent white Alabamians established the "American States Rights Association," an organization dedicated to maintaining segregation ("the only insurance against racial mongrelization") and rooting out those "subversive agents" who had infiltrated Southern schools with "socialism, communism, and race intervention."

Two wealthy Birmingham businessmen proved to be the real driving force behind the ASRA.

William Hoover, a young self-taught pharmacist and insurance salesman, had organized the Employees Insurance Company of Alabama in 1921 and later developed an office and housing complex in a semi-rural area south

Left, William Hoover. Right, Sid Smyer. Both Birmingham, 1954.

of Birmingham. With the profits from his company and a series of shrewd real estate ventures he became rich enough to indulge his racist fantasies. In one newspaper interview, Hoover outlined his grand design: "What we are going to have to do is abolish the public schools [in the South] and set them up as private. . . ." If this failed to stem integration demands, he warned, "white people will have to get together and send fifteen million Negroes back to Africa."[140]

Hoover set up the newly created ASRA rent-free in an office in downtown Birmingham and directed Olin Horton, personnel director of Hoover's insurance company, to become "Executive Secretary" of the new organization.

Sid Smyer, a Cherokee County country boy who had become one of Birmingham's most prominent attorneys, proved equally important in the founding of the anti-integration group. He had been a key figure in organizing the "Methodist Laymen's Union," which hounded racially moderate ministers from their pulpits and pressured church leaders to speak out in support of continuing segregation within Southern churches.[141] He saw the ASRA as an organization that could present a more respectable face to the public and, at the same time, lead less sophisticated lower-class whites to follow their betters rather than the Klan that tended to have a more toxic image and a tendency to engage in counter-productive violence.

The successes of the ASRA proved somewhat more modest than its charter suggested. Horton dutifully compiled statistical data showing the disparity between Black and white venereal disease and illegitimate birth rates and clipped examples of racial conflict in the North, distributing such materials to newspaper editors throughout the state, to little effect.[142] He did persuade the Birmingham Girl Scout Council to adopt a resolution condemning the national Scouts' handbook for making positive statements about the United Nations. And after pressure from the ASRA, the Birmingham school board fired a high school teacher for her "subversive teachings" praising the UN (a second teacher saved her job by promising to avoid any mention of the international organization in her classroom). Volunteers recruited for the ASRA's "Educational Committee" also "found a book in a school library that we thought was subversive," Horton told the *Birmingham News,* "and we had to have that removed."[143]

If the witch-hunts bagged only a handful of troublesome moderates, it was part of the larger and generally successful effort to create a climate in which any whites who questioned segregation or supported any liberal causes learned to remain silent.

For Asa Carter, the American States Rights Association was an opportunity to reach a larger audience and to establish himself as one of the prominent voices of white resistance. On February 28, less than a week after the organization had officially incorporated and opened its office, Carter introduced himself to Smyer and presented several taped recordings of his Yazoo City political commentaries. He impressed both Smyer and Hoover with his wide-ranging knowledge of conservative and far-right anti-communist and racist thinkers, something that distinguished him from the typical segregationist. Carter, who vaguely described himself as having

1954 newspaper ad promoting Carter's radio commentaries broadcast on Birmingham station WILD.

"attended" the University of Colorado, was the voice they sought: an intellectual who was also a man of the people.

In early March 1955, the States Rights Association hired Carter to produce a series of radio commentaries, "The History You and I Are Making," to be broadcast from WILD in Birmingham, a high-powered AM station that reached much of central Alabama. Well before the Supreme Court's 1954 *Brown* v. *Board of Education* decision outlawing segregation, white Southern political leaders like South Carolina's Strom Thurmond, Mississippi's James Eastland, and Georgia's Herman Talmadge had begun to emphasize what they saw as the links between Communism and the "integrationist movement." When Carter described the ASRA's mission in a fundraising letter, he quoted the three men and promised the organization would lead the fight for the "death of Communism and the protection of our race."[144]

Linking anti-communism with the struggle for white supremacy proved to be a strategic choice. As early as 1946, as the Soviet Union dominated much of Eastern Europe and threatened to take over Greece and Turkey, Americans had become convinced that their World War II ally posed a strategic threat to the United States and its allies in Europe. And with the disclosure that a number of Americans had acted as Stalin's spies, the first post-war wave of anti-communism swept the nation. In an effort to head off more extreme legislation, President Harry Truman established a sweeping "loyalty" program that required government agencies to undertake a background review of all its employees, dismissing those that had been affiliated with "totalitarian, fascist, communist, or subversive" organizations. Truman had hoped to politically outflank the growing right-wing claims of communist subversion in the federal government, but his actions only set the stage for the rise of anti-communist extremists like Joseph McCarthy, who was at the peak of his power when Carter was hired in 1954.[145]

At a time when the median family income was less than $75 a week, Carter demanded—and received—a monthly salary of $800 plus a "travel allowance" that allowed him to drive around the state.[146]

At age twenty-nine, Carter's years of obscurity seemed behind him.

5

Riding High

"In defeat the [white] Solid South was born . . . the mystique of prideful 'difference,' identity, and defensiveness. . . . In the moment of death the Confederacy entered upon immortality."[147]

— Robert Penn Warren

Less than two weeks after the American States Rights Association hired Asa Carter, he moved his family from Yazoo City to an apartment in downtown Birmingham less than three miles from radio station WILD. The small studio sat in the shadow of the city's landmark fifty-six-foot tall cast-iron statue of Vulcan, Roman god of fire and forge, originally constructed as the centerpiece of Alabama's exhibit at the 1904 World's Fair in St. Louis. After thirty years of fundraising, the city fathers placed the semi-nude Vulcan atop Red Mountain overlooking Jones Valley and downtown Birmingham. An iron forger's apron decorously covered his front while his bared buttocks mooned the middle-class suburb of Homewood.

Five days a week, Carter drove to his office at WILD and spent the morning typing his fifteen-minute commentary—"The History You and I Are Making"—which he broadcast at 12:30 and again at 6:15 p.m. As the ASRA expanded the number of stations broadcasting his commentary, he soon drew a listening audience across central Alabama and eastern Mississippi.[148] Unlike the more bombastic voices of an earlier generation of radio announcers, commentators, and politicians, he spoke into the microphone as though he were having a casual conversation with a friend, combining homespun humor with what appeared to be a deep knowledge of historical subjects and contemporary political issues. Rather than raising his voice in outrage, he relied upon ridicule and sarcasm to attack the enemies of the white South: the "Northern news media," the left-wing—and communist—racial agitators and the naive white moderates who counseled caution in the face of the growing menace of integration.

Carter may have been uninterested in history as a high school student, but the Civil War and its aftermath dominated the historical memories of most white Southerners. During the 1950s, the lessons of the past—particularly of Reconstruction—became one of the foundations for his call to arms in the struggle to maintain what he and others increasingly were describing as the "Southern way of life."

Nationally bestselling novels like Thomas Nelson Page's *Red Rock* (1898), Joel Chandler Harris's *Gabriel Tolliver* (1902), and Thomas Dixon's *The Clansman* (1905) laid the foundation for a story of brutality and resistance as white Southern apologists created a vivid morality play that depicted an Old South of beauty and graciousness, of courageous men who fought against overwhelming odds during the war and faced defeat, only to be ruled by corrupt Southern white "scalawags," rapacious Northern carpetbaggers and ignorant Blacks. But this was more than a tale of a fall from grace. Its undercurrent was always a frightening threat to Southern white women from savage Black men unleashed from the wholesome restraints of slavery and intoxicated by dreams of social equality.

Fortunately (as Carter told the story), battle-hardened Confederates led the struggle to overthrow these barbarous governments. It was no accident that in a region steeped in the language of sin and salvation, whites used the word "Redemption" to describe their escape from nightmare of Black domination.[149]

With whites once again in command, the nation could be reunited, but *only* if Northerners allowed the South to work out its own problems. Once "the great Anglo-Saxon race, which is dominant, and the Negro race, which is amiable," were freed from outside interference, wrote Thomas Nelson Page, the "old feeling of kindness . . . will once more reassert itself."[150]

But it was filmmaker D. W. Griffith's 1915 silent film classic, *The Birth of a Nation,* that dramatically shaped almost all white Americans' view that the Reconstruction Era was a nightmare in which beleaguered white Southerners struggled under the corrupt rule of vicious carpetbaggers,

Left, poster for Griffith's film, which is regarded as a classic of movie-making but contains racist fictional scenes like the screen shot, below, of an ex-slave legislator eating a chicken leg, while another props his bare foot on a desk in the South Carolina state capitol.

scalawags, and bestial Black rapists. To the project, Griffith brought path-breaking innovations in cinema, driven by vicious racism. The pioneering film director adapted Dixon's novel, *The Clansman,* a racist saga that tossed in every element of the Reconstruction mythology, with a special emphasis on Black men's propensity to rape white women. Dixon had reached tens of thousands of readers, but more than fifty million Americans watched *The Birth of a Nation.* In one scene Griffith depicted illiterate Black legislators in the South Carolina General Assembly placing their dusty bare feet on their roll-top desks, drinking whiskey from open bottles, and gnawing chicken bones as they leered at white women in the balconies while voting to end the ban on interracial marriages. The most inflammatory part of the film depicted white Southerners' darkest nightmare: the rape of Southern women. In one scene, a virginal maiden leaped off a cliff to her death to avoid rape by "Gus," a brutish Black soldier in South Carolina's Reconstruction militia. In retaliation, Ku Klux Klansmen cornered and then lynched Gus. Finally came salvation as the Klan rescued the heroine, a different white maiden, from the clutches of the power-crazed and sexually aroused mulatto lieutenant governor and then overthrew the corrupt regime, restoring white rule.[151]

In Dixon's novel, "Gus" does rape the beautiful sixteen-year-old Marion. In shame, she and her mother commit suicide and her brother, the grand kleagle of the recently created Klan, mobilizes his followers to hunt down the rapist, castrate, and kill him. Censors would later demand that a more acceptable form of revenge (lynching) replace the original castration scene. The problem was not its barbaric cruelty, but its sexual content.[152]

It also led to the creation of a new twentieth-century Ku Klux Klan. William Joseph Simmons, a failed preacher in Atlanta affectionately described by friends as someone "amiably fraudulent who managed to be equally at home leading prayer, preaching, taking a dram, or making a fourth a poker." Inspired by the overwhelming response to the movie, Simmons cobbled together some material on the original KKK and on Thanksgiving of 1915 convened thirty-four men to inaugurate his new fraternal organization, the Knights of the Ku Klux Klan. Later that evening, fifteen members climbed Stone Mountain just outside Atlanta and ignited a fifteen-foot kerosene-soaked wooden cross. The "Invisible Empire" had been "called from its slumber of a half-century," Simmons told his followers. (Reconstruction Klansmen had never used a burning cross; that was imagery from *The Birth of a Nation*. Simmons may have been a failure in his earlier careers, but he knew the value of showmanship.) The KKK would reach its peak membership with somewhere between three million to four million members before declining in the late 1920s. Despite its reduced numbers, various national and state Klan groups would continue into the twenty-first century.[153]

Dixon's book and Griffith's film dramatized the Lost Cause mythology that emerged in the late nineteenth and early twentieth century and became a powerful weapon used to eradicate class differences among whites by uniting them in a common commitment to defend white supremacy, using legal means if possible, and violence if necessary.[154]

While Carter embraced the broad outlines of this melodramatic tale of good (white, Southern) and evil (Black, white turncoat, Yankee) there were revealing variations in his commentaries. Most popular novels and dramas of the Civil War gave only a passing nod to the "common folk" who made up the backbone of the Klan. In *The Birth of a Nation*, plantation owner and former Confederate Colonel Ben Cameron organized and commanded the Klan, and white elites took center stage. Twenty years later, when *Gone With the Wind* captivated American moviegoers, once again the central characters, Ashley Wilkes and Rhett Butler, came from the planter and wealthy merchant classes. The Slatterys represented poor whites, a family so degraded they were seen as inferior to loyal Black slaves.

But Carter's heroes were not the aristocratic gentlemen of novels and films. They were working people, descendants of generations of Anglo-Saxons, men who traced their heritage to the "fierce Scot blood that sounded the bagpipe of battle . . ." Many members of the wealthy and effete elites of the South, he told his listeners, had in fact cooperated with their Yankee overlords while privately dismissing with disdain the "'red neck' and 'wool hatter,' 'cracker,' and 'hillbilly'" working-class Southerners. Despite the veiled contempt from their "betters," it was these hard-working men of the soil who formed the backbone of Klans across the region and ultimately overthrew the tyrannical rule of "negro-carpetbag-scalawag" governments that had raped a defeated and broken South.[155]

In his tales of Civil War battlefield courage, Carter seldom mentioned the gallant cavaliers like Robert E. Lee, who "retired on silver and lace" after the Civil War. Instead, he celebrated the rough-hewn and often crude men of action: John Mosby, whose brutal guerilla tactics in Northern Virginia earned him the title of the "Gray Ghost"; Brigadier General John Bell Hood, commander of the Texas Brigade, personally courageous and reckless in battle; and J. E. B. Stuart, commander of the First Virginia Cavalry and Lee's master of reconnaissance.[156]

The bravery and aggressive tactics of these Confederate cavalry officers made them heroes of the Lost Cause. Carter reserved his greatest admiration for Nathan Bedford Forrest, the semi-literate antebellum slave trader who became one of the Confederacy's most brilliant calvary generals. Forrest's blunt and sometimes crude language and his disdain for more-polished Southern leaders drawn from the region's elites earned Carter's admiration. "I ain't no graduate of West Point, and never rubbed my back up against any college," Forrest said at one point, but his slashing attacks on Union forces, and his ruthless tactics, proved to Carter that the only response to the enemies of the white South was "when cornered, attack, never retreat."[157] The infamous slaughter under Forrest's command of surrendering Black solders at Fort Pillow and his role in leading the post-Civil War Ku Klux Klan only increased Carter's admiration.[158]

Nathan Bedford Forrest, 1864.

Unlike more aristocratic leaders who acquiesced in the new order, said Carter, "General Nathan B. Forrest, the only true redneck in the army, went back to the mountains to figure out how to keep on fighting, and organized the Ku Klux Klan."

As so often, Carter created a history more attractive than reality. The Mississippi-born slave trader and landowner Forrest was born in a log cabin and he may have been a bit coarse, but by the start of the Civil War he had become a wealthy man, and his response to defeat reflected his lifelong pragmatism.

When Robert E. Lee and Joseph Johnston surrendered the bulk of the South's forces, Mississippi Governor Charles Clarke convened a meeting of Confederate officials, including Forrest, to outline a plan to continue the struggle by retreating into the mountains and waging guerilla war. Within minutes, Forrest abruptly stood and interrupted the discussion. "Men, you may all do as you damn please," he said, "but I'm agoin' home." When former Tennessee Governor Isham Harris demanded that Forrest take the field against the Yankee invaders, Forrest reminded him that his calvary unit would soon be outnumbered ten to one. "To make men fight under such circumstances would be nothing but murder," he argued. Glowering at Harris, he added: "Any man who is in favor of a further prosecution of this war is a fit subject for a lunatic asylum."[159]

The Confederate guerilla commander John Singleton Mosby, another of Carter's heroes, famous for his behind-the-lines surprise attacks upon Union forces before disappearing into one of his many Shenandoah Valley hideouts, may have been a dashing (and ruthless) cavalryman, but he joined the Republican Party after the war, becoming a hated "scalawag." After hearing a post-war Southern politician insist that "states' rights" had been the cause of the war, Mosby reacted with sarcasm: "Why not talk about witchcraft . . . . ? I always understood that we went to war on account of the thing we quarreled with the North about. I never heard of any other cause of [that] quarrel than slavery."[160]

Like most white Southerners of his generation, Asa Carter had numerous connections to the war: three of his great-grandfathers and at least six great-uncles served in the Confederate army. In April 1862, just north of the Mississippi-Tennessee line, one of his great-uncles fell near Shiloh Church on the first day of the bloodbath. Another died at Gettysburg and a third was trapped with Confederate General John Pemberton's thirty thousand troops in General Ulysses Grant's siege of Vicksburg. Just weeks before Pemberton's surrender, the uncle died of dysentery, weakened as rations dwindled to a handful of rice and—as a horrified Southern matron discovered when her maid went to market—"mule-meat and dressed rats."[161]

But Carter never drew upon any of the actual experiences of his Confederate ancestors. Perhaps it was because his father, Ralph, bluntly acknowledged that the fourth of Asa's great-grandfathers had used every possible tactic to unsuccessfully avoid serving in a war he regarded as a "rich man's fight."

The most oft-repeated family stories of Confederate service came from Asa's great-uncle, Gerald Weatherly, and his great-grandfather, James Anderson Weatherly. Both regaled their family with tales that were more comic than heroic. The latter quickly rose through the ranks to become a lieutenant and briefly served as an adjutant to Alabama Brigadier General John Tyler Morgan (not the more illustrious John Hunt Morgan, as Carter claimed). But during the lull after one battle, he got drunk, put on a horse collar, and danced around the company campfire singing off-color drinking songs. The next day, he was court-martialed and reduced to private, a rank he held until the end of the war.

Gerald Weatherly's accounts of war-time service were even less inspirational. With a bemused smile, he would often confess to his children and grandchildren that he was little help to the cause since "I always closed my eyes before I pulled the trigger."[162]

Larry, Asa's youngest brother, was the more reliable family historian. Growing up, "Bud" as Asa was called, had never been interested in family history. Perhaps it was more accurate to say that he was not interested in factual stories about his own family because ignoring them let him create a more colorful and politically appealing history. In later years, Carter repeated one story on at least a half dozen occasions. In radio broadcasts and in speeches, he vividly described the tragic story of a great-uncle who had served with guerilla general John S. Mosby. When Union General Philip Sheridan's troops captured the great-uncle and gave him a choice between hanging or revealing the hide-outs of his comrades, he and his friend William Overby walked unafraid to the scaffold, according to Carter. "My last moments are sweetened by the reflection that [for] every man you murder this day, Mosby will take a tenfold vengeance," said a defiant Overby as the rope was placed around his neck. As Carter made clear, his "blood connection" to Confederate patriotism and courage in the face of death placed him directly in the line of courageous and unyielding Southern patriots.[163]

In a well-known Civil War account, union troops did hang a man whose last name was Carter. But Asa Carter's dramatic narrative had little resemblance to the far more complicated story of violence and brutality that marked so much of the war.

In late September 1864, a detachment of Mosby's Rangers attacked a Union ambulance wagon train near Front Royal, Virginia, as it moved north to a Washington field hospital. According to survivors, the 120 Confederates easily overwhelmed the thirteen accompanying soldiers from the US 2nd Cavalry and began firing indiscriminately into the wagons filled with the wounded. After killing or seriously wounding nine of the union guards, Mosby's men captured the young officer in charge, Lieutenant Charles McMaster, and three of his fellow cavalrymen. They stripped them of their belongings, then shot the four before moving through the wagons, stealing anything of value until a lookout warned of an approaching Union battalion. The dying McMaster survived long enough to tell of the execution of his men.

The next day, a detachment of the US 2nd Cavalry led by Major T. A. Tolbert surprised a small force of Mosby's men, killing thirteen and capturing the remaining seven. When Tolbert approved the execution of the captured guerillas as retaliation for the murder of McMaster and his men, enraged members of his command shot several of the men "to pieces," one Union soldier recalled.

Because of their youth, the junior officer in charge interrupted the executions and gave the seventeen-year-old Overby and a sixteen-year-old soldier, identified only as "Carter," the option of cooperating with the Union Cavalry in the hunt to locate Mosby's men. When they pleaded for their lives and insisted they knew nothing of the unit's location, union solders threw two ropes over a large walnut tree on a hill overlooking Front Royal, Virginia, and unceremoniously hanged them. A Baltimore newsman invented Overby's heroic final words long after the war had ended.[164]

While most historical accounts described the younger soldier only by his last name, the 1899 Front Royal monument erected to honor the executed Confederate prisoners identified him as H. C. Carter. The sixteen-year-old resident of nearby Warren County—no relative of Asa Carter—had joined Mosby's Raiders only days before his hanging.[165]

Carter's imagination seemed limitless. In his writing, his broadcasts, and his speeches, he described how one of his great-grandfathers survived the war, became Calhoun County's Klan grand dragon, and led the battle to free Alabama from Black Reconstruction. The twelve volumes of testimony by the 1872 congressional committee investigating Klan activities as well as the work of local historians identify the two men who served in that position after the Civil War. Neither was related to Carter.

Myths, by their nature, are often more appealing than facts.[166]

I had my first history lessons on our front porch as I sat listening to my grandfather. His stories focused on colorful bygone days, but they seemed devoid of race or even politics. Claudius Quintillus Carter—or C. Q. as he was called—was ruggedly handsome even when I knew him in his eighties, despite a crooked nose that came from dozens of fracases in which, he proudly told me, he had proved to be the best bare-knuckle fighter in Florence County, South Carolina.

For hours I would sit on our front porch with him. He always dressed the same: dark pants and a starched white dress shirt, often with a tie in the summer heat. Many of his accounts reflected the hardships of rural life in the late nineteenth and early twentieth century. He and the three oldest of his five sons cross-cut pine trees from the family farm during the winter break from cultivating cotton and tobacco, dragged them by mules down to the Lynches River, lashed them together, and poled their crude floating barges downstream into the great Pee Dee River and to the port city of Georgetown for sale before making the trip back—fifty miles on foot.

None of his stories fascinated me more than his accounts of his own father's experiences during the Civil War. In June 1861, just weeks after his seventeenth birthday, my great-grandfather Theodore enlisted in South Carolina's 14th Infantry regiment. Over the next three and a half years, his unit fought in most of the bloodiest battles of the Civil War: the Seven Days

Battle in 1862 that turned back McClellan's assault on Richmond; from there to Second Manassas, Gettysburg, Cold Harbor, Chancellorsville, the Battle of the Wilderness and Spotsylvania Courthouse before Theo turned in his rifle at Appomattox and, over the next eight days, walked the 265 miles home to South Carolina.

The highlight of grandfather's stories was always the drama of Pickett's Charge, the last day of the decisive Battle of Gettysburg. As he talked, I could feel the heat of that July day in 1863 as Theodore and two of his cousins, Giles and Sidney, joined a mile-wide arc of Confederates marching in quick-step two thousand yards across an open field through a wall of cannon and musket fire coming from entrenched Union forces atop Cemetery Ridge.

Forty-five minutes later, a shattered army retreated past the dead and dying. Unlike 40 percent of his unit, great-grandfather Theodore had survived without a scratch. But late on the evening of July 3, in one of the chaotic field hospitals, he found his cousins Giles and Sidney—Giles with a leg wound that left him with a limp for the rest of his life and Sidney dying in agony from a Minie ball in his stomach. In the hours before my great-grandfather rejoined the retreating Confederate army, he wrote down his cousin Sid's last words to his wife, removed his wedding ring and pocket watch, then kissed him goodbye. After the war, great-grandfather Theodore married, had five children, and lived to be eighty. By all family accounts he was a shell of the confident, outgoing young man who had marched off to war in 1861.

Over the years, I was surprised to read family letters published by a distant cousin and discover that, however much they were vivid recreations of a master storyteller, my grandfather's accounts were essentially accurate. But I also learned an important lesson about memory.

Grandfather proudly told me that, at the young age of twenty-seven, he had become postmaster of my rural community. This responsible and relatively well-paying position was widely sought in that relatively impoverished community. Until my son did research, however, I had not considered that my grandfather had been appointed postmaster by a Republican president in 1897, at a time when virtually all whites had closed rank within the Democratic Party. In this small, close-knit community, he had almost certainly been recommended by the local African American leadership and trained by his predecessor, a Black political activist named Frazier Baker. After my grandfather's appointment, Baker moved from Effingham to a larger post office in Lake City thirteen miles away. A year later, a white mob murdered Baker and his infant daughter for daring to keep what had become a "white man's job" in the late 1890s. This I learned from my son's research for his history honors thesis. But I had heard nothing about Baker's story from my grandfather.[167]

Silence, as I discovered, can be as deceptive as falsehood.

Carter's daily broadcasts may have included folksy family stories and historical accounts, but all were in the service of promoting his views on race. In his role as an intellectual defender of segregation, he reassured white listeners that they were not bigots; "irrefutable scientific research" proved there were basic differences between the "superior white race and the inferior nigra race." With a series of pithy quotes, Carter would summarize the writings of Madison Grant, the opponent of "non-Nordic" European immigration whose influential 1916 book, *The Passing of the Great Race*, became a handbook for white supremacists in the United States and abroad. (Adolf Hitler wrote Grant an admiring letter, calling his book "my Bible.")[168]

The American States Rights Association and the promotion of Carter's broadcasts reflected the growing sense of uneasiness among white Southern leaders. Through the 1940s, the Supreme Court slowly but inexorably chipped away at the "separate but equal" doctrine of the *Plessy* decision, exposing the reality of pervasive inequality for African Americans in southern and border state educational institutions. Knowledgeable white Southern political leaders prepared for the worst.[169] Beginning in 1951, several governors in the region supported increased expenditures for Black schools in an attempt to strengthen their defense of segregation by reducing some of the most marked inequalities in public education. That year, South Carolina enacted a three-cent sales tax and spent nearly one billion dollars (corrected for inflation) over the next six years with 60 percent of that amount directed toward school construction and modernization for Black South Carolinians. In a similar attempt to forestall court challenges to the "separate but equal" doctrine, Georgia, and to a lesser extent, Mississippi, approved increases for Black schools. But most other Southern governors made little effort to boost expenditures for Black education, and the great majority of African American children in the region continued to attend dilapidated schools with crowded classrooms and poorly paid teachers.[170]

The modest improvements in a few states were all for naught. In May 1954, the Supreme Court issued its famous *Brown* v. *Board of Education* decision, concluding nine to zero that racial segregation in public schools violated the Fourteenth Amendment, which prohibited the states from denying equal protection of the laws to its citizens.

A few Southern community leaders expressed confidence that, over time, the issue of school segregation would be resolved peacefully and without conflict. And most Southern politicians called for calm and restraint, emphasizing that the Supreme Court had failed to describe a timetable or method for ending racial segregation.[171] The measured response seemed to rest upon the assumption that the court's decision would be implemented over a generation and would have little effect upon the region for years to come.

May 17, 1954. *I was an eighth-grade student in my small rural school in eastern South Carolina, already looking forward to the summer break when, only a half-hour before the last bell of the day, our teachers marched us into the school auditorium. We knew Marion Anderson, our school principal, as a smiling presence when he wandered through the halls. But, as he stood on the stage that day, he was somber and seemed at a loss for words. The United States Supreme Court, he told us, had issued a ruling calling for an end to separate schools for the races. He pointed out that nothing would change in the immediate future. His main concern seemed to be that the issue might lead to conflict with Black friends since we lived in a rural community where contacts between Blacks and whites were common. If so, he said, we should avoid any discussion or argument about the issue and act as "young ladies and gentlemen."*

Beyond that, I cannot recall what he said. What I remember most vividly was that, rather than employing the polite white Southern term "Nigra," or "Colored." Mr. Anderson referred to Blacks as Negroes ["knee grows"], a correct pronunciation I had only heard on radio or film.

*Even by this age, I was an avid reader of the local newspaper as well as the magazines that came into our house—*Life, Look, Reader's Digest, *and the* Progressive Farmer. *Legal segregation, so much a part of my life but seldom discussed, had existed to one degree or another since the 1880s and had been given official approval in 1896 in the Court's famed (or infamous)* Plessy v. Ferguson *decision. I feel certain that I would have read about the* Brown *decision, but I have no recollection of my reaction, perhaps because little seemed to change in its aftermath.*

In the summer months of 1954, as I had since I was ten, I spent five days a week on our tobacco farm and that of our neighbors working alongside Black and white men, women, and young boys and girls like myself. Too young to be a "cropper" (that would come the following year), for twenty-five cents an hour I drove a mule-drawn sled through the tobacco fields to be filled by stooped men, racially integrated, toiling in the sweltering heat for forty-five cents an hour. Once my "drag" was full, I made the short trip from field to shed where I unloaded the tobacco. There, younger children handed three leaves at a time to women who deftly tied them to four-foot sticks to be hoisted at the end of the day into the three-story barns. Over the coming week, oil-fired stoves slowly increased the barns' temperature to 130 degrees, turning the green leaves to a golden brown.

At the end of the long harvest summer, one of the landlords for whom I worked would stage a "last cropping" dinner for his workers. With the tobacco securely hung in the barns, we would go over to the hand-powered water pump to freshen up, while the landowner and his wife spread out the meal: fish stew, a mixture of freshwater bream and redbreast cooked in a spicy tomato base and poured over rice, which would be washed down with sweet iced tea and loaf after loaf of soft, sliced "white bread." I still remember the smell of the wood fires under the black pots of stew and the pungent sweetness of the barns, saturated from past generations when oak wood fires cured the tobacco. As I sat with the other children, teenagers, and womenfolk and finished off the evening with a bowl of hand-churned ice cream, I watched the men as they drifted out under the trees and began passing Mason jars of corn whiskey, laughing nervously like small boys, away from the censuring eyes of womenfolk and respectability.

I saw nothing strange about the mixing of Blacks and whites or the absurdity of the unwritten but always understood rule that—since the sky was overhead—we could eat side by side in a way that would have triggered a riot in one of the handful of restaurants in nearby Florence. And when the two jars of whiskey were passed—one for Blacks and one for whites—it was simply the natural order of things.

That was the summer of 1954. Only later did I recall that this was the last year in which Blacks and whites gathered and ate a meal together. Even outdoors.

Two years later, my high school principal announced he would run for the elected position of superintendent of education in Florence County. In his declaration of candidacy, he called for a calm and "responsible" response to the growing crisis over the issue of school integration. He wanted us not to see segregation as a "problem" but as a challenge. And whatever our feelings on the subject, he said, "we must recognize that the Supreme Court's decision is the law of the land." He lost by a two-to-one margin.[172]

In the weeks after the *Brown* decision, as Carter and other committed white supremacists warned of the coming dangers of race conflict, Alabama's James E. Folsom faced off against six opponents in an attempt to regain the governorship he had held from 1947 to 1951. During his first administration, Folsom emerged as one of the most colorful figures in twentieth-century American politics. His personality matched his size (6'8", 280 pounds) and gave him his nickname: "Big Jim." He gained a well-deserved reputation for his equally colorful marital (and extra-marital) history. In 1944, his wife died leaving him a widower with two children. Months later he embarked on a brief affair with a Birmingham hotel cashier and fathered a son before meeting seventeen-year-old Jamelle Moore at a campaign rally when he successfully ran for governor in 1946. After their marriage, they had seven children and remained married until his death in 1987.

His hard drinking was no secret. British Ambassador Lord Inverchapel made a courtesy call to the Governor's Mansion in 1946 and was a bit taken aback when greeted by one of Folsom's barefoot assistants. The governor, the aide explained, made it a policy to greet guests without wearing socks and shoes. Somewhat awkwardly, Lord Inverchapel detached his socks from his formal garters and removed his shoes just in time to hear a drunken Folsom shout as he staggered down the stairs, "Where's this goddamn limey? Let's get him fed and out of here." He did get him fed, but not before he managed to tip the table, spilling food over his British guest. In what might be one of the understatements of modern diplomacy, Inverchapel later described Folsom as "one of the most interesting men I have ever met."[173]

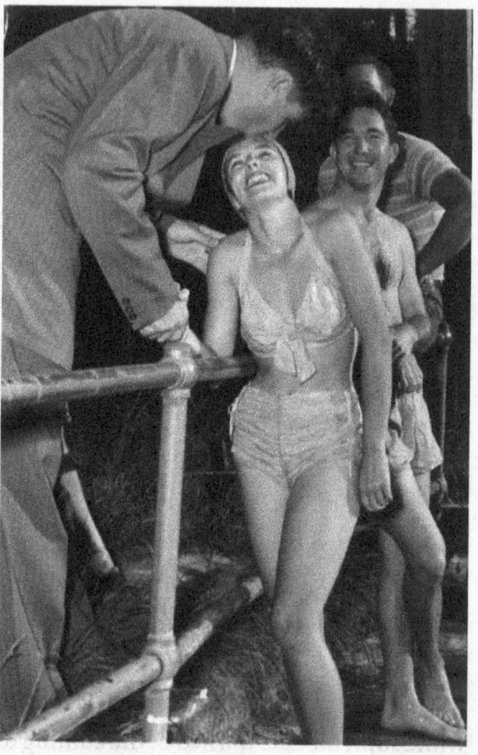

James E. Folsom, 1946.

Despite this behavior (or perhaps because of it) nothing seemed to shake Folsom's connection to the working-class white voters of Alabama. At that time, Alabama governors could not succeed themselves. When he sat out four years and sought reelection in the 1954 campaign, rivals accurately attacked him for corruption during his first administration. Folsom was ready. "Sure I did some stealing when I was your governor," he told adoring crowds. "But the crowd I worked with, the only way you could get . . . [things done] was to steal it."[174]

Even his sympathy for African Americans did not hurt his prospects. "Big Jim" was no integrationist, but he was a hardcore FDR Democrat who believed that all the "hullabalooing" about race was a political diversion. The "Ku-Kluxers, the race-baiters, and some of the selfish interest groups" would always be present, he warned. They would be "spreading their filth, their lies, their old and ancient hatreds . . . trying to boil up hatred by the poor white people against the Negroes . . . trying to keep the poor white from progressing by keeping the Negro tied in shackles."[175]

As governor, he fought—unsuccessfully—to end a judicial system that allowed local officials to arrest and prosecute African Americans for minor offenses and then collect the fees awarded for each conviction. Those corrupt practices meant that "a Negro doesn't stand a Chinaman's chance of getting fair and impartial justice on an equal footing with white men," Folsom complained to the state legislature. In his 1949 Christmas radio broadcast to the people of Alabama, he described the underfunded schools, the lack of college and professional post-graduate training programs, and the unfair laws and customs that victimized "colored Alabamians." Where were their opportunities for "better health, greater earning power, and a higher standard of living?" he asked his listeners. And at a time when only a tiny minority of African Americans in his state and the Deep South could vote, he quietly but doggedly sought to appoint county registrars who would allow Blacks to register and vote.[176]

Folsom's racial apostasy seemed to have little impact on his campaign, even in the aftermath of the *Brown* decision. As the June 5 primary approached, several of Folsom's opponents accused him of being soft on segregation. Folsom generally ignored the issue of race in his speeches and, at a time when there seemed little pressure for immediate desegregation, his critics sensed that the race issue gave them little traction. The rivals attacked what they called his record as a corrupt spendthrift who would bankrupt the state. But on election day, Folsom overwhelmed five opponents in the Democratic primary and avoided a runoff with more than 50 percent of the vote. In a de facto one-party state, he had become governor-elect.[177]

The election of Folsom as well as the call by regional leaders for "calm" and "moderate" responses to the *Brown* decision confirmed the fears of hard-line segregationists. Asa Carter repeatedly compared the months that followed to a domestic version of the "phony war" of late 1939 and 1940 when few major military operations between Britain and France and the Axis powers took place. "But wake up," Carter warned in one of his broadcasts. "The war is coming."[178]

6

From Propaganda to Direct Action

> *"This is 'Brotherhood Week' . . . sponsored by the National Conference of Christians and Jews that purports to create better understanding among . . . all groups, races and creeds. . . . [It] favors federal law for the suppression of the right of racial separation. The National Council of Christians and Jews uses its offices as a sounding board to advocate dictatorial civil rights legislation, first drawn up by the Communist-fronters . . . ."*
>
> — Asa Carter, Radio Broadcast, 1955[179]

Initially, Carter's radio commentaries stayed within the mainstream of conservative racism in the region, but in "Integration: The Communists Trojan Horse," one of his first broadcasts after the *Brown* decision, he angrily rejected the call for compliance with the US Supreme Court's edict and introduced an argument that was becoming central to white Southern segregationists: Few Black Southerners favored integration. Instead, alien forces within the United States, working hand-in-hand with international communism, saw integrationism and racial amalgamation as a way to divide and weaken the nation.[180]

Communists had infiltrated all levels of the federal government, he complained, but the Supreme Court was the Party's most powerful weapon in the campaign to destroy American society. The Supreme Court had faithfully followed the Marxist plan to create a centralized all-powerful national government that would control the lives of Americans "down to the smallest detail," he told his listeners. "Freedom," he said, inevitably requires "freedom from such government."

When Washington, D.C., schools integrated in September, there were examples of racial conflict between students in the newly integrated schools. But Carter painted a far more frightening picture, claiming that young white boys and girls lived in an atmosphere of intimidation and terror and that no restroom was safe from Black thugs who extorted money from terrified white youths. In at least two broadcasts that fall, he described in detail a nonexistent epidemic of sexual assaults against white girls by Black predators. "Racial mongrelization is staring us in the face. That is the whole goal and purpose of the so-called 'racial moderates.'"[181]

Two quite different individuals furnished Carter's major arguments for white supremacy and Black inferiority.

The first was a Yale-educated Mississippi circuit court judge who considered himself an "intellectual." Sporting a Thomas Dewey-style mustache, horn-rimmed glasses, bow tie, and the tailored three-piece suit of a New York banker, Tom Brady hardly fit the profile of a traditional rabble-rouser. But in a lengthy speech in the fall of 1954, soon expanded into a hundred-page book, he wrote the blueprint for white Southern resistance to the Supreme Court's *Brown* decision.[182]

Thomas Brady, 1954.

The book's title, *Black Monday,* came from the high court's 1954 decision on Monday, May 17. Brady summarized what was quickly becoming the main argument of white resistance: that the *Brown* decision was an "unconstitutional" usurpation of the rights of the states by the federal government, promoted and led by communists and their socialist and liberal allies. Peace and harmony in the South could only exist by maintaining segregation, which was "good for both races." Brady's most practical suggestions outlined what would become the organizing principles of the emerging white Citizens' Council movement. The natural leaders of the region should make certain that respectable middle- and upper-income whites led the movement, disassociating the Councils from violent "Klan-type" leaders and emphasizing political, economic, and legal resistance while appealing to Northern conservatives skeptical of federal interference in local and state issues. As one Southern newspaper editor acknowledged, some of Brady's recommendations were"a bit impractical": the impeachment of all nine Supreme Court Justices and their replacement by popular election, the legal eradication of the NAACP through prosecution by special court panels, the replacement of public with private schools, and the exile of African Americans to a newly created state that would be purchased from Mexico.

When Brady finished his manuscript in January 1955, he donated its publishing rights to the newly created Citizens' Council of Mississippi. Over the next two years, the Council published and sold more than 260,000 copies of the work, and Brady became a celebrity within the growing white resistance movement. Newspapers from Maine to San Francisco (and abroad) ran articles on the Mississippi judge, describing (without detail) *Black Monday* as a "handbook" for organizing the Citizens' Council movement in the South. With the exception of several articles in the Black press, a piece by Anthony Lewis in the *New York Times* and another by James Desmond in the *New York Daily News*, none included specific references to his vicious racism.[183]

The heart of the book was not Brady's constitutional arguments or his recommendations on organizing white resistance, it was his obsession with the threat of impure Black blood, a threat which evoked a visceral fear in the former judge. He referred to the danger of "negro blood" more than a dozen times in the first eight pages of *Black Monday*. Drawing heavily upon James Denson Sayers's 1929 racist manifesto, *Can the White Race Survive?*, Brady argued that racially pure Caucasian and Asian civilizations had changed and developed to higher forms, but "the negroid man, like the modern lizard," remained "one-half step from the primordial brute." It might be possible to "dress a chimpanzee, housebreak him, and teach him to use a knife and fork," but he would still consider the caterpillar and cockroach a delicacy. "Likewise the social, political, economic and religious preferences of the negro remain close to the caterpillar and the cockroach."[184] In Brady's version of the history of race, Aryan India, Rome, "pure-blooded Mayan civilization, Spain, Greece, and ancient Egypt became victims of "the mark of the beast"—racial amalgamation with the Negro. "Whenever and wherever the white man has drunk the cup of black hemlock, whenever and wherever his blood has been infused with the blood of the negro, the white man, his intellect and his culture have died."[185]

He warned that encouraged by communists, socialists and liberals, Blacks—unable to progress on their own—would seek to mongrelize America through intermarriage. And there was always the threat of the forced sexual violation of the "purest of God's creatures," the "well-bred, cultured Southern white woman" and her "blue-eyed, golden-haired little girl."[186]

If Carter relied heavily upon *Black Monday*, he also turned to Wesley Critz George, retired chair of the Department of Anatomy and professor of histology at the University of North Carolina, Chapel Hill. George had little training in genetics, but his position as a respected scientist and his passionate and public commitment to "racial purity" made him one of the most widely quoted scientific racists of the 1950s.[187] Although his political activities centered on North Carolina, George enthusiastically supported and endorsed the American States Rights Association and the growing Citizens' Council movement.

In the wake of *Brown*, he published the first of several articles and books defending scientific racism: *The Race Problem from the Standpoint of One Who Is Concerned about the Evils of Miscegenation*. "All the evidence that we have indicates that the negro races [are] on the average definitely below the white races in intellectual ability and creativeness." George dismissed the overwhelming scientific consensus that there was no basis for superiority and inferiority based on racial typologies. Such nonsense, he wrote, was the product of "left-wing ideologues." On the basis of Carter's recommendation, the American States Rights Association printed and distributed more than twenty-five thousand copies of *The Race Problem* to white Southern community leaders.[188]

Like Brady, Carter always saw himself as an intellectual whose goal was not simply to promote white supremacy but to educate the masses by presenting scientific evidence, buttressed by vivid anecdotes describing the threat posed by inferior races. In his 1950s broadcasts, he repeatedly attacked German-born anthropologist Franz Boas and the "Swedish socialist" Gunnar Myrdal.

It is doubtful that many of Carter's radio listeners had ever heard of Boas, the influential anthropologist who challenged the widely held racism of nineteenth- and early twentieth-century scientists. Nor were they likely to be familiar with the 1944 two-volume work of Myrdal, the Swedish economist and Nobel laureate. In *An American Dilemma: The Negro Problem and Modern Democracy,* Myrdal described a vicious historical cycle in which white Americans, gripped by racial prejudice, oppressed Black Americans, denying them educational and economic opportunities and then justifying their oppression by pointing to the failure of Blacks to match the achievements of whites.[189]

In his escalating attacks against the federal government, and particularly the Supreme Court, Carter had powerful allies. Ten days after the *Brown* decision, Mississippi's powerful senior senator, James Eastland, took to the floor of the Senate to condemn the Supreme Court for "fomenting revolution in the South." Like some caricature of a Southern demagogue, the heavy-set, balding Southerner, a wealthy Sunflower County plantation owner, peered out at his many enemies from his owlish glasses with a scowl, cigar in hand. Newspapers in the Deep South inevitably described Eastland as "courtly," a behavior strictly limited to whites. When Black witnesses opposing segregation came before his Senate committee, he regularly berated them, addressing them by their first names, or simply as "boy."[190]

James Eastland, 1954.

From his election to the Senate in 1942 until his retirement in 1978, three great passions drove Eastland: the ever-present danger of communists at home and abroad, the need to maintain absolute white supremacy in Mississippi and throughout the South, and a commitment to maintaining federal agricultural subsidies that propped up his cotton landholdings. Anti-communism proved a useful political tactic, and federal price supports were a matter of economic self-interest, but the senator's racism reflected authentic fanaticism. "Jim Eastland could be standing right in the middle of the worst Mississippi flood ever known," Lyndon Johnson told one of his friends, "and he'd say the niggers caused it, helped out by the Communists."[191]

As early as 1945, Eastland had described any civil rights measure as "part of the Communist program to . . . sovietize our country." In the wake of the *Brown* decision he railed against these new alien carpetbaggers. "Everyone knows that the Negroes did not themselves instigate the agitation against segregation," Eastland told his fellow senators. In an attack that would become standard fare for segregationists, he lashed out at members of the Supreme Court. Hugo Black, Sherman Minton, William Douglas, Stanley Reed, and Felix Frankfurter, he claimed, had close ties with many "communist front organizations." In view of their associations, charged Eastland, "a presumption of tainted justice becomes inevitable." As he said in a floor exchange with a supportive Joseph McCarthy, the *Brown* decision proved that a "majority of the [Supreme] Court is being influenced by some secret, but very powerful Communist or pro-Communist influence. . . ."

More than three dozen senators sat on the floor listening to Eastland's speech. None rose to defend the justices or challenge the Mississippi Democrat.[192]

But Eastland did more than speak out against his enemies. As chair of the Senate's Internal Security Sub-Committee, Eastland slandered as "communists" or "communist dupes" anyone in the South sympathetic to civil rights. In hearings held in New Orleans in the early spring of 1954, as chairman of the Senate Judiciary Committee he had targeted white Southern liberals.[193]

Throughout the 1950s, FBI Director J. Edgar Hoover proved a valuable ally in Eastland's campaign of slander against integration. Hoover shared Eastland's hostility to civil rights and obsession with Communism, and he sent Eastland a steady stream of "proof" of the links between integrationists and communists, information that Eastland used in his floor speeches, committee reports, and in leaks to friendly newspapers. All these seemed to give official federal verification to claims that the Communist Party was the source of civil rights agitation. (The friendship with Hoover also protected Eastland from possible prosecution after the FBI learned from reliable sources that the Mississippi senator had been receiving money under the table from the notorious Dominican Republic dictator, Rafael Trujillo.[194])

In vain, civil rights leaders leaned over backwards to avoid any connection to the small number of American communists that remained active in the 1950s. "I'm getting sick and tired of people saying that this movement has been infiltrated by Communists," complained Martin Luther King Jr. "There are as many Communists in this freedom movement as there are Eskimos in Florida."[195] But claims that communists spearheaded the movement for racial equality resonated with white Southerners. Over the previous century they had blamed abolitionists, carpetbaggers, and meddling Northerners for rousing docile Blacks and manipulating them into raising irresponsible demands for racial equality. Communists were simply the latest in a historical line of outside agitators.[196]

Eastland was only one among the many powerful segregationists in the United States Senate and House where seniority rules placed long-serving white Southerners in positions of enormous power. In the House, congressmen from the region chaired twelve of nineteen major committees, including the House Rules Committee where the chair, Virginia Congressman Howard Smith, served as gatekeeper to prevent the introduction of civil rights legislation.[197]

While most white Americans outside the South may have balked at the claim that the Supreme Court was under the direct control of the Communist Party, Carter's argument drew strength as the nation's anti-communist fervor grew in the 1950s. By linking civil rights activists to the international communist conspiracy, white Southerners were able to influence many Northern whites uneasy about the more unsavory aspects of segregation—voter repression and white-on-Black violence—but frightened over the possibility that the Soviet Union might use American Blacks as a secret weapon in the Cold War. By the 1960s, national polls showed that well over half of all white Americans believed that the Communist Party played a role in the civil rights movement.[198]

In the wake of *Brown*, Carter's sponsors expanded his broadcasts, creating a statewide radio network of twenty AM stations.[199] Through the summer and fall of 1954, exposing these "agents of amalgamation" became a major theme of Carter's "Liberty Essays" as he described how foreign-born "pro-communist integrationists" like Boas and Myrdal had placed white Americans on the defensive with their "pseudo-scientific" writings.

As his audience expanded across Alabama, Mississippi whites—inspired by Judge Brady's call to arms—launched the Citizens' Council movement that would prove so critical in mobilizing white resistance in the Deep South. Within a year, councils had sprung up across the region, enlisting more than sixty thousand white Southerners. With a membership drawn primarily from the middle-class white community's service clubs, chambers of commerce, and established churches, these local organizations played a critical role in organizing regional resistance to integration. As Brady had hoped, they were the kind of "respectable" folk that gave greater legitimacy to white resistance.

State Senator Sam Engelhardt became the leading organizer in Alabama. Engelhardt entered state politics in 1950 after he discovered that Governor Jim Folsom had appointed a registrar who was allowing Blacks to sign up to vote. Engelhardt, a planter, merchant, and cotton-gin owner, cultivated more than 6,500 acres of prime cotton land on his Macon County plantation less than fifteen miles from Tuskegee, home of the famed Tuskegee Institute and the three hundred-bed Veterans Administration hospital for Black patients. In a town that was more than 90 per cent Black, the two institutions attracted a large educated, middle-class Black population that the wealthy Engelhardt found particularly threatening. "[If] you have a nigger

Sam Engelhardt, 1946.

tax assessor, what would he do to you?" he asked a reporter. "What would a nigger sheriff do to you? What would a nigger judge do to you?"[200]

Most white Southern politicians described themselves simply as segregationists ("for the good of both races"). In 1950, Engelhardt felt no need for such euphemisms. In his successful run for the Alabama House, he printed "I Stand for White Supremacy" on his campaign cards. For the next four years in the state legislature, he struggled to convince fellow Alabamians of the danger of the federal courts and the national government chipping away at the region's white control over the Negro. He had been one of the founders of the American States Rights Association—the same organization that had hired Asa Carter as radio spokesman—but the balding state senator was always conscious of the limited appeal of an organization funded by a handful of wealthy Birmingham businessmen with little public support. As he watched the emerging Citizens' Councils in Mississippi, he saw a much broader movement of white Southerners as the only way to create political counter-pressure.

Engelhardt had attended Washington and Lee University during the Great Depression for two years before dropping out. Despite owning a large plantation, collapsing cotton prices in the 1920s and early 1930s left his family near bankruptcy and his parents unable to afford the school's annual $450 room, board, and tuition. After the death of his father, he took over the 6,500 acres left to him in 1932. Ironically, the federal government he came to hate so much poured out hundreds of millions of dollars in subsidies to cotton growers over the next six years, allowing Engelhardt to expand his landholdings and business interests.[201] Among his white friends—members of the "gentry" and the county's small middle class—he gained a reputation for his self-deprecating sense of humor and his open-handed hospitality. Few state politicians had not attended one of the dove shoots on his vast acreage or spent a lively evening sharing cocktails at his plantation in Shorter, Alabama, in Macon County. Respectable whites admired him for his ability to balance public calls for "peaceful means" to defend segregation and his public insistence that he was not driven by race hatred. "I like Negroes," Engelhardt told a *New York Times* reporter in a 1955 interview. "I ought to, I owe 98 percent of my living to them."

Away from the national limelight, he was more candid. "Damn niggers stink," he indiscreetly told a friendly reporter. "They have no morals; they're just animals. . . . Give him the opportunity be near a white woman, and he goes berserk!" In a chilling defense of biological racism, he argued that the "nigger isn't just a dark-skinned white man. He's a separate individual altogether."[202]

Inspired by the rise of the Mississippi Citizens' Councils, Engelhardt issued a call for a "mass meeting" in Selma to organize the state's first Citizens' Council. He found a receptive audience in Dallas County, where Blacks outnumbered whites three to one. In late November 1955, more than six hundred men signed the Selma Citizens' Council charter and whites in four nearby counties joined in the creation of local Councils. But Dallas, Hale, Macon, Marengo, and Perry counties were in the heart of the Black Belt,* where whites had always been a fearful minority. Across the rest of the state, Engelhardt and his Black Belt political allies found little enthusiasm for the creation of a Council movement. Back from one gathering in north Birmingham when less than a dozen whites showed up, a frustrated Engelhardt complained that "nobody was interested" because they believed that Blacks in the state could not effectively challenge segregation.

There was reason for white Alabamians' self-confidence.

A little over a year after the *Brown v. Board* decision, the Greenville, Alabama, chapter of the NAACP petitioned the local school board to begin drawing up plans for phasing out segregated schools. An angry crowd of eight hundred whites gathered at the Butler County Courthouse the following week and created a local Citizens' Council that included the most prominent figures in the white community. The school board swiftly dismissed the petition without comment, and after white leaders (including the county sheriff) warned those who had signed the petition to avoid "causing trouble," all but a handful of the petitioners withdrew their signatures and the local NAACP collapsed. But so did the local Citizens' Council. Fewer

* The Black Belt is a geologic region with rich, dark topsoil, particularly suited for growing cotton, that stretches across the Deep South from South Carolina to Texas, notably encompassing a dozen counties in central Alabama that had majority slave populations and later total segregation, legal and cultural.

than 150 whites showed up for the next Council meeting, which adjourned without plans for future meetings.

Petitions from a half dozen NAACP chapters across the state—mostly in Black Belt counties—met the same fate.[203]

Although a number of Southern newspapers called for "calm and reason" in response to Brown, *almost none failed to express condemnation. The editor of my hometown newspaper proved an exception. Jack O'Dowd, a Florence-born former Marine had only recently assumed the editorship, but his first editorial on the issue described segregation as an "expediency" that could not be defended on moral grounds. And he bluntly told his readers: "The question is no longer whether or not segregation is proper, the present question is what the state is do in the face of the court's decision." In a lengthy editorial, he expressed concern that the growing opposition to integration would create a climate that would lead to violence and division. Apart from the moral questions involved, he also based his editorial on economic self-interest. New technology and the industrial development of the future required an "educated labor supply; an orderly state government and an expansion of state functions." Already, he said, politicians were talking about replacing public education with private schools, a move that he warned would cripple the South's growing economic progress.*

O'Dowd was hardly a radical. In that and following editorials, he argued for a cautious and slow dismantling of segregation. To his closest friends, O'Dowd's views on African Americans reflected a fundamental human decency that sprang from his deep religious convictions. His willingness to take a stand also seemed to stem from his disdain for the racial demagogues who had long plagued Southern politics.[204]

As a sixteen-year-old, I heard family and neighbors complaining that the editor of the Morning News *was out of touch with local opinion. I have no recollection of my own reaction; I feel certain that I would have agreed. I do recall the appearance of South Carolina Governor George Bell Timmerman on NBC's* Meet the Press *during that period. My father had just purchased our first television set and the family gathered around to watch our governor defend the South from badgering Yankee journalists, particularly the show's founder, Lawrence Spivak, with his horn-rimmed glasses, insufferable bow tie, and, to my South Carolina ears, abrasive New York accent.*

Timmerman was firm but on his best behavior, describing South Carolina's equalization program and emphasizing constitutional arguments against the Supreme Court's decision. Black and white Southerners strongly supported separating the races, he insisted. While he went on the offensive pointing to riots and racial conflict in the North that proved "racial mixing" only resulted in violence and conflict, he promised to use every peaceful means to maintain the Southern way of life.

I was impressed: here was an articulate white Southerner explaining that we as white Southerners were not barefoot bigots but were simply fighting for our constitutional rights.[205] *Of course such rhetoric was strictly for national consumption. Back home, the governor abandoned abstract issues of states' rights as he attacked "mongrelization" and red-baited the NAACP and any individual who questioned segregation. Even his insistence on* Meet the Press *that white Southerners would engage in peaceful resistance took a different turn once out of the national spotlight. If the federal government failed to give the (white) people what they demand, he told one local South Carolina reporter, "the public sometimes takes the law into its own hands."*[206]

O'Dowd and his staff at the Morning News *could attest to the willingness of members of the public to take the law in their own hands. Shortly after receiving a death threat in late November 1955, O'Dowd managed to outrun four Klansmen who tried to force his car off the road. Unknown whites—presumed to be Klan members—slashed the car tires of* Morning News *staffers, and, in one case, Klansmen beat a reporter as he covered one of their rallies.*[207] *As angry letters and opposition grew, O'Dowd's editorials became more cautious and less biting.*[208]

But his swerve to the center was too late. When the county Democratic convention met in March 1956, members overwhelmingly passed a resolution condemning the Florence Morning News *as part of the "carpetbagger press." Shortly afterwards, in a nationally publicized editorial, O'Dowd wrote his last biting editorial. Newspapers that refused to advocate "sedition, bigotry, white supremacy and incitement to legislative violence are not accepted," he declared. Given the climate of opinion, he felt he had no choice but to "retreat from reason" and end editorials on racial issues.*[209]

Two months later he resigned. In the increasingly hysterical response of white Southerners to the Brown *decision, it was clear that even heroes had limits. During the next thirty years before his untimely death at fifty-nine, Jack O'Dowd lived in Chicago, directed Northwestern University's public relations department and periodically wrote reviews and essays for the* Chicago Tribune *on media issues. When he died in 1986, the* Tribune *and the* Sun-Times *described his career in Chicago but made no mention of his role as a Southern newspaper editor in the 1950s.*[210]

Neither the Florence Morning News *nor any other newspaper in the state or region ran an obituary.*

Within a year after the *Brown* decision, Alabama's neighbors in Georgia and Mississippi had moved to enact a series of anti-integration measures, including the elimination of the state's compulsory school attendance laws. But "Big Jim" Folsom continued to resist the Council movement and to oppose additional legislation. When pressed by critics, he responded with an ingenious parody of the calls for white supremacy. "All I can say is what I told the good colored people of this state during my campaign," he told a reporter, "that they wouldn't have to go to school with us white folks." More bluntly he called out Engelhardt and his supporters. "When politicians start hollering 'whip the nigger,'" Folsom warned, "then you know damn well they are trying to cover up dirty tracks."[211]

Despite the absence of a sense of crisis, Carter's WILD listening audience grew through 1954 and into the spring of 1955. Publicly he continued to present himself as the self-styled intellectual voice of white resistance as he cited scientific experts and described what he called the "explosion" of Black crime and violence in integrated schools in the North. If Carter expressed frustration over the passivity of the state's white population, he remained hopeful that they could be persuaded to take a stronger stand. Whites may have been divided on just how far to go in opposing integration, but the overwhelming majority supported segregation in the public schools and in public accommodations. The most complete survey of white

Southern attitudes on the eve of the *Brown* decision found that four out of five white Southerners *strongly* supported racial segregation. A second poll two years later showed that the percentage of whites strongly opposing the *Brown* decision had increased six percentage points, from 80 to 86.[212] At the same time, widespread gerrymandering and malapportionment in the region meant that rural and small-town communities—the home of white Southerners most adamant in supporting segregation—dominated the region's politics.[213]

And white attitudes were all that counted. Black Southerners favored the court's decision, but they had little to no power. In Alabama, less than 5 percent of eligible African Americans had been able to register to vote by the mid-1950s, and in no Southern state did Blacks constitute more than 10 percent of the registered voters. Whites, who in 1950 made up two-thirds of the population of the former Confederacy cast 94 percent of the votes in the 1952 and 1956 presidential elections.

But just as his reputation was growing across the state, Carter blundered into the first setback in his steady rise as a star among the region's growing number of segregationist leaders. While antisemitism remained central to Carter's world view, he knew the pitfalls of openly attacking Jews, particularly in his broadcasting base, Birmingham, where the city's small but influential Jewish community had spent seventy-five years developing strong connections to the overwhelmingly Christian population.[214]

Fifteen years after the 1871 incorporation of Birmingham, Jewish arrivals laid the cornerstone for the city's first synagogue, Temple Emanu-El. When the city struggled to pay its water, sewer, and electricity bonds during the depression of the 1890s, two Austrian-born Jewish bankers guaranteed the city's outstanding bonds for five years, letting the city avoid bankruptcy. By the early twentieth century, Loveman's, Pizitz, Blach's, Parisian, Bromberg's, Burger-Phillips, Tillman-Levinson, Porter's, and Jobe-Rose department stores—all Jewish owned—dominated the city's downtown retail district. The 1908 construction of Loveman's seven-story store—the largest in the Southeast—reflected the role of Jews in the city of coal and steel.

Birmingham's Jewish community had become integrated into the city's civic life through extensive philanthropy, participation in various charitable and community aid organizations, and ties with several mainline Protestant churches. Emanu-El's long-time rabbi, Morris Newfield, taught Hebrew to seminary students at the local Baptist college, regularly lunched with Protestant ministers, and became close friends with the young (and liberal) Presbyterian minister, Dr. Henry Edmonds.

Despite continuing efforts to blend with their Christian and heavily Protestant white communities, at critical moments Jews found themselves in the familiar role of scapegoats in situations that made them conscious of their precarious position in a South dominated by Protestant evangelicals.

In 1908, Leo Frank, a New York-born, Cornell-educated engineer, moved to Atlanta to manage his uncle's pencil factory. He quickly became an influential member of the Jewish community and an active participant in various "social uplift" charities in the city. His Georgia-born wife was the granddaughter of Levi Cohen, founder of the city's first Reform synagogue. But in April 1913, the Black night watchman at the pencil factory reported that he had discovered the bloody body of factory worker Mary Phagan, a thirteen-year-old white girl. Frank, the last person known to have seen her alive, found himself the chief suspect. Goaded by public anger and the anti-semitic ravings of former Populist leader Tom Watson, a jury of twelve white Atlanta Christians convicted Frank on the basis of the perjured testimony of a drunken Black factory janitor who had almost certainly killed Phagan.

Two years later, when the governor of Georgia concluded that Frank was innocent and commuted his death sentence, two dozen of the most prominent citizens of Marietta, Georgia, Mary Phagan's hometown, drove 120 miles through the night to the state penitentiary in Milledgeville. With only feeble resistance from prison guards, the self-styled "Knights of Mary Phagan" seized Frank from his cell and returned to Marietta where they lynched him on a tree overlooking the girl's childhood home. A Marietta grand jury refused to indict any individuals, an unsurprising finding since seven members of the grand jury had participated in the lynching.[215]

Several of the lynchers became part of the KKK revival which began just outside Atlanta only months later. Within a decade, an estimated four million to six million white Protestants had joined the secret order. While the majority of Klan members lived in the midwest, Alabama's Klan became the largest in the South. Klansmen across the state were more likely to assault "immoral" whites, Catholics, and African Americans, but the Jewish community in Alabama would learn it was not exempt from the reach of the hooded order. When the twenty thousand Klan members in Birmingham swept the 1918 elections, the new mayor and city council immediately dismissed the Jewish long-time city comptroller Louis Levy without a public explanation. Birmingham's Jewish community never doubted the cause of Levy's firing.

Levy's firing provoked neither headlines nor protests. But when Klan leaders in the Birmingham suburb of Woodlawn discovered that Chester Bandman, the principal of the local high school was Jewish, they demanded that the Jefferson County School Board fire Bandman lest the children in his school "fall under the spell of a Jew." Unlike the Levy case, the city's morning and evening newspapers as well as at least half a dozen regional newspapers reported details of the controversy.

Although Bandman was a prominent member of Temple Emanu-El, the Reverend Roy Hershey, pastor of the Woodlawn Presbyterian Church, led the defense of Bandman. Hershey did not defend Bandman on the basis of freedom of religion, nor did he attack the bigotry of the Klan. Instead, he sought to draw the popular principal into the circle of whiteness. At a rally attended by students and local residents, he assured the crowd that he had "never met a whiter, cleaner, purer and safer man than Chester A. Bandman. . . . " While the county school board fell one vote short of removing the popular principal, one of the members angrily condemned the failure. It was understandable that good Christians should oppose Jewish teachers, he said. If "we want Christ and the Bible in our schools, then we must have Christ-like people to teach. . . . " At the end of the school year, Bandman resigned and accepted a teaching position in Pittsburgh.[216]

Popular memory of the Klan of the 1920s has been shaped by the most extreme examples of lawless violence, but no gang of outlaws could have gained such broad support from millions of Protestant, white Americans. Despite references to the organization as an "Invisible Empire," it differed from the Reconstruction-era Klan: it was neither invisible nor secretive. "Klannishness," as one historian has shown, was a thoroughly mainstream aspect of the culture of the 1920s, as local klaverns (chapters) sponsored public events, endorsed political candidates, and skillfully used the new mass media of radio and motion pictures to spread their message. There was no space for Jews in this white Christian movement.[217]

The Leo Frank lynching of 1915 had shaken the entire Southern Jewish community, but the infamous Scottsboro Boys case of 1931 left an even deeper impression upon Alabama's Jews. After a sham trial, an all-white jury in Scottsboro, Alabama, sentenced eight innocent Black teenagers to death and a thirteen-year-old to life in prison for supposedly raping two white women.

The International Labor Defense League (ILD), the Communist Party's legal arm, seized control of the case from a bumbling NAACP and retained several of the nation's leading appellate attorneys to carry the case all the way to the United States Supreme Court. In the first of two landmark decisions, *Powell v. Alabama,* the high court ruled seven to two that defendants in capital cases were entitled to effective legal counsel (at the trial, one of the teenagers' court-appointed lawyers was senile and the other was drunk).

In a decision that had fateful consequences for Alabama's Jewish community, the ILD retained famous New York attorney Samuel Leibowitz for the defense in the new trials scheduled in the spring of 1933. Leibowitz was no Communist, but he was definitely the *other*: Jewish, with a pronounced Brooklyn accent and little concern for the niceties of Southern race relations. In one of the most dramatic trials in American history, Ruby Bates, one of the two alleged victims, recanted her earlier claim of rape, and Leibowitz mercilessly exposed the lies and contradictions of the second alleged victim, Victoria Price.

But in closing arguments, Morgan County prosecutor Wade Wright told the jury he had not been able to follow the arguments of Leibowitz and fellow counsel Joseph Brodsky because it was in the "Jew language." He dismissed the testimony of key defense witness Lester Carter, a white hobo who had been on the train at the time of the alleged attack. In his summation to the jury, Wright referred to Carter as "Carterinsky" and sneered that he was "the prettiest Jew" he had ever seen. (Carter was not Jewish.) Wright said, "If he had been with Brodsky [Leibowitz's co-counsel] another two weeks he would have been down here with a pack on his back a-trying to sell you goods." The issue was a simple one, he shouted to the twelve white jurors: "Is justice in the case going to be bought and sold in Alabama with Jew money from New York?"[218]

Despite overwhelming evidence that the charge of rape was false, despite a charge to the jury from presiding Judge James Horton that heavily favored the defense, the jury returned a verdict of death in the electric chair. As one Black Belt newspaper editor told his readers, he and white Southerners were sick of those "kike lawyers who are excellent examples of the scum of humanity."[219]

Charles Fiedelson, an editorial writer for the *Birmingham Age-Herald* (and a prominent member of Montgomery's Temple Beth Or) spent two days at the trial conversing with white residents who listened to his native Georgian accent and assumed that he was "one of them." He was stunned to discover that most "took for granted that a Jew was a Communist" or were "at least in secret sympathy with the reds."[220]

Throughout the retrials, Alabama's Jewish community generally kept a low profile; those who didn't quickly felt the consequences. After Joseph Gumbiner's ordination at Hebrew Union College in 1931, Selma's Temple Mishkan Israel called him to lead the small, but influential congregation in the Black Belt city. Convinced that the Scottsboro defendants were innocent, he delivered a controlled but passionate sermon calling upon his congregation to remember *tzedakah*—Hebrew for the Jewish obligation to speak for justice and righteousness. The response from the Selma congregation was swift and overwhelming "Where does Judaism mix in with race relations" asked the Temple president. "Tell us about Abraham, Isaac, and Rebecca. Stick to Judaism." When told that he would not be allowed to speak on racial issues, Gumbiner left for a congregation outside the South.

Montgomery's Temple Beth Or did not give Rabbi Benjamin Goldstein that choice. The California native had come to the Temple in 1929 and was soon recognized and admired by the largely Christian community in Montgomery for his public lectures on social and religious topics. A few critics expressed concern over sermons in which he publicly defended the right of labor to organize and spoke of the unfair conditions of Alabama's

African Americans. Still, the handsome and gregarious Goldstein retained the support of Temple Beth Or, in no small part because he was popular in the largely Christian community. The editor of the *Montgomery Advertiser* repeatedly praised Goldstein for his lecture series that drew distinguished speakers to Montgomery from across the nation.

As with Gumbiner, Scottsboro was Goldstein's downfall. When he spoke to a mostly Black group of supporters of the Scottsboro defendants in late March 1933, Goldstein criticized the "hatred and bigotry" that had led to the unjust convictions of the "Scottsboro Boys." Two days later, the president of Temple Beth Or presented Goldstein with an ultimatum: he could remain silent on "sensitive" issues of race and politics or he could resign. Goldstein, realizing he had lost the support of his congregation, agreed to leave at the end of his contract. But another six months of Goldstein's presence in the city proved unacceptable to Montgomery Mayor William Gunter. After a tense meeting in his city hall office, Gunter accused Goldstein of being a Southern agent for the ILD and warned him that he was subject to the city's recently adopted "criminal anarchy ordinance" which made it a felony to promote the "subversive doctrines" of criminal anarchy by "word, sign or writing."[221]

The following week, Goldstein left town.

Antisemitism in the South had a peculiarly ambiguous heritage. Over the years, many Southern evangelicals professed great admiration for the "people of the book" and often paid tribute to the piety and knowledge of the scriptures attributed to Jews. But Jews were most valued when they were seen as the ancestors of the *real* Messiah, Jesus Christ. At its most extreme this tolerance of Jews was rooted in millenarian theology which envisioned the creation of the Jewish state in modern-day Israel as a precondition to an apocalpytic Second Coming of Christ in which most Jews would be destroyed and the remainder converted to Christianity.[222]

Given those ambivalent attitudes, the lesson Southern Jews learned remained unchanged. The greatest protection against antisemitism lay in maintaining close relationships between the Jewish and Christian community and business elites *and* avoiding a stand on racial issues. As a group of Jewish leaders would argue during the civil rights era in a widely circulated memorandum: Jews ought to stay out of the desegregation fight on the ground that it was a 'Christian problem' between whites and Negroes. . . ."[223]

World War II and the horrors of the Holocaust pushed antisemitic rhetoric to the margins of American political life, but well before the war there had been attempts to oppose antisemitism and other religious bigotry. In the midst of the bitter 1928 presidential contest between Catholic Democratic candidate Al Smith and Republican Herbert Hoover, a coalition of Birmingham's Jewish, Catholic, and mainline Protestant leaders became the first Southern community to create a chapter of the newly formed National Conference of Christians and Jews (NCCJ), an organization devoted to promoting ecumenical relations between the two communities.[224] During the 1930s, as part of its outreach program, the NCCJ established "National Brotherhood Week," a time when religious leaders were encouraged to sponsor public events to highlight the dangers of religious and racial bigotry and to promote "understanding and respect through conflict resolution, and education." After languishing through the 1930s, post-war revelations of the Holocaust gave a dramatic boost to the organization, and in 1953 newly elected President Dwight Eisenhower agreed to serve as honorary president of the NCCJ.

In the South of 1955, however, even cautious declarations of brotherhood teetered on the edge of apostasy. NCCJ's Southern regional director, William A. Stewart, made it clear that while he opposed the Klan and other violent groups, he was equally contemptuous of the "pro-integrationists and [civil rights] extremists" who were damaging the region's national image.[225]

While Northern and Southern chapters diverged in their views on racial—as opposed to religious—brotherhood, there was one subject on which most Americans agreed: the growing conflict between the United States and the Soviet Union and its communist allies was a religious as well as an economic and military struggle. By the mid-1950s, the United States was in a religious revival, with half of all Americans regularly attending church or synagogue services, the highest percentage in American history. The issue that guaranteed ecumenical solidarity was the war against Godless communism.

In April 1954, President Dwight Eisenhower unveiled a postage stamp depicting the Statue of Liberty, under which was engraved "In God We Trust," the first time a religious message had been used on an American stamp. Two months later, by voice vote and without debate, Congress voted to insert a new phrase into the pledge of allegiance: "One nation, *under God*, indivisible, with liberty and justice for all."

In early 1955, the National Conference of Christians and Jews sounded its theme for the year. "The moral struggle is against the onslaught of Communism and war begins with your congregation."[226] For Sunday, February 20, the culmination of National Brotherhood Week, the conference urged churches and synagogues to present sermons extolling ecumenical relations as a way of bolstering the struggle against communism.[227]

Whatever the NCCJ's promotional success across the nation, its plea had only a mild impact in Alabama. Governor Jim Folsom and mayors in a handful of towns in Alabama signed the NCCJ's proclamation declaring February 13–20 as "National Brotherhood Week," but a review of Sunday sermon topics for February 13 and February 20 in Alabama's nine largest newspapers shows only one instance in which a minister spoke indirectly on the subject.

Despite their limited influence, organizations like the NCCJ infuriated Carter and other antisemitic far-right activists. Since they believed that the communist menace sprang directly from the link between communism and a world-wide Jewish conspiracy that sought to undermine racial purity, Jews—the "Christ killers"—had no place in America because whiteness and evangelical Christianity were inseparable. Such ideas easily connected with earlier forms of Southern populism that saw Wall Street enemies—the moneyed classes—as dominated by Jews.

Within months after Carter began broadcasting on WILD in 1954, the Birmingham office of NCCJ received reports of his bitter hatred of Jews. On one occasion, the director personally followed Carter and eavesdropped nearby as he called the office of a local Jewish physician from a downtown pay phone and shouted about "filthy kikes." When the director passed on a warning memo to the southeastern office of the Jewish Anti-Defamation League (ADL), the Atlanta-based staff of that organization recruited sympathetic Christian allies to investigate Carter. One unnamed source who developed close ties with Carter met him for lunch at Birmingham's popular southside restaurant, Michael's Sirloin Room, in the fall of 1954. The source's memo to the ADL described at length Carter's "ravings" about the Jews.

By early 1955, the ADL Atlanta office became concerned enough to launch an elaborate operation to expose Carter's extremist views. ADL officials recruited two Atlanta men who approached Carter and pretended to be Arabs. They told him they were interested in buying WILD and giving him a larger role than simply broadcasting his "Liberty Essays." Dressed in turbans and robes with awkwardly fake "Arab" accents, they greeted Carter in their Birmingham hotel room with a concealed tape recorder and a bottle of Jack Daniels. Once they made clear their contempt for Jews in general and Israel in particular, Carter launched into a diatribe, condemning the treacherous alliance between "Kikes, Communists and niggers."[228] When news of the elaborate sting reached national headquarters, ADL leaders shut down further operations, fearful that disclosure of Carter's entrapment would only ignite more anti-Jewish hatred. [229]

But they never had to use the audio tape.

The day after "Brotherhood Sunday," Carter sat down at his desk at WILD, wrote, and then broadcast his bi-weekly "Liberty Essay," which he called "The Key Weapon." Carter drew his inspiration and much of the language from Francis Yockey's 1948 pro-fascist/antisemitic manifesto *Imperium: The Philosophy of History and Politics* and magazines by antisemitic publishers such as Conde McGinley (*Common Sense)* and Gerald L. K. Smith (*The Sword and the Cross*).

But Carter was aware that, to be most effective, he would have to avoid crudely overt antisemitism. Instead, he described how the NCCJ used the appealing phrase of "brotherhood" to conceal a false doctrine promoted by "communists, communist-fronters and socialists with their fellow travelers." Repeatedly using the phrase "National Conference of Christians and Jews," he told his listeners that Southern Jews were well aware that the national organization had endorsed the "dictatorial civil rights legislation" drawn up by the communist-fronters on Truman's Civil Rights Commission. At the same time, the NCCJ had attacked the founding fathers as "filled with hatred and promoted films that fostered race mongrelization," all under the "dulcet tones of brotherhood." Christians, duped by the soothing rhetoric of "brotherly love" had unwittingly endorsed the steps that would lead to "racial integration and mongrelization."

Equally dangerous, in Carter's view, was NCCJ's support for the United Nations 1948 Treaty on Genocide. Privately, Carter was an early Holocaust-denier, but he was astute enough to use a different argument. The US Senate's approval of the treaty would "restrict free speech, censor the press, force Americans into foreign courts and place them at the mercy of race amalgamators," he told his listeners.[230]

While Carter believed he had made his argument without overt anti-semitism, three days later the American States Rights Association issued a terse statement announcing the termination of their relationship with the broadcaster. Carter publicly accused the "rich Birmingham Jews" of pulling strings to have him fired, but he was well aware that the most effective opposition came from the Birmingham office of the National Conference of Christians and Jews. James Head, a Methodist layman and the well-to-do owner of a large regional office supply business based in Birmingham, had been one of the founders of the local chapter of the NCCJ, and he remained the organization's most influential member. A passionate New Deal supporter in the 1930s, a moderate on racial issues and a friend of several Jewish business associates, the self-made entrepreneur had gone on to build one of the largest office supply companies in the Southeast. Despite his well-deserved reputation as, by Southern standards, a racial liberal, the tactful, congenial, and wealthy Head maintained close connections with his more conservative business counterparts. He directly approached William Hoover, the insurance company executive and real estate tycoon who financed the ASRA and warned that Carter was likely to cause more problems in the days to come.

ASRA backers like Hoover were reluctant to abandon their new hire. They not only agreed with Carter's racial views but shared his contempt for labor unions ("dominated by the communists," he said on one broadcast) and found in him a link to white working class Alabamians that they desperately sought. Sidney Smyer, closely tied to the ASRA, was particularly unhappy at the prospect of losing the voice of Carter. The wealthy realtor and attorney, a passionate believer that the end of white supremacy would lead to a racial Armageddon, had been a key architect of the 1948 Dixiecrat bolt from the Democratic Party that led to the nomination of third-party candidate Strom Thurmond.

But, over two days, Head rounded up support from other non-Jewish business leaders and the ASRA leadership reluctantly decided Carter had to go. Despite his public claims that "Jews" led to his dismissal, Carter was well aware of Head's role. In a private meeting when the ASRA board announced his firing, Head was the only nonmember of the board present, and a furious Carter stood, pointed at him, and shouted, "You're the known communist I've been talking about," before stomping out of the meeting.[231]

Despite his anger, except for a few sniping remarks Carter made no public comments in the days that followed. Perhaps it was because ASRA director Hoover "loaned" him $3,000 ($27,500 in 2023 dollars) to help him get back on his feet. Retired admiral John Crommelin, a passionate antisemite, made a similar $3,000 payment. And there was no attempt to isolate or denounce Carter by Birmingham's power elite.[232]

Asa Carter's firing did not lead to his disappearance from the campaign to maintain segregation in the region, but in the months that followed, even as he maintained connections with mainline segregationist groups, he began to plan secretly for more extreme forms of resistance. Perhaps this shift simply reflected his conviction that only radical actions could galvanize sleeping white Southerners. More likely, just as Carter's abrupt dismissal from his naval officer's training program seems to have been a major factor in his embrace of right-wing ideas, the loss of his public radio platform pushed him deeper into a growing network of violent white supremacists.

7

Riding the Wave: 1955–56

Oh, I know the politicians talk about [white] Southerners being last in this and that. But we're not last in what counts: a love of freedom, a spirit of liberty, a love of God and a willingness to fight for it. Those are the things that count anyway. Those are the everlasting values that determined men hold. That's why we're number one. And that's why the liberals and the communists hate the South with a bitter hatred.

— Asa Carter, 1956 "Liberty Essay"[233]

Although he lost his position and salary from the American States Rights Association, twelve months on the air had established Carter's statewide reputation and connected him to other die-hard segregationists across the state. The $6,000 from Hoover and Crommelin made it possible for Carter to lease a full-service garage and gas station in suburban Birmingham.[234] Anxious to establish a business that would support his passion for politics, he came to work early each morning, manning the gas pumps and often joining his mechanic in the work pit to help with repairs or perform routine maintenance. Friends later recalled that during these early months he often returned in the evening to complete unfinished repairs.

But by the late summer of 1955, Carter's business had become stable enough that he could establish a new routine. At 5 p.m., he drove to his nearby apartment, cleaned up from the day's work, grabbed a quick meal, and took to the road, traveling across north-central Alabama to meet angry whites frustrated by the cautious response of state leadership to the threat of integration. Carter may have lost his radio platform, but he had come a long way from the previous year when he loaded his family in a clapped-out

Ford and left behind his poorly paid radio job in Mississippi. Behind the wheel of his late-model Packard, he drove to speak to groups of followers in Birmingham's blue-collar suburbs. By the fall, he had given talks in small towns and communities from Northport, west of the city, north and east to Jasper, Pell City, Warrior, and his home turf of Anniston and Oxford, with crowds growing at each stop. Followers distributed handbills and bought radio announcements on low-cost country-music AM stations to advertise Carter's upcoming speeches, gatherings that were always marked by requests for contributions to "support the cause." And Carter began a practice that would continue throughout his career as a right-wing activist: he kept strict financial control of these contributions. And he made certain that he was generously compensated for his expenses.

As he spoke, he often expressed admiration for the historical Klan but avoided references to the contemporary hooded order since most middle-class white Southerners gave at least lip service to the notion that there was no longer a place for the modern Klan. Beginning in the mid-1920s and continuing into the 1950s, several Southern newspaper editors received the Pulitzer Prize for their editorials condemning the Klan, and Citizens' Council leaders in the 1950s insisted they had no use for the organization.

Carter certainly did not reveal that he had secretly joined Ensley Klavern No. 31 based in East Birmingham.[235] The Ensley Klan was not the most notorious in the area. That distinction belonged to Birmingham's Eastview Klavern, and particularly to the hardcore Cahaba River Bridge group, a name taken from their secret meetings under an old bridge trestle where they planned their bombings and assaults. Keeping track of the various splinter Klans proved difficult, even for the FBI record keepers. Both the Ensley and Eastview klaverns were part of Alabama's largest Klan organization in the mid-1950s, the U.S. Klans, Knights of the Ku Klux Klan, led by the Reverend Alvin Horn. He was so alarmed by the critical publicity given to the two Birmingham groups that he placed them on "probation" in December 1955.[236]

If not *the* most violent, the Ensley Klavern came close. In choosing to make that connection, Carter stepped into the shadowy world of modern American terrorists, a motley assortment of racist sociopaths who left a trail of assaults, bombings, and murders across the region. For more than a decade, the FBI tried to keep track of what one agent called a "redneck version of Damon Runyon characters": J. B. ("the gimp") Stoner, Charlie Cagle, the "Bowling Boys" (two brothers from Atlanta who specialized in randomly assaulting Black Southerners and in planting explosive devices for Stoner), Bill "Lucky" aka "Daddy" Collins, the "Cash Brothers" (Herman and Jack), Bobby Frank Cherry, Thomas "Pops" Blanton, John Wesley "Nigger" Hall, Lewandoski "the Polack," Arthur "Sister" White, and police officers like Birmingham's Floyd "Fat Daddy" Garrett. Runyon, a raffish newspaperman of the 1930s, wrote short stories featuring professional gamblers, conmen and hustlers with colorful names like Madame La Gimp, Harry the Horse, Good Time Charley and Dream Street Rose, but there was nothing humorous about the white terrorists the FBI tracked.

The most ruthless activists were J. B. Stoner and Robert Edward "Dynamite Bob" Chambliss. Stoner, an Atlanta lawyer and fanatical neo-fascist, roamed across the region. FBI agents described him as the "go-to guy" in coordinating the bombing of Black churches and homes. Stoner often worked with Chambliss, a racist psychopath and one of the men who would plant the deadly 1963 bomb that killed four Black girls at Birmingham's 16th

Above, with microphone at KKK rally, J. B. Stoner, 1956; right, Robert Chambliss, 1963.

Street Baptist Church. Chambliss also maintained close ties to Birmingham's infamous police commissioner, "Bull" Connor.[237]

Few members of this violent brotherhood were as intelligent or articulate as Carter. A fair number were criminals and alcoholics, and many were classic social losers, marginal and pathetic except when they vented their uncontrolled rage against Jews, Blacks, and white liberals (or "communists" as they were usually described.) To embittered Klansmen, these enemies threatened a social order that protected their most powerful asset: the color of their skin. Even though Carter affected a more "intellectual" tone, he somehow managed to establish close ties with many of these men.

If Carter joined the Ensley Klavern, he made no effort to assume leadership. An FBI informant reported that he only occasionally came to meetings and when he did, said little. In time, it would become apparent that he had joined to identify the most dedicated Klansmen and to gain their personal support and loyalty as part of his long-term plan to build what he called a "cadre" of shock troops for the coming struggle.

While violent segregationists could be found across the South, the heart of this dark underground lay in Birmingham. The presence of a well-developed mining industry meant that dozens of men were familiar with mining explosives and skilled in their use. In the late 1940s, they would put this knowledge to use.

Six months before the outbreak of World War II, President Franklin D. Roosevelt signed into law Executive Order 8802, a measure that prohibited racial discrimination by contractors involved in any war-related work. While often ignored by smaller employers, the order forced large-scale coal and steel operators around Birmingham to begin grudgingly allowing Black workers to move up the ladder from menial positions into higher-paying skilled and semi-skilled jobs. And with better wartime pay came the opportunity for some Black workers as well as Black teachers, professionals, and small business owners to move out of dilapidated Black housing areas, often edging into white working-class neighborhoods.

In 1947, a Black drill operator at the Ishkooda Ore Mines just outside Birmingham used his life savings to purchase a frame house on the edge of the white working-class community of Fountain Heights. Before he could move in, the local Klan destroyed the uninsured house with an estimated six sticks of dynamite.[238] In the coming years, white extremists would dynamite or burn the homes of more than thirty Black families that tried to move into white neighborhoods. And year after year, the investigative reports had the same notation at the conclusion of their investigation: "failed to reveal sufficient evidence to make an arrest." For the most part, there seemed to be a tacit understanding among the city's leaders as well as law enforcement. As long as the bombers and arsonists destroyed empty houses, or struck when Black homeowners were absent, there was little attempt to end the bombings.[239]

BUT AS BLACK RESISTANCE began to take shape in the early 1950s, white supremacists moved beyond property damage and began to attack African American activists across the region. One of the first prominent targets was Harry Moore, a teacher in the Titusville, Florida, "colored school," who proved a tenacious civil rights activist during the 1930s and 1940s. In 1947, after the all-white school board fired him and his wife, Harriette, for their political activities, the national NAACP made him the first paid organizer for the organization. Despite continuous tension with the national office, Moore went on to become president of the Florida NAACP, increasing membership to 10,000 and spearheading registration efforts that increased the number of Black Florida voters to more than 115,000, the highest percentage of Black registration in the South.

For most Americans, Florida's image was that of America's developing vacation paradise, but the state was also home of some of the most brutal racial exploitation and violence in the South. Well into the twentieth century, the turpentine camps across north Florida were often (as one historian described them) "slavery by another name." And Florida was second only to Mississippi in the number of Black lynchings per capita.[240]

In 1949, after a string of Black deaths at the hands of local police and Klan activists in central Florida, Moore became involved in the infamous "Groveland" case in which four Black teenagers were accused on the flimsiest of evidence of raping a young white woman. Before the case ended, a large "posse" chased down one of the four and riddled him with four hundred bullets and shotgun pellets. Another was killed in cold blood by Lake County Sheriff Willis McCall, and a third was critically wounded. The case went on for years, but Harry Moore would not survive to see the outcome. His involvement proved to be the last straw for local Klansmen.

In the fall of 1951, white supremacists (who were never identified) raised $5,000 ($53,000, in 2023 dollars) to pay local Klansman Earl Brooklyn to assassinate Moore. Brooklyn used half the money to pay off his home mortgage, then recruited three other Klan members, Edward Spivey, Joseph Cox, and Tillman "Curly" Belvin, an experienced "blast man," to carry out the murder. Collecting the explosives proved no problem. As an FBI investigator later wrote in his report, "Getting dynamite all over central Florida was like buying chewing gum."[241]

On December 25, 1951, Moore and his wife celebrated the twenty-fifth anniversary of their marriage as well as Christmas Day before going to bed a little after 9 p.m. An hour later, while the others kept watch, one of the four Klansmen planted a bomb estimated at ten sticks of dynamite under the bedroom of the Moores' home and lit the fuse. The blast threw Harriette and Harry Moore into the ceiling of their house and shattered windows a half block away. Moore's brother-in-law, home on leave from Korea, hurried to the house, lifted the Moores into his car, and raced thirty-two miles to the nearest hospital that treated Blacks. Moore died on the way. His wife, Harriette, critically injured, lived another thirteen days.[242]

J. Edgar Hoover had no interest in involving his agency in "political" investigations, but U.S. Attorney General Howard McGrath gave clear instructions that the case was to be investigated as a civil rights crime. However reluctant, Hoover sent a team of agents to Florida who conducted more than a thousand interviews and wire-tapped the main suspects (who were quickly identified). But Cox committed suicide three months later, while Brooklyn and Belvin died of natural causes within a year. Nothing ever came of the investigation.[243]

The "Moore incident" soon disappeared from the headlines, but the assassination of the two civil rights leaders marked a new phase in what one Black leader called "dynamite terrorism." While the bombing of Black homes continued in Birmingham, civil rights activists and the sites of civil rights activities increasingly became the object of white violence. From 1948 to 1959, explosives and firebombs shattered more than 250 Black churches and homes in the region, a pattern of mayhem and murder that continued into the 1960s as white supremacists increasingly struck the homes of civil rights leaders and houses of worship, including the 1963 bombing of Birmingham's 16th Street Baptist Church. During the 1964 Freedom Summer campaign in Mississippi alone, terrorists bombed or firebombed twenty-nine homes and thirty-five Black churches. Not all the terrorist acts were bombings. In the most infamous case, a Philadelphia, Mississippi, deputy sheriff led a mob that assassinated two white and one Black civil rights activists, Andrew Goodman, Michael Schwerner, and James Chaney, then buried their bodies in a Mississippi dam. During the long search for their bodies, the bodies of three other murdered young Black men were discovered in the Mississippi and Big Black rivers. Their deaths attracted little attention. And even though the majority of these assaults and murders took place in the Deep South, there were numerous attacks in the border states as well.[244]

While the campaign of beatings, shootings, and more genteel forms of political and economic intimidation continued, dynamite remained the preferred weapon of white terrorists. The failure of law enforcement to apprehend bombers was never a testament to the operational skills of the Klansmen. It reflected a pervasive moral failure within the so-called "respectable" segregation leadership in the Deep South. As the Klan and other violent groups began their campaign of bombing in Birmingham in the late 1940s, Alabama Attorney General Albert Carmichael had bluntly described the role of so-called respectable business leaders. Tennessee Coal and Iron (the Birmingham division of United States Steel), coal operators, and other wealthy interests were not-so-secret supporters of the Klan and other violent groups, often employing high-profile attorneys to defend bombers on the few occasions when they were arrested, said Carmichael. "The Alabama *Klan IS* unquestionably and undoubtedly directed from tall buildings" in the city, Carmichael told his friend, Alabama Senator Lister Hill.[245]

Even if Carmichael exaggerated the role of wealthy interests, anti-union corporate leaders based in Birmingham certainly tolerated the Klan's obsession with white supremacy since it limited class solidarity between Black and white workers.[246] But the underlying problem went much deeper than a conspiracy of wealthy industrial leaders. As long as the bombers and night-riders directed their violence against bona fide integrationists, as long as the main result was property damage and intimidation, respectable whites saw the bombings as little more than a public relations embarrassment. Police seldom faced pressure to bring the guilty to justice. Instead, white voters continued to support politicians from James Eastland to George Wallace who routinely blamed the victims, often claiming that the deadly explosives had been planted by civil rights activists in order to discredit the white South, arguments that proved particularly effective for defendants in the few cases when police arrested and tried to convict them.

As Sam Engelhardt moved up from the state house to the state senate in 1955, Jim Folsom laid out an ambitious second-term program of economic development, increases in social welfare and education appropriations, repeal of the state's right to work law; reapportionment of the legislature (which was dominated by the Black Belt, with large proportions of Black population but few to no registered Black voters), and the creation of a state-funded public defender's office for the poor and equal rights for women. For Black Belt Alabama whites, however, there was only one issue: segregation. Within days of the legislature's opening session, Engelhardt introduced a range of segregationist measures, several of which the state legislature adopted. While Folsom vetoed many of Engelhardt's initiatives, describing the legislation as unjust, unfair, and undemocratic, others passed. "I would like to remind you that we always hear more noise from those who are guided by prejudice and bigotry than is ever the case with those who try to think through and be fair in their approach." Nobody was excited about the segregation issue except a few hell-raising extremists, Folsom insisted.[247]

He was not altogether mistaken. There was no crisis atmosphere in Alabama through the spring and summer of 1955, but Engelhardt and his allies proved far more skillful than Folsom had anticipated in persuading the legislature to focus on racial issues at the expense of the new governor's liberal agenda. That summer, Folsom sent an intermediary to pass on a message to the man who had become his nemesis. You tell Sam Engelhardt, said Folsom, that if he continued his opposition, "I will get a new board of registrars in Macon County and register every damn nigger in the county." It was enough to enrage Engelhardt, who represented a county that was 80 percent Black.

Publicly, Engelhardt took the high road, reporting the threat to friendly reporters while piously complaining that such underhanded methods would only "jeopardize the good feelings that exist between the people of both races in Macon County." Privately, he declared war on the sitting governor. Folsom was a budding dictator, he told his friends. "He'll make Huey Long look like a Sunday School teacher."[248]

Engelhardt's vendetta reflected his fear that Folsom's promise was not an idle threat. Only a handful of African Americans voted in most Black Belt counties, but during his first administration Folsom had appointed a loyalist who registered more than eight hundred and fifty African Americans in and around Macon County's Tuskegee Institute and the Black Veterans' Administration Hospital. They represented 30 percent of the registered voters in the senator's home county.[249]

However threatening Engelhardt found these developments, the Citizens' Council Movement lagged well behind neighboring Mississippi and drew limited support, even in Alabama's Black Belt. The lack of any significant challenge to segregation allowed whites in Alabama to maintain the illusion that change would come only after years of delay.

Frustrated over the limited growth of the Citizens' Council movement, Engelhardt decided that the organization needed to move beyond the loose-knit structure established during its first year. In October 1955, he created four regional divisions within the state: the Central (Black Belt) Alabama Council with the largest number of chapters would be based in Selma, the North Alabama Council in Birmingham, the South Alabama Council in Mobile, and the West Alabama Council in Northport, just outside Tuscaloosa, home of the University of Alabama.

And then he had turned to Asa Carter.

Engelhardt had been one of the original organizers of the American States Rights Association, and he came to see Carter's hair-trigger temper, intemperate language, and violent public relations gestures as a potential threat to more respectable segregationists. If he was leery of Carter's judgment, he realized he had little talent for enlisting the white working class, the mechanics, miners, steel workers, and grocery store clerks who seemed drawn to the tough-talking former radio announcer. Asa Carter was a "genius at appealing to [white] working people who have never been inside a country club," said one of Engelhardt's friends, "but by God, he knows how to deal with niggers."[250]

In November 1955, with the encouragement of Sid Smyer and other members of the ASRA, Engelhardt hired Carter as an organizer for the Citizens' Councils of Alabama, paying him $150 a week plus $50 for expenses ($2,100 in 2023 dollars).[251] Carter rented an abandoned movie theater in Bessemer and made the upstairs office the center of his operations.

A plywood sign below the faded marquee of the old Central Park Theatre read "Alabama National Citizens' Council." Technically Carter was simply the paid regional coordinator of the North Alabama Citizens' Council. But he soon made it clear that he was personally in charge of the Citizens' Councils he organized. And unlike other regional Councils, members of his groups had to "affirm their belief in the divinity of Jesus Christ," a provision that excluded Jews from membership.

Carter also retained authority for policy announcements of the groups and kept complete control of the finances. In addition to his salary and expense check from the state organization, he began withdrawing additional "traveling expenses" from money that came into the North Alabama Citizens' Councils. A dissident member of Carter's organization showed a magazine reporter a copy of the constitution that Engelhardt had drawn up for all regional Councils. In the version approved by Carter, the section that prohibited officers from receiving any salary or other funds had been crossed out.[252] With income almost entirely in cash contributions, he issued no financial reports.

And just as Asa Carter began his personal organizing campaign in the late fall of 1955, two events reshaped the landscape of race and politics in Alabama.

WHO DOES NOT KNOW the story of Rosa Parks, the Montgomery seamstress who refused to give up her seat on a segregated bus in Montgomery, Alabama, on December 1, 1955? In celebrating the ultimate success of the Montgomery boycott, we often overlook that her defiance ignited a violent white backlash, particularly in Alabama. In the first eight weeks after Parks's arrest, local whites (including uniformed police officers, according to eyewitnesses) threw acid on the cars of nineteen prominent Black activists, snipers fired on the near empty buses at night (badly wounding a pregnant rider), and local Ku Klux Klansmen bombed more than a half dozen Black homes, including that of Martin Luther King. Concerned that the rising violence had spiraled out of control and threatened the city's national image, Montgomery police arrested and charged a group of Klansmen for several bombings in the state's capital after uncovering a trove of incriminating evidence. Detectives even persuaded two of the men to confess.

John Blue Hill, Montgomery's most prominent criminal defense attorney, convinced the men to plead not guilty. Given the "right" arguments, a jury would never convict, he promised. And he had the right argument. "A guilty verdict," he told the all-white jury, would be, "a victory for Martin Luther King and his imps who seek to destroy our Southern way of life." "Negro goon squads," he assured the jurors, planted the bombs in an effort to gain sympathy from Northerners. It took the all-white jury less than ninety minutes to find the Klansmen not guilty on all counts. As the foreman began reading the verdict, reported the *Montgomery Advertiser*, "rebel yells and screams of approval" from the packed courtroom drowned out his last words.[253]

On the heels of the Montgomery bus boycott came a second and even more threatening challenge to segregation in Alabama.

AUTHERINE LUCY HAD GRADUATED from the historically Black Miles College in west Birmingham in 1952. That summer, in an audacious move prompted by her closest college friend, Pollie Ann Myers, the two young women decided to apply to the University of Alabama in Tuscaloosa. A fiery speaker and a leading NAACP activist at Miles College, Myers openly chafed at the Jim Crow system in which she lived as well as the cautious

Autherine Lucy, 1956.

leadership of her all-Black school. More sophisticated than Lucy, she realized the challenges they would face and called Arthur Shores, one of the few Black attorneys in the state. Impressed by his interviews with Myers and Lucy, Shores contacted Thurgood Marshall, chief counsel of the NAACP Legal and Defense Fund, and his co-counsel, Constance Mobley. The NAACP agreed to support their entrance and any legal appeals with Shores acting as local attorney.

In August, Lucy and Myers submitted their applications: Lucy for admission to the undergraduate library science program, Myers for admission to the journalism MA program. To the surprise of the two young women and their NAACP attorneys, their letters of application brought a swift response from the dean of women, asking for a modest deposit before assigning them to dorm rooms. Two days later came a form letter from the president warmly welcoming them. They would find the university a "delightful place to live and work." Even though their materials had included transcripts from Miles College, a fifty-seven-year-old Black college only fifty miles east of Tuscaloosa, their applications apparently raised no red flags. Only days before they were scheduled to begin classes in mid-September did an embarrassed dean of admissions realize his mistake and alert university officials that the two applicants they had so warmly welcomed were African American.[254]

Legally, Myers and Lucy had a strong case for admission. In 1950, the US Supreme Court unanimously concluded in *McLaurin* v. *Oklahoma State Regents* and *Sweatt v. Painter* that racially separate graduate and professional programs for Black students were inherently unequal under the equal protection clause of the Fourteenth Amendment. None of Alabama's Black institutions of higher education offered a graduate program in journalism or an undergraduate degree in library science. While the *McLaurin* and *Sweatt* decisions did not explicitly overturn the 1896 *Plessy v. Ferguson* decision that upheld racial segregation, most legal observers—including white Southern politicians—correctly foresaw the death knell of the *Plessy* doctrine.[255]

When told of the mix-up, President John Morin Gallalee, a humorless and passionate segregationist, seemed unworried. The university had developed a broad range of tactics to block qualified African American applicants. In some cases, officials simply ignored applicants known to be Black. If they persisted, the university contacted local whites who warned them and their families that they would face unnamed but "unwelcome" consequences if they continued. When these tactics failed, law enforcement officials or private detectives launched investigations into the background of Black applicants and their families to gain leverage or to release defamatory information to a cooperative white press.

In the case of Pollie Ann Myers, the strategy worked. The university learned that Meyers had given birth to a child only six months after her marriage. Pregnancy out of wedlock had long been used by the university as a bar to admission. Although Myers was married when her child was born, officials smugly noted that she had obviously engaged in premarital sex. The NAACP, fearful of both the public relations and legal consequences, dropped Myers from the lawsuit and cut off all communications with her.

Unable to discover anything negative in Autherine Lucy's background, the university could only use delaying tactics. Federal District Judge Harlan H. Grooms, a former Birmingham lawyer appointed by President Dwight Eisenhower, had been on the bench for less than two years but had already established a consistent anti-civil rights record. He had supported the City of Birmingham's refusal to allow Black applicants to take the police examination, and in another case he rejected the complaint of Black homeowners whose property had been seized under eminent domain and then used to build whites-only housing.

For two years he found ways to delay Lucy's case, but he eventually bowed to appellate and Supreme Court orders, ordering her admission at the beginning of the spring semester of 1956.[256] By this time Oliver Carmichael had replaced Gallalee as the university's president. Carmichael, a 1911 graduate of the university, left his prestigious positions as president of the Carnegie Foundation for the Advancement of Teaching and chairman of the Board of Trustees for the New York University system to return to his alma mater. Intimidated by a fiercely segregationist board of trustees, he did little to prepare the university for the February arrival of Lucy beyond arranging for a handful of Tuscaloosa police officers to join the small campus force.

As apprehensive whites read of the successful bus boycott in Montgomery and followed the approaching integration of the university, Carter remained on the road. Between the first of December and the end of January, he spoke to more than thirty rallies and public gatherings in north Alabama, particularly in Tuscaloosa and the surrounding small towns, often describing to audiences the looming threat of integration at the University of Alabama.

The day before Autherine Lucy's admission, the owner of a Birmingham Black beauty salon styled Lucy's hair and helped her lay out her best outfit: a pale cream coat for the wintry weather, a white blouse with matching pink skirt, short jacket, and pillbox hat. While NAACP attorneys reviewed the admissions procedure and the questions she would likely face, Lucy listened intently, occasionally interrupting with questions. Her parents, under pressure from white officials, opposed her decision, but the soft-spoken young woman showed a steely determination, reinforced with constant prayer, to go ahead despite her fear.

Her first class on Friday, February 3, 1956, went without incident. In her second—a course on children's literature—two white coeds smiled and purposefully crossed the room to take their seats next to her. Earlier at the bookstore, several female undergraduates also welcomed her, and one seemed concerned about her safety. Another told her, "I hope everything turns out for you here."

Despite the support and the concerned response from a minority of students, most of the all-white student body opposed Lucy's presence on campus, and within hours quiet hostility crystallized into bitterness. The complaints were many: She had been hand-picked by the NAACP (in fact, she and her friend Pollie Ann Myers had decided to apply before any contact with the NAACP). She had arrived in a Cadillac (attorney Arthur Shores's aging Chevrolet had refused to start on the cold morning and a local Black funeral director loaned them his car). The NAACP had dressed her "to the nines" (her outfit was her own). She "whipped out" a crisp $100 bill to pay her tuition (Shores, concerned that the university would not accept a check, had told her to use cash). She did not have to wait in line to register for classes (the admissions office, fearful of problems if she mixed with students on the first day, had insisted that a staff member collect her class cards). As historian Culpepper Clark concluded, Lucy's every act was viewed through the prism of racial bigotry and anger. For most students and most whites in Alabama, the quiet and unassuming Lucy had been transformed into a despicable tool of the NAACP.[257]

On Friday night, a group of more than a thousand mostly male students gathered on campus to watch the burning of a small, improvised cross.

Whites protesting the integration of the University of Alabama, 1956.

One of those most angered by Lucy's enrollment was a nineteen-year-old sophomore, Leonard Wilson.

From an early age, Wilson could best be described as a fanatical "neo-Confederate." Raised by a doting single mother, he grew up on a farm north of Birmingham before the two moved to Selma in the heart of the Black Belt. Academically precocious and passionately right-wing in his political views, he became obsessed at an early age with the notion that white civilization faced racial extinction. Friends said he would sit for hours in the family's small apartment living room, compiling his scrapbooks on segregation, and staring at a large Confederate flag his mother had mounted on the wall.

At sixteen, Wilson attended the first Alabama Citizens' Council Meeting in Selma in the fall of 1954, where Council leader Sam Engelhardt urged him to become more involved. They needed young people. During his last year in high school, as a delegate at the state's "Youth Legislature" in Montgomery, he introduced a resolution calling for the "repatriation" of all Black Alabamians to Africa. His freshman year at the university only strengthened his far-right convictions. He joined the John Birch Society and watched with disgust as his professors tried to "brainwash" students who remained silent, dutifully repeating their "liberal drivel" on exams to get the grades and degrees they needed for future jobs.

But it was Asa Carter who made the greatest impression on the youthful segregationist. Sometime after Carter began organizing white resistance groups in the late summer of 1955, he met and befriended Wilson after a meeting in Tuscaloosa. The former radio announcer passed on racist books, magazines, and pamphlets, including *Common Sense* and *The Sword and the Flag*. FBI informants documented the pair's friendship, and newspaper accounts made it clear that Wilson was Carter's protégé.[258] Carter had chosen well. The young student proved remarkably adept at mobilizing support for Carter. In December and January alone, he organized five local Councils with well over a thousand members in the West Alabama division of the Citizens' Council.[259] He would remain a fanatical advocate of racist causes for the rest of his life. After the Citizens' Councils declined in the 1970s and 1980s, Wilson was a key figure and the first president of an equally racist organization, the Council of Conservative Citizens.[260]

Wilson's Friday night speech made him the leader of the resistance to Lucy's admission, and he embraced his new role. The following night he led an even larger group of students estimated at more than two thousand. He warmed up the crowd with a series of racist jokes and then urged what were now his followers to stop cars driven through the town by Negroes and ask if they believed in segregation. "If they say no, make them believe in it!" he shouted. More ominously, he told the crowd the precise time and location of Lucy's first Monday morning class and, without specifically calling for violence, urged them to resist the integration of the campus. Although Wilson would later deny taking orders from Carter, FBI informants insisted the two were in regular communication.

On Monday morning, a crowd of up to three thousand gathered outside the building where Lucy was to take her first class. Local Klan members including "Dynamite Bob" Chambliss joined the crowd of students. Carter and his assistant, Jesse Mabry, merged with the crowd, and police saw them talking to several dozen workers from the B. F. Goodrich Tire and Rubber Plant and ironworkers from Tuscaloosa's Holt Foundry, a source of many of Carter's followers. Although police stopped the two for questioning, they made no effort to arrest them.

As Lucy and two officials emerged from the classroom building after her first class, the mob greeted them with shouts of "there they go" and "hit the nigger whore." Clearly prepared, they pelted the three with rotten eggs and rocks.[261]

After a frightening drive to a nearby building, university officials and Lucy remained holed up for an hour and a half as the growing mob chanted racist slogans. Fearful the mob would break through the front doors, Jeff Bennett, the university president's assistant, rushed Lucy out a back entrance where a state trooper—with Lucy lying down on the back seat—left the campus at high speed for the relative safety of Birmingham.

Four hours later, President Carmichael announced that the university's board of trustees had voted to suspend Lucy as a student. Judge Grooms, who reluctantly ordered her admission, quickly approved Lucy's permanent expulsion on the grounds that she had made "unfounded charges of misconduct" by claiming that the university had failed in its duty to protect her.

Leonard Wilson's assessment was far closer to the truth. In an opinion article widely disseminated by the Associated Press, Wilson boasted that the demonstrations proved "integration will not work." And, he added ominously, if she returned, so would the riots. A student leader who supported Lucy's right to attend the university agreed. "Let's face it," he said, the university and its trustees had yielded to violence. "The mob has won." Looking back on the surge in the Citizens' Council movement in the winter and spring of 1956, Sam Engelhardt would acknowledge that the growth would not have come "if it weren't for the bus boycott and Autherine Lucy."[262]

The pattern was set: whenever violence took place, the fault lay with the victim. As University of Alabama Trustee John Caddell succinctly described Autherine Lucy, she "came in a Cadillac automobile, she had a chauffeur, and walked in such a way as to be obnoxious and objectionable and disagreeable." In fact, any Black person in Alabama who challenged segregation was automatically "objectionable and disagreeable."

In a few short months, Rosa Parks and Autherine Lucy ended what Asa Carter had called the federal government's "phony war" against segregation and set the stage for the angry resistance of whites in Alabama and across the region.

The Montgomery Advertiser

Montgomery, Ala., Saturday Morning, February 11, 1956 — 16 Pages

Throngs Pack Coliseum For Eastland's Address

HUGE CROWD HEARS EASTLAND

Senator Hits NAACP Move At Rally Here

By BOB INGRAM

U.S. Sen. James O. Eastland (D-Miss) told a cheering throng at the State Coliseum last night he was sure that "you and Alabama are not going to permit the NAACP to take over your schools."

This remark, in obvious reference to rioting on the University of Alabama campus earlier this week, came at the outset of his address when he mentioned he was an alumnus of the University.

"I am sure you are not going to permit the NAACP to control your state, and you are not going to permit that organization to use your little children as pawns in a game of racial politics," Eastland told the crowd.

RECORD CROWD

Eastland spoke at a Citizens Council rally which attracted the largest crowd in history to the huge coliseum. Coliseum Manager Tom Reid estimated the crowd at

Above, local coverage of James Eastland at 1956 rally in Montgomery. Right, antisemite war hero John Crommelin ran for a Senate seat from Alabama.

8

On His Own

> The Southern Manifesto, *March 12, 1956: [In Brown v. Board of Education] the Supreme Court of the United States, with no legal basis for such action, undertook to exercise their naked judicial power and substituted their personal political and social ideas for the established law of the land. . . . It is destroying the amicable relations between the white and Negro races that have been created through ninety years of patient effort by the good people of both races. It has planted hatred and suspicion where there has been heretofore friendship and understanding. . . . [O]utside agitators are threatening immediate revolutionary changes in our public school systems. . . . We decry the Supreme Court's encroachments on rights reserved to the states and to the people, contrary to established law and to the Constitution.*
>
> — 97 OF THE 122 MEMBERS OF THE SOUTHERN CONGRESSIONAL DELEGATION[263]

FOUR DAYS AFTER A mob drove Autherine Lucy from the campus of the University of Alabama, whites filled Garrett Coliseum in Montgomery as national and local television crews set up their cameras, and more than thirty newsmen, including correspondents from the *New York Times* and the *Chicago Tribune,* interviewed local officials. By 7 p.m., the crowd had exceeded the building's ten thousand-seat capacity, and an estimated two thousand stood in the aisles and around the main floor. At 7:20, Mississippi Senator James Eastland, seated in the back seat of an Alabama State Police cruiser, slowly rolled onto the crowded floor. The Montgomery Alcazar Shriners' brass band struck up "Dixie," the local color guards began waving large Confederate battle flags, and—in one reporter's words—"the coliseum thundered" in wave after wave of rebel yells.

As Eastland climbed the steps to the speaker's platform, Alabama Citizens' Council leader Sam Engelhardt, William Patterson, head of Mississippi's Citizens' Councils, Georgia Attorney General Eugene Cook, Montgomery's mayor, and a dozen other local politicians and Citizens' Council leaders surrounded him in what an elated Patterson called "the largest segregation gathering in the recent history of the South." Although Asa Carter was head of the North Alabama division of the state's Citizens' Council, Engelhardt pointedly failed to invite him to sit on the platform.

Much was familiar in Eastland's thirty-five-minute attack on the US Supreme Court ("illegal, immoral, dishonest and a disgrace"). While he called for Southern leaders to avoid overt violence, he urged them to fight to the last breath in their opposition against the "judicial tyranny" that sought to bring about "integration and the amalgamation of the races." If they grew weak, they could get strength from the fact that the "Anglo-Saxon" people of the South had always "held steadfast to the belief that resistance to tyranny is obedience to God."

Georgia's attorney general dismissed any concerns about violence as he called for "defiance, nullification and a refusal to obey illegal court decisions." The NAACP and their "communist leaning" allies sought to "strike down all racial barriers, including laws prohibiting interracial intermarriage, a step that would lead to the racial suicide" of the white South.[264]

Several local Citizens' Councils had set up tables to enroll new members and hand out materials before and after the rally. These included the standard racist literature such as Tom Brady's book, *Black Monday*, and Cook's pamphlet, "The Ugly Truth About the NAACP." There were also broadsheets from Asa Carter's North Alabama councils, one of which began with a crude parody of the opening lines of the Declaration of Independence: "When in the course of human events it becomes necessary to abolish the negro race, proper methods should be used among these are guns, bows and arrows, sling shots and knives. . . . [We] hold these truths to be self-evident. That all whites are created equal with certain rights: among these are life, liberty and the pursuit of dead niggers. . . ." Another leaflet handed out by

Carter's followers included the kind of over-the-top racism that "moderate" segregationists sought to avoid: The "unbearably stinking niggers" had oppressed and degraded whites. Unless whites woke up these "head hunters, and snot suckers . . . , these African flesh eaters" would soon place Martin Luther King in the White House."[265]

This was hardly the image that Engelhardt wanted to portray. Fortunately, the news media dutifully headlined Eastland's call to use legal means of resistance and avoid violence in the struggle ahead. There would be no mention of the handouts or the presence of hundreds of audience members wearing buttons saying, "A Proud Klansman."

Buoyed by the success of the Tuscaloosa mob in driving Lucy from the University of Alabama campus, the enormous outpouring of support at the Montgomery rally, and the growing regional resistance against even minimal desegregation, Engelhardt convened a meeting of Council leaders from across the state to launch a new phase in the campaign for white supremacy. Increasingly distrustful of Carter's independent control of his local Councils, he initially declined to invite Carter. After several local leaders objected, he reluctantly included him in the gathering. Still smarting from having been cold-shouldered by Engelhardt at Garrett Coliseum, Carter sat almost silently through the five-hour meeting, smoking one cigarette after another with a grim scowl that unnerved several participants who correctly sensed his contempt for his fellow Council leaders. "All the political big shots were there," Carter later told his followers, "and they named themselves state officers. I requested that we take it back to the Councils and let the people vote on it, but they wouldn't."[266]

Engelhardt had reason to be concerned. Even before the Tuscaloosa riots, with no coordination or communication with the state Council movement, Carter had launched a whirlwind effort at organizing additional Councils, all tightly under his personal control. In the midst of his tours Carter and his close friend/assistant Jesse Mabry began publishing their magazine, *The Southerner*. While racist in content, *The Southerner* bore little relationship to the semi-literate mimeographed broadsheets usually distributed by Klan groups. The Carter/Mabry publication featured Carter's vivid prose, stirring accounts of Confederate heroism during the Civil War, hard-hitting "exposes" of interracial gatherings in the South, and bitter attacks on the region's mainline segregationist leadership.

Often accompanied by Mabry, his brother Doug, Retired Admiral John Crommelin, and Birmingham's "Bull" Connor, Carter spoke to groups as small as thirty or forty and as large as five hundred whites, mostly men, galvanized by the events in Montgomery and Tuscaloosa. By March 1956, an estimated sixty-five thousand Alabama whites had signed on to the Councils; an apprehensive Engelhardt estimated that as many as ten thousand belonged to groups that Carter had created and tightly controlled.

As one who always carried a whiff of brimstone and menace, Carter posed a growing threat to the image that the other leaders of the Citizens' Council movement sought to portray. For Council leaders like Engelhardt, no criticism stung more than the taunting description by young Birmingham reporter Edward Harris: "Klansmen in business suits."

The phrase stuck. Liberal critics of the Council, including a fair number of Southern moderates like Ralph McGill and Hodding Carter, seized upon variations of Harris's phrase, describing it variously as "a hood-less Klan," "an uptown Klan," and a "country club Klan." Even Grover Hall, the conservative editor of the *Montgomery Advertiser*, initially expressed his scorn for the group. With the night-riding and violence of the 1920s an "abomination" to the public, "the bigots have resorted to a more decorous, tidy and less conspicuous method—economic thuggery."[267]

During the initial response to the *Brown* decision, every racist crackpot across the nation seemed to crawl out from under rocks and into bed with the Council movement, and their enthusiasm made it difficult for the organization to maintain its claims of respectability. The original Mississippi Citizens' Council had a rocky beginning in late 1954 when it distributed a list of suggested readings that included such violently anti-Black and antisemitic publications as Gerald L. K. Smith's *The Cross and the Flag*, the openly fascist *White Sentinel*, and other far-right publications. Hodding Carter, one of the few relatively moderate Southern newspaper editors, was accustomed to traditional anti-Black racism, but he was stunned to read the list of the Council's recommendations, many of them violently antisemitic.

He described the list as "one of the most shameful collection of bigoted publications ever compiled." The Council ignored his complaints.[268]

It wasn't just the hangers-on. Tom Brady, the Yale-educated Mississippi jurist and author of *Black Monday,* the manifesto that laid out the blueprint for organizing the Council movement, railed against the prominent role of "Jewish names in the ranks of Communist fronts" and warned Southern Jews to "stop this disloyalty and sometimes outright treason."[269]

But Brady's foray into antisemitism paled beside that of retired admiral John Crommelin. During World War II, Crommelin had a distinguished Navy record, participated in eighteen major battles, and was decorated with the Silver and Bronze stars. Four of his brothers also served as Navy pilots; two died in combat. But in 1950, his Navy superiors forced Crommelin to retire after he condemned the Truman administration's plan to create a defense secretary with control over all the armed services. He not only attacked his military superiors in a series of public statements, he leaked confidential naval correspondence. His war against combining the military services went far beyond disagreement over policy. He had always seen the handful of senior Jewish officers in the Navy as key members of the cabal who had betrayed the Navy by accepting the administration's consolidation of the armed forces under a single cabinet member. And he attributed his forced resignation to their influence. In 1950, only months after his retirement, he challenged Alabama's popular US Senator Lister J. Hill and drew 24 percent of the vote as an independent candidate. In this campaign, he vaguely referred to "alien forces" at work in the highest level of government, often referring with a smirk to Jews as "Eskimos." But by the mid-1950s, he no longer used such vague language and publicly complained that "jewlattos" were the real source of the South's racial problems.[270]

In 1955, a North Carolina journalist interviewed Crommelin and was surprised by the frankness with which the fifty-nine-year-old expressed his hatred of Jews. Over coffee in the family's plantation home north of Montgomery, Crommelin—surrounded by stacks of antisemitic literature—insisted that he had no hostility toward Blacks. After genially dismissing an older Black employee with instructions to wait outside, he told James

Cook with a smile: "See that boy out there? Why I don't feel any more hostility toward him than I do toward a good bird dog." To Crommelin, the Negro was simply a pawn for those agitating for racial equality, and there was no question who "those" might be. "The Negro is the malarial germ," he explained, "but the *Jew* is the mosquito."[271] Over the next five years, he would become one of Carter's strongest supporters.[272]

Initially, William Patterson, the head of the Citizens' Council regional and national propaganda apparatus, brushed off accusations of anti-Jewish extremism. In a circular letter responding to complaints by Jewish Southerners and some of their white Christian allies, Patterson refused to condemn his antisemitic allies. "Lenin always told his party people: 'Never attack the Left,'" explained Patterson. "I never attack the right." (Lenin never made this statement, and except for the brief "Popular Front" period in the 1930s, Communists repeatedly attacked socialists and liberals.) Like it or not, he said, it was a fact that Arthur Spingarn, "a Jew," had been president of the NAACP for more than twenty years. And it was a fact that B'nai B'rith, the Jewish service organization founded in 1843, supported the NAACP. "I am not antisemitic," insisted Patterson, "but I am against any man or group [that] aids and abets the NAACP which is trying to destroy our way of life."[273]

By early 1956, Citizens' Council leaders had eased out some of their most disreputable fellow travelers and had stopped recommending openly antisemitic publications, but only because the negative publicity had made it more difficult to attract Northern conservatives to the cause. As part of the Council's attempt at respectability it also no longer called for organized boycotts against "integrationists," since openly endorsing such measures would have seemed embarrassingly hypocritical in view of the Council's efforts to enact legislation outlawing Black boycotts.

The public disclaimer of economic coercion also proved to be a public relations exercise. Local Council leaders repeatedly published the names of Black civil rights activists or petition signers and then encouraged individual whites to determine an "appropriate" response. This meant refusing them credit and firing them if they worked for whites. In many rural areas in the Black Belt, when sharecroppers signed petitions supporting integration, landowners replaced them with more pliant workers.[274]

If Council leaders publicly emphasized their commitment to legal tactics against segregation and the maintenance of "law and order," they made little or no effort to use their considerable influence to rein in violent individuals and groups that struck out against civil rights activists. That was clearly true in the case of Engelhardt. After arrests for some of the explosions during followed the Montgomery bus boycott, he used his considerable influence to arrange top-flight legal representation for the Klan bombers.[275]

As the Council movement grew, Carter remained Engelhardt's chief problem. Unwilling to risk the loss of the ten thousand Council members who supported Carter, Engelhardt continued to acknowledge him as the director of the North Alabama Citizens' Council division even as he launched a stealth campaign to discredit the more extreme Carter.

Carter seemed unconcerned and convinced that the stage was set for direct and violent confrontation with the forces of integration as white opposition to integration steadily grew. As other Deep South states had, the Alabama legislature introduced more than a dozen extreme pro-segregation measures. One launched an investigation to show that the NAACP was "substantially directed, dominated or controlled by communists." A related bill authorized local school boards to fire any Black teacher who "belonged to or sympathized with" the NAACP. Other proposals called for an end to subsidizing Negro students in out-of-state graduate programs and the termination of appropriations for Tuskegee Institute, which offered Blacks graduate training in engineering, veterinary medicine, and nursing. Most extreme (and meaningless) was the resolution calling on Congress to provide funds to relocate Black Southerners into Northern cities "where Negroes are wanted. . . ."[276]

A Gallup poll of the former Confederate states showed that only 16 percent of whites approved of the *Brown* decision.[277] In November 1955, *Richmond News Leader* editor James J. Kilpatrick had created a bogus constitutional doctrine of "interposition," claiming that "sovereign" states had a right to "interpose" their authority between the federal government and the citizens of their respective states. However meaningless (and unconstitutional) it was, Virginia's general assembly adopted a resolution in early February 1956 "interposing the sovereignty of Virginia against encroachment upon the reserved powers of this State. . . ." Five Southern states swiftly enacted similar resolutions.

But under pressure from Engelhardt and the Citizens' Council of Alabama, the state legislature issued an even more radical measure. Rather than "interposing" the state between the federal government and its citizens, as Kilpatrick had suggested, Alabama's resolution reached back to South Carolina's 1833 "nullification" ordinance authored by John C. Calhoun. By large majorities, lawmakers declared that the Supreme Court's *Brown* decision was "null, void and of no effect in Alabama."

Alabama Governor Jim Folsom described the nullification measure as "claptrap . . . like a hound dog baying at the moon and claiming it's got the moon treed."[278] Folsom was right. If there was anything the Civil War had settled, it was the supremacy of the union and the Supreme Court as the final arbiter of law. But the governor's former supporters were no longer listening to his plaintive insistence that—like it or not—the decision was the law of the land.

SHORTLY AFTER ALABAMA PASSED its nullification measure, newspapers across the nation and the region headlined the release of a document condemning the Supreme Court and attacking its *Brown* decision. In March 1956, Virginia's ultra-conservative Howard Smith, chair of the House Rules Committee, introduced what came to be called the "Southern Manifesto." In overturning segregation, said the authors of the document, the Supreme Court had exercised "naked judicial power and substituted their personal political and social ideas for the established law of the land." The result was chaos in the South. The court's decision had planted "hatred and suspicion" and destroyed "the amicable relations between the white and Negro races that have been created through ninety years of patient effort by the good people of both races."

Despite such harsh language, cooler heads modified the Manifesto to include a paragraph urging white Southerners to use "lawful means" to reverse *Brown*. And the revised document ended with an "appeal to our [white] people not to be provoked by the agitators and troublemakers invading our States and to scrupulously refrain from disorder and lawless acts."

Strom Thurmond (then a Democrat) had drafted the first version of the Manifesto, but he was a newly elected and marginal figure in the Senate. The real leaders of the Southern resistance were savvy Democratic senators like Georgia's Richard Russell, John Sparkman of Alabama, and Sam Ervin of North Carolina. All were committed to fighting the court's decision, but they had concluded that a policy of strategic delays and legal roadblocks would prove far more effective than intemperate and violent resistance which might lead to a groundswell of Northern support for the decision. This meant throwing support to the so-called "respectable" segregationists and isolating flame-throwers like Carter whose rhetoric might repel sympathetic Northern conservatives.

With these modest changes, a number of wavering border-state lawmakers signed onto the Manifesto. Only three congressmen from North Carolina refused to join Southern senators and congressmen from the heart of the old Confederacy: Virginia, the Carolinas, Georgia, Alabama, Mississippi, Arkansas, and Louisiana. And two of the three were defeated when they ran for reelection.[279]

Equally critical to the congressmen and senators was their desire to protect their personal careers and the strength of the white South within Congress. White Southern lawmakers had long held outsize influence in the nation's capital. During the first half of the twentieth century, congressional committee chairs were selected on the basis of their seniority. With almost no Republican opposition in the one-party Democratic South, voters consistently reelected incumbents, who, as a result, chaired the major committees when the Democratic Party was in power.[280]

But in the 1952 election, Republican candidate Dwight Eisenhower had won four Southern border states and almost carried the Carolinas and Louisiana. Senator Russell feared that a growing Republican vote would lead to the replacement of key Southern Democrats (who chaired most of the major Senate and House committees) by Republicans. Not only would the Democrats' reelections be in danger, but the loss of their chairmanships might lead to the adoption of meaningful civil rights legislation. The Manifesto was an attempt to thread the needle: maintaining the role of mainline leaders as defenders of segregation while avoiding violent resistance that would accelerate the actions of the Congress and the federal courts.[281]

Such nuances were lost on Carter. He saw the emphasis on legal resistance as a "milksop" attempt to conceal the South's surrender in the face of the growing war against segregation. Through January and February 1956, the conflict between his followers and more respectable (and cautious) Council leaders played out in a series of mass meetings held in Montgomery, Birmingham, and other Alabama cities.

At a January rally in suburban Birmingham attended by more than fifteen hundred whites, Carter shared the platform with his close friend retired admiral John Crommelin and with state senator Walter Givhan, a long-time state legislator closely associated with Engelhardt.

Most of the news coverage focused on Senator Givhan's speech. He outlined his organization's strategy: to delay, delay, delay, "log-jamming" the federal courts with lawsuits until public opinion turned against the communists' plot to "mongrelize the Anglo-Saxon Southern white . . ." Only once did he arouse the crowd when he shouted that the Council was committed to keeping "those little white boys and those little white girls pure!" Still there was the caveat: "We're going to do it legally." Violence would discredit the movement, particularly outside the South. "And we need the goodwill of the nation."

There was polite, but tepid applause at the end of his talk.

The lengthy report of an FBI informant and the notes taken by reporter Edward Harris (who was not assigned to cover the rally) give a quite different picture from the news media coverage of the rally. After Givhan completed his speech, Crommelin, the notorious antisemite, warned that Russian plans were well underway, with the cooperation of communist traitors in the federal government, to set up a Black republic encompassing Georgia, South Carolina, Alabama, and Mississippi. "Whites were to be sent away from our beloved Southland to Minnesota and Alaska to prison work camps."

But it was Carter who most unnerved Harris, again and again bringing the audience to its feet with shouts and rebel yells. The reporters for the *Birmingham News* and the associated morning newspaper, the *Post-Herald,* described the audience's enthusiastic response to Carter's "fiery talk" but did not include a single quote from either Carter or Crommelin.

The failure to quote Carter was no accident. The *News*, largest of the city's two newspapers, had once been a supporter of the New Deal and organized labor, with some of the best reporters in the state. By the mid-1950s the paper was run by Executive Editor Vincent Townsend. After Townsend killed a story, written by a new reporter, that had exposed a widespread housing scam in nearby Ensley, he summed up his newspaper's philosophy. "We don't do exposes," he warned the young reporter. "We make a lot of money as things are." And his power was extensive. Not only did Townsend control the *News*, his newspaper company also owned the radio station with the largest state audience and the local television affiliates for both NBC and CBS.

A racist of the old school, Townsend embraced the "respectable" white Citizens' Council movement and consistently used the *News* to discredit challengers like Carter. [282] Even the editor of the *Montgomery Advertiser*, who had initially attacked the Council, admitted to a reporter that the pressure on his paper became too great. "We had to back down," said Grover Hall, and he was soon defending Engelhardt in the Council's internal fight.[283]

Despite the failure of the state's newspapers to downplay the January 1956 rally's most inflammatory rhetoric, the notes of Harris and the FBI informant describe Carter's blunt calls for defiance. "Law and order," he said sarcastically. It was the "cop-out" of phony politicians. "The time for talk is over," he shouted. "The time for action is now!" With an unmistakable swipe at Givhan and the top leadership of the state's Council movement, he warned of the danger that came from following "political leaders" more interested in protecting their respectability than "taking the fight to the communists and integrationists."[284] To Carter, the forced removal of Autherine Lucy from the University of Alabama campus proved that the timid law-and-order rhetoric guaranteed defeat. The cowards who "hide in their corners," rightly feared the true Anglo-Saxon working men who "demanded a fight with the forces of integration." Rather than "prattling on about law and order," White Southerners needed to learn the lessons of their forefathers who had overthrown the Reconstruction regimes. Only those who gave the integrationists "no quarter," had any chance to "chase the mongrelizers from our land."[285]

Equally unsettling to Harris was Carter's description of the threat posed by wealthy bankers and their allies who "control the negro." And who were the wealthy elites? Carter never explicitly described them as Jews, but his message was clear as he called out their names: New Yorkers like Kivie Kaplan, the Jewish philanthropist who served on the NAACP board of directors, and Birmingham's most prominent Jewish businessmen, Louis Pizitz, Harold Blach, Mervyn Sterne, Lenny Salit, and Emil Hess. Pillars of the business community, they had spent a lifetime working to disarm their white Christian friends. As merchants vulnerable to public boycotts, they feared an antisemitic backlash and carefully avoided taking any public position that might be considered anti-segregation.[286] This meant little to Carter. As he off-handedly told a Montgomery journalist, they were all a "bunch of nigger-loving kikes."[287]

Any doubts about Carter's relationship with the larger Council movement ended in early March when he called a "mass protest meeting" for Birmingham's municipal auditorium, sharing the stage with John Crommelin, by then a candidate for the United States Senate, running against the long-time incumbent Lister Hill.

Crommelin called upon the estimated five thousand gathered in the auditorium to begin a revolution to "overthrow the alien forces that have captured our government." While the crowd applauded Crommelin's attacks on the Supreme Court justices ("Pro-Communists who should be investigated and removed from the bench"), they saved their wildest cheers for Carter, who spoke for an hour and a half, lashing out first at the newspaper reporters uneasily gathered at the front of the hall: a bunch of "pink-shirted pencil-pushing sops" who lied about those who fought hardest for segregation. As Carter stalked back and forth in front of a platform draped in Confederate battle flags, the audience often drowned out him with what one reporter described as "foot-stomping rebel yells."

Gone was the indirect criticism of Engelhardt and other state leaders of the Citizens' Council. Engelhardt talked a good game, said Carter, but all he "cares about is keeping his taxes down and making sure that his niggers are satisfied working for twenty-five cents an hour."[288] Engelhardt and the other leaders of the state council movement were "cowards." We need leaders who would say to the contemptible Supreme Court: "These are our public schools and the first Negro that sets foot in a white school will be arrested and placed in jail" along with anyone else who "conspires with the NAACP . . . and breaks our segregation laws. . . ." "We don't want peace in our time, we want the trouble now," he shouted as the audience came to its feet. "We want to bring it on now!"[289]

Since the previous year, application forms for Carter's Council had included the requirement that members should confirm that they were Christians, but, with lines drawn between the two men, the exclusion of Jews gave Engelhardt the needed opening. In a series of press releases and a hastily called news conference, he described the North Alabama Citizens' Council leader as a renegade and a loose cannon who threatened the unity of white Southerners. In their coverage, local reporters and the national press described the split as a direct consequence of the mainline Council leadership's opposition to Asa Carter's antisemitic statements.[290]

With no apparent attempt at irony, Engelhardt insisted that the Council welcomed Southern Jews in the battle against mongrelization. The Citizens' Council was "not interested in religious bias or prejudice, but is concerned only in maintaining segregation." So long as Jews supported segregation, Engelhardt seemed to suggest, they were honorary white people. He announced that the Citizens' Council of Alabama had formally expelled Carter.[291]

There is no evidence that Engelhardt held passionate antisemitic views, but only weeks before their split, he and his closest ally, Senator Walter Givhan, sat at the same table with Carter and Crommelin at a Birmingham dinner honoring retired general Van Horn Moseley. The decorated World War I hero had become a notorious pro-fascist spokesman in the 1930s and had flirted with the idea of a military coup against Franklin Roosevelt. Well into the 1950s, Moseley continued to call for the "purging" of Jews from American society.

Engelhardt and Givhan may not have recognized the American neo-fascists and antisemites who dominated the gathering, but Moseley's views on the subject were well known. Less than four years earlier, when the president of Georgia's Piedmont College accepted funds from Moseley and invited him to speak, the faculty revolted and forced the near collapse of the college. The controversy led to widespread news coverage throughout the region describing the ex-general's antisemitic and pro-fascist views.[292]

For Council leaders, the "Jewish issue" was simply a matter of practical politics. As Givhan told a reporter, Carter's campaign against the Jews was a "tactical mistake" that would leave fellow segregationists wandering down "blind paths or into any unwise actions" alienating national conservatives.[293] Attacking Carter on the issue served as a convenient public explanation for the break with the North Alabama Council leader.

As always, Carter responded with the lesson he had learned from his hero, Nathan Bedford Forrest: "Attack!" He told several reporters that his organization welcomed Jews who had converted to Christianity. The demagogic accusation of antisemitism by Engelhardt and other simpering "politicians" (the worst epithet in Carter's broad vocabulary of vituperation), simply because his Councils required that members believe in the divinity of Jesus Christ, was an "utterly fantastic and hate-mongering charge." To raise the issue was a time-tested tactic used by anti-Christ, atheistic communist ideologues who used slander to "cut the heart from the American Anglo-Saxon." When a reporter asked him about the excommunication of his organization, he replied with a rare smile. "Actually," he said, "I'm thinking about expelling Engelhardt and his crowd."[294]

CARTER DIDN'T LET UP in the weeks that followed. Twenty-four hours after he and the larger Council movement had officially separated, he spoke to a Birmingham rally of more than 2,500. To handclaps, shouts, and cries of "Amen!" he paced the stage, his right hand in a tight and often raised fist as he accused Engelhardt and other Council leaders of serving as "cowardly political henchmen" for Governor James Folsom who should be impeached for having connived with federal officials to admit Autherine Lucy.[295] (In reality, a stressed-out Folsom had gone on a fishing trip/drinking spree during the critical days of the crisis at Tuscaloosa.) Carter also demanded the immediate dismissal of the "spineless administrators" who had passively accepted the integration of the university.[296]

As Carter gained increasing notoriety, Engelhardt and his allies skillfully moved to weaken his "North Alabama Citizens' Councils," even at the expense of losing the members who backed Carter. With the quiet support of Engelhardt, Givhan, and other mainline segregationists, some individuals within Carter's Councils began organizing dissenters and encouraging them to engage in a series of resignations and public protests against Carter's "dictatorial leadership," all extensively covered by the *Birmingham News.*[297]

Unnamed representatives from the Council also leaked stories to the *New York Times* and the *New York Post* that Carter was welcoming Ku Klux Klansmen into his Councils, a charge that Carter dismissed. When questioned by a *New York Times* stringer in Birmingham, Carter acknowledged that there might be Klansmen in the ranks of his organization. "We cannot keep them out, but we try to see that they do not gain positions of leadership." There was a certain droll humor in Carter's last remark; he was scheduled to preside over the regular monthly meeting of his newly formed Klan group the day after his interview.

Even before the open split with Carter, Engelhardt had begun a series of confidential meetings with agents in the FBI's Birmingham office. He warned that Carter was highly prone to violence, skimmed money from his followers for personal use, and was "possibly a Communist." And he emphasized that Carter hated FBI Director J. Edgar Hoover, a claim by Engelhardt that ensured his complaints reached the top of the agency. He had unsuccessfully tried to collect information that would totally discredit Carter among his followers and asked the FBI agent for any information that might be useful. The agent declined to offer any but assured him that Carter was "on the agency's radar."[298]

As Carter's role in the Council movement became more problematic, he found a new way to gain headlines. A week after the break with Engelhardt, he issued a public statement condemning Birmingham City Commissioner James Morgan for "aiding and abetting the Un-American and Un-Christian forces of immorality and integration in allowing the use of City Auditorium for indecent and vulgar performances by Africans before our white children."[299]

Asa Carter had found a new enemy.

9

The War Against 'Jungle Music'

"When white youth . . . begin to think as a Negro, to talk as a Negro, to accept the Negro's moral standard and his 'culture,' to idolize Negro performers, then the white youth is on the level with the Negroid race and integration is already accomplished in the mind and spirit. The physical implementation is a mere formality."

— Asa Carter[300]

Several months after the States Rights Association fired Carter, his friend and financial supporter John Crommelin introduced him to Emory Burke. Burke, just released from a Georgia prison, achieved modest national notoriety in the late 1940s when he and New Yorker Homer Loomis formed an overtly pro-fascist organization, the Columbians. Based in Atlanta, Burke modeled his followers' uniforms on the Nazi SA Brown Shirts (*Sturmabteiling*) with lightning bolt insignia copied from the uniforms of Hitler's protective guards, the Black-shirted SS (*Schutzstaffel*). Initially members provoked more curiosity than hostility as they marched through the streets of the city in a ghostly replay of 1930s newsreels, but they soon gained a reputation for organized street assaults on young Black men in racially mixed neighborhoods. Growing opposition came from politicians and mainline religious groups as well as Klan leaders on the right who resented the organization's success in poaching some of their most dedicated members.

After the local press reported the Columbians' role in the bombing of several Black homes in formerly all-white working-class neighborhoods,

Atlanta prosecutors charged Burke with "inciting to riot," possession of unregistered explosives, and direct involvement in the beating of a Black man who had been targeted while walking in a predominantly white neighborhood. Burke's conviction and four-year sentence at Georgia's Reidsville State Prison did nothing to diminish his political passions. In 1955, he returned to his home state of Alabama, joined Crommelin's senate campaign, and took up the struggle once again.

Burke, who had long called for the forced removal of all Jews to Madagascar and the relocation to Africa of Black Americans, read widely from the leading racist and antisemitic authors of the era. He became obsessed with the notion that Jews held financial control of the motion picture and music industry and had launched a "colored colonization" of American culture. Black entertainers were promoted to replace the more elevated forms of white entertainment with the "sex-crazed jitter-bug of the African [and] . . . the savage tom-toms of the Congo."[301]

Fears over the impact of rock and roll were hardly restricted to racists in the Deep South. Elvis Presley's success in taking rock and roll/rhythm and blues mainstream unnerved traditional and religious Americans who saw his gyrating hips and "sensual leers" as debased and "vulgar." Samuel Stritch, Roman Catholic archbishop of Chicago, condemned rock 'n' roll as a "throwback to tribalism that cannot be tolerated for Catholic youths. When our schools and centers stoop to such things as 'rock and roll' tribal rhythms, they are failing seriously in their duty."[302]

The uninhibited sensuality of rock lyrics and performances also led a number of Protestant leaders like Billy Graham to attack the new music. In some cases, churches sponsored dramatic bonfires against sin, encouraging young evangelicals to bring their records and throw them in the flames.[303] Conservatives also recoiled against the racial and gender-bending look of many performers.[304] Elvis Presley was heterosexual, even a bit homophobic, but he bought his clothes from Meyer Lansky, a Memphis haberdasher who sold to Black and white entertainers and gay clients. Instead of the conservative men's styles of the period, Lansky featured leather jackets, body-hugging slim sport coats and suits, and extravagantly colored sport shirts. In 1955, when a young Richard "Little Richard" Penniman walked into Specialty

Records Studio to record his first major hit, "Tutti Fruiti," he stunned the producer. His hair was in a pompadour a "foot high," said Bumps Blackwell, and his shirt "was so loud it looked as though he had drunk raspberry juice, cherryade, malt, and collard greens and then thrown up all over himself."

The look required more than clothes. Instead of a manly casual appearance, performers went to great lengths to make sure their hair was in place and their outfits flamboyant, at times almost feminine. Presley appeared on the Grand Ole Opry in 1954 and shocked even the worldly guitarist Chet Atkins. "I couldn't get over the eye shadow he was wearing," said Atkins. "It was like seein' a couple of guys kissin' in Key West."[305]

In many ways, attacks on the new music reflected a broader generational conflict that had emerged in post-war America. A more affluent and independent generation of young people embraced values that challenged traditional relationships between themselves and their parents. As two historians of the anti-rock and roll movement pointed out, the embrace of their "own" music seemed to "defy their elders . . . to mock their ideals, to break away from adult control. . . ."[306]

Particularly in the South, race remained the most powerful point of contention. Primarily beginning in the 1940s, nearly fifty Black-oriented AM stations sprang up across the region and gave white listeners access to Black musicians and their performances over unsegregated airwaves. In January 1956, RCA Victor released Presley's "Heartbreak Hotel," which quickly sold more than a million copies and simultaneously topped the charts of pop, rhythm and blues, and country and western music. Presley was not the first white rock and roll performer, but his musical style drew heavily upon the emotional power of earlier Black gospel and rhythm and blues performers. A number of critics complained that Presley and other white performers exploited Black music, which was certainly true. But as white audiences embraced Presley and white rock and roll groups, they also turned to the "race music" that had once been safely isolated from mainstream American culture, welcoming performers like Little Richard, Ellas "Bo Diddley" McDaniel, Chuck Berry, and Fats Domino.[307]

Carter had never expressed views on the perils of Black music until he and Emory Burke began working together in late 1955. Only then did he begin his campaign against "degenerate negroid music." "Turn on your radio and listen to the rock and roll death song of America and the white race," Carter told his followers at a meeting in January 1956. "They are as dangerous as the worst of the civil rights agitators."

His attacks against this "degenerate music" began after half-page Birmingham newspaper ads promoted a "Big Rhythm & Blues Show, with two performances, one for Whites, one for Colored." The star-studded line-up included some of the most prominent Black and white performers of the 1950s: Bill Haley and the Comets, Bo Diddley, the Drifters, La Verne Baker, and the Platters. (White and Black performers performed in separate but equal sets.) The concerts proved so successful that both Birmingham newspapers gave prominent coverage to a scheduled March performance at the city's memorial auditorium, featuring B. B. King, Hank Ballard and the Midnighters, the Five Royals, and a half dozen other rhythm and blues performers. Only this time, ads described the performers as "Rock and Rollers." Sponsors marketed the event for Blacks, with $2–$2.50 tickets; in one of the many ironies of the Jim Crow South, whites could only sit in the balcony. While the main auditorium for Black patrons was 80 percent sold out, white teenagers packed the balcony with several hundred turned away.[308]

In his magazine, *The Southerners,* a disgusted Carter claimed he had stood near the end of one row and watched "young white girls swoon to the sensuous negro music, timed to the jungle beat, accompanied by words shocking in their filthiness." As the "sweating blacks pounded their heavy beat, the white children's conversation flowed around the auditorium, replete with the coarse negro phrases; the teenagers were white, but if one closed his eyes the negroid conversations would convince him otherwise." The words of the Black singers were unprintable, Carter told his readers: "the entire moral structure of man, of Christianity, of spirituality in Holy marriage . . . of all that the white man has built through his devotion to God; all this, was crumbled and snatched away as the white girls and boys were turned to the level of the animal." On the stage and in the worn seats of the Birmingham Municipal Auditorium, the battle for the racial survival of the Anglo-Saxon race was being fought—and lost.[309] (There is no evidence that Carter actually attended.)

"Unprintable lyrics"? Attacks on the "moral structure of man, of Christianity, of spirituality in Holy marriage"? The concerts Carter claimed he had attended in January headlined white rock and rollers Bill Haley and the Comets, but Haley and his band had taken care not to appear on the stage side by side with Black performers. However, the March show was by all Black musicians whose music marked a departure from the chaste rhythms of Pat Boone and Perry Como. But the lyrics from Big Joe Turner ("Shake, Rattle and Roll"), LaVern Baker ("Jim Dandy to the Rescue"), and Smiley Lewis ("I hear you Knocking") were never explicitly salacious. Even Bo Diddley, known for his risque songs, made certain that there was nothing offensive in his Birmingham performance.

It was less the lyrics than the Black rhythms and the uninhibited emotional responses of white listeners to Black performers that outraged Carter and conservative Americans.[310] At a deeper level their fears were justified. Rock and roll music promiscuously combined Black jazz traditions and rhythm and blues, Black and white "Holy Roller" emotionalism, white and Black gospel music, and white country music—it was musical miscegenation.

For Carter, the most dangerous of the Black performers was Nat King Cole. By the mid-1950s, the singer-pianist was at the height of his national popularity and one of a handful of Black performers who drew predominantly white audiences. Born in Montgomery, Alabama, Cole grew up the son of the prominent minister of downtown Chicago's True Light Baptist Church and made his reputation in the 1940s as lead pianist and singer in his jazz trio. Although the trio continued to perform, in the 1950s Cole signed with a major record label and began incorporating orchestral backgrounds by "easy listening" arranger Nelson Riddle. A balladeer closer to Frank Sinatra than the first generation of Black rock and roll singers, Cole had seven hit records on *Billboard*'s pop charts in 1955.

Given Carter's constant attacks on Black "be-bop music," the assault on Cole seemed odd. Cole started his career as a serious jazz pianist and singer, but by the 1950s he was performing stylized romantic ballads with lush string arrangements that hardly reflected the latest trends in Black rhythm and blues or rock and roll. For Carter, however, Cole was an example of how Jewish subversives stealthily worked to undermine white culture. He felt Jews

Nat King Cole, center, with his trio, in **Billboard** *magazine, 1947.*

had subverted the motion picture industry by producing popular films which glorified moral corruption and "anti-Christian" values. Black "jungle" music that fostered licentious interracial sex marked the second stage of their campaign. It was only a "short step from the sly, nightclub . . . vulgarity of Cole, to the openly animalistic obscenity of the horde of Negro rock'n rollers."[311] Carter made sure *The Southerner* included photographs of Cole performing with white female singers. One issue featured the white, blonde artist June Christy standing behind Cole at the piano, with her hands on his shoulders.

In late February 1956, in the midst of Carter's crusade, Cole began a nationwide series of concerts with a line-up that included Christy, Londoner Ted Heath's famous "big band," the Four Freshmen, and comedian Gary Morton (all white). During the tour's first week, the show grossed $110,000 (over $1 million, in 2023 dollars). Even though Cole generally avoided performances in the South, toward the end of his tour he added concerts in Houston; Winston-Salem, North Carolina; New Orleans; and Jackson, Mississippi, as well as three concerts in his native state, one in Mobile and two in Birmingham.

Publicly, Cole made no attempt to challenge Jim Crow; he carefully deferred to each state's segregation laws. "I've always set myself apart from controversy or anything political," he told a white reporter. "I've never known any kind of violence because of race," he explained. "For this reason I never did get a complex about this business of being colored."[312]

Despite his public statements, Cole always resented the discriminatory treatment he had received in his early career. In 1948 he integrated the affluent (and all-white) Los Angeles Hancock Park neighborhood and refused to move despite angry responses from white neighbors and the burning of a cross on his front lawn. Once he became a major star in the Las Vegas casinos in the early 1950s, he demanded that he and his band be allowed to stay at the hotels and eat in the casino restaurants. Even as he refused to take a public position on racial issues, he quietly raised money for the NAACP and sent two checks to the Montgomery bus boycott committee.

Like other early Black performers who had begun to appeal to white audiences in the early 1950s, his low profile on civil rights was a practical response to the threat of boycotts. After his first two concerts in Jackson, Mississippi, and New Orleans, Cole did slyly point out to one reporter that many of his white fans seemed unconcerned about segregation requirements. In New Orleans, he recalled, "we were playing to an all-colored audience and two hundred white people were clamoring to get in." In Jackson, whites were "storming around the place wanting to get in, not caring who they sat next to."[313]

As he was a native son who respected the South's segregation laws, Alabama newspapers wrote glowing articles about Cole and praised his "modest behavior." He sold out his first concert in Mobile as Black and white fans cheered from their separate sections. The demand for tickets for his April 10 Birmingham concert proved so great that the promoters scheduled two shows. The first beginning at 7 p.m. was for whites only; the "colored" show was to follow at 9 p.m.

A week before Cole's scheduled performance, Carter asked representatives from the Councils he still controlled to gather in Birmingham to issue a "joint statement" attacking the music which "promotes integration of the races and demoralizes children." At the end of the four-hour meeting, most of the members left, but Carter met with a smaller group and appointed an "action committee" to be led by Kenneth Adams.

Adams seemed a genial good-natured Anniston, Alabama, businessman. By the mid-1950s he had become co-owner of Adams Oil Company and operated one of its several service stations. He supported local baseball and football teams through the 1940s and 1950s, furnishing team uniforms and often cheering on his sponsored athletes from the sidelines, occasionally with too much enthusiasm. After a referee penalized Adams's sponsored team fifteen yards and loss of down for unnecessary roughness, Adams charged onto the field and beat the hapless referee so badly he had to be hospitalized.[314]

In the late 1930s, Adams had excelled in sports at Calhoun County High as a track star, amateur boxer, and All-State center of his football team. But even when he was a high school student the local newspaper's coverage alternated between his athletic achievements and his involvement in drunken brawls. By the mid-1950s, his police record stretched over two pages: drunk while discharging a firearm in the city of Anniston (1939); petty larceny (1940); assault and battery (1940); drunk, resisting arrest, assault and battery on a police officer (1941), disorderly conduct (1941); drunk and disorderly conduct (1946); transporting moonshine whiskey (1949, 1950); assault and battery with a knife (1951); assault with intent to murder (1953).[315] In most of these cases, Adams plea-bargained charges down to payment of a fine and probation. His only jail time had come in 1950 when police caught him after a high-speed chase and found his car's trunk filled with bootleg whiskey. The arrest took place while he was on probation from an earlier conviction and after he had solemnly promised the presiding judge that he would end his involvement in the illegal whiskey business. He seemed to be a classic example of W. J. Cash's "helluva fellow," an outrageous young Southern man who aroused scorn from the respectable, and bemusement from others, for his willingness to flaunt convention. Brandy Ayers, publisher of the *Anniston Star,* closely followed Adams's career and was not amused. He was, said Ayers, a "personable sociopath."[316]

Kenneth Adams, 1956.

In the aftermath of the 1954 *Brown v. Board of Education* decision Adams turned from general hell-raising toward the violent racism that would mark the rest of his life. There is substantial evidence that his relationship with Asa Carter, dating back to their high school years, led Adams to embrace both hardcore racism and antisemitism. Shortly after Carter returned to Alabama in 1954, he reconnected with Adams in an uncharacteristically close friendship, since Carter generally trusted no one outside his immediate family. The two became so close that when Adams's wife kicked him out of their house at one point in 1955, he spent nearly three months living with the Carter family.

Nothing impressed Carter more than Adams's willingness to take forceful action when dealing with Blacks. In early 1956, when three Black men returning from work made the mistake of stopping at Adams's service station in downtown Anniston, they were unaware of the posted sign ("White Customers Only") when they pulled up to the station's air compressor to inflate a slack tire. According to Adams's statement to the police, Early Vaughn got out of the passenger's side, pulled a "switch-blade," and without provocation advanced on him. In "self-defense," Adams explained, he fired his .38 pistol and shot the young man in the left leg. The driver of the car and the third passenger insisted that Adams fired without warning, but their testimony counted far less than Adams's, who was on a first-name basis with Anniston's police chief and most of the city's police force. Three days later—with Vaughan in a wheelchair—the recorder's court judge fined the twenty-five-year-old Black man $100 and sentenced him to fifteen days in jail for disorderly conduct and carrying a pocketknife.[317]

Four days before the Cole performance, Adams convened a late-night meeting at his service station. He and Jesse Mabry, Carter's co-editor of *The Southerner*, outlined an audacious, if ambitious, plan to four dedicated followers: They would mobilize 100 to 150 of Carter's followers to attack Cole. One group would rush Cole out of the auditorium and temporarily kidnap him, while Adams would seize the microphone and denounce the evils of Black music.[318]

A few hours before the concert was to begin on April 10, 1956, Adams, Mabry, and the four most loyal members of Carter's Klan group—Orliss Clevenger, Mike Fox and the Vinson brothers (Edgar and Willie)—gathered in the back room of Adams's main service station. Clevenger, only eighteen years old, brought a pair of brass knuckles and a lead-filled blackjack. His comrades threw two loaded shotguns, a 30-06 rifle, and two .38 caliber pistols into the trunk of Mabry's '49 Chevy and set out on the ninety-minute drive to Birmingham.

JANIE GRANTHAM GREW UP in the 1940s and 1950s in the small town of Tupelo, Mississippi, birthplace of Elvis Presley. She and her close friend Susie Beam were passionate fans of jazz musicians, particularly Dave Brubeck, June Christy, and Nat King Cole. When the owners of the local music store invited the two teenagers to make the three-hour drive to Birmingham for Cole's concert, "it was like manna from heaven," said Grantham—a chance to see and hear some of her favorite performers, opening with vocalist June Christy singing her signature song, "Something Cool." "I knew the words and felt incredibly superior to everyone around me," she recalled.[319]

John Birchard, a Vermont native, was also a jazz fan. As a teenager, he collected the 1940s and early 1950s recordings made by the Nat King Cole trio. Straight out of high school, he joined the Air Force in the summer of 1955, hoping to receive an assignment in Europe. Instead, he found himself stationed at Craig Air Force Base outside Selma. "I had wanted to see the world," said Birchard. "Well, for me, south Alabama was as much another world as I could have imagined." He saw an ad for the Cole concert and persuaded a fellow airman and jazz buff from New Jersey to join him for the two-hour drive to Birmingham. As he joined the crowd pouring into Birmingham's municipal auditorium, Birchard felt at home for the first time. Despite the Deep South accents surrounding him, the audience seemed in good spirits, and he found it heartening to see young white Southerners so enthusiastic about a Black performer headlining a stage filled with Black and white musicians. More surprising was the appearance of Birmingham Mayor Jimmy Morgan to welcome Cole and his performers to the city.[320]

Outside the auditorium, under Adams's command, Carter's strike force arrived early to be able to park just behind the auditorium at the planned rendezvous site to wait for the "150 reinforcements." Ten minutes after the concert began, only one person had appeared.

Whatever the plans had been at Adams's filling station, the final escapade became a product of booze-fueled rage and chaotic improvisation. The youngest of the group, Orliss Clevenger, was assigned to have the car ready for a getaway. At the last minute, Mike Fox volunteered to remain with Clevenger.

Jesse Mabry followed behind Adams and the two Vinson brothers when they shoved aside the usher at the main doors as Cole began his set's third song, "Little Girl," a forgettable ballad he had recorded with his trio in 1947.

Janie Grantham and Susie Beam heard a "loud noise from the back of the auditorium like some sort of thunder" and turned with the rest of the audience in time to hear Jesse Mabry shout "Let's go get that coon." Adams and the Vinson brothers charged down the aisle while a bewildered Cole stopped singing as the band played on.

Birmingham police had received a tip of possible trouble and two plainclothes detectives stood in the wings in addition to the four policemen in the hall always assigned to sell-outs at the auditorium. As Willie Vinson leaped over the footlights, yelling "Drag the son-of-a-bitch off the stage!," he shoved the microphone into Cole's face and slammed the slender singer over the top of his piano bench and onto the floor. Adams, 5'11", 195 pounds, piled on top. In the semi-darkened auditorium, two policemen—who had not been told that plainclothes officers would be present—momentarily grappled with the detectives while another uniformed policeman seized Edgar Vinson.

As officer R. N. Higginbotham used his nightstick to place Edgar in a chokehold, Willie Vinson released Cole, picked up a Coke bottle from the floor next to the piano, and smashed the bottle into Higginbotham's face. (Surgeons at the University of Alabama medical school hospital would spend two hours repairing his broken nose and wiring a fractured jaw.) That was enough for Higginbotham's fellow officer, H. E. Schatz. With, as he described it, "a little help from my nightstick," Schatz knocked Willie Vinson off the stage and five feet down into the orchestra pit.

When Adams continued to resist, Schatz, 6'2" and 212 pounds, turned, grabbed him by the shirt collar, and threw him into the pit next to Vinson. English musicians from the Ted Heath orchestra had been trying to maintain some semblance of order by playing "God Save the Queen," since none knew the American national anthem. As Adams and Vinson landed among the

Nat King Cole, on the stage in Birmingham after the KKK assault.

music stands, orchestra members scrambled to safety.

The brawl completely unnerved Vermont-born John Birchard and his New Jersey friend as the crowd began shouting and the fighting sprawled across the stage. There we were, he said, "a couple of Yankees in a strange land . . . scared that the all-white audience might be calling for Cole's blood."[321] But he quickly realized that the crowd was shouting at the attackers.

Within minutes a shaken Cole had been taken back to his dressing room, and the three attackers were handcuffed and placed under arrest. Mabry had taken a page from Carter's playbook, maintaining a discreet distance from the mayhem, but he began haranguing police for "arresting those white boys rather than the nigger." Police cuffed him as well, and an arriving squad car saw Clevenger and Fox parked at the back door of the theater with their engine running. After a quick search the two policemen found the sawed-off shotgun and other weapons, put the two in handcuffs, and carted them off to the Birmingham jail. The lone reinforcement who initially joined the attackers had fled at the first sign of trouble.

Cole, who had suffered a split upper lip and a strained back muscle, returned to the microphone, and after an extended ovation from the all-white audience, he assured them that he had not been trying to make a political statement. He was born in Alabama, he told the hushed crowd, with the clear implication that he was no stranger to the etiquette of Southern race relations. "I just came here to entertain you," he said. "That was what I thought you wanted."[322]

On the long ride back to Tupelo, Janie Grantham and Susie Beam sat silently. Even at age seventeen, both were aware of how many Americans viewed white Southerners. "[I was] just so disappointed and sad and ashamed of the South," Grantham said. "I wanted to go hug Nat King Cole and tell him how sorry I was."[323]

Asa Carter was nowhere to be seen that night, a pattern he had followed since his presence in the mob during the Autherine Lucy riot. Until the general public was aroused enough to act decisively, he acknowledged to journalist John Bartlow Martin, he would remain in the shadows and deploy his most dedicated "cadre" of followers to engage in direct action. Despite Carter's absence, journalists quickly discovered that he had approved the assault by Adams and Mabry, co-planners, and members of the North Alabama Citizens' Council group.

For mainline segregation leaders like Sam Engelhardt, already in full battle mode against Carter, the assault on Cole became a convenient weapon to denounce Carter's conduct as "damaging to the cause of segregation. If we find any members like these in the Citizens' Council of Alabama," promised Engelhardt, "they will be thrown out. . . ." He cautioned the people of Alabama against "joining the wrong Citizens' Council," a clear slap at Carter's group.[324]

When a *Birmingham News* reporter spoke to him, Carter made no effort to hide his connection to the attackers. He said his followers had planned to attend as "observers" until a Negro in the rear of the auditorium "knocked a camera" from one of his followers, and it "made him mad, and he ran down the aisle toward Cole who was just another Negro to him." And what about the cache of weapons in Mabry's car? Two of the men were "on their way turkey hunting," he responded.[325]

It was a vintage Carter performance. No Black spectators had been admitted to the strictly segregated auditorium, and none of his followers had a camera. But reporters were not so tasteless as to question Carter's account or to suggest that it was unusual to hunt crafty wild birds with .38 caliber revolvers, even in Alabama. Carter had learned from his earlier dealing with reporters that their coverage seldom directly contradicted his statements, however outlandish.

Carter subsequently established a "White People's Defense Fund," headed by his brother Doug, and then filled the pages of his magazine with a defense of the brave white men who were "mercilessly beaten" by Birmingham policemen "after negro singer Nat 'King' Cole fell over a piano stool at the City Auditorium." In Carter's telling, the real responsibility for the Cole incident rested upon the shoulders of the "negroid promoters," all of whom had Jewish names. These promoters had deliberately set out to use Black music to "drive the white to the Negroid level, culturally, mentally, spiritually and finally physically."[326]

And why the uproar? Mrs. Orville Clevenger, the mother of the youngest accused, bitterly complained about the double standard of the press in her fundraising appeal to pay for attorney's fees. "When a White does something to a Negro it makes front page for two or three days and . . . when two or three Negro men raped that white woman a few weeks ago, there was only one small article about it. . . ."[327]

For white adolescents in the segregated South, there often came a moment which revealed the explosive and dangerous connection between race and sex. As a rural farm boy of the 1940s and the 1950s, I looked forward to few events more eagerly than the annual county fair. Since I raised Jersey cattle on our farm and showed them in the livestock exhibition, it meant a week away from school. I often slept in the cattle barns and slipped away during the afternoons for walks through the carnival booths and rides. The highlight of these excursions on the sawdust-covered midway was to move to the edge of the crowd at one of the two "girlie shows" in which a dozen skimpily clad young women paraded across the platform to the constant patter of the barker who promised a far more revealing look inside the tent to those who paid their fifty cents. ("Men only, over the age of eighteen.") There were two shows; one was white, and the other was Black, or "colored" as it was called.

The Saturday after fair week, I spent the afternoon fishing on a small creek with my cousin and two young Black teenagers who lived on a nearby

farm and were a little older than us. One would say they were "boys" except for the painful meaning that word had for young Black men. All of us, I discovered, had been to the fair. It did not occur to me that it was peculiar that there was a single "colored day" set aside for Black patrons. That was the world I accepted without questions.

I began talking about how beautiful I had thought the "colored girls" were at the fair. I was not conscious of my comments as predatory; I thought of them as a compliment. I, as a white boy, recognized the beauty of an "inferior" race. I do not remember what my cousin's Black friends said, but I distinctly remember that both recoiled as though physically struck. They stood and simply walked away without saying a word.

Afterwards, bewildered, I told the story to my mother. She groped for some way to help me understand their reaction. Finally, she said: "What if they had started talking about how beautiful the white girls were at the fair?"

Of course, that was impossible since the white burlesque closed on "Colored Day." But, dimly, I had begun to understand the taboo that lay at the heart of white resistance.

In the next issue of *The Southerner,* Carter illustrated his defense of the six arrested men with photographs purportedly of white women kissing Black servicemen at an officer's club dance at Fort McClellan just outside Anniston; the photographs actually were of several young French women and Black American GI's taken in France in 1946 and constantly recirculated among white supremacy groups in the 1950s. Lest anyone miss the meaning of the connection between Cole and these scenes, Carter explained that integrationists had developed a master plan to use Black "jungle music" to get white youth to "think as a Negro, to talk as a Negro, to accept the Negroes' moral standard and his culture. . . ." Once that was accomplished, said Carter, sexual amalgamation became a mere formality.[328]

Respectable white conservatives defended Cole by emphasizing that he had scrupulously followed the state's segregation laws, was no politician, and had always been "cool toward the NAACP." Two days after the attack, Cole—well aware of the danger of angering many of his white followers—told an Associated Press reporter, "I can't understand it. . . . I have not taken part in any protests. Nor have I joined an organization fighting segregation. Why should they attack me?"[329]

In a more candid conversation with a British reporter, Cole drew a direct link between his appearance as a Black performer performing with white entertainers. It was all part of the "segregation business," he said, "part of the fuss over Autherine Lucy at the University of Alabama and the bus boycott in Montgomery." Only two weeks after his assault—responding to Black activists who criticized him for praising Birmingham police and performing before segregated audiences—Cole publicly announced that he had taken out a life membership in the NAACP and would perform several benefits for the organization. After that Spring 1956 tour, he refused to appear in Southern segregated venues.[330]

Birmingham's district attorney initially indicted Kenneth Adams and Willie Vinson with "intent to murder," a felony that could have resulted in a five-year jail sentence. But Cole's public declaration of support for the NAACP cooled the prosecutor's enthusiasm. In December, he accepted a plea bargain in which Adams paid a $50 fine for simple assault and Vinson twice that amount because he had assaulted a police officer. The other four paid $25 fines.[331] The Cole "incident" (as local reporters described it) soon disappeared from the state's newspapers. Nat King Cole, the NAACP life member, was not as appealing a victim as Nat King Cole, the home-grown observer of regional racial etiquette.

But Carter had made little progress in his campaign to eradicate rock and roll. And the largest Alabama newspapers editorially condemned the incident, primarily because of the embarrassment it brought to the state. At least temporarily, however, such criticism raised Carter's standing among hard-line segregationists. Over the next two months he drew large crowds at rallies in the Birmingham area and in north Alabama, often side by side with John Crommelin, whose announced campaign for the Senate had attracted far-right activists from all over the nation.

Crommelin had played a critical role in supporting Carter through the years. He enthusiastically supported the decision of the American States Rights Association (ASRA) to hire Carter to begin with, and he renounced the well-heeled coalition of right-wing businessmen who fired Carter after his antisemitic radio remarks. He became convinced that Carter was one of the few anti-segregation leaders who understood the links between Jews, Communists, and integrationists. Over the next five years, Crommelin repeatedly aided the fiery crusader, loaning him funds and defending him publicly. At the same time, he introduced Carter to a variety of far-right extremists operating across the nation, notably a New Jersey-born activist named John Kasper who—like Carter—would achieve brief nationwide fame.

THE SON OF A successful MIT-educated engineer, Kasper drifted through a half dozen private and public schools during his adolescence, repeatedly dismissed for his emotional and erratic outbursts. Finally completing high school, he spent more than a year in a Philadelphia psychiatric hospital but recovered enough to win admission to Columbia University, where he proved to be an excellent student, graduating in 1952. As a sophomore majoring in philosophy, Kasper fell under the spell of the disgraced American poet Ezra Pound. Controversial but highly regarded, Pound had spent much of his early career in Europe as a pioneering figure in the emergence of free verse. He published more than twenty volumes of poetry and an even larger number of prose works. He also became a fanatical anti-communist, a passionate antisemite, an indiscriminate racist, and an opponent of representative democracy.[332]

During the 1920s, while living in Rapallo, Italy, Pound became an admirer of Benito Mussolini's fascist state. In 1939, still in Italy, he began reading "essays" on Italy's radio network, supporting Mussolini and Hitler in their struggle against the corrupt English empire. (England had "let in the Jew and the Jew rotted your empire," he said in one broadcast directed to a British audience.) After the United States entered the war in December 1941, he became even more passionately pro-fascist, broadcasting more than two hundred pro-Axis broadcasts from Rome.[333]

Arrested after the war, he narrowly avoided a trial for treason for his wartime pro-fascist broadcasts. With the help of Pound's literary admirers in the United States, he was instead diagnosed as "mentally ill" and detained in St. Elizabeths Psychiatric Hospital outside Washington, D.C. There, with the cooperation of hospital officials, Pound lived in a comfortable suite, regularly

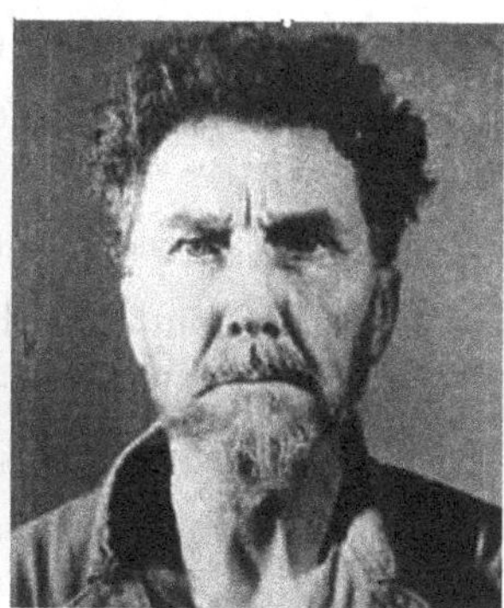

Left, John Kasper, 1956. Right, Ezra Pound mug shot, 1945.

welcoming visitors to his quarters for literary and political discussions.[334]

When Kasper wrote Pound an admiring letter in 1951, he was thrilled to receive a warm response. Over the next five years, Kasper corresponded with and visited Pound whenever possible. The brilliant but disgraced poet became Kasper's hero, surrogate father, and intellectual mentor. After graduation from Columbia in 1953, Kasper opened the Make It New bookstore in Greenwich Village, selling "intellectual" works on a wide variety of left- and right-wing subjects.[335]

As Kasper's correspondence with Pound evolved and he continued what he called his "pilgrimages" to St. Elizabeths, he soon embraced his mentor's poisonous antisemitism. If he was clear about the threat posed by Jews, his racial ideas initially remained a muddle. At times he wrote admiringly of African culture, and friends later recalled that he attended interracial dances, had Black friends, and was particularly close to what he called a "brilliant" young Black woman who worked at his bookstore and shared his antisemitism.

But under Pound's tutelage he had already begun his journey toward classical racism. In November 1955, he closed his Greenwich Village store and leased the Cadmus bookstore in Georgetown to be closer to Pound, the man he had come to call "Master" and "Grandpaw." Cadmus soon became the main source of far-right books and pamphlets in the Washington area and a meeting place for antisemites and racists like George Lincoln Rockwell, head of the American Nazi Party.[336]

Shortly after the United States Senate censured Joseph McCarthy for "conduct contrary to Senatorial traditions," John Crommelin traveled to New

York as the headline speaker at a massive pro-McCarthy rally in Madison Square Gardens. During the visit, a mutual friend introduced him to the impressionable Kasper.

Kasper, the intellectual, had never been involved in politics, nor did he know much about the American South. But he sensed in Crommelin the embodiment of the intellectual as political activist as he listened to the ex-admiral describe his political campaign to unseat Alabama's long-time incumbent Senator Lister Hill. With Pound's blessing, Kasper turned over the management of the bookstore to a friend and left for Alabama to work in the campaign leading up to the May 1, 1956, primary. He wrote Pound that he had found a political candidate willing to openly confront the threat facing the nation: the "kike behind the nigger."[337]

Within days after Kasper arrived in Alabama, Crommelin brought the New Yorker around to Carter's Bessemer theater and over the next six weeks, the two bonded in a way that was unusual for Carter. With Carter's encouragement, Kasper began speaking to Crommelin supporters and quickly found his voice. Despite his New York accent, he discovered that working-class audiences welcomed the support of what one admirer called the "Yankee rebel."

Crommelin lost, but undaunted he financed Carter in a new and ambitious organizing venture. He gave Carter and Kasper funds to begin recruiting allies in the Washington, D.C., area, and he paid Doug Carter "traveling money" and enough to set up an office in Dearborn, Michigan, near the massive Ford River Rouge auto assembly plant. It would be a trial run for recruiting Northern white blue-collar workers to the cause of white supremacy.

If any city in the North was prime recruiting ground for Carter's efforts to expand outside the South, it was suburban Detroit. Between 1945 and 1965, suburban residents, often in heavily working-class areas, created more than two hundred all-white neighborhood associations devoted to excluding Black residents. On several occasions in the late 1940s and early 1950s, white mobs had attacked Blacks who sought to purchase homes in white neighborhoods.[338] In an article published in *The Southerner*, Doug Carter claimed to have met hundreds of disgruntled whites angry over the movement of African Americans into their working-class communities. He claimed (without evidence) that he had organized a half dozen Northern versions of the Southern Citizens' Councils under the name of the "Homeowner's Association of Michigan."

While Doug continued his efforts in Detroit, Asa made the thirteen-hour trip to Washington, staying in a boarding house and using Kasper's Georgetown bookstore as the unofficial staging office for their combined effort to expand a militant version of the white Citizens' Council movement into Washington and the surrounding communities in Maryland and Virginia.

Alvin Miller, a college student and part-time Cadmus clerk, initially found Carter fascinating. He could be an ingratiating performer, said Miller. He often set himself up in a corner of the store and held forth with humorous stories and anecdotes for an appreciative audience. If he could be charming and humorous, he could also suddenly become grim and enraged, railing against Blacks while giving mini-lectures about his favorite racist authors.

One afternoon, Carter began praising the Germans' "solution" to the "Jew problem." For Miller, it was enough. "That's Nazi talk," he told Carter. Without warning, Carter jumped to his feet, "charged like a bull," and decked Miller. For what seemed like forever but was really only a few minutes, Carter kicked and punched Miller through the bookstore aisles, knocking over displays and shelves until several customers persuaded Carter to stop. As Miller ruefully recalled: "I was almost six feet tall, weighed 180 pounds and was in good shape. But he cleaned my clock."[339]

Miller found another part-time job.

Carter, far more experienced in grassroots organizing, guided Kasper as in forming two Washington chapters of what they decided to call the "Seaboard Citizens' Councils." The new organization would have nothing to do with the mainline Citizens' Council movement, which they denounced as "soft on integration." Membership forms required all who joined the Seaboard Citizens' Council to declare, "I am white, 18 years of age, believe in the separation of the races, in upholding racial segregation, am loyal to the United States of America and believe in the divinity of Jesus Christ." On the first page of the recruiting materials, Carter and Kasper warned of the "alien gangsters" who had "gained control of the major newspapers, publishing houses, radio and T.V. networks and Hollywood." Remember, read the handout: "Brotherhoodism + Equalityism [sic] = Communism." To make clear the reference to "alien gangster," the application form included a cartoon caricature with a hook-nosed Jew pouring lies of "brotherhood" into the brain of the sheep-like "John Q. Public."[340]

By this time, Doug Carter's Detroit organizing campaign had collapsed, in part because of a tone-deafness to Northern variants of white racism. In an interview with the *Detroit Free Press*, he explained his goal: to alert Northern whites to the threat of race mongrelization. "When I stepped off the plane in Detroit," he said, "I felt like I was in a foreign country" with "Negroes and white people dating and eating together." In efforts to organize local workers, he distributed the latest issue of his brother's magazine *The Southerner,* containing lengthy article that described an epidemic of Black rapists in the Motor City. A "negro raped a little 3-year-old White girl . . . breaking most of her bones and leaving her for dead," wrote his brother. "Another negro raped a little 5-year-old White girl, slit her throat and placed her in a garbage can. One negro, apprehended for slaying a 64-year-old White woman and raping her as she died, testified that he was a member of a pack of negroes who roamed the streets [of Detroit] searching for white women to assault."

Carter fabricated these and other stories of Black men's "animalistic lust for white women." But even though Northern working-class whites often expressed racist fears about Black crime, they seemed more concerned about economic competition by Black workers and the collapse of property values that supposedly came when African Americans moved into their neighborhood. In late June, the owner of the building where Doug had rented his office filed an official eviction notice, claiming that he had been misled about the purposes of the organization.[341]

In Washington, Kasper and Asa Carter initially operated without publicity, quietly meeting small groups of segregationists. But on June 14, 1956, they publicly unveiled their plans to Maryland and District press as well as WTOP-TV, Washington's flagship CBS station. At a town meeting held in suburban Maryland, more than two hundred white men packed a local community center to hear Carter and Kasper describe their new organization.

Kasper introduced himself as the "executive secretary" of the "Seaboard Citizens' Councils" and claimed that six local Council groups had already been organized in the Virginia and Washington areas. With boyish enthusiasm, he described his guest speaker, Asa Carter, as the man whose followers had "prevented the entrance of Autherine Lucy to Alabama University" and single-handedly destroyed a Birmingham interracial council by exposing these race traitors who stood in a circle before every meeting, "held hands, white and colored alike, and recited the oath of allegiance to the Communist Party."

Only three years away from a dead-end disc jockey job in Yazoo City, Mississippi, Carter had become a national celebrity, with cheering crowds, reportage from the Birmingham press, even requests for quotes from the hated *New York Times* and an interview by *Newsweek*.[342] During a time before the television networks provided extensive news coverage, millions of Americans watched the Fox Movietone News weekly in theaters across the nation. Beginning in the spring of 1956, Movietone News featured Carter in eleven segments, interviewing him or showing films of his speeches.[343]

Washington's WTOP-TV recorded long sections of the two-hour panel featuring lengthy monologues from Kasper and Carter interspersed with questioning from reporters. For a long-time radio broadcaster, Carter seemed oblivious to the impression he created on television. In his speeches, he moved back and forth between describing Black people as "Nigras" or, more often, simply "niggers." While print reporters back in Alabama dutifully transposed such references to "Negroes" in their newspaper copy, there was no filter for the film footage when several segments were shown on WTOP's evening news. Most area viewers must have been jarred by Carter's sneering references to Benjamin Mays, the respected president of Morehouse College, as an "Atlanta nigger," or to his repeated insistence that America was a "Christian nation"—followed by scowling listing of "communist" politicians with suspiciously Jewish names like New York Senator Herbert Lehman, or "lying journalists like the *New York Daily News* Milton Berliner who, I understand, is not a Christian. . . ."

Nor could there have been any doubt about Carter's violent intentions. The "pink shirted poodle dog crowd" could talk about law and order, but that was simply a recipe for ultimate mongrelization. "People worry that I'm going to step on some toes," Carter emphasized as he slammed his right hand into his left palm. "Well, I'm not going to *step* on them," he warned. "I'm going to stomp them!"[344] The crowd interrupted Carter repeatedly with applause exceeded only by their shouted approval when self-appointed marshals grabbed a Black student who had come to observe the meeting and shoved him out the door.

Despite their claims of success in organizing chapters in Washington and the Maryland and Virginia suburbs, Kasper and Carter were never able to establish permanent Councils. Carter argued that more fertile ground lay in Charlottesville, Virginia, where the threat of integration was imminent. The city had decided to become the first school system in Virginia scheduled to integrate in the wake of the *Brown* decision.

When the Charlottesville Human Relations Council met on August 23, 1956, as part of the community's preparation for a peaceful desegregation, Kasper and Carter appeared. While Carter sat silently, Kasper stood up, interrupted the meeting, and attacked the biracial (and predominantly female) group as a bunch of "flat-chested highbrows" who were "defying the state law tonight with that nigra sitting there," he said, pointing at the editor of the local Black weekly. His friend Asa Carter had successfully shut down a Birmingham biracial committee, Kasper told the group, and he and his newly formed "Seaboard Citizens' Council" would not stop until they had "run you people out of town."[345]

A week later, at a rally attended by more than three hundred men, Carter called on the crowd to ignore the courts and the politicians. The "so-called" Human Relations Council in Charlottesville sought to "mongrelize the Anglo-Saxon race with the Negro," he shouted. Like Kasper, he called on the crowd to "run them out of town." While he spoke, local white segregationists held aloft posters listing the names, addresses, and telephone numbers of the members of the HRC.

The "flat-chested highbrow" on the Charlottesville Council that most annoyed Kasper and Carter was Sarah Patton Boyle, a forty-nine-year-old descendant of one of Virginia's "first families." Boyle had just published an article in the *Saturday Evening Post*, arguing that once white Southerners had overcome their irrational fears they would accept integration.[346]

The night of Carter's August 23 speech, Boyle heard noises on her front lawn, saw light through her bedroom window, and a sound she described as a "crackling noise, almost like dry leaves being raked." Less than twenty feet from her front door stood a burning six-foot-tall cross. Later that morning she examined the charred cross, beautifully constructed with graceful proportions and carefully beveled supports. The loving care with which a skilled craftsman had constructed the cross seemed to depress her more than the burning itself.[347]

Earlier, Kasper had bragged to an FBI informant that he and his friend Asa were heading down to Charlottesville, and everyone would "soon read about burning crosses in the yards of two Charlottesville women." But the FBI decided not to inform local police, fearful that disclosing the information would jeopardize their informant.[348]

During the days that followed, every Charlottesville Human Relations Council member received threatening telephone calls and letters, but most of the attacks were directed against Boyle, perhaps because her *Saturday Evening Post* article had made her a national figure. A member of the Virginia House of Delegates introduced a bill to have her husband, Roger Boyle, fired from the faculty of the University of Virginia. Although the bill died in committee, she quickly learned to leave the phone off the hook much of the time as callers screamed

Sarah Boyle with burned crosses, 1956.

obscenities or warned that her home would be "blown sky high." And she tried to ignore the hate mail she received.

Despite the painful consequences for outspoken individuals like Boyle, Charlottesville was no Birmingham. This was not the "Virginia way," declared the head of the Virginia Defenders of State Sovereignty, an anti-integration organization that overshadowed the small Virginia Citizens' Council. Kasper and Carter were "violence-prone outside agitators," and Virginia had no need for rabble rousers. Virginia would defend segregation legally.[349]

Even as the Charlottesville school board planned to integrate, Governor Thomas Stanley convened the General Assembly on August 27 and called for the withdrawal of state funding to any school district that accepted integration. That same afternoon, US District Judge John Paul indefinitely stayed his earlier order for the desegregation of Charlottesville schools.[350]

The struggle had entered a new phase: massive resistance. If a single Southern school district desegregated its schools even on a limited scale, went the argument, the tide of integration would sweep across the region. Stanley had warned the General Assembly that "a little integration" would inevitably lead to its "sure and certain insidious spread through the entire commonwealth," and ultimately the "destruction of our schools." The only hope for the white South, agreed Senator Harry Byrd, was "absolute and unconditional massive resistance" to integration in every Southern state. Under orders from Virginia's attorney general, the Charlottesville school board abandoned the plan for integrating the schools.[351]

Confident that they had played a part in turning back the first break in Virginia's wall of resistance, Asa Carter returned to his home in Alabama for the first time in several weeks. But John Kasper had no time for rest. Rising just before dawn on August 24, he loaded his dilapidated 1947 Chevrolet with a change of clothes and a box of anti-integration pamphlets and began the twelve-hour drive from Washington to the small Appalachian mountain community of Clinton, Tennessee.

10

What Goes Up Comes Down: The Clinton Debacle

I tell you. It's the hardest thing in the word to live a Christian life. I want to treat the nigger right, and I know I ought to, but . . . you know there's something in the blood that's agin mixing. We can talk all we want to—justice, equality, all that sort of thing, talking—but when we come right down to it, that's what it's all about: a nigger marrying your sister or your daughter.

CLINTON, TENNESSEE, RESIDENT, SEPTEMBER 1957[352]

LATE SUMMER, 1956: CLINTON, Tennessee, a small Appalachian community of fewer than four thousand residents, seemed an unlikely place for racial violence. In a county that was 98 per cent white, their Black elementary students attended a one-room schoolhouse in Clinton while the small number of Black high school students were bused to the nearest Black high school in Oak Ridge. After a successful legal challenge to the city's segregated school system, the local board of education unanimously agreed to admit twelve Black students on Monday, August 27.

Although civic leaders in the small town accepted the prospect of limited school integration, many whites in the surrounding rural areas resented the court-ordered changes. Only twelve miles away, the Oak Ridge nuclear facility, established in 1942 as a "secret city" devoted to enriching uranium for the atomic bomb, had nearly doubled Anderson County's population. While Oak Ridge had attracted a core of well-educated scientists, it drew much of its overwhelmingly white work force from across the South. These

First African American students entering Clinton High, August 1956.

new arrivals, like many whites in Appalachia, shared traditional attitudes toward segregation and white supremacy.

John Kasper, Asa Carter's comrade in the effort to organize Citizens' Councils in Virginia and Maryland, arrived on the scene just three days before the scheduled school opening; he did not know a single person in the community. After spending the night sleeping in his car, he walked the streets of the town all day Saturday, an itinerant evangelist for bigotry, handing out leaflets and urging people to come down to the courthouse that afternoon to hear him outline a plan to stop the communist plot to undermine the white race. Town officials, notified of his presence, asked him to leave and, when he refused, charged him with vagrancy and threw him into one of the town's three cell jails. With Kasper behind bars, the Monday desegregation of schools passed without event.[353]

On Tuesday, convinced that the crisis had passed, the local justice of the peace dismissed Kasper, who promptly walked to Clinton High School and angrily accused principal David Brittain of being a "race traitor." He then stood across from the school as classes ended, quickly recruiting two dozen sympathetic white students. He urged the them to "drive the niggers out."

The initial integration had gone smoothly; Black students were relieved that they received little more than hostile stares while several white students smiled and spoke to them. The all-white teaching staff seemed particularly welcoming. But Kasper had done his work well. On Wednesday morning his student recruits moved through the halls, shoving several of the twelve Black students and shouting, "Nigger go home if you know what's good for you." That afternoon Bobby Kane, one of the twelve, walked alone out of the school on his way to Foley Hill, the small Black neighborhood a half mile away. As he passed through the parking lot, students and several young men surrounded Kane and began shoving and kicking him. Two Clinton policemen parked outside the school stopped the attackers, placed Kane in their squad car, and drove him home. But they made no effort to break up the mob which quickly moved to the front of the building and cornered three other Black students. They were rescued only when Jeffrey Shattuck, the seventeen-year-old president of the Clinton High School student body, recruited several of his fellow football teammates to surround the three and escort them back into the school, untouched but surrounded by shouts of "nigger lover, nigger lover."

Six decades later, Shattuck acknowledged that he held fairly traditional Southern ideas on race. "I didn't ask for integration," he said, but he believed that the decision was "the law of the land" and had to be obeyed. And watching the rowdy bullies, he had felt an instinctive sympathy for the beleaguered Black students.[354]

Small, grainy photo is only known image of John Kasper agitating Clinton crowd of 1,000, 1956.

Over the next two weeks, despite the efforts of principal Brittain, schoolteachers, and a handful of sympathetic white classmates, the twelve Black teenagers were constantly harassed and assaulted. Inside the school the abuse was mainly verbal. Outside, protestors physically attacked the

Black students, throwing rocks, rotten eggs, spoiled tomatoes, and sticks. "The rocks are what I remember the most," Jo Ann Boyce recalled. "I can remember the rocks whistling as they passed your ear. That's how close they would get. . . . You didn't dare turn your head. You just didn't dare."[355]

By nightfall on Wednesday, August 29, more than a thousand protestors had gathered in front of the Anderson County Courthouse to hear Kasper. As he began to speak, two federal marshals handed him an injunction issued by US District Judge Robert Taylor, ordering him to cease from "hindering, obstructing, or in any way interfering" with the integration of Clinton High School. Kasper took the document and accused Taylor of "betraying the white people of the county." One member of the audience pointed to the marshals and shouted "kill them." The marshals quickly left as the crowd cheered.

Earlier, Kasper had learned that Brittain spent the day in the school halls, disciplining white students for their harassment of the Black students. While segregation supporters held up placards listing Brittain's home telephone number, Kasper called on the crowd to telephone Brittain at "all hours of the day or night." And he told his white listeners to do whatever was necessary to "run the Negro students out of the school." Over the next two weeks, Brittain received more than a dozen written and telephoned death threats. In one letter, the unsigned writer promised to throw acid in the faces of his children.[356]

Kasper's time with Carter traveling across Alabama had prepared the handsome 6'8" New Yorker to speak with a language familiar to his audience. "It simply does not hold that the white race, as the majority in the United States, should turn their civilization over to a group of people only eighty years removed from slavery and separated from the jungle by a hundred years," he told Clinton whites. In language lifted directly from Carter, Kasper spoke of the courage of white Klansmen in overthrowing "Black rule" after the Civil War. Without their willingness to act with force, he said, "everyone here today [in the South] would be a mulatto."[357]

Like his mentor, Kasper captured the frustration of angry mountaineers who saw the rising civil rights upheavals as a challenge to the white world in which they lived. He attacked the Anderson County sheriff and Clinton police chief as lacking the "guts" to arrest the Negro students and their parents for breaking state laws against integration. Unlike Carter, Kasper spoke in a conversational tone and seldom raised his voice, but he still projected a passion that led his audience to erupt into applause and cheers, again and again. More than forty years later, one Clinton resident still remembered Kasper. He may not have "yelled," but his voice was intense, his eyes gleaming with the fire of the true believer. "He was the most hate-filled man I've ever run across. . . . He had eyes you'd never forget."[358]

Under the influence of his idol Ezra Pound, Kasper had abandoned Black friends from his New York days and become a passionate racist. The white race, he said, quoting Pound, "is the great race and the only race which has fought for free institutions." Carter's greatest influence on Kasper was not racial rhetoric and language, but the importance of building a movement based upon a contempt for "elites" of all kinds. Despite Kasper's Columbia University degree, despite his voracious reading in history, literature, and political ideology, Carter had taught him to "distrust any man with a college education." Working class [white] people were the only remnants of the white race who had the "intelligence and the courage to maintain their racial integrity." The "intellectual" was always trying to imitate life from reading books while maintaining a distance from true Americans who had "horse-sense and independent thought."[359]

The Clinton police force consisted of seven uniformed officers, but Chief Francis Moore seemed convinced that his men could restrain the crowd by quiet persuasion. After all, they knew many of the individuals. Before and after Kasper's talk, Moore and his officers wandered through the crowd, exchanging good-natured remarks. They made no effort to disperse the crowd. Moore's strategy seemed to work; by 9 p.m. the crowd had peacefully left the courthouse square.

On Friday morning, however, Judge Taylor ordered the New Yorker segregationist into his courtroom in nearby Knoxville. Taylor asked Kasper why he had failed to abide by the earlier injunction. A grim Kasper ignored the question and demanded that the judge halt the integration of Clinton's high school. "Do you still think that I have the power to go against the law of the United States Supreme Court?" asked an incredulous Taylor.

You're nothing but a "vassal" for the integrationist forces, retorted Kasper. With the slam of his gavel, the furious Taylor ordered him jailed for contempt of court.[360]

Twenty miles away, Knoxville's two country music radio stations, WNOX and WKVL, broadcast news of Kasper's arrest. Through that Friday afternoon, Clinton Mayor W. E. Lewallen helplessly watched carloads of sullen white men drive into town and began milling around the courthouse square.

After Carter heard of Kasper's arrest, he gassed up his '54 Buick, picked up his brother, Doug, and began the five-hour drive up the Tennessee Valley, through Knoxville, and into a tense and crowded Clinton. By early evening, a crowd estimated at more than a thousand had filled the streets facing the Anderson County Courthouse, chanting "Free John Kasper! Free John Kasper! Free John Kasper!"

Just after 7:30 p.m., a black-suited Carter climbed the steps of the courthouse and turned to face the crowd. "I'm Ace Carter," he said. "I'm from Alabama." By this time, Carter had become a well-known figure to segregationists across the region, and the crowd roared its applause. Unlike his radio broadcasts, there was little conversational in Carter's speaking style. "I came here," he shouted, "because I have four children." Today the

Asa Carter in Clinton, Tennessee, 1956.

courts were trying to "take a white child and a Nigra child and mongrelize our children." Because Kasper resisted, he was under political arrest at the hands of a "carpetbagging judge." Make no mistake, he told the crowd, Clinton was part of a broader campaign to silence the voices of those who defended white civilization.

And who were the traitors who enabled them? Carter's voice rising, he answered his question: the "get-along, go-along compromisers" and the "lying news media" who had defamed the "God-fearing, working-class people who are simply trying to protect the purity of their children."

These are difficult days, he said. Whites made up only 30 percent of the world's population, but even in the South with a large "colored population," whites sprang from an undiluted racial background. The communists might call for a one-world government and a one-world race, but these were the Anglo-Saxon patriots who have "stood up and told the nigras, 'You must operate, you must conduct yourself from a separate station.'"

Here was the problem, he said. For the last generation "we haven't been white men." Instead, rich and powerful "so-called" leaders betrayed their birthright by refusing to take action while organizations like the NAACP took over the country. This will not stand, he shouted. "We are here to protect our wives and our daughters." Remember the Ku Klux Klan of our forefathers, said Carter. The "reason we don't have banana-colored skin, kinky hair, and thick lips is because of leaders like Nathan Bedford Forrest!"

As the crowd cheered him on, Carter smacked his right fist into his open left palm and, one by one, listed the Supreme Court justices, each name followed by the crowd's shout: "Traitor!" Now "act like white men," he said as he ended his speech.[361]

As Carter descended the steps of the courthouse, an estimated three hundred members of the crowd surged through the streets to Highway 24W, the main north-south highway from Cincinnati, Ohio, to Knoxville, Tennessee. They allowed whites to pass, but blocked the cars of Black motorists and began attacking them with clubs, rocks, and baseball bats. The rioters, mostly teenagers and young white men in their twenties and thirties, shattered the windows and smashed the sides of an estimated twenty to thirty cars with Black passengers, including families from Michigan and Ohio.

Rioters in Clinton assaulting Blacks after Carter's speech, 1956.

After a half dozen men failed to turn over one car containing five Black passengers, the car began backing up and two members of the mob opened the door and began pulling the driver out into the street. Bill Middlebrooks, the burly United Press International bureau chief in Knoxville, abandoned his neutral status as a journalist-observer, charged into the crowd, punched one of the surprised attackers and shoved the driver back into the car. As the family escaped down the highway, Middlebrooks ran for safety toward the courthouse followed by shouts, "There's a nigger lover in the crowd, get him."

During the melee, Homer Clonts, staff writer for the *Knoxville News-Sentinel,* was busily taking notes during the disorder when an overalls-clad man grabbed his arm, looked him in the eye, and in a low voice said: "I may have to kill you before the night is over if you don't print the truth." Mob members also directed their rage against the local newspaper. Horace Wells, editor of the *Clinton Courier-News,* had repeatedly reminded his readers that the court order was the "law of the land" and had to be obeyed. When angry whites began demanding that reporters show their press IDs to prove they did not work for the *Courier-News,* the newspaper's two reporters retreated to the safety of the county courthouse.

On Saturday morning, Clinton's local government woke up to a public relations disaster. Headlines of the riot and the assaults on passing motorists dominated the front pages of newspapers across the nation. Anderson County Sheriff Glad Woodward and his predecessor hastily assembled fifteen active and former deputies to supplement the small Clinton police force while Mayor Lewallen deputized forty young men in the town—many World War II and Korean military veterans—asking them to walk the streets, unarmed, and "talk down" the crowd to prevent further violence.[362]

Fearful of further violence, Sheriff Woodward had no illusions that his small force could control a large mob. Through much of Saturday he struggled to reach Tennessee Governor Frank Clement to plead for backup from the state police and a National Guard unit. Clement, the politically ambitious national Democratic Party's 1956 keynote speaker, knew a no-win crisis when he saw it. If he supported Clinton authorities, he would anger the state's most passionate white supporters of segregation. If he failed to act, he would draw the ire of other white Tennesseans who disliked mob rule even more than integration. As the crisis escalated, Clements made himself unavailable to the sheriff and to reporters who besieged his office.

As dusk fell, John Moore, one of the local community leaders deputized by the mayor, joined fellow "deputies" wearing armbands and began patrolling the street in front of the courthouse only to encounter a replay of the events of the night before. With Kasper in jail, and a federal injunction threatening lengthy imprisonment to those who interfered with the desegregation of Clinton's High School, Carter had made a hasty exit, returning home to Alabama. Despite the absence of Carter and Kasper, a coalition of right-wing organizations led by the "Tennessee Federation for Constitutional Government" had called for "patriots" to gather at the courthouse that Saturday evening. Well before speakers could mount the steps, the crowd that filled the town square had become a disorganized mob.

For ninety minutes, members screamed threats at the community volunteers who sought to restore order. World War II vet John Moore would always remember one woman, baby in arms, who showered him with spit and a torrent of obscenities "I'd never heard in the Navy." Just after 9 p.m., what appeared to be shots sent the deputy-volunteers fleeing toward the courthouse. (It was actually the sound of breaking glass from rocks thrown through the courthouse windows.) As he scrambled up the steps, Moore looked up to see what he would always remember as "a glorious sight": flashing red lights from fifty state police cars that had driven the 150 miles from the state capitol in Nashville. As the lead car pulled up in front of the courthouse, Greg O'Rear, the 6'8" head of the Tennessee State Highway Patrol, stepped out of the passenger side with a double-barreled shotgun over his shoulder. "All right, boys," he said to the crowd in a booming voice. "It's all over."

Reluctantly, and with considerable ill grace, Governor Clement had finally realized that a blood bath in Clinton would endanger his political future more than would calling out the state highway patrol. Twenty-four hours later a contingent of six hundred national guardsmen arrived to take up police duties in the town.

Moore never forgot that evening. He had served in combat during World War II, but Clinton was "the most terrifying experience of my life," he said. "I vowed when I got home later that night, that if they ever called for volunteers again, I was gonna hide under the bed."[363]

If the threat of mass violence had been averted, conflict over desegregation continued. In the months that followed, a small group of white students formed their own high school "Citizens' Council" and continued to harass, threaten, and (outside the school building) assault Black students despite the best efforts of principal Brittain. When a local white Baptist minister escorted the twelve Black students to school to protect them, four men later cornered the Reverend Paul Turner as he returned to his church, knocked him to the ground, and beat him senseless. Other "unknown persons" set off five dynamite blasts in the Black community that fall. Two years later—in the midst of desegregation turmoil across the South—three massive back-to-back explosions of seventy-five to one hundred sticks of dynamite leveled the high school that had been the scene of Tennessee's first desegregation. It would be another decade before significant school integration took place in Clinton.

Unlike Kasper, who seemed to court jail time with the zeal of a first-century Christian martyr, Carter had no desire to spend the next year in a Tennessee prison. His notable absence during the second day of demonstrations characterized his behavior. What was unusual was Carter's continued support for Kasper. He usually insisted on complete independence from other individuals and groups, and the only person he seems to have fully trusted was his brother, Doug. But the six months he had spent with Kasper created a close bond of more than convenience—a shared form of populism. Both men hated Blacks and Jews and seemed equally contemptuous of the upper-class whites who remained passive in the face of this growing threat. The nearly penniless Kasper made it a point to stay with working-class people, and they readily welcomed this Columbia University graduate and philosophy major as one of their own. In one of his trials, Kasper attacked the composition of the jury that would judge him. He had come South to defend the rights of poor white people, he complained, but the jurors selected to judge him were dominated by "foremen, overseers, professionals, executive-type people. . . ."[364]

The Appalachia-born novelist Wilma Dykeman seemed particularly attuned to the class dimensions of his appeal. In his travels through the region as a non-stop agitator, Kasper made a point of not only dividing Blacks and whites, Dykeman wrote in the *New Republic.* His "chief success has been in dividing the white South within itself," by puncturing the image of sober legality and white unity led by respectable middle-class and well-to-do Southerners.[365]

Carter's description of the whites who had attended the Nat King Cole concert in April 1956 reflected the same disdain—even hatred—for the "high-hat" Southerners, the moneyed class interested only in profits and comfort where "the almighty dollar takes precedence over all else." As police beat the brave men with "work-hardened hands" who had attacked Cole and dragged them out of the auditorium, they looked back on the "fur-bedecked crowd of Cole admirers, resplendent in their dinner jackets, their white-puttied flabby faces, angry and pouting."[366]

In fact there were no dinner jackets among that crowd of mostly middle-class young whites in casual dress, and it's even more unlikely that any of the young women were "fur-bedecked" since the temperature that day reached eighty-one degrees. But his words captured Carter's contempt for "respectable" middle- and upper-class elites, obsessed with propriety and retreating into cowardly calls for "law and order."

They responded in kind. Carter was a "loathsome would-be Fuhrer," wrote the editor of the *Montgomery Advertiser* the summer of 1956. His paper "cherishes the hope that Carter and his mob choke," said Grover Hall, "For they and their breed are the worst possible enemies of the South at this time. They sicken potential sympathizers."[367] Most of the region's major newspapers routinely described Kasper and Carter in language that was hardly neutral. The two men seldom "spoke" to their followers but "harangued" their audiences. Shortly after the Clinton riot, a reporter for the *Knoxville News-Sentinel* described Carter in a front-page news article as a "professional agitator" who had assembled followers similar to "Adolf Hitler's fascists." In news columns as well as the editorial pages, Kasper was a "trouble-maker," a "violent agitator," and a "vicious racist," presumably in contrast to white Citizens' Council leaders who were non-vicious racists. "It is not considered Christian to wish ill of anyone," one editor wrote of Kasper, "but the hope remains that if he cannot be restrained, he will somehow be removed from this planet."[368]

Throughout much of the 1950s, there was a gentleman's understanding among journalists that, even when politicians used the "N" word, reporters would substitute "Negro" in their reports. Not so in descriptions of Asa Carter the Alabama organizer and particularly his New York ally. "I used to think all our problems would be solved if every nigger killed a kike," ran one news account of Kasper, "but I find I overestimated the nigger mind."[369]

After supporters bailed out Kasper, Carter greeted him and announced plans to raise funds for the New Yorker's legal defense beginning with rallies in Anniston, Montgomery, and Mobile. When Sam Engelhardt quietly persuaded officials to withhold approval for use of city-owned auditoriums, Carter immediately arranged a talk at his Bessemer theater, but less than forty men showed up to hear Kasper.[370]

As the Clinton demonstrations wound down, Kasper continued his racist evangelism, traveling across the region for the next eighteen months, escalating his rhetoric with threats of violence, and praising white supremacists who bombed, burned, and assaulted. Carter remained in touch with his friend, but—short of cash—he had returned to his radio broadcasts. Although he no longer had access to the network created by the American States Rights Association, he found a half dozen AM stations willing to broadcast his "Liberty Essays," and he produced and sold the first of what he hoped would be a series of LP records of some his essays.

If Kasper's repeated arrests made him a hero to white supremacists, his earlier bohemian life in Greenwich village came back to haunt him. In the wake of events in Clinton, a reporter for New York's *Amsterdam News*, the nation's oldest Black newspaper, interviewed those who had known him before he headed South. The *News* claimed that Kasper had a Black male lover while other New York friends insisted that he had never shown any racial prejudice, welcoming Blacks to late-night parties in his bookstore.[371]

The accusations initially achieved little traction in the white press and Carter continued to support his friend. But after a series of Kasper speeches in Florida, calling for violent resistance to integration, a special committee of the state legislature subpoenaed him. During two hours of questioning by the committee's chief counsel, Kasper admitted that he had a number of close Black friends in the early 1950s and had dated a young African American college student who worked part-time in his bookstore. As Southern newspapers widely reported the news, Carter broke off connections with his friend and gave the final verdict: "That will about fix it for Kasper in the South."[372]

The US Constitution gave Congress control over the District of Columbia and, after the integration of Washington's public schools in the fall of 1956, Georgia Congressman John C. Davis saw an opportunity to discredit what he called the "mixing of white and colored students." As chair of the House's District of Columbia committee, he had the authority to convene special hearings on the impact of the new policy. Davis had no interest in providing a balanced report on the impact of integration. He had repeatedly claimed that the goal of the NAACP and the civil rights movement in integrating schools was ultimately the "intermarriage and complete mongrelization of the American people, the identical goal of the Communist Party."[373] In hearings dominated by a chief counsel who shared the views of Davis and

Mississippi Representative John Bell Williams, the staff described the horrors of integration, describing terrorized white teachers and students, and marauding Black teenagers.

Four years later, *Washington Post* education editor Erwin Knoll analyzed police and school reports and found that Davis's committee vastly exaggerated and even fabricated incidents of violence in the integration of the city's schools.[374] But the hearings became grist for segregationists and particularly for Carter as he described "jungle conditions just like Africa" in which, at best, white students suffered extortion and beatings from "100 percent Negroid degenerates," or worse, those Blacks repeatedly cornered young white girls in bathroom stalls and raped them.[375]

Even though Carter's threat to the larger Citizens' Council movement seemed to be declining, Engelhardt remained intent on destroying his opponent. In late April 1956 the Selma planter had contacted J. J. Gleason, the senior agent in the Mobile FBI field office. Engelhardt handed over a series of newspaper clippings and leaflets. Carter, he said, deliberately sought to provoke violence that would lead to widespread bloodshed. In fact, Engelhardt told Gleason, Carter's constant attacks on wealthy community leaders had led him to suspect that he was some sort of "secret communist."[376]

Even before Engelhardt contacted Gleason, the FBI had elevated Carter from a "subject of interest" to a "potential violent extremist." The Bureau had never seemed particularly concerned about his threats of violence and mayhem against Blacks or white integrationist (or even Jews). But in a February speech at a rally in Anniston, an Army G-2 intelligence officer from nearby Fort McClellan was present and took notes as Carter urged his listeners to pressure Governor Jim Folsom into supporting soldiers who refused to serve under Black officers. According to the agent's notes, Carter said:

> We must stand up and set an example for all States of the Union. There is . . . too much at stake: our Christianity, our morals and our children. We want a Governor who says publicly to every boy in Alabama: If you are in the Armed Forces and serving under a Negro Corporal or a Negro Sergeant, and if you are being degraded and forced to eat and sleep with them, you just come home and it will be all right.[377]

The Birmingham FBI office sent the officer's report as well as statements from their own informant and an audio copy of the speech obtained from a local radio station to US Attorney General Herbert Brownell. Brownell referred the case to Assistant Attorney General William Tompkins requesting that he advise whether the activities of Carter "constitute a violation of the Sedition Statutes. . . ."[378]

The audio transcript was consistent with the notes of the G-2 agent, but Carter had carefully avoided a direct call for GIs to desert. Instead, he expressed his wish to have Governor Folsom make such a statement. Tompkins, a no-nonsense prosecutor, had built his reputation convicting organized crime figures knew a losing case when he saw it. To convict under the sedition statutes required proof than an individual directly incite "rebellion against the authority of the state." And, as Tompkins concluded, given the political climate in Alabama, it would be difficult to convince a jury that Carter violated the law.[379]

While the decision to drop the case against Carter may have been a reprieve, the investigation increased the FBI's level of monitoring him. His name had occasionally appeared in bureau reports before 1956, but in the months to follow the sedition investigation, the "Asa Carter" file grew steadily. In a reflection of the anti-communist paranoia that existed in the 1950s, the FBI initially seemed preoccupied with the claims of Sam Engelhardt and Mississippi Senator James Eastland that the fiery activist was, in Engelhardt's words, a "secret Communist provocateur." Agents repeatedly passed on claims that Carter either had been, or still was, a member of the Communist Party. In one report, agents cited a "reliable" informant who claimed that Carter had admitted to a group of followers that he was a Party member.

Of course this was nonsense. Carter occasionally used Party lingo in discussing "cadres" or calling for "a mobilization of the masses of working people," but his repeated use of such phrases—often associated with Communist Party rhetoric—came from his voracious reading of the literature of political protest movements and his oft-expressed contempt for wealthy community leaders.

And despite Engelhardt's frustration, Carter's threat to the mainline

Council movement had begun to fade. Preoccupied with his newfound national celebrity status, Carter had given twenty-five speeches outside Alabama in the summer and early fall of 1956. Increasingly, leaders of local Councils chafed under Carter's dictatorial leadership. And the refusal of Carter to allow oversight of his Council's finances provoked a growing suspicion that he was raking off funds for his personal use. His North Alabama Citizens' Councils began to collapse or break away, with many chapters formally announcing their affiliation with Engelhardt's state Council.[380]

Whether out of necessity or because he was more comfortable with a close-knit (and more easily controlled) group of followers, Carter soon turned most of his energies to the creation of a new and secret organization based in Bessemer, Alabama, the working-class suburb of Birmingham.

11

The Brotherhood

> *And [after the war] when it seemed the end had come, the Southerner lifted himself from a starving, crippled and bleeding South where hope lay like a skeleton beneath the heel of an occupying army. He spat in the face of the odds with a bone hard stubbornness that snatched victory from the most desolate of defeats to save the seed of his breed, his womanhood, his children, the Book, the fireside, the Prayer, the Code. . . . We have full faith that this spirit shall not die. . . . We shall come together in our small groups of the Brotherhood to fuel it with our stubbornness and to bring victory for the Cause.*
>
> — Asa Carter[381]

Through the summer and fall of 1956, Carter continued to describe himself as the head of the North Alabama Citizens' Councils. Secretly, he was recruiting hardcore followers for a new group that he called the "Original Ku Klux Klan of the Confederacy." By day Bessemer's Central Park Theatre remained the headquarters of the North Alabama Citizens' Council. By night, it was the home of his new Klan group.

In the Calhoun County High School yearbook, classmates had noted Carter's flair for drama, a talent he used in the ceremonies surrounding the birth of his new Klan. Under tight security, the group's first meeting took place on October 19, 1956. With the lights dimmed, Carter's most trusted aide, Exalted Cyclops Jesse Mabry, walked onto the stage of the semi-darkened theater—illuminated only by a row of burning highway "smudge pots"—threw a Confederate sword on the floor, then stepped up to the Klan "altar" and plunged a bowie knife into an opened book of Klan rituals.

A hooded Carter then stepped dramatically out of the darkness wearing a distinctive red Klan robe, Sam Brown cartridge belt, and an antique, long-barreled .38 at his side. This Ku Klux Klan, he told his followers, bore no relationship to the rudderless Klan groups infiltrated by the FBI that did nothing but talk. The Ku Klux Klan of the Confederacy would be based upon the principles (and the organizational structure) of the Reconstruction Klan led by Nathan Bedford Forrest. Like its nineteenth-century predecessor, they would make no effort to be a "political organization," he told the group. They would, instead, use "direct action" under the cloak of absolute secrecy to drive the modern-day scalawags and carpetbaggers from the region, restoring absolute white supremacy.

Although he emphasized the precepts of the new Klan and the dramatic nature of the multi-colored robes they would wear—complete with a white helmet with a large spike in the center for officers—he did not overlook practical matters. Dues would be $10 a year ($90, in 2023 dollars). And members would have to purchase their regalia directly through Carter's Klan: robe and hood: $17.50.[382]

Despite the hefty fee, more than fifty men gathered a week later in an open field twenty miles north of Birmingham to swear allegiance to the Original Ku Klux Klan of the Confederacy, The FBI informant who met with agent Charles Stanberry two days after the gathering remained shaken, fearful that his identity would be exposed. Despite the masked hoods that covered the Klansmen's faces, he recognized many of Carter's close supporters, including Kenneth Adams (who had led the attack on Nat King Cole). With some understatement, the informant described the men as "pretty rough." Almost all the new recruits wore holstered revolvers as they knelt at the crude "altar" for their initiation.

While Carter presided in his red robe, arms crossed, Exalted Cyclops Mabry handed a razor-sharp knife to the men. One by one, they were told to make a cut in their arms and sign, with blood, a "death oath" in which they pledged to fight, and die if necessary, as blood brothers. At the conclusion of the initiation ceremony, the men gathered around a bonfire ringed with skulls and threw their blood-signed oaths into the fire.

The informant found it all, at best, childish and a bit absurd. But he thought that most of the men seemed genuinely moved as they joined the ranks of what Carter called "proud Aryan soldiers" embarked on a heroic, but dangerous crusade to save their world from the evils of the hated integrationists and their "Jew allies."[383]

Carter had learned much about self-promotion in his years in broadcasting. At some level, he realized that most middle-class white Southerners were ready to do battle against the Yankee integrationists and civil rights agitators, but still shied away from what one Alabama conservative called that "Ku Klux herd of albino swine." After *Montgomery Advertiser* editor Grover Hall linked Carter with the hooded order, Carter complained of "leftist newspaper smears" and filed a $150,000 lawsuit against Hall claiming that he was "humiliated, embarrassed, and caused to suffer great mental anguish" by the accusation that he was a Klansman.[384] A local judge promptly dismissed the suit. Through the mid-1950s, Carter learned to mask the worst aspects of his antisemitism, maintaining a semblance of public legitimacy, but his passion was clearly reserved for his Klan organization. He had used his earlier membership in the Ensley klavern to carefully recruit trusted followers. Now his dwindling Council groups became a similar screening mechanism to identify potential recruits to his new Klan. This was the "cadre" that would initiate blows against the enemy until the larger white community was ready to join in the violent struggle.

The Autherine Lucy, Nat King Cole, and Clinton, Tennessee, incidents had set the pattern. Publicly Carter would avoid direct participation in violent activities, but in speeches and in *The Southerner,* he would support the "strike forces" as "Southern heroes." From the campus of the University of Alabama to the streets of Clinton, Carter never encountered a violent act defending segregation that he did not approve.[385]

Such tactics cemented Carter's appeal to the most hardcore racists, but his violent rhetoric reinforced the hostility of main-line segregationists. During the period when Carter and Kasper worked closely together, Mississippi's attorney general, no wallflower on defending segregation, told reporters that there was "no room in Mississippi" for the two men. Governor J. P. Coleman warned that they would be arrested if they sought to speak in Mississippi, a message echoed by public officials across much of the South.[386] Carter and Kasper proved convenient foils for Southern segregation leaders who could insist they were even-handed, reining in outside agitators on the right (Carter and others) as well as on the left (the NAACP, Martin Luther King and anyone who challenged racial segregation).

Through the late fall and into the winter of 1956, Carter's secret Klan group met each Tuesday night, slowly expanding to more than a hundred tight-knit members. But even among his most loyal supporters, dissent grew over the over the usual issues: money and control.[387]

IN LATE JANUARY 1957, some sixty Klan members gathered in one of the darkened corridors of the Bessemer theater and donned their regalia. Because of Carter's insistence on secrecy and the separation of the membership into isolated cells, the men brought flashlights, dressed in darkness, and wore their hoods during the meeting. While many knew each other, the precautions minimized the opportunity for suspected FBI informers to learn the identify of all of Carter's Klansmen.

Most came armed with pistols or bowie knives or both. Instead of the all-white robes of rank-and-file Klansmen, Carter's top aides wore a set of uniforms that reflected the military structure of his new organization, with various chevrons and colored sashes to identify their authority. Carter wore red, three top aides donned black hoods, while six Klansmen had white skulls on red diamond backgrounds sewn to their hoods to indicate their authority as the group's security force.

The January 22 meeting began with the usual mumbo-jumbo in the theater, dimly illuminated by a row of burning smudge pots, with a Confederate battle flag as a backdrop. Carter had set up a reel-to-reel recorder to play back one of his many speeches describing the growing threat of communist mongrelization and the treacherous compromises of local politicians. His followers had heard the message many times before, and there was a constant hum of conversation in the auditorium. At the end of the recording, when Carter began speaking directly to the group, the topic suddenly veered from communism, mongrelization, and cowardly local politicians to money.

During his brief time in the Ensley Klavern, Carter had recruited J. P.

Tillery, a twenty-four-year-old Birmingham aircraft maintenance worker. Present at the initial organizational gathering of Carter's group the previous summer, Tillery never missed a meeting. Carter soon promoted him to lieutenant of the "bloody platoon," an internal security group given the task of enforcing discipline against recalcitrant or disloyal Klan members. Despite his commitment to the Confederate Knights, Tillery had become frustrated by Carter's authoritarian style and constant pleas for additional contributions, funds that were collected, deposited, and controlled without oversight by members.

As Carter spoke, Tillery stood and interrupted to call for an accounting of the group's finances.

Tillery was not alone in his frustration over Carter's refusal to allow anyone else to oversee the financial records. The secrecy of the Klan—many lieutenants knew only the code names of their platoons—intensified paranoia. In early January, Tillery and several members received identical unsigned, typed letters in plain envelopes claiming that Carter was siphoning cash for his personal use. It is likely that an FBI agent sent the document in an effort to provoke division in the group, a tactic that resurfaced later in COINTELPRO (Counter Intelligence Project). Under Hoover's direction, the Bureau generally directed such divisive tactics against leftist and civil rights groups, but the Klan was also on the FBI's hit list.[388]

Carter defended his leadership from Tillery's question and called for support from his followers. If "you men will stand by me," he said, "I'll lead you. I'll guide you. Now has anybody got anything to say?"

A nervous but determined Tillery insisted there should be a committee to examine the financial records of their Klan organization. "I was there when we were formed," he told Carter, and "it was agreed we would be run by a group instead of by one."

Carter, at the end of his patience, shouted down at Tillery: "Are you telling me I'm trying to run it?"

"No," replied Tillery, "But I believe it should be run like we first set it up. I'm merely stating facts."

It was enough for the mercurial Carter, who leaped from the stage to the theater aisle, shouting "I'll show you!" Three security men wearing their distinctive hoods with bright red skull patches surrounded and then grabbed Tillery. "Bring that man to me," Carter ordered.

Tillery pulled back, falling between the seats with his legs in the aisle. When the men began kicking him, he reached under his robe and pulled out his snub-nosed .38 revolver.

What next happened in the darkened theater would always remain unclear. When later questioned by police, the Klansmen suffered a complete loss of memory. Only two described the events and that was because they were Birmingham police officers who had become active members of Carter's Klan. Under pressure from their boss, they agreed that at least five or six men had drawn their weapons, but they claimed to be on the other side of the darkened theater, and they disagreed over who fired first. One of the two insisted that Klan security guard Harold McBride fired the first shot, hitting J. P. Tillery in the upper chest. But the other police offer reported that Tillery got off the first shot and missed McBride; he believed that one of the security guards, Ira Evans, then returned fire, wounding McBride in the left shoulder.

Whatever the sequence, over the next twenty seconds at least eight shots rang through the theater. Tillery took a second shot in the right buttock and a third in the back of his knee. Charles (Chad) Bridges, a fifty-four-year-old member of the group and one of the few unarmed men in the theater, had the misfortune to be standing next to Tillery. As he leaned over to help Tillery, he was shot through each buttock with both bullets lodging in his lower bowel. In a state of shock, Bridges felt no immediate pain, but he suddenly realized he was covered in blood. "Look at that," he told the first Klansman to reach him, "The durned fools done shot my heart out."

Carter had leaped off the stage, drawn his revolver, and come within five feet of the struggling melee when gunfire erupted, In the semi-darkness, a confused security Klansman had yelled: "They've shot Ace. Give me a pistol and I'll kill the son of a bitch." But Carter was unhurt. With the first shot, the two policemen present who were Klansmen saw him drop to the floor and then jump to his feet, bolting up the aisle into the vestibule of the theater, pulling off his gun belt, robe, and hood as he ran.

Most of the Klansmen had fallen to the floor to escape the flying bullets, but they quickly recovered. ("Little hoss," one Klansman told his best friend as they lay face down between the seats, "let's get out of here.") They were soon scrambling up the aisles, through the swinging doors to the lobby, and out into the streets. The critically wounded Bridges, leaving a trail of blood on the faded carpet, crawled out of the theater where a sympathetic Klansman loaded him into his car, drove him to the nearby West End Baptist Hospital, and dumped him out at the emergency room entrance.

A little over a block away, a young Bessemer policeman making his rounds had just checked the front door of Chicken in the Rough, a local restaurant. When James Parsons heard the unmistakable sound of gunfire, he ran down

Top left, bloodstained floor of the Central Park Theatre after the melee; top right, police officers inspecting blood trail; above, Carter (right) being brought in for booking after his arrest; all January 1957.

The Birmingham News

36 Pages—3 Sections BIRMINGHAM, ALA., WEDNESDAY, JANUARY 23, 1957 ★

Citizens Council leader—

Asa Carter is accused after 2 Klansmen are wounded

Klan meeting fight erupts

Asa Carter was charged today with shooting two robed Ku Klux Klansmen here last night. Carter is head of the Alabama Citizens Council.

The Klansmen were shot at the Central Park Theater meeting of the Ku Klux Klan of the Confederacy.

Two warrants charging Carter with assault with intent to murder were sworn out by Det. J. W. Jones.

Carter appeared at police headquarters at 11 a.m. today and was questioned for more than an hour before the warrants were served on him.

Police said he would be questioned further this afternoon before being take to City Jail on the charges. Police said bond would be fixed at $10,000 on each of the two assault with intent to murder counts.

THE TWO wounded men were identified as J. P. Tillery, 24, of 1313 25th-st, n, and Charles Bridges, 54, of 119 60th-st, s.

Before he arrived at police headquarters today, Carter denied to a Birmingham News reporter that he had anything to do with the shooting. He said he left the KKK meeting before it happened.

OFFICERS SAID the meeting of the secret, hooded order had been blanketed in mystery and most of their information had come from the wounded men.

According to Homicide Sgt. M. H. House and Det. V. T. Hart Tillery apparently was left on the floor of the Central Park Theater "for dead."

Bridges, they said, had managed to crawl from the building and was taken to a hospital by an unidentified passerby.

FROM THE operating table at West End Baptist Hospital, Tillery told officers that the shooting occurred during a row over what he called "one-man rule"

ASA CARTER
. . . Arrives at City Hall

In news coverage the next day, Carter was named as a "Citizens Council leader" and quoted as not being present during the shootings, which was not true.

the street in time to see the last of dozens of white-sheeted men running in every direction.[389] Bridges had already been removed and Patrolman Parsons found the theater empty except for a semi-conscious Tillery, who had been left for dead. Someone had stripped Tillery of his robe and taken his pistol and keys and driven away in his prized light blue '52 Buick Roadmaster.

From the outset, police were hampered by the fact that everyone in the theater wore hoods. And there was the blood oath committing all the Klansmen to secrecy. However, after interviewing Tillery, Bridges and the two policemen who were KKK members, the three detectives investigating the case began to put together the sequence of events. Carter, they concluded, was not the main shooter, but they believed he had drawn his gun and instigated the shoot-out. Their suspicions were strengthened when Carter refused to talk with them and instead issued a press release to the two Birmingham newspapers that was, from any perspective, ludicrous.

He insisted that he was not a member of the Original Ku Klux Klan of the Confederacy even though both local newspapers and the Associated Press confirmed that his signature was on the group's 1956 incorporation charter registered with Alabama's Secretary of State. Carter told an AP reporter that because one of his great-grandfathers had fought with General John Hunt Morgan's "Raiders" during the Civil War, he had been approached by Klan members who wished to rent the theater and have him as a guest speaker. At the last moment, however, he had received a call from a Tuscaloosa man who asked him to drive the fifty-five miles to help organize a local Citizens' Council. For that reason, he had recorded his speech on a large reel-to-reel recorder and placed it on the stage to be played during the meeting. He insisted he was not present when the fracas took place.

TWO DAYS AFTER THE shooting, and facing an arrest warrant, Carter reluctantly met with detectives Vernon Hart and Connie Pitts, with his attorney R. B. Jones present during the four-hour interrogation. Carter acknowledged that he had not actually met anyone in Tuscaloosa. ("He didn't show up.") And he couldn't remember the name of the individual who had called.

Frustrated by what he regarded as Carter's absurd alibi—at least seven Klansmen had told police and newspaper reporters that Carter was present—Jefferson County Solicitor Emmett Perry charged him with assault with intent to murder and placed him in the county jail under a $20,000 bond. Within twenty-four hours, two of Carter's close supporters had come up with the $2,000 bondsman's fee to obtain his release.

Identifying the individuals who had shot Tillery proved more difficult, but the evidence pointed to three men in their late twenties and early thirties. Louey C. Curry, Ira N. Evans, and Harold W. McBride were all officers of the "inner guard"—klarogos in the nomenclature of the Klan. Birmingham city police detectives quickly rounded up Curry and Evans and issued an all-points bulletin for the missing McBride.[390]

A week later, Carter, still out on bail, accompanied McBride to the

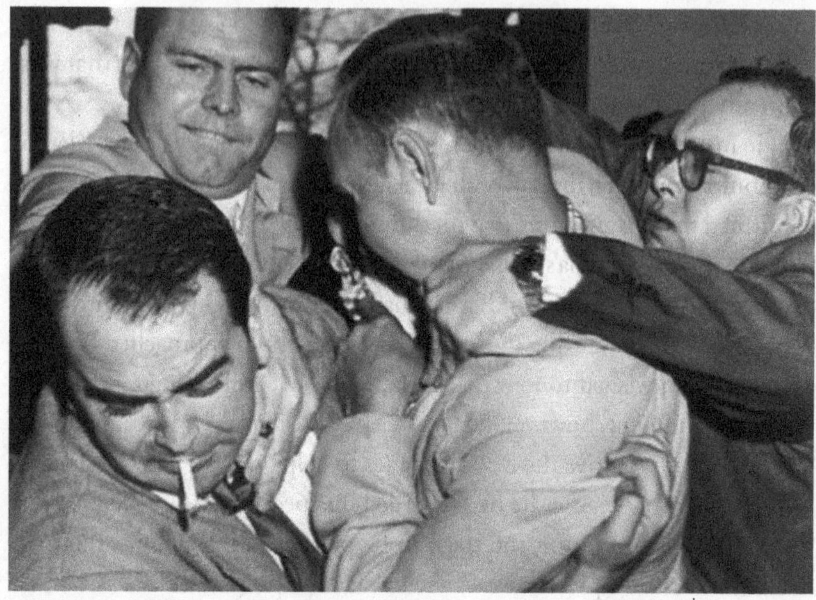

A week after the shootout, Carter (front left) struggled with Detectives Connie Pitts (upper left) and Vernon Hart (right) to wrest Harold McBride (center) from their control while McBride screamed in pain from the wound in his left shoulder.

Jefferson County Courthouse to surrender him to Sheriff Holt McDowell. The city had issued arrest warrants, but Carter and his lawyer believed McDowell would be more sympathetic to Klansman McBride than Birmingham Commissioner of Public Safety Robert Lindbergh.

When two city detectives showed up to claim the city's right to arrest McBride, Carter slugged one of the officers and began fighting with the second, a brawl captured by a photographer from the *Birmingham News* and spread over the newspaper's afternoon edition. Arrested and charged with assault (along with his brother Doug, who joined the fray), a defiant Carter posted another bond within hours and was back on the street.[391]

Given the gunshot wound to McBride and statements by the two gunshot victims, the city's prosecutor was convinced that they had enough evidence to unravel the truth and persuade some of the Klansmen involved to turn state's evidence. They were aided by the discovery of Carter's secret check-in book at the theater that gave the names of all those present at the gathering.

But the Klan oath proved far more powerful than a couple of inquisitive Birmingham detectives. In one interview after another, Klansmen stonily refused to respond to questions. Off the record, one detective told an Associated Press reporter there had been death threats against any Klansmen who considered cooperating with the police. He was right. Even Bridges, who had challenged Carter's leadership and been shot by the Klan's security guards, told the detectives that, despite his original statement implicating five Klan members in the fracas, he actually couldn't remember what had happened.

R. B. Jones, the attorney for Carter and his followers, had long developed a technique for protecting his clients: delay. As he had seen in the Nat King Cole case and in similar incidents, officials initially promised dire consequences for lawbreakers, but time eroded their resolve. So long as white lawbreakers stuck together and refused to testify, prosecutors remained reluctant to bring cases to trial, aware of the difficulty of persuading all-white juries to convict defenders of segregation.

In a brief trial in city recorder's court that foreshadowed the future, the city judge heard the case growing out of what newspapers called the "battle of the Jefferson County Courthouse," but he dismissed the serious charges against Asa Carter and his brother Doug of assaulting a police officer. Instead, he found them guilty of an insignificant misdemeanor—disorderly conduct—and fined them $25.[392]

THE SHOOTING TRIAL WAS far more serious. Late that May, in a courtroom packed with Klan supporters, the first of the defendants went on trial. Newspaper reporters expected the state to open its case against Carter, but Assistant Solicitor Cecil Deason felt he had a stronger case against Klan security guard Ira Evans. One of the two shooting victims, Charles Bridges, had positively identified Evans as the man who shot him. And the head of Carter's "security forces," Eugene Thomas Coleman, was a twenty-four-year-old Birmingham motorcycle policeman who decided his job was more important than his Klan Oath. He had witnessed the shooting and was positive that Evans was the gunmen.

But once on the stand, the injured Bridges ignored the prosecutor's first question and told the jury he had no idea who shot him. He later admitted that his memory had been affected by a telephone call warning him that any testimony he gave would be "the last damn thing you do."

Klan defense attorney Jones was ready for Coleman, but he was apparently caught by surprise when the state called to the stand M. J. Abernathy, one of the few men present that night who had been willing to talk with police detectives despite warnings from his fellow Klansman. In dramatic testimony, Abernathy told the jury that he was standing less than five feet to the side of the two victims when the first shots rang through the theater. It was Evans, he said, who shouted, "They've shot Ace; give me a pistol and I'll kill the son of a bitch." Evans, said Abernathy, grabbed a pistol from one of the other guards, pulled up his face mask to see better, and began firing at Tillery, wounding him as well as Bridges. Coleman, the Birmingham policeman and Klan member, was standing directly behind Evans. He agreed with Abernathy that Evans was the shooter.

Jones went after the two state witnesses with his usual tenacity. Coleman was only testifying to save his job, Jones suggested in his cross-examination. He made the policeman put on a Klan robe over his uniform, supposedly to illustrate the difficulty of seeing anything through the two eyeholes of the hood. When Jones questioned Abernathy, he repeatedly asked if it were not true that he had sworn an oath of silence when he joined the Klan, suggesting that he could not be trusted to keep his word.

Unable to shake the testimony of either man, Jones put on a string of character witnesses and Klansmen who testified that they were certain that Evans was not the shooter. One Klansman insisted that he was lying on the floor next to Evans when the shooting erupted; another claimed that Evans was on the opposite side of the theater from the commotion. When the prosecutor read back sworn statements to the grand jury that contradicted their trial testimony, both claimed to have remembered things more accurately in the wake of their grand jury appearance. As one Klansman explained, everything he told the grand jury was the truth "but I told only part of what happened."[393]

Their newly discovered recollections were enough for the jury. The twelve men deliberated less than two hours before finding Ira Evans not guilty. The next day's newspapers showed a triumphant Carter leading a group of fellow Klansmen as they congratulated Evans.

Assistant Solicitor Deason, who had handled the case for the prosecution, insisted that Evans could still be tried for shooting bystander Bridges. And he pointed out that indictments remained in force against Carter, McBride, and Louey Curry. No one took him seriously. Seven months later, the county solicitor quietly dropped the remaining indictments.

By then, Carter's position among respectable segregationists in the campaign for white supremacy had become increasingly tenuous, but the most painful fallout for Carter came not from the legal system but from his mother. Several news stories printed details of the Klan incorporation, including the fact that Asa had listed his younger brother, Larry, as secretary of the group. Larry, a student at Alabama Polytechnic Institute (now Auburn University), knew nothing of Carter's group, was not outspoken on racial issues, and certainly had no use for the Ku Klux Klan.

Neither did his mother, Hermione. Nearly fifty years later, Larry Carter remembered the bitter confrontation between Hermione Carter and her son. "I can't tell you what to do or run your life or have any influence on what you do, but you're not going involve him [Larry] or me in this Klan business," she told her oldest son. She was "quiet but firm, no yelling," said Larry, "but Mama could cut you in two with her eyes and she cut him in two." Her husband, Ralph, continued to support his son, but the relationship between Asa and his mother was never the same.[394]

12

Mayhem: Part One

> *Gus rose to his feet and started across the cave as if to spring on the shivering figure of the girl. . . . He still wore his full Captain's uniform, its heavy epaulets flashing their gold in the unearthly light, his beastly jaws half covering the gold braid on the collar. His thick lips were drawn upward in an ugly leer and his sinister beady eyes gleamed like a gorilla's. A single fierce leap and the black claws clutched the air slowly as if sinking into the soft white throat.*
>
> — Thomas Dixon, *The Clansman* (1905)[395]

After the Bessemer theater shootings and Carter's courthouse brawl with Birmingham City detectives, his Klan group splintered into a half-dozen factions. Many of his followers joined Robert Shelton's Alabama Knights of the Ku Klux Klan, but the most loyal regrouped under the slightly altered title of "Knights of the Ku Klux Klan of the Confederacy." All but a handful of the twenty-five members had been associated with Carter through his earlier Klan group.

In early February 1957, out of jail on a $20,000 bond while still under indictment for the Bessemer shootings and his confrontation with Birmingham detectives, Carter announced his candidacy for Birmingham Commissioner of Public Safety. In a race between the incumbent Robert Lindbergh and former Police Commissioner Theophilus Eugene "Bull" Connor, there is no evidence that Carter believed he could be elected, but he was driven by his anger at Lindbergh whom he blamed for his arrest and "persecution" in the Bessemer incident. Without specifically referring to his own indictment, Carter attacked what he called "automatic convictions" in city courts.

His decision to join the field angered the leading challenger, "Bull"

Connor. The two men had worked closely together in the past and Connor feared that his one-time friend would siphon away the hard-line segregationist vote. But Carter was seldom one to place loyalty above his own interest. He told his brother that he believed a well-run campaign would improve his public image and restore his reputation as something other than a violent troublemaker.

In his campaign he described himself as the man most committed to maintaining segregation. Although the US Supreme Court handed the Montgomery bus boycott movement a victory in December 1956 that ended segregated municipal bus seating across the state, Carter argued that as public safety commissioner he would continue to oppose the dictates of the federal courts. He proposed that citizen "Minutemen" would ride buses. If Black riders "insulted" a white woman—presumably by sitting next to her—the volunteer would "relieve the tension," thus restoring "good race relations." Since these individuals would not be city officials, they would not be subject to court orders. He also proposed the creation of a city commission, armed with subpoena power, that would investigate and prosecute unscrupulous real estate companies that were "blockbusting" by selling homes to "Negroes in white areas."[396]

Through the late winter and early spring of 1957, undeterred by the long odds, members of Carter's Klan devoted their energies to working for his election. Over four weekends in March they built a small twenty by thirty-foot building down an unmarked dirt road on a secluded section of land north of Birmingham. The crude concrete block building—the "lair" as Carter grandiloquently named it—had four windows, a battered door, a dirt floor, and no electricity or running water. Lit by two kerosene lanterns, its only furnishings were a crude rostrum constructed of unfinished pine, a few shelves against one wall, and a rickety trestle table that held a hand-operated printer for producing Carter campaign materials and Confederate Klan literature. The nearest house stood more than a hundred yards away.[397]

The new Klan continued many of the rituals and practices of Carter's earlier group. But the group with fewer than thirty followers was a far cry from the thousands who had joined his Citizens' Councils or the much larger Klan that met in the old Bessemer theater.

BIRMINGHAM POST-HERALD FRIDAY, APRIL 12, 1957

WANTS POLICE JOB—Asa E. (Ace) Carter is a candidate for commissioner of public safety in the May 7 election. His wife and four children are shown in the background at their home.

Meet Your Candidates—

Asa Carter Admirer Of Confederate Heroes

This 1957 news story contains the only known photo of Asa Carter and his family: wife, Thelma "India," with, from left, Asa Jr., Ralph, Bedford, and Tara.

During March and April Confederate Klan members printed nearly ten thousand leaflets promoting Carter's candidacy and distributed them primarily to church parking lots in white working-class districts across the city. In the run-up up to the May 7 election, however, Carter failed to show up for several joint appearances with other candidates. He gave one newspaper interview and raised enough money to broadcast a fifteen-minute television advertisement on a Birmingham station on the eve of the election, but—compared with his early fiery speeches—he gave a tepid performance. He attacked incumbent Lindbergh, but he also dismissed Connor as one of the "so-called" segregation candidates who were tied in to "respectable" community leaders. Whatever Carter's intentions, by running a more radical anti-segregationist campaign, he may well have helped Connor by making him appear slightly less extreme.

Not surprisingly, Carter ended in last place.

With his trial on hold after the May acquittal of fellow Klansman Ira Evans, Carter disappeared from public view, but he continued to direct his Klan organization through Jesse Mabry, former co-editor of *The Southerner* and one of the participants in the 1956 attack on Nat King Cole.

Mabry, Carter's friend for more than five years, had never finished high school, but he proved to be a surprisingly skilled polemicist, writing publicity releases and articles for the North Alabama Citizens' Council while serving as co-editor of *The Southerner.* As the relatively well paid foreman of the Birmingham's Perfection Mattress Manufacturing Company, he owned a comfortable three-bedroom home, drove a late-model car, and served as the respected secretary of the "Foreman's Club," a fraternal organization that brought together working-class factory supervisors in the Birmingham area. Unlike many of Carter's Klansmen, his only brush with the law had come with his involvement in the 1956 attack on Nat King Cole.

Although Mabry remained close to Carter, he lacked the force of personality—or recklessness—to lead the Klan group into action. That position fell to Joe Pritchett, a newcomer to Carter's group. In the early summer of 1957, the thirty-five-year-old unemployed construction worker approached his neighbor, James Abercrombie, about the possibility of joining Carter's

Klan. Pritchett knew that Carter had recently promoted Abercrombie's son-in-law, John Griffin, to the position of "lieutenant" in charge of recruiting new members. In an organization riddled by informers, personal contacts verified the reliability of would-be members, proving critical in avoiding FBI infiltration.

Often dressed in suit and tie, the clean-cut Pritchett could easily be mistaken for a local businessman or professional. Gregarious and cordial, he was quick to smile and offer a helping hand to friends and neighbors. But at any mention of Black men, he would become "agitated" and "upset" said one neighbor and obsessed with the belief that every Black man was a potential rapist. The only way to protect white women, he told Abercrombie, was to "castrate them all." Abercrombie had not been surprised by his remarks, since, at one time or another "most men" he knew said that "all of them ought to be done that way."[398] After several conversations and a further background check, Carter appointed Pritchett "grand cyclops" in early August and authorized him to wear the red robe of authority. Despite his recent enrollment, members of the klavern deferred to him, as much out of fear as respect.

Two weeks after Pritchett's appointment, Mabry set up a 16-mm projector at his home to show *The Birth of a Nation* to Carter's Klan members. Viewing the film had by then become a common practice in recruiting and indoctrinating Klan members.

Despite his personal struggles and diminished group of followers, Carter took heart as the growing threat of school integration led to increasing white solidarity. In an unsuccessful effort to stop the 1957 Civil Rights Act from passing, South Carolina's Strom Thurmond took to the Senate floor on August 28 for twenty-four hours, still the nation's longest uninterrupted filibuster. However limited, the 1957 Act was the first federal measure since Reconstruction designed to protect civil rights, establishing the Civil Rights Division in the Justice Department, and empowering federal officials to prosecute individuals who denied citizens the right to vote.

And five days later, Little Rock, Arkansas, provided a second flash point to inflame white resistance throughout the South. On Sunday, September 2, Arkansas Governor Orval Faubus held the last of several meetings with

US District Judge John Miller in which Faubus urged him to postpone the scheduled admission of nine Black students to Little Rock's Central High School the following day. At 10:15 that evening, Faubus ordered the state militia to surround the school and block the entrance of the nine students. Given what he claimed was the threat of violence, he said that law and order could only maintained by blocking "forcible integration" and maintaining the schools "on the same [segregated] basis as they have been operated in the past."[399]

The next day, the Faubus speech claimed front page on virtually every newspaper in the nation. Most headlined their coverage with neutral headlines (*New York Times:* "Militia Sent to Little Rock; School Integration Put Off.") Several Deep South newspapers referred to "race-mixing" in their headlines and praised the governor for his defiance.

If events in Little Rock dominated news coverage around the nation, Carter and his fellow Klansman were most enraged by events close to home.

In late August 1957, the Reverend Fred Shuttlesworth, Birmingham's most militant civil rights activist, submitted a petition to the city school board insisting that students be allowed to attend those schools nearest their homes. He announced that he and the other petitioners would seek to enroll their children in all-white schools, a move that drew bitter condemnation from the city's two newspapers and warnings that his actions could only "inflame a situation already troubled and dangerous."[400]

Early civil rights arrest mug shot of Fred Shuttlesworth, 1956.

If Shuttlesworth, one of the 1957 founders of the Southern Christian Leadership Conference, worked closely with Martin Luther King, he was cut from a different cloth. Educated at the small Black Baptist Selma University and Alabama State College for Negroes,

Shuttlesworth was an "old-time" preacher who drew working-class as well as middle-class Blacks to his north Birmingham church.

He had accompanied Autherine Lucy during her brief integration of the University of Alabama in 1956 and initially served as membership chairman for the Alabama chapter of the NAACP. Dissatisfied with the cautious policies of NAACP, he formed the Alabama Christian Movement for Human Rights, which ultimately drew together more than fifty Black churches to support lawsuits, demonstrations, and boycotts. Nothing infuriated white supremacists more than Shuttlesworth's willingness to engage in direct confrontation with segregated institutions during the time when massive resistance reached its peak in the Deep South.

That anger had long placed Shuttlesworth in jeopardy. On Christmas night, 1956, a blast from as many as sixteen sticks of dynamite thrown under his house exploded almost directly under the bed where he was resting after a busy day. The blast shattered the floor, collapsed one wall and lifted him and his mattress into the air. Miraculously, he had no serious injuries.

"I knew in a second, [a] split second, that the only reason God saved me was to lead the fight," Shuttlesworth told his family. For Shuttlesworth, this providential intervention just "brought the Bible back up to date," he would later tell his congregation. "You don't have to go back to Daniel in the lion's den or the boys in the fiery furnace" to have God's protection.

Just in case, armed members of his congregation began around the clock protection of the church parsonage.[401]

But Shuttlesworth would not be the first victim of Carter's Klansmen. Instead they chose a hapless thirty-five-year-old Black handyman, with no involvement in the civil rights movement, as a warning to the troublesome Shuttlesworth.

As headlines reported the growing racial tension across the nation, a dozen members of Carter's Klan met at Mabry's home north of Birmingham. Because it was Labor Day, Mabry scheduled the meeting for late afternoon rather than the normal 7 p.m. gathering time. He followed his usual pattern of deference, in this case standing quietly aside while Pritchett took charge. Eleven Klansmen were present, including Charles Bridges, one of the men shot in the Bessemer theater fracas the previous year, but Pritchett dismissed

Joe Pritchett, seated, with his attorney Norman Moon, 1957.

six of them from the night's assignment. In addition to Mabry, he ordered three "lieutenants" to stand by.

Grover McCullough had served in the army for eight years. He had a checkered career after leaving the military, although his offenses and misdemeanors—bootlegging, public drunkenness and resisting arrest—were relatively mild compared to the records of many Klansmen. The forty-five-year-old McCullough described himself as a welder and automobile body shop repairman. In reality, he had never held a job for more than six months and was unemployed.[402]

The two remaining "lieutenants," William Miller and John Griffin, friends for more than eight years, worked as stock clerks at a small independently owned grocery store in Homewood, a Birmingham middle-class suburb. Both were married; Griffin had three small children, and neither man had a criminal record or a history of violent behavior. Miller in particular hardly fit the profile of a battle-hardened Klansman. With thick "Coke-bottle" glasses, he suffered from night blindness and had to depend on his wife or friends to drive him after dark. Everyone who knew Miller described him as quiet and timid. Despite Miller's visual handicap, Carter rewarded his loyalty by appointing him as "Chief Intelligence Officer." Miller proudly accepted the appointment and promotion.

John Griffin's father-in-law had vouched for Pritchett when the hard-drinking unemployed carpenter sought membership, but the Griffin family's initial friendship with Pritchett soon cooled. Griffin's wife, who also worked at the Homewood grocery store, shared her husband's opposition to integration, but she distrusted Pritchett and resented his late-night telephone calls peremptorily ordering her husband out on secret assignments. Despite tensions at home, Griffin was present on the night of September 2.

Bart Floyd, the last member of the group, desperately wanted to become a member of Carter's inner circle, but he remained untested and on trial. The handsome thirty-one-year-old electrician, with a sweeping pompadour and a wife eight months pregnant, worked at a Birmingham aircraft assembly plant. He had no police record and fellow workers described him as dependable and extremely skilled in his job. But even in the racially charged climate of 1957, he unnerved those around him with his hatred for Blacks. Grand Cyclops Pritchett saw him as someone who would not flinch at taking forceful action.

As the six remaining Klansmen shared a cigarette break in Mabry's back yard, Floyd pleaded with his fellow Klansmen to support his promotion to captain. Everyone understood that Carter was the final authority on all matters, but it was clear that Pritchett would decide whether to recommend Floyd. He explained that Floyd would have to prove his worthiness by getting "nigger blood on his hands." Floyd stood proudly before the group; he was ready and willing.[403]

At 8:30, as dusk turned to darkness, the six men divided into two cars and left Mabry's north Birmingham home. Labor Day marked the last weeks of summer, but a blazing sun during the day had pushed the temperatures into the low nineties with little cooling in the early evening. They first stopped at Alley Drugs, one of the few Birmingham pharmacies open after 6 p.m. Floyd, driver of the lead car, purchased a package of single-edge razor blades and a bottle of medicinal turpentine. As Floyd opened the back door, Mabry slid into the driver's seat.

Griffin, driving his 1955 powder blue and white Chevy, took the lead. Pritchett, barking instructions, ordered Griffin to drive ten blocks to an unpaved alley where several Black families lived. When the men spotted an older woman sitting on her front porch, the two cars stopped in front and a smiling Pritchett ambled up the steps. "Auntie," he explained, he was "looking for a colored person to cut some grass." It seemed an outlandish gambit: six white men in a Black neighborhood at 9 p.m. looking for someone to "cut grass"? Not surprisingly the "auntie" assured him that there were no men in her house and she was certain there were no men available in the neighborhood.[404] McCullough then suggested the Klansmen ride six blocks to a main street where he had earlier "noticed a lot of colored people right in front of the bus stop."[405]

But the stop was deserted when they arrived, and a frustrated Pritchett ordered the driver of the lead car to pull into a nearby filling station. He explained that he "wanted to make a report." The others assumed the call was to Asa Carter. Ten minutes later, Pritchett walked back to Griffin's car. He took a sixteen-inch tire tool and a large wrench out of the trunk and handed them to Floyd.

From there, the group drove two miles northwest through a series of unpaved alleys on the perimeter of the Birmingham airport before stopping at the Cabin Club, a well-known "honky-tonk" where a jukebox, legal beer, and illegal bootleg whiskey drew local Black residents for dancing and drinking late into the night. This was not a night spot frequented by whites, but Pritchett prided himself on his fearlessness in dealing with Blacks. His courage was helped by the fact that—in the words of several of his fellow Klansmen—he had been "drinking quite a bit" that night. He walked across the gravel parking lot and into the Club. It impressed his friends, but after he failed to return for more than a quarter hour, they uneasily got out of the car and had begun walking toward the club when Pritchett stepped out the front door and ordered them back to their cars. Police later learned that he had looked around the dance floor and then demanded that the owner allow him to use the Club's telephone to make his second call of the evening. He talked for about ten minutes; no one stood close enough to overhear his conversation.[406]

With Pritchett barking out new instructions, the two cars left the Cabin Club, winding again through back alleys and unpaved streets until they reached the Tarrant City/Huffman Highway and turned eastward. In the 1950s, this was still sparsely populated countryside, with houses scattered along large stretches of rural roadside. After turning onto the highway, the two cars slowly drove past the local Zion African Methodist Episcopal Church. As they reached the church cemetery, the three men in the lead car—Griffin, Pritchett, and McCullough—saw a Black couple walking in the same direction on the opposite side of the road. It was just before 10 p.m. They were less than a mile from Mabry's home.

Although journalists, basing their reporting on police records, identified the man as "Edward Aaron," his actual name was *Judge* Edward *Arone.* Since Southern whites generally refused to use the honorifics Mr., Mrs., or Miss when referring to Black men and women, it was not uncommon for African Americans to subtly mock the system by naming a son "Captain," "Major," or, in this case, "Judge," all titles held by whites. The police never bothered to check the spelling of Arone's name, and he was identified in court proceedings, news reports, and later historical accounts as "Aaron." Only Montgomery's Black weekly newspaper, the *Alabama Tribune*, correctly spelled his name.

An army veteran from rural Barbour County, Arone had served as a stevedore in England and the Philippines during World War II. He lived with his mother and picked up odd jobs as a house painter and handyman, earning less than a thousand dollars a year. He did not own a car. For some time, he had been "going together" with Cora Parker, a neighbor and friend of Arone's mother. On this warm September night, the two were walking to a nearby country store to buy a soft drink when the Klansmen spotted them.

As the lead car drew closer, Pritchett ordered Miller to turn off his lights and stop on the opposite side of the road. The second car dropped back and slowed to a crawl. Pritchett and McCullough calmly walked across the road. To Arone, the men seemed friendly. He thought they were lost and simply asking for directions. Suddenly, McCullough and Pritchett "swarmed on me like wasps," said Arone, and yelled at Cora Parker to "get gone." At that moment, the thirty-five-year-old army veteran realized he was in the kind of danger that every Black man feared. "What do you want? What have I done? What do you want with me?" he asked.

"We want you," Pritchett said, "you black son-of-a-bitch. You're the one we've been looking for." They dragged Arone back to the second car driven by Mabry where they blindfolded and threw him face down on the floor of the backseat. The abduction was over in a less than two minutes.

After hiding in the nearby underbrush, Cora Parker ran back onto the road and flagged down a young white couple. She frantically explained what had happened, but after listening for a moment, they looked at each other and drove off without saying a word. She then ran nearly a half mile past her house to the nearest Black neighbor with a telephone. He called the state highway patrol and reported the abduction and pleaded with them to send an officer to investigate. The dispatcher passed the call on to the county sheriff's office, but it was well over an hour before two officers arrived, one from nearby Tarrant City's police department, the other a deputy sheriff from Jefferson County. (There was some question over whether the incident had taken place within the Tarrant City limits or in unincorporated Jefferson County.) Neither lawman seemed concerned; they briefly listened to Parker's story, scrawled a few notes, and left. They never filed a report.[407]

While Parker waited for police to arrive, the Klansmen had driven northeastward, Mabry's car in the lead with the nearly blind Miller at his side. Floyd sat on the back seat, his foot planted on Arone's back, a pistol in one hand, the wrench in the other. From the front seat, either Mabry or Miller (Arone could not tell who was talking) began barking questions. Did he go to church? Was he married? Did he have any children? Did he want to mix with whites? Was he a member of the NAACP? "No sir," replied Arone to each question. But there was one question asked again and again: did he know the Reverend Fred Shuttlesworth? As Arone replied with the same answer, "No, sir," Floyd would strike Arone with the five-pound wrench.

As his questioners railed against Shuttlesworth ("he tried to enroll nigger children in white schools") they added an ominous threat. They were going to "do something" to Shuttlesworth, "like they going to do me," said Arone. Twenty minutes later the two cars reached the Klan shack in Chalkville.

After the three men pulled the blindfolded Arone from the car, they donned their Klan hoods. "Make like a dog," Floyd ordered as he forced his victim to crawl on his hands and knees through the graveled parking area. As Arone reached the threshold of the cinder block building, once again Floyd struck him in the head with the wrench and he heard another voice: "Go on into the slaughter pen."[408] While the men lighted a kerosene lamp, Arone, still blindfolded, kneeled on the floor desperately trying to hear the men as they whispered. Finally, Pritchett—his white robe worn under a scarlet red "cyclops" pointed hood—pulled off Arone's blindfold and then raised his own mask. Do you know me, he asked?

"No, sir," insisted Arone, "I never saw you before."

You're lying, he said, and kicked Arone in the face and onto his back.

Get back on your knees, one of the men shouted at him, "the boss is talking. . . ." Two Klansmen dragged Arone back to a kneeling position where he was once more interrogated about Shuttlesworth and Arthur Shores, a Black Birmingham attorney who had long been active in civil rights cases.

When asked again if he knew the civil rights leader, Arone mumbled "No, sir," only to be kicked again in the mouth by Pritchett. Repeatedly the men asked the same question; with each "No, sir," he received blows to the head with the wrench and shouts of "You're lying."[409]

Suddenly the beating stopped, and Pritchett told him that

> they going to let me go back alive and wanted me to carry a message back to them, wanted me to tell them not to try to integrate any nigger children in white schools, or they going to do them like they going to do me, do some more like they going to do me. . . .

"To do me."

It took only a moment before Pritchett gave him the choice: "We are going to kill you or cut your balls out. Which one you want?"[410]

"I don't want neither one," said Arone.

Shaw slammed the tire iron into the side of his head and told him to stand up. As he lurched to his feet, Arone heard Pritchett repeat "they going to cut my nuts out."

Stunned, Arone first followed orders to drop his trousers and underwear to his ankles, but then began flailing at two men who grabbed each arm. Floyd slapped him across the face with his pistol and then slammed the wrench against the back of Arone's head. This time, mercifully, he became unconscious.

"Captain, do your duty," Pritchett told Floyd, who knelt with a razor blade in his right hand. While a fellow Klansmen held the kerosene lamp, Floyd severed the testicles of Judge Edward Arone and placed them in a Dixie paper cup.

Griffin, who had been designated as sentry, looked up in surprise as Floyd walked out holding up his razor blade in the full moonlight. "I've got a souvenir," the grinning Floyd told Griffin,who walked into the building and saw Arone lying on the floor covered in blood. To the amusement of Pritchett and McCullough, Miller staggered against one wall and began vomiting. He would later claim that he thought they were going to "scare" Arone and did not really believe they would castrate him.[411]

As Arone slowly returned to consciousness, his first thought was of the excruciating pain in his groin. When he opened his eyes, he saw Floyd pouring turpentine over his "privates" and then calmly wiping the turpentine and blood from his hands on a rag. Griffin and Mabry pulled up Arone's pants, which were soon soaked in blood.

"I believe he's dying," Pritchett told the other Klansmen. "Let the son-of-a-bitch die."[412]

Roughly, four of the men picked him up and threw him in the trunk of Griffin's car. After Pritchett dismissed Floyd, the five men sped away on the same Tarrant City/Huffman Highway, this time westward toward Tarrant City near where they had seized their victim. At one point in the twenty-minute ride, Pritchett held up the paper cup with Arone's testicles and jokingly asked each of the men if they "wanted to eat them."[413] After turning onto a connecting street and then to a smaller side road, they stopped on a deserted stretch crossing over Five Mile Creek, a meandering stream that passed through the old Warrior Coal fields north of Birmingham.

"Let's throw the Black son-of-a-bitch out here," said Pritchett. As they raised the trunk, however, they saw the headlights of an oncoming car and crouched behind the back of the car until it had passed. Roughly, they threw Arone to the ground then raced off a little over a hundred feet before suddenly stopping.

"I thought they was coming back to finish killing me," said Arone. Still bleeding heavily, he crawled down the side of the embankment, down into the shallow waters of the creek and then back under the highway overpass to the opposite side of the road, where he hid for several moments. Just as he started to crawl up to the road, one of the kidnappers' cars returned and stopped on the bridge. When the men had dumped Arone from the car's trunk, Pritchett had absentmindedly placed the cup containing the mutilated testicles beside the road. He retrieved the cup and ordered Griffin to drive him back to his home, stopping long enough to dump the grisly evidence at another creek crossing.

After waiting several more minutes, Arone began crawling on his hands and knees up the bank and down the three hundred yards back to the main highway, stopping several times as he passed in and out of consciousness. When he reached the intersection and the more heavily traveled Springdale Road, he collapsed as he tried to pull himself up beside a metal sign advertising "DRINK PEPSI, BE SOCIABLE."

"I was too weak. I couldn't go no further," remembered Arone.[414]

Arone was clearly visible on the side of the road. Over the next fifteen minutes cars drove by and several slowed. None stopped. One motorist did make an anonymous call to the Tarrant City police department to report that a "bloody negro" was at the intersection of Clow and Springdale roads. Rookie police officer James Reid was unprepared for what he found when he arrived just before midnight. "His pants and shirt were soaked in [blood]," he reported. And when he helped Arone to his feet, Reid saw "he was bloody from the waist down; I mean like he had been dipped in a tub of blood." Before the ambulance arrived, Reid gently lowered Arone's pants and confirmed what Arone had feared: he had been castrated.[415]

Edward Harris, a Birmingham-Southern College student and part-time reporter for the *Birmingham Post-Herald*, was in the newsroom's skeleton Labor Day crew when a friendly police contact tipped him off to the Arone assault. While senior reporters interviewed police officers, Harris drove to Birmingham's Hillman Clinic, the emergency facility used for indigent patients at the University of Alabama School of Medicine. There he interviewed one of the two emergency room physicians who had given Arone four pints of blood and spent the next two hours treating his injuries. Still shaken by the experience, the younger of the two doctors told Harris he had never seen such an injury; it was certainly not something taught in medical school.

As he walked the halls outside the Hillman Clinic's emergency room, the young reporter also talked to employees and hospital visitors. "He must have been doing something really bad," one white man told Harris. Added another: "Probably was screwing some white woman and they caught him." In the days that followed Harris heard rumors that Arone had castrated himself to receive an increase in veterans' benefits. "The white imagination knows no bounds with regard to the intentions of black folk," Harris bitterly concluded.[416]

Newspapers across the nation gave brief coverage to Judge Edward Arone's brutal mutilation. My hometown newspaper, the Florence Morning News, *published an initial page one account and three lengthy follow-up stories that fall.*[417] *But even though I was a passionate newspaper reader during these years and carefully read the* Morning News *each day, I have no memory of reading anything about the Arone case. Perhaps it was simply parochialism; what happened in Alabama was far away. Perhaps I have simply forgotten. But I am inclined to believe that it was more a matter of willful selection, just as most newspapers in the South found it inconvenient to look too closely at such a horrendous example of white brutality.*

I was far more attuned to Black misdeeds. Less than two years earlier, I had closely followed a series of stories concerning (as he was always described) the Black "controversial pastor" Joseph A. Delaine, who had taken up a church in Lake City, just eleven miles from my home.

Within weeks after his arrival at his new church, the troubles began. In mid-September, the local newspaper ran its first article on Reverend DeLaine. A brief account reported that he had complained to Lake City police and the county sheriff that whites had repeatedly thrown rocks through the windows of his parsonage. Less than a month after that first story, DeLaine became front page news, not only in the local press but across the state and in several national newspapers. On October 5, 1955, a fire swept through Delaine's Lake City church while he was away at a minister's conference in Charleston.

Only a week after the fire, the Morning News *headlined: "Sheriff Hunting Negro Pastor: Warrant Charges Shooting Assault." Four local whites reported that, as they returned home after work and drove by the minister's home on the evening of October 10, Delaine had fired a rifle shot that hit the roof of their car. Two days later, a grand jury returned an indictment of attempted murder against DeLaine, who had fled to New York the night of the shooting.*[418] *There, reported the South Carolina press with some indignation, he told gullible supporters that he had been terrorized for months and had defended himself only after the four men fired on his home.*

And I knew the inside story. Shortly after Delaine fled to New York, I had sat in the neighborhood general store with my father and a half-dozen local men, listening to Florence County Deputy Sheriff Heyward Myers. This "NAACP colored preacher" was no victim, Myers told us. He had a long history of troublemaking including arson. Before DeLaine came to Lake City, said Meyer, he had burned his home in Clarendon County for insurance, and then, after moving to Lake City, arranged for an accomplice to set fire to his church while he was out of town and conveniently had an alibi. It was all a scam to collect the insurance on the building. Proving arson would have been difficult, said Deputy Myers, but DeLaine had made a mistake when, unprovoked, he shot at innocent locals driving by his home. What's more, added Myers, the FBI agents brought into the case agreed with him.

Over the years I taught African American and Southern history and become far more aware of Delaine's important role in the struggle for ending segregation. In the late 1940s and early 1950s, Delaine mobilized African American parents to sue the state of South Carolina over the wretched conditions of Black schools in Clarendon County. That lawsuit, Briggs v. Elliott *(1952) became a critical part of the court case that every American had come to recognize:* Brown v. Board of Education.[419]

I assumed that the description of DeLaine I had heard at age fifteen was exaggerated and reflected the racial prejudices of the era. Still, I thought, South Carolina was not Mississippi or Alabama.

I was wrong. Shortly after I began teaching at the University of South Carolina in 2000, I went through the FBI file on Reverend Delaine, his personal papers at the University library, and the detailed newspaper coverage in my hometown newspaper, the Florence Morning News.

In the spring of 1955, when an arsonist burned his home just outside the small town of Manning, city firemen called to the scene by a neighbor sat and watched the home burn. The fire chief explained that it was one hundred feet outside the city limits. A state fire marshal investigated the case, but, on orders from Governor George Bell Timmerman Jr., he was told to seal his report.[420]

Concerned over Delaine's safety, the A.M.E. bishop who oversaw DeLaine's church moved him thirty miles away to Lake City, South Carolina. Although DeLaine kept a low profile after he moved to Lake City, the harassment began within weeks after his arrival. On several occasions, a group of whites, led by the owner of the local Esso service station, shouted threats to his wife as she walked downtown, and the taunts and verbal abuse escalated through the late summer of 1955. Early that fall, he received a detailed death threat, warning that he and his wife would suffer the fate of Frazier Baker, the Black postmaster who had been murdered by a Lake City mob in 1898 after he refused to give up what was considered a "white man's job."

DeLaine repeatedly filed complaints with the Lake City police and county sheriff's department, describing how cars had driven by his home throwing rocks through his front windows while yelling racial threats. In one case he was able to write down the license number of the car.

The Lake City police and the county sheriff's department dismissed his complaints. When he turned to the FBI for help, J. Edgar Hoover personally wrote a memo identifying Delaine as "a controversial figure in racial segregation matters in South Carolina." Hoover told local agents that they should not acknowledge Delaine's complaints "since he might be able to use this to his own advantage at some later date."[421]

Within a week after the burning of his church by arsonists, four white men, well known to local officials for their hostility to Delaine and his family, drove by his house late one evening. Although they claimed that they were innocently returning from work, the gas station had been closed for over an hour and none of them lived at addresses near the Delaine house. Reverend Delaine had seen the men drive by earlier and he loaded his rifle, prepared to stay on guard all night. When the men drove by a second time, they shot into his house and he fired back, striking the roof of the car before it sped away. He would later insist he had no intention of wounding or killing the occupants. "I wanted to mark the car so there would be no question of its identity." But he quickly realized that whatever, the provocation, he would be charged by local police. Hurriedly he sent his wife and daughter to a neighbor's home, packed a small suitcase, and drove north to friends in New York city.[422]

Two days later a Florence County grand jury returned an indictment for attempted murder against DeLaine. Within hours, South Carolina Governor Timmerman issued a request for extradition from the state of New York.[423]

After an extensive review of the evidence in the case, a New York state judicial panel recommended that Governor Averell Harriman deny extradition. The charges were politically motivated, the panel concluded, and driven by racial bias. Given the climate of opinion in the area, it would be impossible for the Reverend Delaine to receive a fair trial in South Carolina.

As I read the death threat letter in his papers and followed the nightmare of the DeLaine family; as I reviewed the complete failure of local law enforcement to protect him, his wife, and their two children, I once again reflected on how the feverish defense of white supremacy in the mid-1950s blinded so many white Southerners.

It had certainly blinded me.

13

Mayhem: Part Two

> *There has never been a case in all my years of law practice and ten years on the bench that has shocked me as this one has. I'm sorry. There's no pleasure for me in sending a man to prison . . . but there's just no justification for your act from the testimony presented in the case. . . . Because of the very seriousness of this, I do not think anything but the maximum would suffice. . . . Therefore, I sentence you to twenty years.*
>
> — Judge Alta King, October 31, 1957[424]

The morning after the assault on Judge Edward Arone, John Griffin slept in; he was not scheduled to work that day at Hill's Grocery. But his wife, Mary, had the morning shift as one of the check-out cashiers, and she was angry. She had stayed up until after midnight the night before and, when her husband finally came in, she "raised sand" with him over his Klan activities. Her husband had increasingly refused to talk about his activities once Joe Pritchett became head of the group. Pritchett would call at all hours of the night and demand her husband leave home for undisclosed purposes, evidently not simply passing out "anti-integration literature." Before she left for work, she called the Klan leader and asked if he been with her husband the night before.

Oh no, he said, "I was at a friendly little poker game." Angrily, she told Pritchett that her husband was going to "get out of the Klan or I'm going to divorce him."

Shortly after noon, a delivery truck deposited the city's afternoon newspaper in front of the Homewood grocery. As she read the *Birmingham News* account of the assault on Arone, she remembered she had seen a large wrench and tire iron on the passenger's side floor of their Chevy that morning. After work, she systematically went through the car, where she found a billfold with Pritchett's driver's license and several other cards under his name in the glove compartment. When she called him a second time, he acknowledged that the billfold and "some metal objects" were his.

After another stormy confrontation that night, her husband agreed to resign from the Klan but he insisted that he had nothing to do with the assault on Arone. She was not convinced. He refused to tell her anything about what he had done with his fellow Klansmen on the previous night, and he clearly was worried, said Mary Griffin. "I knew something was wrong."[425]

In the seventy-two hours after the assault, sheriff's deputies worked non-stop, aided by the ineptness of Carter's "strike force" and the critical assistance of special state policeman Ben Adams. In the 1960s, Adams would become an architect of some of the most repressive investigative tactics George Wallace's administration used against civil rights activists. Like many traditional white Southerners, however, he prided himself on his affection for Blacks who knew their place. And one of the first things he told his boss was that Arone was a "humble darky" who had never been involved in any form of civil rights activities.

Although Arone remained in serious condition, he gave Adams and sheriff's deputy Tom Ellison a description of his attackers and managed to draw a crude sketch of the site of his mutilation. With his extensive files and network of contacts in the Klan, it took Adams only a few hours to learn the names of the men and then find the weak links in the group. Friday afternoon, Ellison arrested John Griffin and William Miller as they worked at their grocery jobs. Both seemed resigned to their fate and it required neither threats nor promises to persuade them to confess. Although Griffin insisted that he had never been in favor of more than a "whipping" for Arone, his decision to turn state's evidence had little to do with remorse. "I was involved in something pretty deep," he admitted. "I didn't want to get shot and be left dead as a member of that organization." Despite three telephoned death threats to Griffin's wife over the next twenty-four hours, both Griffin and Miller agreed to testify against their fellow Klansmen.[426]

With Miller's directions, Ellison, Adams, and three more deputies arrived at the Klan "lair" just after dusk and discovered that Arone's attackers had made no effort to conceal their crime. Dried blood covered a large section of the dirt floor, and the smell of turpentine permeated the shuttered building. Arone's blindfold lay on the floor, the group's distinctive Black Klan hoods had been stacked neatly on a shelf, and the blood-stained cloth that Floyd had used to clean his hands lay in plain sight next to the small, hand-operated printing press. A *Birmingham News* reporter invited to accompany the police photographed a stack of personal letters written to Carter, and the printer, he noted, had been used to reproduce copies of Carter's speeches. The *News* ran photographs of the interior of the Klan building, and the large front-page photo focused on a stack of Asa Carter street signs and campaign literature from his unsuccessful campaign for Birmingham City Commissioner. The connection between Carter and the Klansmen could not have been clearer to readers. By the end of the weekend, all six of the men were in custody.

Arone's mutilation shocked and infuriated Birmingham's Black community; the incident primarily seemed to embarrass whites. Stories in both the *News* and the *Post-Herald* described the link between Arone's mutilation and Fred Shuttlesworth's integration efforts and made it clear that the assault was intended as a personal warning. Shuttlesworth's only response was to express concern about Arone and to issue a statement to the press explaining that he planned to exercise his "constitutional rights" to have

Items linked to Carter, photographed inside the KKK building where Arone was mutilated, 1957.

his children attend the school nearest their home—all-white Phillips High School in downtown Birmingham rather than the more distant Parker High School for Blacks.

Parker High, built in 1900 as Industrial High School for Negroes, offered the best secondary school education for Blacks in Alabama through the 1930s and 1940s. Even though it had a distinguished roster of graduates, no one would confuse it with Phillips High as a facility. The latter's striking beaux art building, constructed in the 1920s at the height of Birmingham's post-World War I prosperity, had a two-thousand-seat auditorium, a gymnasium with galleries, a swimming pool, laboratories for general science and physics, manual training shops, domestic science and art rooms, a library and a huge study hall, an infirmary, and a state-of-the-art cafeteria able to serve five hundred students at a time.

Over the weekend of September 7 and 8, 1957, a week after the Arone assault, Shuttlesworth explained to his two daughters, Ruby Frederika, twelve, and Patricia Ann, fourteen, that they would have to take the lead and present themselves for admission on Monday morning. They dutifully agreed. But friends pleaded with him to step back. "Fred, there ain't any point in going down to Phillips. You won't do nothing but get in trouble," warned his attorney, Oscar Adams. And "you may get your head beat up. . . ."[427]

After his Sunday worship service, Shuttlesworth instructed his daughters on how to respond nonviolently if they were assaulted. Reluctantly, his close friend the Reverend J. S. Phifer agreed to drive. Shuttlesworth and his wife, Ruby, would ride in the front seat with Phifer while his daughters and two other Black applicants would sit in the back. To prevent a preemptive arrest, Shuttlesworth waited until early the next morning to notify city police (and two local television stations) that he would arrive at Phillips High at 10:15 a.m. to present four students for enrollment.

Carter's Klan members monitored police radio traffic and quickly mobilized their members and other supporters. As Reverend Phifer pulled to a stop in front of Phillips High, the six passengers saw two television cameramen on a nearby sidewalk and a mob of fifteen to twenty shirt-sleeved whites carrying baseball bats and links of heavy chain. Shuttlesworth recognized Bobby Frank Cherry, who had been involved in several bombings in the area and had belonged to Carter's Klan. Despite Shuttlesworth's notice to the police department, only four police officers were present, two of whom would remain seated in their patrol car several hundred feet from the entrance of the school. Fearlessly, if somewhat foolishly, Shuttlesworth stepped out of the car. Within seconds, the blow of a baseball bat knocked him to the ground. As he scrambled to his feet and lurched down the street he could hear the howls of the mob: "This is the son of a bitch. If we kill him it'll be over." Twice he went down as a bat-wielding older man kept screaming, "Kill the motherfuckin' nigger."

One of the two policemen watching the assault stood back from the

The Reverend Fred Shuttlesworth was long a target of white extremists. Left, moments before he desegregated Birmingham city buses, 1956. Below, the aftermath of the bombing of his home at Christmas, 1956.

mayhem, laughing, as he mockingly calling out to the crowd: "Now y'all ought not to bother him." Alone, Lieutenant E. T. Rouse charged into the crowd swinging his night stick in a futile attempt to rescue Shuttlesworth. Shoved backward by the mob, he saw two men pulling Shuttlesworth's wife, Ruby, from the car, and he rushed back in time to push her back in the car and handcuff I. F. Gauldin as he wielded a twelve-inch link of chain. In the confusion, Rouse did not even realize that another member of the mob had stabbed Mrs. Shuttlesworth in the upper thigh.

Meanwhile Reverend Shuttlesworth was on his own. Repeatedly kicked and beaten, he scrambled on his hands and knees through his attackers back to the car as his wife opened the door. He managed to crawl into the front seat and Reverend Phifer slowly forced his way through the crowd as members of the mob shattered the car windows and kicked and pounded the hood and sides with bats and chains.

Always aware of the way Birmingham policed used traffic infractions to harass civil rights activists, a groggy Shuttlesworth told his friend, "Don't run the stop sign!"[428]

At Birmingham's University Hospital, one of the emergency room physicians who had treated Arone the previous week took one look at Shuttlesworth's battered face (most of his skin had been scraped off on one side) and rushed him to the x-ray room. He was stunned to discover that, though his patient was covered in massive bruises, abrasions, and cuts, there was no sign of a skull fracture. The "Lord knew I lived in a hard town," Shuttlesworth explained, "so he gave me a hard head."[429]

If Shuttlesworth expected his beating to create a sympathetic backlash against white violence, he was badly mistaken. Crowds of students at Phillips and other white schools in the city paraded through the streets carrying Confederate battle flags and shouting slogans condemning Shuttlesworth's attempt to desegregate the city's schools.

"What a deplorable move it was for the Reverend F. L. Shuttlesworth to go to Phillips High School yesterday to seek to have Negro students enrolled," said the *Birmingham News* in an editorial the following day. While the physical attacks were "regrettable," said the *News*, they were the inevitable consequence of Shuttlesworth's foolish actions which "menace the welfare of the people as a whole." The *News* editorial pointed to the ongoing Little Rock Crisis in which the federal courts had rejected efforts by officials to suspend integration there. The "disturbance" at Phillips High was further evidence that state and local officials should be given the power to "act in behalf of peace and order." Tactics on "both sides"—the Klansmen who mutilated Arone and the Black preacher who tried to integrate an all-white school—were "lamentably wrong."

Mayor James Morgan did not even bother to issue bromides about "both sides." In a statement released the following day, Mayor Morgan declared that "Negro agitators sought to create a condition of general disturbance at Phillips High School, but the good citizens stood up and the guilty were punished." Nothing, he said, has occurred to "unduly disturb our happy existence in this beautiful valley."[430]

Two weeks after the assault, police stopped Shuttleworth's friend, the Reverend J. S. Phifer, claiming that his rear license plate was "partially obstructed." When they searched his car, they found a small .25 caliber pistol in his brief case which he readily acknowledged was his. He had received numerous threats to kill him or bomb his house; armed members of his congregation had set up a nightly watch to guard his home. "I can't go out with empty hands," he told the police. Forty-eight hours after his arrest, a city judge sentenced him to 180 days in jail and a fine of $100 for violating the state firearms law and an additional $25 fine for driving a car with an obstructed license plate.[431]

Police did charge three men they had handcuffed at the scene of the assault on September 9, and Shuttlesworth, his wife, and Reverend Phifer identified the three assailants from a lineup. Gauldin had used a chain in his attack; Herbert Frank Cash had hit Shuttlesworth repeatedly with brass knuckles; and J. E. Breckinridge had leaped on Shuttlesworth, knocking him to the ground. During the brief trial, the assistant solicitor asked the Shuttlesworths and Phifer only a handful of questions, and he declined to introduce extensive local televised film footage of the mob during the assault including one vivid section that showed Cash and a smiling Bob Cherry (who was not arrested) beating Shuttlesworth with brass knuckles.

When the city judge levied fines of $50 on the three men for misdemeanor assault, Klan attorney George Rogers appealed the fine and insisted that his clients be bound over to a grand jury for possible indictment on the far more serious charge of assault with intent to murder. He was confident no white jury would indict the three men for attacking Shuttlesworth. He was right. On October 5, the all-white grand jurors met for twenty-seven minutes before unanimously dismissing all charges. Six years later, Cash and Cherry would join two other men in planting the bomb that killed four girls at the 16th Street Baptist Church.[432]

The acquittal of the men who assaulted Shuttlesworth in broad daylight seemed to embolden local bombers. In June 1958, terrorists planted dynamite at Shuttlesworth's Bethel Baptist Church. Alerted by a passing resident that there was "something burning" next to the church, Will Hall, a sixty-two-year-old volunteer watchman, grabbed a paint can packed with fifteen to twenty sticks of dynamite. Hall raced to the middle of the street, placed the can down and ran. A moment later the massive explosion blew a two-foot hole into the pavement and shattered windows in the church and surrounding residences.[433]

THE TRIAL OF JUDGE Edward Arone's assailants took a different turn. In the days after news broke of the attack, the press emphasized that Arone was not part of any "racial or integration movement."

Solicitor Emmett Perry would normally have left the prosecution of those who mutilated Arone to his assistant, Cecil Deason, but he took personal charge. When the first case, against Joe Pritchett, went to trial, the theme was set: Judge Edward Arone was the victim of an "unprovoked attack," a "humble Negro," in the words of one of the prosecutors, a "harmless colored handyman" who had never been involved in civil rights activities.

Thus Perry moved to disarm the usual Klan defense that aimed at discrediting and blaming the victims. Here was a chance for respectable white Southerners to prove they were not the barbarians of Northern propaganda. In a sermon the Sunday before the trial began, the pastor of Birmingham's largest Methodist church responded to the "stupid and cruel treatment of an innocent Negro man" as evidence of "recklessness and Godless living, too many drinking parties, too many homes threatened by loose living. . . ." Far

Judge Edward Arone and Cora Parker, waiting to testify, 1957.

worse was the way in which this incident had "struck a cruel blow against the South."[434]

From the outset, Judge Alta King gave the Klansmen's defense lawyers no leeway as the state presented its witnesses. The young doctor who treated Arone and the policemen who investigated the case methodically laid out their evidence. Cora Parker, who had been walking with Arone on the night of the assault, pointed without hesitation to Joe Pritchett as one of the two men who had seized her boyfriend. Despite a fierce cross-examination by Pritchett's lawyer, she remained calm and unflustered. And Arone, the state's star witness, gave a soft-spoken but powerful description of his ordeal to the all-white jury and a courtroom audience composed mainly of African Americans. At the conclusion of Arone's testimony, at the insistence of the prosecution, and after women had been cleared from the courtroom, he had to lower his pants, lift his penis and show the all-male jury the scars from his emasculation. (Alabama law barred women from juries until 1966.)

Klan attorney Norman Moon cross-examined Arone about the possible contamination of his identification of the Klansmen by conversations with sheriff's deputies, but after a brief exchange, Judge King brusquely told Moon to move on. Repeatedly, and occasionally with sarcasm, King dismissed repeated objections from the Klan defense attorney, who seemed frustrated by such treatment in a white-on-Black case.

Even when cross-examining John Griffin and William Miller, the two Klansmen who had turned witnesses for the state, Moon stumbled against the objections of the prosecutor and the judge. In the end, he could only fall back on the usual defense in such a case: the men had violated their Klan oath not to reveal secrets of the organization. As one reporter wrote, this was hardly a declaration of Pritchett's innocence.

The jury deliberated less than fifty minutes and came back with a guilty verdict for "mayhem," a crime that gave the judge unusual latitude, allowing him to sentence the convicted for any period from two to twenty years. When it came time for King to pass judgment on the man whom newspaper reporters described as "Klan Boss Joe Pritchett," he was scathing as he handed down the maximum sentence.[435]

The trials of the other three defendants continued into December, as Klan attorneys tried a variety of defenses that had always worked in the past. They introduced bogus alibis; they attacked the investigation; they had their clients testify they were simply passive observers. But even the usual tactics of intimidation failed. During a break before his damning testimony in the trial of Bart Floyd, John Griffin went to the men's room to find a message scrawled on the wall: "Be my oath broken, then be I broken." This was from the Klan oath never to betray a member of the organization, and it was an unmistakable threat to kill anyone who testified against a fellow Klansman.[436]

Fearful for the safety of his wife, Griffin knew that testifying for the state was his only chance of avoiding serious jail time. He repeated his testimony from the Pritchett trial, and the jury deliberated less than ninety minutes before convicting Floyd of mayhem. In swift successive trials, juries convicted Jesse Mabry and Grover McCullough for the same offense. After each verdict, Judge King handed down the maximum twenty-year sentence. If anyone doubted the extent to which Carter's men had misjudged public opinion, King made it clear that larger issues were at stake. The defendants had disrupted the "friendly relations here between the races" and "drawn the attention of the entire world."

Asa Carter was not on trial, but his name repeatedly surfaced in jury selection as prosecutors questioned potential jurors as to whether they had any connection to the well-known segregationist. Day after day during the trials, his name appeared, dutifully reported by the press. Prosecutors never *directly* implicated Carter but emphasized in their examination of the two Klansman testifying for the state that Carter personally appointed all members of his Klan.

From the beginning, Birmingham detectives never doubted that Carter had instigated the assault. But only Mabry and Pritchett had direct links with Carter, and neither was ever willing to betray him. During the trials, he helped raise funds for the defendants but kept a low profile, publicly insisting that he not been involved. According to an FBI informant, however, he told several friends that he supported the "warning" to local Blacks.

One person who knew Carter well had no doubts about his role in the affair. Jack Shows, chief of detectives in Montgomery, had entered the police force in 1948 and quickly worked his way up through the ranks, propelled by a keen intelligence and what one reporter called his "extraordinary ability to play departmental politics." Amiable—the quintessential good ole boy—he also established strong connections with Montgomery's modest Black and white underworld. From pool halls to houses of prostitution on Pollard and Columbus streets in Montgomery, he could be seen amiably greeting prostitutes, bookies, and small-time crooks. Even after he had helped to put some of them away, he often drove to Kilby Prison in Montgomery to bring fresh sandwiches and cigarettes for a visit and gossip. Once released, many of the ex-cons became his sources in the years that followed.

In much the same way, Shows maintained contacts with KKK members and often enjoyed fresh seafood at the Seven Seas Restaurant, a favorite hangout of leading Klansmen, including Asa Carter when he was in town.[437] When Shows was asked if Carter could have been uninvolved in the Arone mutilation, there was a long pause and rumbling laughter. "You're kidding, right?" Carter "was smart, I'll give him that," said Shows. "When bad things happened, he always seemed to find a way to stay out of the line of fire." But listen, he said, Mabry and those other followers of Carter "didn't unzip to take a leak without checking with Ace."[438]

Even if his close followers refused to implicate him, anyone following the highly publicized trial would have assumed that Carter was involved in the crime. The case basically finished him as a respectable public defender of segregation and white supremacy. As many of the Citizens' Councils he had created repudiated him, his income dwindled. He still had enough supporters to campaign for Alabama lieutenant governor in the spring of 1958, running a series of advertisements in at least a half-dozen state newspapers and broadcasting two half-hour television "call-ins." But though he campaigned across the state, the news media essentially ignored him. On May 13, with more than a half million ballots cast for the five candidates, he came in last with a humiliating total of fewer than 36,000 votes.[439]

While Sam Engelhardt celebrated the loss and isolation of his bitter enemy, he had no illusions about the damage his former hire had done to the reputation of the state's mainline Citizens' Councils movement. Other factors were at work. Riven by class divisions between working-class members and the traditional corporate and small-town elites and Black Belt planters, the Citizens' Council of Alabama had begun a steady decline in membership that would continue through the rest of the decade. But Engelhardt wasn't mistaken when he sat for an interview in the mid-1960s with historian Neil McMillen. Carter's violent acts tainted the organization's reputation and the "respectable element" had gradually withdrawn its support, said Engelhardt. In his view, Asa Carter "killed the Council dead."[440]

INITIALLY TREATED FOR HIS injuries at the local Veterans Administration hospital, Judge Arone was soon on his own, half-crazed by recurring nightmares. "I'd wake up in my sleep crying and scared, and I'd see them robes standing around me just a-itchin' to cut me. Or sometimes I'd wake up all ashamed, and I'd see myself standing up there in front of all them jurors with my pants down."[441]

His injuries required expensive long-term hormone injections, but he had no medical insurance. As a World War II veteran, he tried to obtain his injections at the Birmingham VA hospital. Because the injuries were not "service-connected," the local VA hospital denied treatment. A white minister helped him apply for a small disability pension under the Social Security Disability Insurance program (SSDI), but the Birmingham Social Security office summarily rejected his application with a one-sentence explanation: He was not "totally and permanently disabled," and therefore he was physically able to obtain employment. In a plea mailed out by a local Black citizens committee, Arone plaintively wrote that "nothing worse could have happened to me, and I need the help of others. I do not like to talk about what this experience has done to me. No one can really know. Can you help me?"

In 1960, Birmingham minister C. Herbert Oliver led a group of Black citizens documenting police brutality and violence against African Americans in the city. After learning that the unemployed Arone had been denied VA and Social Security benefits and was unable to afford medical treatment, Oliver took up his cause. He learned that the Veterans' Administration had a program that gave a non-service pension to medically disabled former veterans whose income was less than $600 a year. Once again, the local Birmingham VA office dismissed Arone's application. Frustrated and angry, Oliver wrote to every member of the Alabama congressional delegation asking for help. Not one replied. Finally, through a friend, he contacted New York's moderate Republican Senator Kenneth Keating, who personally called John Gleason, administrator for the Veteran's Administration. Within two weeks, the VA granted Arone an $85 a month pension ($805, in 2023 dollars).[442]

After Alabama writer William Bradford Huie wrote about the case in *True: The Man's Magazine* and donated his $3,000 author's fee to the victimized man, Arone was able to move to a Dayton, Ohio, subsidized housing apartment where he supplemented his disability pension as a baby-sitter for working parents until his death in 1993.[443]

14

Down and Out: 1958–60

> *He was a very violent person as far as the way he would speak, a frightening person, very controlling. I think even as a child, I was always afraid around him. It just seemed like he was consumed with power. He controlled the room you were in, he controlled the conversation. He controlled your opinion.*
>
> —Jimmy Carter, Asa Carter's nephew[444]

At 3:30 a.m., November 12, 1958, a massive explosion awakened sleeping residents of Atlanta's Ansley Park neighborhood. Fifty sticks of dynamite had shattered the Hebrew Benevolent Congregation Temple, the city's largest Reform synagogue, causing more than $200,000 in damages ($1.9 million, in 2023 dollars).

Individuals who closely followed the news might have assumed that terrorists only struck the homes of civil rights leaders, activists, and Black churches. But a year before the Atlanta Temple Bombing, terrorists in the region had broadened their attacks to include Jews as well as African Americans. For the most part, news coverage seldom linked these events.[445]

In mid-October 1957, while forty women members of the Temple Sisterhood met in Charlotte's Temple Beth El, an unknown individual placed six sticks of dynamite with a twenty-foot fuse on the outside wall of the meeting room. The fuse sputtered out only inches from the detonating cap, sparing the group from a deadly explosion. In a reflection of the vulnerable position of Southern Jews during the civil rights era, Rabbi Melvin Helfgott pleaded with the Charlotte police chief to keep the press from reporting the investigation, fearful it would provoke other antisemitic terrorists. A month later, when an anonymous policeman told a *Charlotte Observer* reporter about the attempted bombing, Rabbi Helfgott dismissed the problem as a "minor thing that's been taken care of."[446]

Over the following year, attacks on Jewish institutions continued. In Gastonia, just twenty-two miles west of Charlotte, terrorists planted an even more destructive bomb, with thirty sticks of dynamite, against the wall of Temple Emanuel in February 1958. As in the Charlotte bombing attempt, Gastonia's Jews were spared by the incompetence of the attackers. In both cases, the bombers had wrapped the dynamite so tightly in a canvas overnight bag that the lack of oxygen extinguished the last few inches of the burning fuse, a mistake that convinced investigators that the same assailants had been involved in the two attacks.[447]

Other Jewish organizations were not so fortunate.

On March 16, almost simultaneous explosions severely damaged Miami's Temple Beth El and Nashville's Jewish Community Center. Another set of attacks took place the following month, only hours apart at the Jacksonville, Florida, Jewish Center and at Birmingham's largest synagogue. The Jacksonville center suffered extensive damage, but the fifty-four sticks of dynamite outside Birmingham's Temple Beth-El failed to explode when an unexpected rain shower extinguished the twenty-one foot fuse only seventeen inches from the blasting cap. Had the dynamite gone off, said an army explosives expert, it would have leveled the synagogue and shattered the exteriors of at least a dozen surrounding buildings.[448] Frustrated police across the South tried to coordinate their investigations after laboratory tests showed that the dynamite used in all attacks had come from the same source.

In mid-summer 1958, officials from the six Southern cities met in Miami to exchange information and to plead with the FBI to become involved in what was clearly a conspiracy of antisemitic terrorists operating across interstate lines. Traditionally, local police officials went out of their way to maintain good relations with J. Edgar Hoover and the FBI. But in a press conference following the gathering of police chiefs, Miami Police Chief Walter Headley bitterly complained that the Bureau had ignored the request to send Bureau investigators and coordinate the investigation."[449]

Perhaps because the Atlanta Temple Bombing came only a week after terrorists had destroyed the recently integrated Clinton, Tennessee, High

School, or perhaps because of the withering editorials of *Atlanta Constitution* editor Ralph McGill, the role of the national government dramatically shifted. President Dwight Eisenhower ordered an FBI team to join local state and police officials in Georgia and he called on Hoover to support local officials in investigating the crime.

Georgia's US Senator Herman Talmadge and a handful of hardcore segregationists argued that communists had set the bomb to discredit the "Southern cause," but most white and Black community leaders in Atlanta united in condemning the bombing and pointing the finger at white extremists. There was one discordant note. While Annie Moore expressed her sympathy for members of the Temple, she reminded readers of the *Miami News* of the Christmas Day 1951 bombing that had killed her father and mother, Harry T. and Harriette Moore. Despite the fact that Harry Moore was head of the Florida NAACP, or perhaps *because* he was head of the state's leading civil rights organization, no rewards were offered, no governor spoke, and no president ordered the FBI to investigate their deaths. Could the difference be, asked Moore, that "the Jew, while hated, is nevertheless white?"[450]

In fact, under pressure from the national press, the Truman administration ordered the FBI to undertake a quiet investigation of the death of her father and mother, but her bitterness was understandable. Even though the Bureau presented compelling evidence implicating four local individuals, the local district attorney refused to bring charges. And the daughter's larger complaint about the lack of interest in attacks on Black activists was well taken. An incomplete survey of newspapers in the region showed that there had been well over sixty anti-Black bombings and firebombings between January 1957 and the Temple bombing. The majority of regional newspapers ignored or gave only the briefest accounts of the individual incidents. When Birmingham's Fred Shuttlesworth pleaded with the FBI to investigate the widespread arson and bombing attacks, the Bureau did not respond to Shuttlesworth's letter to Director Hoover.

Meanwhile, the FBI's newly active role in investigating such violence against Jewish Southerners raised Asa Carter from what the Bureau called a "subject of interest" to the far more ominous description: "potential bomber."

The FBI had no direct information linking Carter to the bombings, but his close association with white supremacist and antisemite J. B. Stoner and other known (but unconvicted) bombers increased their suspicions. Interviewed within hours after the Atlanta synagogue's explosion, Chester Griffin, an Atlanta Klansman, told city detectives that he had overheard fellow Klansmen discuss plans for planting the explosives. According to Griffin, Stoner was to pick up the dynamite from KKK contacts in Anniston. The "two Bowling boys [brothers Richard and Robert] would plant the dynamite and one of Ace Carter's men from Birmingham would set the fuse to it."[451]

Less than forty-eight hours later, agents Charles Stanberry and Byron "Ron" McCall arrived unannounced at Carter's small three-bedroom home in the middle of a rundown Birmingham commercial strip.

Stanberry, born in the mountains of east Tennessee, had been in the Birmingham office for most of his career, while McCall had only recently transferred from his midwestern assignment to Alabama. Reluctantly, Carter admitted the two men. Although Stanberry had conducted several interviews with Carter over the previous two years, McCall took the lead. When he began by asking Carter his whereabouts on the night of the Atlanta bombing. Carter jumped to his feet. You "can't talk to me like this in my own home," he yelled. As the two men shouted over each other, Stanberry intervened and calmly told Carter to sit down. If he wished, said Stanberry, they would be glad to leave. (Stanberry later suggested that Carter's reaction may have been caused by Agent McCall's mid-western accent, since the fiery Alabamian had a "deep-seated antipathy towards Northerners.") While they talked for a few more moments, both men agreed that Carter was too angry to have a productive interview.

But two weeks later, he returned a follow-up call from Stanberry and agreed to come to the FBI's Birmingham office. That exchange also did not go smoothly. To Stanberry, Carter seemed "emotionally unstable, particularly in connection with any discussion of the segregation question. . . ." After an outburst, he would suddenly become perfectly calm. Stanberry found it difficult to know whether he was responding with genuine anger or pretending outrage.

While Carter warned that, should further harassment continue, he would "expose" agents in a forthcoming book, he did arrive carrying his appointments calendar, a list of his whereabouts and the names of alibi witnesses for the Atlanta synagogue bombing as well as other recent attacks. To the surprise of the agents, he also volunteered to take a polygraph test and allowed them to record his voice to compare it to the unidentified spokesman for the "Confederate Underground" who had called and warned Janice Rothschild, the wife of the Temple's rabbi, that her house would be destroyed. Mrs. Rothschild, an amateur actress with an ear for accents, later listened to the recording and firmly insisted that the mystery caller was not Carter.[452]

Stanberry and McCall concluded that Carter was probably not directly involved in the Atlanta bombing. They were less impressed by his insistence that he knew nothing about other individuals with whom he had close connections. In a memo to FBI headquarters, Stanberry recommended that, because of Carter's erratic behavior, his connection to known terrorists, and his tendency toward violence, he remain on the agency's list of prime suspects in racial and antisemitic bombings.[453]

THESE WERE ALREADY HARD times for Carter. Without an income after his Klan group disintegrated, he had also lost control of the North Alabama Citizens' Councils that paid him a salary. Just before Christmas 1958, when Carter was unable to pay the rent on his Birmingham house, his father purchased a seventy-acre tract in the small rural community of White Plains, north of the original family farm. In the weeks that followed, Ralph Carter divided his herd of 130 cows between the two farms in an attempt to help his son get back on his feet.

It soon became apparent that Asa Carter had little taste for planting hay and milking cows.[454] He leased a dry-cleaning business in Oxford, but operated it only a few months. Instead, he spent much of his time writing and broadcasting additional versions of his "Liberty Essays" on two low-power Calhoun County AM radio stations; this earned him a minimal income.

He also told his neighbors that he was writing radio scripts for "Life Line," a program financed by the Texas oil billionaire H. L. Hunt. "Life Line" ran on more than five hundred AM stations with an audience estimated at five million listeners. The central theme of the programs—the role of Communists in fomenting racial unrest and internal subversion—was certainly consistent with Carter's views. In other ways it reflected the growing paranoia of America's far right, promoting fear that, in the words of one Texas journalist, "the foe is everywhere, subversive and conspiratorial." While there is no direct evidence of his claim that he worked for Hunt, later events suggested that he did have connections with the Texas oil man during this period.[455]

Between 1959 and 1961, Carter alternated between rage and resignation at what he saw as ongoing persecution by the FBI. In the wake of the Atlanta Temple Bombing, President Eisenhower—not noted for his advocacy of civil rights—had urged Congress to adopt modest civil rights legislation. Under pressure from New York Senators Kenneth Keating and Jacob Javits, US Attorney General William Rogers agreed to add a provision to the administration's 1960 civil rights legislation that made it a federal crime to transport or possess any explosive material with an "intent to damage a building or property."[456]

Even before the passage of the measure, the FBI had begun to shadow bombing suspects, and their investigations repeatedly involved Carter. After each new explosion, FBI agents interviewed him and many of his neighbors in an attempt to verify his whereabouts at the time of the attacks. The FBI's Anniston-based agent, Clay Slate, periodically parked at the end of the road to Carter's rural home on Route 6 in White Plains and then followed him when he drove to work or shopping, a surveillance that outraged local supporters of Carter who saw it as another example of federal harassment.

If the Bureau was never able to link Carter directly to bombings that continued into the 1960s, Stanberry and Slate were positive that he was directly involved in a demonstration of Klan strength in the early spring of 1960. On the night of March 26, some fifty Klansmen spread across Calhoun County, burning more than one hundred crosses at major intersections, on remote dirt roads, and in full view of Anniston's Black community. One attacker firebombed a Black home with a homemade kerosene molotov cocktail. (The family managed to extinguish the blaze.)

An Anniston police informant described to Slate how Carter had worked closely with his follower Kenneth Adams in organizing the cross burnings. Although there was no evidence that Carter ordered him to undertake the firebombing, the suspected arsonist was an ex-member of Carter's Klan. While Carter remained in the background, Adams made no effort to conceal his role. He bluntly told a reporter that the burning crosses were meant "to serve notice the KKK is here."[457]

While Slate felt certain that Carter was involved in the cross burnings, he had to tread carefully. His Anniston city police informant warned him that Calhoun County Sheriff Roy Snead and Anniston Police Chief J. L. Peek worked directly with the Klan and gave them free rein to operate in the county. Quite apart from the fact that Peek was suspected of corrupt financial dealings, he repeatedly protected white extremists like Adams. In a statement to the Anniston newspaper, Peek promised to "work around the clock to bring the offenders to justice." However, according to Slate's police informant, Peek told his police officers to do "nothing whatsoever" about the cross burnings and other Klan activities unless they resulted in the deaths of individuals.[458]

If the local authorities gave Carter and his friends a pass, the FBI did not, at least when it came to attacks on Jews in Alabama. Twenty-four hours before the flurry of cross burnings, a young neo-Nazi attacked the dedication of a new education annex at the Gadsden, Alabama, Beth Israel synagogue thirty miles north of Carter's home. In the midst of the Friday night dedication ceremony, the assailant threw a firebomb through a window in the synagogue and then shot two members of the congregation as they ran outside. It took only hours to arrest Hubert Jackson, a sixteen-year-old well known at Gadsden High School for his diatribes against Jews and his praise of Adolf Hitler. (Five months later, out on bail, Jackson fired five shots at high school band members while they practiced. As he fled in his car, he lost control, crashed into a tree, and died.[459])

When witnesses mistakenly told police that there was a second person in the teenager's getaway car, the FBI immediately interrogated Carter about both the cross burnings and the Gadsden synagogue attack. Carter had an alibi for the Gadsden firebombing and insisted he was at home and asleep on the night of the cross burnings.[460]

After a blast ripped through a Black elementary school in Atlanta on December 12, an FBI informant claimed that one of Carter's former Klan members was involved. Agents showed up on Carter's doorstep the next evening, asking for proof of his whereabouts. A frustrated Carter pointed out that the blast had occurred in the middle of the night while he was asleep with his wife. Of course he had no alibi. [461]

As the FBI continued to follow Carter and periodically show up unannounced for interviews, he faced additional pressure after the Bureau suggested that the IRS look into his income tax returns. Carter had always operated on a cash basis, and the agency's audit pointed to a significant discrepancy between his living expenses and the limited income he had reported between 1955 and 1957. The IRS suspected that he had been pocketing money from Klan and Citizens' Council initiates without reporting it as income. But Carter had always avoided leaving a paper trail. While the IRS levied two liens against his property in 1959 and 1960, his attorney, R. B. Jones, negotiated a sharply reduced payment and avoided penalties.[462]

But all the pressure proved too much for Carter. When agents returned to his White Plains home in mid-January 1961, they found an empty house. The local Choccolocco post office reported that his father periodically picked up his mail but Carter had left no forwarding address. Since Carter had promised Slate that he would notify him of any change in his residence, the disappearance set off alarm bells. After being rebuffed by local residents who refused to answer questions, a regular informant passed on a rumor that Carter had taken a position at the Choc-O-Loc Bottling Company in Grand Prairie, Texas, just west of Dallas, where Frank Carter, one of his father's numerous brothers, had established a small and struggling soft-drink bottling company a few years earlier. Never able to break into the larger supermarkets, Carter's uncle Frank directly distributed his inexpensive chocolate drink to rural and small-town general stores west of the city. Despite his title of "delivery foreman," Carter was simply a salesman and driver.

The Birmingham FBI office, responsible for maintaining surveillance of Carter, passed off his file to the Dallas office, urging it to "put Carter under close observation, "since he was potentially violent and likely to be involved in racial affairs."[463]

By mid-summer, Choc-O-Loc teetered on the verge of bankruptcy, occasionally missing payrolls for the company's thirteen employees, including Carter. In late June a Dallas FBI agent had visited Carter's rental home in a working class neighborhood three miles from the small bottling plant. The three-bedroom house where the family lived looked unpainted and dilapidated. While the Dallas agent was unable to interview Carter, a gossipy next-door neighbor was more than willing to give background on the family. A week earlier she had seen a Southern Bell technician disconnect the Carters' telephone for nonpayment. Even though the previous tenant had left behind a working window air conditioner, the unit remained unused even on the hottest Texas days, apparently to save money. Tara, the Carters' thirteen-year-old daughter, was "sweet" and pleasant, but beyond a curt nod, Asa and his wife, India, refused to speak and kept to themselves—she never saw any visitors at the house. She found the Carters' three sons, Asa Jr. (ten), Ralph (eight), and Bedford (six), particularly offensive. They were "rowdy and difficult," loudly shouting "ugly words"—profanity and "nigger"—as they played in the back yard of their home.[464]

After missing two weekly paychecks, Carter took a position with the "National Write Your Congressman Club" that contracted with small businesses to furnish information on pending state and national legislation and underwrite lobbying at the state level. He was to be paid by commission. Neighbors reported that he left early each morning, apparently calling on local businesses from a list furnished by his employer.

Just three weeks after beginning his new job, the city of Dallas placed its police force on high alert as eighteen Black students prepared to integrate four Dallas elementary schools. Fearful that Carter might become involved in anti-integration violence, the Dallas FBI office placed him under twenty-four-hour surveillance. Just before 7 a.m. on the morning of September 7, an agent followed Carter, accompanied by his wife, India, as they drove eighteen miles to the William Travis Elementary School, one of the four schools that had integrated without incident the previous day. When Carter got out of the car carrying a briefcase and walked around the perimeter of the school, the agent radioed the Dallas police dispatcher. As Carter drove away, two detectives in an unmarked police car turned on their siren. When he accelerated, rather than stopping, they forced his car to the side of the road and placed him under arrest, leaving India to drive back home.

They found nothing in his briefcase except materials from his employer, but he refused to explain the purpose of his visit to the school. Over the next sixteen hours, he talked with two Dallas detectives who described him as emotional and "unhinged." Much of what he told them reflected his tendency to treat the truth with disdain. At one point he bragged that he been a middle-weight boxing champion in the Pacific fleet in World War II before attending and graduating from the University of Colorado in 1949. He also told the two men that his younger brother, Larry, was a star player on the Auburn football team. None of this was true.

Even more frustrating to the investigators were his statements that contradicted the FBI report that had been passed on from the Alabama office. Was he still in communication with the notorious racist and antisemite John Kasper? Carter insisted he had never had *any* connection with Kasper although he "may" have met him when he gave a speech in Clinton, Tennessee. What about his Klan affiliations? He eventually acknowledged that he had "spoken" to a few Klan groups but had never joined the organization. After the "trouble" when gunfire broke out at a Klan meeting where he was a guest speaker in 1957, he had "lost everything he had and his wife had become emotionally upset." He insisted he had given up any involvement in political or racial matters.[465]

Unable to find evidence that would allow Carter's continued detention, the Dallas police released him just after midnight with a warning that he would remain under surveillance. Ten days later, he rented the largest U-Haul trailer that could be towed behind his 1957 Chrysler and returned to the Alabama farm he had left months before. Carter's father made a few repairs to the old house on the property and his children enrolled in the local White Plains elementary and middle school.

Only three years has passed since Carter was a national celebrity, featured in the regional press and interviewed by national reporters. When Larry Carter came home from his Auburn studies over the Christmas holidays that year, he found his older brother depressed and withdrawn. "I had never seen him like that," said Larry. He just seemed "beat down."[466]

After the family's return to White Plains, they spent more time with Carter's brother, Doug, his sister-in-law, and his nephew and niece Jimmy and Kaye, who lived in nearby Oxford. Over the next three years, the two youngsters regularly visited their cousins on the White Plains farm. Kaye looked forward to time with her older cousin, Tara, despite the prospect of the long walk down the overgrown path to the outhouse (there was no indoor toilet), particularly after one visit when a king snake slithered across the floor as she closed the door. "I would hold it till I had to go. And then I'd say, don't take me, don't take me to that place."

Kaye and her brother did remember happy times. "Aunt Thelma [as India was called by family] and Uncle Asa used to come over to the house," said Kaye. Thelma/India would get out her guitar, and Kaye's mother and father would join Carter as they sang Gospel hymns and "old time" Southern music until late into the night. When her Uncle Asa was in a good mood, he was always joking and "a lot of fun to be around." At times, agreed Jimmy, "[Uncle Asa] could be a jovial person. He wasn't always dark and brooding."

Still, an overshadowing tension overrode such moments and permeated Carter's home. Every subject was secretive, said Jimmy. Asa, India and all the children lived in a constant state of paranoia in which no one outside the immediate family was to be trusted, and peace came only when everyone deferred to Carter as head of the house. "I think it was the most dysfunctional family you can have," said Jimmy. The "domineering way that he kept control" was even more destructive than his racism. To Carter's nephew, the house itself reflected those tensions. Despite the fact that there were no curtains, in memory it seemed dark and "spartan," without pictures on the walls or decorative objects anywhere, the few surfaces broken only by books and right-wing pamphlets.

And there was always the fear of what might come next, particularly when Carter began drinking. Even as a ten- or eleven-year-old, said Jimmy, "I was very frightened. . . . It just seemed he was consumed with power" and whether he was pleasant or angry, "he controlled the room . . . he controlled the conversation . . . he controlled your opinions."

"I was always intimidated by him," agreed Kaye. "He ruled the house with an iron fist." And nothing unnerved her more than one visit. From their marriage on, Carter had insisted that India leave her hair uncut. As it reached below her waist, she began wearing it in a time-consuming bun. For years, she had tried to persuade her husband to let her have her hair cut. One evening when Kaye was visiting and India complained about the time it took to deal with her hair, Carter walked into the kitchen, came back with a pair of shears, and grimly hacked off her hair just above her shoulders.

Perhaps because he was gay, closeted, and repressed in his teenage years, Carter's nephew Jimmy remained an outsider, more an observer than a participant in his visits. Even as Carter's behavior horrified him, he didn't see his uncle as some kind of "monster." For all his faults, said Jimmy, "I think he loved his children." He saw himself as protecting his family by creating a world that allowed them to escape the contamination of their racial heritage and culture by outside forces. Somehow, in Carter's mind, said his nephew, he saw these as the ultimate "Christian virtues."

But that protection and support extended only insofar as those around him faithfully embraced his views. Jimmy knew from conversations with grandmother Hermione that she was uneasy about Carter's extremist politics. His mother, Helen, definitely did not share the strong racist views of her husband, Doug, and her brother-in-law, Asa. But Hermione and Helen were Southern women of a time and a culture when it was assumed they would defer to their husbands, particularly on any subject of importance.

India's sister, Claudia Walker, had an even stronger reaction to Carter. Married to an abusive alcoholic who repeatedly beat her, Claudia remained with him until her children were grown, then struck out on her own. Deeply religious, she explained that she inherited her father's views that "colored people" were brothers and sisters, "children of God." She also found Carter's views on Jews offensive. "He hated the Jews and the Jews is God's chosen people," she said with exasperation. Worse, he demanded that we "hate the ones he hated."

When Claudia timidly expressed her views, Carter accused her of being a communist. She wasn't sure what a communist was, she said, but she knew it was bad. On the last visit Claudia ever made to Asa and India's house, she said she had just returned from having a permanent that turned out a little too "frizzy." When she walked into the house Carter looked up. "Oh, here comes the little nigger," he said. What are trying to do,"get just like the niggers? You ought to be ashamed of yourself."

It was the last time she ever spoke to her brother-in-law.

She wanted to believe that India did not share Asa's darkest views, and she was heartbroken that her sister "married somebody that had so much hatred in his heart." But to Asa's younger brother, Larry, whether India secretly agreed or disagreed was irrelevant. "She became a nonentity, just an extension of Bud's [Asa's] authority."[467]

That was certainly the way it appeared on the surface. In reality, India shared Carter's views and served as an important sounding board for his ideas. After her husband's death, she wrote to one of his closest friends, and the three letters that survive show a lively intelligence, excellent writing skills, and a shrewd, tough-minded business sense.[468]

IN THE MONTHS THAT followed the family's return to Alabama, Anniston FBI agent Clay Slate—who monitored Carter—saw no evidence that he was involved in local political activities. In the absence of such political extremism, Slate wrote a memo suggesting that the Bureau drop Carter from regular monitoring.[469]

15

The Resurrection of Asa Carter

Today I have stood, where once Jefferson Davis stood, and took an oath to my people . . . . [F]rom this Cradle of the Confederacy, this very Heart of the Great Anglo-Saxon Southland . . . we sound the drum for freedom. In the name of the greatest people that have ever trod this earth, I draw the line in the dust and toss the gauntlet before the feet of tyranny . . . and I say . . . segregation now . . . segregation tomorrow . . . segregation forever.

—George Wallace, January 14, 1963[470]

By 1961, Carter had reached the lowest point of his adult life. His anti-segregation activities in the mid-1950s made him a well-known figure in Alabama and throughout the Deep South. But his leadership of the men who castrated Judge Edward Arone in 1957 made him a pariah in Alabama politics. Still, as it turned out, Carter was not too toxic for a rising Alabama politician named George Wallace.

In his early years as a state legislator and circuit court judge, Wallace had a reputation in Alabama as a "Folsom man," a follower of the state's two-time governor "Big Jim" Folsom, probably the most liberal politician ever to hold statewide office in Alabama. After Wallace decided to run for governor in 1958, he parted company with Folsom but still positioned himself as a candidate for the "little man" and, by the standards of the time, a racial moderate.

As the campaign began, the most knowledgeable observers of state politics saw Wallace and south Alabama businessman Jimmy Faulkner as the leading candidates. But Faulkner soon faded, replaced by the state's youthful attorney general, John Patterson, an opponent who proved far more formidable. In 1954, Patterson's father, Albert, had won the Democratic Party's nomination to become the state's attorney general after promising to destroy the loose coalition of gangsters who had turned Phenix City, Alabama, into an open city for prostitutes, gamblers, loan sharks, and bootleggers, all catering to soldiers at the US Army's sprawling Fort Benning, just across the Chattahoochee River in Columbus, Georgia. But a week after the elder Patterson won the June 1954 primary, a professional hit man walked up to him as he left his law office, shoved a gun in his mouth, and fired three times. Riding a wave of sympathy, the son, John, captured support from the state's Democratic leaders and was appointed to replace his father on the November general election ballot.

After Patterson's election as attorney general, Allied Artists produced a popular film, *The Phenix City Story,* that critics compared to *On the Waterfront* and *All the King's Men.* Character actor Richard Riley portrayed John Patterson as he courageously confronted the mobsters who had assassinated his father. While George Wallace's television ads showed him standing awkwardly behind a podium and reading a series of talking points, Patterson hired a major advertising firm to produce dramatic campaign ad spots, with swelling background music and vignettes that seamlessly blended voice-over recollections by the candidate ("Whenever I take a law book off of my shelf, I get soot on my hands from where the gangsters tried to burn me and my daddy out. . . .") and excerpts from the dramatic if grossly inaccurate film that depicted the son facing down gangsters at great risk to his own life.[471]

As the 1958 campaign for the governorship began, Patterson made white supremacy the core of his message. As attorney general, he had tried to use an obscure and seldom-enforced law to obtain the membership rolls of the state's NAACP. In several speeches, he boasted that the NAACP, so hated by whites, would collapse after the state exposed the names of the state's Black members. While the US Supreme Court ultimately overturned Patterson's order, his continued litigation campaign against the NAACP and his attacks on Black voting rights established his ruthlessness in the war against outside agitators and home-grown integrationists. He also worked closely with Robert Shelton, head of the state's largest Ku Klux Klan, and promised his followers that, if the federal courts ordered the integration of a single school in Alabama he would "close the state's schools rather than allow them to admit one Negro student."[472]

Wallace was no slouch in defending segregation as "best for both races" and boasted of his resistance to federal intervention into Alabama's voter laws. But in his 1958 campaign he distinguished his views from Patterson. Before a large crowd of supporters, he assured them he would approach racial issues "from a background of Christian faith based on love and understanding." No problem is "ever solved by violence, hatred, malice and ill-will.[473] Instead his platform, like that of his old mentor Jim Folsom, promised increased appropriations for schools ("colored and white"), farm-to-market highways, and higher state pensions, as well as revisions in the tax code that would reduce the burden on working-class people.

As the campaign drew to a close, Wallace sharpened his attacks on the attorney general's embrace of the Klan and warned that a Patterson administration would give the green light to the "bedsheet crowd." "Patterson chatters about the gangster ghosts of Phenix City," Wallace told a crowd of Montgomery supporters, even while he "is rolling with the new wave of the Klan and its terrible tradition of lawlessness." In one of his few television ads, Wallace stiffly stood before a gray backdrop and talked about his record as a circuit court judge. "I want to tell the good people of this state, as a judge of the Third Judicial Circuit, if I didn't have what it takes to treat a man fairly, regardless of his color, then I don't have what it takes to be the governor of your great state."[474]

Patterson won decisively. In 1958, there was no place for a half-hearted white moderate Alabama politician. To recycle the oft-quoted phrase of Texas populist Jim Hightower, there was nothing in the middle of an Alabama highway in the mid-1950s but yellow stripes and road-kill possums. Patterson had no illusions about the primary reason for his victory over Wallace: "I beat him because he was considered soft on the race question at the time." Wallace too had learned his lesson, a political education he described in more colorful language to three friends on the night he lost. "John Patterson outniggered me," he said, "and I'm never going to be outniggered again."[475]

Well before he officially announced his candidacy in the 1962 governor's race, Wallace laid the groundwork for his second campaign. It would be based squarely on the issue that guaranteed Patterson's decisive win. "Vote right—vote white—vote for the fighting judge," became the campaign slogan. When *Florence Times* editor Louis Eckl confronted Wallace over his exploitation of race, he shrugged. "I started off talking about schools and highways and prisons and taxes and I couldn't make them listen," he told Eckl. "Then I began talking about niggers—and they stomped the floor."

FOR THE CANDIDATE, IT was politics, but Asa Carter convinced himself that George Wallace could turn the tide against integration by uniting white Southerners in an uncompromising campaign of resistance.

The two had met on several occasions during the 1950s; Wallace had even joined Carter on the platform at a meeting of one of the Citizen's Council chapters in 1957. As the 1958 campaign got underway in January, Carter attended a Wallace rally held at the Calhoun County Courthouse square. With a blustery light rain and cold temperatures, fewer than two dozen locals gathered under store awnings to hear Wallace as he stood under an umbrella on the courthouse steps. Perhaps because of the weather, perhaps because Wallace was always at his best before an enthusiastic crowd, several of the listeners soon wandered away. Carter's brother, Doug, had attended and thought it was a "pretty lackluster" performance. Afterwards Wallace walked over to Asa Carter, shook his hand, and asked, "how you are gettin' along?" Carter handed him a folder, recalled Doug, saying: "I've written something for you and there's a phone number on there. When you get time, read it. If you don't like it, throw it away. If you like it, call me."[476]

Within hours after reading the material, Wallace summoned four of his closest advisers—Glen Curlee, Oscar Harper, Ray Andrews, and Seymore Trammell, for a late-night meeting in nearby Gadsden.

Curlee, long-time prosecutor for Alabama's Nineteenth Judicial District, had been one of Wallace's closest friends since their first days as law students at the University of Alabama. Curlee's classmates, who remembered him for his less than stellar law school record (straight C's and C-'s), rumpled suits, and ever-present drug store cigars, seemed amused by his fanatical loyalty to Wallace. He was constantly telling anyone who would listen that the slight, wiry country boy from Clio, Alabama, was destined to be governor of the state.

Montgomery businessman Oscar Harper built his small financial empire on no-bid state contracts, steered in his direction by politicians who welcomed his generous political contributions. He had supported John Patterson in 1958, but the state constitution barred an incumbent governor from running for a second consecutive term. In 1962, he hitched his wagon to Wallace.

Ray Andrews officially worked as a state purchasing agent, but he spent most of his time as a political operative. Watching Carter in action in the mid-1950s, he admired his ability to fire up audiences and coin memorable political phrases. He also believed Carter's ties to the declining but still critical Klan membership could be an asset in a close race.

The fourth member of the group, former south Alabama prosecutor Seymore Trammell, would ultimately become Wallace's closest aide. He never questioned Carter's skills as a rabble-rouser, but he hesitated. He reminded Wallace and the other three men that even though prosecutors had not indicted Carter in the 1957 assault on Judge Edward Arone, the press had highlighted Carter's leadership of the small Klan group that carried out the mutilation. Whatever Carter's talents as a writer and his valuable links to Alabama Klan groups, a public appointment to the candidate's entourage would be, he said with some understatement, "a little awkward." "I could

Seymore Trammell, right, confers with State House Speaker (and future governor) Albert Brewer, 1963.

already see the headline," said Trammell: "George Wallace Hires Castrator as Speech Writer!"

But Harper assured Wallace that Carter would remain in the shadows, and he agreed to hire him as an employee with no duties except that of speechwriter and advisor. Prying newspaper reporters could pore through the state records as much as they liked. Carter's name would never appear.[477]

The following morning, the phone rang, remembered Doug Carter, and his brother picked up the receiver to hear the unmistakable voice of George Wallace. "When can you pack your bag?" he asked. "[I like your speech suggestions and I] want you to write more of it."[478]

As the campaign began, Carter proved his usefulness. Wallace had only one enemy in 1962: "Washington." The candidate himself had proved no slouch when it came to coining invective description of the federal government, particularly federal judges he memorably described as "integratin', scallawaggin', carpetbaggin' liars!" But the former Klansman contributed some of Wallace's most angry lines of political defiance.

On the campaign trail, Wallace soon whipped audiences to a frenzy, with his attacks on the "lousy, federal court system, bent on destroying our schools, our government, our unions, our very way of life." Journalists covering the campaign began comparing Wallace's hard-hitting speeches with his performance in 1958, an improvement that his closest aides and friends attributed to their new speechwriter. "I could always tell when George was giving a speech Ace had written," said Oscar Harper. "Listeners were on their feet rather than sitting on their hands."[479]

George Wallace easily defeated seven opponents during the 1962 Democratic primary, a victory tantamount to election in one-party Alabama.

FOR SOMEONE TOTALLY DOWN and out, the job proved remarkably lucrative for Carter. Harper paid him $12,000 a year plus a generous car allowance and picked up the bill for rooms in Montgomery at the Jefferson Davis, Governor's House, or Diplomat hotels, where Carter variously stayed during the week. The package totaled well over $115,000 per year in today's dollars (plus expenses), for what was a part-time job with few daily responsibilities. With his new salary and $25,000 he made from publishing the 1963 official inauguration book, he was able to secure a low-interest loan from the Farm Security Administration, purchase the White Plains farm where he had been living, and completely renovate its rundown farmhouse.[480]

The Wallace victory also proved to be a good investment for Harper. Within weeks, his firm received dozens of no-bid contracts from the new administration.

In late August of that summer, as Wallace aides had begun preparation for the incoming new governor's administration, Trammell read in the *Montgomery Advertiser* that Carter would be the headline speaker for the "National Convention of the States Rights Association" meeting in Montgomery the following month.[481]

He was not pleased.

Despite its relatively innocuous name, the National States Rights Party—founded by chiropractor Edward Fields—could only be described as extremist. As a fourteen-year-old high school student from an upper-middle class Atlanta family, Fields had joined the neo-fascist Columbian order in 1946. Through the Columbians, he met and was inspired by many of the major post-war antisemitic activists. Strikingly handsome and always immaculately turned out in tailored suit and tie, Fields struck a reporter as well spoken, "the kind of guy you'd meet at the local Kiwanis." The US Navy had been less impressed. When Fields attempted to enlist after the outbreak of the Korean War, a shaken Navy psychiatrist described him as paranoid and dangerous, "one step away from being totally insane." Fields was rejected for service. After first enrolling in then dropping out of an Atlanta night law school, he finally graduated from a small chiropractic college, an achievement that allowed him to refer to himself as "Dr. Fields" even though he seldom practiced his profession. Instead he threw himself into promoting American-style fascism.

In the summer of 1958, Fields and his fellow Atlantan J. B. Stoner brought together more than one hundred "delegates" from far-right splinter groups across the nation to officially form the National States Rights Party (NSRP). While the original organizers dreamed of a future American version of Nazi Germany, they were practical enough to avoid openly embracing fascism in the organization's founding document. Instead, their call to arms focused on the "task of saving America and the White Race and the preservation of the pure blood of our forefathers. . . . "We will not allow the blood of our people to be polluted with that of Black, yellow, or mongrel peoples."[482]

Organizers hailed the September meeting as the largest gathering of the NSRP in its history, claiming that nearly fifteen hundred delegates from twenty-seven states assembled in Montgomery's City Auditorium. The FBI report on the meeting estimated the crowd at less than five hundred.

As the rally began, Carter led a delegation of speakers up the steps to a stage flanked by large banners: "Our Leader, Jesus Christ," a Confederate battle flag, an American flag, and, most prominently, the emblem of the National States Rights Party: a thunderbolt, derived from Nazi Germany's dreaded Schutzstaffel (SS). Several of the nation's leading antisemitic neo-fascists joined Carter on the platform, including Robert DePugh, Willis Carto, Edward Fields, John Crommelin, and J. B. Stoner.

Only months earlier, DePugh, a wealthy Missouri manufacturer of patent medicines for dogs, had organized the "Minutemen," a violent paramilitary organization of secret groups that stockpiled weapons (including machine guns and anti-tank bazookas) while they trained in preparation for a counter-revolution against America's complete takeover by Jews and Communists. We are "not radicals," DePugh had insisted, but we are preparing and training an "armed, dedicated and patriotic population," for the "time will come when we will be forced to stand and fight."[483]

Willis Carto, an admirer of Hitler, had just begun his rise to prominence as a far-right activist and early Holocaust denier. In his newly created magazine, Liberty Essays, Carto emphasized the role of communists in fomenting racial discord, but under the pseudonym "E. L. Anderson" he published the antisemitic magazine *Right,* which promoted "Aryan" racial supremacy by seeking to unite former Nazis, fascists, and newly aroused white Southern segregationists.[484]

Before the cheering crowd, one speaker after another rose to sound the alarm against the threat of an alliance between "international Jewry," Communists, and left-wing politicians who controlled the American government.

Fields: Look at the leadership of the "pinko" and communist organizations seeking to mongrelize America. "They're all Jew names."

Admiral Crommelin, Carter's long-time supporter: "The greatest challenge facing America" is to help whites understand the "origin, nature, purposes and aims of the Communist-Jewish conspiracy now bent on the destruction of the White race and White Christian civilization through economic strangulation, fratricidal wars, mongrelization and political slavery."

While Carto agreed that communism posed a major threat to the United States, he briefly referred to the Jewish threat and then warned that all of the western world faced a broader threat from the "expanding colored world." Americans were particularly vulnerable to an influx of aliens from Mexico and Central America, he said, and their growing numbers would soon fundamentally alter the racial composition of the United States and threaten its identity as a "white Christian nation."

Carter, the last speaker on the program, introduced himself as "Mr. White Supremacy." Perhaps remembering he had lost his lucrative radio job when he suggested that Jews were behind the integration crisis, Carter was the only speaker who avoided explicitly antisemitic remarks, making only a passing reference to Supreme Court Justice Felix Frankfurter ("an Austrian Jew"). Instead, he relied upon traditional themes of Southern white supremacy as he railed against Black rapists and defended "Anglo-Saxons" as the only group capable of self-government. "No negro has the right to vote," he shouted to his audience which responded with the night's only standing ovation.[485]

The one person on the speaker's stand who remained silent was the most sinister of all, J. B. Stoner, co-founder of the NSRP. FBI and law enforcement officials knew him as the mastermind behind at least a half dozen bombings directed against Black political activists. A victim of childhood polio, Stoner had a pronounced limp that led his critics to compare him to Joseph Goebbels, the club-footed Nazi minister of propaganda. Stoner embraced the comparison since he worshipped Goebbels. Like others at the rally, Stoner saw the threat of Blacks ("only a half step away from apes") as a side-show to the real threat: the Jews. In an earlier interview with reporters, he had dismissed Adolf Hitler as "too moderate." When his anti-Jewish party came to power, Stoner boasted, they would execute every Jew in America with gas chambers, electric chairs, firing squads, "or whatever seems appropriate."[486])

For Wallace's chief of staff, Seymore Trammell, Carter's appearance could have been worse. Willis Carto's *Right* and the NSRP's *The Thunderbolt* included extensive remarks from the evening, but of the mainstream media, only the Montgomery newspapers gave accounts of the meeting. The *Montgomery Advertiser* story, buried on the obituary page, briefly summarized the speakers' anti-communist emphasis. The afternoon *Alabama Journal*'s nine-paragraph article did little more than list the speakers and, like the *Advertiser*, highlighted the anti-communist remarks. Neither mentioned the antisemitic speeches.

In spite of this limited news coverage, Carter's return to the public eye raised the possibility that an enterprising reporter might begin to probe his connections to the incoming Wallace administration. Trammell summoned Carter to a private meeting and made it clear that his role as Wallace speechwriter and adviser was in jeopardy unless he agreed to remain out of the spotlight. Well aware of his financial dependence on Wallace, Carter promised he would avoid future public appearances. And he did remain in the background during the weeks that followed. All seemed forgotten in the wake of his success with Wallace's inauguration speech in January 1963. Trammell later said Carter had been right in bragging about the impact the speech would have: "There must have been two or three hundred news stories" about the governor.

Trammell did not exaggerate. While not every US newspaper headlined Wallace's speech, there were 523 news stories about it from Maine to California. In retrospect, what seems surprising is how little is remembered of Wallace's 1963 words beyond his futile promise of "segregation forever." Ignored at the time, and now forgotten, are the themes that Carter wove into Wallace's remarks, ideas he had developed during twenty years of immersion in America's scattered community of racist white Christian nationalists.

Carter's political rhetoric always rested on the familiar foundation of white Southern victimization, with its lurid accounts of the horrors of "Black rule" during the Reconstruction era, the rise of communist-inspired Black integrationists and their white liberal allies, and the vicious treatment of white Southerners by a bigoted "Yankee" press. At the same time, his reading of right-wing literature over the year drew him to a larger vision.

If he began, while in the Navy, with the writings of Gerald L. K. Smith, his reading broadened to include many of the standard far-right works of the era including Francis Parker Yockey's eccentric 1948 book *Imperium*, a "spiritual" ode to the values of the Third Reich that read like the jottings of a mental patient. According to a classmate during Carter's brief time as a student at the University of Colorado, he was even more impressed by Madison Grant's 1918 pseudoscientific anti-immigration book *The Passing of the Great Race: Or, The Racial Basis of European History*.[487]

Grant awakened Carter to the dangers posed by the rise of nonwhite people around the globe. White Christian western civilization stood at the crossroads. Close to home, the major increase in visas for Mexican farm workers (which often led to citizenship) and the migration of brown-skinned Puerto Ricans (who were American citizens) to the mainland in the 1950s, enraged Carter. "The immigration flood has ridden upon the propaganda of the Communists and has been spurred by the near-sighted sentimentalists and made political capital by the liberal politicians, almost as fervently as the suicidal theory of immigration," he warned in one of his radio broadcasts.[488]

Early in his political life, Carter had expressed his admiration for Adolf Hitler. According to his brother Doug, Carter found *Mein Kampf* "a powerful book" that "had a real impact on him."[489] But he did not broach the "Jewish" issue, having learned from his firing as a radio broadcaster that it was still dangerous to publicly focus upon the threat of the worldwide Jewish conspiracy. And he saw little political traction in the immigration issue and seldom featured it in his speeches.

But Black Americans were fair game. Although most white Americans outside the South gave at least lip service to opposing the disenfranchisement of Black voters, in Carter's inauguration speech for Wallace he sarcastically dismissed the "illegal Fourteenth Amendment" which had granted equal protection of the law to emancipated slaves. The forced imposition of this constitutional change set the stage for Reconstruction and, in more recent times, allowed the growth of "insipid bloc voters" (i.e., Black voters). To Carter, nothing was more irresponsible than the misguided belief that "everyone has voting rights." If anyone doubted the threat, he raised up the greatest nightmare for generations of white Southerners: the "communistic" plan for racial amalgamation which would replace a "race of honor" with a "mongrel unit" under the control of an all-powerful federal government.

Focused on their struggle to maintain white supremacy in Alabama, some of Wallace's listeners may have been bewildered by his discussion of the international context of the racial struggle. "AROUND THE WORLD," Carter had written in capital letters, the "international racism of the liberals seek to persecute the international white minority to the whim of the international colored majority . . . but the "Belgian survivors of the Congo cannot present their case to a war crimes commission," he wrote.

The "Belgian survivors of the Congo"?

For later generations, that paragraph seems irrelevant to the issues of the time. But those who followed the news in the early 1960s understood the reference. In 1960, when the Belgian government abruptly handed independence to one of its colonies, violence spread throughout the new Republic of Congo. The Belgian government's failure to develop an education system or a functioning Congolese civil service exacerbated long-time friction between various ethnic groups and factions that erupted into indiscriminate violence, including against white colonizers. The greatest victims of the following civil war proved to be the people of the Congo, in particular women as—not for the first time—rape became a widespread weapon of war. Marauding groups, many of them former members of the native colonial army, raped and killed thousands of native Congolese women.

The *New York Times* correspondent in Africa made some attempt to explain the complex origins of the violence, but newspapers in the Deep South focused on the white victims. As the New Orleans schools moved toward token integration in the midst of news reports from the Congo, Louisiana political kingpin Leander Perez brought the crowd at a New Orleans Citizens' Council rally to its feet as he compared the rape of white women in Africa with the imminent threat to white girls and women in America: "Now!" "Act now!" he shouted. "Don't wait until your daughter is raped by these Congolese burr-heads." More than forty newspapers in the South reported his speech.[490]

At the same time, the white South African government officials seized on the opportunity to deflect growing criticism of its increasingly rigid system of apartheid. Not only did it secretly transfer money to the Citizens' Council movement, a South African information officer visited the region and appeared in newspapers in Mississippi, Georgia, and Alabama, explaining the violence in the Congo as an inevitable product of "Communist agitation combined with a foolish effort to create a twentieth-century state out of a primitive people. . . . "[491]

Most astonishing was the coverage of the collapse of Belgian colonial rule in *Life* magazine. In a section filled with photographs of the fleeing Belgian colonial officials, *Life* included an article by South African author Stuart Cloete, one of the most published white African writers of the era and a racial paternalist seemingly unhinged by the collapse of colonial rule in the Belgian Congo. It would be disastrous, he wrote, to turn over colonial (white) rule to the "savage Blacks, worshipers of the fetish and the juju" who lived in filthy huts "under the thrall of the witch doctor and the chief." Worst of all, Cloete intimated, was the fate of the members of the heroic Belgian colonial civil service who had to suffer at the hands of these "savage and cannibalistic tribes. . . . What is the state of a man's mind who has seen his wife raped twenty times?"

For Southern defenders of white supremacy, the coverage by this "Northern, liberal magazine" was welcome news. The four largest Alabama newspapers (as well as sixteen others across the region) reprinted the *Life* article.[492]

Southern (and Northern) newspapers widely covered (if in discreet language) the assaults on white Belgian women but seldom mentioned that most of the victims were Black Congolese. Carter included this segment of Wallace's inaugural speech because he believed that recounting the atrocities would revive the sexual obsessions that had served as a major justification for the disenfranchisement of Black voters in the region and the lynching of thousands of Black men in the years after the Civil War.

This was the speech that launched George Wallace into the national spotlight. But an examination of more than forty-nine regional and national newspapers showed a consistent pattern in reporting the speech. All led with the "segregation forever" quotation. None reported the more explicitly racist and inflammatory sections.[493]

ALTHOUGH CARTER WAS ASSIGNED a small office in the basement of the capitol, well away from the governor's office, he usually drafted his speeches in his hotel room. Even daily communications were often routed through Ray Andrews, and when Wallace and Carter got together, Andrews arranged an evening meeting away from reporters, capitol visitors, and most state workers.[494]

Carter wrote or co-wrote a number of George Wallace's best-known speeches in the years that followed, including his remarks at the "Stand in the Schoolhouse Door." But his main contribution was to furnish barbed phrases and cutting lines that Wallace incorporated in his off-the-cuff remarks.[495] Several reporters in Alabama knew of Carter's role in writing Wallace's inaugural remarks, but they followed the unwritten journalistic understanding of the era: politicians wrote their own speeches and speechwriters did not exist, even when they were as toxic as Carter.

Meanwhile, J. Edgar Hoover soon learned of Carter's position in the new administration. It would have been risky to spy on Wallace, but closely monitoring Carter proved a way of collecting information on the newly elected governor. Always alert to the ways in which political intelligence could be useful leverage in navigating the shifting winds of politics, Hoover sent a memo to the Birmingham FBI office ordering agents to collect all information showing the connections between Wallace and Carter. Such reports, said Hoover, were to be copied directly to his desk.

If Hoover remained preoccupied with political intelligence, it was Carter's penchant for violence and extremism that most alarmed local FBI agents.[496] Agents knew that Carter's first act after Wallace's inauguration was to press for the release of the four men given twenty-year prison sentences for the castration of Judge Edward Arone. In Alabama prisoners received paroles only after serving at least half of their terms, making the four eligible to be considered for release after 1968. Despite the pleas of the prosecutor and the presiding judge in their trials, the Alabama Board of Pardons and Paroles soon released the men. As the board explained, Jesse Mabry, Carter's close friend and Klan associate, had an "excellent reputation" and he and the other men involved in the case "have demonstrated that they are good prospects for rehabilitation."[497]

More interesting to Hoover was a meeting Carter convened in Alabama two weeks after Wallace's inauguration with two prominent figures in the region's fight against integration, Robert "Bobby" Shelton of the United Klans of America and Edward Fields of the neo-fascist National States Rights Party, as well as a half-dozen of their lieutenants. The gathering was at the back of Montgomery's Chester's Restaurant, which was a favorite gathering place for the two groups and was owned by a member of the NSRP.

In the late 1950s, Shelton, an Air Force veteran and B. F. Goodrich tire salesman in Tuscaloosa, joined and quickly became a promising (and ambitious) member of the Alabama-based U.S. Klans, Knights of the Ku Klux Klan, Inc. (generally referred to as the United Klans of America, or the UKA). Only a year after taking over the UKA, Shelton managed to absorb the Georgia-based "Invisible Empire, United Klans, Knights of the Ku Klux Klan of America" into his organization. As head of the enlarged UKA, he would eventually recruit more than thirty thousand members with an even larger number of sympathizers.

Fields, head of the National States Rights Party, was also present with two of his aides, although the NSRP had begun to decline from its noisy but relatively small place among right-wing racist organizations. Divided by rival factions, its meetings had been reduced to paranoic ramblings by neo-Nazis and lengthy lectures on the Communist-Jewish conspiracy to destroy the health of the white race by removing the nutritional value of prepared foods, adding poisonous fluoridation to the water supply, and weakening the minds of whites through the promotion of mental health programs.[498]

While Carter remained in contact with NSRP leaders, he increasingly turned to the Klan groups that he knew best. Between October 1962 and April 1963, he convened more than twenty meetings with attendance as high as three hundred as he outlined elaborate plans for the creation of what he called an "anti-integration militia." Like his earlier Klan organizations, the new project reflected his grandiose ambitions and his infatuation with grand titles and semi-military organizations. Operating under his leadership, he explained, sub-commanders in north and south Alabama would create a telephone chain link using coded language to mobilize supporters in "mass demonstrations" against any move to integrate a public school, college, or university in Alabama.

His vague references to mass mobilization did not always satisfy advocates of more forceful action. In a Montgomery gathering of one hundred, mostly Klansmen from just north of the city, several members of the audience seemed skeptical that such demonstrations would accomplish anything. Carter replied that for legal reasons he could not advocate violence, but if someone wants to "put a .45 pistol on his hip," that would be his business." Kenneth Adams, Carter's passionate acolyte who had led one of the assaults on Freedom Riders two years earlier, was even more direct about the need to act decisively. "The way to end a desegregation attempt at a school is to kill off the relatives of the student one at a time . . . ," he told the crowd. Carter paused a moment before repeating his earlier comments. "He could not advocate violence," reported the FBI informant, "but if that is what he thought should be done, that was up to him."[499]

ONLY WEEKS AFTER WALLACE's inauguration, Carter persuaded the new governor to meet with a delegation of citizens on the Capitol steps to announce the formation of "Volunteers for Alabama and Wallace" (VAW). He instructed the Klansmen and NSRP members to "wear business suits, shirts and ties and give the impression of being businessmen." James L. Croft, who described himself as a "young businessman," read from a text prepared by Carter. Their group had no connections with other organizations; they were simply patriotic citizens who wanted to prevent their children from attending schools that would quickly become like the "integrated jungle of the Washington [D.C.] school system." Wallace thanked the men, but he promised only that "Alabamians will replace fear with courage" in their fight against integration.[500] Carter also tipped off Montgomery's Associated Press correspondent, who reported the gathering in newspapers across the state.

With a court order directing the University of Alabama to integrate in June, Wallace remained intent on keeping federal officials uncertain about how far he might go in resisting court orders for desegregation. But the last thing he wanted was an outbreak of violence that would discredit him nationally. "I told [Asa] that he could talk about it all he wanted, but the governor was not going to endorse such an organization," said Wallace aide Seymore Trammell. Though Carter nodded in apparent agreement, the exchange only reinforced Trammell's view that they had, in his words, "hired a loose cannon."[501]

While Carter's willingness to shut down the "Volunteers for Alabama and Wallace," temporarily reassured Trammell, it provoked a bitter response from Carter's former ally, John Crommelin. An informant for the Mobile FBI office obtained a copy of a letter Crommelin sent to supporters, accusing Carter of betraying the cause. Carter, claimed Crommelin, might very well be a Communist agent in view of his "constant attacks on rich people."[502]

In late April, five weeks before the scheduled integration of the University of Alabama, Attorney General Robert Kennedy and Assistant Attorney General for Civil Rights Burke Marshall visited Governor Wallace in an effort to obtain a firm promise that he would agree to a peaceful integration of the university. As the two reached the state Capitol, several dozen demonstrators mobilized by Carter greeted the two men with hand-lettered signs: "Kosher Team: Kennedy/Kastro/Kruschev [sic]," "Christians Wake Up!" "Mississippi Murderer," "No Kennedy Congo Here." Once inside the building, Kennedy turned to speak to two women employees who had smiled and welcomed him to Alabama. A grim-faced state trooper stepped between the women and Kennedy, placed his nightstick against the stomach of the attorney general of the United States, and shoved him backwards.

"It's like a foreign country here," an unnerved Kennedy said to Marshall as he left the frustrating and inconclusive meeting with Wallace.[503]

If his personal views were more radical than Wallace's, Carter dutifully followed the orders passed on to him by Trammell. When questioned off-the-record by one reporter about his not-so-secret meetings with Klan groups, Carter insisted that he was urging them to stay away from the Tuscaloosa campus and let the governor deal with the federal authorities, a claim that was supported by later events. Three days before US Deputy

Attorney General Nicholas Katzenbach faced off on June 11, 1963, with Wallace in the infamous "Stand in the Schoolhouse Door," Carter learned that six members of a renegade Klan group were on the way to Tuscaloosa with two carloads of weapons and ammunition. A friendly Klansman told Carter that the men were intent on violently resisting the admission of African Americans Vivian Malone and James Hood. Carter immediately called Charles ("C. B.") Stanberry, an FBI agent who had interviewed him several times. He was unaware that the FBI already knew about those plans from their star Klan informant, Gary Thomas Rowe. The Bureau had arranged for a reluctant state police unit to stop the Klansmen on the outskirts of Tuscaloosa and turn them over to the Tuscaloosa County sheriff's department. (Despite the existence of an illegal machine gun in their possession, the local sheriff freed the six men and returned their weapons.[504])

Carter was disappointed but not surprised when Wallace later removed the most inflammatory sections of the "Stand in the School House Door" speech, but he told friends that Wallace probably had made the right decision since his stand on "constitutional principles" gained him positive coverage from conservatives across the nation.

Through the summer and fall of 1963, Carter may have been frustrated by the need to remain in the background, but he reveled in his new role as adviser to a man he was convinced could gain enough national support to turn the tide against racial integration. Even after the September 15, 1963, bombing of Birmingham's 16th Street Baptist Church that left four Black girls dead and another critically injured, Carter seemed relaxed and confident as he met with Agent Stanberry. Despite the murders, which had placed Wallace on the defensive, Carter was poised and on-message as they chatted over lunch. He remained a strong segregationist, he told Stanberry, but was "more mature" now, and he expressed concern over the fallout from the bombing. It had been "damaging to both Governor Wallace's prestige and the overall cause of the segregation movement."

The bombers were probably Communists, Carter told Stanberry, but when the agent pushed back, he acknowledged that they "could be" renegade members of the National States Rights Party or some other extremist group.

While Carter insisted he had no connections with the NSRP, Stanberry knew from bureau informants that Carter had repeatedly visited the organization's Birmingham headquarters. Nor was he impressed when Carter blandly denied earlier Klan membership, a claim contradicted by documentary evidence and dozens of informers' reports from the 1950s.

Anniston's FBI agent Clay Slate disagreed with his fellow agent. While he acknowledged that Carter had remained in touch with radical white supremacists, he insisted that "Asa seems to have withdrawn" from his violent activities since he began working with Wallace.[505] Stanberry recommended that the Bureau remove Carter from its list of active bombing suspects, but—mindful of Hoover's interest—he added that Alabama agents would continue to monitor Carter's activities.[506]

16

His Master's Voice: 1964–68

"If Congress passes Lyndon Johnson's so-called 'Civil Rights' law you can forget about your job seniority. The government will tell your boss that, if he's got 100 Japanese-Lutherans working for him and there are 100 Chinese-Baptist unemployed, he's got to let some of the Japanese-Lutherans go so he can make room for some of the Chinese-Baptists."

— 1964 Wallace speech written by Asa Carter[507]

Encouraged by the thousands of letters of support George Wallace received from around the nation after the "Stand in the Schoolhouse Door," Asa Carter began arguing that the governor should enter several Democratic presidential primaries and run as an alternative conservative candidate against John F. Kennedy.

It was not the first time he had raised the issue of a presidential run. Shortly after Wallace's election, Carter joined Seymore Trammell at Montgomery's historic Greystone Hotel in an unpublicized meeting with Mississippi Governor Ross Barnett, Louisiana Judge Leander Perez, and James Gray, a wealthy Georgia media figure and chair of that state's Democratic Party. The agenda: promoting a presidential run by a white Southern candidate, either in the Democratic primaries or as a third-party candidate.[508]

"I'm your boy," Wallace had told the group, then, as usual, he hesitated. But five days after Kennedy's assassination on November 22, 1963, in Dallas, the nation's new president, Lyndon Johnson, spoke to a joint session of Congress: "No memorial oration or eulogy could more eloquently honor President Kennedy's memory than the earliest possible passage of the civil rights bill for which he fought so long," he told the still-stunned lawmakers.[509]

A week later, Wallace took to the road on a speaking tour that stretched from Boston to Tacoma, Washington, attacking the civil rights measure as a "fraud, a sham and a hoax" that would destroy individuals' property rights, impose racial quotas, and lead to the destruction of America's public schools.

While he furnished a number of Wallace's best lines,. Carter seemed to have a tin ear for appealing to whites outside the South. Just weeks before Kennedy's death, Carter and Wallace's legal adviser, John Kohn, jointly prepared a speech for the Alabama governor to deliver at Harvard University. The remarks Kohn prepared amounted to a somewhat dull defense of state sovereignty and the dangers of overreach by the federal government, without any mention of race.

Carter's contribution was a bit different. "When you speak of the Negro in the North," he wrote, "the image before your eye is the mulatto and he constitutes a very small percent of your population." But when we "speak of the Negro in the South, the image in our minds is that great residue of easy-going, happy, unambitious, incapable-of-much-learning African who constitutes 40 per cent of our population." Such people were quite different from the "highly educated" mulattos who attended Harvard. And to argue that the "Negro with whom we deal has the capacity of the white man is to argue that the mud and straw huts of Africa are equal to the cathedrals of France."[510]

Wallace, who *did* have a keen sense of his audience, struck through the sections Carter had written, briefly summarized Kohn's constitutional argument, and then began to disarm his audience with self-deprecating jokes and quick-witted but good-natured responses to hecklers. (Smiling: "You cut that out, fella, you made me lose my place.")

During the question and answer period, a young white man walked to the microphone. "How do you square what you say about civil rights with your police brutality?" he asked in a soft Southern accent.

"Oh, I know you," Wallace said, "you're Bob Zellner, and you are a renowned Alabamian. In fact, you have been in a number of jails in Alabama." When several students seemed to applaud Zellner, Harvard law professor Arthur Sutherland stepped to the microphone and scolded Zellner for asking a "Have you stopped beating your wife?" type of question.

One Georgia-born graduate student present at the speech ruefully recalled the reaction of Harvard students. "They didn't exactly follow the example of the atheist who attended the revival to scoff and stayed to pray," said Irwin Hyatt, but most seemed disarmed by the Alabama governor's repartee with the hecklers. Wallace received extended applause at the end of his remarks, and the president of Harvard's Young Democrats expressed pride at the students' response. "The overwhelming support of the Governor's right to talk is a glowing testimony to our university and the fact that our motto—*Veritas*—lives on."

William Bradford Huie, the Alabama journalist-novelist, was less impressed. He could understand how the rich supported Wallace's anti-government rantings; he could understand the fears of poor whites and working-class ethnics. "What I will never forget or forgive is the sight of the well-bred supposedly intelligent sons and daughter of Harvard University and Radcliffe College laughing and applauding the cleverness of George Wallace."[511]

While Carter was not alone in urging Wallace to run for president, he proved to be one of the most passionate supporters of the idea as the Alabama governor hesitated. But in early March 1964, the potential candidate flew to Madison, Wisconsin, to speak to students at one of the most liberal universities in the country.

That spring, I was frantically trying to finish my MA thesis at the University of Wisconsin, when I saw a group outside the student union waving signs, "We Shall Overcome" and "End Racism in Alabama." Inside the auditorium, a small group of students began singing freedom songs to greet the Alabama governor as he took the stage. By the time I entered the auditorium, there was standing room only. After his four-month speaking tour across the North, Wallace appeared at ease as he began by expressing gratitude for the chance to "see new beard styles." In the question and answer period after his brief remarks, many of the students, prepared for a vicious race-baiting demagogue, seemed uncertain over how to respond to a hillbilly humorist. I was not alone in my frustration at his skill at deflecting difficult questions and his willingness to lie to his audience with what seemed to be

earnest conviction. At one point, he insisted that all "qualified" Negroes in Alabama were able to vote without difficulty. Claims to the contrary were simply the administration's efforts to appeal to gullible voters. Disarmed by his "Southern charm," wrote the editor of the campus newspaper, his jokes had the audience in "perplexed convulsions."

Like Huie, I was not amused and apparently others shared my frustration. That night, unknown students had mixed a solution of red Kool-Aid and, in four-foot-high letters, spelled out "FUCK WALLACE" *on the frozen ice of Lake Mendota.*

Lloyd Herbstreith and his wife, Dolores, drove from their home in Oshkosh over a hundred miles on two-lane roads in a steady snowfall to hear Wallace speak. For months, they had traveled the state, drumming up support for a "Liberty Amendment" to the Constitution that would eliminate the power of the federal government to enact an income tax. His success in taming the unruly students and his skill at pitching the issue in "constitutional" rhetoric confirmed the Herbstreiths' belief that this conservative Southerner was the man who could save the nation. After Wallace agreed to meet them the next day, the Herbstreiths—leading members of Wisconsin's John Birch Society—urged Wallace to enter the Wisconsin Democratic Primary. The would arrange all the paperwork, and in the lead-up to the election they promised to mobilize Birchers and the thousands of angry and discontented voters disgusted by Lyndon Johnson's left-wing policies.

The governor's press secretary, Bill Jones, was convinced that the visit of these passionate supporters tipped the balance. Wallace agreed to run against Wisconsin's Democratic governor, John Reynolds, who—along with Democratic politicians in other Democratic primaries—had agreed to run as a stand-in candidate for the president. Encouraged by the response Wallace received on his first campaign trip in Wisconsin, he registered for primaries in Indiana and Maryland.

After Wallace had rejected the hard-line racist remarks Carter had written for the Harvard speech, the latter quickly adjusted, replacing his hardcore racist rhetoric with carefully coded language. And Wallace was the perfect voice for this new message. "If every politician is an actor," said novelist

Norman Mailer, "only a few are consummately talented. . . . Wallace is talented."[512] In time it would be difficult to disentangle Carter's rhetoric from Wallace as their relationship deepened.

Wallace's primary campaign itself proved to be an exercise in chaos and improvisation. The governor had no real campaign staff and few connections in the states where he had decided to run. The Herbstreiths kept their promise and formed the nucleus of his Wisconsin run.

Klan leader Robert Shelton had little use for Asa Carter, in part because he felt Carter had stolen members from his organization in the 1950s and in part because he seemed to believe that Carter's constant attacks on wealthy Southerners were motivated by "communistic tendencies." But the two white supremacists declared a truce and jointly set up an operation in Indiana, with an "office" in the back room of an Indianapolis service station owned by a sympathetic Klansman. Shelton's group, now the United Klans of America, had more than thirty thousand members, and even though the majority were in Alabama and the Deep South, he had strong connections to William Chaney, grand dragon of the Indiana Ku Klux Klan, the largest Klan group remaining in the North. While the John Birch Society reached out to middle-class Indiana voters, the Klan proved critical in mobilizing working-class members to vote for Wallace.[513]

In Maryland it was white activists of the Citizens' Councils and John Birch Society who formed the core of Wallace's support, setting up an organizational structure that mailed out pamphlets, arranged radio advertising, and scheduled rallies across the state.

Robert Shelton, undated.

The press as well as Democratic politicians initially dismissed the Wallace campaign as "hopeless" and even "nonsensical." Wisconsin Governor Reynolds publicly predicted that Wallace would draw less than 10 percent support. Privately, he told friends that Wallace would not receive half that amount in the Wisconsin Democratic primary. But on April 7, more than a third of the Democratic voters pulled the lever for Wallace. In the weeks that followed, 30 percent of Democratic primary voters in Indiana and nearly 50 percent in Maryland voted for the Alabama governor. (If it hadn't been for "the nigger bloc vote [in Baltimore]," Wallace told his aides "we'd have won it all.")[514]

The Barry Goldwater surge in the Republican Party soon overshadowed Wallace's 1964 foray into national politics, but Wallace's unexpected strength convinced Carter and other advisers that large numbers of white Americans were ripe for joining white Southern opposition to the growing civil rights movement. In Indiana he had met with hundreds of supporters, and they loved Wallace, said Carter. "Those folks were starved for the truth. . . . They could see the dragon in Washington breathing down their necks" and taking from them their "the most precious thing any of us own—freedom."[515]

Exhilarated by his access to power, Carter convinced himself that Wallace was not a typical political opportunist, but a true believer. While the white South and a large number of voters in Indiana and Wisconsin might be receptive to reshaping the nation into a true white Christian nation, it would take time for non-Southerners to take the next critical step. As Carter had concluded from his early studies of communist organizational models, it was important to carry on the struggle at two levels: publicly and underground. In the meantime, he had work to do.

But Carter's enthusiasm for Wallace made him blind to the governor's willingness to shift direction for political gain. Even during the famous "Stand in the Schoolhouse Door," Wallace had begun to back away from the hard-line racist language that had marked his 1963 inaugural address. Carter's version of Wallace's schoolhouse door speech was filled with apocalyptic warnings that integration would lead to all-out racial war in the South. And for a time during the days before the confrontation at Tuscaloosa Wallace seemed to embrace Carter's hard-line position, even suggesting at one point that, if US Assistant Attorney General Nicholas Katzenbach tried to place him under arrest, "I'm going to hit him." But cooler heads prevailed, and Wallace's legal adviser, John Kohn, reminded him of the possible consequences. Your political career will be ruined, said Kohn, and "the Kennedys will put you in jail with two hundred niggers." As at Harvard, Wallace struck much of Carter's extremist rhetoric and replaced it with Kohn's turgid appeal to the rights of the "sovereignty of the states" and the "usurpation of power by the Central Government."

During Wallace's brief 1964 presidential campaign, Carter contributed the usual warnings of communist infiltration and helped Wallace focus on cultural values that involved both race as well as pocketbook issues. The Alabama governor was not the first but he was clearly the most effective politician of his time in shaping coded language that avoided explicit racism while skillfully exploiting the prejudices of white Americans across the nation. Repeatedly he attacked the shiftless and undeserving poor—who white voters identified with inner-city Black Americans. As Carter wrote in one of Wallace's speeches, "I'm sick and tired of seeing hardworking Americans pay for welfare recipients who are too lazy to get out from in front of their television set and go to work!"

One Carter-penned speech delivered by Wallace in Milwaukee warned that Lyndon Johnson's civil rights law would establish quotas requiring the hiring of a specific number of "Chinese-Baptists" and "Japanese-Lutherans." It was not the most skillful instance of the Alabama governor's use of coded racist language, and it is fair to assume that members of the audience discerned that the hyphenates threatening their jobs were place-markers for the real enemies.[516]

Carter came even closer to Wallace in 1965 as Wallace faced the prospect of leaving the governorship because Alabama's 1901 state constitution prohibited its governors from succeeding themselves. When a small opposition group in the state senate blocked a repeal of the one-term limitation, Wallace hinted that he might get his wife to run in his place. The suggestion dumbfounded his friend Tom Johnson. Like many Wallace aides, Johnson admired Lurleen Wallace, but he found her the "most unlikely candidate imaginable." He told Wallace, "It is as difficult to picture her in politics as to envision [stage and movie star] Helen Hayes butchering a hog." Most of Wallace's advisers agreed. John Kohn and press secretary Bill Jones dismissed the idea. So did Finance Director Seymore Trammell—"I thought it was a harebrained scheme," he later admitted.[517]

Carter was one of a handful of Wallace advisers who urged him to follow his instincts. He persuaded Texas oilman H. L. Hunt to send Wallace a memo outlining how Texas governor James "Pa" Ferguson had gotten his wife, Miriam, to run successfully in his place in 1925, after he was impeached and barred from office.

At one meeting with Wallace and his advisers, Carter threw up his hands in frustration. "What political science books have y'all read?" he demanded. "She can win. If she doesn't, she can get a million dollars' worth of publicity and it'll help the governor nationally." Political aide William White was present at one of these heated sessions and was convinced that it was Carter's persuasive and relentless promotion of Lurleen Wallace that played a critical role in persuading her husband to put aside his misgivings. Wallace crony Oscar Harper agreed: "If anybody can be credited with talking George into running Lurleen for governor, it was Ace."[518]

In Lurleen's successful campaign to replace George, Carter wrote her standard stump speech, which concluded with a stilted recognition of her symbolic role: "I am grateful to be the instrument whereby you, the people of Alabama, have an opportunity to express yourself on the record compiled by the Wallace administration."

Lurleen Wallace, 1966.

When her husband then stepped up to the speaker's platform, Carter had his chance to furnish more biting rhetoric and to make clear Wallace's national ambitions. "I want to stay in public life so I can continue this campaign throughout the nation" to fight the "judicial dictatorship," the "liberals and beatniks and socialists" who want to create a "government bureaucracy run by folks a thousand miles away with beards and goatees." Just remember, he said, pointing to the Confederate Battle Flag, "Whenever you see the Confederate flag flying, you will see people who will fight for their country," and you won't find "college students taking up money for the Vietcong and giving blood to the Vietcong or burning draft cards."[519]

Political observers saw Lurleen Wallace as the clear frontrunner, but with nine male candidates opposing her, they expected a runoff. Instead she swept the field with 55 percent of the votes cast in the Democratic primary, a nomination that insured she would become Alabama's first woman governor.

Before Lurleen Wallace's untimely death of cancer in 1968, journalists often saw, but never reported, Carter's constant presence at her major campaign appearances. He became a devoted supporter, seeing in Lurleen Wallace the perfect Southern lady with a gentle personality, who was always publicly deferential to her husband. Carter seemed unaware that she knew about his violent background and remained uneasy about his presence in the campaign.

And when Carter wrote her January 1967 inaugural address, she rejected his first draft. "That's not the way I talk," she said. Even though the final version included several swipes at the federal courts and the "intrusive" national government, Carter dutifully followed her instructions, revising the text to reflect what she called her "special concerns" in caring for the sick, the elderly, and the handicapped and making certain that there was adequate funding for schools, hospitals, and community facilities. After an emotional visit to one of the state's wretched mental institutions during the campaign, she underlined her insistence that these facilities "must receive additional attention."[520]

Well before Lurleen Wallace took office, Carter began looking to 1968, encouraging George Wallace to consider running for president, not as a Democrat but as a third-party independent candidate. In 1967, as part of his plan to expand Wallace's national reputation (and to supplement his income) Carter wrote a two-hundred-page Wallace "autobiography," *Stand Up for America: The Story of George C. Wallace*. The Alabama governor and Carter agreed to split the royalties 50-50.[521]

Carter and Willis Carto were first acquainted when Carto came to Alabama in 1956 to support John Crommelin's unsuccessful challenge to incumbent Senator Lister Hill. Carter and Carto hit it off immediately, in part because of their shared (and private) antisemitic beliefs. Only twenty-nine, the World War II Purple Heart veteran Carto had begun his lifelong political activism in 1950, working for the notorious California racist, Aldrich Blake.[522] Five years later, never one to concern himself with ethical considerations, Carto secretly copied Blake's mailing list and established his own organization: Liberty Lobby. While his new organization initially attracted few members, he doggedly traveled across the country making connections with McCarthyites and other right-wing activists.

But Liberty Lobby grew quickly after the passage of the 1964 Civil Rights Act and even more so after it became an unofficial arm of Barry Goldwater's run for the presidency that year. As part of his pro-Goldwater campaign, Carto published *LBJ: A Political Biography*, suggesting among other crimes that Lyndon Johnson had arranged the murder of three of his critics. It sold fourteen million copies.

Between 1964 and 1965, Carto's conservative radio program ("This is Liberty Lobby") quickly grew to a broadcasting network of more than four hundred stations. As he became a popular figure within America's expanding far-right movement, the man who had once been seen as a crank suddenly became respectable in the eyes of conservative Republican politicians who called him to testify before congressional hearings more than a half-dozen times to support their claims that communists had successfully infiltrated American institutions.[523]

Wallace continued to discuss Carter's third-party scheme with several of his advisers. While he refused to commit himself, he authorized his speechwriter to assemble (discreetly) some of his strongest supporters. On the night of Lurleen Wallace's inauguration in January 1967, Carter and Dallas County Sheriff Jim Clark—notorious for his "Bloody Sunday" attack on civil rights activists at Selma's Edmund Pettus Bridge—convened a meeting of more than a dozen Wallace supporters in the private dining room of Montgomery's Woodley Country Club. During their four-hour meeting, the group sketched out the foundation for a third-party run by Wallace in 1968.

The "Woodley Conference," as it came to be called, included several second-tier white supremacists like Sheriff Clark, but—in addition to his old friend Carto—Kent and Phoebe Courtney also accepted Carter's invitation.

Kent Courtney, the second-most influential member at the Montgomery meeting had become well known in ultra-conservative circles by the mid-1960s. In the late 1940s, he began his far-right activism, serving as chairman of the "counter-subversive" program of the American Legion in Louisiana. From there he moved on to participation in the Citizens' Council of New Orleans before establishing his own organization, the Conservative Society of America (CSA) in 1961. He struggled, without success, side by side with his wife, Phoebe, whom he called the "tigress of the right," to create third-party movements in 1956 and 1960.

The Courtneys' influence also rose as they hitched their organization to the Goldwater movement, with active membership expanding from 9,000 in 1961 to 220,000 in 1965. With growing contributions from small donors and wealthy backers, Kent launched a weekly radio program, "The Independent American," and Phoebe created a voter guide that graded members of congress on their devotion to "Americanism." With a range of views that combined "America First" foreign policy, limited government, and not-so-covert racism, they worked closely with Robert Welch and the John Birch Society as well as a number of ultra-conservative religious leaders, particularly right-wing televangelist Billy James Hargis's "Christian Crusade."[524]

The Courtneys threw their organization behind Goldwater, even though they believed that communists and liberals (interchangeable in their minds) controlled the two major parties. But the Arizona senator's conservative economic views and his opposition to the Civil Rights Act of 1964 led them to put their misgivings aside. If the Courtneys seldom used overt racist language in CSA publications, their views were hardly a secret. "We've got niggers living in the next block to us and that's all right," Phoebe Courtney told one reporter. But we're not racists, she insisted, "we're against the civil rights bill because it destroys property rights and freedom of choice."[525]

Like Carto, the Courtneys promised to back any future Wallace candidacy.

Carter had also invited Robert Welch to attend. He declined, explaining that the John Birch Society would lose its tax-exempt status as an "educational organization" if it openly endorsed a political candidate. But in a personal and "private" letter to George Wallace, he furnished the names of key Birch Society leaders around the country.[526]

By the end of the four-hour meeting in Montgomery, the group had created an outline for how such a presidential run might bring together far-right groups from across the nation in support of a Wallace candidacy.

In the following months, the Courtneys and Carto—working through Carter—played key roles in laying the foundation for a Wallace third-party run in 1968. Carto persuaded Doubleday, a major press, to publish a Wallace "autobiography" (*Stand Up for America*) written by Carter. With the backing of an anonymous donor, Carto mailed 175,000 copies to potential supporters and gave 150,000 copies to the campaign to be sold at campaign rallies and events.[527] And with a $50,000 grant from another unnamed benefactor, ($375,000 in 2023 dollars), Carto launched the Youth for Wallace organization, placed ads in virtually every college newspaper in the country, and ultimately created a mailing list of more than forty thousand pro-Wallace college activists.[528]

The Courtneys also worked closely with Carter and Wallace's 1968 campaign coordinator, Tom Turnipseed. They made their Conservative Society of America an adjunct of the campaign, using contacts from all over the country and creating a "Wallace for President News," that was included in the group's regular newsletter. As early as July 1966, Courtney passed out "Win with Wallace in '68" buttons at a Boston "God, Family, and Country" rally. In the months that followed, the CSA distributed not-so-subtle racist, anti-communist, and law-and-order pamphlets and handouts to help Wallace reach beyond his Southern base and connect with a growing network of national right-wing organizations. Reporters briefly mentioned that Kent Courtney introduced Wallace at his first national rally, but they gave no background beyond describing him as the head of the Conservative Society of America.[529]

Two months before the 1968 presidential election, *Los Angeles Times* reporter Jack Nelson described the critical importance of these and other far-right groups to the Wallace campaign in a lengthy article. A native of Alabama who grew up in Mississippi, Nelson painstakingly researched the background of the hundreds of official "electors" for Wallace's American Party. He discovered that the overwhelming majority belonged to the Courtney's Conservative Society of America, the John Birch Society, the Citizens' Council, the National States Rights Party, Robert DePugh's right-wing Minutemen militia group, and various Ku Klux Klan organizations and splinter far-right and neo-fascist groups.[530] His extensively researched article received little coverage beyond the *Los Angeles Times*.

By then, Wallace's campaign had begun to falter. As late as a month before the election, Wallace drew the support of more than 20 percent of the voters in three national polls, but on election night he received less than 14 percent of the vote, still a respectable showing for a Deep South third-party candidate. What was more important was the effect his candidacy had for the future. A shift of less than 1 per cent of the vote in New Jersey or Ohio from Nixon to Humphrey would have meant that neither candidate had a majority of electoral votes, and Wallace would have been (as he said) "in the catbird seat" and able to extract concessions for his forty-six electoral votes. It would have led Nixon to turn further right on racial issues during his administration.

But Carter was no longer a major actor in the process he had begun.

DURING WALLACE'S FIRST ADMINISTRATION, Carter furtively emerged from his small, isolated office in the Capitol for evening meetings with his boss, but the governor had always avoided being seen in public with Carter and fellow Klansman Robert Shelton. (Years later, he would insist that Asa Carter was never his speechwriter, that he barely knew him.)[531]

Whatever Wallace's feelings, his advisers had grown increasingly uneasy about their fiery employee. Just two weeks before Lurleen Wallace's inaugural in January 1966, a drunken Carter profanely (and loudly) confronted Montgomery city detective Jack Shows in Jack Cash's Barbecue, a Birmingham watering hole for both Klansmen and local businessmen. Shows, investigating a Montgomery case with Birmingham connections to some of Carter's former Klansmen, had long shown an unusual willingness to go after violent white supremacists. In the wake of the 1963 bombing of the home of Martin Luther King's brother, A. D.

King, Shows continued to bring in Klansmen for grilling about the King bombing, even though he suspected members of his own police department had been directly involved. A decade later he would become the chief investigator in bringing the first of the 16th Street Baptist Church bombers to trial and conviction.

When Shows sat down to eat, Carter, sitting at a table with several of his friends, stood up. "I could tell he was into the sauce," said Shows, as he watched Carter charge across the dining room with the "stiff-legged roll of a practiced drunk." You "leave my men alone," he told Shows. While dozens of diners listened intently, Carter yelled that he would "beat the shit" out of him if he did not stop his investigations. "Ace was a regular bush hog when he was drunk," the Montgomery detective recalled, and he was more amused than intimidated. When Carter continued his tirade, Shows smiled, and suggested they step out to the parking lot and "stop disturbing folks trying to have their supper in peace." Carter's friends, who knew Shows's reputation as a tough, no-nonsense cop, pulled him away.[532]

While the incident went unreported in the press, it became the talk of insiders in the close-knit world of Alabama politics, and Seymore Trammell worried that Carter's public tirade would lead reporters to look closely at the connection between Wallace and his Klan-defending speechwriter.

Nor was Trammell reassured when he read in the *Birmingham News* that Carter called a public meeting only days after the inaugural of Lurleen Wallace to raise money for his friend and long-time fellow Klansman, Kenneth Adams. After a series of violent acts including his involvement in the 1961 burning of the Freedom Riders' bus in Anniston, his attack on Nat King Cole, and numerous assaults on Black victims, a federal district attorney indicted Adams for hiding a massive cache of explosives and ammunition stolen from Anniston's Fort McClellan. Despite extensive evidence of Adams's involvement, an all-white jury refused to convict him, to the disgust of the presiding judge. Although he avoided prison time, Adams found himself responsible for almost $10,000 in legal fees. In a gathering of over three hundred men, mostly

Klansmen, Carter passed around baskets collecting contributions for his long-time friend.[533] The *Birmingham News* covered the meeting and described Carter as the "organizer." Although the reporter did not link him to the governor or identify the group as a Klan gathering, the press attention alarmed Trammell.[534]

Equally frustrating was the *Birmingham Post-Herald*'s publication of a vague (and inaccurate) account of the "Woodley Conference." Wallace had given his approval for the gathering, but he emphasized that it should remain confidential since it was premature to discuss a possible '68 presidential race. Once the two stories appeared, Governor Lurleen Wallace's press secretary, Ed Ewing, issued a two-line statement saying that former governor Wallace "knew nothing of the meeting."[535]

Carter was always a self-promoter, said Trammell, who suspected he had been bragging to individuals who passed on the news to the Birmingham journalist.[536] Their speech writer had been useful in the early 1960s, but it was time to reduce his role in the administration.

If Wallace and his staff increasingly became uneasy about the role of their hired ex-Klansman, Carter became equally disenchanted with the man to whom he had hitched his wagon. Racial issues drove George Wallace's political campaigns in the 1960s, but after he moved to the national stage and subtly shifted his rhetoric, he seldom mentioned racial segregation, instead attacking "busing" or "bloc voting" or "ghetto rioters" or "inner-city welfare cheats." After Wallace launched his 1968 third party campaign for the presidency, reporters soon began to lip-sync his claim that he had "never made a statement attacking anyone on the basis of race or religion."

Initially supportive of Wallace's approach as a "tactical" measure, Carter began to complain to friends that his boss was no longer the man he had followed as the savior of the white race. When FBI agent Clay Slate met with Carter in early 1967, he detected Carter's cynicism in his reference to Wallace as a "politician," about the most damning word in his vocabulary. At the same time, FBI informants described Carter's growing interaction with far-right groups and former associates, a shift that led the agency to return him to the status of "possible violent activist."[537]

And just as Wallace's campaign began in early 1967, Tom Turnipseed learned from an old law school friend that the US Justice Department was investigating complaints that Carter had established his own "Wallace for President" campaign fund, pocketing the proceeds to finance his personal expenditures. Using a federal statute that prohibited interstate "fraud by wire," the Justice Department launched an investigation. The department dropped the case after concluding that the amounts involved were not substantial, but Carter's escape from a federal indictment further weakened his standing in the Wallace administration.[538]

Weeks after Turnipseed learned of the FBI investigation, a Mississippi friend told him that Carter had signed on as the campaign manager for Jimmy Swan, who had just decided to run for governor in the state's 1967 race. In the Hattiesburg, Mississippi, country singer, Carter had found a candidate who left no doubt about his support for white supremacy. That was enough for Wallace and his advisers. Oscar Harper told Carter that, "regretfully," he would no longer pay his salary as "consultant" and Seymore Trammell told Carter to remove his belongings from his small office in the basement of the capitol.

After Carter continued to call and offer advice to campaign officials, Tom Turnipseed had the unpleasant task of ending all connections between Carter and the '68 presidential campaign. When Carter talked with Turnipseed a last time, he was subdued but bitter. "George used me and when I was no longer useful to him, he dropped me." The Alabama governor, he said, had "abandoned the cause."[539]

17

Politics: End Game

> *"The riots we have seen in the North are heading South. We all know that the communists are responsible for the riots, howling mobs, burning looting and murder. And if we give every nigra in Mississippi the right to vote, it will make savagery the equal of civilization. There has to be a superior race, which is the white race."*
>
> Asa Carter, 1967 speech for Jimmy Swan[540]

Country singer Jimmy Swan grew up in Birmingham, Alabama, in the 1930s and "damn near starved to death," he recalled, before he moved to Mississippi to play country music in bars and honky-tonks. While he never became a major performer at the Grand Ole Opry, he wrote and recorded popular songs in the early 1950s including "I had a Dream" and "The Last Letter," the latter a tribute to Jimmy Rodgers whom he had known as a teenager. Unwilling to abandon his old-style singing for the new Nashville sound of the late 1950s and 1960s, he instead became a successful businessman, owning a radio station and broadcasting as a disc jockey. He still performed weekly on the Hattiesburg, Mississippi, television station and around the state for listeners who preferred his hard-edged country music.[541]

During his early life, Swan had an ambivalent attitude toward Blacks. He shared the views of the most whites of the day who saw segregation as a central part of the "Southern way of life." But he loved Black music, particularly groups like the Golden Gate Quartet, one of the first successful Black gospel groups. All that changed when his station began broadcasting retired Air Force Major Robert Bennett's program, "Know Your Enemy."

Bennett became well known among right-wing, antisemitic activists in 1950 when he published a sixty-page pamphlet, *Know Your Enemy,* an "expose" of what he described as the Jewish-Communist infiltration of all levels of American government. Bennett claimed to have worked at the highest levels of US Army Air Forces intelligence during World War II. He actually served as a low-level coordinator of weather forecasts for European bombing sorties and was discharged in 1950 for his outspoken racism and antisemitism while in uniform. Despite Bennett's fraudulent credentials, his claim of inside information on national security and his vivid description of the infiltration of American institutions by Communists and Jews (who manipulated ignorant Blacks) led white supremacy groups to embrace and widely distribute his pamphlet.[542]

Although Swan said little in public about the "Jewish question," he became convinced that a Communist/Jewish cabal sought to destroy American society through the "mongrelization" of the races, a catastrophe that would lead to the nation's moral, cultural, and ultimate economic collapse and a complete takeover by the Soviet Union. As Swan watched Mississippi Governor Paul Johnson's grudging acceptance of limited court-ordered integration in 1965, he decided to run for governor.[543]

At the end of the 1950s, Black citizens in Mississippi made up nearly 40 percent of the population, but decades of voter suppression and violence meant that only 4 percent of African Americans had been able to exercise the right to vote. In the two years after the passage of the Voting Rights Act of 1965, federal officials registered more than one hundred thousand Black voters, enough to lead most candidates to begin softening the hard-line segregationist rhetoric that had dominated the state's politics since the *Brown* decision.[544]

The 1967 governor's race would be the first test of this new political landscape, not only in Mississippi but across the Deep South.

During George and Lurleen Wallace's campaigns in 1962 and 1966, Swan performed at several of their rallies, and Lurleen recognized him as a special guest when she took the oath of office in January 1967. At a small reception on inauguration day, Carter—then still in the good graces of the Wallaces—introduced himself and told Swan he had heard that he was considering a run for governor of Mississippi. Carter reminded him that Louisiana's Jimmie Davis, composer of "You Are My Sunshine" and other country music hits, pioneered the route from guitar-picking to the governor's mansion, winning in 1944 on a campaign of "peace and harmony." But in his successful 1960 campaign for the governorship, Swan repeatedly warned of the dangers of the "minority bloc vote." And he promised to close the state's public schools if federal courts issued integration orders.[545] Unlike Davis, Swan had no political experience, but Carter assured Swan that his years as a musical performer and disc jockey had established statewide name recognition and showcased his natural ability to connect to an audience. More critical, said Carter, was the failure of other candidates to emphasize the all-out defense of the white South. Their silence created a perfect opening for a "true segregationist." Carter told Swan he wanted "to come and work with you," describing (and exaggerating) his role in Wallace's 1962 campaign and his continued influence as a major adviser.

It took little to convince Swan. From the moment they met, Swan later said, he was convinced "Asa Carter was one of the sharpest men you've ever seen in your life," a true "intellectual and political genius."[546] One of Swan's supporters soon hired Carter as a tax-deductible "consultant" for his Hattiesburg construction company and furnished him a late-model Cadillac. Carter then began traveling around Mississippi, reconnecting with local white Citizens' Councils and Klan contacts. Over the months that followed, Swan gave Carter complete control over the campaign.[547]

As the campaign for the August 1967 Democratic primary began in Mississippi in late 1966, most observers assumed that the winner would emerge from three leading candidates: ex-governor Ross Barnett, who had bumbled his way through the violence surrounding James Meredith's 1961 integration of Ole Miss; William Winter, popular state treasurer; and former congressman John Bell Williams. Winter ran as an outspoken "moderate" (unusual in the state) and had the overwhelming support of new Black voters. Even Williams, who originated the phrase "Black Monday" to condemn the Supreme Court's 1954 *Brown* decision, made little mention of racial issues as he launched his campaign. Instead, he emphasized the importance of economic development and the need to improve the quality of education in Mississippi.

Barnett had been expected to carry the banner of the state's most passionate white segregationists, but he soon dropped from serious consideration after floundering his way through meandering speeches and a sea of malapropisms ("My opponent is one of those scorpions you see sitting on a fence, changing colors"). As Barnett's support declined, Swan emerged as a serious contender.

Carter's first campaign manager hurdle came when he prepared a hard-hitting speech for his candidate to deliver as Swan officially announced his candidacy. Swan could be relatively articulate in casual conversations, but he had never gone beyond the eighth grade, and he struggled through a reading of the speech, often pausing and mispronouncing Carter's best lines. Fortunately, Swan's years as a singer had made him adept at quick memorization, and Carter spent hours with him patiently rehearsing phrases and explaining a political platform that revolved around segregation, anti-communism, and an ambitious plan to replace public education with "free, private segregated schools for every white child in the State of Mississippi." As one newspaper reporter who closely followed the campaign remembered, Carter controlled every aspect of the campaign to the point of telling Swan "how to stand and what to say."[548]

Swan needed little prodding to make white supremacy the centerpiece of his campaign. In that opening campaign speech, he described himself as a disciple of the late governor and senator Theodore Bilbo (1877–1947), Mississippi's most notorious demagogue in a state that set a high bar for race-baiting. If elected governor, Swan told voters, he would ensure that the school children of Mississippi would not "be sacrificed on the filthy, atheistic altar of integration."[549]

In speeches written by Carter, Swan warned of even more insidious threats to the nation and particularly to the Anglo-Saxon South. "A Communist revolution is taking place in America today," he told a crowd of several hundred in northwest Mississippi, "a revolution which has already destroyed over 50 percent of our freedom. . . ." In his standard stump speech, Swan described the growing racial conflict in Northern cities as a warning of what was to come in the South. Hiding in the background, communists sought to carry out their sinister plot, said Swan, by fomenting "riots, howling mobs, burning, looting, and murder." Granting equal rights to the state's Blacks would make "savagery the equal of civilization," he told a cheering crowd of several hundred whites in Hattiesburg. "There has to be a superior race, which is the white race."[550]

One reporter claimed that it was difficult to find a pick-up truck in heavily white areas of rural Mississippi without a Swan bumper sticker. His personal "bodyguard" was a leading member of the state's Klan, and through Carter, Swan openly courted the support of the hooded order.[551]

With a candidate finally willing to express Carter's political views openly and unapologetically, he arose each Monday before dawn and made the grueling six-hour drive from his home in White Plains to the Swan headquarters in Jackson. He filled the rest of his week with fourteen-hour days before he collapsed each night in his room at the Sun-n-Sand Motel. On most Saturdays he would drive back to White Plains to be with his family for thirty-six hours before returning to Jackson.

INITIALLY, THE STATE'S NEWSPAPERS downplayed the growing crowds of his enthusiastic supporters and dismissed Swan's chances in the August 8 primary. But halfway through the campaign, the state's leading newspaper columnist suggested that Swan, the only all-out segregationist, might make it into the run-off against John Bell Williams or William Winter. That was enough for the savvy Williams, undefeated since his election to Congress in 1946. He tacked to the right, publishing a letter in every major newspaper in Mississippi: "I am probably a more ardent advocate of segregation now than ever before, after having seen the disastrous results that have followed in the wake of forced integration of our schools throughout the country."[552] What followed, said long-time Mississippi reporter Curtis Wilkie, was the last of the full-blown racist campaigns in the state, as Williams outdid Swan in his blistering attacks on Black voters. In the last weeks of the campaign, the former congressman circulated leaflets headlined "Awake White Mississippi," warning that the "NEGRO MINORITY BLOC VOTE" could "insure negro domination of

Mississippi elections for generations to come." Even Bill Winter, who had studiously avoided references to race, half-heartedly defended segregation as he struggled to maintain some support from whites.[553]

When voters went to the polls, Swan carried seventeen mostly rural north Mississippi counties and captured nearly 20 percent of the state's votes. He ran well ahead of the bottom four candidates, but he still finished third behind Winter and Williams. Carter approached campaign managers for the two candidates and offered to "deliver" the Swan vote for the right price. Neither campaign responded, knowing that most of the Swan votes would almost certainly shift to Williams, who easily defeated Winter in the runoff later that month.[554]

Swan's loss was a bitter defeat to Carter, especially since he no longer had his financially lucrative position with George Wallace. He remained in Mississippi for several months, speaking more than a dozen times with different chapters of Americans for the Preservation of the White Race (APWR), a Mississippi group established in 1963. With only twenty local chapters of mostly working-class whites, the group became increasingly embattled after six of its members admitted to police in early 1964 that they had brutally beaten a white farmer for allegedly failing to support his family and then fired into the homes of two white families considered friendly with their Black neighbors. More bad publicity came when the APWR set up a booth at the Mississippi State Fair and distributed mimeographed pamphlets describing how to create home-made bombs.[555]

In one of the many political miscalculations that would mark his life, Carter convinced himself that the extremist APWR, despite its relatively small membership, was a potential replacement for the more respectable Citizens' Council. In the months after Swan's defeat, the two men headlined fundraising dinners to pay the legal fees of Mississippi Klansmen indicted for various violent crimes against civil rights activists. The federal government had launched a vendetta against "white Christian citizens," said Carter, who praised the convicted men for their courageous defense of white civilization. There is "no middle of the road" on this struggle, agreed Swan. "You are either on one side or the other." Both insisted that much of the violence blamed on white Mississippians was the work of communists.[556]

In the midst of the APWR fundraising campaign, an all-white Mississippi jury convicted seven of the men who had murdered civil rights workers James Chaney, Andrew Goodman, and Michael Schwerner in 1964, in the "Mississippi Burning" Case. It was a mixed victory for justice, since US District Judge Harold Cox dispensed brief sentences. As Cox later explained, the seven defendants "killed one nigger, one Jew, and a white man—I gave them all what I thought they deserved." (Actually both Schwerner and Goodman were Jewish.)[557]

Any conviction, no matter how mild the sentence, infuriated Carter and members of Americans for the Preservation of the White Race. The organization labeled the twelve white jurors "traitors to the white race," and, in early December 1967, donors funded a half-hour broadcast on Mississippi's largest television station. Seated in front of a large Confederate battle flag, Carter attacked Judge Cox and praised the APWR as an organization composed of "good, solid, decent people," the very same "type of men that signed the Declaration of Independence." As he had in earlier talks, Carter blamed the racial violence in Mississippi on communists seeking to discredit the segregation cause. There may have been some "unfortunate acts" by whites, but only because they had been "goaded into it."[558]

In 1968 most Mississippi whites still supported segregation, but the defense of the most violent white activists proved a bridge too far. Concerned as always about Mississippi's "image," state officials viewed the APWR as an embarrassing public relations problem and an unwelcome competition to the Citizens' Council. Working through the infamous Mississippi State Sovereignty Commission, state officials undermined and discredited the APWR. Within weeks, the organization collapsed, although many of its members simply moved back into Klan organizations.[559]

UNDER PRESSURE FROM THE Johnson White House, J. Edgar Hoover expanded the Bureau's role in infiltrating and attacking white supremacist groups. Still, he placed little emphasis on the burning and bombing of Black churches that had begun in the 1950s and continued through the next decade. There were exceptions. The national media publicized some of the more spectacular attacks, notably the 16th Street Baptist Church

Sam Bowers worked with Carter during the Swan campaign. He later served a life sentence for murders of civil rights activists.

blast in Birmingham, to which the Bureau sent more than a dozen agents to investigate. But in most cases attacks on Black churches and ministers received limited coverage.[560]

But then came a renewed round of attacks on synagogues and Jewish leaders in Mississippi and across the region. The cycle began with the bombing of Jackson's Temple Beth Israel on September 18, 1967. For local police and the FBI, the prime suspect was Sam Bowers, head of the Mississippi White Knights of the Ku Klux Klan, and owner of the "Sambo Amusement Company" a string of coin-operated machines across the state. Bowers had been involved in the 1964 assassination of the three Mississippi civil rights workers and had ordered the assassination of Vernon Dahmer, a Black Hattiesburg civil rights activist in early 1966. Describing Bowers as a fanatical antisemite as well as a racist, one agent concluded that he was the "most unasylumed lunatic in Mississippi."[561]

Washington authorized the Jackson FBI office to place Bowers under a twenty-four hour watch beginning in 1967. The fact that Bowers was in Jackson, staying at a motel the night of the Beth Israel bombing, reinforced the Bureau's belief that he was involved. As a later investigation revealed, Bowers did not order the bombing, but he was close to two young fanatical antisemites, Kathy Ainsworth and Thomas Tarrants, who had told Bowers that "something important" would happen the night of the bombing. FBI and Meridian, Mississippi, police later lured the two into a trap when they attempted to plant a bomb at the home of a prominent Jewish businessman. Ainsworth died in the shoot-out that followed; Tarrants was badly wounded.

Unaware that Bowers was under surveillance, Carter, along with J. B. Stoner, visited him only three hours before the bombing. As the Jackson, Mississippi, FBI office reported, the three "known Klansmen and suspects in the . . . [Beth Israel] case left the motel room at 10:10 p.m." The bombing occurred at 10:40 p.m. The connection to Bowers and Stoner was enough to place Carter at the top of the list of bombing suspects.

Three days later, when agents arrived unannounced at Carter's farmhouse, he admitted that he had joined Stoner in visiting Bowers, but he insisted they had simply been discussing political developments in Mississippi. Skeptical that Carter's visit minutes before the bombing was coincidental, FBI agents in Mississippi and Alabama undertook what they called an "intensive investigation" into his possible role. They eventually concluded that they could find no hard evidence that Carter was involved directly in the bombing, but the Bureau "reactivated" his name to the list of "prime suspects" in this and other related violent activities.[562]

The two-hour interrogation left Carter shaken. From that moment, he assumed that he was under constant surveillance, a conviction that strengthened his paranoia. In the weeks that followed, he instructed friends and associates never to discuss anything of importance on the phone since the FBI had wiretapped him.

CARTER HAD RETURNED FROM Mississippi to his home in White Plains, once again broke and without financial support beyond his family. He persuaded two local AM stations to hire him as an announcer and commentator, but his income was based on his success in selling advertising spots to local merchants. Later that year he did find a sponsor for a weekly broadcast on Montgomery's WMGY and Birmingham's WLPH, but the money was hardly enough to support his wife and four children, two of whom were attending nearby Jacksonville State University.[563]

To add to his misery, he had returned to Alabama just as the IRS launched another investigation of his possible unreported income. The IRS requested extensive financial records for the previous five years and informed him that he would be audited and should be prepared to document all income and all expenditures, including cash payments for his work as a political consultant. When he learned of the investigation, he began a frantic series of property transfers to his wife and children in an effort to shelter his hundred-acre farm. Although the investigation seemed to trail off, it left him convinced (correctly) that this was part of the FBI's attempt to destroy him.[564]

Clay Slate, the FBI agent stationed in Anniston, concluded that Carter's financial difficulties left him little time for involvement in violent acts or political activities beyond his radio broadcasts. In fact, said Slate, Carter seemed to have little interaction with neighbors beyond attending D'Armanville Methodist Church on Sunday, and running out to record his broadcasts and to solicit local businesses for station ads. The Asa Carter who had once appeared regularly in the state's newspapers and on television seemed to have disappeared.

No one was more surprised than Slate when he read in the Anniston newspaper that Carter had announced his candidacy in the upcoming gubernatorial race. Twelve years earlier, Carter had mounted a quixotic race for lieutenant governor, finishing last in the field of five candidates and drawing only thirty-one thousand votes. Now in 1970, running as an overt racist, he seemed even further out of touch with the state's voters.

In 1966, Lurleen Wallace had successfully run as George Wallace's stand-in with the expectation that her husband would then return to the governor's mansion in four years. But with her death from cancer only fifteen months into her administration, Lieutenant Governor Albert Brewer became governor. As the Alabama House of Representatives leader, Brewer had dutifully supported George Wallace over the years, but even Black Alabama opponents saw Brewer as a man of uncommon decency and administrative ability. When Wallace announced that he would oppose Brewer, political observers assumed that the former governor would easily win. But the soft-spoken Brewer seemed transformed as the race began. Inspired by broad support from newspapers, business and labor leaders, and college students from across the state, Brewer began bringing audiences to their feet with the slogan "Full time for Alabama," and the un-sexy rhetoric of competence, honest government, and an "open door for all Alabama's citizens," an oblique invitation to Black voters to become part of his campaign.

As Brewer surged, Wallace desperately embraced an openly racist campaign, describing Brewer as a captive of "left-wing *bloc voters*" [Translation: *Black voters*.]

Even though the press focused on the battle between Brewer and

Wallace, the state's newspapers gave surprisingly extensive coverage to Carter's campaign after he raised a substantial war chest, much of it from Dr. Buford Sanders, a wealthy Birmingham ear, nose, and throat specialist. Sanders, a passionate antisemite as well as a traditional anti-Black racist, had been quietly pushed out of his position at the University of Alabama Medical School in the early 1960s because of his extremist views. He would go on to become a financial supporter of the Knights of the Ku Klux Klan founded by David Duke in 1974. Carter's fundraising (and a reckless decision to mortgage his farm) allowed him to broadcast seven half-hour television shows and to publish full-page political ads in the Mobile, Montgomery, and Anniston newspapers. Carter promised voters that he would "clean the movie screens of the filth produced by the Red movie writers of Hollywood who are intent on destroying the Christian home.[565] The centerpiece of his campaign was a copy of his Mississippi scheme to repeal the state's sales tax and replace "government" schools with a statewide "Free Enterprise" school system that would put "true textbooks" and the Bible back in the classroom. It was all to be funded through a "school stamp" program so bizarre, convoluted, and unworkable that the media generally ignored it.[566]

While Carter repeated his usual warnings of the catastrophic effects of integration, racist voters already had a clear choice: Brewer the moderate or George Wallace. After Brewer refused to lean on state contractors for support, he ran out of money as the primary drew closer. Meanwhile, President Richard Nixon, anxious to eliminate Wallace as a third-party candidate in 1972, secretly funneled $400,000 dollars in cash to the Brewer campaign.[567]

In the May 3, 1970, Democratic primary, Brewer led Wallace but narrowly failed to reach the 50 percent threshold that would have reelected him. As Brewer's lead steadily grew that night, UPI correspondent Tony Heffernan asked Wallace's brother, "What are you going to do now?" Gerald Wallace turned to Heffernan with a smile: "We'll just throw the niggers around his neck." Another aide agreed: "We're going to promise [voters] the moon and holler nigger."[568]

The May primary result for Carter proved to be even more humiliating

Carter in a television appearance during his fruitless 1970 campaign.

than his earlier campaign for lieutenant governor, as he received fewer than fifteen thousand votes. Why had he run in the first place? Tom Turnipseed, who worked with Carter during the early days of the first Wallace administration, never had any doubts. "He hated Wallace. He lost a well-paying job and [had] the humiliation of being dismissed." Worse, Carter felt "duped" as he realized that "Wallace never really gave a damn about race except as a political issue."[569]

Bitter and humiliated by his last-place finish, Carter began asking well-heeled backers for money to buy television time during the week before the run-off between Wallace and Brewer. While Carter said he would not directly support Brewer, he would tell the people of Alabama about his close ties to Wallace and what he had learned: the former governor was a "phony segregationist" who had used the race issue only to get elected. When Wallace aides learned of Carter's plans, they panicked. Ray Andrews kept in touch with his old friend Carter. Andrews was an employee in the Brewer administration, but he had concluded that Brewer would lose, and he quietly kept contact with the Wallace organization. In the discussions that followed the primary, said Andrews, the "Wallace people were . . . , I could say they were scared witless, but more accurately something that rhymes with witless."[570]

Cecil Jackson, a top Wallace operative, ordered Andrews and another Carter friend, Howard White, to "get a hold of Ace and try to keep him from doing this TV thing." Within days White arranged a meeting between Carter, State House Clerk John Pemberton, and Reuben King, commissioner of the Alabama Department of Pensions and Security. Pemberton and King had discreetly raised money for the former governor. It was a straightforward proposition, said White. "Asa wanted money. They gave him money." The payoff allowed Carter to repay the mortgage on his farm.[571]

Carter cancelled plans for his television shows and, two weeks before the runoff, issued a brief statement to the state's newspapers, announcing his support for Wallace. "You don't bring in a Negro bloc in large numbers unless you have made deals," said Carter, and Brewer had definitely "made deals." Unlike Governor Brewer, "George Wallace didn't go behind the door to make deals with the bloc vote."[572]

In the June runoff, more than a million Alabama voters went to the polls. Wallace beat Brewer by fewer than thirty thousand votes.[573]

ALABAMA NEWSPAPER REPORTER WAYNE Greenhaw ran into Carter on inauguration day in January 1971. Incoming Governor George Wallace delivered a lackluster speech that contained his signature attacks on the federal government but avoided racial issues. He pledged at one point that government should be administered "for the weak, the poor and the humble as well as for the powerful. Alabama belongs to all of us—Black and white, young and old. . . ." As if to highlight the transition from his 1970 campaign to a more "moderate" racial position, Wallace welcomed Black marching bands to the traditional inaugural parade for the first time since 1954, and he approved the selection of Alabama-born Black opera singer Robert Brewster to perform for the concert following the ceremony.[574]

On the edges of the inaugural crowd, Carter and a dozen of his still-faithful followers created a forlorn picket line holding up their signs during the ceremonies: "Wallace Sold Out." "Free Our Children." "Defend White Alabama." "Wallace is a Bigot." They were joined by a half-dozen other demonstrators: young Black men who flanked the Capitol steps and held up clenched fists—the salute of the "Black Power" movement.

As the crowd dispersed, Greenhaw joined Carter, sitting alone on the back steps of the Capitol. His head down, Carter talked nonstop. "Wallace is a no-account liar, a cheat who has stolen integrity from the office of the governor, a phony filled with the hot air of hypocrisy." I believed in him, Carter told Greenhaw. "I believed deeply that he was the great man we had been waiting for. But as his popularity grew, "I think he has found himself getting too close to the White House. . . ." He thinks that, if he's seen as a racist, he'll fail to win the presidency. "I am a racist" and "I fight for a cause I hope to win." But if we don't win? "If we keep on the way we're going, with the mixing of the races, destroying God's plan, there won't be an Earth on which to live in five years." He stood and walked toward a car where his friends were waiting and turned. "Farewell," he said as he slipped into the passenger seat.

Two decades later, Greenhaw remained unsure what to make of the encounter. Carter seemed genuinely distraught; he even had tears streaming down his face. But there was something that seemed "a little like a performance," said Greenhaw, as he shook his head. "You know, he was good at that."[575]

18

The Last Days of Asa Carter: 1970–72

"I'm through with all that stuff. I'm gonna make myself some money."

— Asa Carter to Attorney R. B. Jones[576]

In early 1970, a McComb, Mississippi, committee of concerned white citizens invited Asa Carter to speak to a "town hall" gathering. Many of the individuals had worked with Carter in the 1967 Jimmy Swan campaign, but even though he remained on good terms with Swan, he declined. Instead, he recommended as his replacement Ray Burgess, a Calhoun County friend and state representative best known for his fanatical segregationist rants, less so for his oratorical skills. When Burgess hesitated, Carter shared one of his standard stump speeches calling on whites to elect staunch segregationists and stand up against communist-led integrationists.

Back in Anniston, Burgess described the repeated shouts and standing ovations from the crowd that had greeted his remarks. "Ace, I don't understand you," he said. "If I could write a speech like that, I wouldn't let anybody give it but me." Carter shrugged. "To give a speech like that," he told Burgess, "you've got to believe that shit."[577]

Carter had not lost his passion for white supremacy, but Swan's defeat in 1967 and his own disastrous run for the Alabama governorship in 1970 convinced him that the political struggle was over. There was no way to restore the South as it was before *Brown*. And he had been genuinely shaken by the FBI's aggressive investigation of the synagogue bombings during the late 1960s and the Bureau's deep knowledge of his close ties to many of the bombers. There was only one last, desperate alternative. Defenders of segregation would have to create their own white communities, completely separate from an increasing tide of government-forced integration. On one level, the process had already begun in the 1960s with the creation of private white "academies" across the region, but Carter had more ambitious plans.[578]

In the spring of 1970, the small town of Andalusia, Alabama, twenty miles north of the Florida panhandle, agreed to integrate the city's swimming pool. The town council concluded that it did not have the resources to fight a losing and expensive battle against a court order obtained by Black residents. Ron Taylor, a local country and western singer who shared Carter's racism and far-right politics, invited him down to Red Level, Alabama, to advise a group of forty local residents on overturning the town's decision.

Over a two-day weekend at Taylor's home, Carter argued that the national battle had been lost. The only hope for white Southerners was to expand the fight beyond hopeless skirmishes at the local level. They would need to create private institutions free from the tyrannical dictates of the federal government, similar to the burgeoning private school movement but on a much more elaborate scale. Carter came prepared with a blueprint for "The Southerners," a new statewide organization with six "divisions" named after Confederate heroes. Within six months, he created more than a dozen chapters, often led by Klansmen or former Citizens' Council members disenchanted by the organizations' weak response to integration. Alabama newspapers ignored the new group, publishing only a handful of brief stories, all vague and generally inaccurate.[579]

Ready to launch a statewide campaign, Carter called reporters at the Mobile, Montgomery, Birmingham, and Anniston newspapers to announce the details of The Southerners, with more than fifteen local "assemblies" already in place. Despite this effort to drum up publicity to attract recruits, only his hometown newspaper, the *Anniston Star*, ran a short article. As one reporter recalled years later, "It was pretty well accepted by then that you couldn't believe a damn thing Asa said even if he swore it on a stack of Bibles."[580]

For once, Carter was only mildly exaggerating, but the FBI soon greeted his announcement with concern.

BY 1970, THE SEVENTY-FIVE-YEAR-OLD J. Edgar Hoover had run the FBI for nearly a half century, through eight administrations. From the 1930s through the 1950s, he systematically cultivated links with friendly journalists who created an image of the FBI as an incorruptible crime-fighting organization of fearless G-Men who brought down mobsters from John Dillinger in the 1930s to Mafia leaders in the 1960s. And in movies, novels, and newspapers the FBI became the force that protected the United States from gangsters and communist internal subversion.

The first serious challenge to Hoover's FBI came in 1964 when investigative journalist Fred Cook published *The FBI Nobody Knows,* a bestseller that described a breathtaking range of illegal actions by the Bureau: warrantless wire-taps, clandestine searches without warrants, and a willingness to protect informants even after they committed violent acts while undercover. He drew a particularly devastating portrait of Hoover, describing how the head of the nation's primary law enforcement agency smeared individuals as "communists" or "communist-sympathizers" with little or no evidence.

Over the years, Hoover had created an overwhelmingly white bureau with almost no Jews and only a handful of low-level Black agents. Many agents prized their relationships with Southern law enforcement officials far more than any concerns about the attacks on Black and white civil rights activists. Well into the 1960s, Hoover secretly furnished damaging information on civil rights activists to right-wing Southern politicians like Mississippi's Senator James Eastland, who—in turn—used Bureau materials to "document" the role of individuals as willing tools or dupes of the Communist conspiracy.[581] Hoover had always been a racist, and on his long list of enemies, he personally despised none more than Martin Luther King—the "burr-head," as he privately called the civil rights icon. Hoover had once assured Lyndon Johnson's top aide, Joseph Califano, that King was "under active and tight control of the communists."[582]

Through the 1960s, the once sacrosanct FBI increasingly became the target of journalists, liberal politicians, internal FBI rivals, and even some members of Richard Nixon's administration. Under pressure, Hoover had shifted the agency's resources in the early 1960s to investigating what he saw as domestic radical groups, but his definition of "radical" mainly led to the monitoring (and undermining) of "left-wing" subversive organizations: Students for a Democratic Society, Southern Christian Leadership Conference, Student Nonviolent Coordinating Committee, as well as the more militant Black Panthers and the violent Weather Underground.

After Mississippi Klansmen murdered Schwerner, Chaney, and Goodman in June 1964, the Johnson administration ordered the FBI to include the KKK in its investigations of "radical" organizations. Hoover dutifully ordered his Southern offices to expand their network of Klan informants, but he resisted expanding the role of the FBI in bringing charges against white terrorists in the region.

As journalists disclosed his widespread snooping into the private lives of thousands of Americans, Richard Nixon—like John Kennedy and Lyndon Johnson—increasingly saw Hoover as a political liability. But like his predecessors, Nixon hesitated to fire him. Hoover remained popular among hardcore anti-communist conservatives and there was always the fear that he would release damaging information from his famous "secret files" that would ruin the reputations of dozens of Washington figures, including members of the Nixon administration.[583]

Obsessed with his anti-communist crusade, angry over attacks, and preoccupied by turf wars within the FBI, Hoover showed little interest in investigating armed groups of right-wing racists beyond the Klan. When journalists and local law enforcement officials expressed their concern over the growth of such armed anti-government organizations as the Order, the Minutemen militia, and the Posse Comitatus movement, Hoover decried "rumor mongering" over "paper organizations." In testimony before a congressional committee in September 1966, he again dismissed the threat posed by right-wing organizations. The American Communist Party (reduced to less than four thousand mostly aging adherents) "wields an influence and constitutes a security danger far out of proportion to its members." Communists, Hoover concluded, remained the nation's greatest internal threat.[584]

But the following month, an informer for the New York City police department's anti-terrorist unit alerted his handler to an imminent plot by the Minutemen to use three seven-member teams to firebomb what they claimed were "left-wing" summer camps in upstate New York and western

Connecticut. In a coordinated four-hour sweep, city police and New York and Connecticut law enforcement officers arrested twenty members of the group. They quickly found that the Minutemen had secretly planted more than a dozen firebombs at one camp, ready to be ignited on a moment's notice. Even more alarming, police discovered an enormous cache of automatic rifles, mortars, an anti-tank bazooka, more than a million rounds of ammunition, crossbows, and eight homemade "garottes" (piano wire with handles, used for swiftly executing victims). The most lethal military equipment apparently had been stolen by sympathetic reservists from the Staten Island Armory of the 11th Special Forces Reserve Unit and passed on to the Minutemen.[585]

Anniston Agent Clay Slate knew his boss well. "You know the old gospel hymn, "His eye is on the sparrow and he watches over me"? Well "Hoover's eye," he said, "was always on the sparrow."[586] Embarrassed by watching the New York City police department upstage the Bureau just days after he had dismissed militia groups as unimportant and had referred to one of their targets as a "camp for Communist youth," Hoover ordered his agents to infiltrate the Minutemen and any group that had begun arming themselves for what they saw as an inevitable war to overthrow the federal government.[587]

That new concern over armed right-wing groups soon returned Carter to the FBI's attention. In February 1971, an ex-Klansmen stopped by the Bureau's Birmingham office to describe Carter's new organization, The Southerners. He told one of the agents that he had heard that Carter ordered members of his new group to "arm themselves with rifles." Carter's "new outfit is of the Minutemen type," he warned.

The information was, to put it mildly, suspect. The individual (whose name was redacted in the FBI report) acknowledged that he had no use for Carter: he had heard about the arming of The Southerners second-hand from an individual he refused to name.[588] Still it was enough for Washington to order agents to reopen Carter's file and begin monitoring his new group.

A month later, Carter unknowingly invited one of the Bureau's Klan informants to a meeting of the organization's "top commanders" at Huntsville's Albert Pick Hotel. The informant reported to Birmingham Special Agent Robert Klare that he believed Carter had organized The Southerners to take "violent action against the Black Panthers and/or to seek out other Blacks responsible for atrosities [sic] against whites, particularly white women." Members, he reported, are "said to be armed or can be armed with M-14 rifles." There was nothing concrete in his report, but warnings from two informants was enough for Bureau to expand the probe of The Southerners from the level of monitoring to a "high-priority investigation."[589]

Alabama and Mississippi FBI agents soon recruited at least three other informants, one of whom was the head of Huntsville's "Nathan Bedford Forrest" chapter of The Southerners, with more than fifty members. Not satisfied with close surveillance, Hoover ordered the Birmingham office to take "further action," giving very specific information on how to disrupt The Southerners by dividing its leadership. Hoover ordered the Birmingham agents to prepare a letter, typed on unmarked stationary with a manual typewriter ("to protect the Bureau"). The letter, mailed "anonymously" to Carter, warned him that his "associate," Robert Shelton, was attempting to destroy the new group by telling fellow Klansmen that "Carter can't keep his hands out of the till."[590]

THE LETTER WAS PART of an illegal series of FBI COINTELPRO operations that dated back to 1956. Using wiretaps, anonymous mailings, and disruptive insiders, the Bureau infiltrated and discredited communist and left-wing groups considered by Hoover to be a threat to national security. By the 1970s, the various KKK organizations had begun to splinter and diminish in numbers, but FBI tactics were often effective in demoralizing klaverns whose members had always tended toward paranoia.[591]

In Carter's case, the letter proved an exercise in incompetence.

During George Wallace's brief presidential run in 1964, Robert Shelton, head of the United Klans of America (primarily centered in Alabama), may have reached a temporary truce with Carter, but he hated the man he always saw as his rival, feelings that were reciprocated. Carter must have shaken his head in bewilderment when he received the letter referring to his "associate" Robert Shelton. He knew the source and he warned members of his group that the FBI was attempting to infiltrate and disrupt the organization by such fake mailings and the spread of false rumors.[592]

Over the next year and a half, various informants spied on The Southerners, filing over seventy reports, many of them detailed accounts of meetings and Carter's remarks. Aware that "stool pigeons" were likely present, Carter repeatedly emphasized that the use of violence would destroy the new organization. In all the informant reports, Carter never once sanctioned the arming of The Southerners.

Washington Bureau leaders (including Hoover) essentially told local bureau agents to look harder, insisting that they investigate various rumors: three hundred "Southerners" were training in the hills of north Alabama near Carter's home; the group had purchased $10,000 worth of semi-automatic rifles; Carter had obtained "a bazooka and several machine guns." Through late 1971 and into 1972, agents interviewed more than four dozen individuals. When Carter heard of the Bureau's investigation, he voluntarily spoke with Birmingham and Anniston FBI agents, acknowledging that some members of the group might have purchased rifles as individuals, but there was no "cache" of weapons. He had insisted that members of The Southerners avoid any violence, he said, since it would only strengthen the "orchestrated plot" to discredit his organization.

After months of fruitless investigations, Slate expressed his frustration in a report to superiors. He had long known Carter and had interviewed him on numerous occasions. But the Calhoun County native had avoided activism of any kind in the Anniston area for some years, apparently to prevent problems for his family. Nor, despite dozens of interviews, had Slate discovered evidence of armed groups in northeastern Alabama. He urged the investigation be closed. The Birmingham office agreed.[593]

Despite the recommendations, Hoover ordered the surveillance to continue. Between April 2, 1971, and June 15, 1972, the Mobile, Birmingham, and Anniston offices received more than a dozen directives from the Bureau, in several cases directly from Hoover.

If the FBI collected information on the erroneous belief that Carter's new organization was a violent militia group, the detailed accounts by informants over a three-year period furnish a remarkable inside view of what was to be Carter's last struggle for white supremacy. The one-time fire-breathing activist never conceived of The Southerners as an armed resistance.

Carter believed that the only hope for the survival of white Southerners was to build separate communities with white-only private schools, churches, *and* businesses where families could protect their children from integrated schools and live their lives completely separate from Black people. It was no accident that one of the few news reports referred to the Mobile chapter of The Southerners as a "commune."

While Carter managed to create groups in more than a half-dozen communities across the state, he concentrated on creating the first all-white community in Mobile. As he told a reporter in one of the few articles published on the group, Carter selected Alabama's port city as the first site "because we can generate more power by starting where the heat is. . . ."[594]

There was plenty of heat in Mobile. School desegregation in Alabama had moved at a snail's pace through the 1960s, but in June 1969 the US Fifth Circuit Court of Appeals ordered the Mobile County school system, the largest in Alabama, to abandon its "freedom of choice" plan and carry out the immediate integration of thirty thousand Black and forty-five thousand white students. The overnight implementation of the decision made some Black parents uneasy. Most whites were furious, an anger reflected in the overwrought language of the city's daily newspaper, the *Mobile Register*. "This is an outrage, a stench in the nostrils of justice . . . ," wrote segregationist publisher George Cox. The South was "singled out for persecution with the Blackjack of forced integration as all other regions pursue their segregated ways without coercion or penalty."[595]

As the first stages of desegregation took place at the start of the 1969–70 school year, sporadic demonstrations and occasional violence erupted, including several fights between Black and white students. In an all-white rural school outside Mobile, white parents assaulted three Black teachers on opening day at a formerly all-white rural elementary school. By the fall of 1970, Mobile's two daily newspapers regularly reported (and often exaggerated) racial tensions within the county's integrated schools. Black community activists complained that the real problem was continuing racial discrimination in the curriculum, racist comments by white teachers, and the reluctance of white administrators to crack down on white racist students.

But the greatest resistance came from whites. As Vanderbilt political scientist Richard Pride concluded in his study of the desegregation of Mobile's schools, many white parents saw the dissension as evidence of a larger problem. The educational system was under siege from everywhere: "militant Blacks, socialists and communists, drugs, sex and rock'n' roll." The white parents wanted a return to segregated white Christian schools that shared their values.[596]

In November 1970, with little more than word-of-mouth to spread the news, more than four hundred parents showed up at a rural church just south of the Mobile airport for Carter's first organizational meeting. After outlining the purpose of The Southerners, Carter laid out the first challenge: The group would need to recruit at least five hundred members and raise $25,000 ($160,000, in 2023 dollars). On behalf of The Southerners, a newly established church—"The Assembly of Christian Soldiers"—would purchase property west of the city and build a school in a location that would draw students from a ten-mile radius. Aware that many of the rural working-class families lacked the ability to pay private tuition, Carter explained that the school would be financed by building a self-sustaining economic community with a church, grocery store, service station, and family clothing store as well as a social "Lodge."

The new church would be critical to the enterprise. By having the church own and operate the businesses, Carter explained, there would be tax advantages as well as less intrusive interference from the state and federal government. He had talked with experts, said Carter, and they assured him that chain groceries, burdened with tax payments and other government restrictions, had a gross profit margin of 18 to 25 percent. With a supermarket, and later a filling station, clothing store, and social lodge, half of the profits would fund the new school with only minimal tuition payments.[597]

Carter's claims skipped between illegality and fantasy. Traditionally, state, local and federal taxing agencies cautiously dealt with churches, fearful they would be accused of persecuting religious groups. But the US Internal Revenue Service had long required that churches earning more than $1,000 in gross receipts from an "unrelated business" file an "Exempt Organization Business Income Tax Return." By the 1960s, state and local governments followed the IRS guidelines, taxing businesses run by churches, nonprofit agencies and charities. And there was no chance that his new organization would escape notice from the Internal Revenue Service. Birmingham's FBI agent in charge reported Carter's speech in a memorandum to the IRS Intelligence Division describing Carter's proposals and suggesting it might want to "look into" his plans.

As for the enormous profits Carter promised? Economic and marketing research going back to the 1930s consistently showed that the average supermarket profit margin was between 1.9 and 2.4 percent. Even small neighborhood groceries seldom generated profits of more than 5 percent.[598]

Through the late winter and early spring of 1971, desperate parents signed up, initially contributing $12 to become members of The Southerners, with several members ceremoniously offering a hundred dollars ($680, in 2023 dollars). Public meetings at the local National Guard Armory and the American Legion Hall consistently drew from three hundred fifty to five hundred attendees. One informant overheard Carter tell a high-ranking member of The Southerners that well-to-do supporters of the project, included Dr. Buford Sanders, the prominent Birmingham physician who had financially backed Carter's 1970 run for governor. Sanders along with another anonymous supporter had each contributed well over a thousand dollars ($7,500, in 2023 dollars). In June 1971, Carter announced the good news to an audience of more than five hundred. The organization's church had purchased seven acres of the abandoned Mobile livestock market in a rural area west of the city. He did not disclose the cost or the size of the mortgage on the property, only that the property was held by Assembly of Christian Soldiers, a white supremacist Christian Identity church created several months earlier by Jesse Thrift. On behalf of the church, Thrift—a former grand wizard of Carter's Original Knights of the Ku Klux Klan—obtained a state charter as a nonprofit corporation.[599]

At fundraising and organizational meetings, Carter regularly spoke to parent groups, feeding the flames of what he called "the heat" of white resistance. Racial fear was always the foundation for his enterprise. In one of the earlier meetings, a Carter assistant distributed cards asking individuals to report their name, address, and blood type. If any dues-paying member of the new organization needed a transfusion, The Southerners would quickly arrange to have a white member furnish blood so that "you can be sure you are getting white and not nigger blood."[600]

To anyone who had followed his career, Carter's speeches repeated familiar themes, particularly the role of Communists in spearheading the campaign for the federal government to take over schools and enforce integration. The mixing of Black and white would not only remove God from the classroom but inevitably lead to the "mongrelization of the races and the death of Anglo-Saxon civilization." At several meetings, he read dramatic accounts of the nightmare of school desegregation in Washington, D.C., interweaving those stories with lurid accounts of what he claimed was an epidemic of violence by Blacks against whites in Mobile's recently integrated schools. At a meeting in mid-June, Carter claimed to have confirmed evidence that "over 100 white women have been raped and brutally assaulted by niggers in the city of Mobile." The victims, he shouted, included white girls as young as fifteen.

According to Carter, the Black Muslims, the Black Panthers movement, and other radical Black groups had already begun the first stage of their plan to seize areas of the Deep South and turn them into Black-only reservations. At a July meeting, he claimed to have proof that the federal government had channeled hundreds of thousands of dollars to Black Muslim groups, allowing them to buy land in Virginia, Georgia, and Alabama. Secretly buried in these Black Muslim properties were "ammunition dumps [and] staging areas for the fight to come."

However absurd such claims, Carter tapped into widespread apprehension throughout the state after the Nation of Islam purchased a thousand-acre farm forty miles north of Birmingham from Ray Wyatt, a former state senator and local auto dealer. The organization stocked the property with 250 registered (and very expensive) Black Angus cattle. A Black Muslim spokesman explained that the group hoped to establish a slaughter program that would allow them to produce and sell Halal meat to their members.

The state's newspapers headlined the purchase of the farm by Elijah Muhammad's followers; they gave considerably less coverage to the violent response that followed. After a leading member of the Alabama John Birch Society and the minister of a local Baptist church called an emergency meeting, more than two thousand whites gathered to express their opposition to the "anti-Christ, anti-white" Muslims. Within days, the harassment began and Ray Wyatt became the first victim when he arrived at his car dealership to find sulfuric acid poured over a dozen new cars on his lot. Two weeks later "unknown arsonists" burned his showroom and repair shop to the ground.

During the same period, snipers firing from adjacent property leased by Robert Shelton's Alabama Klan killed twenty five cattle. On three other occasions gunmen fired rifle shots through the front window of the home of the farm manager, who was a member of the local Black Lutheran church. (There were no Black Muslims working on the farm). According to Wyatt and the farm manager, the local sheriff did nothing to investigate these attacks. After thirty-four cows died drinking from a watering trough poisoned with arsenic, the Black Muslims sold the property, but Carter continued to claim that their announcement was a ploy, that the Black Muslims secretly were buying property with traitorous white go-betweens and storing their cache of weapons at scattered locations around the state.[601]

In late June 1971, only weeks after the purchase of the abandoned stockyard, a local contractor (and member of The Southerners) set up his transit level and laid out the foundation sites for a grocery store and church. Carter announced that the new school would soon be constructed and named the "Admiral Semmes Academy" in honor of Raphael Semmes, the Mobile-born captain of the *CSS Alabama*, the Confederate raider that seized or burned sixty-five Union merchant ships during the Civil War. The Semmes Academy would have no difficulty finding "first-rate teachers," he told his followers, because of the dangerous violence in integrated schools.

Through the hot Alabama summer, volunteers arrived each Saturday to pour foundations, lay concrete-block walls, and build truss roofs before installing windows and doors in the two larger buildings and a small service station. In mid-August, with store cabinets and cash registers yet to arrive, Carter announced the grocery store would be open for business on August 29. Over the next two weeks, volunteers hastily painted the cinder-block interior, purchased two used freezers for frozen goods, and built crude temporary shelves to hold vegetables as well as canned and packaged goods.

On the day of the grand opening more than a hundred cars filled with supporters from across south Alabama (and a few from Mississippi) assembled at a large parking lot on the east side of Mobile Bay. With Confederate and American flags flying, the convoy followed a Mobile police department motorcycle escort, drove through the Bankhead Tunnel from Mobile Bay into the city, then westward twenty-four miles to The Southerners' site on Schillinger Road. Local members who had worked late into the night before, greeted supporters with a "barbecue and country music" grand opening. FBI informants estimated a crowd of more than a thousand emptied the shelves of the $34,000 inventory by 5 p.m. Afterward, women and teenagers began clearing the debris.

From that celebratory moment, Asa Carter's "Anglo-Saxon community" began to unravel.

Even before the grand opening, Carter repeatedly pleaded for more contributions, a reflection of the precarious economic condition of the venture. At one meeting, as Carter warned of the growing threat of a "Nigger Communist Nation" in the South, one of the organization's marshals—identified by their armbands—shouted and pointed to a young man conspicuously recording the proceedings. Another marshal pulled out a chrome-plated .38 revolver, grabbed the "hippie" and roughly shoved him out the door. The FBI informant standing at the back of the auditorium walked out and saw the young man go to his car, place his recorder in the trunk, take off his brightly colored jacket, and return to a seat on the back row.

Desperate pleas, like the staged "hippie" drama, failed to bring in enough money. Financial shortfalls mounted, exacerbated by an audit showing that the manager of the grocery store had been siphoning funds for personal use. Wholesalers, frustrated over long delays in receiving payment, demanded reimbursement before delivery. As the deadline for the arrival of the temporary school building moved further into the fall, Carter pleaded with parents to keep their children out of public schools.

In November the school did open, in a poorly heated galvanized steel structure, filled with battered desks in noisy classrooms created by hastily thrown-up partitions. The seventy students discovered that there were only a handful of texts and, while they had graduated from college, none of the three teachers had teaching certificates or any experience in the classroom.

One informant who talked to several parents concluded that the lead teacher's primary qualification was his repeated harangues over the threat of Blacks.

The project struggled through the winter and into spring with one setback after another. Once, the grocery store's major supplier removed all the stock because of a bounced check. A frantic fundraising campaign in February–March 1972 brought in enough cash to keep the store in operation, but the "elders" of the Assembly of Christian Soldiers discovered that, far from furnishing profits to subsidize the school, the grocery store was barely breaking even. Meanwhile, the newly constructed gas station sat empty. The cost of installing pumps and underground tanks had proven prohibitive.

Carter, already under tremendous pressure, was soon overwhelmed by one crisis after another. For years he had heard nothing from the Internal Revenue Service about the 1967 investigation into his failure to pay his taxes. But in mid-February 1973 the IRS filed a tax lien against Carter for 1967–1968 for almost $8,000 ($60,000 in 2023 dollars), claiming that he had substantially under-reported cash income for these years. His attorney, R. B. Jones, assured him that, given the fact that it would be difficult to precisely prove the amounts he had received, they would be willing to settle for substantially less.[602]

They did, but Carter's problems continued. While still a student at White Plains High School, his youngest son, Bedford, had already established a reputation for fighting and general "trouble-making" according to an Anniston policeman. For reasons that were never clear, the seventeen-year-old became involved in an argument with other teenagers at a service station just outside the small town of Talladega, southwest of his home. When the argument escalated into a fistfight, the attendant called for help. Two deputies arrived to find a drunk and belligerent Bedford. Told to hand over a pistol openly tucked into his waist, one of the deputies reported that Bedford refused and "sassed him." The two deputies slammed him to the ground and handcuffed him. After treatment at a local hospital for multiple bruises and abrasions, authorities charged him with resisting arrest, driving while intoxicated, and carrying an unregistered pistol with the serial number filed off.

Less than a week after Carter bailed him out of jail, Bedford drove back to Talladega's shopping center, looking for the same teenagers he had confronted a week earlier. After fruitlessly searching through the stores, he got in his pickup and promptly drove into the rear of a car at the shopping center's exit stop sign. Accelerating in reverse, he then slammed into the car behind him. When the driver opened his door, Bedford pulled out a pistol and warned him to get back in his car before racing off at high speed.[603] Since one witness knew Bedford and had written down his truck's license number, it took only minutes for Talladega Sheriff Gene Mitchell to call Calhoun County Sheriff Ron Snead, and ask him to arrest Bedford when he returned to his home in White Plains.

A half hour later, Snead and one of his deputies parked out of sight on the Choccolocco Road near Carter's home. When Bedford drove by, Snead turned on his blue light and siren. Instead of stopping, Bedford accelerated, pulled into his father's driveway and ran into the house. When he stepped out of his car, Sheriff Snead saw a pistol on the truck's front seat. Just as he and his deputy pulled out their guns, Carter and (Snead assumed) Bedford, kicked out a couple of window screens and "threw shotguns on us." Unwilling to risk a shoot-out, the two men backed off, got in their car and drove back to the sheriff's office in nearby Anniston.

Snead was, if not a close friend, well acquainted with Asa Carter. Rather than returning with greater force, he called Carter and explained that he was simply acting on behalf of the Talladega County sheriff who had a warrant for Bedford's arrest.

"Well, what can we do about it?" asked Carter.

We'll "work something out," he assured "Ace," as he called him. After a conversation with Sheriff Mitchell in Talladega, authorities there agreed to drop the arrest warrant if Carter would drive down to Talladega and post a bond for his son.

Later that afternoon, Snead drove out to White Plains to explain that all was well. Over coffee, he and Carter ended up talking for a couple of hours. Carter described a book he was writing about a "rebel outlaw" named Josey Wales. (Snead said that when the book was published, he read it and "bought several of them and gave them away for Christmas presents that year.") Two weeks later the Talladega district attorney dropped all felony charges against Bedford, reducing them to a misdemeanor, leaving the scene of an accident. Carter paid his son's fine.[604]

But nothing else seemed to go right for Carter.

On May 7, he brought his son Asa Jr. to the emergency room of Anniston Memorial Hospital with a gunshot wound to the leg. When an Anniston policeman arrived to investigate the gunshot wound, Carter told him that Asa Jr. had shot himself in the leg while cleaning his pistol. At a meeting of The Southerners and in conversations with friends he gave a more colorful version of the incident. A would-be "assassin" had attempted to kill him, explained Carter, but the bullet had hit his son.[605]

As Asa Jr.'s condition worsened, Carter told supporters in Mobile that his son lay in a hospital bed for a day and a half before he received medical treatment. Dr. Joseph Harner, the surgeon on call, was on the golf course when the hospital admitted his son. Harner, said Carter, told the hospital he would see the patient on his regular rounds the following Monday.

The hospital's version of events was quite different. According to Dr. Walker Reynolds, there was a delay, but a very brief one. It was true that Dr. Harner, the surgeon on call, had refused to operate when he learned that the victim was Asa Carter's son. Dealing with anyone around Asa Carter would lead to nothing but trouble, he told his colleague, Dr. Reynolds, who stepped in within two hours, not two days. When he removed the bullet, Asa Jr. had a high temperature and Reynolds found gangrene in the surrounding tissue with sepsis already underway. He did not believe the family had brought Asa Jr. into the hospital immediately after the accident but had waited until the infection spread. Despite intensive antibiotic treatment for thirty-six hours, Reynolds and Harner concluded that amputation of the leg offered the only hope for the survival of Asa Jr.

Within days after his son's release from Anniston Memorial, Carter filed a $2 million lawsuit against Dr. Reynolds.[606]

Shortly after his son's accident, Carter published a new version of his 1950s magazine, *The Southerner.* Unlike his earlier magazine, he had been forced to print the 1972 edition on a borrowed mimeograph machine. It reflected the ravings of someone unhinged. For thirty-two pages, Carter railed against his enemies: the "communist NAACP"; Black radicals and the "scalawags" who supported them, particularly Alabama's newly elected (and liberal) Attorney General Bill Baxley; and the head of the State Highway Patrol, Walter Allen. Under a federal court order, Allen had begun admitting Black applicants to the patrol's training program. "SOON," warned Carter, "you can expect your wife or daughter to be pulled over to the side of the road by one of these Ubangi or Watusi tribesmen, wearing the badge of Anglo-Saxon law enforcement and toting a gun . . . but as uncivilized as the day his kind were found eating their kin in the jungle."

His attacks on his former boss, George Wallace, were even more vituperative. Carter said Wallace had begun his career in politics as a "negrophile" and campaign manager for the "degenerate Jim Folsom." For a time it seemed Wallace had changed, that he had "seen the light . . . that he believed in the Cause," but that was simply a temporary detour before returning to his first love, the left-wing philosophy that is killing our nation and our people." Wallace, wrote Carter, cared nothing about the "little white girl with broken ribs and punctured lung from being stomped by Black savages in a Jefferson County school; nor the two little white girls in a Mobile hospital stabbed and slashed by the knives of Blacks; nor the little white girls who have been raped [by Blacks] and ruined for all their lives." The Bible tells us that "a dog will return to its vomit," he concluded. "George Wallace has apparently returned."[607]

Carter met no pushback when he distributed the crude magazine to members at the March and April meetings of The Southerners. But on May 15, 1972, John Hinkley shot Wallace five times in Laurel, Maryland, as the Alabama governor campaigned for the presidency. Ten days after the shooting, as Americans from right to left expressed their sympathy and concern for the fallen governor, Carter brought copies to the meeting of the Mobile Southerners. The leaders of the group refused to distribute the material.

To add to the problems of The Southerners, several members came to Carter's friend Ron Taylor to report that one of their key leaders had been sexually assaulting his own fourteen-year-old daughter. While the group quickly removed the accused, rumors spread through the community.[608]

All these events seem to have convinced Carter that The Southerners had become a lost cause. Although he never officially withdrew, through the summer and fall the chair of the "Admiral Semmes" chapter in Mobile, repeatedly apologized for Carter's failure to appear. He had "car problems," he was "ill," and once he was "delayed" while out of state. When Carter appeared, for the first time in months, at an August meeting, an FBI informant described him as subdued, disheveled, and with a three-day stubble of beard. Although Carter seemed sober, he had bloodshot eyes and all the signs of someone suffering from a serious hangover. While he sporadically continued to attend meetings of the Southerners' "state board" in Montgomery, he made only one trip to Mobile over the next six months as his grand experiment unraveled.

THROUGHOUT HIS LIFE, ASA Carter had struggled with alcohol, particularly when he came under intense pressure. In late August 1972, a Gadsden, Alabama, city patrolman stopped Carter as he drove erratically across the white line on Highway 431, thirty miles from his home. His attorney, R. B. Jones, persuaded the city prosecutor to drop the charges, and the news media did not pick up the story.

A month later, his luck ran out. After a Montgomery meeting with the state board of the Southerners in early October, Carter hit the city's bars, drinking steadily into the night until he became so loud and abusive that the bartender of one dive called city police. Arrested for public drunkenness, police threw him into the "tank" to sober up with nearly thirty other drunks rounded up over the weekend. The next morning, Carter stood, his head down, as the city attorney read out the charge of public drunkenness.

"All those who want to plead guilty, raise your hand," said the city judge, "and I will sentence you to another day in jail." The alternative was a $25 fine, which Carter paid and left, but not before a local reporter covering municipal court recognized him and printed an account that appeared in the state's newspapers.[609]

In January 1973, Carter appeared before the board of The Southerners. In his report, the FBI's informant seemed stunned at the rambling incoherence of Carter's remarks, perhaps because he was clearly intoxicated. Between complaining that the hotel had used "nigger cooks to prepare the food" and demands that the organization do a better job of distributing copies of his pamphlet, he kept returning to the "crisis" facing the nation.

The brave sons of God must realize "there is a time for war, a time for peace, a time for love, and a time for hate." Now, he said, was the time for hate. When the federal government strips individuals of their guns that is the "last step taken before a country is taken over by the Communists" We know that the "nigger is a beast," he rambled on, but the "anti-Christ Jew" would be the winner from this conflict since "the Jew is against everything that is natural and according to God's law." The "Jew man is effeminate, and the Jew woman is masculine" which is why the Jews are "all for pornography and homosexuality." As board members awkwardly looked down, he began a lengthy discussion about reincarnation and Nathan Bedford Forrest. Even though the Confederate general and Ku Klux Klan leader had only a third-grade education, said Carter, he has "come back in another body and probably as a genius in another body."[610] It was his last appearance at any of the group's meetings.

There was still the matter of his pending medical malpractice lawsuit scheduled for trial in mid-April 1973.

On the night of March 23, less than three weeks before the trial was to begin, Dr. Walker Reynolds and his wife sat in their Anniston living room watching television when they heard a shotgun blast and the sound of broken glass. He walked outside to find the windows of his car shattered. The Anniston police, he would later complain, did nothing except write a report. Despite the lack of hard evidence, Reynolds and his wife feared that either Carter or one his sons "came through the woods and shot at us. The shooting was a warning shot that we better settle." Within weeks, the insurance underwriters agreed to pay Carter $75,000 ($450,000, in 2023 dollars) plus lawyer's fees.[611]

The same month that Carter received his lawsuit settlement, the Assembly of Christian Soldiers formally closed the Admiral Semmes Academy and liquidated the property that had been Carter's dream of an all-white enclave. The FBI's chief informant reported that the organization had collapsed and Carter no longer had any role in its leadership.[612]

19

Becoming Forrest

If the individual wishes, he can add touches to his clothes to make them a costume, expressing whatever he feels at the moment. With the magic deftness of stage sorcery, a headband can produce an Indian, a black hat a cowboy badman.

— Charles Reich, *The Greening of America*[613]

With financial stability restored, Carter took his first steps in a remarkable transformation that he believed would let him leave his past life behind.

In June 1973, Carter called a family gathering at his parents' home in Oxford, Alabama. Present were his parents Ralph and Hermione and his two brothers, Larry and Doug. His sister, Marie Bonner, director of psychiatric nurses at the University of Alabama School of Medicine, stayed away. She had no use for Carter's racial ideas and knew she would not be welcome (Carter had gone into a rage when she suggested once that he needed psychiatric help).

In broadcasts, *The Southerner,* and his hundreds of speeches he had promoted his extremist ideas, but they were often wrapped in appealing stories and narratives that could be used to avoid the mine fields of antisemitism and explicit racism. Yet he realized that his personal history would make it impossible for any major press to publish his work, and it would never be safe to write under a pseudonym. His future as a novelist depended upon creating a completely new identity with an appealing background that would attract publishers and a reading audience much larger than the AM radio broadcasts and magazines he had published.

With an instinct that proved remarkably prescient, he decided to become an Indian.

Carter was hardly the first to assume a fake Native American identity. Ogala Sioux author Vine DeLoria described the versatile role Indians have played in American culture. Columbus had brought back news of a new world inhabited by Southeast Asian Indians, and Europeans immediately created exotic visions: a fountain of youth, seven cities of gold, and a world of strange animals and stranger people. The absence of elephants, noted DeLoria, apparently failed to alert the early explorers they weren't in India. But by the time they discovered their error, "instant knowledge of Indians was a cherished tradition." And because "people can see right through us," said Deloria, white Americans could create Indians as they would like them to be. "To be an Indian in modern American society is, in a very real sense, to be unreal."[614]

As white settlers moving westward, the native peoples of North America were usually seen as troublesome obstacles, at worst a war-like and barbarous people. In an 1868 speech to the US House of Representatives, Minnesota Democrat James Cavanaugh used a phrase common among frontier settlers: "I will say that I like an Indian better dead than living. I have never in my life seen a good Indian (and I have seen thousands) except when I have seen a dead Indian."[615] But there was always a counter-narrative. Nineteenth-century author James Fenimore Cooper's several volumes of "Leatherstocking tales" (1827–1841), and Henry Wadsworth Longfellow in his lengthy poem "The Song of Hiawatha" (1855), joined other romantic writers in shaping a more benign mythology of the Noble Savage: perhaps a bit primitive, but brave, honorable, and at peace with the natural world. By the end of the nineteenth century, with the majority of Native Americans safely dead or dispossessed of their lands and forced onto reservations, whites began to appropriate Indians to their own purposes.[616]

Archibald Stansfeld Belaney, born in 1888 in East Sussex, England, became fascinated with North American Indians from an early age and moved to Canada at seventeen. Calling himself "Grey Owl," he claimed that his mother was an Apache, his father a Scotsman. He became one of the great conservationists of his generation, writing five books and dozens of articles and appearing in nature films throughout the 1930s.[617]

At least two African Americans became famous as Indians: "Long Lance"

(Sylvester Long, son of a Winston-Salem, North Carolina, janitor) starred as a native American in silent films, served as an adviser on Western films, and gave lectures around the country before a reporter exposed his past. Disgraced, he later committed suicide. "Red Thunder Cloud" (Cromwell West of Newport, Rhode Island) was more successful throughout his lifetime in maintaining fake credentials as a Catawba Indian from the Carolinas. He learned enough of the language to become a linguist and ethnographer, recording materials for the Smithsonian Institute.[618]

Italian American Espera Oscar de Corti became even more famous as "Iron Man Cody," serving as a "Native American consultant" to Cecil B. DeMille, John Ford, and other producers of Western films from the 1930s to the 1960s. As an actor, he starred in over two hundred films, but is best remembered for his role in an emotional sixty-second conservationist ad first broadcast on Earth Day, 1971. As the camera panned over trash, litter, and industrial pollution sullying the landscape, Cody sat in his canoe, sadly staring into the distance as a tear coursed down his cheek.[619]

Over the years, the roster of counterfeit Indians grew: from academics falsely claiming Native American ancestry (Ward Churchill, Rachel Dolezal, and Susan Taffe Reed) to novelist Margaret Seltzer, writing as Native American Margaret Jones.[620] Beginning in 1969, "Jamake Highwater" (Jewish, Jackie Marks) wrote more than two dozen books, winning several awards including the Newbery Medal. Even after Native Americans raised questions about Highwater's background, he convinced PBS to create and broadcast a documentary based on his bestselling 1983 book, *The Primal Mind: Vision and Reality in Indian America.*[621]

For a fanatical racist like Carter, his embrace of "Indianness" might seem incongruous, but once Indians had been reduced to a handful in most of the Old South, whites found it useful to draw a distinction between the brave and independent "red man" and inherently inferior Blacks. South Carolina's "Pitchfork" Ben Tillman, one of the region's most rabid race-baiting politicians, explained to his fellow US senators that white Southerners "respect the Indians because they were too brave to ever consent to be made slaves while the negroes have submitted to slavery and seemed to thrive on it."[622]

Individuals had different reasons for assuming Native American identity, but underlying their appeal to whites was the belief that Indians maintained an authentic connection to an earlier, simpler time before our modern but sterile world became alienated from nature.[623] For Asa Carter, the role of Indian had an additional resonance: The federal government had brutally destroyed the Indians' way of life, just as Carter believed communists, Jews, and Blacks sought to erase authentic Anglo-Saxon white Christian culture.

Nor was it an accident that he described himself as an Indian cowboy. More than a third of the men who rode the open range of the post-Civil War era were either Black Americans or Mexican and Mexican American "vaqueros" or Native Americans. But there was no place for them in popular culture. Historian Heather Cox Richardson has described how the "myth of the American cowboy was born of Reconstruction . . . ; he was a hardworking white man who started from nothing, asked for nothing, and could rise on his own"; such men needed no "regulations or a handout; they were individualists, working to make it on their own." In Carter's writings, the two mythologies blended, so long as the Indian served as the Lone Ranger's Tonto.[624]

Carter's parents and brother Doug reluctantly accepted his decision. Younger brother Larry responded with enthusiasm, pleased that Carter was "getting away from his political stuff." You could become a "real Mickey Spillane," said Larry. Carter—clearly annoyed—rejected the comparison between his writing and that of the popular author of crime-noir detective stories in the 1950s and 1960s. "I want to be a Hemingway, not a Mickey Spillane," he retorted.[625]

He just "pulled up out of the Choccolocco Valley, tanned himself up, grew a mustache, lost about twenty pounds and became Forrest Carter," said his friend Ron Taylor.[626] But even before the days of social media and an increasingly skeptical public, creating a new identity was no easy task for someone who had been constantly and recently in the news.

There was historical precedent. In the years before the Civil War, Frederick Law Olmsted, the father of American landscape architecture, traveled as a young man through the American South. Riding through the worn-out cotton lands of Virginia, Georgia, and the Carolinas, he saw dozens of abandoned homesteads marked by a scrawled "GTT" [Gone to Texas].

Thousands of struggling farmers and some large-scale planters sought a more promising future in the still-rich cotton lands of east Texas. And not all emigrants came voluntarily. "It would amuse you very much, could you hear the manner in which people of this country address each other," William DeWees wrote to friends back in Arkansas from his new home in Texas. "It is nothing uncommon of us to inquire of a man why he ran away from the States, but few persons feel insulted by such a question. They generally answer for some crime or other which they have committed. . . ."[627]

Asa Carter had decided to establish a new identity in Texas.

Methodically, he set about putting his finances in order and covering his tracks. In mid-July, he and India transferred their farm to their children without entering a deed in the courthouse. By using them as go-betweens, he hoped to block inquiring reporters from following a paper trail. Weeks later he made an agreement to rent, with an option to buy, a beach house on the Gulf of Mexico barrier island of St. George, just south of Apalachicola, Florida. Although modest in size, the three-bedroom, two-bath frame house sat just behind the dunes of the Gulf beach with a wide front porch looking out to the sea. Again, he filed no documents in Florida's Franklin County Courthouse.[628]

Forrest Carter emerges, 1974.

The next step was the creation of a Texas background, and no one would prove more important in building that back story than Don Josey, a Texas oil millionaire whose friendship Carter had cultivated during his years in the Wallace administration. During the 1950s and 1960s, everyone in central Texas seemed to have heard stories about Josey's colorful personality and his impulsive generosity. When Fred Hickman, the maître d' of Josey's favorite New Orleans restaurant, stepped down, rather than contributing a modest retirement gift, Josey told

Hickman that he would be receiving a lifetime $50 monthly check (more than $500 a month, in 2023 dollars).[629]

In central Texas Josey was best known for the "come one, come all" free rodeo he hosted at his one thousand-acre ranch ten miles north of Dallas. Josey moved into a four-room suite at the Adolphus Hotel and welcomed friends for drinks and partying for two days before driving out to his ranch to greet as many as sixteen thousand spectators on hand to watch the nation's best rodeo performers. Old timers remembered his grand entrance as he stepped out of his chauffeur-driven limousine, smiling as he waved his trademark Stetson cowboy hat to the crowd.[630]

He was never one of the wealthiest of Texas oil magnates, a distinction reserved for the "Big Rich," men like H. L. Hunt, Roy Cullen, Clint Murchison, and Sid Richardson. These and other Texas oil millionaires are remembered for their flamboyant and often garish lifestyles, but, like Josey, their most important mark on American politics was their financial support for America's growing far-right movement. Even if they worked the political system with Democrats and Republicans alike, their enemy remained the

Don Josey, 1962.

same: a grasping federal government that stole their hard-earned money with a rapacious tax system that penalized the deserving rich and pandered to the undeserving poor.[631]

If Josey was a step below the richest Texas oil men—one reporter estimated his wealth at more than $20 million (about $1.2 billion, in 2023 dollars)—he shared their right-wing politics with an extra dash of racism.[632] His outbursts against Blacks eventually isolated him from his large family and his own mother would not speak to him in later years, said his nephew, Lenoir Davis. "When his name was mentioned, "Grandmother Mildred Josey would pointedly display a huge frown. . . . "[633]

Josey donated $10,000 ($85,000, in 2023 dollars) to George Wallace for his abortive 1964 Presidential campaign. A year later when Dallas County Sheriff Jim Clark joined Alabama state troopers in assaulting John Lewis and other demonstrators on the Edmund Pettus Bridge, Josey impulsively sent a $5,000 gift to Clark. If Josey publicly kept his racism under wraps, he agreed with George Wallace's defense of segregation, and he saw Wallace's opposition to the civil rights movement as critical in promoting his anti-government, ultra-conservative economic views. When Wallace, term-limited from running for reelection for governor in 1966, came up with the plan to have his wife, Lurleen, run as his proxy, Josey was first in line with a $20,000 campaign check.

The Texas oilman met Carter during George Wallace's 1964 presidential foray, and they became friends during Lurleen Wallace's 1966 campaign. Josey joined her on the campaign trail for a swing through north central Alabama where he spent long hours with Carter and the two men bonded over their veneration for the Confederacy, a shared hostility to Black people, and disdain for liberalism in all its forms. Over the years, they remained in contact, and when Carter fell on hard times in the late 1960s, Josey gave him a sizeable (and never repaid) "loan."[634]

During a visit to Texas in 1972, Carter told Josey about his plans to become a writer and the need to conceal his past. Josey seemed particularly amused when Carter told him that his new name would be "Forrest" Carter, an homage to his long-time hero, Nathan Bedford Forrest. Like the incriminating document left openly on a mantel in Edgar Allan Poe's "The

Purloined Letter," Carter's violent past would be flaunted in plain sight.

Together, Carter and Josey worked out the backstory. Supposedly, Forrest Carter, a Cherokee teenager educated by his grandparents, left his east Tennessee home in the early 1940s and traveled west, "wrangling horses" and working as hired help across central and west Texas. In the 1950s, "almost starved to death," he visited Josey's ranch-house just north of Dallas and asked for work. The owner offered him a meal, but Forrest proudly insisted he "wouldn't take it without working first." According to their cover story, that was the beginning of Forrest's long friendship with Don Josey. Over the next six years, Josey invited reporters out to his spacious ranch home, decorated with valuable Confederate memorabilia, and told them about his old friend, Forrest, who had been his best cowhand over the past twenty-five years, even "if a bit unreliable at times" since the horse wrangler often disappeared on spiritual pilgrimages to reconnect with his Indian forefathers.[635]

BY MID-JULY, FORREST CARTER, his wife India, and their youngest son, Bedford, had settled into their new home on St. George Island. He began writing after 11 p.m., working through the night revising his Josey Wales manuscript. After sleeping until noon he walked on the beach, developing a weathered bronze tan that would make his claim to be Native American plausible.[636]

While St. George remained his home base, Carter established a Texas identity by choosing Abilene as the location of his new life as a Texas cowhand turned writer. Some three hours west of Dallas, the smaller city of ninety thousand not only lacked the major media outlets that might lead to his exposure, it had other advantages. Founded in 1881 on the Texas & Pacific railroad, Abilene quickly became the major railhead for cattlemen in western Texas shipping their animals north for slaughter. But by 1970 it was no longer a "cow town." The adjacent oil-producing region and the steep rise in oil prices had a spillover effect on Taylor County. Abilene became the hub of a nineteen-county area with a regional medical center, the best bookstore in west Texas, and three universities. In the 1970s, a young Ohio reporter arriving at the *Abilene Reporter-News* quickly discovered that the city and its leadership wanted to be perceived as a "wine-sipping sophisticated community" rather than a stereotypical Texas "beer-drinking, hot dog, rodeo, country-music kind of crowd."[637]

Originally Comanche country, its tribal members had been forcibly removed to Oklahoma well before the creation of Abilene. In a city with shallow roots in the past, most residents knew little about the Native Americans who had lived there for centuries and almost nothing about the quite different history of the Cherokees beyond the fact that they were forced west on the "Trail of Tears." With the city growing rapidly, Carter convinced his two oldest sons, Ralph and Asa Jr., to move to Abilene in January, leasing for them a service station—renamed "Carter Auto Service"—with gas sales and repair services. Over the years that followed, Forrest Carter could sometimes be seen pumping gas at what he called his "nephews'" business, staying in their homes for long periods.

At the end of the summer, he mailed the first hundred pages of the manuscript he called "Gone to Texas." Without an agent or connections to the publishing world, he sent copies to more than a half-dozen publishers and agents. From an unknown and unpublished author, it seemed unlikely that "Gone to Texas" would receive a reading. Major publishers and agents received dozens of such unsolicited manuscripts each month. At best the works got a cursory glance before the "I'm sorry to inform you" letter went out. In Carter's case, the submission was mostly ignored; one agent responded that the author would never find a publisher for a book about a "vicious criminal."

But Carter sent one submission to the "Literary Department" of the William Morris Agency that proved critical to his later success. In the 1960s and '70s, the West Coast-based Morris agency was best known for representing Hollywood talent, but it maintained a small New York literary office to review books and manuscripts that might have movie potential. Michael Peretzian, who began his career in the agency's New York mail room in the early 1970s, quickly found himself offered a job in the literary department. "None of my fellow trainees were interested in representing writers," he said. They wanted to represent movie stars.[638] And Carter was convinced that "Gone to Texas" would make a great Western film.

In 1973, Rhoda Weyr became the first female editor in the agency's small literary department. The daughter of Garrett Ackerson, an American diplomat who served in Eastern Europe before and after World War II, she had been born in Budapest in 1937. Her father served as the American chargé d'affaires and quietly supported his wife Rhodita when she began hiding Jewish refugees after the war began in Europe in September 1939. During the McCarthy Era, Ackerson showed equal courage when he refused Joe McCarthy's demands that he fire two staff members who were supposedly "left-wing," even though it limited his future in the State Department.[639]

Rhoda Weyr, 1973.

Rhoda attended schools in Europe before returning to the United States to graduate from Barnard College. After she married free-lance journalist Tom Weyr, the two returned to Europe where he worked on various assignments while she worked as a free-lance literary "scout" for foreign and American publishers, in part because of her proficiency in several languages. In 1967, she had her first major success, securing the rights to the memoir of Joseph Stalin's daughter, Svetlana Alliluyeva.[640]

Over-qualified for the position at the William Morris Agency, as a woman in what was still primarily a man's world, she was grateful for the job even though her boss assigned her to read dozens of unsolicited manuscripts by would-be authors in the search for what she called "gems among the slush." In the late summer of 1973, she picked up the "Gone to Texas" manuscript and read the cover letter. Forrest Carter explained that, as an unpublished American Indian who had been writing for years, he really didn't know how to go about this "publishing business." He would appreciate some help.

The letter caught her attention, and then she began to read. "He was a good writer, and the pacing was terrific," she recalled. She had a disdain for most "Western" novels, but if Forrest Carter could "make me care what happens," she decided, "he's gotta have something going for him." On the basis of the first one hundred pages, she wrote back. She made no promises, but she told Carter how much she liked his work and encouraged him to send a final manuscript.[641]

When Doug Carter visited his older brother on St. George Island in early September, Asa seemed elated by Weyr's positive response. Well after he had gone to bed, Doug could hear his brother out on the porch overlooking the night-time Gulf waters, pounding away on his Underwood portable. By mid-October, Carter had mailed a final draft to Weyr, but instead of waiting for her response, he borrowed $4,000 from a cousin and paid Birmingham's Oxmoor Press, the printing company for the *Progressive Farmer* and later *Southern Living* magazines, to produce a thousand copies of his work with a lurid cover set against the background of a Confederate flag. He called it *Gone to Texas.*[642]

He mailed the first copy to Don Josey, inscribed: "Josey Wales is named for you. Without your help, this book would never have been written. Your friend, Asa Carter." Josey had been a key figure in his transformation to "Forrest" Carter. It is also true that Carter's paternal grandmother was Josephine "Josie" Taylor Carter and his maternal grandfather was "Wales" Weatherly. Good stories had a long shelf life and could be recycled for multiple purposes.

He also mailed a copy of the crudely printed novel to Clint Eastwood's Malpaso Productions with a lengthy and personal letter to the Hollywood actor. After watching Eastwood in his "spaghetti Westerns"—*A Fistful of Dollars, For a Few Dollars More,* and *The Good, the Bad and the Ugly*—Asa believed that no other actor could better capture his vision of Josey Wales.[643]

"I am part Cherokee, and Cherokee and Creek friends helped me print a few copies of the enclosed book," he wrote in his cover letter to Eastwood. He was a forty-eight-year-old Texas horse wrangler who had written a great deal over the years, he said, "but only to be read at Indian Council gatherings in the custom of storytelling." As someone unfamiliar with the ways of Hollywood, we know you are a "very important and busy man . . . but if you could find time to read the book you could tell us if it has merit."[644]

While he heard nothing from Eastwood, other good news arrived in early December. Not only was the William Morris Agency willing to represent him for a possible movie sale, Weyr had sent a copy of the manuscript to Eleanor Friede, an independent editor at Delacorte, a Dell Publishing imprint. Weyr believed that the release of the book by a major publishing house would make it a more attractive prospect as a movie project, and Friede proved equally enthusiastic. Only two weeks after receiving the manuscript, she mailed Carter a standard author's contract offering an advance of $5,000, ($25,000, in 2023 dollars), a generous offer for a first-time author.[645]

Weyr's main goal was to swing a movie deal, and she agreed that Eastwood's Malpaso film studio was the best place to shop the project. Unaware that Carter had already mailed his privately printed book to Eastwood, she sent a telegram to Bob Daley, Eastwood's long-time friend and co-producer, and explained that Carter's manuscript was in the mail. Weyr had learned from her agency's Los Angeles office that the best way to pitch a project to Eastwood was through Daley. Born in Chicago, Daley's family had spent a few years in Texas when he was a child, but he was very much a Californian. A graduate of UCLA film school, a book lover, and a collector of first-editions, he was hardly typical of Eastwood's friends. But he had been Eastwood's best man for the actor's first marriage and worked with him from the creation of Malpaso Productions in 1967. In Weyr's telegram, she argued that the Josey Wales book was a "natural" for Eastwood, and she urged Daley to read the manuscript once it arrived.

Two weeks later, when Daley turned the last page sometime after midnight, he called Eastwood at his home in Carmel, California. "This better be good," said Eastwood, waking from a sound sleep. It was better than good, said Daley. It was the story they needed for their next film. "God, this has so much soul to it." Within twenty-four hours, Eastwood read Carter's novel and agreed. The forty-four-year-old actor had made his reputation in Western television and movie roles. "I've always liked [Westerns], even as a kid, and that's the only way I ever judge a film." The story of Josey Wales, he believed, would go far toward establishing his reputation as a serious filmmaker.[646]

THE JOSEY WALES STORY begins in 1858, with the young Missouri farmer plowing in the new ground of his recently acquired homestead. Hearing gunfire, he looks up to smoke in the direction of the family's log cabin and desperately runs to find the cabin ablaze and in it the blackened bodies of his wife and daughter, brutally murdered by a band of anti-slavery abolitionists who called themselves "Kansas Redlegs." It was the beginning of the bitter struggles that would set the stage for the Civil War as pro-Northern and pro-Southern forces battled over whether Kansas and Missouri would become slave states.

Driven by a need for revenge rooted in "generations of the code handed down from the Welsh and Scot clans" and burned into his being," Wales became, in Carter's words, "filled with a cold hatred and bitterness," and driven by the Biblical call for an "eye for an eye, a tooth for a tooth," his desire for revenge always driven by the atrocities of infamous abolitionist "Redlegs."

The peaceful Wales transformed himself into a deadly gunfighter and, when the Civil War began, joined Confederate raiders led by William Quantrill and "Bloody Bill" Anderson. After five years of ruthless warfare, the war was over. But Wales refused to surrender and was soon "gone to Texas" with a $3,000 reward on his head and bounty hunters, Union soldiers, and Pinkerton detectives hired by the hated Union government in close pursuit.

As he rode hard across southern Kansas, through the Oklahoma territory's "Indian Country," to Texas on his way toward safety in Mexico, Wales seemed to fill the cemeteries along his route with would-be bounty hunters, murderous desperados, and hapless members of carpetbag/scalawag militia forces intent on collecting a reward that kept increasing. With each encounter, he gained new companions: Lone Watie, a Cherokee who had fought for the Confederacy; "Little Moonlight," a "Comanche squaw" rescued from a thuggish rapist; and an elderly Arkansas woman and her beautiful young granddaughter, Laura Lee, (again) rescued from a violent would-be rape by half-breed "Comancheros" from northern Mexico who pillaged their way across Texas and the New Mexico and Arizona territories.

Ultimately there was a happy ending as Wale's friends convinced a Texas Ranger and a Pinkerton detective that the man the man known as Josey

Wales died in a gunfight in Monterrey. Assuming a new identity as "Mr. Wills," he married the beautiful Laura Lee.

Carter's political causes lay at the heart of the book. Wales's first bank holdup after the war is succinctly justified: "Carpetbag bank, Yank Army payroll." Scattered through the book are scornful descriptions of Yankee carpetbaggers and traitorous white Southern scalawags. "The effects of the vulturous greed and manipulation of the politicians were everywhere" as they "settled like locusts over the land."[647]

But Carter had been right when he wrote to Eastwood that he was unfamiliar with the ways of Hollywood. He was equally unfamiliar with the notion of exclusive contracts. By submitting directly to Malpaso, he set off what the urbane Daley later described as a "royal clusterf—k." His independent mailing to Malpaso potentially cut Weyr and the Morris Agency out of the movie contract.

However much Eastwood liked the Josey Wales book, his eye was always on the bottom line. When he learned Malpaso had earlier received a copy of the book from Carter, his response to Daley was immediate: "Why the hell should we get involved with William Morris?" "[Carter] sent the damned thing to us directly." Known for his penny pinching, Eastwood believed that he could cut a direct deal at a lower cost with an unknown author. In the flurry of exchanges that followed between the lawyers for Malpaso and the William Morris Agency, Daley acknowledged that no one at Malpaso had actually read Carter's crudely printed paperback. Eventually, Eastwood agreed to a contract through Weyr for $25,000 with another $5,000 if production began and a final $15,000 if the film showed a profit (nearly $240,000, in 2023 dollars). With a total budget of less than $4 million, it was a surprisingly generous offer to an unpublished author and a reflection of the enthusiasm of both Daley and Eastwood.[648]

Nearly two decades before he wrote *Gone to Texas*, Carter had delivered at least four radio broadcasts describing the desperate struggles in "Bloody Kansas" between pro- and anti-slavery factions before and during the Civil War.[649] His dramatic accounts always revolved around Frank James and his younger brother, Jesse,who began their career riding with William Quantrill and "Bloody Bill" Anderson, the two most notorious

Confederate guerilla leaders and eventually the best-known outlaws after the war. Driven by lurid newspaper accounts in the 1870s and 1880s, the James brothers, particularly Jesse, became the subject of dozens of books, films, and a Republic Pictures movie serial in the 1930s. While the portrait of Jesse and Frank differed in each portrayal, few accounts had any relationship to historical reality.

Frank James was part of Quantrill's band that descended on the abolitionist stronghold of Lawrence, Kansas, in August 1863. For twenty-four hours, they looted, burned, and slaughtered more than one hundred sixty unarmed men and boys, some as young as twelve. A year later, Jesse joined Frank as they enlisted in "Bloody Bill" Anderson's "bushwhackers" and robbed a train near Centralia, Kansas. When they discovered two dozen unarmed Union soldiers in a passenger car, many of them furloughed because of their war injuries, Anderson's Confederate guerillas executed, scalped, and mutilated their bodies.[650]

The political justifications for pro-Union and pro-Confederate guerillas often seemed little more than an excuse for looting and indiscriminate bloodletting, but popular writers of the period and later filmmakers seldom described the atrocities that marked both sides during the conflict.

To Asa Carter, the James brothers were brave Southerners, fighting to protect their lives and property against the hated abolitionist "Jayhawkers," "Bushwhackers," and Kansas Redlegs. And after the war, the brutal oppression of federal soldiers who supported the Yankee carpetbaggers, traitorous white Southern scalawags, and ignorant Blacks during the Reconstruction era forced the two men to take up arms again, he told his listeners in a broadcast he made in the mid-1950s:

> This was the bloody period of Reconstruction in the Southland. The years when the southerner was pushed to the brink of savagery and where hope was almost abandoned. . . . The South lay crippled and starving, crushed by an all-powerful army and occupied by nigra and Yankee troops and carpetbag militia. It was then that the name of Jesse James came into prominence. . . . His name began to appear in the newspapers. Jesse James had raided a carpetbagger bank; Jesse James had stopped the train run by the hated rich

> Yankee. . . . What he was doing, of course, was proving that the all-powerful national government was not all powerful. He spit in the face of the mighty and he returned to do it again and again and again. He became a symbol of hope to the barefooted southern woman digging sweet root from the ground. He became the angel of miracles to the southern man that they could rise up and achieve victory over tyranny, over military occupation. . . . He became a spirit of resistance, as other men have become in other wars. He didn't have a uniform. He had no metals, no prestige. But he was no outlaw.[651]

Nothing infuriated Carter more than books and articles that began to appear in the 1940s and 1950s describing the Jameses as ruthless bandits and dismissing the popular notion that they were modern day Robin Hoods. Such "trash" was written by "pseudo-intellectual liberal, revisionist historians," said Carter in one of his broadcasts. James was a "true Confederate." And that was certainly true, as T. J. Stiles showed in his prize-winning biography *Jesse James: Last Rebel of the Civil War.*[652]

Both Josey Wales and Carter's model, Jesse James, were what one film critic called the "apotheosis of a [movie] subgenre" where the Confederate avenger is the hero and "the villains are soldiers who fought to end slavery and maintain the Union." From the 1930s to the 1960s, with the moral issues of slavery still absent from popular culture, ex-Confederate heroes became a Hollywood staple: John Wayne, *The Lonely Trail* (1936, *The Undefeated* (1969), *True Grit* (1969); Clark Gable, (*Gone With the Wind,* 1939); Gary Cooper (*Vera Cruz,* 1954); Rod Steiger (*Run of the Arrow*, 1957), and Jimmy Stewart (*Shenandoah*, 1965).[653]

For Eastwood, the great attraction of *Gone to Texas* was less the political content than the fast-paced narrative, with adventures, danger, violent shootouts, and a crude but typical Western hero who combined a fast six-gun, loyalty to his friends, and a thirst for vengeance as he dispatched despicable villains. Like many of Eastwood's films, the saga of Josey Wales is the story of a central character constantly on the move toward or away from danger. In his earlier films, particularly Sergio Leone's "spaghetti Westerns," the central character—often called the "man with no name"—emerged without a past and no suggestion of a future. To Eastwood, the deeper backstory of

Josey Wales and why he became a gunfighter created a character with more depth, complexity, and even a bit of humor.

Eastwood also explained to one interviewer that he had been attracted to the "whole treatment of war in general and how it not only destroys the lives of people in combat, but those around him. While he never saw the Civil War story as a direct parallel to the Vietnam War, he recognized some resonance between the two. "I think the dislocation could be the same after every war," he said.[654]

A quarter-century after the release of the film and the exposure of Carter's past, Eastwood defensively told an interviewer that he had kept the pro-South, anti-North emphasis of the book, but he "stripped the book of much of its political ideology." A comparison of the novel and the movie script shows that he did downplay some of the overtly political message of Carter's book, but in a promotional interview with film critic Roger Ebert, Eastwood made it clear that he also shared, on a much less visceral level than Carter, his generation's common assumptions about the excesses of abolitionists and the evils of Reconstruction. The Kansas Redlegs were "a lot like carpetbaggers," he told Ebert. While abolitionists might praise them as heroic, "they were just as much renegades as [William] Quantrill."[655]

And Eastwood certainly shared Asa Carter's general anti-government philosophy.

If the strength of Carter's work, his timing, and his ability to "sell" himself had made his gamble successful, it was also the result of chance. Rhoda Weyr's presence at the William Morris Agency and the fact that she had vouched for him with Eleanor Friede and with Malpaso Productions had proved the critical link between obscurity and national prominence as a writer.

With that success came increasing mental pressure as the likelihood grew that someone would unmask Carter's new identity.

20

The Making of a Con Man

Carter was very, very smart. I always knew that. I never thought of him as an innocent. Once I met him, I knew that, except when he was drunk, he knew what he was doing at every minute. And he was handling me, he was handling the publishing world, he was handling Clint Eastwood, he was handling our Los Angeles office. . . . We weren't handling him.

— Rhoda Weyr, Asa Carter's movie agent[656]

Once settled in Abilene, Carter methodically began to make the connections he would need for his new life. A visit to Chuck and Betty Weeth's bookstore in March of 1973 was his first stop even though Delacorte's publication of his Josey Wales manuscript was nearly a year away. The handsome Indian author captivated the Weeths, and Chuck was soon on the phone with the publisher's book representative to arrange a future book-signing. Weeth interviewed Carter for his weekly television program on Abilene's CBS affiliate, KTXS, and invited him to dinner. And over several meals, the Weeths introduced him to Abilene friends who shared their passion for history and literature.

He was "so convincing an actor," said Chuck Weeth, "that we took him at face value, because that's what you do in West Texas." What attracted the Weeths was Carter's personality: "The stories that he told acted as a magnet to people and just drew us all in happily, joyously, to find out all we could about this man and the story he was telling."[657]

Other than his friend Don Josey, no one Carter met would prove more important to establishing his new identity than Lawrence Clayton, a cultural historian and folklorist at Abilene's Hardin-Simmons University. From day one, Carter captivated the usually skeptical Clayton, who specialized in "cowboy culture" and Western history. "I've studied a lot of storytellers in my time," said Clayton. With his "expressive baritone voice he could spin a yarn that had you on the edge of your seat. . . . I liked him from the start."[658]

Although Clayton's books and articles were academic rather than popular, he was an influential figure among Western writers and historians, serving as president of the West Texas Historical Association, the Southwest Popular/American Culture Association, the Texas Folklore Society, and the Western Literature Association. With connections throughout the Southwest, he was soon Carter's unofficial promoter, inviting him to speak to classes, signing him up for talks and autograph parties, as well as arranging for his appearance at various conferences and "literary" gatherings in Texas and nearby states.

As Carter settled into Abilene, Rhoda Weyr and Eleanor Friede promoted his work. Weyr had discovered "Forrest" Carter and made it possible for him to become a published writer, but his literary agent, Eleanor Kask Friede, would spend the next five years—and more—tirelessly promoting him.

Born Eleanor Kask, she and her two younger brothers grew up in a modest house on Long Island. Her father, a seaman for a transatlantic shipping company based in New York, spent long years away. "Distant and austere," as she described him, he seemed to ignore her most of the time while her mother focused attention on Eleanor's brothers. After graduating from Glen Cove High School in 1938, she enrolled in Long Island's newly created Hofstra College. Although her home was only eight miles from the college, she moved into a boarding house near the campus and seems never to have looked back. She seldom spoke of her family and neither of her surviving younger brothers was listed in her obituary.[659]

Always described as "glamorous," Kask excelled in athletics and academics. Her 1942 classmates voted her "Most likely to Succeed."[660] And with the men away at war, she found a job as a copyeditor for World Publishing Company. Driven and career-focused, Kask seemed, in the admiring words of one of her editors, "completely devoted to her work" as she moved up in the publishing world to senior marketing director at Macmillan, one of the nation's most prestigious publishers. But at age thirty, her life changed when she met Donald Friede, a literary agent and sometimes publisher who had inherited a fortune from his father in the early 1920s. Twenty years her senior, Donald Friede had a well-deserved reputation for womanizing. During (and between) his two earlier marriages, he had a number of well publicized romantic relationships including a brief fling with the glamorous movie star Jean Harlow. But in 1950 Friede met the beautiful young Eleanor Kask at a charity event and was, as he later said, "absolutely smitten." He swept her up in a whirlwind courtship of flowers and dinners at upscale New York restaurants and within three months they had married. When Donald Friede died in 1965, Eleanor inherited his still considerable fortune, took up flying, bought her own private plane, and lived comfortably in their large Manhattan apartment.

But she remained fiercely devoted to her career.

Her professional breakthrough as editor came in 1969 when she persuaded Macmillan to publish a much-rejected manuscript about an adventurous seagull. Written by former Air Force pilot Richard Bach, *Jonathan Livingston Seagull* was a fable filled with pithy observations that captured the self-affirming spirit of the 1960s and '70s. ("You have the freedom to be yourself, your true self, here and now, and nothing can stand in your way.") The novella sold more than three million hardback copies and led to Friede's own imprint at Delacorte Press, giving her leeway to publish almost anything she liked.[661]

Like Weyr, Friede had been enthusiastic about Carter's manuscript. Within months after signing *Gone to Texas,* she was equally enthralled with its colorful "Indian" author. Over the next five years, in lengthy telephone conversations and long letters, Carter became

Eleanor Kask Friede, 1973.

more than a literary client. At one point, she casually mentioned that her father had emigrated from Estonia. In his next letter, Carter had obviously done some research on the history of Estonia and described the achievements and heroism of its people. She seemed bemused but also touched by his efforts to find a deeper connection. Soon her letters were as much personal as professional. Much of his correspondence was filled with colorful stories she found entertaining and sometimes moving. At the same time, his apparent lack of sophistication (and his Indian background) made her willing to overlook a drinking problem that was obvious in many of his telephone calls. In early 1975, she confided to him about her struggles growing up with a distant father who was always away and a mother who often ignored her. Carter responded with a long letter filled with sympathy and manufactured tales of friends he had known who dealt with the same problem.

Rhoda Weyr was never sure whether Friede and Carter were simply close friends or more, despite the fact they had not actually met. What Weyr did know from conversations with her friend Friede was that "he made her feel like a woman. He made her feel attractive."[662]

However close her relationship with Carter, Friede found nothing more frustrating than her difficulty in staying in touch with him at critical times. In one letter he would be "up with my Cherokee friends in Ducktown [Tennessee]"; in others, "camping in the hills" of north Texas or "fasting with my Indian brothers at the Creek Council House" in Muskogee, Oklahoma. Once he explained he would be beyond contact for weeks on a "spiritual fast" in Oklahoma's Wichita Mountains, where the Apaches had once hunted buffalo.

In reality, he spent most of his time at his St. George Island home or operating out of Asa Jr.'s home in Abilene. He created tales of his journeys into the wilderness for "spiritual renewal" by sending letters to Friede through friends in southeast Tennessee, Oklahoma, and north Texas. They would mail them from isolated post offices with a return address: "General Delivery: Forrest Carter." When Friede responded with letters to Ducktown, Tennessee, North Carolina's Eastern Cherokee Reservation, the Cookson Hills, near Tahlequah, Oklahoma, and other sites of Carter's "pilgrimages," friends picked up her letters and mailed them to Carter on St. George

Island, or more often to Abilene where he spent much of his time building his new identity.

In the spring of 1975, Friede became particularly frustrated over her inability to connect with him. In one telephone call, he agreed to sign a contract for his latest manuscript, an account of his childhood as a Cherokee-American boy in the mountains of eastern Tennessee. She needed his signature, and she also wanted to brief him on plans to promote the Josey Wales book. When he called her from Ducktown, Tennessee, which he described as "north of Atlanta" (three hours north, to be precise), she insisted they meet. She had made plans to pick up her plane in Florida, where she had stored it for the winter, and fly it back to New York. Initially reluctant, he called the next day and invited her to join him at his home on St. George Island. He suggested that she fly into Bear Creek, Georgia, where a local businessman had opened a small airport south of Atlanta. The Bear Creek airport was a strange choice, since there was a commercial airport in Apalachicola, less than twenty miles away from his island home. But Friede's sense of Southern geography seemed as deficient as her knowledge of characters like Carter.

Apprehensive about meeting Carter for the first time, she invited Faith Hubley to join her. Hubley, along with her husband John, was an Oscar-winning Hollywood animator who had moved from Hollywood to New York in 1970 and soon became one of Friede's few close friends.

In early 1973, Carter had sent a photograph of himself, standing in a shaded forest, and she was surprised, even a bit shocked, when she stepped out of the cockpit and saw him for the first time. In an interview twenty-five years later, she never used the word "dissolute," but his appearance unsettled her. He looked much heavier than his picture, and he had the look of someone who had been drinking far too much.

But "Forrest" proved as charming in person as his letters had suggested. On the long drive down to St. George Island, he regaled Friede and her friend with stories of his colorful past growing up in the mountains of east Tennessee and later wrangling horses across the Southwest. For Hubley, who had never been south of Washington, D.C., the roadside vistas of rural shacks, open fields, and occasional grand antebellum homes proved as fascinating as a visit to some exotic foreign destination. When they

Forrest Carter 1973 photo from The Education of Little Tree *book jacket, 1976.*

arrived on St. George, India was nowhere to be seen and was never mentioned over the next two days. At the time, Friede was unsure if he was married and did not ask.

As they arrived, Carter introduced them to "Ron" and "Rusty." Over two days, neither Friede nor Hubley learned their last names (Ron Taylor and Rusty Thornhill). In 1970, Taylor had worked closely with Carter in organizing the racist group, The Southerners. In 1978, Thornhill, a Nashville musician, would become a key figure in Carter's efforts to produce a film sequel to his first book.

As Faith Hubley walked into the modest three-bedroom house, the first thing she saw was fourteen pairs of small sneakers lined up against the wall. Forrest explained that each year, he arranged for fourteen Navajo children to come and spend two weeks with him. He described to Friede and Hubley how he had taken them out on the shore to wade into the sea for the first time. "See, these are desert children," he explained, and they would all "put their fingers in the sea and then in their mouth," gesturing as he described their wide-eyed wonder. It was beautiful, Hubley recalled. "This is something people can't make up."[663]

But of course it was made up.

Over the next thirty-six hours, Friede—an excellent cook—whipped up several meals while Forrest and his two friends made sure they had plenty to drink. Thornhill played his guitar and Carter performed Cherokee chants. Mostly the three men regaled them with colorful stories of a land far, far away from Manhattan. Carter drank steadily but remained pleasant, often dominating the conversation as he entertained Friede and Hubley with humorous, but outlandish tales of his life as an Indian. Only later did Friede reflect that, in dozens of telephone conversations and letters and in her island visit, Carter often described colorful accounts with his Indian and cowboy friends, but he said nothing about his personal life.[664]

As Carter made the six-hour drive back to Bear Creek Airport, he suddenly stopped by the side of the road next to a wooded area, picked up two pine cones and got back in the car.

These are to remember you by, he told Friede and Hubley. "I'll probably never see you again." And then he began weeping.

"I loved this man," said Hubley.

DESPITE HIS SHIFTING LOCATIONS, between the late fall of 1973 and early spring of 1975, Carter mailed both Weyr and Friede three manuscripts: *The Outlaw Josey Wales,* self-published as *Gone to Texas*; *The Vengeance Trail of Josey Wales*; and *The Education of Little Tree.* He also gave Friede an outline of what would be his fourth book, a fictional biography of the Apache chief Geronimo.[665]

The speed of his writing stunned Weyr and Friede. They did not know

Carter with a fan at a 1975 book signing in Abilene, Texas.

that Carter had begun working on the first three of his books a decade earlier.

In the years that Carter worked for George Wallace, the governor's entourage remained divided on the merits (and usefulness) of their speechwriter and Klan conduit. Seymore Trammell, one of Wallace's closest advisers, described him as a "hand grenade with the pin pulled out most of the way." He admired Carter's writing skills, but never trusted him. Despite Trammell's skepticism, Ace Carter had his supporters in the Wallace administration, and few were closer to him than Howard White, a state purchasing agent who seemed to spend much of his time as a political operative. The two had met in 1963 and bonded over their passion for Southern history, often sharing books and articles and visiting the state archives together to research local and state history.

When White paid a 1967 visit to Carter's White Plains home, the piles of books and historical materials surrounding a cluttered desk were impressive. With Carter's duties reduced after Lurleen Wallace took office, he had more time on his hands which he spent writing at his White Plains farmhouse. While the two sat and talked during White's visit, Asa pointed to a large pile of hand-written manuscript pages. "It's the story of a man named Josey Wales," Carter told him. There was also some other material about an Indian boy growing up in the mountains of east Tennessee. "I'm going to be a writer," Carter confided. White only skimmed through the material; he would realize later that the hand-written manuscripts were the first drafts of *Gone to Texas, The Vengeance Trail of Josey Wales,* and *The Education of Little Tree.* Carter's close friend Buddy Barnett also insisted that he had read a draft version of *Gone to Texas* in the late 1960s.[666]

As Carter began research on his fictionalized biography of Geronimo, he finished a revision of what he originally called "Gone to Mexico" but ultimately published as *The Vengeance Trail of Josey Wales.* He mailed it to Eleanor Friede and to Rhoda Weyr in late February 1975. Although Friede tactfully suggested that the draft needed additional polishing, she assured Carter that Delacorte would be offering a generous contract. Weyr immediately sent a copy to Clint Eastwood's partner, Bob Daley, arguing it would be an excellent sequel to *The Outlaw Josey Wales.*

Normally, studios kept authors at a distance as they converted book to movie, but Daley began a series of telephone calls and exchanges of letters with Carter, intrigued and attracted by what he called Carter's "folksy innocence." Daley's first hint that things might not go smoothly came after Carter called from Dallas in mid-May. Carter explained that he would be in Los Angeles the next day and would "like to drop in and meet him and Clint." Eastwood, who visited Los Angeles only when necessary, was relaxing at his home in Carmel-by-the-Sea, but Daley offered to send a driver to meet Carter at Los Angeles International Airport.

Carter never arrived, and early the next morning Daley received a call. "I got in a little fracas with some friends after we had a few too many," he cheerfully confided, and "ended up spending the night in jail." He assured Daley he would be there the next day and gave him his flight arrival time.

Art Ramus, Malpaso Productions' security man and driver, was there to greet Carter as he staggered through the gate, "drunk as a brewer's horse." After he propped Carter on a stool at the airport bar, he walked across the passageway to a pay phone and called Daley, explaining the problem. As they discussed what steps to take, suddenly Ramus interrupted. "Oh God, he's taking a whiz in the middle of the Satellite Lounge carpet." The studio driver rushed over to apologize just as an airport security officer arrived and began to arrest the unresponsive Carter—his fly still open—for public indecency. The quick-witted Ramus explained that Carter suffered from epilepsy that left him "confused and disoriented." Officer, he said, as he wrapped his arms around the drunken Carter, "I'll take care of him—he's my father." (Ramus was only ten years older than Carter.) After a night sleeping it off, Carter arrived at the studio, said nothing about his arrival in Los Angeles, and after a few minutes of chit-chat, abruptly stood: "Well I guess I ought to be getting back to Abilene."

Convinced that the episode the day before stemmed from Carter's fear of flying (which was real), Daley urged him to stay over another couple of days. He had an unbreakable commitment that evening, but he arranged to have Ramus and his secretary, Carol Rydall, take their out-of-town guest to dinner at a Los Angeles restaurant near Carter's hotel. Rydall had been intrigued by Daley's exchanges with this exotic Native American and was anxious to meet him. A bit uneasy after hearing Ramus describe Carter's arrival in Los Angeles, she persuaded another secretary on the Warner Brothers lot to join them for dinner.

It did not go well. Carter was drunk when he arrived at the restaurant and became more so as the evening wore on. In contrast to some of Carter's "mean drunk" episodes, he seemed in good spirits, intent on impressing the two attractive young women with stories of his colorful cowboy/Indian past. Then, without warning, he reached down to his boot, pulled out an eight-inch Bowie knife and held it to Rydall's throat. "I love you," he said. "If you don't marry me, I'm going to kill you and then kill myself." Ramus remembered how calm Rydall remained as she looked him at him intently and without expression for what seemed minutes but probably was only a few seconds. Without prompting, Carter gave a drunken smile and replaced the knife in his boot. The dinner was over. Despite her controlled reaction that evening, Rydall made it a point to be out of the office when Carter twice returned to Los Angeles over the next year.[667]

21

The Big Time with Barbara Walters

In the Great American Indian novel, when it is finally written, all of the white people will be Indians and all of the Indians will be ghosts.

— Sherman Alexie, "How to Write the Great American Indian Novel"[668]

Unaware of Carter's misadventures in Los Angeles, Rhoda Weyr and Eleanor Friede worked to arrange a full-scale roll-out of the Josey Wales book. Although *The Outlaw Josey Wales* would not appear in movie theaters until the following year, their plan was to promote the book in tandem with the forthcoming film. Like many publishers, they hoped to have their author interviewed on NBC's *Today Show*, the most watched early morning television show in America, with as many as twenty million viewers. The show was co-hosted by Barbara Walters, the first woman to hold such a position on national television. After meeting with Friede, the *Today Show*'s executive producer expressed interest in having Carter as a guest, but hesitated.

When Friede described her inability to get a firm commitment, Carter moved into action. In early June, he told Friede and Weyr that he had arranged for Chief Edward Evans of the Florida Muscogee-Creek tribe and Oklahoma Comanche Chief Nevaquaya to send telegrams to Barbara Walters, urging her to interview "their brother" Forrest Carter.

It was a classic Carter operation. After he moved into his home on St. George Island in 1973, he introduced himself to Evans, who lived just across the bay on the mainland. Widely respected in the small Indian community,

Evans held the honorific title of "Chief" because of his work on behalf of the Muskogee-Creek tribe but never held an official position. The previous year, Carter had prepared a statement endorsing *Gone to Texas.* Always ready to support a fellow Indian, Evans, who could barely read and write, signed it. Carter excerpted a section of the endorsement and sent it under Evans's name as a telegram to Walters at the *Today* show.[669]

The second telegram supposedly came from "Chief Nevaquaya." Unlike Evans, Joyce Lee Nevaquaya was a nationally known Indian celebrity. Through the 1940s and 1950s, the Oklahoma artist and musician had revived the art of the traditional Comanche wood flute and recorded for Folkways Records. Nevaquaya proved to be one of the most popular artists performing at the annual National Folk Festival and later appeared at venues around the nation including the Kennedy Center.[670] Earlier in June, Carter had written to Clint Eastwood's co-producer, Bob Daley, describing what he claimed was a twenty-year "personal and close friendship" with Nevaquaya. "We have rode together here to yonder and many times camped in the Wichita Mtns."[671]

In the telegram, Nevaquaya, who described himself as "Chief of the Penateka Band of Comanches," told Walters that Carter's was the first book that "accurately shows the character, the spirit and the morals of the Comanche. . . ." We want to share this with America," he said as he closed the telegram with a poetic tribute to his friend. "You will find Forrest Carter a person of depth, humor and perception, as I have found him over the years as we rode together and where we camped the wind was always soft and the water was sweet."[672]

But the Comanche artist never described himself as a "chief." Nor is there any evidence that he and Carter had ever met, let alone been fast friends.[673] The real giveaway came in the last sentence in the telegram: "where we camped the wind was always soft and the water was sweet." In an autographed copy of *Gone to Texas* he gave to Dallas columnist Bob St. John, "Forrest" had written: "Across the trails we've traveled, the fire has been warm, the wind soft, the water sweet."[674]

Despite being bogus, the telegrams worked. Only days after receiving endorsement by the two Indian "chiefs," NBC scheduled the interview for June 29. Though Carter had worked hard to obtain the interview, he seemed to hesitate when Rhoda Weyr called to give him the good news and to confirm his flight and hotel arrangements for the trip to New York. He wasn't sure if he would be able to answer Barbara Walter's questions without making a fool of himself. And, as an Indian, he plaintively asked her, "Will the hotel let me in?"

"Of course they're going to let you in," replied Weyr, "This is New York."

Concerned over her client's lack of sophistication and experience, she impulsively added: "You can come and stay with us." She, her husband, and their four daughters had a large Manhattan apartment, she explained. It would be more restful to be with the family on the evening before the NBC interview than to stay alone in a hotel.

When she told her husband that Carter would be staying with the family, he warned her: "You know, Indians often have a problem with liquor. Do you think I should offer him a drink when he comes?"

He's our guest, she had replied, "Of course you offer him a drink."

When the downstairs doorman called to say that Carter had arrived, Rhoda, her husband, and their four daughters (ages fourteen to four) waited for his arrival. She opened the door to see him for the first time: "tall, dark-complexioned," with a neatly trimmed mustache, dressed in blue jeans, cowboy boots, a denim jacket, a shirt with a bolo tie, and a large black cowboy hat. His opening line surprised Weyr. "Wow, that's some big nigger you got running that thing," he said as he nodded toward the elevator operator. But he smiled, introduced himself to the girls, and handed each a pair of Indian moccasins.

After Weyr sent her two youngest daughters up to bed, Carter settled into the living room with her husband and the two older girls. The conversation was mostly "chit-chat," remembered Weyr's husband, Tom. Carter gave a vivid description of his recent trip to see his "close friend Clint" [Eastwood] in Los Angeles and the positive reviews of *Gone to Texas.* He also seemed nervous and fearful about his coming interview with Barbara Walters.

While she made last-minute preparations for their dinner, Weyr could barely hear the conversation in the next room, but when her fourteen-year-old daughter came into the kitchen, she said that Carter had put his arm around her on the sofa and said, "You're really a looker. You all are, but you're really a looker." She seemed uncomfortable, but shrugged it off.

During dinner Carter switched to wine and continued drinking. Steadily. When the Weyrs' ten-year-old daughter began asking him questions about growing up as an Indian, he tried to answer, but slurred his words and his remarks took on a vaguely threatening tone. "I felt like I was dealing with a cobra or something," said Rhoda Weyr. "I thought he was dangerous."

Anxious to end the evening, she moved the five back into the living room. Weyr's two older daughters sat down on the sofa. Suddenly Carter lurched out of his seat, sat between them and again started talking about how beautiful they were. He didn't use the words, said Weyr, but "nubile and desirable" sprang to her mind as she watched him leaning forward talking to each of them.

Frightened, but furious, she told the girls to "say good night to Mr. Carter" and hustled them into the bedroom where they were sleeping together to give a private room and bath to their guest. "I was really scared," she said. She instructed them to place a chair in front of their door. She became even more unnerved when Carter revived and began insisting they all "go out and do the town."

Fortunately, he soon passed out on the sofa, where he spent the night. He got up the next morning with hardly a word, drank a cup of coffee, and went downstairs to meet the driver from Delacorte Press who picked him up for the short ride to the *Today Show* studio downtown in the Rockefeller Center's RCA Building.

As her husband walked out the door on the way to work, he asked, "Is he going to stay another night?"

"No way in hell is he staying here tonight," she told him.[675]

As Eleanor Friede met Carter in the *Today Show* make-up room, she assured him he would be fine. Privately, she feared a disaster. "I wanted to sell books," she said, and she had seen Walters dismantle interviewees. "Barbara Walters is a tough lady. She always asks the questions everyone wanted to know and wouldn't dare ask. And she could be nasty if she didn't like you." Despite her assurances that things would go well, Carter remained unnerved. As he and Friede sat in the green room waiting to go on camera, he kept murmuring, "She's going to skin me alive. She's going to skin me alive."

Barbara Walters and Frank McGee on the Today show studio set, 1975. No image of Walters with Carter exists because those tapes were reused in later years.

When Walters entered the green room, Carter nervously rolled the brim of his Stetson around and around while looking down at the floor. Whether to calm him or because he evoked in the host what Friede called a "motherly instinct," Walters put her hand on his knee and softly told him: "You're going to be fine. I promise, you're going to be fine."

Weyr and Friede knew Carter was frightened, but they had no way of understanding that his real terror was that he would be recognized by viewers as Asa Carter, destroying the identity he had so carefully constructed over the previous two years. When the interview began, said one friend, he "had his black hat pulled way down. He had tanned himself up, grew a mustache, lost about twenty pounds." Oscar Harper, who had put Carter on his payroll during the Wallace years, was on edge as the interview started, anxiously "hoping [Walters] wouldn't ask him about the Ku Klux Klan."[676] Watching a monitor in the green room, Friede gradually began to relax as Walters "rolled over like a pussycat." Her questions were gentle and open-ended, allowing Carter to retell a story that he had been shaping for years.

Although there is no video of the fourteen-minute interview—the networks in that era often taped over earlier recordings to save money—it went well. And despite his fears of exposure Carter had called several close friends in Alabama to tell them about his upcoming appearance. "Hell, I think half of Montgomery had heard he was going to be on television," said Seymore Trammell. Most enjoyed Carter's ability to "pull a good one" on the Queen of Yankee media.

Montgomery Circuit Judge Richard Emmet remembered how the former Klansman and Wallace speechwriter modestly but skillfully sketched his colorful background as a cowboy horse wrangler and storyteller to the Cherokee Nation. Ray Andrews, who had worked with Carter in the 1960s, recalled little more than Walters's opening question. "Are you a real cowboy, Mr. Carter," she asked? "Yes, mayam," said Carter, the "mayam" stretching into two elongated syllables. Andrews just shook his head as his old friend—a polished radio announcer—drawled his way through the interview with "aint's" and an "aw shucks" delivery. "I literally got down on the floor laughing," said another Alabama friend. "Asa had pulled it off. He had fooled them."[677]

Unlike Carter's friends, Alabama viewers who had tangled with him were not amused. Within hours, the NBC switchboard received dozens of long-distance calls from viewers complaining that the network had given publicity to a known Klansman and violent segregationist. Weyr also began receiving calls at her office. Her reaction? "Well, that's ridiculous!" She had always believed that Carter used poetic license to write about his childhood with his Indian grandparents, but she never doubted that they were real. "After all, he clearly was an Indian." And despite his casual use of the "N" word when she first met him, "I was such an unknowing racist that I just couldn't conceive that he was an anti-black Indian racist. I just dismissed it."

So did Eleanor Friede. She assured Weyr that there were simply a "lot of people who did not want him to succeed and they were trying to discredit his book." Rhoda Weyr's husband captured Carter's power to override any second thoughts about his legitimacy. "He looked the part," said Tom Weyr. "He acted the part. He talked the part. He moved the part. He was very persuasive."[678] Once his Abilene friend Lawrence Clayton learned that Carter was actually an Alabama ex-Klansman, he looked back and marveled at the ability of "Forrest" to remain the "master of his identity." While he told slightly different versions of his life, said Clayton, there was "rarely, if ever, a slip in the facade he maintained."[679]

Neither Weyr nor Friede mentioned to Carter the angry telephone calls they, as well as NBC had received in the days after the Walters interview.

WITH THE *Today Show* interview safely behind, Carter began working in earnest on his Geronimo manuscript. He had always been drawn to the story of the extraordinary Chiricahua Apache leader who had mounted a successful and bloody war during the early 1880s against Mexican and American soldiers. Moving back and forth across the border between the New Mexico territory and the northern Mexican state of Chihuahua, Geronimo emerged from his hideouts in the northern Sierra Madre Mountains, to outmaneuver, outfight, and frustrate larger American and Mexican forces.

As early as the late fall of 1973, Carter had appeared at the public library in Sweetwater, Texas, forty miles west of Abilene and in the weeks that followed, rented a small apartment a few blocks away. Each morning, he arrived as the library opened, spreading out his writing materials and taking notes on yellow legal pads.

From his first day, said librarian Darlene Walker, he looked like no other patron who had ever entered the Sweetwater library. With high-heeled cowboy boots, he stood six feet tall and wore a fringed buckskin leather jacket and a wide-brimmed Stetson with a feather in the hatband. On that first visit, "He let us know that he was part Indian," said Walker, and talked about his research for his biography of the Indian leader, Geronimo. He captivated Walker and all the library staff as he described his recent success as a self-taught writer and entertained them with fictional accounts of his Indian heritage and his equally fictional close friendship with Clint Eastwood and other celebrities.

Somehow, Walker said, he never seemed boastful but modest and self-deprecating as he dismissed the suggestion that he was an important writer. "He was so gentle, you know, sweet." The library staff went to great lengths to obtain books or materials he requested. And she saw that he enjoyed "all the ladies" surrounding him and listening to his every word. "He was a big fish over here in a little pond as compared to Abilene. . . . We showed him a lot of attention and we asked him questions and he liked all that."[680]

Despite claims to reporters that he had done extensive original research, including interviewing "several Apaches on the reservation, including some of the tribal historians," the Sweetwater library proved adequate for his research.[681]

In 1970, the University of New Mexico Press had published the journal of Dr. Leonard Wood, a physician who accompanied army soldiers in their last exhausting campaign against Geronimo. In his diary-like account, he vividly described the day-by-day events that led to the final surrender of Geronimo in 1886. A year later, Western writer (and leading national conservationist) Alexander Adams published the first carefully researched study of the Indian leader's life. Although Adams was a self-taught scholar, professional historians and reviewers praised his generally sympathetic treatment of Geronimo as well as his carefully researched description of the "connivances, blunder, savagery and heroism that characterized the removal of the Apaches from their New Mexico lands."[682] Carter's other major source material came from *Geronimo: His Own Story.* Compiled by an Oklahoma school superintendent and published in 1907, the Indian leader's reminiscences had long been out of print when E. P. Dutton republished the book in 1970 with an extended introduction by American historian and naturalist Frederick W. Turner III. A close reading of Carter's Geronimo biography shows that he combined details from these three works with his vivid imagination.[683]

As he worked long hours on his epic tale of Geronimo, he wrote Bob Daley outlining his ideas for promoting the upcoming filming of *The Outlaw Josey Wales.* During that summer of 1975, Eastwood was on the road, promoting his latest film, *The Eiger Sanction,* with print and television interviews. Pointing to the success of the *Today Show* interview, Carter urged Daley to arrange appearances on the popular Merv Griffin and Johnny Carson television shows. He could bring along one "authentic" Apache and a Comanche friend to promote *Gone to Texas.* They could also talk about Eastwood's planned film version of the book.

Daley responded evasively only to have Carter fly out to Los Angeles to strengthen his pitch for television appearances. Daley managed to sidetrack the proposal. Malpaso wanted to concentrate all promotion efforts during the year of the film's release, he explained. When Carter left, Daley heaved a sigh of relief. "The last thing Clint or I wanted was for Forrest and his friends to appear on the [Johnny] Carson or [Merv] Griffin shows. It would have been the Little Big Horn and Custer all over again. The networks would never have survived."[684]

As the film production date neared, Carter bombarded Daley with letters and calls, offering suggestions on everything from Indian costumes to Union Army ordinance, to the smoke signals of various tribes, to the silent hand signals used by soldiers in their maneuvers. He actually would have been useful, conceded Daley, since he seemed to have a deep knowledge of the history, costumes and armaments of the period. But had Carter been involved, said Daley, there would have been one overwhelming problem: "We never knew when he was going to show up roaring drunk, morning noon,or night." And when he was drunk, said Daley, he was volatile and dangerous to himself and others."

Eastwood planned to shoot outdoor segments of the film amid the striking sandstone rock formations of Utah's Coyote Buttes and "town" portions on a widely used "Old Tucson" film lot in Arizona four hundred miles to the south. But Carter was convinced that only the Big Bend region of south Texas, near the border with Mexico, was true to the book. If Eastwood did the filming there, Carter said he would arrange for his friend Don Josey to round up Texas oil roustabouts and wildcatters for crowd scenes. And his Comanche friends could organize an expedition of three hundred to five hundred "authentic" members of the tribe to appear in the film for a nominal fee. "All we needed was three hundred to five hundred full-blooded Comanches," said a horrified Daley, particularly if they shared Carter's affinity for whiskey and partying.[685]

Despite his constant references to his "friend Clint," Carter had only met Eastwood in person on one occasion, which seemed to go well. But as Carter continued to call and write, making suggestions (and polite criticisms), Eastwood finally agreed to talk with him by phone. By this time in his career, Eastwood had developed a low threshold for any form of conflict and an expectation of deference from his employees and those around him. He never told Daley the substance of the conversation, but afterwards he was emphatic in his instructions. Daley and his staff were to make certain that he was *never* to have a conversation or any interaction with Forrest Carter. "*Never,*" he repeated to Daley.[686]

Malpaso Productions had been relatively generous in Carter's contract, particularly for someone as parsimonious as Eastwood. But by December, with the film in mid-production, Carter was constantly calling Daley to request his second payment even though it was not due until the film had been completed.

In early 1976, without informing Rhoda Weyr (who was supposed to handle all negotiations on film issues), he called Daley asking why Malpaso was stalling on signing an option for *The Vengeance Trail of Josey Wales,* a sequel to the first book. He also sent a manuscript of *The Education of Little Tree* to Daley to see if he was interested in it as well.

Despite his personal distaste for Carter, Eastwood authorized Daley to explore an option for Carter's sequel in case *The Outlaw Josey Wales* should prove particularly successful at the box office. But in a conversation with a friend who was an agent in Los Angeles, Daley discovered that Carter already had signed a movie option for *The Education of Little Tree* with a well-known producer, Danny Arnold. Unnerved, he began calling around and discovered that, in addition to Carter's agreement with Arnold, Carter had signed *two* other options for the film rights to *The Education of Little Tree.* With Carter constantly demanding more money, and Malpaso anxious to be rid of him, Eastwood personally paid the last $15,000 on the *Josey Wales* contract, even though the film had yet to be released and Carter's last payoff was not due until gross profits had exceeded $4 million.[687]

Even after his disastrous conversation with Eastwood, Carter continued to write Daley, promoting a high-profile premiere in Dallas or Fort Worth. His wealthy and well-connected Texas friends would put on a "helluva show" and drum up lots of publicity. Daley was well aware of Carter's drinking problems, but he was particularly struck by one of the last letters he received in early June as they wrapped up the editing of the film. In it Carter repeated his claim of a close friendship with Nevaquaya and rambled on about gathering hundreds of Indians for a grand opening of the film. What struck Daley was the letter itself, hand-written in a barely readable scrawl.

And Eastwood had no interest in a red-carpet premiere. He was annoyed that though he was now a movie actor *and* a director he continued to be dismissed by critics who saw him only as the star of Sergio Leone's "spaghetti westerns." "I will never win an Oscar," he told his friends. "First of all because I'm not Jewish. Secondly, because I make too much money for all those old farts in the Academy. Thirdly and most importantly, because I don't give a fuck."[688]

Despite his claim that he cared nothing about the Hollywood establishment, Eastwood did want to establish his reputation as a serious actor and director. He agreed to premiere *The Outlaw Josey Wales* at a national conference on western films to be held at the Sun Valley Center for the Arts in Ketchum, Idaho, in late June 1976. Only weeks before the conference, Gail Lichtenstein wrote a lengthy piece, "What Made Hollywood Hop Back in the Saddle Again," in the *New York Times* describing the sudden resurgence of grand-scale western films after television had become the major outlet for the genre in the 1950s and 1960s.[689]

At Ketcham, Eastwood sat patiently for hours with the nation's leading academic film scholars and historians as they discussed Western film's "semiotics"—symbols and their use or interpretation. In one panel, Eastwood joined Jenni Calder, author of *There Must Be a Lone Ranger*; Siew-Hwa Beh, an early feminist critic; and Dartmouth professor Will Wright, whose book *Sixguns and Society* explored "abstract structural theory" to explain how the mythology of the Western film and the Western hero reflected the "social institutions and attitudes that have created and continued to nourish the myth."

Although critics' views varied, they agreed that the emergence of a new generation of filmmakers marked the death of the traditional western hero. "The frontier did not want to be civilized," said Calder, but at the same time, it spawned a hero to tame it." When that happened, the heroic figure could "no longer function in a new society and since he cannot adapt, is no longer a hero."

Siew-Hwa Beh, a feminist critic, emphasized the limited role of women in western films. Perhaps, she said, this was because women "try to deal within the community and within the self to resolve conflict" while the male heroic figure "seldom can join a community and is generally seen riding into the sunset at the end."

Eastwood listened politely and responded briefly. The 1953 film *Shane* remained the classic American western, and the form was not really that complicated. It could be reduced to a hero who recognizes that "everybody longs for vengeance and justice," said Eastwood. And almost every successful film ends in retributive violence. So long as westerns remained true to their past, they would continue to appeal to audiences in the future.[690]

For the most part, *The Outlaw Josey Wales* received positive reviews. One exception mattered most to Eastwood: Richard Eder, the newly named film and theater critic for the *New York Times* wrote that in this "soggy attempt at a post-Civil War western epic," the characters are established by "worn and dribbly" devices and "overact beyond belief":

> A hard-luck but winsome Indian girl repeatedly gets knocked off her feet or worse; a sneaky boatman cringes and leers; a spry old woman bustles about with a broom, shrills out hymns and grabs a rifle to shoot marauders; a doe-eyed young woman opens her eyes reindeer-size to convey fear, passion or bashfulness; a young follower of the outlaw [Josey Wales] manages three distinct and radiant deathbed scenes on one bullet hole.

Alone among reviewers, Eder identified pro-Confederate political themes in a storyline in which "every Unionist is vicious and incompetent, whereas Wales, despite his [tobacco] spitting, is really a perfect gentlemen." To the degree that a movie is embedded in the historical past, said Eder, "it should at least attempt to do it fairly."[691]

The general public did not share the viewpoint of the Harvard-educated film critic. With a production cost of less than $4 million, box office receipts totaled more than $32 million.[692]

Carter's erratic behavior and his tendency to sign multiple options for the same film convinced Daley that there were too many pitfalls to maintain a professional relationship. Over a two-year period, Daley had grown extremely fond of Carter despite their difficulties. At one point he had told Forrest about the painful last days of his father as he died of terminal cancer. In response, "Forrest wrote me some of the most wonderful, heartwarming and comforting letters I ever received."

But when Daley tried, as tactfully as possible, to explain that Eastwood was not interested in producing a sequel, Carter exploded with rage and sent Daley the last letter he would receive from his former friend. Daley found it hard to believe it came from the same person as he read Carter's words: "insulting, awful, and bigoted—racist, antisemitic. . . ." The Jews were stealing all his money, raged Carter. Daley and Eastwood had double-crossed him; they were worse than the "lowest nigger" in their dealings.[693]

Back in Abilene, Asa bitterly told Lawrence Clayton that Eastwood had refused to pay him his final payment and, as a result, he had decided not to allow Malpaso to film *Vengeance Trail*.[694]

BY THAT SUMMER, FORREST Carter had a far greater problem than the premiere of *The Outlaw Josey Wales* or movie options on his various books. A young Montgomery, Alabama, reporter threatened to unravel the identity he had so carefully constructed over the past three years.

It was not the first time he had faced the threat of exposure. Two years earlier, he learned from former neighbors in Alabama that FBI agents had interviewed them in an attempt to locate his whereabouts. He immediately returned to Alabama and visited the FBI agent in Anniston. He had written a western novel, he explained, and it would be "embarrassing to him if the FBI attempted to locate him. . . ." He gave the agent the telephone number of his friend Ray Burgess, a member of the Alabama legislature. If they should ever wish to contact him, said Carter, they should call Burgess. He was "about to make some money for the first time in his life," he said, and the last he wanted was something to go wrong.[695]

The Bureau closed its file on Carter.

Wayne Greenhaw proved a far greater threat. The thirty-year-old journalist gained something of a national reputation when he broke the first news of the My Lai massacre, even before Seymour Hersh's better-known stories that captured a Pulitzer Prize.[696] In early January 1976, Greenhaw had written a brief but generally positive review of *Gone to Texas* for the *Montgomery Advertiser.* John Pemberton, clerk of the Alabama House of Representatives teased Greenhaw, showing him a copy of *Gone to Texas* autographed by Asa Carter as well as a letter in which Carter talked about his contract with Delacorte. Embarrassed by his failure to see the connection since he had interviewed Carter several times, Greenhaw looked closely at the author photograph on the book jacket. Forrest Carter was not as heavy as Asa Carter had been in the 1960s and was darker in complexion, with a mustache and cowboy hat that made him appear a different individual on first glance. But it was Asa. By early August, Greenhaw had collected strong evidence of the double identity. Unable to reach "Forrest" Carter, who was in England promoting *Gone to Texas*, Greenhaw called Eleanor Friede and asked for her reaction.

She rejected his claim out of hand. The "loving and gentle giant I know as Forrest Carter would never have been a segregationist, much less a Klansman and definitely not antisemitic," she responded before hanging up. Still, Friede knew that an article accusing Forrest Carter of a Klan background (however false) was a potential public relations disaster. She urged him to call Greenhaw as soon as he returned from England.

At his desk in Montgomery, Greenhaw picked up the telephone late one afternoon to hear the unmistakable voice of Asa Carter. With airline announcements in the background, Carter opened the conversation. "Hey, old buddy, you don't want to hurt old Forrest, do you?" he said in a growling low-pitched "phony voice." For several minutes, the two verbally sparred as Greenhaw laid out his evidence: the autograph Carter had signed as "Asa" for Pemberton, the fact that the copyright for *Gone to Texas* listed the same address as that of Asa Carter, and most telling of all, the acknowledgment of Asa Carter's Montgomery attorney, R. B. Jones, that the two men were the same.

"Forrest" insisted that he was a cowboy and an Indian. He was the "nephew" of Asa Carter, a "mean and cruel man" who had divorced his wife, India. "Forrest" had married her after her divorce from Asa and become stepfather to their four children.

"Aw, cut out the bull," Greenhaw interrupted, "I know it's you." But Carter refused to back down and within hours sprang into damage control. He called Don Josey to give him a heads-up in case he was contacted by the press, and he talked to other friends in Montgomery, pleading with them to deny any connection between "Asa" and "Forrest." And a furious Carter was soon on the phone to Jones, threatening enough violence to send the Birmingham lawyer scrambling to withdraw his remarks. "Lay off the story,"

Jones warned Greenhaw, "you're going to ruin the shit out of me if you keep digging." I'll "sue your ass," he added, "if you get me involved in this."[697]

On August 26, after multiple rewrites and cuts to Greenhaw's piece, the *Times* finally published his story on an inside page with the headline: "Is Forrest Carter Really Asa Carter? Only Josey Wales May Know." Instead of giving the Montgomery journalist a byline, the *Times* labeled it, "Special to The New York Times."

Carter had scheduled a heavy round of promotional appearances in early September for *Gone to Texas* as well as his forthcoming book, *The Vengeance Trail of Josey Wales*, beginning with an interview with the *Dallas Morning News* book editor, an appearance at the annual "International Campfire Cook-off" in Texas, and opening-night remarks to start the Western Writers Book Show in Abilene. But just before the first event, he called Lawrence Clayton, clearly too drunk to function. Clayton covered for his friend, telling the organizers that Carter would not be able to attend since he was "writing a new book" and had to stay in the north Georgia mountains to work.[698]

Still concerned that Eleanor Friede might question his background, Carter sobered up enough to write two letters which he mailed, one signed by his wife, India and the other by his younger brother, Doug Carter.

India's letter told Friede about her tragic marriage to a "mean and cruel" Asa Carter. Fortunately, she had met Asa's nephew, Forrest, who was "bright and kind and generous. She had fallen in love with him, divorced her husband in Alabama, and eloped to begin a new life with Forrest.

In Doug's letter (actually written by Asa), he explained to Friede that Forrest was the brother of Asa Carter. In 1972, Asa was "stricken with failing health," Doug's letter said, and entered a Birmingham hospital, "the corridors filled with blacks." Sadly, his brother Asa had "gone incognito" ("we cannot locate him"). It was a bitter Asa who had "instituted this false story to gain publicity for himself," enlisting his "drug addicted" attorney, R. B. Jones and "certain political associates in Montgomery who advantaged themselves of an opportunity to capitalize on a family's tragic past and get their name in the paper." Doug's letter insisted that Forrest and Asa had the same last names, but they were not related. Forrest ("a man of great honor") had simply been a former employee of Asa who had generously and selflessly "sent funds to relieve my brother's medical burden." As was often the case when he was on a bender, Carter seemed to have forgotten that he had told both Greenhaw and Friede that he was the nephew of Asa.[699]

Despite such inconsistencies, Friede attributed the confusion to Carter's problems with drinking and assured her friend Rhoda Weyr that it was a fake controversy. And what seemed to be a disaster soon passed almost unnoticed. The *New York Times* story was ambiguous enough in its conclusions that it failed to gain traction. And articles in the Montgomery and Anniston newspapers that seemed to confirm Greenhaw's link between the two men never reached beyond the state. With no internet social networks to spread and develop the mystery of Forrest Carter, the story was soon forgotten.

Over the next few months, Carter disappeared from the public life he had created in Texas. After the publication of the *Times* story, he retreated to his St. George home, spending hours walking the beaches. And drinking. With one exception, he had few close contacts with other islanders. Ron Bloodworth, the owner of an Apalachicola, Florida, cement plant spent a great deal of time at the small St. George marina, constantly working on his thirty-foot sailboat. He had heard about Forrest and knew he was an author, but it was only in the early fall of 1975 that Carter, walking down by the marina, introduced himself to Bloodworth.

When Forrest was home, they often talked often about the history of St. George Island, but also about Carter's past, growing up with his Indian grandparents. "He never seemed to have a have an ego at all. And he never put on any airs about being more successful than anybody else." He did describe what he claimed were close friendships with actor Robert Mitchum and other Hollywood personalities, said Bloodworth but, oddly enough, he never mentioned Clint Eastwood.

Bloodworth introduced himself to India Carter when he saw her at the island's convenience store, and she seemed pleasant, "nice," but was clearly not interested in small talk. He heard from a neighbor that one of Carter's "nephews" (his son, Bedford) was living with him and had been in a fight at the small local bar. But beyond stories of his childhood with his Indian grandparents, Carter never talked about his family.[700]

In the spring of 1978 Carter returned to Abilene and resumed interviews and personal appearances, mainly in Texas, but also in nearby Oklahoma and New Mexico. Ever more expansive and factually careless in his newspaper interviews, he told a Texas reporter that Eastwood would start production in 1979 on a film version of *The Vengeance Trail of Josey Wales* (not true), that Eastwood had asked him to stand in for him for the London premiere of *The Outlaw Josey Wales* (the trip was arranged by Doubleday to promote his book; there was no movie premiere in England), that he had only gone to school for six months (obviously not true), and that he and his Creek Indian wife, "Annie" were married but he couldn't be sure of the date. "Annie remembers them things—I don't."[701]

Presumably his wife, India, did not read the Texas press.

Of all these invitations, none was more prestigious than the annual Book Author Benefit Luncheon sponsored by the Wellesley College Alumnae of Dallas. Held in the ballroom of the Sheraton-Dallas Hotel, the elegant ceremony featured awards to local and national authors and raised thousands of dollars for scholarships. It also drew considerable media coverage.

At the September 30 luncheon, Carter shared the spotlight with Barbara Tuchman, author of ten books and winner of the Pulitzer Prize for *The Guns of August* (1963) and for *Stilwell and the American Experience in China* (1972). In later years, no one could recall much about the remarks of Tuchman. They certainly remembered Asa Carter.

Following Tuchman's remarks, Carter lurched to the podium. In minutes it was clear to everyone that he was, as one of the organizers recalled, "three sheets to the wind." He had been drinking since the night before, having stayed up until 2 a.m. carousing in the hotel bar with his friend, Dallas newspaper columnist Bob St. John. Together they had entertained the customers, performing a "Cherokee War Dance," and singing repeated stanzas of "Red River Valley." St. John was too hung over to attend the luncheon, but, with a bit of the "hair of the dog," said St. John, Carter was off to the occasion.[702]

Despite the ripple of uneasiness in the audience, Forrest initially proved to be an entertaining, if highly intoxicated speaker. He drew upon his colorful Cherokee-cowboy background as he amused the audience with a self-deprecating account of his encounters with the strange ways of the white man. His New York editor had taken him to three cocktail parties in New York," he told the crowd. At the third one, as a guest approached him, his editor whispered: "He's gay." Of course I greeted him warmly, said Carter. "Howdy, Mr. Gay, I'm Forrest Carter."[703]

Jokes about homosexuals were hardly off-limits in 1978, but then he leaned forward and smiled at Tuchman, who sat just to his right on the dais. "I'm honored to be on the platform with this good ol' Jew gal," he said. (While Tuchman was not particularly religious, she was Jewish, and she and her well-to-do father had been outspoken supporters of Israel since its 1948 founding.)

Hester Parker, sitting at a table only a few feet away from Tuchman, remembered that she looked bewildered. It was so unexpected, she said, that it took a moment for Tuchman to absorb the offensiveness of the remark. Carter then turned back to the audience and pointed to Stanley Marcus, founder of the famous Neiman Marcus department stores and the major sponsor for the event. Marcus was not only a successful businessman, philanthropist, and bibliophile, but a strong supporter of the United Nations and an outspoken advocate for Black causes, positions that were not particularly popular in Dallas, Texas, in the 1960s. Like Tuchman, Marcus was not a devout Jew. He once joked to his friends that he would never visit Israel because he was afraid that he might be converted. Still, he embraced his Jewish background and financially supported the largest synagogue in the city.

"Now Stanley," Carter said, his arm waving awkwardly, "there's a good ol' Jew boy." There was a ripple of awkward laughter before he slumped back into his seat. In the silence that followed, Marcus grimly stared at Carter, clearly not amused. While several newspapers covered the event, none mentioned Carter's remarks about Tuchman and Marcus.[704]

A wealthy Dallas investment adviser had invited the speakers and luncheon organizers to a catered dinner that evening at his home in the city's prestigious Preston Hollow neighborhood. Carter arrived late and headed straight for the open bar where he downed several drinks before he began mingling with guests. Camilla Graves, one of the luncheon organizers, quickly realized that things were not going well when he sloshed a drink on one guest and began swearing about an insult he claimed to have received earlier in the day. Fortunately, their troublesome guest collapsed into a chair and passed out. As the guests filed into the large dining room for dinner, Graves, with the help of two caterers, discreetly piled him into a cab and sent him back to the Sheraton.[705]

22

Out of Control

"Oh what a tangled web we weave,
When first we practice to deceive!"
— Sir Walter Scott, *Marmion, Canto XVII*[706]

Only days after Carter's drunken speech in Dallas, Delacorte published *The Education of Little Tree.* The first pre-publication review was not auspicious. Writing for *Library Journal,* poet Judith McPheron had little use for the book. She found Carter's comparison between "the fatuous whites and freedom-loving Indians" so filled with stereotypes, its narration "so heavy-handed, so larded with sentimentality, pseudo-naivete, and cracker-barrel philosophy that all serious intentions are rendered bathetic."[707]

Those individuals who had a deep knowledge of Cherokee culture were less caustic but convinced that the book was inauthentic. David Scott, a well-known artist who spoke only Cherokee until he was thirteen, found the book far more a description of white mountaineer life than an account of Indian culture in eastern Tennessee. Freeman Owle, a member of the eastern band of Cherokees who spoke the language fluently and was an authentic storyteller to the tribe, found parts of the book "charming" and insightful in its description of the cruelties of Little Tree's boarding school. Owle's father had described how he had been beaten repeatedly with a leather strap and "saw children beaten until blood flowed from their backs" because they clung to their "heathenish" Cherokee ways at a similar "civilizing school."

But like Scott, he found the rest of the book bewildering. The Cherokee words Little Tree used to identify the animals of the mountains of eastern Tennessee seemed totally created by Carter. *Awinageehi* (or *ahwi*) was the Cherokee word for deer not *awusdi*; *go-ga* was the crow, not *kagu*; *guque*, was the quail hen, not *mine-e-lee,* and *tawodi*—sometimes *tsiwodi*—was the hawk, not *talcon.*

Repeatedly, Owle found minor incongruous details such as the reference to the family wearing deer-skin moccasins. By the early twentieth century, even in more remote communities, the Cherokee people had replaced moccasins with store-bought shoes, said Owle. And Carter had described his grandfather's skill in making moonshine whiskey even though Cherokee moonshiners were almost unknown, in part because they were "kept out of the business by the Scotch-Irish."

Most disconcerting was Little Tree's description of his physical and spiritual environment. In the book, Forrest Carter often described nature in poetic language, but always with a vagueness inconsistent with Cherokee life. My people, said Owle, were intensely attached to place. Where you lived, "every hill, every stream and every mountain has a name." None of that was present in Carter's book. And to Owle, the author's discussion of the "body-living mind" and the "spirit-living mind" as well as his references to "Mother Earth, "*Mon-o-lah,*" seemed "New Age-speak" that bore little relationship to the spiritual world of the Cherokee.[708]

While a number of prominent Indians praised the book, none were knowledgeable about Cherokee language and culture. And for the most part, the book received positive (if sometimes patronizing) reviews. A few readers expressed their belief that, given his age at the time of the events he described, much of the book was (as one reviewer said) a "creative" memoir. It sold fairly well, thirteen thousand copies in hardback and another twenty thousand in paperback. Eleanor Friede believed in the book and tried to get Carter to "sell" it with appearances, but he was in no position to engage in extensive promotion in the months after publication.[709]

CARTER HAD BEEN A heavy drinker for most of his life. By 1978, one of his closest Abilene friends sadly concluded he had become a full-blown alcoholic. Louise Green knew the signs. She had separated from, though never divorced, her husband when he drifted into alcoholism in the 1960s. Green, the strikingly beautiful fifty-eight-year-old owner of a local advertising agency, was well-known in West Texas, serving as host of a half-hour television

Louise Green publicity photo, 1967.

show broadcast on twenty-two stations across the region. She interviewed book authors, celebrities, and what she believed were "interesting people." A passionate believer in astrology, she also published a weekly column ("What the Stars Tell Us") in the Abilene newspaper.[710]

Green first met Carter in September 1975 at the annual "Cowboy Campfire Cook-off" in Abilene where more than eleven thousand book lovers and fans of Texas chili gathered over three days to sample the food prepared by Western writers and to listen to readings followed by book-signings.[711] As a TV host, Green was always on the lookout for subjects. She was never particularly interested in Western fiction (or "cowboy stories," as she dismissively called them), but she thought Carter was the star of the cook-off, a quietly dramatic speaker, with a rich voice and an intensity that made his brief reading from *Gone to Texas* come alive. Later that afternoon, she saw him sitting alone on the edge of the empty speakers' platform, smoking a cigarette. He had the look of a "personality," she said: handsome, dark-skinned, with his ever-present black cowboy hat and (a phrase often used by those who met him) an "unmistakable presence." Within minutes after introducing herself, Carter told her that he was half-Cherokee and had been writing for years before finally publishing his first novel. Most of their conversation revolved around his life as the grandson of Cherokee grandparents, growing up close to nature in the east Tennessee mountains. Years later, Green, a passionate environmentalist and something of a New Age mystic, remembered Carter's intense account of how his grandparents had taught him to enter a trance, then listen as the trees talked to each other.

A week later, she interviewed him for her television show and arranged a dinner party with a dozen members of the Abilene "book set." They were equally entranced. Many of his stories seemed to come straight from the long tradition of "tall tales" as he described his various humorous encounters with "one arm this" or "no guts that." He could also shift suddenly to a description of the spiritual world of the Cherokee, a world shaped by "creation spirits" where those who drew closest to nature could be instructed by dreams and visions.

Green seemed an unlikely friend to Carter. She joked that she was one of a "baker's dozen" of white Abilene voters who voted for George McGovern in 1972, and she described herself as a "Yellow Dog liberal Democrat," someone particularly outspoken in her condemnation of the anti-Black, anti-Latino racism that still marked Texas daily life. One of her young friends was not surprised by her friendship with Carter. Green's "compassion for drunks and people down on their luck was legendary in a small town that often ostracized anyone who was different," said Kelley Garrett, a geologist who became one of her best friends despite their age difference.[712]

In the three years after meeting Carter, in long conversations at her home and over dinner at Abilene's Saddle and Sirloin restaurant, Green became closer to him than any other Texans except the handful of individuals like Don Josey who knew his true identity.

Carter often arrived in town unannounced. Green was somewhat exasperated, but not surprised, when she received a call in May 1978, explaining that he was in Abilene meeting a couple of friends. With no advance warning, he wanted to know if they could come over that night for dinner. "Typical Forrest behavior," she said with a smile.

With little notice, she invited a dozen of her friends—most of whom had met Carter—and began preparing a buffet dinner. As was also typical of Carter, he arrived late with his friends Larry Malone and Rusty Thornhill. And two bottles of Jack Daniels, one of which was already severely depleted. "He wasn't drunk," said Green, but he seemed "anxious to remedy that" as the evening went on. Despite his steady intake of the Tennessee whiskey, he seemed in good spirits and, as usual, became the center of attention, reading poetry and describing in detail his (nonexistent) meetings with

Clint Eastwood. It was 2 a.m. before the party finally broke up.

Two hours later, Green's telephone rang, waking her from a sound sleep. "I'm in trouble," said Carter. "Can you come and get me at my motel." It was 4 a.m. in the morning, she told him, but he seemed so unhinged that she agreed to bring him back to her apartment. Since Barbara Sutton, her friend from Dallas, was spending the night in her guest room, she warned him he would have to sleep on the sofa.

"I don't care," he blurted out. "Please come and get me."

Unnerved, she woke up Sutton, and the two drove across town to the Sunset Lodge near Abilene's airport. They knocked on the door of his room and he came lurching out, black Stetson in hand, overflowing with cash. As he got into her car, clutching his hat, he said, "I'm scared" and then seemed to pass out during the twenty-minute drive back to her apartment. She and her friend managed to shake him awake so that he could stagger inside and over to the sofa where he lay down and passed out again.

Still asleep as she left for work the next morning, she returned late in the afternoon to find him sitting at her kitchen table, still drinking, and surrounded by piles of cash which he was counting with some difficulty. She helped him; it was precisely $7,000 in $100 and $20 bills. At first, he said it was from a poker game with friends the night before, but in the rambling and sometimes incoherent conversation that followed, he changed his story. It was "seed money" to make a movie of his book, *The Vengeance Trail of Josey Wales.* He had given up on his negotiations with Eastwood and the "Hollywood types."

"They talk so damn fast, and they're so crooked you know you're being screwed, but you're not exactly sure how they are screwing you," he told her. Instead, he was going to create a production company, hire filmmakers and actors, and produce his own movie version of *Vengeance Trail.* The cash came from a couple of "investors," presumably Malone and Thornhill who had come with him the night before. When she asked why he had been so upset, Carter explained that he was "very concerned about the financial backers, and he said something like, 'They expect their investment to make money and they don't take no for an answer.'"

She became even more uneasy when he explained that he wanted to stay over another night; his plane was leaving in the morning. After dinner, with her friend no longer in the house, he began drinking again and "got a little amorous and tried to kiss me." Her first thought was: "God, am I going to have to fight this drunk?" "We're friends," she said. "Let's don't disturb that."

After she went to bed, she heard a knock on the door. With some reluctance, she opened the door. Carter stood there. And then he began weeping. "I mean crying." Again and again, he kept saying: "I'm sorry, I'm sorry. I just need somebody to listen to me." For more than two hours, he lay on her bed beside her as he rambled on about how lonely he was, that he was at the end of his rope. "He didn't think he could live anymore. No one knew the pressure he lived under." It was the "Indian in him," he told her. The white man's civilization was overwhelming. He couldn't adapt to "civilization, all this concrete between man and the good earth." When he was in the mountains, he could place his bare foot on the soil and let the earth recharge his soul. But since he became well-known, he didn't have a kindred soul with whom he could talk. "I have to put on a monkey suit and be nice to people that don't deserve being nice too." But you, he told Green, "you're my salvation. I can talk to you about anything, and you'll understand."

"I think it's one of the most marvelous visits we ever had," said Green.

After she discovered his double identity, she had a different interpretation of his emotional breakdown. "I think . . . he was afraid he was going to be caught out. That he was living a lie."[713]

On the way to the airport, he asked her to stop at a local discount store where he bought a cheap plastic briefcase to place his film "seed money." "It was strange, standing around in the parking lot, looking around while he stuffed money into the case," said Green. But then things were often strange when dealing with Forrest Carter.

IT'S IMPOSSIBLE TO FULLY understand what was going on with Carter during this period. What is certain is that he fabricated the story of his fearful flight from Malone and Thornhill. Far from being afraid of the two men, it was Carter who had threatened the two, or more precisely, Rusty Thornhill.

When the three men returned to their motel after dinner at Green's apartment, Carter may have had a lot to drink, but Malone found him all business as they began to discuss plans for a film of *The Vengeance Trail of Josey Wales.* Malone, a Texas businessman, was a newcomer to the project. Rusty, his wife's uncle, assured Malone he would make a fortune if he backed the film. As an enthusiastic fan of Carter's books and Eastwood's Josey Wales film, Malone signed onto the project and agreed to put up $35,000 ($180,000, in 2023 dollars). Thornhill had flown to Abilene to bring a first installment from Nashville investors.

But when Carter opened the large manila envelope, he immediately saw that it was less than the $20,000 promised. Carter "took the wad of cash money and threw it across the room. You lied to me," he yelled at Thornhill as he "got in his face" and seemed on the verge of assaulting him. "Are you a bunch of liars? Are you good at your word or not?" Rusty became frantic, said Malone. "I'm sorry, I'm sorry," he explained as he went over and put his arm around Carter.

"Don't hug me like that," yelled Carter. "You think I'm a queer?"

Thornhill sat on the bed and "started crying like a baby," said Malone.

Carter would have been even more infuriated if he had known that Thornhill had successfully collected the $20,000 "seed money" from Nashville investors, but promptly gone out and purchased a $7,000 Buick Riviera while keeping another $6,000 for "wardrobe and living expenses." As he defensively explained later, he had to make a good impression if he was going to get people to invest in the project.

The motel escapade gave Malone second thoughts about his investment. "This could a great opportunity," he told another Dallas investor, "but I don't know whether these dummies can handle it or not."[714] But he wasn't really shocked or surprised by Carter's violent outburst. Carter, he said, saw Thornhill's disregard for their agreement as a personal insult. And that, he could not tolerate.

The belt line. For fourteen-year-old boys in my small rural school in the 1950s, it was a frightening test of "manhood." The fall that my class graduated from grades 1–7 in our elementary school, we moved to the adjacent combined junior high and high school. And on the first Monday after classes

began in September, I joined the male members of my eighth-grade class as we anxiously waited in the wooded "smoking" area as the boys in grades nine through twelve formed two lines. "No buckles," a senior would shout, as the forty or so upper-classmen removed their belts.

One by one, we were to run the gauntlet with belts raining down across our backs, buttocks and upper legs. (If you were to be a "real" man, you had to walk rather than run.) Through the summer of 1954, I dreaded the beginning of school. Until I blurted out my fears one late summer day, my mother had been unaware of the practice. Appalled, she threatened to talk to the principal. My father was no fan of this brutal rite of passage, but—though he never said anything directly to me—I think he believed that those brief moments of fear and pain would soon disappear. If I refused (or, God forbid, my mother interfered to protect me), I would always see myself as a coward in the eyes of my classmates. Grimly, my mother said nothing.

I think the fear was greater than the pain that came with the ordeal, and I when I came home that afternoon, I insisted to my mother that it really wasn't so bad, but I carefully made sure that she did not see the raised whelps and blue bruises that covered my back. The next year, despite the jibes of a few classmates, my cousin Glenn and I, as well as one other of my ninth-grade classmates, refused to join the belt line. Two years later it ended.

Is violence a "Southern thing"? The raw statistics seem to suggest that is the case for both Black and white, but for different reasons. I'm not certain that it is a question that can be answered, but I do believe there is, as a number of historians, sociologists, and social psychologists have seen, an embrace of violence by white Southern males as a test that required a man to defend his "honor" at all costs—with violence if necessary—and cowardice was the ultimate humiliation. Today we would describe the cruelty, the violence, the desperate need to avoid "dishonor" as a form of "toxic masculinity."

I simply accepted it as normal.[715]

Lawrence Clayton had known Carter since just after the Alabamian arrived in Abilene and saw firsthand his problems with alcohol. Twice he had covered for Carter when he went on drinking binges and failed to show up for scheduled appearances. For the most part, said Clayton, such "benders"

One of the last images of Carter, though of unknown origin, about 1979.

were followed by periods in which Carter would cut back his alcohol intake and go on crash diets (his weight fluctuated dramatically during the 1970s). By 1978, said Clayton, he seldom saw a completely sober Carter.

Throughout his adult life, Asa Carter had been prone to violent outbursts, particularly when he had too much to drink. One of the worst episodes came in the fall of 1978, just months after his overnight stay at Green's home. During the five years he had lived on St. George, Carter had come to know, at least superficially, a number of island residents. Each seemed to see a different side of his personality. Several enjoyed his stories and welcomed him as a local celebrity, but Larry Hale, a wounded Vietnam vet confined to a wheelchair, had a different reaction. He ran a small real estate office on the island and found Carter pleasant enough most of the time. But when he was drinking, said Hale, "he could be a pain in the ass, like a two hundred-pound bomb with a one-inch fuse." He detested Carter's racial views. Some folks on the island described Carter as "conservative," but when he became drunk, it was clear that he wasn't conservative, said Hale. "He was bigoted. He was absolutely a white supremacist." Mixed in with racial slurs, he repeatedly bragged about his Cherokee heritage, which made no sense to the vet whose Vietnam friendships with Black soldiers had led him to reject what he said were his often-unconscious racial prejudices. Hale began avoiding Carter whenever possible.[716]

Ron Bloodworth had met Carter in 1975 and perhaps was his closest friend on St. George Island. Bloodworth saw him walking on the beach through the late summer and into the early fall of 1978, but Carter made no effort to renew what had been a fairly close relationship.

On the last day of September, Bloodworth walked the short distance from his house to the island's only bar for a drink. Minutes after he arrived, India Carter walked over to him. "Ron, I need your help," she said. "Would you help me get Forrest out of the Captain's Lounge? He's drinking and he's bothering people and I'm afraid he's going to start a fight. . . ."

Bloodworth had seen enough of Carter to know that persuading him to do anything when he was drunk was impossible. Since it was after 11:30 p.m., he told India, "I'll ask the bartender to run the clock to 11:55 [legal closing time]. We'll pass the word that we're closing up and we all have to get out and go home."

When the bartender made the last call, Ron walked over to the table where Forrest was sitting. He was "ranting about someone that had insulted his cowboy friend that had a broken leg." He demanded another drink from the bartender and then yelled out to the small crowd that he was offering $5,000 for the name of the person who had insulted his friend.

"Forrest, I don't know anything about that," Bloodworth said. "We gotta get out of here, the sheriff will be here in a few minutes . . . and we can't be here after twelve o'clock."

Suddenly Carter grabbed his friend by the shirt and shouted, "I think you're the one that did it."

"And he hit me and knocked me down," recalled Bloodworth. Stunned by the unprovoked attack, he tried to de-escalate the quarrel by backing out of the lounge as the two shoved and pushed each other. But once outside, Carter pulled out the large knife he seemed to carry everywhere and Bloodworth, a regular jogger, hit the street running. "He'll probably just pass out," he optimistically thought to himself. After waiting a few minutes, "I made the mistake of jogging back by his car, and Carter stepped out and pulled out his pistol."

Spectators who had been watching the show from just outside the bar entrance scrambled back inside and locked the door. In the semi-darkness, the drunken Carter thought Bloodworth had also fled into the bar, and he walked over to the window just as one patron raised her head to see what was going on. The young woman found herself "looking right down the barrel of the pistol," said the bar's co-owner, Arlene Henderson. "She fainted."

Somehow, India managed to get her husband back into the car and drove off. Relieved, Bloodworth went back into the lounge. Although he had nothing to do with Carter's departure, "everybody was patting me on the back like I was the hero who got him out of there."

After a drink to steady his nerves, Bloodworth began walking home. On the way, he saw the lights at the house of the two friends he planned to take hunting the next morning, the first day of duck season. The men were in bed asleep, but the wives were cleaning up the kitchen.

Still a bit shaken by his experience, he said, "You won't believe what's been happening to me. A man has been chasing me around the Captain's Lounge with a knife."

One of the women looked over his shoulder and calmly said. "I believe that's him coming in the front door." And there was Carter standing in the doorway with his knife. Outside, he seemed a bit less agitated, but he told Bloodworth he was going to kill him.

Bloodworth awkwardly smiled and said, "Well, could you wait about three days? Let me get my business taken care of before you knock me off?"

"I'll give you three days," Carter responded. Then, abruptly: "Would you come smoke the peace pipe with me?"

Of course, said Bloodworth, as he walked up to Carter. And then "he hit me again and knocked me down."

In the short scuffle that followed, Carter fell head-first into the bumper of a parked car, rolled over on the ground, lay there bleeding, and passed out. By this time India returned in her car. Together, with the help of a next-door neighbor, they bandaged Carter's head, took him home, and loaded him into his bed. ("Damn, he was awfully heavy.")

Despite that awful night, said Bloodworth, he regretted the whole episode "because I wanted to get back [with Forrest] and shake hands and get this thing past us." But that was the last time he ever saw his friend. "We never did get to resolve it."[717]

In November 1978, less than a month after his drunken encounter with Bloodworth, Delacorte published Carter's book, *Watch for Me on the Mountain: A Novel of Geronimo and the Apache Nation.* Writing in the *New York Times Book Review,* Webster Schott saw in Carter an ability to create a spirit world, "a mystic fusion with wind and wild animals" that lifted his novel to poetry. Western novelist Larry McMurtry praised Carter's fictional biography of Apache leader Geronimo as a work of great power and insight. The Native American author was, said McMurtry, the "Iliad of the Southwest," a writer of "extraordinary skill and sensitivity who had come closer than anyone to writing the great American novel of the Indian." And Dee Brown, author of the 1970 bestseller *Bury My Heart at Wounded Knee,* agreed. In *Watch for Me on the Mountain,* said Brown, Forrest Carter had created a portrait that "comes as close any ever will to recreating the real Geronimo."[718]

Despite such positive reviews, Carter ignored pleas from his publishers to make promotional appearances. Encouraged by the substantial payoff from Eastwood's film, he had become convinced that the money was to be made in the movies, not his books. He would have the last laugh on the Hollywood thieves; he would make his own sequel to *The Outlaw Josey Wales.*

IN 1965, RON TAYLOR, from Red Level, Alabama, recruited four musicians to create "Country Brand," a country-music band that lasted until 2008. Although the group recorded a few singles on an obscure label, the "rebel from Red Level" and his friends mostly performed as a cover band for major stars, playing at occasional country-music jamborees and at Taylor's own nightclub, The Barn. The band also performed at Confederate reenactments and memorial services promoting the glorious history of Confederate heroes. Taylor's friendship with Carter in the 1960s became particularly close during the two years he and Carter formed The Southerners.

Despite, or perhaps because of, Taylor's lack of experience in moviemaking, he and his friend Rusty Thornhill would prove to be the central figures in the disaster that followed. Thornhill, the Nashville country singer who showed up at Louise Green's house in Abilene, had never been a close friend of Carter until he was brought into the project because of his promise to raise money from silent partners in Tennessee. He described himself as a record "producer," though he had put together only two albums for an obscure label. And while Thornhill had no other employment besides occasional gigs at a Nashville Holiday Inn, he often flashed a roll of large-denomination bills.

Neither Thornhill nor Taylor could be described as typical "movie moguls."[719]

Finally, there was Carter's old friend from north Alabama, Buddy Barnett, whose experience in the "entertainment business" was a twenty-five-year career as a bouncer in several country music bars and honky-tonks where his main skill was swinging a baseball bat at unruly customers and anyone who crossed him. The great thing about working in a bar when most people are drunk, bragged Barnett, is that you can "reach over there and pop somebody on the head [with a baseball bat] and 90 percent of the customers won't notice." By the early 1990s, a criminal record two pages long showed Barnett had been charged with and in some cases served time for multiple assaults, rape, moonshining, gun running, wholesaling marijuana, and organizing cockfights. In one incident, a Calhoun County grand jury indicted him for murdering a customer after an altercation in the bar where Barnett served as bouncer. Prosecutors dropped the case after their only cooperating eyewitness turned up with a broken nose, several lacerations, and a statement that he could no longer remember the events he had described in his grand jury testimony. As Brandy Ayers, publisher of the *Anniston Star* ruefully observed, Barnett was a classic example of a "thug for hire."[720]

His duties surrounding the film project remained vague and undefined.

In January 1979, Mickey Grant, a Dallas television cameraman, received a telephone call from Florida banker Larry Melton. He explained that he was acting on behalf of a group preparing to produce a film based upon Forrest Carter's book, *The Vengeance Trail of Josey Wales.* Melton was a major investor. Manuel ("Manny") Malone, a well-known Dallas entrepreneur who had established a chain of "Cost Plus" grocery stores and was one of Carter's greatest fans, had also become a partner in the project.

Malone's involvement impressed Grant, who had worked as a television cameraman in Dallas for several years and held undergraduate and graduate degrees in film. When Grant explained that he had done a number of short documentaries but had no experience in full-scale production, Melton assured him that they had found a seasoned Hollywood professional, Cheyenne Rivera, as the film's producer, but they needed someone who was more knowledgeable about the technical end of filming. Was he interested in serving as co-producer?

The call from out of nowhere seemed a bit surreal to Grant; it should have set off alarm bells. But he agreed to read *The Vengeance Trail of Josey Wales* as well as a script that Carter had written. The script needed a great deal of work, concluded Grant. "It was not visual at all and very wordy," but he saw the book as natural for a film. And what thirty-year-old could turn down the chance to make a movie, he said, a reaction he might later have amended to include: "only one who was pretty naive."

In the sequel to *The Outlaw Josey Wales,* the former guerilla fighter/gunslinger has settled down to a peaceful life in south Texas with his wife, Laura Lee, and their newborn son, as well as his entourage, Laura Lee's mother, his faithful Indian companion, Lone Watie, and Watie's bride, Little Moonlight. Then comes news that a vicious band of *Rurales*—Mexican mounted police, more bandits than law enforcement—had crossed the Rio Grande. Led by a psychotic and cruel captain, Jesus Escobedo, the *Rurales* had murdered and raped Wales's close friends in a border town.

Even more than Carter's first book on Josey Wales, the explicit violence and brutality in *The Vengeance Trail of Josey Wales* reflected the broader culture's embrace of a new popular culture of more blood, more guts, more gore. But Carter's western novels were more than an exploitation of cultural changes. His political agenda remained embedded in many ways, notably his obsession with protecting the virginity of white women and the pleasures of violent retribution against the "other"—in this case, dark-skinned half-breed Mexicans.

> *With one hand, [Captain Jesus] Escobedo held the neck thong, and now with the other, he stroked [the young Apache girl's] belly feeling for the pubic hair. It had only begun its growth. . . .*
>
> *He placed himself carefully at the virgin opening and moved into her. . . .*

Suddenly he plunged, throwing himself hard into her . . . venomously, and watched the thin body rise in an ecstasy of pain. . . . Blood fountained from her. . . .

— Forrest Carter, *The Vengeance Trail of Josey Wales*[721]

For more than a century, white Southern men had created and manipulated the fear of Black rapists in order to intimidate Blacks and to remind white women of their frailty and vulnerability. Carter's obsession with sexual violation in his three novels would have been unthinkable in the traditional Western. But the celebration of sadism, vigilantism, and blood-spattered screen violence reflected the distance between director George Stevens's classic 1953 film, *Shane*, starring Alan Ladd, and Sam Peckinpah's 1969 feature, *The Wild Bunch*, with William Holden and Ernest Borgnine. That shift in American popular culture in the 1960s and 1970s allowed Carter to combine his passion for such violence with his underlying political views. In all the reviews of both of the Josey Wales novels, not one critic pointed out that, with a single exception (a Union soldier), the rapists whose brutal acts are described with lingering detail are sociopathic Mexican "half-breeds," repeatedly described as "swarthy" or dark-skinned.

Mickey Grant, whose views were generally liberal, was not interested in a political message; he wanted to make an exciting action Western. And his meeting with Ron Taylor and Rusty Thornhill went well. If they lacked experience, Grant admired their enthusiasm and their willingness to give him a relatively free hand in beginning the project. With Clint Eastwood unavailable for such a follow-up portrayal of the well-known character Josey Wales, Grant argued that obtaining a recognized star for the film would be the key to success. Taylor off-handedly suggested actor/singer Michael Parks. He had read somewhere that Parks, unlike most Hollywood bleeding-hearts, was in favor of the death penalty, but was unaware that Parks was in other respects a typical Hollywood liberal.[722]

Parks had been a rising television star in the 1960s, reaching his greatest success as Jim Bronson, a disillusioned reporter who quit his job and wandered across America on his Harley-Davidson, often encountering similarly colorful angst-ridden characters. NBC's "Then Came Bronson" quickly developed a cult following (and sparked a surge in Harley sales to middle-aged buyers). Despite respectable ratings, the series only ran one season, 1969–1970. It turned out that Parks's on-screen "James Dean" personality was a faithful mirror of his difficult behavior during production as he quarreled with his directors and sometimes walked off the set in disgust. NBC did not renew the series. In later years, promoted by auteur Quentin Tarantino, Parks's career would rebound, but in the mid-1970s he had hit a low point.[723]

To Grant's surprise, when he approached Parks to play the role, he agreed.

From there, it was all downhill. Rivera, the "seasoned" co-director, had worked as a stuntman on a handful of films, but—as Grant quickly learned—he knew nothing about filmmaking, was a compulsive liar, and "seemed most interested in womanizing and ingesting various mind-altering substances."

One strange turn followed another. Shortly after Grant began working on the project in early 1979, he asked Taylor to arrange a meeting with Forrest Carter. For reasons he never understood, Taylor told him that Carter had died.

Working seven days a week, twelve to sixteen hours a day, the inexperienced Grant struggled to handle the complex logistics of production, first securing a site for the filming in Bracketville, Texas, where John Wayne had built a full-scale nineteenth-century village for his 1960 film *The Alamo.* Although Grant had some contacts from his television career in Dallas, it was difficult to line up the needed dozens of technical and creative staffers and secondary actors. Perhaps the most daunting challenge was recruiting nearly a hundred horsemen to play the "Comancheros" in the film's climactic gunfight.

Most of the backers seemed reputable. One was a bank president in Florida, another a major manufacturer of mobile home fittings. But at least one of the major film backers had a distinctly shady background. In conversations with Grant, the south Alabama owner of a "catfish farm" bragged that his investment came from marijuana grown on his farm with the paid-for-cooperation of the county sheriff.

After production began in the early summer of 1979, Grant found the financing of the film unorthodox, to put it mildly. "They would often give me attaché cases with nothing but hundreds totaling fifty thousand or more . . . bank wires well over fifty thousand. Cash." The secretiveness of the financial backers and their preference for cash gradually convinced Grant that the money men were members of the "Dixie Mafia." And they were not just dishonest, said Grant. They were "dangerous people."

"Dixie Mafia" evokes comparisons with *The Godfather*, but the Southern version was never more than a loose-knit group of pre-war white bootleggers who moved into the more lucrative fields of prostitution, organized car theft, pornography, and drug smuggling and sales after World War II. They were sometimes violent. FBI and local police attributed more than forty assassinations to the group, including the killing of a Biloxi, Mississippi, judge who sought to shut down illegal gambling in the city. But even though these criminals sometimes cooperated in dividing up areas for criminal activities, they would never be confused with Vito or Michael Corleone's professional soldiers.[724]

As filming drew toward a close that fall, the regular valises of cash suddenly ended, the money men disappeared, and no one would answer Grant's desperate calls for additional funds. With suppliers and extras demanding immediate payment, a dispirited Grant became depressed. He was at his wit's end and drinking at a fearsome rate. After downing five pre-mixed Screwdrivers on the set one afternoon, he woke up that night to the sound of his assistant yelling at him to run—dozens of the hundred Mexican and Mexican American horsemen in the film were at the site, angry and demanding to be paid. There was nowhere to go but into the desert that surrounded the movie set. In the darkness, Grant hid from the yelling horsemen in a shrub thicket of chaparral for what seemed hours until they left. Barefoot, he began walking back to his tent, breaking into a run as he confronted a pack of feral javelinas, a piglike and sometimes dangerous animal that roamed the arid areas of south Texas.

Concerned over the secretive behavior of the individuals involved in the project, Grant became increasingly paranoid. In the middle of a legal battle with Ron Taylor over who should do the final editing of the film, a pickup truck followed him as he left a favorite bar on his motorcycle and repeatedly tried to force him off the road. "I turned off the highway and I went through someone's back yard. . . . I managed to get away. But I became really nervous at this point." Less than a week later, two "rough looking" men pushed their way into a friend's home where he had been staying. They finally left after they searched the house. (When Grant heard one of the men shouting demands to know if he was there, he climbed out a back window.)[725]

A film on the making of *The Vengeance Trail of Josey Wales* (originally to be titled *The Return of Josey Wales*) could have been a hilarious black comedy, said Grant, had it not been so terrifying. Once Taylor and the financial backers succeeded in gaining control of the unfinished film, Grant left Texas for New York to become a documentary filmmaker. The following year, Taylor hired a film editor to piece together an amateurish one hour and twenty-minute version of the movie. Never released in theaters, it went straight to the emerging VHS market.[726]

23

The Last Days of Forrest Carter

Eulogies, June 11, 1979

Forrest really believed in living close to the earth. He never spoke negatively about anyone. He was concerned about the Indian, the forgotten American [and] donated a percentage of his royalties to various Indian nations.

— Ron Taylor

The English writer Rudyard Kipling paid tribute to the spirit of the Southern fighting man when he wrote: "There in the Southland lives the greatest fighting breed of man in the world . . . That was my cousin Forrest, a fighter, a warrior . . . We were proud of our Southern roots and our struggle against socialism, mongrelization and communism."

— Wayne Bennett[727]

Carter had set *The Vengeance Trail of Josey Wales* film in motion, but once he received a $75,000 payment under the terms of its contract, he seemed to realize that the project was doomed and moved on to others with greater potential. With the 1979 publication of *Watch for Me on the Mountain,* he began contacting Hollywood producers. In one of his earlier trips to California to visit Bob Daley at Eastwood's studio, he had introduced himself to Danny Arnold. The red-headed ex-Marine wrote scripts and starred in two Dean Martin/Jerry Lewis movies before moving on to producing television shows, including the 1969 ABC comedy sitcom *My World and Welcome to It*, for which he won an Emmy. Carter remembered that Arnold had said he was interested in more serious projects, so he sent him a copy of *Watch for Me on the Mountain.* According to Carter, Arnold "loved the book."

In a later interview, Arnold confirmed Carter's claim. He found Carter's portrait of Geronimo evocative and powerful and the story seemed a natural for film or television adaptation. Still, he hesitated. He was always bouncing around dozens of ideas, and while he found Carter intriguing, he was accustomed to writers and agents making a persuasive pitch. His conversations with Carter proved a letdown. "He seemed an ordinary guy . . . with long silences . . . ," a characteristic Arnold attributed to Carter's Indian background. "You didn't come away from the conversation inspired by having talked to him."

But in January 1977, Americans embraced the blockbuster television series based on Alex Haley's book *Roots: The Saga of an American Family.* Over eight weekly episodes, viewers followed the story of Kunta Kinte—abducted from his African village and sold into slavery in America—and the generations that followed. Week by week, the audience grew to become one of the largest in the history of television. As Arnold considered what he called the "Geronimo project," he became convinced that *Watch for Me* had the potential to become a "Native American" television series that would mirror the success of *Roots*.[728]

Eleanor Friede negotiated a modest original option of $10,000 for the film rights, but with a possibility of far greater returns to Carter. If a film was produced, his "Cherokee Corporation" would receive a payment of $62,500. If the book was adapted for a television series, he would receive more: $90,000 (more than $850,000, in 2023 dollars). With that potential payout, it is easy to see why Carter had decided that television and movies were his future.[729]

Even as Friede began negotiations, Carter was contacting other producers about a possible film of *The Education of Little Tree.* When he drew no takers, he seems to have become convinced that a screenplay adaptation might entice backers. In late 1978, he had proposed to his friend Louise Green that she write a script based on *Education*. "I looked at him like had asked if I was interested in flying a jet plane," said Green. "I told him that I had no experience in writing movie scripts." But Carter knew that she had served as a copywriter for local programming on Abilene's KRBC-TV as well as a scriptwriter for five medical documentary films produced by the West Texas Rehabilitation Foundation. He insisted that she had a "real feeling for the spiritual aspects of Little Tree" and he promised to pay her $25,000 for a draft script. Even if it had to be rewritten, he told her, it would show producers that the book was movie material.

Green agreed to try her hand. "I *had* written a few scripts," she laughed, "but this was just a bit different." With a copy of *The Education of Little Tree* and a mail order book on how to write a screenplay, she spent the next few weeks blocking out scenes and writing dialogue, much of it taken directly from the book.[730]

In April 1979, Carter returned to Abilene. "He showed up at my house in a cab in mid-afternoon without calling, which I didn't care for," said Green. When she saw him, however, she felt only concern. "I don't know how to describe him. He had bags under his eyes, he had put on a lot of weight and, well, he dressed . . . kind of slovenly."

She asked if he wanted to look at the script. He glanced through a few pages, told her he liked it, and put it in his small suitcase. Nothing was said about his earlier offer of $25,000. Still uneasy over his appearance and what seemed to be an absence of "affect," she suggested they go out to dinner. ("I didn't have much in the house.") After they arrived at the Saddle and Sirloin Restaurant, he began drinking heavily. When a Black couple came in and took a seat, he complained loudly. "I hate to use the N-word," said Green, but it was "all about how the niggers couldn't be trusted and they were parasites . . . They lived on welfare and had their nigger babies who grew up and raped white women."

Stunned, Green tried to calm him down and when he continued, she told him, "Forrest, I'm leaving. I know people here and I don't want to be associated with that kind of talk." He ended his outburst, but she never saw him again after that night. "It was an awful way to end our friendship. I really cared for him. He was a tortured individual, but he could be so kind and gentle. I just don't understand it."[731]

TWO MONTHS LATER, ON Thursday, June 7, 1979, Forrest Carter again flew into the Abilene airport. He had arranged to stay with his son Ralph, daughter-in-law Geneva, and two grandchildren before flying out to Los Angeles on Monday to make a pitch for the *Little Tree* project with several producers whose names Arnold had given him.

When his oldest son, Asa Jr. (or Earl as he was called in Abilene), arrived to pick him up, he saw his father stagger down the ramp from the small commuter plane. "I could tell that he was pretty intoxicated." Carter went straight into the small airport bar and ordered a double whiskey while Asa Jr. kept trying to get him to leave. Geneva had prepared dinner and the family was waiting, he told his father. But he was "drunk and he wanted to stay at the airport and drink some more." After a half-hour argument, his father finally agreed to make the four-mile drive to Ralph's double-wide trailer just outside the city limits.[732]

When they arrived, Ralph, Geneva, and the two children were waiting at the table, but the meal ended within minutes. Carter sat down and angrily scowled at his two sons. You're both "bums," he told them. Asa Jr. tried to play the peacemaker, but Ralph began arguing with his father who continued to curse and shout. Finally, Ralph had enough: "I told him to get out." When Carter stood unsteadily, Ralph pushed him toward the back door. As Geneva grabbed the two children and fled into a back bedroom, Asa Jr. begged the two men to calm down, but they ignored him as they pushed and shoved each other. When his father fell to the floor, Asa Jr. had enough. He walked outside and drove away.

After his father seemed to have passed out, Ralph dragged him to the back porch for air, but Carter managed to get back to his feet and charged forward, fists swinging. "I moved off of the porch to stay away from him," said Ralph, but as he backed up against his pickup, "he then hit me in the mouth." No slouch at fighting since his teen years, Ralph gave his father three hard punches: one to his eye, a second to his neck, and a third to his stomach that sent him to his knees. Carter kept mumbling, "I'm going to kill you," but the fight was over.

Back in the house, Carter insisted on sitting down at the dinner table even though Geneva and the two children remained locked in the bedroom.

"He would take a bite of food and then stand up and tell me he was going to kill me," said Ralph. "He would then sit back down and eat." Minutes later, Carter fell out of his chair and lay on the floor "gasping for breath."

Ralph removed his father's false teeth and called Geneva out of the back bedroom. She went next door to her neighbor, Barbara Poor, explaining that her father-in-law had "suffered a heart attack." Poor, a registered nurse, had lived next to Ralph and Geneva for two years, but she later told sheriff's deputies that she had never been acquainted with the family; they kept to themselves. Nevertheless, she gathered her medical kit and went into the trailer, where she found Carter lying on the floor. She quickly cleared his air passage and, when she could find no pulse, began to administer cardiopulmonary resuscitation. As the fifty-nine-year-old nurse rhythmically pushed on Carter's chest, she ordered Ralph to try mouth-to-mouth resuscitation. She could hear a faint gurgling, but there was no heartbeat or any evidence that Carter was breathing on his own. Despite the lack of a response, she continued until an ambulance arrived twenty minutes later. Poor later told investigators that she believed Carter was dead when she arrived.

The paramedic confirmed Carter's death, but he and the ambulance driver refused to transport Carter to a funeral home because of his obvious injuries. Shortly after the ambulance left without the body, Brenda Putnam, the night dispatcher for the Taylor County Sheriff's Department, logged a call from a "Mrs. Ralph Carter." There had been a death in the family, she reported, and she specifically requested that "Justice of the Peace Roland Dunwoody be sent along with a deputy." The caller seemed calm as she gave the location of her home on Highway 36 just south of Abilene's city limits.

Twenty minutes later, deputies Richard Wimberly and Robert Jones and Dunwoody arrived, to find several people from the trailer park standing around outside the steps of the front door. Geneva Carter's husband, Ralph, led the way as they walked into the living/dining room to find a heavyset white male lying on the floor next to the dining room, his body covered by a blanket. That's my father, Ralph said, "Bedford Forrest Carter."

Wimberly began jotting down his notes: "The deceased is lying on his back with his face to the ceiling. [He] has a small laceration above his left eye and his right eye is swollen shut. There is a strong odor of alcohol. . . . The deceased does not have a shirt on, but is wearing blue, plaid pants and some brown western boots."

Wimberly told the family that he would be requesting an autopsy and he would be questioning everyone involved the following day.

BY 10 A.M. FRIDAY, Abilene pathologist Dr. Joseph Hall had completed his autopsy; his findings were consistent with Ralph's description of the fight with his father. The coroner's test showed extremely high alcohol levels—0.156 percent—even though he had not been drinking for well over an hour before death. As medical texts on alcoholism point out, such levels can cause "aggression, reduced sensations, inappropriate social behavior, slurred speech, lack of balance and lack of reasoning."[733]

While Carter had suffered a number of minor injuries, the pathologist found only three significant blows to his body, one to his right eye that left the eye bloodshot and swollen shut, a visible contusion on the lower left chest, just above the abdomen, and a cut on the interior of the right side of his mouth caused by a blow to the jaw. Death came from "strangulation," caused when Carter "regurgitated blood and vomit that blocked his air passage to the lungs."[734]

Although the evidence corroborated Ralph's account, at least one of the deputies, Richard Wimberly, remained concerned about inconsistencies and what he regarded as "unanswered questions."

When Carter collapsed, Ralph had called out to his wife who went next door to Nurse Poor. But how long did they wait before going next door to Mrs. Poor? he asked in his report. By the neighbor's own account, it was at least five to ten minutes before she arrived to examine Carter. And why did the family wait until after Mrs. Poor came into the mobile home before calling for an ambulance, a timeline confirmed by the 911 dispatch records and by Geneva Carter's statement?

Geneva and Ralph told Poor and Wimberly that they believed "Forrest" had suffered a heart attack since he had a "heart condition" and was on medication. But the other officer on the case went through all of Carter's suitcases and found no medication. The autopsy confirmed that his heart was in excellent condition for a man his age.

Even more bewildering was the confusing relationship of Ralph and Earl (Asa Jr.) to "Forrest Carter," whose name was variously spelled as "Forest" and "Forrest" by the family. In his sworn written statement, Ralph Walker Carter wrote that "my father, Bedford Forest [sic] Carter" had arrived from Florida early Thursday evening, June 7. "My brother, Asa [Earl] Carter, picked up our father and brought him to the house."

But when Deputy Wimberly called Earl (Asa Jr.) Carter to arrange a time for an interview and referred to Forrest Carter as Earl's father, "he immediately informed me that 'Bedford' Carter, the man who had died the night before, was not his father, nor was he Ralph Carter's father." Their father had died several years earlier, Earl told Wimberly, and Bedford Carter was a "cousin" who had been like a father to him and to Ralph. When Wimberly arrived the next day to write out an account of the Saturday events, Earl described the dead man as "Forrest," not "Bedford." In this second interview, Earl said the deceased was his "uncle" (not his cousin). He had "raised me with my brother, and he was like a father to us."

Wimberly acknowledged that individuals in shock often responded in different ways. But he was concerned about the contradictory statements and the "demeanor" of Ralph and Geneva Carter. During the investigation, said Wimberly, "neither the complainant [Ralph Carter] nor his wife seemed upset about this ordeal."

None of these inconsistencies alone pointed to criminal behavior, but they convinced Wimberly that reconciling the conflicting accounts required an extensive investigation and the further interrogation of all the individuals involved. He remained particularly interested in establishing how long it had taken for the family to notify their next-door neighbor and to call 911. But two days later, Justice of the Peace Dunwoody (the individual Ralph Carter's wife, Geneva, had specifically requested come to the house) closed the investigation without contacting the sheriff's office or referring the case to the local district attorney.

Judge Samuel Matta, the first Latino Taylor County justice of the peace, reviewed the investigative reports in 1991. "I don't like to second guess, but if I had been in charge of this case, I would definitely have referred it to the district attorney on the basis of the preliminary evidence. And I would never have halted the investigation."[735]

THE ABSENCE OF ANY significant interest in Forrest Carter's death was somewhat surprising. While Carter was no household name, he had published four successful books, one made into a major Hollywood film. The *Abilene Reporter-News*, which had covered him extensively during the 1970s, received a call on Saturday morning, June 9, 1979, that Carter had died of an "apparent heart attack" while visiting a nephew on his way to Los Angeles.

Bill Whitaker, a young Ohio-born reporter working at the *Abilene Reporter-News,* had interviewed Carter on two occasions, and he said he called Roland Dunwoody for further details, but "Dunwoody didn't seem to find it [Carter's death] particularly suspicious." Nor did Dunwoody correct him when Whitaker he said he had heard that Carter died of a heart attack. With a deadline looming, he quickly filed a four-paragraph story for the Saturday afternoon newspaper. The brief obituary gave a brief sketch of Carter's life but few details of his death beyond the statement that he had died of an apparent heart attack. That story appeared in the Sunday edition of the *Abilene Reporter-News*. "Popular western/Cherokee American novelist Forrest Carter died of a heart attack on June 7, 1979, while visiting his three nephews in Abilene. His body is to be returned to Georgiana, Alabama, for burial."[736]

Louise Green learned of Carter's death from Abilene artist Robert Miller, who had painted a portrait of Carter and had been one of his friends. There would be a visitation on Sunday afternoon at Abilene's North's Funeral Home, he told her. In the South and Southwest, the proper response to a death is a casserole. Miller and his wife, Ruth, had driven over to Asa Jr.'s home Sunday morning, but no one answered the door, and they had left their food on the back stoop. Early that afternoon, chicken tetrazzini in hand, Green knocked on Asa Jr.'s door. After a long wait, he appeared.

Asa Jr. hardly seemed welcoming as she placed the casserole on the kitchen counter. Awkwardly, she smiled and asked, "is there anything else

I can do?" Then, she said, "he grabbed me" and sneered, "'Oh, come off it. You're one of Daddy's whores,'" as he pushed her out the door.[737]

Shaken, but determined to pay her respects at the funeral home, Green called Ruth Miller. Together they went to the funeral home to find an almost-empty viewing room where an attendant explained that "Mr. Carter died of a heart attack." When Green signed the condolence book, she saw that a handful of Carter's Abilene friends had been there earlier, but no family seemed present. As she looked into the pine coffin at Carter in his blue denim suit, she said to Miller, "He must have died in terrible pain because that is the most unpeaceful-looking corpse I have ever seen." Well, he didn't die of a heart attack, said Miller. Her husband had learned from a friend in the sheriff's department that his son had killed him in a fistfight, but "it was an accident."

MEANWHILE, NO BURIAL IN Georgiana, Alabama, was ever intended. Back in St. George Island, Florida, India had heard the news from her sons and immediately called Carter's friend Ron Taylor, who volunteered to take on the delicate task of conducting a funeral that would pay respects to "Asa" while concealing the connection with "Forrest." In a brief statement released to the press, and appearing in the *Abilene Reporter-News*, the family explained that Forrest Carter's body would be flown to Georgiana, Alabama, for burial in the "family plot." Asa Carter had no connection to the small south Alabama town, but Taylor knew the local funeral home director, who agreed to maintain a discreet silence about the unusual circumstances. The "burial in Georgiana, Alabama" was simply a cover story to deflect attention from Anniston.

Despite Taylor's best efforts, the planning nearly went awry.

The morning after Carter's brief obituary appeared in the *Abilene Reporter-News* and was distributed by the Associated Press, the city desk received a request from Atlanta's AP office. "They wanted to know whether the dead man was Forrest Carter, the Western novelist, or a fella named Asa Carter, who was a fiery segregationist of whom I had never heard," said Bill Whitaker. He went to the "viewing" at North's Funeral Home, only blocks from the newspaper's editorial offices. And like Louise Green, he was surprised to see only a handful of mourners. He walked over and looked in the casket. "Sure enough, it was Forrest Carter, still in that blue denim suit that I saw when I interviewed him some months earlier." As far as he was concerned, it was an "either-or question." Was the dead man Forrest Carter or Asa Carter? From his office he called the AP regional news desk. "I told them . . . that I didn't know about this Asa Carter guy, but Forrest Carter, the Western novelist, was the man in the casket." What he didn't know was that "there were two Carters in that box," he said wryly a quarter-century later. "I had accidentally kept his secret going."[738]

There was no follow-up to the Associated Press obituary of "Forrest" Carter's death that appeared in newspapers across the country, and no mention of "Asa" Carter.

By Monday morning, June 11, 1979, the body was on a plane from Abilene to Atlanta where a driver for the cooperative Georgiana funeral home loaded the casket into a hearse and began driving westward the ninety miles to the cemetery across the road from the D'Armanville Methodist Church outside Anniston.

Although it was almost 4 p.m. when the hearse arrived, the sun "was still blazing like a furnace," recalled Carter's youngest brother, Larry. A handful of members from the church who had known "Forrest" as "Asa" were there as well as three of his friends, Ron Taylor, Buddy Barnett, and a second-cousin, Wayne Bennett. Mostly it was family: Asa's mother, Hermione; his wife, India; their daughter Tara and her husband; Asa's youngest son, Bedford; as well as his brothers Doug and Larry, and his nephew, Jimmy, and niece Kaye. There were also a handful of members of Hermione's church. Neither Asa's sister, Marie, who was dying of cancer, nor his sons Ralph or Asa Jr. came to the funeral.

India remained stoic during the graveside service; not so, Carter's mother Hermione. She had recently lost her husband, Ralph, and she knew that her daughter, Marie, had only weeks to live. Even though Asa had not been in touch with the family for over a year, her other sons would always remember the devastation on her face. As they stood at the open grave, Hermione saw the brass marker, "Forrest Carter, 1925–1979," and turned to her son, Larry. "I wish they could have used his real name," she whispered. For someone who greeted most disagreements by withdrawing into grim silence, she had confronted her daughter-in-law earlier in the day. Her young grandson, Jimmy, was unclear why this was such an important argument. "I guess my grandmother thought that somehow Jesus wouldn't be able to find him without a tombstone with his correct name and he couldn't go to heaven," he said dryly. "You know, there's not much you can argue with that."

Hermione did win one argument. Against India's wish, she insisted that the coffin be opened so she could see her son for the last time. While the funeral home had used heavy cosmetics, a close look showed one eye was swollen and there were bruises on the left side of his face as well as a poorly concealed injury on his cheek.[739]

The graveside service lasted less than thirty minutes. Buddy Barnett said only a few words, perhaps aware that many of the mourners knew his extensive criminal background.[740] Ron Taylor extolled "Forrest" as a man obsessed with the tragic fate of his Native American ancestors. A gentle man, he had lived a life of extraordinary generosity, said Taylor. He "never spoke negatively about anyone" and always donated part of his book royalties to various Indian nations as he "worked to unite the tribes to preserve their heritage."

Wayne Bennett ended the graveside service by describing his closeness with his cousin, telling stories, with long emotional pauses, of their childhood. "We had the same Cherokee-American grandmother," he said. He too spoke of his cousin's generosity to various Indian causes, but his eulogy veered off-script. Taylor had praised "Forrest" as a warm-hearted man who loved all people. Bennett insisted that, despite their "shared Indian blood," they were proudest of their Southern roots and their fight against the federal government's embrace of "socialism, mongrelization, and communism."

In that battle, he said, his cousin was a fierce warrior, the embodiment of the men praised by the English writer Rudyard Kipling: "There in the Southland lives the greatest fighting breed of man in all the world."[741] It seemed fitting that Carter's service ended with a particularly ironic counterfeit quote. Carter had used it repeatedly in his writings and broadcasts. But Kipling never wrote a tribute to white Southerners. The actual barroom ballad that Carter turned upside-down referred to the nineteenth-century

Black Sudanese warriors who ferociously resisted the British army in the late nineteenth century and earned the grudging admiration of the victorious English: "So ere's to you, Fuzzy-Wuzzy, at your home in the Soudan; You're a pore benighted 'eathen but a first-class fightin' man."[742]

After a benediction from the local minister, the small gathering silently stood for several minutes. Finally, four members of Carter's former group, The Southerners, stepped forward from where they had been waiting some distance from the service. With ropes, they lowered the simple wooden casket into the ground. It was as Carter had insisted: "No vault, dust to dust."

The entire ceremony was surreal. Everyone present knew that the individual lying in the coffin was Asa Earl Carter. But Ron Taylor worried that some outsider might be present. Even though Bennett had not stayed on message, Taylor at least referred to Carter as "Forrest."

A funeral already fraught with tension became even more difficult when Taylor cornered India Carter as they walked out of the cemetery and began insisting that it was critical that he talk with her about the film of one of Carter's books that was in mid-production. (She had earlier signed an agreement with Mickey Grant on behalf of her husband, giving Grant full control of the film.) Her brother-in-law, Larry, was bewildered. "Who the heck is this guy," he thought, "and what does he want." Although India kept nodding, Larry politely told Taylor it was neither the time nor place to talk about such things. When Taylor ignored him, Larry Carter had enough. He leaned in inches from Taylor's face. "You damn well better leave her alone."

Taylor left.[743]

A month after the funeral, the local *Anniston Star* interviewed several individuals who had been present and suggested that there were strong similarities between the Western writer and the former resident Asa Carter. But the headline "Death Fails to Resolve Mystery" reflected the success of Carter's family in maintaining Forrest Carter's fake identity. By the fall, it was old news.[744]

Coda

All Is Revealed

By 1985, Asa Carter's three novels and his childhood memoir were out of print and his former agent, Eleanor Friede, could not find a trade press interested in reprinting his books. But she was convinced that there was an audience for the work she loved the most: *The Education of Little Tree.* In 1970, Freide had fought the scepticism of every editor at Macmillan Publishers over *Jonathan Livingston Seagull,* a book about a bird expelled from his flock for lifting his eyes toward flight rather than scrambling for daily scraps. Through the wisdom of a wise seagull named Chiang, Jonathan ascends to a place where the gulls have reached unlimited freedom by being true to themselves. Critic Roger Ebert was convinced that the book was "so banal that it had to be sold to adults; kids would have seen through it."[745]

Despite the disdain of Ebert and other cynics, and with minimal promotion by Macmillan, the book climbed to the top of the *New York Times* bestseller list and stayed there for thirty-seven weeks. Through the 1980s, books vaguely described as "New Age" exploded, as a generation of Americans embraced personal self-improvement through "self-actualization," "enhanced consciousness," "crystal healing," or spiritual awakening through the exploration of ancient traditions. And what could be more perfectly suited for this changing culture than the pithy wisdom of Little Tree's Indian grandfather? As Carter's former movie agent said, the reprinting of Carter's memoir was perfect timing: "Indians were hot."[746]

Frustrated by her inability to find a commercial publisher, Friede finally approached the University of New Mexico Press. She frankly acknowledged she knew nothing about university presses. She chose the UNMP because of its reputation for printing books on archaeology, Latin American history, and "indigenous studies." The press agreed to reissue the work and paid an advance of five hundred dollars to Carter's widow. The first paperback edition print run was two thousand copies.[747]

Over the next five years *The Education of Little Tree* became one of the more remarkable publishing stories of the decade. Sales steadily increased, driven by the enthusiasm of readers and bookstore owners. In January 1991, the title became the first recipient of the American Booksellers Association's ABBY award, a prize established to recognize the "hidden treasures" bookstore owners recommended most to their customers. By the end of August, UNMP had printed more than six hundred thousand copies of Carter's book, and had another two hundred thousand on order. In mid-September, the memoir reached number one on the *New York Times* list of paperback bestsellers.[748]

By then I had known the true identity of "Forrest Carter" for more than two years, and, while I have always believed that writers should be free to create stories and describe experiences that go beyond their ethnic or racial background, I saw *The Education of Little Tree* as something quite different. By claiming Cherokee heritage, Asa Carter had engaged in cultural theft, expropriating the culture and identity of American Indians to sell books.

When I called the *New York Times* about the possibility of an article to expose Forrest Carter, the op-ed page editor responded skeptically. But after I faxed extensive evidence that "Forrest" and "Asa" were one and the same, in early October 1991 the *Times* published my opinion piece: "The Transformation of a Klansman."[749] I wrote:

> Adolescent and adult readers have warmed to the uplifting story of how this well-known writer of westerns—author of "The Rebel Outlaw: Josey Wales" and "Cry Geronimo" and friend of Clint Eastwood—came to know the wisdom of his Cherokee ancestors. In the wake of the success of "Dances With Wolves," there is even talk of a Hollywood film.
>
> Unfortunately, "The Education of Little Tree" is a hoax. The carefully constructed mask of Forrest Carter—Cherokee cowboy, self-taught writer and spokesman for Native Americans—was simply the last fantasy of a man who reinvented himself again and again in the 30 years that preceded his death in 1979.

"Forrest" Carter, I went on, was in reality, Asa Carter, a white supremacist, Klansman, and secret speechwriter for Alabama Governor George Wallace.

Within hours after the publication of the piece, the University of New Mexico Press and Eleanor Friede told inquiring reporters that they were familiar with these groundless scurrilous rumors. But as reporters from the *Times,* the *Washington Post,* and more than a dozen other newspapers confirmed that "Forrest" was, in fact, "Asa," it became impossible for anyone to maintain their denials. Faced with overwhelming evidence, India Carter finally confirmed that Forrest Carter was her late husband, Asa Carter.[750]

Understandably reluctant to abandon a book that had been so important to the University of New Mexico Press, director Elizabeth Hadas insisted that labeling the book as a hoax was a "meaningless and stupid statement." She dismissed Carter's political activities in the 1950s and 1960s as an "unfortunate stage" in his life. She said it was "hard to believe that these stories were faked. If he was a bad man, he took on a new identity and became a good man." That became the refrain of conversations, telephone calls, letters from fans, and several news stories.[751]

But he didn't become a good man. Asa Carter remained a virulent racist until the end of his life.

Understandably, members of the family were less than pleased by the exposure of Carter's background, since they were then negotiating with several movie producers for film rights to *The Education of Little Tree.* When Dallas journalist Donna Rubin contacted Carter's brother, Doug, he explained that he had read somewhere that I might be related to their family. (I am not.) "You tell [Dan Carter]," said Doug, "if I ever see him, he'll be a *late* member of the family." Perhaps, suggested Rubin to me with a laugh, "you might get a mirror on a pole to check your car before you start it in the morning."[752]

I wasn't terribly concerned about Doug Carter, but I was disconcerted by the responses from readers, particularly young ones. By 1991, *Little Tree* had become widely assigned, primarily in the curricula of middle-school classes across the nation. When some teachers told their students the truth about the author's background, several sent me packets of notes and letters written mostly by adolescents who felt betrayed or simply bewildered. "I loved Little Tree," wrote an African American eighth-grader in New Jersey, "but now I learn that he hated black people. It doesn't make sense."

I tried to respond to each letter and on three occasions spoke by telephone hook-up with middle school classes. I told readers that they should feel free to enjoy *Little Tree* as a story. The book they loved did not reflect the racism that was clearly part of Asa Carter's personal feelings. But at the end of every session, I felt like the Grinch who stole Christmas.

When Henry Louis Gates published an article in the *New York Times Book Review* on "The Real Meaning of Little Tree," he pointed out that fiction writers, to some degree or another, are "cultural impersonators." What novelists write is always mediated through their life experiences. There was never a straight line between our own past lives, our "heritage" (racial or otherwise), or our ideologies and what we write or say. The controversy over *Little Tree* was "only the latest embarrassment to beset the literary ideologues of authenticity. . . ."[753]

I agreed. I was far more skeptical about the argument of other critics that the underlying beliefs and views of an author are of little significance. By the 1960s, a number of influential literary scholars had begun to "decenter" the importance of the author by arguing that the intent of a writer, his or her ideas and background, was far less important than the way in which readers respond—as it was described, "reader response theory." From Jacques Derrida to Stanley Fish and onward came a torrent of literary jargon—"animate," "authorial audience," "discourse community," "signifier and signified," and on, and on, and on. Whatever subtleties literary critics might see, I found it all an over-elaborate explanation of a commonsense observation: there is always a complex interaction between a writer's work and the response of the reader. (Often, it is less an interaction than a chasm, an observation easily confirmed by teachers who read their students' book reviews.)

Asa Carter hardly reflected upon the latest literary theories, but he knew the appeal of "authenticity," and he was perceptive enough to understand the shifting views of Americans, including white Southerners. To be a successful author, he would need to write books for a broader audience than the fanatical followers who embraced his racist speeches, articles, and pamphlets in the 1950s and 1960s. But if he managed to modify (and often conceal) them, his underlying beliefs were always present, particularly in his three Western novels. He never abandoned his belief that America should be cleansed from the influence of "pseudo-intellectual sophisticates" and wealthy elites who lacked the courage to resist Black Americans, Jews, brown immigrants from south of the border, and other "racial degenerates" who represented a threat to what he saw as the nation's core identity. As Carter knew, the Cherokee were among the most race-conscious of the five "civilized" tribes of the Southeast.[754] Far more important was the connection he made between white Southerners' defense of a world of white supremacy and the willingness of American Indians to engage in violent resistance to a federal government that sought to destroy their culture.

In Carter's skillful hands, the reshaped Western novel and the story of the American Indian melded the disparate strains of the political left and right. Millions of Americans could find common ground in the celebration of the Noble Savage who lived by a personal code that needed no government to achieve a life of meaning and fulfillment.

Clint Eastwood's film *The Outlaw Josey Wales* tampers with several portions of the plot of Asa Carter's novel, but it is no accident that the most climactic scene in the movie and the book are the same. When Josey Wales

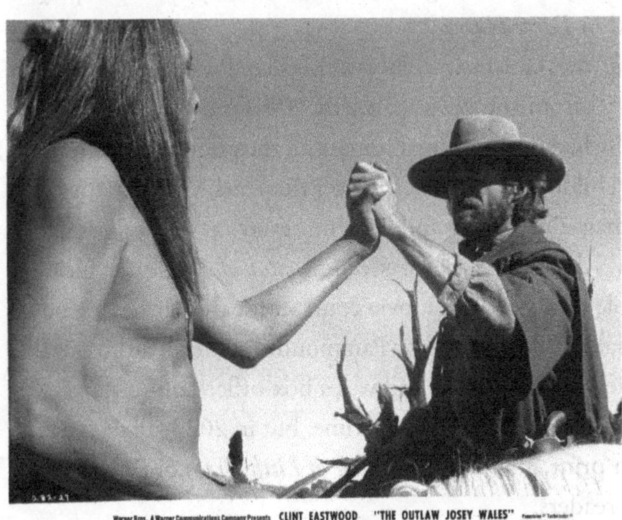

Publicity still from* The Outlaw Josey Wales, *1976.

tries to persuade the Comanche chief, Ten Bears, that they should stand together, his plea rests upon his hostility to the very notion of government: "What ye and me cares about has been butchered . . . raped," Wales explains to Ten Bears. "It's been done by them lyin', double-tongued snakes thet run guv'mints. Guv'mints lie . . . promise . . . back-stab . . . eat in yore lodge and rape yore women and kill ye when ye sleep on their promises." Even in the gentle story of *The Education of Little Tree,* the Cherokee youth learns the fundamental lesson: "The law" should be despised, and those who carried out its dictates were "powerful monsters who had no regard for how folks had to live and get by."[755]

In his lifetime, Asa/Forrest Carter moved from Klan rabble-rouser to speechwriter for George Wallace's white backlash to successful author as his writings found a more congenial popular culture. An earlier generation might feel a sense of loss at the end of the frontier, but few questioned the role of Western heroes to replace the savage world of the desperado with a civilized community governed by law. In the 1970s and 1980s, a worship of the individual unfettered by social bonds or obligations, a hostility and contempt for government, and an embrace of extravagant violence became the theme song of popular culture. *High Noon*'s Marshal Will Kane (Gary Cooper) is a world away from the vigilante detective Harry Callahan, played by Clint Eastwood in *Dirty Harry*.[756]

Beyond forcing the University of New Mexico Press to remove the label "A True Story" from the cover page, the 1991 exposure of Carter's background initially had only minimal impact on the popularity of his fake memoir of Indian childhood. Periodically over the years, Carter's story was "rediscovered" in magazine articles and academic essays as well as in a highly regarded 2012 ITVS documentary, *The Reconstruction of Asa Carter*. Eleanor Friede was even able to negotiate a movie contract for the Little Tree book with Allied Filmmakers (distributed by Paramount Pictures), although the 1997 movie received mixed reviews and was a box-office failure.[757]

As with most books, sales decline over time, but in 2023, all of Carter's books remained in print, and *The Education of Little Tree* continued to be assigned to young readers.

Epilogue

Reflections

> *Brainwashed by the pro-communist anthropologist Franz Boaz, near-sighted sentimentalists have become convinced that immigration is a good thing, while liberal politicians welcome these arrivals as ignorant and loyal supporters. Make no mistake. The introduction of vast numbers of Mexicans and other colored people is a recipe for racial suicide. White Christian American will not survive such an onslaught, for these immigrants are incapable of self-government and history has shown that they will blindly follow leaders who offer them something for nothing.*
>
> — Asa Carter, 1959 Liberty Essay Broadcast[758]

> *Now, I know that the left and all the little gatekeepers on Twitter become literally hysterical if you use the term "replacement," if you suggest that the Democratic Party is trying to replace the current electorate, the voters now casting ballots, with new people, more obedient voters from the Third World. But they become hysterical because that's what's happening, actually. . . . Demographic change is the key to the Democratic Party's political ambitions. In order to win and maintain power, Democrats plan to change the population of the country.*
>
> Tucker Carlson, Fox News, April 12, 2021[759]

A half century ago, I began my life as a historian writing about the Scottsboro Case of the 1930s, a miscarriage of justice in which nine Black teenagers were nearly electrocuted and spent the most critical years of their young lives wrongly imprisoned on the false charges of raping two white women. However tragic the story, one could find consolation, even hope, in how that case helped to galvanize a generation of Black Americans into a force that ultimately brought down the legal walls of segregation. Even in my 1995 biography of George Wallace, his political transformation from race-baiting to desperate appeals for Black support in the later years of his life, seemed to reflect a region—and an America—that might confront and then move beyond its past.

Instead, as white Americans across the nation confronted unsettling challenges to the world they had known—or imagined—the response was often the same. In 1968, NBC's Douglas Kiker watched a New York audience stand and cheer George Wallace's not-so-covert racist speech. Kiker was struck, he said, by a sudden, epiphany: "They all hate Black people, all of them. They're all afraid. . . . Great God! That's it! They're all Southern! The whole United States is Southern!"[760]

In the years that followed, with the exception of fringe groups, conservative politicians and political activists abandoned explicitly racist language.[761] But George Wallace had deftly pioneered the use of coded language that allowed politicians to evoke fears of the Black menace even as they responded with outrage when accused of racism. Any student of modern American politics is familiar with the interview that Republican operative Lee Atwater gave in 1981 at the beginning of the Reagan era. "You start out in 1954 by saying, 'Nigger, nigger, nigger,'" he explained, but "by 1968, you can't say 'nigger'—that hurts you. Backfires. So you say stuff like forced busing, states' rights, and all that stuff."[762]

Asa Carter's story seems to come from a different world. His ideas were extreme, even at the height of Southern white resistance to integration. Although he and other far-right racists, antisemites, and fanatical antigovernment activists reached hundreds of thousands with their low-power AM radio broadcasts, sporadic conferences, pamphlets, mimeographed newsletters, and poorly funded newspapers, they were never able to organize a large movement at a time when state and national newspapers and the three television networks dismissed or ignored them as extremists.

But their words and their ideas are more than echoes from the past.

While the use of the N-word may still be frowned upon, the rise of the internet and the growth of social networks have bypassed the traditional information gatekeepers of Asa Carter's generation. If these new forms of communication have proved to be a powerful force in mobilizing groups to oppose dictatorial rule, in the United States and other open societies, they have heightened political divisions and eroded trust in government, media, and critical social institutions while spreading disinformation and normalizing threatening—and often violent—hate speech. Cole Porter's hit song from his 1938 musical suddenly seems up to date: "Anything Goes."

Perhaps Kevin Phillips's 1968 observation remains true. As he explained to journalist and historian Garry Wills, the ultimate secret of a successful politician is "knowing who hates who."[763]

Today's racist and far-right political activists share many of the ideas of Carter and his allies in the 1950s and 1960s, and they have far more powerful tools for reaching millions of Americans and even more targets for scapegoating.[764] Through the years, the list of enemies has grown: feminists, an assertive LGBTQ movement, "baby-killers," Muslims, brown-skinned immigrants from the south replacing traditional white Christian Americans, and intellectual elitists like those educators intent on undermining American patriotism and brainwashing children with "critical race theory."[765] Beyond the grassroots' net of true believers, the nation's growing plutocracy has bankrolled the politics of fear. The super-rich may not be concerned about divisive social and cultural issues, but they welcome anti-government movements that paralyze a national government with the potential to challenge their wealth and their power.

As I finished this manuscript, I remembered the late Milton Mayer's post-World War II interviews with Germans who looked back on their nation's journey to totalitarianism and the Holocaust. None were more powerful than Mayer's conversations with Heinrich Hildebrandt, who described the "gradual habituation of the people, little by little" to take one step and then another into the darkness. "Each act, each occasion is worse than the last," he said, but only a little worse. And so you wait for that one horrific event, thinking that when that shock comes, your fellow Germans will unite and join you in resisting. And then it is too late.

Haunted by his experience, Hildebrandt, a Latin scholar and retired literature teacher, kept remembering the words of Ovid, the ancient philosopher and poet: *Principiis obsta, Finem respice*—"Resist the beginnings, consider the end." But that was the problem, wasn't it, asked Hildebrandt. "One must foresee the end clearly, and how is this to be done by ordinary men or even by extraordinary men?"[766]

IN THE SUMMER OF 1991, I visited the burial place of Asa Carter, east of Anniston. Several years after his death in 1979, Carter's wife, India, had quietly replaced the small brass plaque—"Forrest Carter, 1926–1959"—with a granite headstone: "Asa Earl Carter, September 4, 1926–June 7, 1979." More than thirty years after his death, the D'Armanville Methodist Church cemetery remains a beautiful setting, with tall oaks shading the graves of the families that attended the small church for generations. But there is now a new headstone next to Asa Carter's: "India Walker Carter, June 2, 1925–November 22, 2014." When I last visited, fresh flowers marked the graves.

Asa Carter had come far from the young farm boy who washed out of Navy officer training and then become a college dropout. If he did not become the Hemingway of his generation, for a brief time he became—as he had hoped—famous.

The churchyard seems frozen in time, but in the last decade, a woman pastor with mixed-race children preached from the pulpit of the country church where Asa Carter once served as "Superintendent of Religious Education." On a recent Facebook page, its small congregation gathers on the steps of the sanctuary on a sunlit Sunday morning. A young Black member smiles into the camera and reminds us that, whatever the future, nothing ever truly remains the same.

~

Notes

1 Bill Jones interview with author, August 3, 1990, Jack Nelson interview with author, November 21, 1993, Dan T. Carter research files, Stuart A. Rose Manuscript, Archives and Rare Book Library, Emory University. Hereafter cited as DC.

2 Dick Smith interview, April 30, 1993, Fred Burger Research Papers (digital), Public Library of Anniston-Calhoun County, hereafter cited as FB; *Official Inaugural Program Honoring Governor George C. Wallace, January 14, 1963* (Montgomery: N.P., 1963).

3 Daniel McCabe, Paul Stekler and Steve Fayer, *George Wallace: Settin' the Woods on Fire*, 2000, *The American Experience*, Public Broadcasting System (available on Vimeo.com). Bob Ingram interview with author, July 15, 1988, DC.

4 Montgomery *Alabama Journal*, January 14, 1963.

5 "The Inaugural Address of Governor George C. Wallace," January 14, 1963" (available online on the Alabama Government Digital Archives).

6 Chuck and Betty Weeth Interview, December 12, 2008, Outtake from *The Reconstruction of Asa Carter*, a documentary by Douglas Newman, Laura Browder, and Marco Ricci, 2011. Hereafter cited as RAC Outtakes. DC.

7 Louis Menand, "Literary Hoaxes and the Ethics of Authorship," *The New Yorker*, December 10, 2018.

8 George Wallace to Lawrence Clayton, April 3, 1984, Clayton Correspondence, DC.

9 David Denby, "Out of the West: Clint Eastwood's shifting landscape," *The New Yorker*, February 28, 2010.

10 Carter privately printed his novel under this title, but after Eastwood signed an option to produce a film, Doubleday published the book and renamed it *The Outlaw Josey Wales*.

11 *New York Times*, February 27, April 24, 1991,

12 Iris Origo, *A Need to Testify* (New York: Harcourt Brace Jovanovich, 1984), 17–21.

13 Louis Menand, "The People Who Decide What Becomes History," *The New Yorker*, April 18, 2022, 65.

14 Hilary Mantel, "This Day is for the Living," BBC Reith Lecture 1, 2007 (available on the BBC Programme website).

15 *The Quiet Game* (New York: E. Dutton, 1999), 270.

16 Typescript, "Weatherly Family History," by Gerald Weatherly, June 10, 1960, in the "Pinson/Weatherly Family Genealogy File, Alabama Room, Public Library of Anniston-Calhoun Public Library, Anniston, Alabama, hereafter cited as AC Public Library; Larry Carter interview with Fred Burger, April 10, 1999. FB.

17 G.(eorge)W.(illiam) Featherstonhaugh, *The Slave States: Washington on the Potomac to the Frontier of Texas*, (New York: Harper and Brothers, 1844), 155.

18 James D. Miller, *South by Southwest: Planter Emigration and Identity in the Slave South* (Charlottesville: University of Virginia Press, 2002), 19; Henry D. Southerland Jr. and Jerry E Brown, *The Federal Road Through Georgia, the Creek Nation, and Alabama,*

1806–1836 (Tuscaloosa: University of Alabama Press, 1989).

19 Copy of statement before Probate Judge S. Montgomery affirming facts in Joseph Weatherly Will, November 6, 1852, DC.

20 Charles J. Kappler, *Indian Affairs: Laws and Treaties,* Volume 2 (Washington: Government Printing Office, 1904): 341; *Anniston Star,* June 26, 1955.

21 Ben Forkner, ed., *Audubon on Louisiana: Selected Writings of John James Audubon,* (Baton Rouge: Louisiana State University Press, 2018), 285–86. William W. Winn, *The Triumph of the* Ecunnau-Nuxulgee *(Macon: Mercer University Press, 2015),* 372–379. Michael Green, *The Politics of Indian Removal: Creek Government and Society in Crisis.* (Lincoln: University of Nebraska Press, 1982). Theda Perdue and Michael Green, *The Cherokee Nation and the Trail of Tears* (New York: Viking Press, 2007), 49–73.; Grant Foreman, *Indian Removal: The Emigration of the Five Civilized Tribes of Indians* (Norman: University of Oklahoma Press, 1932); Christopher D. Haveman, "Final Resistance: Creek Removal from the Alabama Homeland." *Alabama Heritage* 89 (Summer 2008): 9–19.

22 Information on the Pinson and Weatherly families is from the 1840, 1850, 1860, 1870 and 1880 census returns and the Weatherly Family History, AC Public Library. Larry Carter interview with Fred Burger, April 10, 1999, interview with Fred Burger, FB.

23 David Bright, *Race and Reunion: The Civil War in American Memory* (Cambridge: Harvard University Press, 2001), 113–122; Allen W. Trelease, *White Terror, The Ku Klux Klan Conspiracy and Southern Reconstruction* (Baton Rouge: Louisiana State University Press, 1995), 389–386; Elaine Frantz Parsons, *Ku Klux: the Birth of the Klan During Reconstruction* (Chapel Hill: University of North Carolina Press, 2016), 71–75; 183–190.

24 Montgomery *Advertiser,* January 27, 1869, July 24, 1867; Howard L. Swint, *The Northern Teacher in the South, 1862–1870* (Nashville: Vanderbilt University Press, 1941), 141–142.

25 Gene L. Howard, *Death at Cross Plains: A Reconstruction Alabama Tragedy* (Tuscaloosa: University of Alabama Press, 1984), 91.

26 *Rome Daily,* July 17, 1870; Gene Howard, *Death at Cross Plains: A Reconstruction Alabama Tragedy* (Tuscaloosa: University of Alabama Press, 1984), 9.

27 *Talladega* (Alabama) *Our Mountain Home,* October 11, 1882; *Union Springs* (Alabama) *Herald,* October 11, 1882; *Anniston Star,* February 13, 1906.

28 Equal Justice Initiative, *Lynching in America: Confronting the Legacy of Racial Terror* (Montgomery: EJI, 2015).

29 Grace Hooten Gates, *The Model City of the New South: Anniston, Alabama, 1872–1900* (Tuscaloosa: University of Alabama Press, 1978), 174.

30 Thirteenth Census of the U.S. (1910), Calhoun County, Alabama, Sheet 4, District 7, 93. Information on Carter's father and grandfather can be found in the Georgia 1880 and 1900 census and the Alabama 1900 and 1920 census. DC.

31 J. W. Weatherly Will, Probated October 10, 1934, copy. DC; Larry Carter Interview with Fred Burger, November 24, 1991, FB.

32 *Anniston Star,* November 11, 1964.

33 Herbert Bright Interview with Fred Burger, 1996 (no exact date). FB; Herbert Bright Interview with author, August 11, 1991, DC. Larry Carter Interview with Fred Burger, February 25, 2003, FB.

34 Larry Carter Interview with Fred Burger, November 21, 1991. FB.

35 Margaret Ruhle Coley Interview with Fred Burger, June 15, 1993. FB.

36 Gerald Bell, *Who's Crazy Now?* (New York: Samuel French, Inc., 1935).

37 Herbert Bright Interview with author, August 11, 1991, DC.

38 Melton McLaurin, "The Images of the Negro in Deep South Public School State History Texts," 6. Department of Education, 1968 Research Paper 168120D, Copy in DC. John Archibald, *Shaking the Gates of Hell: A Search for Family and Truth in the Wake of the Civil Rights Revolution* (New York: Alfred A. Knopf, 2021), 36–37.

39 Kristopher A. Teters, "Albert Burton Moore and Alabama's Centennial Commemoration of the Civil War: the Rhetoric of Race, Romance, and Reunion," *Alabama Review,* 66 (April 2013): 122–52.

40 Albert Burton Moore, *History of Alabama* (Alabama Book Store, 1951 printing of 1934 edition) 352–379, 456–501.

41 Ibid., 306.

42 Ibid., 485–86.

43 Ibid., 513.

44 Albert B. Moore, *Conscription and Conflict in the Confederacy* (New York: MacMillan Company, 1924), 361.

45 Fred Burger interviews with John Jackson, August 10, 2004; Margaret Coley, June 15, 1993; Ethel Sherman Bright, October 26, 1996; and Buddy Barnett, November 9, 1991. FB.

46 Glen Jeansonne, *Gerald L. K. Smith: Minister of Hate* (New Haven: Yale University Press, 1988), 122.

47 John W. "Jack" Coe, *Rear Admiral John G. Crommelin: Naval Hero, Conspiracy Theorist, White Supremacist* (Denver: Outskirts Press, 2021), 218.

48 *Anniston Star,* June 18, 1943.

49 United States Bureau of Naval Personnel, *The Navy College Training Program V-12: 1943 Curricula Schedules and Course Description.* (Sacramento: University of California Libraries, 1943).

50 Larry Carter Interview with Fred Burger, February 24, 2003, FB.

51 *Anniston Star,* November 2, 1943

52 Carol Edgemon Hipperson, ed., *Radioman: An Eyewitness Account of Pearl Harbor and WWII in the Pacific* (New York: Thomas Dunne Books, 2008), 34–35.

53 "Log of USS Appling," Copy. DC.

54 Gordon Lackey Interview with Fred Burger, June 3, 1996, FB.

55 Wilbur R. Robertson interview, June 6, 1996, FB.

56 Gordon Lackey Interview with Fred Burger, June 3, 1996, FB.

57 Lauren Rebecca Sklaroff, *Black Culture and the New Deal: The Quest for Civil Rights in the Roosevelt Era* (Chapel Hill: University of North Carolina Press, 2009), 123–58; Randy Roberts, *Joe Louis: Hard Times Man* (New Haven: Yale University Press, 2012), 218–31.

58 *Birmingham News,* June 23, 1938; *Atlanta Constitution,* June 23, 1938; Columbia (SC) *The State,* June 23, 1938; Montgomery *Advertiser,* June 23, 1938; *Anniston Star,* June 23, 1938. Jackson (MS) *Clarion-Ledger,* June 23, 1938.

59 Asa Carter FBI File, BH 157–4634. Copy in DC; "Individual Order to Adjust Pay Account for absence or Sentence of Court or Both, Carter, Asa Earl, 5/18/44," FB.

60 Office of the Chief of Naval Operations, *Dictionary of Naval Fighting Ships: I, Part A* (Washington: Naval Historical Center, 1991), 58.

61 Willis Robertson interview with Fred Burger, June 6, 1996, FB; David Sears, *At War With the Wind: The Epic Struggle with Japan's World War II Suicide Bombers* (New York: Citadel Press, 2008), 313–59; Donald L. Miller, *D-Days in the Pacific* (New York: Simon & Schuster, 2005), 276–313.

62 Alvin J. Kernan, *Crossing the Line: A Bluejacket's World War II Odyssey* (Annapolis: Naval Institute Press, 1997), 48–49.

63 Ibid., 38.

64 "Mr. Roberts Script," Copy in DC. The quote accurately reflects Heggen's observations in *Mr. Roberts* (Boston: Houghton Mifflin, 1946), but it is a creation of the scriptwriter.

65 Molly Guptill Manning, *When Books Went to War: the Stories that Helped us Win World War II* (Boston: Houghton Mifflin, 2014), 63–65, 138–39; Yoni Appelbaum, "Publishers Gave Away 122,951,031 Books During World War II," *The Atlantic* (September 10, 2014); John Jamieson, ed., *Editions for the Armed Services, Inc.: History of the 1324 Books Published for American Armed Services Overseas* (New York Editions for the Armed Forces, 1948), 21; Jamieson, "Books and the Soldier," *Public Opinion Quarterly*, 9 (1945): 320–332.

66 Ben Bradlee, *A Good Life* (New York: Simon & Schuster, 1995), 67–69.

67 Willis D. Jacobs "Throw it Over Here." *Bulletin of the American Association of University Professors* 32 (Autumn, 1946): 531–32.

68 Jeffrey Lyons, "The Family and Partisan Socialization in Red and Blue America," *Political Psychology*, 38 (2017): 297–312; Drew DeSilver, "The Politics of American generations: How Age Affects Attitudes and Voting Behavior," *FactTank*, July 9, 2014.

69 Sander A. Diamond, *The Nazi Movement in the United States, 1924–1941* (Ithaca: Cornell University Press, 1974); Arnie Bernstein, *Swastika Nation: Fritze Kuhn and the Rise and Fall of the German-American Bund* (New York: Picador Press, 2014); Bradley W. Hart, *Hitler's American Friends: The Third Reich's Supporters in the United States* (New York: Thomas Dunne Books, 2018) .

70 Jeffery M. Dorwart's *Conflict of Duty: The U.S. Navy's Intelligence Dilemma, 1919–1945* (Annapolis: Naval Institute Press, 1983). Dorwart to Author, July 22, 2014. Francis MacDonnell, *Insidious Foes: The Axis Fifth Column and the American Home Front* (New York: Oxford University Press, 1995).

71 Glen Jeansonne, *Gerald L. K. Smith*, 89.

72 Alan Brinkley, *Voices of Protest: Huey Long; Father Coughlin and the Great Depression* (New York: Alfred A. Knopf, 1982), 173; Jeansonne, *Gerald L. K Smith*, 38; Nathaniel Weyl, *Treason: The Story of Disloyalty and Betrayal in American History* (Washington: Public Affairs Press, 1950).

73 Jeansonne, *Gerald L. K. Smith*, 37.

74 Ibid., 58.

75 Ibid., 30–31.

76 From a confidential FBI informant who recorded and transcribed Smith's speech, Copy in DC.

77 Chip Berlet and Matthew N. Lyons, *Right-Wing Populism in America: Too Close for Comfort* (New York: The Guilford Press, 2000), 162–163.

78 Gerald Winrod, *The Jewish Assault on Christianity* (Gainesville, Missouri: Gordon Winrod Publisher, 1935), 22; Kim Phillips-Fein, "'A Fight between Two Systems of Thought': Gerald B. Winrod and the Kansas Senate Race of 1938," 108 (*The Journal of American History*, December 2021): 521–543.

79 Daniel Siemens, *Stormtroopers: A New History of Hitler's Brownshirts* (New Haven: Yale University Press, 2017).

80 Leo Ribuffo, *The Old Christian Right: The Protestant Far Right from the Great Depression to the Cold War* (Philadelphia: Temple University Press, 1983), 25–79. (Asheville, NC) *Mountain Express*, January 28, 2004.

81 *New York Times*, October 28, 1979, 44.

82 Paul Michael Marshall, "The Union Party and the 1936 Election," (PhD dissertation, The University of Sussex, 2013).

83 Bradley W. Hart, *Hitler's American Friends: The Third Reich's Supporters in the United States* (New York: St. Martin's Press, 2018) 70, 86, 178.

84 Jeansonne, *Gerald L. K. Smith*, 89.

85 Ibid., 23.

86 Ibid., 122.

87 "SAC Birmingham Office Memorandum: Asa Carter Background," November 11, 1956, FBI Files, DC.

88 Larry Carter interview with Fred Burger, February 25, 2004; Doug Carter interview with Fred Burger, September 9, 1999, FB.

89 Jack Shows interview with author, August 9, 1999, DC. .

90 *The Japan Times*, March 14, 2015; Müller, Rolf-Dieter; Schönherr, Nicole; Widera, Thomas, eds, *Die Zerstörung Dresdens: 13,* bis 15. Februar 1945; *Gutachten und Ergebnisse der Dresdner Historikerkommission zur Ermittlung der Opferzahlen* (Gottingen: Vandenhoeck & Ruprecht, 2010), 42.

91 Midshipman First Class Benjamin L. Olivas, "Close Encounters: U.S. Servicemen Engage Japan in War and Occupation 1941–1946, (United States Naval Academy Honors Thesis, 2010), 30; Yuki Tanaka. *Japan's Comfort Women: Sexual Slavery and Prostitution During World War II and the US Occupation.* (New York: Routledge, 2002), 152; Robert Kramm, *Sanitized Sex: Regulating Prostitution, Venereal Disease, and Intimacy in Occupied Japan, 1945–1952* (Berkeley: University of California Press, 2017, 1–17.

92 Kernan, *Crossing the Line*, 166. Asa Carter to parents, n.d. (April-May 1945?) FB.

93 Robert Edson Lee, *To the War* (New York: Alfred A. Knopf, 1968), 162–67.

94 Kernan, *Crossing the Line*, 176.

95 Dana Rubin, "The Real Education of Little Tree," *Texas Monthly*, February, 1992; James G. ("Buddy") Barnett interview with Fred Burger, November 9, 1991, FB.

96 Larry Carter interview with Fred Burger, November 24, 1991, FB

97 Doug Carter interview with Fred Burger, September 9, 1999, FB. Marriage License (copy), Asa E. Carter and Thelma Walker, February 27, 1946, DC.

98 Larry Carter interview with Fred Burger, February 25, 2004, FB.

99 Doug Carter interview with Fred Burger, September 9, 1999, FB

100 Asa Earl Carter Academic Transcript (Copy) University of Colorado, 1947–1948, DC
101 Larry Carter interview with Fred Burger, November 24, 1991, FB.
102 R. John Rath, "The Failure of an Ideal: The Viennese Revolution of 1848," *The Southwestern Social Science Quarterly, 34* (September 1953): 3–20; Rath, *The Viennese Revolution of 1848* (Austin, Texas: University of Texas Press, 1957).
103 Joan M. Jensen, *Army Surveillance in America, 1775–1980* (New Haven, Yale University Press, 1991); Roy Talbert, Jr., *Negative Intelligence: The Army and the American Left, 1917–1941* (Oxford: University of Mississippi Press, 1991; *Final Report of the Select Committee to Study Governmental Operations with Respect to Intelligence Activities, United States Senate. Together with Additional Supplemental and Separate Views.* April 26, 1976. Copy in DC.
104 AC FBI File, Part 4, SAC Birmingham to Director, FBI, November 29, 1954, DC.
105 Richard Hofstadter, "The Paranoid Style in American History," *Harper's Magazine*, November 1964, 85.
106 Jerry Kopel interview with author, March 12, 1997, DC.
107 Ibid.
108 J. Peters, *The Communist Party: A Manual on Organization* (New York: Workers Library Publishers, 1935), 51, 103–04, Thomas Sakmyster, *Red Conspirator: J. Peters and the American Communist Underground* (Urbana: University of Illinois Press, 2011), xiii, 39–51.
109 Jerry Kopel interview with author, March 12, 1997, DC.
110 Jerry Kopel to author, November 12, 2008; Jerry Kopel interview March 12, 1997, DC; Kopel, Jerry. "Asa Carter," *Colorado Statesman*, January 16, 1998.
111 Jerry Kopel interview with author, March 12, 1997, DC.
112 Robert Alan Goldberg, *Hooded Empire: The Ku Klux Klan in Colorado* (Chicago: University of Chicago Press, 1981); Denver *Rocky Mountain News*, November 23, 1999.
113 Robert Alan Goldberg, *Hooded Empire: The Ku Klux Klan in Colorado* (Chicago: University of Chicago Press, 1981); Denver *Rocky Mountain News*, November 23, 1999
114 *The Western Voice*, January 17, 1947.
115 Michael Barkun, *Religion and the Racist Right: The Origins of the Christian Identity Movement* (Chapel Hill: University of North Carolina Press, 2014.
116 William Blessing, *White Supremacy* (Denver: House of Prayer for all People, 1952).
117 Alvin Weinberger, "An Analysis of the [1943] Colorado Labor Peace Act," *Rocky Mountain Law Review, 19* (1946–1947): 359–366.
118 (New York: Harper and Brothers, 1947), 223.
119 R. Douglas Hurt, *The Great Plains During World War II* (Lincoln: University of Nebraska Press, 2008, 48–49 Robert G. Athearn, *The Coloradans* (Albuquerque: University of New Mexico Press, 1976), 276–91, 316–17; Carl Abbott, Stephen J. Leonard, and Thomas J. Noel, *Colorado: A History of the Centennial State* [Fourth Edition], (Boulder: University Press of Colorado, 2011), 266, 294–97; Marshall Sprague, *Colorado: A History* (New York: W. W. Norton and Company, 1984) 157–59; Margaret Pilcher, "Eugene Cervi and Cervi's *Rocky Mountain Journal*: A Study of Post-World War II Colorado," (PhD dissertation, University of Denver, 1986).
120 McCarty, Patrick Fargo "Big Ed Johnson: A Political Portrait" (MA thesis, University

of Colorado, 1958).

121 Jerry Kopel to author, November 12, 2008, DC.

122 SAC New Orleans to SAC Birmingham, April 3, 1956, Part 4. FBI Files, DC.

123 John McDuling, *Quartz,* "The remarkable resilience of old-fashioned radio in the US," April 4, 2014; Clive Webb, *Rabble Rousers: The American Far Right in the Civil Rights Era* (Athens: University of Georgia Press, 2010), 24,

124 Broadcast Pioneers of Colorado: Hall of Fame, Art Peterson," Copy in DC. Art Peterson interview, June 22, 1993. FB.

125 Neal Gabler, *Winchell: Gossip, Power and the Culture of Celebrity* (New York: Vintage Press, 1995), 642–680.

126 Dennis Mazzocco, Networks *of Power: Corporate TV's Threat to Democracy* (Boston: South End Press, 1999) 39–40.

127 *Boston Globe,* November 13, 1961; Ed Cray, *Chief Justice: A Biography of Earl Warren* (New York: Simon & Schuster, 1997), 391.

128 *Los Angeles Times*, August 22, 1966; *New York Times*, August 22, 1966

129 *The Arizona Republic* (Phoenix), August 25, 1966.

130 Joel A. Carpenter, *Revive Us Again: The Reawakening of American Fundamentalism,* (Oxford: Oxford University Press, 1999), 135–139. The *Rocky Mountain News* daily published a complete radio log for the Denver stations. See listings for 1950, 1951 and 1952.

131 11/29/54—SAC Birmingham to Director re. Asa Carter, Part 4, FBI Files, DC.

132 SAC New Orleans to SAC Birmingham, April 3, 1956, Part 4. FBI Files, DC.

133 Albert D. Kirwan, *Revolt of the Rednecks: Mississippi Politics, 1876–1925* (Lexington: University of Kentucky Press, 1951).

134 Rick Bragg, *All Over but the Shoutin'* (New York: Pantheon Books, 1997), 97–99.

135 Moore, *History of Alabama,* 389

136 Ibid., 401, 539, 542.

137 Hundley, *Social Relations in Our Southern States* (New York: Henry B. Price Publishers, 1860), 263–64.

138 Frances Anne Kemble, *Journal of a Residence on a Georgian Plantation in 1838–1839* (London: Longman, Green, Longman, Roberts, & Green, 1863), p. 89.

139 Steven E. Atkins, ed., *Encyclopedia of Right-Wing Extremism in Modern American History* (Santa Barbara, California: ABC-Clio, 2011), 89–90; Morris Fine, ed, *American Jewish Yearbook, 1956* (New York: American Jewish Committee, 1957), 184.

140 *Ocala* [FL] *Star-Banner*, ; Jane Hoover Parish, "The History of the Family of William Henry Hoover, Sr., Founder of the City, Hoover, Alabama." Copy in DC.

141 Glenn Eskew, *But for Birmingham: The Local and National Movements in the Civil Rights Struggle* (Chapel Hill: University of North Carolina Press, 1997), 111–13; William E. Nicholas, *Go and Be Reconciled: Alabama Methodists Confront Racial Injustice, 1954–1974* (Montgomery: NewSouth Books, 2018), 22–25.

142 Heather Bryson, "To Give Racism the Face of the Ignorant: Race, Class, and White Manhood in Birmingham, Alabama, 1937–1970," (PhD dissertation, University of Florida, 2011), 77.

143 Ibid., *Birmingham News*, .

144 Fundraising appeal by Asa Carter, N.D., circa 1954, copy, DC.

145 Landon R. Y. Storrs, "Revisiting Truman's Federal Employee Loyalty Program," in *Civil Liberties and the Legacy of Harry S. Truman,* edited by Richard Stewart Kirkendall. 67–8 (Kirksville, Missouri: Truman State University Press, 2013); Wood, *Black Struggle, Red Scare*, 27–28.

146 Amy Kallio Bollman, "Dangerous Eloquence: Hate Speech Tactics in the Discourse of Asa/Forrest Carter from 1954–1974," University of Oklahoma Dissertation), 2004, 92–94.

147 Warren, *The Legacy of the Civil War* (Cambridge: Harvard University Press, 1961), 14–15.

148 American States Rights Association papers, Department of Archives and History, Birmingham Public Library.

149 Bruce E. Baker, *What Reconstruction Meant: Historical Memory in the American South* (Charlottesville: University of Virginia Press, 2007), 21–43

150 Thomas Nelson Page, *The Negro: The Southerner's Problem* (New York: Charles Scribner's Sons, 1904), 203–04.

151 Craig D'Ooge, "'The Birth of a Nation': a Symposium," *The Library of Congress Information Bulletin,* June 27, 1994.

152 Jennifer Fronc, "'Historical Presentation' or 'Libel to the race'?," *The Journal of the Gilded Age and Progressive Era,*" 14 (2015: 612–615).

153 Wyn Craig Wade, *The Fiery Cross: The Ku Klux Klan in America* (New York: Simon & Schuster, 1987), 142, 145. The literature on the modern Klan is extensive; two of the best relatively recent works are by Nancy MacLean, *Behind the Mask of Chivalry: The Making of the Second Ku Klux Klan* (New York: Oxford University Press, 1995), and Linda Gordon, *The Second Coming of the KKK: The Ku Klux Klan of the 1920s and the American Political Tradition* (New York: Liveright, 2017).

154 K. Stephen Prince, "Jim Crow Memory: Southern White Supremacists and the Regional Politics of Remembrance," in *Remembering Reconstruction: Struggles Over the Meaning of America's Most turbulent Era,* edited by Carole Emberton and Bruce E. Baker (Baton Rouge: Louisiana State University Press), 17–34.

155 This summary is taken from recordings in the Fred Burger Collection. He sometimes reprinted excerpts in his magazine. *The Southerner,* March 1956, 2, 7–8.

156 John Bartlow Martin, "The Deep South Says Never," *Saturday Evening Post,* 229 (June 29, 1957): 56.

157 Christopher Rein, "This Beloved Confederate General Was one of the Worst Military Leaders in History," Slate.com, March 5, 2022.

158 The main source for Carter's writings on Forrest seems to have been John Allan Wyeth's 1908 biography, *That Devil Forrest: Life of Lieutenant-General Nathan Bedford Forrest* (New York: Harper Brothers, 1908).

159 Jason Niles Diary, May 6, 1865, Southern Historical Collection, Wilson Library University of North Carolina Chapel Hill.

160 Blight, *Race and Reunion,* 199, 298.

161 Shelby Foote, *The Beleaguered City: The Vicksburg Campaign, December 1862-July 1863* (New York: Modern Library, 1995); Dora Richards Miller, *War Diary of a Union Woman in the South: 1860–63.* Edited by George Washington Cable. (New York: Charles

Scribner's Sons, 1889), 342.

162 Gerald Weatherly, "Weatherly Family History," Anniston-Calhoun County Public Library; Larry Carter interview with Fred Burger, April 10, 1999, February 25, 2004, FB.

163 Carter based his account of the death of "Overby and Carter" on John S. Mosby's memoirs, Charles Wells, ed., *The Memoirs of Colonel John S. Mosby* (Boston: Little, Brown, and Company, 1917), 301–02.

164 *Baltimore Sun*, April 30, 1901

165 Russell, ed., The Memoirs of Colonel John S. Mosby, 296–303; Robert W. Black, *Ghost, Thunderbolt and Wizard: Mosby, Morgan and Forrest in the Civil War* (Mechanicsburg, Pennsylvania: Stackpole Press, 2008), 79–87; *Baltimore Sun*, May 1, 1899; "Roster of the 43rd Battalion, Virginia Cavalry, Army of Northern Virginia," Copy in DC.

166 United States Congress, Joint Select Committee on the Condition of Affairs in the Late Insurrectionary States, *Report of the Joint Select Committee to Inquire into the Condition of Affairs in the Late Insurrectionary States, made to the two Houses of Congress February 19, 1872*, Vols. 11, 12 (Washington: Government Printing Office, 1872). *The Southerner*, I (April-May, 1956), 5; John Bartlow Martin, *The Deep South Says "Never."* (New York: Ballantine Books, 1957), 117; *The Southerner* [2nd version], 1970, 13.

167 David C. Carter, "Outraged Justice: The Lynching of Postmaster Frazier Baker in Lake City, South Carolina, 1897–98," (honors thesis: Department of History, University of North Carolina, 1992).

168 Jonathan Peter Spiro, *Defending the Master Race: Conservation, Eugenics, and the Legacy of Madison Grant* (Burlington: University of Vermont Press, 2008).

169 Richard Kluger, *Simple Justice: The History of Brown v. Board of Education and Black America's Struggle for Equality* (New York: Alfred A. Knopf, 1976), 331–335.

170 Rebekah Dobrasko, "Upholding 'Separate but Equal': South Carolina's School Equalization Program, 1951–1955." (MA thesis, University of South Carolina, 2005); James E. Robin Thomas Victor O'Brien, "Georgia's Response to *Brown v. Board of Education*: The Rise and Fall of Massive Resistance, 1949–1961." (PhD dissertation, Emory University, 1992); Charles C. Bolton, "Mississippi's School Equalization Program, 1945–1954: 'A Last Gasp to Try to Maintain a Segregated Educational System.'" *Journal of Southern History* 66 (November 2000): 781–814

171 Gareth D. Pahowka, "Voices of Moderation: Southern Whites Respond to *Brown v. Board of Education*," *The Gettysburg Historical Journal*, 5 (2006), 43–66; Anthony Badger, "'Closet Moderates': Why White Liberals Failed, 1940–1970" in *The Role of Ideas in the Civil Rights Movement*, edited by Ted Owenby, 83–112 (Jackson: University Press of Mississippi, 2002), 83–112; Anders Walker, *The Ghost of Jim Crow: How Southern Moderates Used Brown v. Education to Stall Civil Rights* (New York: Oxford University Press, 2009).

172 *Florence* (SC) *Morning News*, March 23, June 9, June 12, 1956.

173 *Tuscaloosa* (AL) *News*, May 26, 2006; Anthony Badger, *Why White Liberals Fail: Race and Southern Politics from FDR to Trump* (Cambridge: Harvard University Press, 2022), 87–88.

174 George Sims, *The Little Man's Big Friend: James E. Folsom in Alabama Politics, 1946–1955*, (Tuscaloosa: University of Alabama Press, 1985) 131–32.

175 Carter, *The Politics of Rage: George Wallace, The Origins of the New Conservatism, and the Transformation of American Politics.* (New York: Simon & Schuster, 1995), 72–73; *New York Times*, November 10, 1990.
176 Sims, *The Little Man's Big Friend*, 165.
177 "Alabama Governor, Democratic Primary, 1954," OurCampaigns.com. Copy in DC.
178 J. Tyra Harris, "Alabama Reaction to the *Brown* decision, 1954–1956: A Case Study in Early Massive Resistance," (PhD dissertation, Middle Tennessee State University, 1978.)
179 Asa Carter, "The Key Weapon," *Common Sense*, May 1, 1955.
180 Jeff R. Woods, *Black Struggle, Red Scare: Segregation and Anti-Communism in the South, 1948–1968.* (Baton Rouge: Louisiana State University Press, 2003), 49–84.
181 AC Liberty Essay (?) 1956, "Washington Schools," DC.
182 Brady, *Black Monday.* (Jackson, Mississippi: Association of Citizens' Councils, 1955). Newport News (Virginia) *Daily Press*, September 3, 1956.
183 "Interview with the Honorable Thomas Brady: Associate Justice, Mississippi Supreme Court" (1972), Center for Oral History and Cultural Heritage, University of Southern Mississippi; Portland *Press Herald*, August 12, 1955; *New York Times*, December 30, 1955, August 25, 1957, October 5, 1957, Minneapolis *Star Tribune*, August 21, 1955; *San Francisco Examiner*, August 21, 1955; *Tampa Bay Times*, August 21, 1955, *Sydney Morning Herald* (Australia), August 27, 1955.
184 Brady, *Black Monday*, 2, 7, 11–12. James Denson Sayers, *Can the White Race Survive?* (Washington: Independent Publishing Company, 1929), dust jacket.
185 Brady, *Black Monday*, 7.
186 Ibid., 45, 64.
187 John Jackson, Jr., "The Scientific Attack on *Brown* v. *Board of Education, 1954–1964," American Psychologist, 59* (September 2004): 532–33; Andrew Winston, "Science in the service of the far right: Henry E. Garrett, the IAAEE, and the Liberty Lobby," *Journal of Social Issues,* 54 (Spring, 1998): 179–210.
188 W. C. George, *The Race Problem from the Standpoint of One Who is Concerned About the Evils of Miscegenation* (Birmingham, Alabama: American States Rights Association, 1955), 4. Copy in the W. C. George Papers, Southern Historical Collection, Louis Round Wilson Special Collections Library, University of North Carolina.
189 Lee D. Baker, "Columbia University's Franz Boas: He led the Undoing of Scientific Racism," *The Journal of Blacks in Higher Education*, 22 (Winter, 1998–1999): 89–96. *An American Dilemma,* Two volumes, (New York: Harper Brothers, 1944).
190 *Montgomery Advertiser*, February 5, 1956.
191 Arthur M. Schlesinger, *Robert Kennedy and His Times* (Boston: Houghton Mifflin, 2002), 234.
192 Maarten Zwiers, *Senator James Eastland: Mississippi's Jim Crow Democrat* (Baton Rouge: Louisiana State University Press, 2015), 24–25; David M. Oshinsky, *A Conspiracy So Immense: The World of Joe McCarthy* (New York: Simon & Schuster, 1983), 497; Senator Eastland speaking, 83rd Cong., 1st sess., *Congressional Record* 100 (May 27, 1954) 7251–7257; *New York Times*, May 28, 1954.
193 Zwiers, *Senator James Eastland*, 117–19.
194 Tim Weiner, *Enemies: A History of the FBI* (New York: Random House, 2012), 217;

Jeff Woods, *Black Struggle,* 85–111; Woods, *Black Struggle, Red Scare,* 86–92, 120–121.

195 "Playboy Interview: Martin Luther King," *Playboy Magazine*, January, 1965.

196 Woods, *Black Struggle, Red Scare,* 12–48.

197 Michael J. Klarman, "Court, Congress, and Civil Rights," in *Congress and the Constitution*, edited by Neal Devins and Keith E. Whittington, 173–197 (Durham, NC: Duke University Press, 2005).

198 Hazel Erskine, "The Polls: Race Relations," *Public Opinion Quarterly,* 26 (Spring, 1962): 137–148; Hazel Erskine, "The Polls: Demonstrations and Civil Rights," *Public Opinion Quarterly,* 31 (Winter 1967–68): 655–677.

199 Leaflets promoting the broadcasts were distributed by the Alabama States Rights Association—see ASRA papers, Birmingham Public Library.

200 Martin, *The Deep South Says "Never,"* 105–06. Robert J. Norrell, *Reaping the Whirlwind: The Civil Rights Movement in Tuskegee* (New York: Alfred A. Knopf, 1985) remains the best description of Engelhardt and his role in Alabama politics.

201 Jerry Pytlak, "The Cotton Economy in Depression," *The New International,* 5 (August 1939):247–50.

202 Joseph Bagley, *The Politics of White Rights: Race, Justice, and Integrating Alabama's Schools* (Athens: University of Georgia Press, 2018), 19; J. W. Peltason, *Fifty-eight Lonely Men: Southern Federal Judges and School Desegregation* (New York: Harcourt, Brace and World, 1961), 58; Thomas Gilliam, *"The Second Folsom Administration:* The Destruction of Alabama Liberalism, 1954–1958," (PhD dissertation, Auburn University, 1975), 104–105.

203 Between July and early September, NAACP chapters in Marion County, Mobile, Gadsden, Bessemer, and Montgomery filed similar petitions which the *Montgomery Advertiser* and the *Birmingham News* reported briefly and without comment. Neil R. McMillen, *The Citizens' Council: Organized Resistance to the Second Reconstruction, 1954–1964* (Urbana: University of Illinois Press, 1971), 42–43.

204 *Florence* (SC) *Morning News,* June 6, 1954.

205 On July 30, the *Greenville News, Florence* (SC) *Morning News, Charleston News and Courier,* and *The* (Columbia) *State* as well as dozens of newspapers across the nation reported Timmerman's television appearance.

206 Orangeburg *Times Democrat,* July 30, 1956; Candace Cunningham, "'Hell is Popping Here in South Carolina': Orangeburg County Black Teachers and Their Community in the Immediate Post-*Brown* Era," *History of Education Quarterly*, 61 (February, 2021): 35–62.

207 Howard H. Quint, *Profile in Black and White: A Frank Portrait of South Carolina* (Washington: Public Affairs Press, 158–60.

208 *Florence* (SC) *Morning News*, May 18, 1954, January 1, 1956.

209 Ibid., March 6, 1956; Eugene N. Zeigler, Jr., *When Conscience and Power Meet: a Memoir* (Columbia: University of South Carolina Press, 2008), 152.

210 *Chicago Tribune*, May 7, 1986; *Chicago Sun-Times*, May 8, 1986.

211 *Saint Louis Post Dispatch*, September 21, 1955; *Huntsville* (AL) *Times,* June 1, 1955.

212 Bartley, *The Rise of Massive Resistance,* 13–14; John Kyle Day, *The Southern Manifesto: Massive Resistance and the fight to Preserve Segregation* (Jackson: University Press of Mississippi, 2014), 65.

213 Malcolm E. Jewell, "State Legislatures in Southern Politics," *Journal of Politics,* 26 (1964), 177–78.

214 Clive Webb. *Fight against Fear: Southern Jews and Black Civil Rights* (Athens: University of Georgia Press, 2001); Leonard Dinnerstein and Mary Dale Palsson (eds.), *Jews in the South* (Baton Rouge: Louisiana State University Press, 1973); Nathan M. Kaganoff and Melvin I. Urofsky (eds.) *Turn to the South: Essays on Southern Jewry* (Charlottesville: University of Virginia Press, 1979). Leonard Dinnerstein, "Southern Jewry and the Desegregation Crisis, 1954–1970," *American Jewish Historical Quarterly,* 62 (March, 1973): 231–241; Howard Rabinowitz, "Nativism, Bigotry and Anti-Semitism in the South," *American Jewish History,* 77 (March,1988): 437–51.

215 Steve Oney, *And the Dead Shall Rise: The Murder of Mary Phagan and the Lynching of Leo Frank* (New York: Pantheon Books, 2003), 561–572; 586–591; Rabinowitz, "Nativism, Bigotry and Anti-Semitism in the South," 437–451.

216 Glenn Feldman, *Politics, Society, and the Klan in Alabama, 1915–1949* (Tuscaloosa: University of Alabama Press, 1999), 57–58, 78.

217 Felix Harcourt, *Ku Klux Kulture: America and the Klan in the 1920s* (Chicago: University of Chicago Press, 2017).

218 James E. Goodman, *Stories of Scottsboro* (New York: Pantheon Books, 1994), 133; Dan T. Carter, *Scottsboro: A Tragedy of the American South* (Baton Rouge: Louisiana State University Press, 1969), 254–261.

219 Dan J. Puckett, *In the Shadow of Hitler: Alabama's Jews, the Second World War, and the Holocaust* (Tuscaloosa: University of Alabama Press, 2014), 22.

220 New York *Daily Worker,* December 4, 1933.

221 *New York Times,* April 10, 1933, New York *World Telegram,* August 19, 1933, Montgomery *Advertiser,* May 11, 27, 28, 1933.

222 Yaakov Ariel, "It's All in the Bible," in Jonathan Karp and Adam Sutcliffe, eds,, *Philosemitism in History* (London: Cambridge University Press, 2011), 257–288,

223 Elovitz, *A Century of Jewish Life in Dixie,* 170–175.

224 Tim Hollis, *Birmingham's Retail and Theater District* (Charleston, SC: Arcadia Publishing, 2005).

225 Stewart to Governor James A. Folsom, August 27, 1957, Alabama Department of Archives and History, Digital Collections.

226 Robert L. Fleegler, *Ellis Island Nation: Immigration and American Identity in the Twentieth Century* (Philadelphia: University of Pennsylvania Press, 2015), 141.

227 *Birmingham Post-Herald,* February 21, 1955.

228 Dianne McWhorter, *Carry Me Home: Birmingham Alabama: The Climactic Battle of the Civil Rights Revolution* (New York: Simon & Schuster, 2001), 100–01; Gordon W. Lovejoy Memo, August 3, 1960, National Conference of Christians and Jews, Alabama Region Papers, Department of Archives and History, Birmingham, Alabama, Public Library, Box 3.

229 Gordon W. Lovejoy Memo, August 3, 1960, National Conference of Christians & Jews, Alabama Region Papers, Birmingham Public Library, Box 3.

230 Asa Carter, "The Key Weapon," *Common Sense,* May 1, 1955; The United States Senate did not approve the United Nations genocide treaty until 1988. *New York Times,* November 5, 1988.

231 McWhorter, *Carry Me Home,* 249; *Birmingham News,* December 22, 2010.

232 "The North Alabama Citizens' Council & Asa (Ace) Earl Carter," from "A Survey of Resistance Groups in Alabama," Southern Regional Council Archives, Archives and Special Collections, Robert W. Woodruff Library, Atlanta University Center, hereafter cited as SRC.

233 Liberty Essay—MP3 recording from 1956 LP Record, DC.

234 "A Survey of the Resistance Groups in Alabama: the North Alabama Citizens' Council & Asa (Ace) Earl Carter," 1956, prepared by the Southern Regional Council, SRC Archives.

235 M[ilton] A. Jones to Mr. [Louis] Nichols, January 22, 1957, FBI Memorandum, Asa Carter File, Part I, Copy in DC.

236 Doug Jones with Greg Truman, *Bending Toward Justice: the Birmingham Church Bombing that Changed the Course of Civil Rights* (New York: All Points Books, 2019), 17–19.

237 Webb, *Rabble Rousers: The American Far Right in the Civil Rights Era,* 2010), 153–209; McWhorter, *Carry Me Home,* 71–75, 132–34.

238 *Birmingham News,* November 20, 1947.

239 Eskew, *But for Birmingham: The Local and National Movements in the Civil Rights Struggle* (Chapel Hill: University of North Carolina Press, 1997), 54–83.

240 Jerrell H. Shofner, "Forced Labor in the Florida Forests, 1880–1950," *Journal of Forest History,* 25 (January, 1981): 14–25; Lauriault, Robert N. "From Can't to Can't: The North Florida Turpentine Camp, 1900–1950," *Florida Historical Quarterly*, 67 (1989): 310–328; Michael Newton, *The Invisible Empire: The Ku Klux Klan in Florida* (Gainesville: University of Florida Press, 1997).; Equal Justice Initiative, *Lynching in America: Confronting the Legacy of Racial Terror* [Third Edition], (EJI: Montgomery, Alabama, 2017), 41.

241 Gilbert King, *Devil in the Grove: Thurgood Marshall, the Groveland Boys and the Dawn of a New America* (New York: Harper Collins Press, 2012), 282.

242 Ibid., 246, 249. *Orlando Evening Star,* December 26, 1951; *Orlando Sentinel,* December 30, 1951; *Miami News,* January 6, 1952.

243 Harry T. Moore, Harriette V. Moore. Notice to Close File No. 144–17M-3164, Civil Rights Division, Department of Justice, Copy in DC; Raymond A. Mohl, *South of the South : Jewish activists and the Civil Rights Movement in Miami, 1945–1960* (Gainesville: University of Florida Press, 2004), 23–29.

244 These numbers are based upon the well-researched pamphlet, "Intimidation, Reprisal and Violence in the South's Racial Crisis," published jointly by the American Friends Service Committee, the National Council of the Churches of Christ and the Southern Regional Council as well as newspaper accounts and FBI reports. Mississippi figures come from John Dittmer's *Local People: The Struggle for Civil Rights in Mississippi* (Urbana: University of Chicago Press, 1994), 251; Seth Cagin and Philip Dray, *We Are Not Afraid: The Story of Goodman, Schwerner, and Chaney and the Civil Rights Campaign for Mississippi* (New York: McMillan Publishers, 1988).

245 McWhorter, *Carry Me Home,* 75.

246 Robert J. Norrell, "Caste in Steel: Jim Crow Careers in Birmingham, Alabama," *The Journal of American History, 73* (December, 1986): 669–694; Thomas R. Pegram, "The Ku Klux Klan, Labor, and the White Working Class During the 1920s," *The Journal*

of the Gilded Age and the Progressive Era, 17 (April 2018):373–396.

247 *St. Louis Post Dispatch*, September 21, 1955.

248 Norrell, *Reaping the Whirlwind,* 87–91; *New York Herald Tribune*, September 21, 1955.

249 Hanes Walton, Jr., Sherman Puckett and Donald R. Deskins, Jr. *The African American Electorate* (Thousand Oaks California: Sage Publications, 2012), 510.

250 Bob Ingram interview with Author, August 11, 1991, DC.

251 Ibid.

252 Douglas Cater, "Civil War in Alabama's Citizens' Councils," *The Reporter* (May 17, 1956), 19–21.

253 *Montgomery Advertiser*, February 11, 1957; J. Mills Thornton, III, *Dividing Lines: Municipal Politics and the Struggle for Civil Rights in Montgomery, Birmingham and Selma* (Tuscaloosa: The University of Alabama Press, 2002), 95-96.

254 The following description of the story of Autherine Lucy's efforts to integrate the University relies heavily upon E. Culpepper Clark's account, *The Schoolhouse Door: Segregation's Last Stand at the University of Alabama* (New York: Oxford University Press, 1993), 1–90.

255 David W. Levy, *Breaking Down Barriers: George McLaurin and the Struggle to End Segregated Education* (Norman: University of Oklahoma Press, 2020); Gary M. Lavergne, *Before Brown: Heman Marion Sweatt, Thurgood Marshall, and the Long Road to Justice* (Austin: University of Texas Press, 2010).

256 Peltason, *Fifty-Eight Lonely Men*, 84–85.

257 Clark, *The Schoolhouse Door,* 58–59.

258 Leonard Wilson Interview with Fred Burger, May 29, 2006, FB.

259 McMillen, *The Citizens' Council,* 48–49.

260 L(eonard) H. Wilson to Enoch Powell, April 25, 1968. Copy in DC, courtesy of Olivier Esteves, author of forthcoming study, *Inside the Black Box of White Backlash: Letters of Support to Enoch Powell, 1968–1969*; Leonard J. Wilson RAC interview, February 2, 2008, DC; David A. Graham, "The White-Supremacist Group That Inspired a Racist Manifesto," *The Atlantic,* June 22, 2015.

261 *Montgomery Advertiser,* Montgomery *Alabama Journal*, February 12, 1956; Thornton, *Dividing Lines*, 191.

262 *New York Post*, January 9, 1957

263 Day, *The Southern Manifesto,* 160–62.

264 Quotes are from the lengthy articles in the February 11 issues of the *Montgomery Advertiser,* the Montgomery *Alabama Journal,* the *Birmingham News* and *The New York Times.*

265 Handbill produced by the Central Alabama Citizens' Council, February 10, 1956. Montgomery, Alabama. Copy in DC. Gary S. Sprayberry, "'Town Among the Trees': Paternalism, Class, and Civil Rights in Anniston, Alabama, 1872 to Present," (PhD dissertation, University of Alabama, 2003), 173.

266 Martin, *The Deep South*, 108.

267 W. Edward Harris, *Miracle in Birmingham: a Civil Rights Memoir, 1954–1965* (Indianapolis, Indiana: Stonework Press, 2004), 33; Dan Wakefield, *Revolt in the South* (New York: Grove Publishers, 1960), 53; McGill, *The South and the Southerner* (Boston:

Little, Brown, 1963), 143; Wyn Craig Wade, *The Fiery Cross: the Ku Klux Klan in America* (New York: Simon & Schuster, 1987), 301; Ann Waldron, *Hodding Carter: The Reconstruction Of A Racist* (Chapel Hill: Algonquin Press, 1993); Carter, *Politics of Rage,* 135.

268 James E. Robinson, "Hodding Carter: Southern Liberal, 1907–1972" (PhD dissertation, Mississippi State University, 1974), 196–197.

269 Tom Brady, *Black Monday* (Jackson, Mississippi: Association of Citizens' Councils, 1955), 27.

270 Coe, *Rear Admiral John G. Crommelin,* 188, 209.

271 Hamilton, Virginia Van der Veer. *Lister Hill: Statesman from the South.* Chapel Hill: University of North Carolina Press, 1987) 192; James Graham Cook, *The Segregationists* (New York: Appleton Century-Croft, 1962) pp 156–57.

272 American Jewish Committee, "Trio of Bigots State Meeting in Louisville," *For Your Information,* 3 No. 2, (February, 1958), DC.

273 Cook, *The Segregationists,* 76, 153–54.

274 Martin, *The Deep South Says Never,* 28–30, 33–34; David Halberstam, "The White Citizens' Councils," *Commentary,* October 1956, 299–300.

275 Thornton, *Dividing Lines,* 95-96.

276 *Birmingham News,* February 27, March 2, 1956; *Montgomery Advertiser,* March 2, 3, 1956.

277 Mildred A. Schwartz, "Trends in White Attitudes toward Negroes," Report No. 119, National Opinion Research Center, the University of Chicago.

278 *Race Relations Law Reporter,* I (April 1956), 437; *Montgomery Advertiser,* January 26, March 4, 1956.

279 Tony Badger, "Southerners Who Refused to Sign the Southern Manifesto," *The Historical Journal* (June 1999): 528–32.

280 George Goodwin, Jr., "The Seniority System in Congress," *American Political Science Review* 53 (September 2013), 421–423.

281 Day, *The Southern Manifesto,* 5, 34–35.

282 McWhorter, *Carry Me Home,* 182–185.

283 Halberstam, "The White Citizens' Councils," 301.

284 *Birmingham Age-Herald,* January 16, 1956; *Birmingham News,* January 17, 1956.

285 *The Southerner, I* (March, 1956), 4.

286 Harris, *Miracle in Birmingham,* 35; *Birmingham News,* February 4, 1956. Webb, *Fight Against Fear,* 106–07.

287 Robert (Bob) Ingram interview with author, August 11, 1991, DC.

288 R. B. Jones interview with author, July 27, 1992. DC.

289 Taken together, the March 10, 1956 issues of the *Birmingham Age-Herald, Birmingham News Anniston Star* and *The New York Times* and the March 15, 1956 issue of the *Christian Science Monitor* give us extensive coverage of the rally. Reports of the split in the organization are detailed in *The New York Times,* March 6, 1956, the New York *Post,* March 12, 1956, and in Douglass Cater's report, "Civil War in Alabama's Citizens' Councils," 19–21.

290 Halberstam, "White Citizens' Council," 300; Sprayberry, "Town Among the Trees,"

180–184.

291 *New York Times,* March 6, 1956; Neil R. McMillen, *The Citizens' Council,* , 49–50; *Birmingham News,* February 29, 1956, March 13, 1956; *Birmingham Post-Herald,* March 1, April 14, 1956.

292 *Atlanta Constitution,* February 20, 1952; "The White Citizen Councils vs. Southern Trade Unions," Memo, H. L. Mitchell to the Southern Regional Council, March 12, 1956, SRC; Steven Weisenburger, "The Columbians, Inc.: A Chapter of Racial Hatred from the Post-World War II South, *The Journal of Southern History.* 69, (Nov 2003): 857–58; *Atlanta Constitution,* January 20, March 3, 21, May 14, 1951.

293 Halberstam, "White Citizens' Council," 300.

294 *Montgomery Advertiser,* March 6, 1956; *New York Times,* March 6, 1956.

295 *Montgomery Advertiser,* March 10, 1956; *Decatur* (Alabama) *Daily,* March 11, 1956.

296 *Anniston Star,* March 11, 1956; *Birmingham News,* March 11, 1956.

297 *Birmingham News,* March 13, 16,17,18.

298 "White Citizens' Council of North Alabama," March 14, 1956, FBI Asa Carter Files, Part 1.

299 *The Southerner,* I (March 1956); Ralph Edwards and Asa Carter to Commissioner James Morgan, May 8, 1956, James W. Morgan Mayoral Papers, Folder # 3.27, Department of Archives and History, Birmingham Public Library.

300 Asa Carter, "Nat King Cole," *The Southerner* (April-May 1956), 6.

301 Weisenburger, "The Columbians, Inc," 830–31.

302 Patricia L. Dooley, *Freedom of Speech: Reflections in Art and Popular Culture* (Westport, CT: ABC-Clio/Greenwood Press, 2017), 60.

303 Randall J. Stephens, *The Devil's Music: How Christians Inspired, Condemned and Embraced Rock 'n' Roll* (Cambridge: Harvard University Press, 2018), 27–64.

304 Bryson, "To Give Racism the Face of the Ignorant," 97–100.

305 Pete Daniels, *Lost Revolutions: The South in the 1950s* (Chapel Hill: University of North Carolina Press, 2000), 152.

306 Linda Martin and Kerry Segrave, *Anti-Rock: The Opposition to Rock 'n' Roll* (Hamden, Conn.: Archon Books, 1988), 13–14; Brian Ward, *Just My Soul Responding: Rhythm and Blues, Black Consciousness, and Race Relations* (Berkeley: University of California Press, 1998), 90–122.

307 Brian Ward, "Race, Politics and Culture: The Cole Incident of 1956," *Race and Class in the American South Since 1890,* 181–208, edited by Rick Halpern and Melvyn Stokes, (Oxford: Berg Press, 1994), 181–208.

308 *Birmingham News,* January 22, 30, March 11, 16, 1956.

309 Musical Treatment," *The Southerner,* March, l956, 5.

310 *Birmingham News,* January 15, 1956.

311 "Nat 'King' Cole," *The Southerner,* I (April-May, 1956), 6.

312 Unidentified newspaper clipping, April 9, 1956.

313 Marcia Cole, with Louie Robinson, *Nat King Cole: An Intimate Biography* (New York: William Morrow & Company, 1971), 122–23.

314 Sprayberry, "'Town Among the Trees,'" 183; *Birmingham News,* April 19, 1956.

315 *Anniston Star,* September 24, 1938, June 26, 1939, June 28, 1939, November 6, 1949,

April 14, 1950, July7, 1953; FBI File, Kenneth Lamar Adams FBI File, 52–71362, 228–29, Copy in DC.

316 *Birmingham News,* April 12, 1956 ; *Anniston Star,* January 18, 1990, March 24, 2009. H. Brandt Ayers, *In Love With Defeat: The Making of a Southern Liberal* (Montgomery: New South Books, 2013), 88–90.

317 *Anniston Star,* February 14, 17, 1956; Sprayberry, "'Town Among the Trees,'" 182–84.

318 Ibid., April 12, 1956; Birmingham *News,* April 13, 1956; Birmingham *Post-Herald,* April 12, 1956.

319 Mary Jane ("Janie" Grantham) Sargent to author, November 4, 2015, DC.

320 John Birchard interview with author, March 11, 2012, DC.

321 Doug Ramsey, "Eyewitness: the Attack on Nat Cole," *Riftides: an ArtsJournal Blog,* May 19, 2006; *Birmingham News,* April 11, 12, 1956.

322 *Birmingham News,* April 11, 12, 13, 1956; *Birmingham Post-Herald,* April 12, 14, 1956; *Anniston Star* , April 11, 12, 1956; Ward, "Race, Politics and Culture," 181–208.

323 Mary Jane ("Janie") Grantham Sargent to author, November 4, 2015, DC.

324 *Birmingham News,* April 12, 1956.

325 Ibid.

326 *The Southerner,* April-May 1956.

327 *Anniston Star,* April 21, 1956.

328 All quotes are from the April-May issue of *The Southerner,* 5–7.

329 *The Huntsville Times,* March 13, 1957.

330 Brian Ward," Civil Rights and Rock and Roll: Revisiting the Nat King Cole Attack of 1956," *OAH Magazine of History,* 24 (April 2010):23; Ward, *Just My Soul Responding: Rhythm and Blues, Black Consciousness and Race Relations* (Berkeley: University of California Press, 1998), 132–34.

331 *Birmingham News,* April 21, December 7, 1956.

332 Ezra Pound, *Jefferson and/or Mussolini: L'idea Statale Fascism as I Have Seen It* (New York: Liveright, 1970 [reprint]), 70.

333 Leonard W. Doob, *"Ezra Pound Speaking": Radio Speeches of World War II* (Westport, Conn.: Greenwood Press, 1978).

334 E. Fuller Torrey, MD, *The Roots of Treason: Ezra Pound and the Secret of St. Elizabeths* (New York: McGraw Hill, 1984).

335 Webb, *Rabble Rousers, 39–71.*

336 Alec Marsh, *John Kasper and Ezra Pound: Saving The Republic* (London: Bloomsbury Press, 2015), p. 46.

337 Professor Marsh generously made available to me nearly one hundred letters between Kasper and Pound that document their relationship. Copies, DC.

338 Thomas J. Sugrue, *Sweet Land of Liberty: The Forgotten Struggle for Civil Rights in the North* (New York: Random House, 2008), 204–05.

339 Alvin Miller interview with author, June 11, 1991.

340 Marsh. *John Kasper and Ezra Pound,* 132; "Membership Application: Seaboard Citizens' Councils," in possession of the author.

341 "Councils Move Toward National Scope," *The Southerner,* April-May, 1956, 1-a; New York *Daily Worker,* July 3, 1956; Detroit *Free Press,* July 6, 1956; *New Republic,* July

30, 1956.

342 *Newsweek,* April 23, 1956.

343 Negative file sheets, (copies), September 26, December 27, 1956, March 11, March 29, May 20, July 8, July 14, September 4, October 1, 1957, October 4, 1958, Fox Movietone Files, Twentieth Century Fox Film Corp, Inc, New York, NY, DC.

344 WTOP TV Transcript, June 14, 1956 Washington D.C. Citizens' Council Meeting, copy, DC. An account of the meeting os also in the *Birmingham News,* June 16, 1956.

345 Charlottesville *Daily Progress,* August 24, 1956.

346 Boyle, "Southerners Will Like Integration," *Saturday Evening Post,* 27, February 19, 1956, 25, 133–34.

347 Boyle, *The Desegregated Heart: A Virginian's Stand in a Time of Transition* (New York: William Morrow Publishers, 1962),

348 FBI Files, John Kasper, Part 1, 36–37, Copy in DC.

349 Robbins L. Gates, *The Making of Massive Resistance: Virginia's Politics of Public School Desegregation, 1954–1956* (Chapel Hill: University of North Carolina Press, 1964), 48–49. Accounts of the Carter-Kasper activities in Charlottesville can be found in the Charlottesville *Daily Progress,* August 22, August 28, August 31`, September 4, September 7, 1956.

350 Charlottesville *Daily Progress,* August 28, 1956.

351 *Richmond News Leader,* August 28, 1956.

352 Wilma Dykeman and James Stokely, "Inquiry into the Southern Tensions," *New York Times Magazine,* October 13, 1957.

353 *Knoxville News-Sentinel,* August 28, 1956.

354 Ibid., August 29, 1956; *Pittsburgh Courier,* September 8, 1956; WATE (ABC) Television Broadcast, Knoxville, Tennessee, January 17, 2018; James Rorty, "Hate Monger with Literary Trimmings: From Avant-Garde Poetry to Rear-Guard Politics," *Commentary,* December 1956.

355 Rachel L. Martin, "Out of the Silence: Remembering the Desegregation of Clinton, Tennessee, High School," (PhD dissertation, University of North Carolina, 2012), 40.

356 Edward R. Murrow, CBS: *See it Now: Clinton and the Law,* CBS Broadcast; "John G. Moore interview on the Desegregation of Clinton High School," *The History of Jim Crow: Teacher Resources,* copy in DC Papers.

357 *Knoxville News-Sentinel, Nashville Tennessean* and *Knoxville Journal,* August 28, 1956.

358 *See it Now: Clinton and the Law,* CBS Broadcast; "John G. Moore interview on the Desegregation of Clinton High School," DC Papers; "Clinton Beauchamp and Amanda Turner interview on the Desegregation of Clinton High School," DC Papers.

359 *Birmingham News,* September 13, 1967.

360 *Knoxville News-Sentinel,* September 1, 1956.

361 Quotes are from the September 2, 1956, accounts by the *Clinton* (Tenn.) *Courier-News, Knoxville News-Sentinel, Knoxville Journal,* and *Nashville Tennessean,* and the 2012 PBS documentary, "The Reconstruction of Asa Carter," Copy in DC.

362 Clinton, Tennessee *Courier News,* September 2, 1956.

363 "John G. Moore on the Desegregation of Clinton High School," Clinton Beauchamp and Amanda Turner, "The Desegregation of Clinton Senior High School," *The History*

of Jim Crow: Teacher Resources, DC.

364 Dykeman and Stokely, "On the Road," 13.

365 In addition to their article, "On the Road with John Kasper," *The New Republic*, December 1, 1958, 13–14, Dykeman and her husband James Stokely wrote several articles on Kasper and the Clinton crisis, including "Clinton, Tennessee: A Town on Trial," *New York Times Magazine*, April 16, 1960, 1, 9, 61–5, and "Inquiry into the Southern Tensions," *New York Times Magazine*, October 13, 1957, 86–8. See also *New York Times*, September 22, 1957, Clive Webb, "Rabble Rousers," 56–57, and June N. Adamson, "Few Black Voices Heard: The Black Community and the Desegregation Crisis in Clinton, Tennessee, 1956," *Tennessee Historical Quarterly*, no. 53 (1994): 30–41.

366 Carter, "Nat King Cole," *The Southerner* (April–May, 1956), 6.

367 *Montgomery Advertiser*, July 10, September 25, 1956; Oak Ridge, Tennessee, *Oak Ridger*, September 27, 1956.

368 *Montgomery Advertiser*, September 16, 1957.

369 Michael Newton, *The National States Rights Party: A History* (Jefferson, NC: McFarland and Company, Inc., 2017), 46.

370 Rorty, "Hate Monger with Literary Trimming," *Commentary*, December 1956; *Birmingham News*, September 14, 1956.

371 Ibid., September 29, 1956.

372 *Montgomery Advertiser*, March 17, 1957; Clive Webb, *Rabble Rousers*, 69–70.

373 Jason Morgan Ward, "The D.C. School Hearings of 1956 and the National Vision of Massive Resistance, *Journal of Civil and Human Rights*, 1 (Spring/Summer 2015): 82–110; Sarah Watson Brown, "Congressional Anti-Communism and the Segregationist South: From New Orleans to Atlanta, 1954–1958," *Georgia Historical Quarterly* 80 (Winter, 1996): 797–816.

374 Erwin Knoll, "The Truth About Desegregation in the Washington, D.C. Public Schools," *The Journal of Negro Education*, 28 (1959): 92–113.

375 John Jackson, Jr., *Science for Segregation: Race, Law, and the Case Against Brown v. Board of Education* (New York: New York University Press, 2005), 76–79; "Liberty Essays by Asa Carter," LP Recording, (1956), DC.

376 AC FBI Files, SAC, Mobile to Director FBI, May 9, 1956, DC.

377 FBI Reports, Asa Carter, "Sedition Memo," March 23, 1956, File 87–94821-4, 3.

378 SAC Report, "Asa Carter, aka 'Ace' Carter: Sedition," July 18, 1956, FBI Files, Asa Carter, 14–79-1, Part 1.

379 William F. Tompkins, Assistant Attorney General, Internal Security Division, to J. Edgar Hoover, "Sedition—Asa Carter," September 10, 1956, FBI Files, Asa Carter, 87–94821-4. Copy in DC.

380 Birmingham *News*, April 18, 20, 1956.

381 *The Southerner*, March 1970, 18.

382 *Birmingham News*, January 24, 1957.

383 SAC Mobile to J. Edgar Hoover, May 9, 1956, Asa Carter file, Part I. DC.

384 *Montgomery Advertiser*, July 13, 1956.

385 *Knoxville* (TN) *News-Sentinel*, December 8, 1956.

386 *Washington Star,* March 28, 1957.
387 The following account is based on coverage in the *Birmingham News* and *Birmingham Post-Herald* from January 23 through February 13, 1957, as well as testimony given in the later trial of one of the Klansmen and reported in the two newspapers. Because the jury acquitted the only defendant tried in the case, the court did not prepare a transcript of the trial, but the two newspapers gave extensive coverage with long excerpts of the testimony.
388 AC FBI Files, SAC, Mobile to Director, FBI, May 9, 1956. DC; John Drabble, "The FBI, COINTELPRO-WHITE HATE, and the Decline of Ku Klux Klan organizations in Alabama, 1964–1971," *The Alabama Review,* 61 (January 2008): 3–47.
389 "James Parson Interview, November 19, 2008, RAC. DC.
390 *Montgomery Advertiser,* January 24, 25, 1957; Montgomery *Alabama Journal,* January 24, 25, 1957; *Birmingham News,* January 23, 24, 25, 1957.
391 *Birmingham News, Birmingham Post-Herald, Montgomery Advertiser,* Montgomery *Alabama Journal,* January 28, 29 and 30, 1957.
392 *Birmingham News, Birmingham Post-Herald,* March 13, 14, 27, 28 and 29,1957.
393 *Birmingham News,* May 23, 1956.
394 Larry Carter interview with Fred Burger, February 25, 2004. FB.
395 Dixon, *The Clansman: An Historical Romance of the Ku Klux Klan,* (New York: Grosset & Dunlap Publishers, 1905), 321.
396 Norman W. Walton, "The Walking City: A History of the Montgomery Bus Boycott," in David Garrow, ed., *The Walking City: The Montgomery Bus Boycott, 1955–1956.* Minneapolis: Carlson Publications, 1989), 43; *Birmingham News,* December, 26, 1956.
397 *Birmingham News,* September 7, 1957.
398 *Joe Pritchett* vs. *The State of Alabama,* 216. The following account is primarily based upon the 1500 pages of trial transcripts included in the 1959 appeals to the Tenth Judicial Court, transcripts deposited in DC: *Grover McCullough v. Alabama; Joe Pritchett v. Alabama* and *Jessie W. Mabry v. Alabama.*
399 Elizabeth Jacoway, *Turn Away Thy Son: Little Rock, The Crisis that Shocked the Nation* (New York: Free Press, 2007), 122–24.
400 *Birmingham Post-Herald,* August 23, 1957; *Birmingham News,* August 23, 1957.
401 Andrew W. Manis, *A Fire You Can't Put Out: The Civil Rights Life of Birmingham's Reverend Fred Shuttlesworth* (Tuscaloosa: University of Alabama Press, 1999), 108–10.
402 *McCullough* v. *Alabama* trial transcript, 170. DC.
403 *Mabry* v. *Alabama* transcript, 53. DC.
404 *McCullough v. Alabama* transcript, 53–77. DC.
405 Ibid., 85. DC.
406 *Mabry* v. *Alabama* transcript, 63–65. DC.
407 Ibid., 87–89. DC.
408 *Birmingham News,* October 29, 1957.
409 *Pritchett* v. *Alabama* transcript, 41. DC.
410 Ibid., 42. DC.
411 Ibid., 109. DC.
412 *McCullough v. Alabama* transcript, 46–49 DC.

413 *Pritchett* v. *Alabama* transcript, 155. DC.
414 Ibid., 33–52. DC.
415 *McCullough* v. *Alabama* transcript, 70–72; *Mabry* v. *Alabama* transcript, 126. DC.
416 Harris, *Miracle in Birmingham,* 48.
417 *Florence* (SC) *Morning News,* September 8, 10, October 31, November 1, 1957.
418 Ibid., October 12, 14, 1955.
419 Richard Kluger, *Simple Justice,* (New York Alfred A. Knopf, 1975), 3–25, 294–95, 527; John Egerton, *Speak Now Against the Day: The Generation before the Civil Rights Movement in the South* (New York: Alfred A. Knopf, 1994), 589–595.
420 *Florence* (South Carolina) *Morning News,* October 6, 1955
421 Herbert Hoover to FBI Savannah Regional Office. Delaine had contacted the FBI after reciving the death threat. (He enclosed a copy in his letter to the FBI). Joseph Armstrong Delaine Papers, South Caroliniana Library, University of South Carolina.
422 Joseph A. Delaine Remarks, Delivered at Bethel AME Church, New York, October 17, 1955; FBI Files, Reverend J. A. DeLaine file # HQ9–28873, Delaine Papers.
423 Joseph A. Delaine to Esso Standard Oil Company, September 19, 1955; H. M. Dreyer, (Manager, Esso Standard Oil Company) to Reverend J. A. Delaine, September 22, 1955, Ibid.
424 *Birmingham Post-Herald,* November 1, 1957.
425 *Birmingham News,* October 30, 1967; *Birmingham Post-Herald,* October 31, 1967.
426 *McCullough* v. *Alabama* transcript, 116–17.
427 Manis, *A Fire You Can't Put Out,* 149–50.
428 McWhorter, *Carry Me Home,* 127–129; Manis, *A Fire You Can't Put Out,* 147–152. *Birmingham News,* September 9, 10, 1957; *Birmingham Post-Herald,* September 10, 1957; Ibid., 150–51; *New York Times,* September 10, 1957.
429 Manis,*A Fire You Can't Put Out,* 153.
430 Statement by Mayor James Morgan Statement, September 12, 1957. Morgan Papers, Collection 266, File 5, Archives Division, Birmingham Public Library.
431 *Birmingham News,* September 23, 25, 1957.
432 *Birmingham News,* September 10, September 20, October 6, 1957; Manis, *A Fire You Can't Put Out,* 158–59.
433 Manis, *A Fire You Can't Put Out,* 168–73; Eskew, *But for Birmingham,* 142–43.
434 *Birmingham News,* September 7, 9, 1957.
435 *Birmingham Post-Herald,* November 1, 1957.
436 Ibid., November 7, 1957.
437 Wayne Greenhaw, *Fighting the Devil in Dixie: How Civil Rights Activists Took on the Ku Klux Klan in Alabama* (Chicago: Lawrence Hill Books, 2011), 31–32.
438 Jack Shows interview with author, August 9, 1991, DC.
439 *Birmingham News,* March 3, May 14, 1958; *Montgomery Advertiser,* May 8, 1958.
440 McMillen, *The Citizens' Council,* 56.
441 William Bradford Huie, *Three Lives for Mississippi* (New York: WCC Books, 1964), 29.
442 Harris, *Miracle in Birmingham,* 48.
443 Huie, "Ritual Cutting by the Ku Klux Klan," *True: The Man's Magazine,* October 1964,

5–9; Interview with William Bradford Huie, conducted by Blackside, Inc. in August 30, 1979, for *Eyes on the Prize: America's Civil Rights Years (1954–1965)*. Washington University Libraries, Film and Media Archive, Henry Hampton Collection.

444 Jimmy Carter interview with Fred Burger, April 20, 1992, FB.

445 King, *Devil in the Grove*, 273–283, 357.

446 *Charlotte* (NC) *Observer,* November 22, 27, 1957.

447 *Tampa* (FL) *Sunday Tribune*, May 4, 1958.

448 Raymond A. Mohl, "'South of the South?' Jews, Blacks and the Civil Rights Movement in Miami, 1945–1960," *Journal of American Ethnic History,* 18 (Winter, 1999): 5–8; Jackson Toby, "Bombing in Nashville: A Jewish Center and the Desegregation Struggle," *Commentary,* 25 (May 1958): 385–389; Nathan Perlmutter, "Bombing in Miami: Anti-Semitism and the Segregationists," *Commentary,* 25 (June 1958): 498–503; *Birmingham News*, April 29, 1958.

449 *Miami News*, June 15, 1958.

450 *Atlanta Constitution*, October 13, 1958; Clive Webb, "Counter Blast: How the Atlanta Temple Bombing Strengthened the Civil Rights Cause," *Southern Spaces*, June 22, 2009.

451 Melissa Faye Greene, *The Temple Bombing* (Reading, Mass.: Addison-Wesley Publishing Company, 1996), 284–85.

452 Asa Carter FBI Summary File, Record Number 495 228C, October 4, 1963. DC.

453 SAC Birmingham to Director, FBI, 10/30/58, FBI Asa Carter File, Part 3 of 4. DC.

454 Anniston SAC Agent to SAC, December 30, 1958; Anniston SAC to Birmingham SAC, February 4, 1959, FBI Asa Carter File, Part 3 of 4. DC.

455 Wayne L. Hays, "Facts About 'Facts Forum,'" August 20, 1954, United States Congress, Congressional Record: Proceedings and Debates, Volume 100, Part 12, 15778–15780. Tom Buckley, "Just Plain H. L. Hunt," *Esquire*, January 1, 1967, 147; Bill Porterfield, "H. L. Hunt's Long Goodbye," *Texas Monthly,* March 1975.

456 *New York Times*, November 7, 1958; United States. Congress. Senate. Committee on the Judiciary. Subcommittee on Constitutional Rights. (195960). *Civil Rights—1959.: hearings before the United States Senate Committee on the Judiciary, Subcommittee on Constitutional Rights, Eighty-Sixth Congress, first session.* Washington: U.S. G.P.O.

457 *Anniston Star*, May 28, 1960

458 Clay Slate interview April 4, 1998, FB; Birmingham SAC Report on Asa Carter, March 30, 1960, AC FBI File, DC; Interview of Former FBI Special Agent Ralph Butler, July 11, 2008, Society of Former Special Agents of the FBI, DC.

459 Jasper, Alabama *Daily Mountain Express,* September 1, 1960.

460 *Anniston Star,* March 26, 1960; Montgomery *Alabama Journal*, March 26, 1960.

461 SAC Interview with Asa (Earl) Carter, December 13, 1960, FBI Files, Part 3, DC; Montgomery *Alabama Journal,* March 26, 1960, *New York Times*, March 27, 1960; *New York Post,* March 27, 1960.

462 R. B. Jones interview with Author, July 27, 1992, DC.

463 Birmingham SAC to Dallas SAC, April 27, 1961, Asa Carter FBI Files. DC.

464 Dallas SAC Report, June 30, 1961, Asa Carter FBI Files. DC.

465 SAC (Special Agent in Charge) to J. Edgar Hoover and SAC, Birmingham, September 7, 1961, "URGENT." Asa Carter FBI Files, DC.

466 Larry Carter interview with Fred Burger, January 26, 1992, February 12, 2002, FB.

467 Jimmy Carter interview with Fred Burger, April 20, 1992, Kaye Carter interview with Fred Burger, March 26, 1991, Claudia Walker Dates interview with Fred Burger, September 28, 2004, Larry Carter interview with Fred Burger, November 24, 1991, January 26, 1994, February 25, 2004, FB.

468 India Carter to Bruce Marshall, July 7, August 4, August 27, 1979, Marshall-Carter Correspondence, 1978–1979. DC.

469 Anniston Special Agent to SAC, Birmingham, December 30, 1959, April 19, 1960, Asa Carter FBI Files, Part 3 of 4. DC.

470 "The Inaugural Address of Governor George C. Wallace, January 14, 1963, Montgomery Alabama," ADAH, Copy in DC.

471 Gene L. Howard, *Patterson for Alabama: The Life and Career of John Patterson* (Tuscaloosa: University of Alabama Press, 2009), 140–149;

472 Carter. *Politics of Rage, 210.*

473 *Anniston Star*, November 7, 1957.

474 *The Union-Banner* (Clanton, Alabama), May 1, 1958; "George Wallace: Settin' the Woods on Fire" (PBS Documentary, Part 1, 2000), transcript. DC.

475 Seymore Trammell interview with author, November 28, 1989, Starr Smith interview with author, June 10, 1988, Starr Smith to author, June 1, 1994, DC. Howard, *Patterson for Alabama,* 140–149; Carter, *The Politics of Rage*, 90–97.

476 James Douglas (Doug) Carter interview with Fred Burger, October 6, 1984, FB.

477 Seymore Trammell interview with author, August 12, 1991, DC.

478 James Douglas (Doug) Carter interview with Fred Burger, October 6, 1984, FB; Birmingham *Post-Herald,* December 31, 1997.

479 Bill Jones Interview with author, August 3, 1990; Seymore Trammell interview with author, February 14, 1989, DC; Harper, *Me'N George,* 29.

480 Warranty Deed, R. J. Carter and Alpha E. Carter to Asa E. Carter and India Thelma Carter, July 5, 1963, Book 1140, Page 44, Calhoun County [Alabama] Probate Court Records.

481 Clay Slate interview with Fred Burger, April? 1998. FB.

482 Steven Weisenburger, "The Columbians, Inc.: A Chapter of Racial Hatred from the Post-World War II South," *The Journal of Southern History,* 69 (Nov., 2003): 857–58; Newton, *The National States Rights Party,* 43–51. FBI investigations and reports, "Extremist Organizations, Part II, National States Rights Party," Copy in DC.

483 *New York Times*, November 26, 1961; J. Harry Jones, Jr., *The Minutemen* (New York: Doubleday and Company, 1968); Eric Beckemeir, *Traitors Beware: A History of Robert Depugh's Minutemen* (N., 2008).

484 *Washington Post,* December 19, 1970; *St. Louis Jewish Light,* July 17, 1974; *The American Israelite*, September 2, 1976. *Roads to Dominion: Right-Wing Movements and Political Power in the United States* (New York: Guilford Press, 1995), 156–57. Frank Mintz, *The Liberty Lobby and the American Right: Race, Conspiracy, and Culture* (New York: Praeger Publishing, 1993), 5, 84–86; George Michael, *Willis Carto and the American Far Right* (Gainesville, Fl.: University of Florida Press, 2008), 85–86, 140–143; John Huntington, *Far-Right Vanguard: The Radical Roots of Modern Conservatism* (Philadelphia: University of Pennsylvania Press, 2021).

485 *Montgomery Advertiser*, September 3, 1958; *Montgomery Journal*, September 3, 1958; *The Thunderbolt*, November,1958; *Anniston Star*, September 3,1958; *Right*, September-October,1958.

486 *New York Times*, April 29, 2005; Stoner, The Gospel of Jesus Christ versus the Jews: Christianity's attitude toward the Jews as explained from the Holy Bible. (Chattanooga, Tenn.: Stoner Anti-Jewish Party, 1946), 58; Michael Newton, *The National States Rights Party: A History* (Jefferson, NC: McFarland & Company, Inc., Publishers, 2017), 15.

487 Jerry Kopel Interview with author, March 12, 1997, DC; Madison Grant, *The Passing of the Great Race* (New York: Charles Scribner's Sons, 1916).

488 José L. Vázquez Calzada, *La Población de Puerto Rico y Su Trayectoria Histórica* (Río Piedras, P.R.: Escuela Graduada de Salud Pública, Recinto de Ciencias Médicas [The Population of Puerto Rico and its Historical Trajectory], Universidad de Puerto Rico, 1988), 286; Francisco L. Rivera Batiz and Carlos Santiago, *Island Paradox: Puerto Rico in the 1990s* (New York: Russell Sage Foundation, 1996), 45; Alex Nowrasteh, "Enforcement Didn't End Unlawful Immigration in the 1950s, More Visas Did," Cato Institute, November 11, 2015; "Editorial," *The Southerner*, September-October, 1957, 2.

489 Larry Carter interviews, April 10, 1999, February 24, 2004, FB.

490 *New Orleans Times-Picayune*, November 16, 1960; *Shreveport* (Louisiana) *Journal*, November 16, 1960.

491 *Jackson* (MS) *Clarion-Ledger*; *Augusta* (GA) *Chronicle*, July 30, 1960; *Selma* (AL) *Times Journal*, July 30, 1960.

492 Cloete, "End of Era with the Threat of the Jungle," *Life*, August 1, 1960, 14–15.

493 See January 16, 1963, news stories in the *Los Angeles Times, The San Francisco Chronicle, The Chicago Tribune, The Philadelphia Inquirer, The New York Times, The Washington Post, The Atlanta Constitution, The Miami Herald*. Most coverage in mid-sized newspapers across the nation reprinted AP or UPI dispatches.

494 Ray Andrews interview, February 1, 2008, RAC Outtakes. DC.

495 Howard White interview, February 3, 2008, RAC Outtakes. DC.

496 Director, FBI to SAC, Birmingham, June 30, 1961, Supplemental addition, 1573535–1, Asa Carter FBI File, Supplementary Files. DC.

497 *Birmingham Post-Herald*, July 11, 1963; *Montgomery Advertiser*, January 17, 1964, January 5, 1965; *Anniston Star*, January 24, 1964.

498 "Data concerning National and State Organization of NSRP," April 30, 1963. Bureau File 105–66233, ASA Carter FBI Files, Part 4 of 4. DC. Newton, The National States Right Party, 111.

499 Ibid. The FBI censors Blacked out the name of the Klansman, but other information in the document indicates that it was almost certainly Adams. Burke Marshall, "Memorandum re: University of Alabama," March 19, 1963, Marshall Papers, Box 17, John F. Kennedy Library and Museum.

500 *Montgomery Advertiser*, February 11, 1963.

501 Director, FBI to SAC, Birmingham, June 30, 1961, Supplemental addition, 157–926-3, Asa Carter FBI File, Supplementary Files. DC. Seymore Trammell interview, February 14, 1988, DC.

502 SAC Mobile to SAC Birmingham, May 24, 1963, Asa Carter FBI File, Part 3 of 4.

DC.

503 Robert F. Kennedy Interview, 518, John F. Kennedy Library, Boston, Massachusetts.

504 Clark, *The Schoolhouse Door*, 34–35.

505 SAC Birmingham to Director, FBI, October 1, 1963, Asa Carter Files, Part 3 of 4. DC.

506 Clay Slate Interview with Fred Burger, April 12, 1988, FB.

507 John Joseph Makay, "The Speaking of Governor George C Wallace in the 1964 Presidential Primary" (PhD dissertation, Purdue University, 1969), 128.

508 Greenhaw, *My Heart is in the Earth,* 45.

509 "President Lyndon B. Johnson's Address to a Joint Session of Congress, November 27, 1963, US National Archives.

510 *Montgomery Advertiser,* November 5, 1963; Joe Azbell interview with author, February 14, 1989.

511 Carter, *Politics of Rage,* 196–198.

512 Rick Perlstein, *Nixonland: The Rise of a President and the Fracturing of America* (New York: Scribner, 2008), 78.

513 FBI Interview with Robert Shelton, Tuscaloosa, Alabama, November 23, 1963, Asa Carter File, Part 4 of 4. DC; Illinois Legislative Investigative Commission, "Ku Klux Klan: A Report to the Illinois General Assembly," Printed by the State of Illinois, October 1976, Copy in DC; William Chaney (Grand Dragon of the Ku Klux Klan, Indiana) interview, June 1972, Indiana University Library, Bloomington Indiana, Media Collection.

514 Carter, *Politics of Rage,* 202–215.

515 Wayne Greenhaw, *Watch Out for George Wallace* (Englewood Cliffs, N.J.: Prentice-Hall, Inc., 1976), 159.

516 *Milwaukee Journal,* April 2, 1964; George Wallace, Wisconsin Speech, April 2, 1964, Alabama Department of Archives and History, Montgomery, Alabama, Speech Collection; Makay, "The Speaking of Governor George C Wallace, 128.

517 Bill Jones, interview with author, August 3, 1990, Seymore Trammell interview with author, January 11, 1989, DC.

518 *Birmingham News,* February 21, 1966, April 23, 1967; Harry Hurt, III, *Texas Rich: The Hunt Dynasty from the Early Oil Days Through the Silver Crash* (New York: W. W. Norton, 1981), 371; Howard White Interview, February 3, 2008, RAC Outtakes. DC; Taylor, *Me 'n' George,* 79.

519 Greenhaw, *My Heart is in the Earth,* 47; Carter, *Politics of Rage,* 283–285; Seymore Trammell interview with author, April 4, 1994, DC.

520 Lurleen Wallace Inaugural Address, January 16, 1967, Papers of George and Lurleen Wallace, SG 031280, Alabama Department of Archives and History.

521 George Wallace, *Stand Up For America.* (New York: Doubleday Publishers, 1976).

522 Blake, *The Civil Rights Revolution: It Pays to be Free* (Waco, Texas: NP, 1955).

523 *LBJ: A Political Biography* (Washington, 1964: Noontide Press). Carto's book was essentially a summary of J. Evetts Haley's *A Texan Looks at Lyndon: A Study of Illegitimate Power* (Amarillo (TX): Palo Duro Press, 1964).

524 Daniel K. Williams, *God's Own Party: The Making of the Christian Right* (New York:

Oxford University Press, 2012); Kent and Phoebe Courtney, *America's Unelected Rulers* (New Orleans: Conservative Society of America, 1962).

525 John S. Huntington, "Right-Wing Paranoid Blues: The Role of Radicalism in Modern Conservatism," (PhD dissertation, University of Houston, 2016), 247, 255.

526 Robert Welch to George C. Wallace, December 6, 1966, Box 45, Wallace Private Papers, Alabama Department of Archives and History; Berlet and Lyons, *Right-Wing Populism in America,* 184.

527 Doubleday publishers would later print a revised edition when Wallace began his last campaign for the presidency in 1976.

528 Michael, *Willis Carto and the American Far Right*, 95–96.

529 Huntington, "Right-Wing Paranoid Blues," 294–300; *St. Louis Post-Dispatch*, February 28, 1968; *Minneapolis Star*, May 24, 1968

530 *Los Angeles Times,* September 17, 1968.

531 George C. Wallace to Lawrence Clayton, April 3, 1984, copy. DC.

532 Jack Shows interview with author, August 9, 1991. DC.

533 Birmingham SAC to FBI Director, August 20, 1965; A[lex] Rosen Memorandum, September 1, 1965; Informant Report: "Meeting with Asa Carter Suggesting Defense Fund for persons prosecuted in racial matters," February 28, 1966, Asa Carter FBI files, Part 3 of 4. DC.

534 *Birmingham News*, January 2, 1966.

535 *Montgomery Advertiser*, January 27, 1967.

536 Seymore Trammell interview with author, August 12, 1991, DC.

537 Clay Slate Interview, April 12, 1998, FB.

538 Asa Earl Carter: Extremist Matters. Summary report of Birmingham FBI Bureau, Jan. 17, 1962; Asa Carter: Wallace for President Solicitation, June 14, 1967, Asa Carter FBI Supplementary Files. DC.

539 Tom Turnipseed interview March 3, 1994, DC: Tom Turnipseed interview, February 15, 2007, RAC Outtakes, DC.

540 Transcript, Asa Carter television speech, Jackson, Mississippi, December 1, 1967. Copy in DC.

541 Bruce Eder, "Jimmy Swan: a Biography," *All Music,* Copy in DC.

542 Major Robert H. Bennett, *Know Your Enemy* (privately published, 1950).

543 Jimmy Swan Interview, March 23, 1977, The University of Southern Mississippi Center for Oral History and Cultural Heritage, Hattiesburg, Mississippi.

544 Neil R. McMillen, "Black Enfranchisement in Mississippi: Federal Enforcement and Black Protest in the 1960s," *The Journal of Southern History*, 43 (August 1977): 370–71.

545 Glen Jeansonne, "Racism and Longism in Louisiana: The 1959–60 Gubernatorial Elections," *Louisiana History*, 26, (Summer 1970), 265.

546 Jimmy Swan Interview, March 23, 1977, USM.

547 Ibid.; SAC, Jackson to SAC Mobile February 1, 1968, "Asa Carter: Bombing Investigations in Mississippi," Asa Carter FBI File.

548 *The Greenwood* (MS) *Commonwealth*, July 28, 1966; Jackson (MS) *Clarion Ledger,* July 28, 1979; Michael Newton, *The Ku Klux Klan in Mississippi: A History* (Jefferson, NC: McFarland Publishers, 2020), 174–75.

549 Curtis Wilkie, *Dixie: A Personal Odyssey Through Events that Shaped the Modern South* (New York: Scribner's, 2001) 170; Michael Newton, *The Ku Klux Klan in Mississippi: A History* (Jefferson, North Carolina: McFarland. Press, 2010) 174–175.

550 The *Greenwood* (MS) *Commonwealth,* July 7, 1967; Jackson (MS) *Clarion Ledger*, July 22, 1967; Jimmy Swan Interview, March 23, 1977, UMS.

551 B. J, "The Mississippi Election Today," *The Harvard Crimson,* August 8, 1967.

552 Bill Minor, *Eyes on Mississippi: A Fifty-Year Chronicle of Change* (Jackson, Mississippi: J. Prichard Morris Books, 2001), 90–91.

553 Wilkie, *Dixie,* 172.

554 Randy Swan Interview, March 13, 2000. FB

555 McComb, *Mississippi Enterprise-Journal,* November 5, 1964; *Memphis Commercial Appeal,* November 29, 1967; "Investigation of the Activities of the Americans for the Preservation of the White Race, December 18, 1964," 6–36-40, Mississippi Sovereignty Commission Online, Mississippi Department of Archives and History.

556 *Jackson* (MS) *Clarion Ledger,* November 12, December 2, 1967, February 29, 1968.

557 Douglas O. Linder, "The Mississippi Burning Trial (U.S. vs. Price et al.)." Copy in DC.

558 *Jackson* (MS) *Clarion Ledger,* December 2, 1967; *Greenwood* (MS) *Commonwealth,* December 2, 1967.

559 Joseph Crespino, *In Search of Another Country: Mississippi and the Conservative Counter-revolution* (Princeton: Princeton University Press, 2007), 24–25, 134.

560 Jack Nelson, *Terror in the Night: The Klan's Campaign Against the Jews* (New York: Simon & Schuster, 1993), 124. Nor did such attacks end in the 1960s. The 1990s saw an upsurge with dozens of Black church burned or badly damaged. Christopher Strain, "Holy Smoke: Church Burnings, Journalism and the Politics of Race, 1996–2006," 71–99 in Yuya Kiuch, *Race Still Matters: the Reality of African American Lives and the Myth of a Postracial Society* (Albany, NY: State University of New York Press, 2016); Michele M. Simmsparris, "What Does It Mean to See a Black Church Burning? Understanding the Significance of Constitutionalizing Hate Speech," 1 *University of Pennsylvania Journal of Constitutional Law* (1998): 127–51.

561 Nelson, *Terror in the Night, 63.*

562 There are numerous communications between local agents and Washington, the most critical of which are dated October 1, 10, 1967 and February 1, 14, 1968 in the Asa Carter FBI files, DC.

563 "Asa E. 'Ace' Carter, Oxford, Alabama," February 1970, Antidefamation League File—Asa Carter Files, Department of Archives and History, Birmingham Alabama Public Library.

564 R. B. Jones, interview with author, July 12, 1993.

565 *Mobile* (AL) *Register,* January 16, 1970.

566 "Asa Carter Candidate for Governor,"campaign pamphlet, in possession of the Author. DC. *Birmingham News,* October 3, 1969; *Anniston Star,* October 2, 1969, March 15, 1970; Montgomery *Alabama Journal,* April 21, 1970.

567 Carter, *Politics of Rage,* 386–395.

568 Tony Heffernan Interview with author, May 25, 1994, DC.

569 Tom Turnipseed interview with author, March 3, 1994; DC; *Montgomery Advertiser,*

May 17, 1970.

570 Howard White interview, February 3, 2008, RAC outtakes , DC.

571 Ibid., Ray Andrews Interview, February 1, 2008, RAC Outtakes. DC.

572 *Montgomery Advertiser,* May 13, 1970; *Birmingham News,* May 13, 1970.

573 Carter, *Politics of Rage*, 381–395

574 *New York Times,* January 19, 1971; *Montgomery Advertiser,* January 19, 1971.

575 Greenhaw, *My Heart is in the Earth,* 48–49; Greenhaw, *Watch Out for George Wallace,* 158–59; Wayne Greenhaw interview with author, September 28, 1993, DC.

576 R. B. Jones interview with author. July 27, 1992. DC. Carter told FBI Agent Clay Slate that he was "about to make some money for the first time in his life. . . ." Clay Slate Memorandum, May 20, 1974, FBI File. DC

577 Brandt Ayers interview, October 12, 2014. DC.

578 Crespino, *In Search of Another Country,* 237–52; Steve Suitts, *Overturning Brown: The Segregationist Legacy of the Modern School Choice Movement* (Montgomery: NewSouth Books, 2020).

579 Anniston *Star*, January 21, 1971; Montgomery *Alabama Journal,* March 14, 1972, Selma *Times-Journal,* June 26, 1972.

580 *Anniston Star,* January 20, 1971; Wayne Greenhaw interview with author, September 28, 1993, DC.

581 Cook, *The FBI Nobody Knows* (New York: The McMillan Company, 1964).

582 Kenneth O'Reilly, *"Racial Matters": The FBI's Secret File on Black America, 1960–1972* (New York: The Free Press, 1989), 289, 355–59.

583 Curt Gentry, *J. Edgar Hoover: The Man and the Secrets* (New York: W. W. Norton & Company, 1991), 541–709.

584 William W. Turner, "The Minutemen," *Ramparts Magazine,* October 27, 1966, 69. James Coates, *Armed and Dangerous: The Rise of the Survivalist Right* (New York: Hill and Wang, 1987), 41–151; Zeskind, *Blood and Politics,* 85–115.

585 *New York Times,* October 31, November 1, 5, 8, December 15, 1966; January 24, 1967; *New York Daily News,* October 31, 1966.

586 Clay Slate Interview, April 1998. FB.

587 David C. Viola, Jr., "Terrorism and the Response to Terrorism in New York City During the Long Sixties," (PhD dissertation, City University of New York, 1977), 93–97.

588 SAC, Birmingham, Subject: "The Southerners," February 17, 1971, Asa Carter FBI File. DC.

589 Robert Klare, "The Southerners," April 2, 1971, Asa Carter FBI File. DC.

590 Director, FBI to SAC, Birmingham SAC, May 17, 1971, Asa Carter FBI File. DC.

591 O'Reilly, *Racial Matters,* 198–99; Drabble, "The FBI, COINTELPRO-WHITE HATE, 3–47.

592 "Information Concerning Meeting of Southerners," May 20, 1971, Asa Carter FBI File. DC.

593 SA Clay Slate, February 28, re. Mobile letter to Birmingham, February 17, 1972, Asa Carter FBI Files. DC.

594 *Birmingham News,* August 29, 1971.

595 *Mobile* (AL) *Register,* July 30, 1970.

596 Richard A. Pride, *The Political Use of Racial Narratives: School Desegregation in Mobile Alabama, 1954–97,* (Urbana and Chicago: University of Illinois Press, 2002), 80–82; *Montgomery Advertiser*, June 11, 1969.

597 The following summary is based upon over seventy FBI memos and informant reports in the "Southerners" section of the Asa Carter's FBI file. DC.

598 United States Internal Revenue Service, "Exempt Organization Business Income Tax Return"; Frances E. McNair and Charles R. Pryor, "Tax Reporting for Houses of Worship," *Journal of Accountancy*, May 1, 2006; Gary Hoover, "Supermarket: One of the Most Important (and least known) American Inventions, *American Business History*, August 2, 2019.

599 Pride, *The Political Use of Racial Narratives*, 217; Chester L. Quarles, *Christian Identity: The Aryan American Bloodline Religion* (Jefferson, NC: McFarland Press, 2004), 67; Incorporation of Assembly of Christian Soldiers, August 13, 1971, DC.

600 Some of the informants used the word "Negro" or "negro" in writing their reports, but several made the same observation: they had never heard any word used in meetings except "nigger."

601 New York *Times,* March 17, 1980; *Montgomery Advertiser*, March 19, 1970; *Anniston Star*, December 13, 1970, August 9, 1971; Montgomery *Alabama Journal*, January 27, March 17, 1970, May 4, 1971; *Montgomery Advertiser*, March 19, 1970, January 29, June 21, July 2, 1971; *Selma* (AL) *Times Journal* March 17, 1970.

602 R. B. Jones interview with author, July 27, 1992.

603 *Anniston Star*, April 2, 10, 1973.

604 Ron Snead Interview, November 19, 2008, RAC Outtakes, DC.

605 D*allas Morning News*, October 10, 17, 1991, Lawrence Clayton interview with author, November 14, 1991; Louise Green interview with author, November 12, 1991. DC.

606 Dr. Walker Reynolds, Jr. interview with Fred Burger, August 15, 2000, FB.

607 *The Southerner* (April 1972), 2, 5, 12–13.

608 Ron Taylor Interview with Fred Burger, November 19, 1998, FB.

609 Wayne Greenhaw Notes, August 23, 1972, DC; Montgomery *Alabama Journal*, October 10, 1972; *Montgomery Advertiser*, October 11, 1972.

610 "Mobile Informant Report of January 28 Meeting," AC FBI Files

611 Dr. Walker Reynolds, Jr. interviews, August 15, August 16, 2000, FB.

612 "General Information on the Southerners," April 26, 1973, Asa Carter FBI Files. DC.

613 Charles A. Reich, *The Greening of America* (New York: Random House, 1970), 236.

614 Vine Deloria, Jr., *Custer Died for Your Sins: An Indian Manifesto* (New York: Collier-MacMillan, 1969), 1, 5–6.

615 *The Congressional Globe: Containing the Debates and Proceedings of the Second Session [of the] Fortieth Congress* (Washington: Office of the Congressional Globe, 1868), 2638.

616 Philip Deloria's *Indians in Unexpected Places* (University of Kansas Press, 2004); Philip Deloria, Playing *Indian* (New Haven: Yale University Press, 1999) Shari Huhndorf, *Going Native: Indians in the American Cultural Imagination* (Cornell University Press, 2001); S. Elizabeth Bird, *Dressing in Feathers: The Construction of the Indian in American Popular Culture* (New York: Westview Press, 1996).

617 Donald B. Smith, *From the Land of Shadows: The Making of Grey Owl* (Saskatoon:

Western Prairie Books, 1990).

618 Donald B. Smith, *Chief Buffalo Child Long Lance: The Glorious Imposter* (Alberta: Red Deer Press, 1999); Ives Goddard, "The Identity of Red Thunder Cloud," *Society for the Study of Indigenous Languages of the Americas Newsletter* (April 2000), 7–10.

619 Iron Eyes Cody, *Iron Eyes: My Life as a Hollywood Indian* (New York: Everest House, 1982); Russell Cobb, "Welcome to the Tribe: Membership Has Its Privileges. Iron Eyes Code and the Making of a Wannabe Nation," *This Land*, August 1, 2014; *Chicago Tribune*, November 21, 2017.

620 *Rocky Mountain News*, June 10, 2005; Scott Jaschik, "Fake Cherokee?" *Inside Higher Education*, July 6, 2015; Scott Jaschik, "Indian Enough for Dartmouth?" *Inside Higher Education*, September 17, 2015.

621 New York: Plume Publishers, 1983). *The Primal Mind* (Public Broadcasting System documentary, 1984); Jamake Highwater, *Shadow Show: An Autobiographical Insinuation* (New York: Alfred Van Der Marck Editions, 1986).

622 Joel Williamson, *The Crucible of Race: Black-White Relations in the American South* (New York: Oxford University Press, 1984), 381.

623 *New York Times*, March 8, 2008; David Treuer, "Going Native: Why do Writers Pretend to be Indians?," Slate.com, March 7, 2008.

624 Kenneth Porter, "Negro Labor in the Western Cattle Industry, 1866–1900," *Labor History*, 10: 346–374; Jonathan Haeber, "Vaqueros: The First Cowboys of the Open Range," *National Geographic*, August 15, 2003; Heather Cox Richardson, *How the South Won the Civil War: Oligarchy, Democracy, and the Continuing Fight for the Soul of America* (New York: Oxford University Press, 2022), 87–88.

625 Larry Carter interview with Fred Burger, February 25, 2004, Doug Carter interview with Fred Burger, September 9, 1999, FB.

626 Ron Taylor interview with Fred Burger, November 19, 1998. FB.

627 Frederick Law Olmsted, *A Journey Through Texas; or, A Saddle-Trip on the Southwestern Frontier* (New York: Dix Edwards & Co., 1857), 124; W. B. DeWees, *Letters From An Early Settler of Texas* (Louisville, Kentucky: Morton and Griswold, 1852), 139.

628 With the help of my friend, Carol Puckett, I have examined land and property records for Calhoun County, Alabama, Franklin County Florida and Taylor County Texas, but it would require a forensic accountant to fully unravel Carter's property transfers that included the creation of at least two shell corporations in order to avoid having his name in the public record.

629 *Lubbock* (TX) *Morning Avalanche*, April 12, 1954.

630 Louisville (TN) *Courier-Journal*, May 6, 1951; *Marshall* (TX) *News Messenger*, May 7, 2004.

631 Bryan Burrough, *The Big Rich: The Rise and Fall of the Greatest Texas Oil Fortunes* (New York: The Penguin Press, 2009); Edward H. Miller, *Nut Country: Right-Wing Dallas and the Birth of the Southern Strategy* (Chicago: University of Chicago Press, 2015), 1–28.

632 *Fort Worth Star-Telegram*, May 16,1969; *Austin* (TX) *American*, February 19, 1969.

633 Lenoir Davis to Dan Carter, September 11, 2009, DC.

634 Lawrence Clayton Notes of Interview with Don Josey, March 15, 1984; Forrest Carter to Don Josey, September 16, 1976, copies furnished by Lawrence Clayton, DC.

635 *Carrollton* (TX) *Star*, March 19, 1975; Tom Turnipseed interview with author, March 3, 1994. Clint Josey, Jr., to author, September 25, 2009, DC; Don Josey Interview with Fred Burger, July 8, 1991, FB. Dana Rubin, "The Real Education of Little Tree," *Texas Monthly*, February, 1992, 95.

636 Doug Carter Interview with Fred Burger, September 9, 1999, FB.

637 Bill Whitaker interview, August 9, 2005, RAC Outtakes. DC.

638 Tony Frankel, "Interview with Michael Peretzian," *Stage and Cinema*, May 4, 2013.

639 *New York Times*, September 16, 1992

640 "Rhoda Weyr: Obituary," *Booth Bay* (Maine) *Register*, May 6, 2021.

641 Rhoda Weyr interview, May 26, 1992, FB; Weyr interview, RAC Outtake, DC.

642 India Carter to Bruce Marshall, August 27, 1981, "Marshall-Carter Correspondence, 1978–79," DC.

643 Ibid.

644 Fred Burger, "Ace Carter: The Tale of the Mysterious Author of 'Josey Wales' and 'Little Tree'," unpublished manuscript. FB.

645 Rhoda Weyr interview February 15, 2007, RAC Outtakes. DC; Eleanor Friede interview, October 30, 1991 transcript. FB.

646 "Hell Hath No Fury: The Making of 'The Outlaw Josey Wales,'" Warner Home Video,1999.

647 *Josey Wales: Two Westerns by Forrest Carter* (Albuquerque: University of New Mexico Press, 1989), 85–86.

648 Bob Daley interviews with Fred Burger, March 29, 1991, May 7, 1993; January 24, 2001, FB.

649 James A. Rawley, *Race and Politics: "Bleeding Kansas" and the Coming of the Civil War* (Philadelphia: J. Lippincott Company, 1969); Nicole Etcheson, *Bleeding Kansas: Contested Liberty in the Civil War Era* (Lawrence, Kansas: University Press of Kansas, 2004).

650 T. J. Stiles, *Jesse James: Last Rebel of the Civil War* (New York: Alfred A. Knopf, 2002), 119–22.

651 From a radio broadcast sometime in the mid-1950s. DC. Asa drew heavily upon John Edward's adulatory (and pro-Confederate) in *Noted Guerrillas, or the Warfare of the Brothers* (Chicago, Bryan and Company, 1877) and Frank Triplett's *The Life, Times & Treacherous Death of Jesse James.* (St. Louis: J. H. Chambers & Co., 1882).

652 Stiles, *Jesse James.*

653 Ben Beard, *The South Never Plays Itself: A Film Buff's Journey Through the South on Screen* (Montgomery: NewSouth books, 2020), 92–93.

654 Richard Schickel, *Clint Eastwood: A Biography* (New York: Vintage Books, 1996), 318–20; Patrick McGilligan, "Clint Eastwood: April, 1976," 26–27 and Christopher Frayling, "Eastwood on Eastwood/1985," 130–33, in Robert E. Kapsis and Kathie Coblentz, *Clint Eastwood: Interviews* (Jackson: University Press of Mississippi, 1999).

655 *St. Louis Post-Dispatch*, April 24, 1978; Lawrence Clayton, "Forrest Carter/Asa Carter and Politics," *Western American Literature*, 21 (Spring, 1986): 14–26.

656 Rhoda Weyr interview, February 15, 2007. RAC Outtakes, DC.

657 Charles and Betty Weeth, July 5, 2005 interview. RAC Outtakes, DC.

658 Lawrence Clayton interview, November 14, 1991. DC.
659 *New York Times,* July 25, 2008.
660 Hofstra College Yearbook, *Nexus-1942.*
661 *New York Times,* July 25, 2008, Eleanor Friede interview, October 30, 1991, Transcript, FB.
662 Twenty-two letters survive of the correspondence between Carter and Friede. See Asa Carter/Eleanor Friede correspondence File, copies DC; Rhoda Weyr Interview, February 15, 2007, *RAC* outtakes. DC; Eleanor Friede interview with Fred Burger, October 30, 1991, FB.
663 Faith Hubley interview with Fred Burger, May 20, 1995. FB.
664 Eleanor Friede interview with Fred Burger, October 30, 1991, transcript, FB; Eleanor Friede to Forrest Carter, n.d. July? 1975, Asa Carter/Eleanor Friede correspondence File, Copies, DC.
665 Forrest Carter to Eleanor Friede, December 31, 1974, University of New Mexico Press files, Copy DC.
666 Howard White interview, February 3, 2008, RAC Outtakes, DC; *Anniston Star,* Oct 16, 1991.
667 Schickel, *Clint Eastwood,* 320–321; Bob Daley, February 16, 2007, RAC outtakes. Bob Daley interviews, March 29, 1991, May 7, 1993; January 24, 2001, FB.
668 *The Summer of Black Widows* (Brooklyn, New York.: Hanging Loose Press, 1996).
669 Asa Carter to Eleanor Friede, August 29, 1974, University of New Mexico Press Files. Copies, DC.
670 Paula Conlon, "Nevaquaya, Joyce Lee "Doc" Tate (1932–1996), *The Encyclopedia of Oklahoma History and Culture.*
671 Forrest Carter to Bob Daley, June (?) 1975, FB.
672 Nevaquaya to Good Morning America, copy of June 16, 1975, telegram. DC.
673 Paula J. Conlon to Dan Carter, November 11, 2019, May 26, 2021, DC.
674 Bob St. John Interview, December 12, 2008, DC.
675 Rhoda Weyr interview, May 16, 1992, FB; Weyr interview February 15, 2007, RAC Outtakes, in DC; Eleanor Friede interview, October 30, 1991. FB.
676 "Seeing the Forrest for the Little Trees," *This American Life,* Broadcast, June 14, 2013, Transcript in DC.
677 Oscar Harper interview with author, August 9, 1991, Seymore Trammell interview with author, August 15, 1989, DC; *Montgomery Advertiser,* October 11, 1991; Ray Andrews Interview, February 1, 2008, RAC Outtakes, DC.; Greenhaw, *My Heart is in the Earth,* 52–54.
678 Rhoda Weyr interview with Fred Burger, May 16, 1992, Tom Weyr interview with Fred Burger, June 15, 1992, FB.
679 Roche, "Asa/Forrest Carter and Regional Identity," 249.
680 Darlene Walker Interview, December 5, 2008, RAC Outtakes. DC.
681 *Abilene* (Texas) *Reporter-News,* December 31, 1978.
682 Jack C. Lane, ed., *Chasing Geronimo: The Journal of Leonard Wood, May-September 1886* (Albuquerque: University of New Mexico Press, 1970); Alexander B. Adams, *Geronimo: A Biography.* New York: G. Putnam's Sons, 1971).

683 S. M. Barrett, *Geronimo: His Own Story* (New York: E. Dutton, 1970).

684 Bob Daley interview with Fred Burger, March 29, 1991, FB.

685 Forrest Carter to Bob Daley, June (?), June 10, 1975, Bob Daley cover note to Fred Burger; Daley to Forrest Carter, August 6, August 7, 1975 FB.

686 Bob Daley interview with author, March 22, 2002, DC; Bob Daley interview, February 16, 2007, RAC Outtake, DC. Clint Eastwood to Author, November 12, 1991. DC.

687 Schickel, *Clint Eastwood,* 321; Robert Daley interview, March 22, 2002, DC; Danny Arnold interview, June 20, 1991, Bob Daley interview, March 29, 1991, FB.

688 Patrick McGilligan,, *Clint: The Life and Legend.* (New York: Harper Collins, 1991) *260.*

689 *New York Times,* May 16, 1976.

690 *The Twin-Falls* (ID) *Times-News,* May 30, June 30, 1976; Pocatello *Idaho State Journal,* June 18, July 1, 1976.

691 *New York Times,* August 5, 1976.

692 *The Numbers: Where Data and the Movie Business Meet,* "The Outlaw Josey Wales," 2022, Copy in DC.

693 Robert Daley interview February 16, 2007, RAC Outtakes. Bob Daley interview with author, March 22, 2002, DC.

694 Lawrence Clayton interview with author, November 14, 1991. DC.

695 SAC Birmingham Memorandum, May 20, 1974, FBI Files.

696 Kendrick Oliver, *The My Lai Massacre in American History and Memory* (Manchester, UK: Manchester University Press, 2006), 43–45.

697 Wayne Greenhaw interview with author, August 9, 1991; copy of Greenhaw's notes, August 1976, DC; Forrest Carter to Don Josey, September 16, 1976, copy furnished to author by Lawrence Clayton, DC.

698 *Abilene News Reporter,* August 29, September 3, 1976; Author's interview with Lawrence Clayton, November 14, 1991.

699 Wayne Greenhaw, "Asa's Secret Story," *Mobile Register Sunday Magazine,* August 23, 1991. India Carter to Eleanor Friede, September 2, 1976, James Douglas Carter to Eleanor Friede, September 4, 1976; copies furnished to author by Lawrence Clayton, DC.

700 Ron Bloodworth Interview, November 20, 2008, RAC Outtakes, DC.

701 *Abilene Press-Register* June 10, 1977.

702 *Dallas Morning News,* October 17, 1991.

703 Ibid., October 1, 1978.

704 Rubin, "The Real Education of Little Tree," 79–80; Rose G. Biderman, *They Came to Stay: The Story of the Jews of Dallas, 1870–1997* (New York: the Eakins Press, 2001), 58–60. Hester Parker interview with author, April 4, 2016, DC; *New York Times,* February 7, 1989.

705 Camilla Graves interview with author, April 22, 2003, DC.

706 Walter Scott, *Marmion: A Tale of Flodden Field* (Boston and New York: Leach, Shewell & Sanborn, 1891), 163.

707 Judith McPheron, "Forrest Carter, *The Education of Little Tree,*" *Library Journal,* November 15, 1976, 29–31.

708 Freeman Owle, February 15, 2007, David Scott, December 15, 2008, RAC outtakes, DC. Will Chavez, "Cherokee Artists Bringing Back Authentic Tribal Art," *Cherokee Phoenix,* October 15, 2010; Christopher Teuton, "Literature Education and 'The Return of the Whippoorwill': A Conversation with Freeman Owle," *Appalachian Journal,* 34 (Winter 2007): 194–205.
709 Eleanor Friede to Elizabeth Hadas, December 6, 1984, University of New Mexico Correspondence, DC.
710 *Abilene Reporter-News,* September 12, 1970.
711 Ibid., Sept 1, 2, 3.
712 Kelly Garrett to Author, September 7, 9, 2009. DC.
713 Louise Green interview with author, November 12, 1991, DC; Louise Green interview with Fred Burger, June 30, 1991, FB.
714 Ronnie Malone, July 2, 1991; Larry Melton, July 2, 1991, FB.
715 Matthew R. Lee, et al., "Revisiting the Southern Culture of Violence," *The Sociological Quarterly* 48 (Spring, 2007), 270; Richard E. Nisbett and Dov Cohen, *Culture of Honor: The Psychology of Violence in the South* (New York: Routledge, 1996); Bertram Wyatt-Brown, *Southern Honor: Ethics and Behavior in the Old South* (New York: Oxford University Press, 1982).
716 Larry Hale Interview, November 20, 2008, RAC outtakes, DC.
717 Ron Bloodworth Interview, November 20, 2008; Ben Bloodworth Interview, December 15, 2008, RAC Outtakes, DC.
718 *New York Times Book Review,* March 18, 1979; *Chicago Tribune,* April 29, 1979; *Newsday,* June 19, 1983.
719 The Nashville *Tennessean,* July 23, September 29, 1972; Montgomery *Advertiser-Journal,* December 15, 1979; Mickey Grant interview with author, June 29, 2018. DC.
720 James Leroy 'Buddy' Barnett Criminal Record, copy, DC; *Anniston Star,* June 20, 1968, April 10, 1969; September 21, 1971, June 24, 1979, September 31, October 1, 1981, October 16, 1999; Brandt Ayers interview with author, October 12, 2014.
721 Forrest Carter, *Two Westerns by Forrest Carter: Gone to Texas & The Vengeance Trail of Josey Wales* (Albuquerque: University of New Mexico Press, 1989), 332.
722 Mickey Grant to author, June 25, 1968, June 28, 1968; Mickey Grant Interview with author, June 29, 2018. DC.
723 Ryan Gilbey, "Michael Parks, *The Guardian* (London), May 19, 2017; Seth Kelley, "Michael Parks, Character Actor in 'Kill Bill' and 'Tusk,' Dies at 77," *Variety,* May 10, 2017; "The Blacklisting of Michael Parks: How a Hollywood Star Was Quietly Shunned, "*The Artifice* (March 12, 2013).
724 Edward Humes, *Mississippi Mud: Southern Justice and the Dixie Mafia* (New York: Gallery Books, 2010); *Orlando Sentinel,* February 16, 1992. *New York Times,* December 18, 1982; *Texarkana News,* December 2, 2013; National Advisory Committee on Criminal Justice, Standards and Goals, *Report of the Task Force on Organized Crime* (December 28, 1976), 37, 215.
725 Mickey Grant to Dan Carter, August 13, 2021; Mickey Grant Interview with author, June 29, 2018. DC.
726 "The Return of Josey Wales," Multi/Tacar Productions, 1980.
727 *Anniston Star,* July 1, 1979, October 31, 1991; Wayne Greenhaw notes, July 3, 1979, DC.

728 Danny Arnold interview with Fred Burger, June 20, 1991, FB; *New York Times,* August 22, 1995; "Forgotten TV Pioneer: Writer/Producer Danny Arnold," *The Life and Times of Hollywood,* September 13, 2020; Wesley Hyatt, *Television's Top 100: The Most-Watched American Broadcasts, 1960–2010* (Jefferson, NC: McFarland Publishing, 2011).

729 Danny Arnold interview with Fred Burger, June 20, 1991, FB.

730 Louise Green Interview with author, November 12, 1991, DC; *Abilene Reporter-News,* June 21, 1965, April 10, 1966, April 8, 1971.

731 Louise Green interview with author (transcript), November 12, 1991, DC.

732 Over the next two days, deputies interviewed members of Carter's family as well as a nurse who lived next door. The following account is based upon the sworn interviews of Asa, Jr., Ralph and Geneva Carter as well as Barbara Poor, a registered nurse who lived next door who had examined and tried to resuscitate Asa. Investigative Reports of the death of Bedford Forest (sic) Carter, June 6, 8 and 12, 1979, copy, DC.

733 Duke University Alcohol Pharmacology Education Partnership, "Blood Alcohol Concentration: Estimates of the Degree of Intoxication." Copy in DC.

734 "Postmortem No. ON 42–79, Carter, Bedford Forest (sic), Autopsy Surgeon Joe D. Hall, M.D., Supervised by Justice of the Peace Roland Dunwoody," copy. DC;

735 Judge Samuel Matta interview with author, November 11, 1991; Author's telephone call to Richard Wimberly, November 16, 1991. DC.

736 Abilene *Reporter-News,* June 9, 1979.

737 Louise Green interview with Fred Burger, June 30, 1991, FB.

738 Bill Whitaker Interview, August 9, 2005, RAC.

739 Larry Carter interview with Fred Burger, February 25, 2004. FB.

740 *Anniston Star,* June 20, 1968; April 10, 1969; September 21, 1971.

741 No reporters were present at the graveside. Debbie Skipper of the *Anniston Star* later interviewed all of the participants and reconstructed the eulogies, a reconstruction that is generally consistent with the later memories of those present. *Anniston Star,* July 1, 1979, October 31, 1991; Wayne Greenhaw notes, July 3, 1979, in possession of the author.

742 Kipling, *Departmental Ditties and Ballads and Barrack Room Ballads* (Garden City: Doubleday, Page and Company, 1911), 150.

743 Larry Carter interview, February 24, 2004, FB.

744 In addition to the *Anniston Star* story (July 1, 1979), the Fort Worth *Star-Telegram* (July 4, 1979) printed a brief story suggesting a "mysterious" connection between Asa and Forrest Carter, but that was the end of any publicity surrounding his death.

745 Ebert, "Jonathan Livingston Seagull," RogerEbert.com, November 8, 1973.

746 Paul Heelas, *The New Age Movement: The Celebration of the Self and the Sacralization of Modernity* (Oxford: Blackwell Publishers, 1996); Robert Basil, ed., *Not Necessarily the New Age: Critical Essays* (New York Prometheus Books, 1988); Wade Clark Roof, *A Generation of Seekers: The Spiritual Journeys of the Baby Boom Generation* (New York: Harper Collins, 1993).

747 Elizabeth Hadas interview, November 25, 2008, RAC Outtakes, DC.

748 *New York Times,* February 27, April 24, September 27, 1991; *El Paso* [Tx] *Times,* October 2, 1991.

749 *New York Times,* October 4, 1991.
750 Calvin Reid, "Widow of 'Little Tree' Author Admits He Changed Identity," *Publisher's Weekly,* October 26, 1991, 16.
751 Elizabeth C. Hadas to Members of the American Booksellers Association, November 1, 1991. University of New Mexico Correspondence, DC.
752 Author's telephone conversation with Donna Rubin, October 22, 1991. DC.
753 Henry Louis Gates, Jr., "'Authenticity,' or the Lesson of Little Tree, *The New York Times Book Review,* November 24, 1991, 27.
754 Halliburton, R. Jr., *Red Over Black: Black Slavery Among the Cherokee* (Westport, Connecticut: Greenwood Press, 1977), 37.
755 Carter, *Gone to Texas,* 177; Motion Picture Script, *The Outlaw Josey Wales,* Copy in DC; Carter, *The Education of Little Tree,* 16.
756 J. David Slocum, "The 'Film Violence' trope: New Hollywood, 'the Sixties,' and the Politics of History," 13–33 and Martin Barker, "Violence redux," 57–80, in Steven Jay Schneider, ed., *New Hollywood Violence* (Manchester: Manchester University Press, 2004); Lee Clark Mitchell, "Violence in the Film Western," in J. David Slocum, ed., *Violence and American Cinema* (London: Routledge Publishing, 2001): 176–191.
757 *The Education of Little Tree (1997): Theatrical Performance,* Box Office Receipts, Copy in DC.
758 Transcript, Liberty Essay, "America's Threat," July (?) 1959, DC.
759 Tucker Carlson, "The truth about demographic change and why Democrats want it," Fox News Opinion, April 12, 2021.
760 Douglas Kiker, "Red Neck New York: Is This Wallace Country?" *New York,* October 7, 1968, 25–27.
761 Right-wing radio began in the 1930s, but with the exception of Father Coughlin, the goal was laissez-faire capitalism and the nightmare was communist infiltration. Race, hovered on the edges. Nicole Hemmer, *Messengers of the Right: Conservative Media and the Transformation of American Politics* (Philadelphia: University of Pennsylvania Press 2016), 46–49.
762 Rick Perlstein, "Exclusive: Lee Atwater's Infamous 1981 Interview on the Southern Strategy," *The Nation,* November 13, 2012.
763 Wills, *Nixon Agonistes: the Crisis of the Self-Made Man* (New York: Houghton Mifflin, 1972), 265.
764 Christopher Caterwood and Joe DiVanna, *The Merchants of Fear: Why They Want Us to be Afraid* (Guilford, Conn:Lyons Press, 2008).
765 Nathanel Persily, ed., *Social Media and Democracy* (Cambridge, England: Cambridge University Press, 2020; Philipp Lorenz-Spreen, et al., "Digital Media and Democracy: A Systematic Review of Causal and Correlational Evidence," November 2021, Copy in DC.
766 Mayer, *They Thought They Were Free: The Germans, 1933–1945* (Chicago: University of Chicago Press, 1955), 166–169, 200.

Bibliography

Books

Abbott, Carl, Stephen J. Leonard, and Thomas J. Noel. *Colorado: A History of the Centennial State* [Fourth Edition], Boulder: University Press of Colorado, 2011.

Adams, Alexander B. *Geronimo: A Biography.* New York: G. P. Putnam's Sons, 1971.

Alexie, Sherman. *The Summer of Black Widows.* Brooklyn, New York: Hanging Loose Press, 1996.

Alliuyeva, Svetlana. *Twenty Letters to a Friend.* New York: Harper & Row Publishers, 1967.

Archibald, John. *Shaking the Gates of Hell: A Search for Family and Truth in the Wake of the Civil Rights Revolution.* New York: Alfred A. Knopf, 2021.

Athearn, Robert G. *The Coloradans.* Albuquerque: University of New Mexico Press, 1976.

Atkins, Steven E. ed., *Encyclopedia of Right-Wing Extremism in Modern American History.* Santa Barbara, California: ABC-Clio, 2011.

Ayers, H. Brandt. *In Love With Defeat: The Making of a Southern Liberal.* Montgomery: New South Books, 2013.

Bagley, Joseph. *The Politics of White Rights: Race, Justice, and Integrating Alabama's Sch*ools. Athens: University of Georgia Press, 2018.

Baker, Bruce E. *What Reconstruction Meant: Historical Memory in the American South.* Charlottesville: University of Virginia Press, 2007.

Barkun, Michael. *Religion and the Racist Right: The Origins of the Christian Identity Movement.* Chapel Hill: University of North Carolina Press, 1994.

Barrett, S. M. *Geronimo: His Own Story.* New York: E. P. Dutton, 1970.

Bartley, Numan V. *The New South, 1945–1980.* Baton Rouge: Louisiana State University Press, 1995.

Basil, Robert, ed. *Not Necessarily the New Age: Critical Essays.* New York Prometheus Books, 1988.

Batiz, Francisco L. and Carlos Santiago, *Island Paradox: Puerto Rico in the 1990s.* New York: Russell Sage Foundation, 1996.

Berlet, Chip and Matthew N. Lyons. *Right-Wing Populism in America: Too Close for Comfort.* New York: The Guilford Press, 2000.

Bernstein, Arnie. *Swastika Nation: Fritz Kuhn and the Rise and Fall of the German-American Bund.* New York: Picador Press, 2014.

Biderman, Rose G. *They Came to Stay: The Story of the Jews of Dallas, 1870–1997.* New York: the Eakins Press, 2001.

Bird, S. Elizabeth. *Dressing in Feathers: The Construction of the Indian in American Popular Culture.* New York: Westview Press, 1996.
Black, Robert W. *Ghost, Thunderbolt and Wizard: Mosby, Morgan and Forrest in the Civil War.* Mechanicsberg, Pennsylvania: Stackpole Press, 2008.
Blake, Aldrich. *The Civil Rights Revolution: It Pays to be Free.* Waco, Texas: NP, 1955.
Blessing, William. *White Supremacy.* Denver: House of Prayer for all People, 1952.
Bradlee, Ben. *A Good Life.* New York: Simon & Schuster, 1995.
Brady, *Black Monday.* Jackson, Mississippi: Association of Citizens' Councils, 1955.
Bragg, Rick. *All Over but the Shoutin'.* New York: Pantheon Books, 1997.
Bright, David. *Race and Reunion: The Civil War in American Memory.* Cambridge: Harvard University Press, 2001.
Brinkley, Alan. *Voices of Protest: Huey Long; Father Coughlin and the Great Depression.* New York: Alfred A. Knopf, 1982.
Brown, Dee Alexander. *Bury My Heart at Wounded Knee.* New York: Holt, Reinhart and Winston, 2008.
Brown, Jerry E. and Henry D. Southerland, Jr. *The Federal Road Through Georgia, the Creek Nation, and Alabama, 1806–1836.* Tuscaloosa: University of Alabama Press, 1989.
Burrough, Bryan. *The Big Rich: The Rise and Fall of the Greatest Texas Oil Fortunes.* New York: The Penguin Press, 2009.
Cagin, Seth and Philip Dray. *We Are Not Afraid: The Story of Goodman, Schwerner, and Chaney and the Civil Rights Campaign for Mississippi.* New York: McMillan Publishers, 1988.
Calzada, José L. *La Población de Puerto Rico y su Trayectoria Histórica [The Population of Puerto Rico and its Historical Trajectory]* Rio Piedras, P. R.: Escuela Graduada de Salud Pública, Recinto de Ciencias Médicas, Universidad de Puerto Rico, 1988.
Carpenter, Joel A. *Revive Us Again: The Reawakening of American Fundamentalism.* Oxford: Oxford University Press, 1999.
[Carter, Asa]. *Official Program Honoring Governor George C. Wallace, January 14, 1963.* Montgomery: privately printed, 1963.
Carter, Dan T. *Scottsboro: A Tragedy of the American South.* Baton Rouge: Louisiana State University Press, 1970.
——. *The Politics of Rage: George Wallace, The Origins of the New Conservatism, and the Transformation of American Politics.* New York: Simon & Schuster, 1995.
Carter, Forrest. *Josey Wales: Two Westerns by Forrest Carter.* Albuquerque: University of New Mexico Press, 1989.
——. *The Education of Little Tree.* Albuquerque: University of New Mexico Press, 1986.
——. *Watch for Me on the Mountain: A Novel of Geronimo and the Apache Nation.* New York: Doubleday/Eleanor Friede. 1978.
Charles A. *The Greening of America.* New York: Random House, 1970.

Clark, E. Culpepper. *The Schoolhouse Door: Segregation's Last Stand at the University of Alabama.* New York: Oxford University Press, 1993.

Coates, James. *Armed and Dangerous: The Rise of the Survivalist Right.* New York: Hill and Wang, 1987.

Cody, Iron Eyes. *Iron Eyes: My Life as a Hollywood Indian.* New York: Everest House, 1982.

Cole, Marcia with Louie Robinson. *Nat King Cole: An Intimate Biography.* New York: William Morrow & Company, 1971.

Cook, Fred J. *The FBI Nobody Knows.* New York: The McMillan Company, 1964.

Cook, James Graham. *The Segregationists.* New York: Appleton Century-Croft, 1962.

Courtney, Kent and Phoebe. *America's Unelected Rulers.* New Orleans: Conservative Society of America, 1962.

Cray, Ed. *Chief Justice: A Biography of Earl Warren.* New York: Simon & Schuster, 1997.

Crespino, Joseph. *In Search of Another Country: Mississippi and the Conservative Counterrevolution.* Princeton: Princeton University Press, 2007.

Daniels, Pete. *Lost Revolutions: The South in the 1950s.* Chapel Hill: University of North Carolina Press, 2000.

Day, John Kyle. *The Southern Manifesto: Massive Resistance and the Fight to Preserve Segregation.* Jackson: University of Mississippi Press, 2014.

Deloria, Philip. *Indians in Unexpected Places.* University of Kansas Press, 2004.

——. Playing *Indian.* New Haven: Yale University Press, 1999.

Deloria, Vine, Jr. *Custer Died for Your Sins: An Indian Manifesto.* New York: Collier-MacMillan, 1969.

DeWees, W. B., *Letters From An Early Settler of Texas/* Louisville, Kentucky: Morton and Griswold, 1852.

Diamond, Sander A. *The Nazi Movement in the United States, 1924–1941.* Ithaca: Cornell University Press, 1974.

Dillard, Philip D. and Randal L. Hall, eds., *The Southern Albatross: Race and Ethnicity in the American South.* Macon, Ga.: Mercer University Press, 1999.

Dinnerstein, Leonard, and Mary Dale Palsson (eds). *Jews in the South.* Baton Rouge: Louisiana State University Press, 1973.

Dittmer, John. *Local People: The Struggle for Civil Rights in Mississippi.* Urbana: University of Chicago Press, 1994.

Dixon, Thomas. *The Clansman: an Historical Romance of the Ku Klux Klan.* New York: Grosset & Dunlap Publishers, 1905.

Doob, Leonard W. *"Ezra Pound Speaking": Radio Speeches of World War II.* Westport, Conn.: Greenwood Press, 1978.

Dooley, Patricia L. *Freedom of Speech: Reflections in Art and Popular Culture.* Westport, Conn.: ABC-Clio/Greenwood Press, 2017.

Dorwart, Jeffery M. *Conflict of Duty: The U.S. Navy's Intelligence Dilemma, 1919–1945.* Annapolis: Naval Institute Press, 1983.

Edward, John. *Noted Guerrillas, or the Warfare of the Brothers.* Chicago: Bryan Brand, and Publishers, 1877.

Elovitz, Mark. *A Century of Jewish Life In Dixie: The Birmingham Experience*. University of Alabama Press, 2016.

Eskew, Glenn. *But for Birmingham: The Local and National Movements in the Civil Rights Struggle.* Chapel Hill: University of North Carolina Press, 1997.

Etcheson, Nicole. *Bleeding Kansas: Contested Liberty in the Civil War Era.* Lawrence, Kansas: University Press of Kansas, 2004.

Featherstonhaugh, G(eorge) W(illiam). *The Slave States: Washington on the Potomac to the Frontier of Texas.* New York: Harper and Brothers, 1844.

Feldman, Glenn. *Politics, Society, and the Klan in Alabama, 1915–1949.* Tuscaloosa: University of Alabama Press, 1999.

Fine, Morris, ed, *American Jewish Yearbook, 1956.* New York: American Jewish Committee, 1957.

Fleegler, Robert L. *Ellis Island Nation: Immigration and American Identity in the Twentieth Century.* Philadelphia: University of Pennsylvania Press, 2015.

Foote, Shelby. *The Beleaguered City: The Vicksburg Campaign, December 1862–July 1863.* New York: Modern Library, 1995.

Foreman, Grant. *Indian Removal: The Emigration of the Five Civilized Tribes of Indians.* Norman: University of Oklahoma Press, 1932.

Forkner, Ben, ed., *Audubon on Louisiana: Selected Writings of John James Audubon.* Baton Rouge: Louisiana State University Press, 2018.

Gabler, Neal. *Winchell: Gossip, Power and the Culture of Celebrity.* New York: Vintage Press, 1995.

Garrow, David, ed. *The Walking City: The Montgomery Bus Boycott, 1955–1956.* Minneapolis: Carlson Publications, 1989.

Gates, Grace Hooten. *The Model City of the New South: Anniston, Alabama, 1872–1900.* Tuscaloosa: University of Alabama Press, 1978.

Gates, Robbins L. *The Making of Massive Resistance: Virginia's Politics of Public School Desegregation, 1954–1956.* Chapel Hill: University of North Carolina Press, 1964.

Gentry, Curt. *J. Edgar Hoover: The Man and the Secrets.* New York: W. W. Norton & Company, 1991.

Goldberg, Robert Alan. *Hooded Empire: The Ku Klux Klan in Colorado.* Chicago: University of Chicago Press, 1981.

Goodman, James E. *Stories of Scottsboro.* New York: Pantheon Books, 1994.

Grant, Madison. *The Passing of the Great Race.* New York: Charles Scribner's Sons, 1916.

Green, Michael. *The Politics of Indian Removal: Creek Government and Society in Crisis.* Lincoln: University of Nebraska Press, 1982.

Greene, Melissa Faye. *The Temple Bombing.* Reading, Massachusetts: Addison-Wesley Publishing Company, 1996.

Greenhaw, Wayne. *Fighting the Devil in Dixie: How Civil Rights Activists Took on the Ku Klux Klan in Alabama*. Chicago: Lawrence Hill Books, 2011.

——. *Watch Out for George Wallace*. Englewood Cliffs, N.J.: Prentice-Hall, Inc., 1976.

Griffin, Robert S. *The Fame of a Dead Man's Deeds: An Up-Close Portrait of White Nationalist William Pierce*. San Francisco California: Internet Archive, 2001.

Gumbel, Andrew and Roger G. Charles, *Oklahoma City: What the Investigation Missed—and Why It Still Matters*. William Morrow Publishers, 2012.

Gunther, John. *Inside USA*. New York: Harper and Brothrs, 1947.

Guptill, Molly. *When Books Went to War: The Stories that Helped Us Win World War II*. Boston: Houghton Mifflin. 2014.

Halliburton, R. Jr. *Red Over Black: Black Slavery Among the Cherokee*. Westport, Connecticut: Greenwood Press, 1977.

Hamilton, Virginia Van der Veer. *Lister Hill: Statesman from the South*. Chapel Hill: University of North Carolina Press, 2004.

Hanes, Walton Jr., Sherman Puckett and Donald R. Deskins, Jr. *The African American Electorate*. Thousand Oaks, California: Sage Publications.

Harcourt, Felix. *Ku Klux Kulture: American and the Klan in the 1920s*. Chicago: University of Chicago Press, 2017.

Harper, Oscar. *Me'n George: A Story of George Corley Wallace and His Number One Crony Oscar Harper*. Pittsburg, California: Greenberry Publishing: 1988.

Harris, W. Edward. *Miracle in Birmingham: A Civil Rights Memoir*, 1954–1965. Indianapolis, Indiana: Stonework Press, 2004.

Hart, Bradley W. *Hitler's American Friends: The Third Reich's Supporters in the United States*. New York: St. Martin's Press, 2018.

Hart, Bradley W. *Hitler's American Friends: The Third Reich's Supporters in the United States*. New York: Thomas Dunne Books, 2018.

Heelas, Paul. *The New Age Movement: The Celebration of the Self and the Sacralization of Modernity*. Oxford: Blackwell Publishers, 1996.

Heggen, Thomas. *Mr. Roberts*. Boston: Houghton Mifflin, 1946.

Highwater, Jamake. *Shadow Show: An Autobiographical Insinuation*. New York: Alfred Van Der Marck Editions, 1986.

Hipperson, Carol Edgemon, ed. *Radioman: An Eyewitness Account of Pearl Harbor and WWII in the Pacific*. New York: Thomas Dunne Books, 2008.

Hollis, Tim. *Birmingham's Retail and Theater District*. Charleston, SC: Arcadia Publishing, 2005.

Howard, Gene L. *Death at Cross Plains: A Reconstruction Alabama Tragedy*. Tuscaloosa: University of Alabama Press, 1984.

——. *Patterson for Alabama: The Life and Career of John Patterson*. Tuscaloosa: University of Alabama Press, 2009.

Huhndorf, Shari. *Going Native: Indians in the American Cultural Imagination*. Cornell University Press, 2001.

Huie, William Bradford. *Three Lives for Mississippi. New York: WCC Books, 1964.*

Humes, Edward. *Mississippi Mud: Southern Justice and the Dixie Mafia*. New York: Gallery Books, 2010.

Hundley, Daniel. *Social Relations in Our Southern States.* New York: Henry B. Price Publishers, 1860.

Hurt, Harry III, *Texas Rich: The Hunt Dynasty from the Early Oil Days Through the Silver Crash.* New York: W. W. Norton, 1981.

Hurt, R. Douglas. *The Great Plains During World War II.* Lincoln: University of Nebraska Press, 2008.

Hyatt, Wesley. *Television's Top 100: The Most Watched American Broadcasts, 1960–2010.* Jefferson, North Carolina: McFarland Publishing, 2011.

Isles, Greg. *The Quiet Game.* New York: E. P. Dutton, 1999.

Jackson, John P., Jr. *Science for Segregation: Race, Law, and the Case Against Brown v. Board of Education.* New York: New York University Press, 2005.

Jacoway, Elizabeth. *Turn Away Thy Son: Little Rock, The Crisis that Shocked the Nation.* New York: Free Press, 2007.

Jamieson, John, ed. *Editions for the Armed Services, Inc.: a History: Together with the Complete list of 1324 books published for American Armed Forces Overseas.* New York: Editions for the Armed Services, Inc., 1948.

Jarvis, Sharon E. *Conservative Political Communication: How Right-Wing Media and Messaging (Re)Made American Politics.* London Routledge Publishers, 2021.

Jeansonne, Glen. *Gerald L. K. Smith: Minister of Hate.* New Haven: Yale University Press, 1988.

Jensen, Joan M. *Army Surveillance in America, 1775–1980*, New Haven, Yale University Press, 1991.

Jones, Doug with Greg Truman. *Bending Toward Justice: the Birmingham Church Bombing that Changed the Course of Civil Rights.* New York: All Points Books, 2019.

Kaganoff, Nathan M. and Melvin I. Urofsky (eds). *Turn to the South: Essays on Southern Jewry.* Charlottesville: University of Virginia Press, 1979.

Kappler, Charles J. *Indian Affairs: Laws and Treaties.* Volume 2. Washington: Government Printing Office, 1904; *Anniston Star*, June 26, 1955.

Kapsis, Robert E. and Kathie Coblentz. *Clint Eastwood: Interviews.* Jackson: University of Mississippi Press, 1999.

Kendrick, Oliver. *The My Lai Massacre in American History and Memory.* Manchester, UK: Manchester University Press, 2006.

Kernan, Alvin J. *Crossing the Line: A Bluejacket's World War II Odyssey*. Annapolis: Naval Institute Press, 1997.

Kirwan, Albert D. *Revolt of the Rednecks: Mississippi Politics, 1876–1925.* Lexington: University of Kentucky Press, 1951.

King, Gilbert. *Devil in the Grove: Thurgood Marshall, the Groveland Boys and the Dawn of a New America.* New York: Harper Collins Press, 2012.

Klarman, Michael. *From Jim Crow to Civil Rights: The Supreme Court and the Struggle for Racial Equality.* New York: Oxford University Press, 2006.

Klein, Adam G. *A Space for Hate: The White Power Movement's Adaptation into Cyberspace.* Sacramento, California, Litwin Books, 2010.

Kluger, Richard. *Simple Justice: The History of Brown v. Board of Education and Black America's Struggle for Equality.* New York: Alfred A. Knopf, 1976.

Kramm, Robert/ *Sanitized Sex: Regulating Prostitution, Venereal Disease, and Intimacy in Occupied Japan, 1945–1952.* Berkeley: University of California Press, 2017.

Lane, Jack C., ed. *Chasing Geronimo: The Journal of Leonard Wood, May-September1886.* Albuquerque: University of New Mexico Press, 1970.

Lavergne, Gary M. *Before Brown: Herman Marion Sweatt, Thurgood Marshall, and the Long Road to Justice.* Austin: University of Texas Press, 2010.

Lee, Robert Edson. *To the War.* New York: Alfred A. Knopf, 1968.

Levy, David W. Levy. *Breaking Down Barriers: George McLaurin and the Struggle to End Segregated Education.* Norman: University of Oklahoma Press, 2020.

MacDonnell, Francis. *Insidious Foes: The Axis Fifth Column and the American Home Front.* (New York: Oxford University Press, 1995.

MacLean, Nancy. *Democracy in Chains: The Deep History of the Radical Right's Stealth Plan for America.* New York: Viking Press, 2017.

Manis, Andrew W. *A Fire You Can't Put Out: The Civil Rights Life of Birmingham's Reverend Fred Shuttlesworth.* Tuscaloosa: University of Alabama Press, 1999.

Manning, Molly Guptill. *When Books Went to War: The Stories that Helped us Win World War II.* Boston: Houghton Mifflin, 2014.

Martin, John Bartlow. *The Deep South Says "Never."* New York: Ballantine Books, 1957.

Martin, Linda and Kerry Segrave. *Anti-Rock: The Opposition to Rock 'n' Roll.* Hamden, Conn.: Archon Books, 1988.

Mayer, Milton. *They Thought They Were Free: The Germans, 1933–1945.* Chicago: University of Chicago Press, 1955.

Mazzocco, Dennis. Networks *of Power: Corporate TV's Threat to Democracy.* Boston: South End Press, 1999.

McGilligan, Patrick. *Clint: The Life and Legend.* New York: Harper Collins, 1991

McMillen, Neil R. *The Citizens' Council: Organized Resistance to the Second Reconstrucation, 1954–1964.* Urbana: University of Illinois Press, 1971.

McWhorter, Dianne. *Carry Me Home: Birmingham Alabama: The Climactic Battle of the Civil Rights Revolution.* New York: Simon & Schuster, 2001.

Menand, Louis. "Literary Hoaxes and the Ethics of Authorship." *The New Yorker.* December 10, 2018.

——. "The People Who Decide What Becomes History," *The New Yorker*, April 18, 2022.

Michael, George. *Willis Carto and the American Far Right.* Gainesville: University of Florida Press, 2008.

Michel, Lou and Dan Herbeck. *American Terrorist: Timothy McVeigh and the Oklahoma City Bombing.* New York: Harper and Row, 2001.

Miller, Christopher. *Imposters: Literary Hoaxes and Cultural Authenticity.* Chicago: University of Chicago Press, 2018.

Miller, Donald L. *D-Days in the Pacific.* New York: Simon & Schuster, 2005.

Miller, Dora Richards. *War Diary of a Union Woman in the South: 1860–63.* Edited by George Washington Cable. New York: Charles Scribner's Sons, 1889.

Miller, Edward R. *A Conspiratorial Life: Robert Welch, the John Birch Society and the Revolution of American Conservatism.* Chicago: University of Chicago Press, 2021.

——. *Nut Country: Right-Wing Dallas and the Birth of the Southern Strategy.* Chicago: University of Chicago Press, 2015.

Miller, James D. *South by Southwest: Planter Emigration and Identity in the Slave South.* Charlottesville: University of Virginia Press, 2002.

Minor, Bill. *Eyes on Mississippi: A Fifty-Year Chronicle of Change.* Jackson, Mississippi: J. Prichard Morris Books, 2001.

Mohl, Raymond A. *South of the South: Jewish Activists and the Civil Rights Movement in Miami, 1945–1960.* Gainesville: University of Florida Press, 2004.

Moore, Albert Burton. *Conscription and Conflict in the Confederacy.* New York: MacMillan Company, 1924.

Moore, Albert Burton. *History of Alabama.* Tuscaloosa: Alabama Book Store, 1951 Reprint, 1934 edition.

Müller, Rolf-Dieter, Nicole Schönherr, and Thomas Widera, eds. Thomas, eds. *Die Zerstörung Dresdens*: 13. bis 15. Februar 1945. [*The Destruction of Dresden: February 13–15, 1945*]. Gottingen: Vandenhoeck & Ruprecht, 2010.

Myrdal, Gunnar, *An American Dilemma: The Negro Problem and Modern Democracy.* New York: Harper & Bros, 1944.

Nelson, Jack. *Terror in the Night: The Klan's Campaign Against the Jews.* New York: Simon & Schuster, 1993.

Newton, Michael. *The Invisible Empire: The Ku Klux Klan in Florida.* Gainesville: University of Florida Press, 1997.

Newton, Michael. *The Ku Klux Klan in Mississippi: A History. Jefferson, North Carolina: McFarland Publishers, 2020.*

Nicholas, William E. *Go and Be Reconciled: Alabama Methodists Confront Racial Injustice, 1954–1974.* Montgomery: NewSouth Books, 2018.

Nisbett, Richard E., and Dov Cohen, *Culture of Honor: The Psychology of Violence in the South.* New York: Routledge, 1996.

Norrell, Robert J. *Reaping the Whirlwind: The Civil Rights Movement in Tuskegee.* New York: Alfred A. Knopf, 1985.

O'Reilly, Kenneth. *"Racial Matters": The FBI's Secret File on Black America, 1960–1972.* New York: The Free Press, 1989.

Olmsted, Frederick Law. *A Journey Through Texas; or, A Saddle-Trip on the Southwestern Frontier.* New York: Dix Edwards & Co., 1857.

Oney, Steve. *And the Dead Shall Rise: The Murder of Mary Phagan and the Lynching of Leo Frank.* New York: Pantheon Books, 2003.

Oshinsky, David M. *A Conspiracy So Immense: The World of Joe McCarthy.* New York: Simon & Schuster, 1983.

Page, Thomas Nelson. *The Negro: The Southerner's Problem.* New York: Charles Scribner's Sons, 1904.

Parsons, Elaine Frantz, *Ku Klux: the Birth of the Klan During Reconstruction.* Chapel Hill: University of North Carolina Press, 2016.

Peltason, J. W. *Fifty-eight Lonely Men: Southern Federal Judges and School Desegregation.* New York: Harcourt, Brace and World, 1961.

Perdue, Theda and Michael Green. *The Cherokee Nation and the Trail of Tears.* New York: Viking Press, 2007.

Perlstein, Nixonland. *The Risa of a President and the Fracturing of America.* New York: Scribner, 2008.

Peters, J. [pseud. Sándor Goldberger*]. The Communist Party: A Manual on Organization.* New York: Workers Library Publishers, 1935.

Powers, Richard Gid. *Not Without Honor: The History of American Anti-communism.* New Haven: Yale University Press, 1998.

Pride, Richard. *The Political Use of Racial Narratives: School Desegregation in Mobile Alabama, 1954–97.* Urbana: University of Illinois Press, 2002.

Puckett, Dan J. *In the Shadow of Hitler: Alabama's Jews, the Second World War, and the Holocaust.* Tuscaloosa: University of Alabama Press, 2014.

Quarles, Chester L. *Christian Identity: The Aryan American Bloodline Religion.* Jefferson, North Carolina: McFarland Press, 2004.

Quint, Howard H. *Profile in Black and White: A Frank Portrait of South Carolina.* Washington: Public Affairs Press, 1958.

Rappoport, Jon. *Oklahoma City Bombing: The Suppressed Truth.* BookTree, Press: Daly, California, 1997.

Rath, R. John. *The Viennese Revolution of 1848.* Austin, Texas: University of Texas Press, 1957.

Rawley, James A. *Race and Politics: "Bleeding Kansas" and the Coming of the Civil War.* Philadelphia: J. P. Lippincott Company, 1969.

Ribuffo, Leo P. *The Old Christian Right: The Protestant Far Right from the Great Depression to the Cold War.* Philadelphia: Temple University Press, 1983.

Richardson, Heather Cox. *How the South Won the Civil War: Oligarchy, Democracy, and the Continuing Fight for the Soul of America.* New York: Oxford University Press, 2002.

Rolph, Stephanie R., *Resisting Equality: The Citizens' Council, 1954–1989.* Baton Rouge: Louisiana State University Press, 2018.

Roof, Wade Clark. *A Generation of Seekers: The Spiritual Journeys of the Baby Boom Generation.* New York: Harper Collins, 1993.

Ruotsila, Markku, *Fighting Fundamentalist: Carl McIntire and the Politicization of American Fundamentalism.* New York: Oxford University Press, 2015.

Russell, Charles Wells, ed., *The Memoirs of Colonel John S. Mosby.* Boston: Little, Brown, and Company, 1917.

Sakmyster, Thomas. *Red Conspirator: J. Peters and the American Communist Underground.* Urbana: University of Illinois Press, 2011.

Sayers, James Denson. *Can the White Race Survive?* Washington: Independent Publishing Company, 1929.

Schickel, Richard. *Clint Eastwood: A Biography.* New York: Vintage Books, 1996.

Schlesinger, Arthur M. *Robert Kennedy and His Times.* Boston: Houghton Mifflin, 2002.

Schneider, Steven. *New Hollywood Violence.* Manchester, UK: University of Manchester Press, 2004.

Settle, Jaime E. *Frenemies: How Social Media Paralyzes America.* Cambridge: Cambridge University Press, 2018.

Sharrett, Christopher, ed., *Mythologies of Violence in Postmodern Media.* Detroit: Wayne State University Press, 1999.

Siemens, Daniel. *Stormtroopers: A New History of Hitler's Brownshirts.* New Haven: Yale University Press, 2017.

Sims, George. *The Little Man's Big Friend: James E. Folsom in Alabama Politics, 1946–1955.* Tuscaloosa: University of Alabama Press, 1985.

Sirgiovanni, George. *An Undercurrent of Suspicion: Anti-Communism in America During World War II.* Brunswick, New Jersey: Transaction Publishers, 1990.

Sklaroff, Lauren Rebecca. *Black Culture and the New Deal: The Quest for Civil Rights in the Roosevelt Era.* Chapel Hill: University of North Carolina Press, 2009.

Slocum, J. David, ed. *Violence and American Cinema.* New York and London: Routledge, 2001.

Smith, Donald B. *Chief Buffalo Child Long Lance: The Glorious Imposter.* Alberta, Canada: Red Deer Press, 1999.

Smith, Donald B. *From the Land of Shadows: The Making of Grey Owl.* Saskatoon, Canada: Western Prairie Books, 1990.

Spiro, Jonathan Peter. *Defending the Master Race: Conservation, Eugenics, and the Legacy of Madison Grant.* Burlington: University of Vermont Press, 2008.

Sprague, Marshall. *Colorado: A History.* New York: W. W. Norton and Company. 1984.

Stephens, Randall J. *The Devil's Music: How Christians Inspired, Condemned and Embraced Rock 'n' Roll.* Cambridge: Harvard University Press, 2018.

Stiles, T. J. *Jesse James: Last Rebel of the Civil War.* New York: Alfred A. Knopf, 2002.

Suitts, Steve. *Overturning Brown: The Segregationist Legacy of the Modern School Choice Movement.* Montgomery: NewSouth Books, 2020.

Swint, Howard L. *The Northern Teacher in the South, 1862–1870.* Nashville: Vanderbilt University Press, 1941.

Talbert, Roy, Jr., *Negative Intelligence: The Army and the American Left, 1917–1941.* Oxford: University of Mississippi Press, 1991.

Tanaka, Yuki. *Japan's Comfort Women: Sexual Slavery and Prostitution During World War II and the US Occupation.* New York: Routledge, 2002.

Thornton, J. Mills, III. *Dividing Lines: Municipal Politics and the Struggle for Civil Rights in Montgomery, Birmingham and Selma.* Tuscaloosa: the University of Alabama Press, 2002.

Trammell, Warren. *Madness in the Magnolias.* Boynton Beach, Florida: WM Productions, 2017.

Trelease, Alan W. *White Terror, The Ku Klux Klan Conspiracy and Southern Reconstruction. New York: Harper and Row, 1971.*

Tuscaloosa: University of Alabama Press, 1985.

Wade, Wyn Craig. *The Fiery Cross: the Ku Klux Klan in America.* New York: Simon & Schuster, 1987.

Wakefield, Dan. *Revolt in the South.* New York: Grove Publishers, 1960.

Waldron, Ann. *Hodding Carter: The Reconstruction of a Racist.* Chapel Hill: Algonquin Press, 1993.

Walker, Anders. *The Ghost of Jim Crow: How Southern Moderates Used* Brown v. Education *to Stall Civil Rights.* New York: Oxford University Press, 2009.

Wallace, George [Asa Carter]. *Stand Up for America.* New York: Doubleday Publishers, 1968.

Ward, Brian. *Just My Soul Responding: Rhythm and Blues, Black Consciousness and Race Relations.* Berkeley: University of California Press, 1998.

Webb, Clive. *Rabble Rousers: The American Far Right in the Civil Rights Era.* Athens: University of Georgia Press, 2010.

Webb, Clive. *Fight against Fear: Southern Jews and Black Civil Rights.* Athens: University of Georgia Press, 2001.

Weyl, Nathaniel. *Treason: The Story of Disloyalty and Betrayal in American History.* Washington: Public Affairs Press, 1950.

Wilkie, Curtis. *Dixie: A Personal Odyssey Through Events that Shaped the Modern South.* New York: Scribner's, 2001.

Williams, Daniel K. *God's Own Party: The Making of the Christian Right.* New York: Oxford University Press, 2012.

Williamson, Joel. *The Crucible of Race: Black-White Relations in the American South.* New York: Oxford University Press, 1984.

Wills, Gary. *Nixon Agonistes: The Crisis of the Self-Made Man.* Boston: Houghton Mifflin Company, 1970.

Winn, William C. *The Triumph of the Ecunnau-Nuxulgee.* Macon, Georgia: Mercer University Press, 2015.

Winrod, Gordon. *The Jewish Assault on Christianity.* Gainesville, Missouri: Gordon Winrod Publisher, 1935.

Woods, Jeff R. *Black Struggle, Red Scare: Segregation and Anti-Communism in the South, 1948–1968.* Baton Rouge: Louisiana State University Press, 2003.

Wyatt-Brown, Bertram. *Southern Honor: Ethics and Behavior in the Old South.* New York: Oxford University Press, 1982.
Wyeth, John Allan. *That Devil Forrest: Life of Lieutenant-General Nathan Bedford Forrest.* New York: Harper Brothers, 1908.
Zeigler, Eugene N., Jr., *When Conscience and Power Meet: a Memoir.* Columbia: University of South Carolina Press, 2008.
Zeskind, Leonard. *Blood and Politics: The History of the White Nationalist Movement from the Margins to the Mainstream.* New York: Farrar Straus Giroux, 2009.

ARTICLES

Adamson, June N. "Few Black Voices Heard: The Black Community and the Desegregation Crisis in Clinton, Tennessee, 1956," *Tennessee Historical Quarterly,* 53 (1994): 30–41.
Appelbaum, Yoni. "Publishers Gave Away 122,951,031 Books During World War II," *The Atlantic,* September 10, 2014.
Badger, Tony. "'Closet Moderates': Why White Liberals Failed, 1940–1970" in *The Role of Ideas in the Civil Rights Movement,* edited by Ted Owenby, 83–112. Jackson: University Press of Mississippi, 2002.
——. "Southerners Who Refused to Sign the Southern Manifesto." *The Historical Journal* 42 (1999): 517–534.
Baker, Lee D. "Columbia University's Franz Boas: He led the Undoing of Scientific Racism." *The Journal of Blacks in Higher Education,* 22 (Winter, 1998–1999): 89–96.
Barker, Martin, "Violence redux," in Steven Jay Schneider, ed., *New Hollywood Violence* (Manchester: Manchester University Press, 2004): 57–80.
Bolton, Charles C. "Mississippi's School Equalization Program, 1945–1954: 'A Last Gasp to Try to Maintain a Segregated Educational System.'" *Journal of Southern History* 66 (November 2000): 781–814.
Browder, Laura. "The Curious Case of Asa Carter and the Education of Little Tree," in Elizabeth DeLaney Hoffman, ed., vol. 2, *American Indians and Popular Culture Literature, Arts, and Resistance.* Santa Barbara, California: Praeger. 2012: 63–79.
Brown, Sarah Watson. "Congressional Anti-Communism and the Segregationist South: From New Orleans to Atlanta, 1954–1958." *Georgia Historical Quarterly.* 80 (Winter, 1996): 797–816.
Buckley, Tom. "Just Plain H. L. Hunt," *Esquire,* January 1, 1967, 144–156.
Cater, Douglas. "Civil War in Alabama's Citizens' Councils." *The Reporter,* May 17, 1956, 19–21.
Clayton, Lawrence. "Forrest Carter/Asa Carter and Politics." *Western American Literature,* 21 (Spring, 1986): 14–26.
Clayton, Lawrence. "The Enigma of Forrest Carter." *Texas Books in Review* 5 (1983): 16–26.

Cloete, Stuart. "End of an Era with the Threat of the Jungle." *Life.* August 1, 1960: 14–15.

Denby, David."Out of the West: Clint Eastwood's shifting landscape," *The New Yorker,* February 28,2010.

Desilver, Drew. "The Politics of American Generations: How age affects attitudes and voting Behavior," *FactTank,* July 9, 2014.

Dierenfield, Kathleen Murphy. "One 'Desegregated Heart': Sarah Patton Boyle and the Crusade for Civil Rights in Virginia," *The Virginia Magazine of History and Biography,* 104 (1996): 251–284.

Dinnerstein, Leonard. "Southern Jewry and the Desegregation Crisis, 1954–1970" *American Jewish Historical Quarterly,* 62, (March,1973): 231–241.

Drabble, John. "The FBI, COINTELPRO-WHITE HATE, and the Decline of Ku Klux Klan Organizations in Alabama, 1964–1971." *Alabama Review* 61 (2008): 3–47.

Drabble, John. "To Ensure Domestic Tranquility: The FBI, COINTELPRO-WHITE HATE and Political Discourse, 1964–1971." *Journal of American Studies,* 38 (2004): 297–328.

Erskine, Hazel. "The Polls: Demonstrations and Civil Rights." *Public Opinion Quarterly,* 31 (Winter, 1967–68): 655–677.

Erskine, Hazel. "The Polls: Race Relations." *Public Opinion Quarterly,* 26 (Spring, 1962): 137–148.

Goodwin, George Jr., "The Seniority System in Congress," *American Political Science Review* 53 (September, 2013): 412–36.

Graham, David A."The White Supremacist Group That Inspired a Racist Manifesto." *The Atlantic,* June 22, 2015.

Haeber, Jonathan. "Vaqueros: The First Cowboys of the Open Range," *National Geographic,* August 15, 2003.

Haveman, Christopher D., "Final Resistance: Creek Removal from the Alabama Homeland." *Alabama Heritage* 89 (Summer 2008): 9–19.

Hofstadter, Richard. "The Paranoid Style in American History," *Harper's Magazine,* November,1964.

Jackson, John P., Jr. "The Scientific Attack on *Brown* v. *Board of Education, 1954–1964." 59 American Psychologist* (September 2004): 532–3.

Jacobs, Willis D. Throw it Over Here." *Bulletin of the American Association of University Professors)* 32 (Autumn, 1946): 521–32.

Jamieson, John, "Books and the Soldier." 9 *Public Opinion Quarterly* (1945): 320–332.

Jeansonne, Glen. "Racism and Longism in Louisiana: The 1959-60 Gubernatorial Elections." *Louisiana History* 11 (Summer, 1970): 259–270.

Jewell, Malcolm E. "State Legislatures in Southern Politics." *The Journal of Politics,* 26 (1964): 177–196.

Kiker, Douglas "Red Neck New York: Is This Wallace Country?" *New York,* October 7, 1968: 25–27.

Klarman, Michael J. "Court, Congress, and Civil Rights," in Neal Devins and Keith E. Whittington, eds. *Congress and the Constitution.* Durham, NC: Duke University Press, 2005: 173–197.

Knoll, Erwin. "The Truth About Desegregation in the Washington, D.C. Public Schools." *The Journal of Negro Education,* 28 (1959): 92–113.

Lauriault, Robert N. "From Can't to Can't: the North Florida Turpentine Camp, 1900–1950," *Florida Historical Quarterly* 67 (1989): 310–328.

Lee, Matthew R., et al., "Revisiting the Southern Culture of Violence," *The Sociological Quarterly* 48 (Spring, 2007): 253–275.

Lyons, Jeffrey. "The Family and Partisan Socialization in Red and Blue America." 38 *Political Psychology,* (2017): 297–312.

Martin, John Bartlow. "The Deep South Says Never." *Saturday Evening Post,* 229 (June 22, 1957): 32–101.

McGurl, Mark. "Learning from Little Tree: The Political Education of the Counterculture." *The Yale Journal of Criticism* 18 (2005): 243–267.

McLaurin, Melton. "The Images of the Negro in Deep South Public School State History Texts," Department of Education, Research Paper 168120D, 1968. Copy in DC.

McMillen, Neil R. "Black Enfranchisement in Mississippi: Federal Enforcement and Black Protest in the 1960s," *Journal of Southern History,* 43 (August,1977): 351–372.

McPheron, Judith. "Forrest Carter, *The Education of Little Tree,*" *Library Journal,* November 15, 1976: 29–31.

Menand, Louis. "The People Who Decide What Becomes History," *The New Yorker,* April 18, 2022.

Mitchell, Lee Clark, "Violence in the Film Western," in J. David Slocum, ed., *Violence and American Cinema.* London: Routledge Publishing, 2001): 176–191.

Mohl, Raymond A. "'South of the South?' Jews, Blacks and the Civil Rights Movement in Miami, 1945–1960, *Journal of American Ethnic History,* 18 (Winter, 1999), 3–36.

Norman W. Walton, "The Walking City: A History of the Montgomery Bus Boycott," in David Garrow, ed., *The Walking City: The Montgomery Bus Boycott, 1955–1956.* Minneapolis: Carlson Publications, 1989.

Norrell, Robert J. "Caste in Steel: Jim Crow Careers in Birmingham, Alabama." *The Journal of American History* 73 (December 1986): 669–694.

Pahowka, Gareth D. "Voices of Moderation: Southern Whites Respond to Brown v. Board of Education," *Gettysburg Historical Journal,* 5 (2006): 43–66.

Pegram, Thomas R. "The Ku Klux Klan, Labor and the White Working Class During the 1920s," *The Journal of the Gilded Age and the Progressive Era* 17 (April 2018): 373–396.

Perlmutter, Nathan. "Bombing in Miami: Anti-Semitism and the Segregationists." *Commentary*, 25 (June 1958): 498–503.

Perlstein, Rick. "Exclusive: Lee Atwater's Infamous 1981 Interview on the Southern Strategy," *The Nation*, November 13, 2012.

Porter, Kenneth. "Negro Labor in the Western Cattle Industry, 1866–1900," *Labor History* 10 (Summer, 1969): 346–374.

Prince, K. Stephen. "Jim Crow Memory: Southern White Supremacists and the Regional Politics of Remembrance," 17–34 in *Remembering Reconstruction: Struggles Over the Meaning of America's Most Turbulent Era*, edited by Carole Emberton and Bruce E. Baker. Baton Rouge: Louisiana State University Press, 2017.

Rabinowitz, Howard. "Nativism, Bigotry and Anti-Semitism in the South." *American Jewish History*, 77 (March 1988): 437–51.

Rath, R. John. "The Failure of an Ideal: The Viennese Revolution of 1848," *The Southwestern Social Science Quarterly. 34* (September 1953). 3–20.

Roche, Jeff. "Asa/Forrest Carter and Regional Political Identity," in Philip D. Dillard and Randal L. Hall, eds., *The Southern Albatross : Race and Ethnicity in the American South*. Macon, Georgia: Mercer University Press, 1999.

Rubin, Dana. "The Real Education of Little Tree," *Texas Monthly*, February 1992.

Shofner, "Force Labor in the Florida Forests, 1880–1950," *Journal of Forest History* 25 (January 1981): 14–25.

Simmsparris, Michele M. "What Does It Mean to See a Black Church Burning? Understanding the Significance of Constitutionalizing Hate Speech," 1 *University of Pennsylvania Journal of Constitutional Law* (1998): 127–51.

Slocum, J. David, "The 'Film Violence' trope: New Hollywood, 'the Sixties,' and the Politics of History," in Steven Jay Schneider, ed., *New Hollywood Violence*. Manchester: Manchester University Press, 2004, 57–80.

Storrs, Landon, R. Y. "Revisiting Truman's Federal Employee Loyalty Program," 67–78, in Richard Stewart Kirkendall, ed., *Civil Liberties and the Legacy of Harry S. Truman*. Kirksville, Missouri: Truman State University Press, 2013.

Strain, Christopher. "Holy Smoke: Church Burnings, Journalism and the Politics of Race, 1996–2006," 71–99 in Yuya Kiuch, *Race Still Matters: The Reality of African American Lives and the Myth of a Postracial Society*. Albany: State University of New York Press, 2016.

Teters, Kristopher A. "Albert Burton Moore and Alabama's Centennial Commemoration of the Civil War: The Rhetoric of Race, Romance and Reunion." *Alabama Review*. 66 (April 2013): 122–52.

Teuton, Christopher. "Literature Education and 'The Return of the Whippoorwill': A Conversation with Freeman Owle," *Appalachian Journal, 34* (Winter 2007): 194–205.

Toby, Jackson. "Bombing in Nashville: A Jewish Center and the Desegregation Struggle." *Commentary*, 25 (May 1958): 385–389.

Turner, William W. "The Minutemen," *Ramparts*, October 27, 1966.

Ward, Bryan. "Civil Rights and Rock and Roll: Revisiting the Nat King Cole Attack of 1956." *Organization of American Historians' Magazine* 24 (April, 2010): 21–24.

Ward, Bryan. "Race, Politics and Culture: The Cole Incident of 1956," in Rick Halpern and Melvyn Stokes, (eds), *Race and Class in the American South Since 1890* (Oxford: Berg Press, 1994):181–208.

Ward, Jason Ward. "The D.C. School Hearings of 1956 and the National Vision of Massive Resistance, *Journal of Civil and Human Rights,* 1 (Spring/Summer 2015): 82–110.

Webb, Clive. "Counter Blast: How the Atlanta Temple Bombing Strengthened the Civil Rights Cause." *Southern Spaces,* June 22, 2009.

Weinberger, Alvin. "An Analysis of the [1943] Colorado Labor Peace Act," *Rocky Mountain Law Review* 19 (1946–1947): 359–366.

Winston, Andrew. "Science in the service of the far right: Henry E. Garrett, the IAAEE, and the Liberty Lobby." *Journal of Social Issues,* 54 (Spring, 1998): 179–210.

Yaakov, Ariel. "It's All in the Bible," in Jonathan Karp and Adam Sutcliffe, eds., *Philosemitism in History*. London: Cambridge University Press, 2011: 257–288.

THESES AND DISSERTATIONS

Bauer, Jordan R. "Domestic Anticommunism in Alabama and the Resurgence of American Conservatism," MA thesis, University of Alabama, Birmingham, 2007.

Bollman, Amy Kallio. "Dangerous Eloquence: Hate Speech Tactics in the Discourse of Asa/Forrest Carter from 1954–1974," PhD dissertation, University of Oklahoma, 2004.

Bryson, Heather. "To Give Racism the Face of the Ignorant: Race, Class, and White Manhood in Birmingham, Alabama, 1937–1970," PhD dissertation, University of Florida, 2011.

Carter, David C. "Outraged Justice: The Lynching of Postmaster Frazier Baker in Lake City, South Carolina, 1897–98." Honors thesis, University of North Carolina, 1992.

Corley, Robert Gaines. "The Quest for Racial Harmony: Race Relations in Birmingham, Alabama, 1947–1963." PhD dissertation, University of Virginia, 1979.

Dobrasko, Rebekah. "Upholding 'Separate but Equal': South Carolina's School Equalization Program, 1951–1955." MA thesis, University of South Carolina, 2005.

Gilliam, Thomas. *"The Second Folsom Administration:* The Destruction of Alabama Liberalism, 1954–1958." PhD dissertation, Auburn University, 1975.

Harris, J. Tyra. "Alabama Reaction to the *Brown* decision, 1954–1956: A Case Study in Early Massive Resistance." PhD dissertation, Middle Tennessee State University, 1978.

Huntington, John S. "Right-Wing Paranoid Blues: The Role of Radicalism in Modern Conservatism," PhD dissertation, University of Houston, 2016.

Makay, John Joseph. "The Speaking of Governor George C. Wallace in the 1964 [Indiana] Presidential Primary." PhD dissertation, Purdue University, 1969.

Marshall, Paul Michael, "The Union Party and the 1936 Election." PhD dissertation, Sussex University, 2013.

Martin, Rachel L. "Out of the Silence: Remembering the Desegregation of Clinton, Tennessee, High School," PhD dissertation, University of North Carolina, 2012.

Matzko, Paul. "No Uncertain Trumpet: Carl McIntire and the Politicization of Fundamentalism," MA thesis, Temple University, 2010.

McCarty, Patrick Fargo. "Big Ed Johnson: A Political Portrait." MA thesis, University of Colorado, 1958.

O'Brien, Thomas Victor. "Georgia's Response to *Brown v. Board of Education*: The Rise and Fall of Massive Resistance, 1949–1961." PhD dissertation, Emory University, 1992.

Olivas, Midshipman First Class Benjamin L. "Close Encounters: U.S. Servicemen Engage Japan in War and Occupation 1941–1946, Honors Thesis, United States Naval Academy, 2010.

Pilcher, Margaret. "Eugene Cervi and Cervi's *Rocky Mountain Journal:* A Study of Post World War II Colorado" PhD dissertation, University of Denver, 1986.

Sprayberry, Gary S. "Town Among the Trees": Paternalism, Class and Civil Rights in Anniston, Alabama, 1872 to Present." PhD dissertation, University of Alabama, 2003.

Viola, David C., Jr. "Terrorism and the Response to Terrorism in New York City During the Long Sixties," PhD dissertation, City University of New York, 1977.

Government Documents

Adams, Kenneth. FBI Files. Copy in Dan T. Carter Collection, Asa Carter Files, Stuart A. Rose Manuscript, Archives, and Rare Book Library, Emory University, Atlanta, Georgia.

Alabama States Rights Association Papers, Archives and Manuscripts Collection, Birmingham Public Library, Birmingham, Alabama.

Carter, Asa Earl. FBI Files. Copy in Dan T. Carter Collection, Asa Carter Files, Stuart A. Rose Manuscript, Archives, and Rare Book Library, Emory University, Atlanta, Georgia.

Final Report of the Select Committee to Study Governmental Operations with Respect to Intelligence Activities, United States Senate. Together with Additional Supplemental and Separate Views. April 26, 1976. Copy in DC.

Mabry, Jessie W. v. *The State of Alabama (*1957). Trial Transcript. Copy in Dan T. Carter Collection, Asa Carter Files, Stuart A. Rose Manuscript, Archives, and Rare Book Library, Emory University, Atlanta, Georgia.

McCullough, Grover vs. The State of Alabama (1957). Trial Transcript. Copy in Dan T. Carter Collection, Asa Carter Files, Stuart A. Rose Manuscript, Archives, and Rare Book Library, Emory University, Atlanta, Georgia.

Pritchett, Joe P. vs. *The State of Alabama* (1957). Trial Transcript. Copy in Dan T. Carter Collection, Asa Carter Files, Stuart A. Rose Manuscript, Archives, and Rare Book Library, Emory University, Atlanta, Georgia.

United States Congress, Joint Select Committee on the Condition of Affairs in the Late Insurrectionary States, *Report of the Joint Select Committee to Inquire into the Condition of Affairs in the Late Insurrectionary States, made to the two Houses of Congress February 19, 1872,* Vols. 11, 12 (Washington: Government Printing Office, 1872).

Civil Rights—1959.: hearings before the United States Senate Committee on the Judiciary, Subcommittee on Constitutional Rights, Eighty-Sixth Congress, first session. Washington: U.S. G.P.O. Copy in DC.

Audio Visual Materials

The Reconstruction of Asa Carter (RAC), PBS Broadcast, 2012. Director Marco Ricci, Producer Douglas Newman, Executive Producer Laura Browder. Interview Outtakes in Dan T. Carter Asa Carter Research Files, Stuart A. Rose Manuscript, Archives, and Rare Book Library, Emory University, Atlanta, Georgia.

See it Now: Clinton and the Law: A Study in Desegregation, Edward R. Murrow CBS Broadcast January 6, 1957.

John G. Moore interview on the Desegregation of Clinton High School," *The History of Jim Crow: Teacher Resources.* Copy in DC.

Huie, William Bradford interview. Conducted by Blackside, Inc, August 30, 1979, for *Eyes on the Prize: America's Civil Rights Years (1954–1965).* Washington University Libraries, Film and Media Archive, Henry Hampton Collection.

Manuscript Collections

Alabama Department of Archives and History, Montgomery, Alabama. (ADAH) Papers of George and Lurleen Wallace.

Alabama Room, Public Library of Anniston-Calhoun County. Anniston, Alabama. (FBC)

American States Rights Association Papers, Department of Archives and History, Birmingham Public Library, Birmingham, Alabama.

Burger, Fred. Research Papers. Public Library of Anniston-Calhoun County (Alabama), Digital Collections.

Carter. Dan T. Research Files. Stuart A. Rose Manuscript, Archives, and Rare Book Library, Emory University, Atlanta, Georgia.

Delaine, Joseph Armstrong. Papers, 1918–2000. South Caroliniana Library, University of South Carolina, Columbia, South Carolina.

Kennedy, Robert F. Interview, John F. Kennedy Presidential Library and Museum, Boston, Massachusetts.

Marshall, Burke. Personal Papers. John F. Kennedy Presidential Library and Museum, Boston, Massachusetts.

Morgan, James W. Mayoral Papers. Department of Archives and History, Birmingham Public Library, Birmingham, Alabama.

Southern Regional Council Collection, Archives Research Center, Robert W. Woodruff Library, Atlanta University, Atlanta, Georgia.

Swan, Jimmy. Interview. University of Southern Mississippi Center for Oral History and Cultural Heritage.

AUTHOR'S INTERVIEWS

[Held in Dan T. Carter Research Files, Stuart A. Rose Manuscript, Archives, and Rare Book Library,Emory University, Atlanta, Georgia]

Ayers, Brandt. October 12, 2014
Azbell, Joe. February 14, 1989
Birchard, John. March 11, 2012
Bright, Herbert. August 11, 1991
Clayton, Lawrence. November 14, 1991
Daley, Bob. March 22, 2002
Grant, Mickey. June 29, 2018
Graves, Camilla. April 22, 2003
Green, Louise. November 12, 1991
Greenhaw, Wayne. August 9, 1991, September 28, 1993
Heffernan, Tony. Interview, May 25, 1994
Harper, Oscar. August 9, 1991
Ingram, Bob. July 15, 1988, August 11, 1991
Johnson, Roland. May 12, 1996
Jones, Bill. August 3, 1990
Jones, R. B. July 27, 1992, July 12, 1993
Kopel, Jack. March 12, 1997
Miller, Alvin. June 11, 1991
Nelson, Jack. November 21, 1993
Parker, Hester. April 4, 2016
St. John, Bob. December 12, 2008
Shows, Jack. August 9, 1999
Smith, Starr. June 10, 1988
Trammell, Seymore. February 14, 1988; January 11, 1989; November 28, 1989; August 12, 1991; April 4, 1993
Turnipseed, Tom. March 3, 1994

Outtake Interviews

for the 2012 PBS documentary, *The Reconstruction of Asa Carter,* Director Marco Ricci, Producer Douglas Newman, Executive Producer Laura Browder [Held in Dan T. Carter Research Files, Stuart A. Rose Manuscript, Archives, and Rare Book Library, Emory University, Atlanta, Georgia]

Allen, Richard. December 15, 2008
Andrews, Ray. February 1, 2008
Ayers, Brandt. November 19, 2008
Bloodworth, Ben. December 15, 2008
Bloodworth, Ron. November 20, 2008
Browder, Laura. April 27, 2008
Burger, Fred. June 4, 2005
Carter, Dan. November 19, 2008
Cowley, Marjorie. February 2, 2008
Daley, Bob. February 16, 2007
Davis, Phil. November 19, 2008
Doster, Charles. February 3, 2008
Ford, Charles. November 19, 2008
Greenhaw, Wayne. June 4, 2005
Hadas, Beth. November 25, 2008
Hale, Larry. November 20, 2008
Hobson, Geary. December 12, 2008
Hodges, George November 20, 2008
Hughes, Ned. November 19, 2008
Marshall, Bruce. July 1, 2005
Mattison, Bill. November 25, 2008
McWhorter, Diane. June 4, 2005
Moulson, Peter. November 25, 2008
Olney, James. February 15, 2007
Owle, Freeman. February 15, 2007
Palmer, Theron. June 5, 2005
Parsons, James. November 19, 2008
Raines, Howell. February 15, 2007
Roche, Jeff. November 19, 2008
Snead, Roy. November 19, 2008
Snider, Charles. June 4, 2005
Sprayberry, Gary. November 19, 2008
Scott, David. December 15, 2008
Sproul, Barbara. February 3, 2008
Stewart, Sam. February 3, 2008
St. John, Bob. December 12, 2008
Treuer, David. April 27, 2008
Turnipseed, Tom. February 15, 2007
Walker, Darlene. December 12, 2008
Weeth, Charles and Betty. July 5, 2005. December 12, 2008
Weyr, Rhoda. February 15, 2007
Whitaker, Bill. August 9, 2005
White, Howard. February 3, 2008
Wilson, Leonard. February 2, 2008
Wood, Ed. November 19, 2008

Interviews conducted by Fred Burger, 1991–2008

[Held in the Burger Collection of the Anniston-Calhoun County Public Library]

Acker, Gerald
Adams, Larry K., Sr.
Adams, Larry K., Jr.
Adams, Moe
Andrews, Ray [2]
Arnold, Danny
Atkinson, Johnny
Barnett, Agnes
Barnett, Buddy
Baxley, Bill
Bennett, Ellen
Blackwater, Eddie
Brady, David
Branton, Gert
Branton, Leo
Bridges, Thomas E.
Bright, Ethel
Bright, Hubert
Burke, Emory
Carter, Doug [4]
Carter, India
Carter, Jimmy [2]
Carter, Kaye [2]
Carter, Larry [4]
Chandler, Wayne
Chitwood, W. O.
Clayton, Lawrence
Coleman, Tom G. Jr.
Collins, John
Crommelin, John

Curlee, Glen
Daley, Bob [2]
Dates, Claudia Walker
Dear, Claude
Deverell, Linion
Downing, Tom Sr.
Dunn, James
Edmond, Cliff
Edmond, Walter, Jr.
Emmerson, Bernard
Emmerson, Faye
Engelhardt, Sam
Ernst, J. D ("Dick")
Everell, Linion
Faulkner, Jimmy
Field, Robert
Fields, Edward
Ford, Johnny
Fox, Al
Friede, Eleanor
Greenhaw, Wayne
Hagler, Bill
Hall, Nan Simpson
Hanes, Arthur, Sr.
Hart, Bob [2]
Hartz, Jim
Henderson, Audrey
Hubbard, A. Pelham
Hubley, Faith
Ingram, Bob
Jackson, John
Coley, Margaret
Jemison, Lloyd
Jones, Bill
Jones, R. B.
Josey, Don
Katzenbach, Nicholas
Kennedy, Olga Shamblin
Kimsey, Anne
Knight, Jimmy
Kohn, Ernest
Kokjer, Tom
Lackey, Gordon
Landers, Joe
Leitke, Charles F.
Lett, Otto
Maddox, Lester
Malone, Ronnie
Mann, Floyd
Mathews, Pete
Mathews, Ruby Harper
McBride, Harold W.
McKinney, Janie
McMillan, Justin
Melton, Larry
Meriwether, Charles
Meriwether, Charles
Miller, Bill
Morgan, Sam
Morris, John Edward
Morrison, Brent
Morton, Gary
Noble, Phil
Parks, Charles L.
Parks, Michael
Patterson, John
Patton, Gen. George IV
Pemberton, John [2]
Peterson, Art
Pettus, Denver
Pfeffer, Jeff
Phillips, Hubert
Potts, Tom
Price, Bobby
Prickett, Diana
Raines, Howell
Rance, Edward
Reynolds, Nimrod Q.
Robertson, Wilbur R.
Rodgers., [Dr.] Gordon A., Jr.
Rollins, Robert Michael
Rose, Bill
Rath, R. John
Scarborough, Lin
Schaefer, Robert H.
Seaborn, Jack
Shaddix, Pat
Shelton, Robert
Simpson, Cecil L.
Sims, Nate
Slate, Clay
Smith, Dick
Smith, Hank
Sproull, Barbara
Sproull, Miller
Stewart, Samuel Linwood
Stoner, J. B.
Swan, Jimmy
Swan, Randy
Taylor, Ron
Thomas, Bernice
Thomas, Cleo, Sr.
Thornton, Thomas H.
Trammell, Asa
Trammell, Seymore
Turner, Thomas C.
Turnipseed, Tom
Valor, Joan
Waldrep, Howard, Jr.
Walker, George P., III
Washington, Lottie Satcher
Watson, Bobby
Weston, Jack Todd
Weyr, Garret
Weyr, Rhoda
Weyr, Tom
White, Howard
White, Howard
Wilson, Emmett
Wilson, Leonard
Wood, Edward

Index

D

T